Managerial Economics

and Business Strategy

FIRST CANADIAN EDITION

Michael R. Baye
Kelley School of Business
Indiana University

Farrokh R. Zandi
Schulich School of Business
York University

McGraw-Hill Ryerson

Toronto Montréal Boston Burr Ridge, IL Dubuque, IA Madison, WI New York
San Francisco St. Louis Bangkok Bogotá Caracas Kuala Lumpur Lisbon London
Madrid Mexico City Milan New Delhi Santiago Seoul Singapore Sydney Taipei

To Orlan and Rich—two teachers who changed my life.

—Michael R. Baye

To my daughter Laila

—Farrokh R. Zandi

Managerial Economics and Business Strategy
First Canadian Edition

Copyright © 2005 by McGraw-Hill Ryerson Limited, a Subsidiary of The McGraw-Hill Companies. All rights reserved. Copyright © 2003, 2000, 1997, 1994 by The McGraw-Hill Companies. All rights reserved. No part of this publication may be reproduced or transmitted in any form or by any means, or stored in a data base or retrieval system, without the prior written permission of McGraw-Hill Ryerson Limited, or in the case of photocopying or other reprographic copying, a licence from The Canadian Copyright Licensing Agency (Access Copyright). For an Access Copyright licence, visit www.accesscopyright.ca or call toll-free to 1-800-893-5777.

ISBN: 0-07-091609-8

1 2 3 4 5 6 7 8 9 10   TCP   0 9 8 7 6 5

Printed and bound in Canada

Care has been taken to trace ownership of copyright material contained in this text; however, the publisher will welcome any information that enables them to rectify any reference or credit for subsequent editions.

Vice President, Editorial and Media Technology: Pat Ferrier
Executive Sponsoring Editor: Lynn Fisher
Economics Editor: Ron Doleman
Developmental Editor: Maria Chu
Senior Marketing Manager: Kelly Smyth
Senior Supervising Editor: Margaret Henderson
Copy Editor: Rodney Rawlings
Production Coordinator: Paula Brown
Composition: Bookman Typesetting Company
Cover Design: Dianna Little
Cover Image: © Marvy/Corbis/Magma
Printer: Transcontinental Printing Company

Statistics Canada information is used with permission of the Ministry of Industry, as Minister responsible for Statistics Canada. Information on the availability of the wider range of data from Statistics Canada can be obtained from Statistics Canada's Regional Offices, its World Wide Web site at http://www.statcan.ca, and its toll-free access number 1-800-263-1136.

Library and Archives Canada Cataloguing in Publication

Baye, Michael R., 1958–
    Managerial economics and business strategy / Michael R. Baye, Farrokh Zandi.—1st Canadian ed.

Includes index.
ISBN 0-07-091609-8

1. Managerial economics—Textbooks.   2. Strategic planning—Textbooks.   I. Zandi, Farrokh   II. Title.

HD30.22.B39 2004   338.5'02'4658   C2004-906398-7

About the Authors

Michael Baye is the Bert Elwert Professor of Business Economics and Public Policy at Indiana University's Kelley School of Business. He received his B.S. from Texas A&M University in 1980, where he won both the University Senior Honors Thesis Prize for best undergraduate thesis and the Alfred Chalk Award for outstanding senior in the economics department. Michael earned a Ph.D. in Economics from Purdue University in 1983.

Michael has won many awards for outstanding teaching, and regularly teaches courses in managerial economics and industrial organization at the undergraduate, M.B.A., and Ph.D. level. He has also taught graduate and undergraduate courses at The Pennsylvania State University, Texas A&M University, and the University of Kentucky, where he also served on the faculty. A prolific researcher, Michael's articles on game theory, industrial organization, and pricing strategy have been published in leading economics journals, including the *American Economic Review*, *Journal of Political Economy*, *Econometrica*, and the *Review of Economic Studies*. His research has been supported by the National Science Foundation, the Fulbright Commission, and other organizations.

Michael has held visiting appointments at Cambridge, Oxford, Erasmus University, Tilburg University, and the New Economic School in Moscow, Russia. He serves on numerous editorial boards in economics as well as marketing, and is the editor of *Advances in Applied Microeconomics*.

Farrokh Zandi is on the faculty in Schulich School of Business, York University in Toronto. He is currently serving as Associate Director of Undergraduate Programs at Schulich School of Business. He received his Ph.D. from Carleton University in 1982 and has more than 20 years' experience in teaching economics at various levels. Professor Zandi teaches courses in the fields of Managerial Economics and Business Strategy, Macroeconomics, and International Economics. His research interests are in the area of International and Public Economics. He is a regular nominee for teaching awards and is the winner of 1998 Teaching Excellence Award, the highest teaching award that can be received by a faculty member at Schulich School of Business.

Brief Contents

Contents

CHAPTER TWO
Market Forces: Demand and Supply

CHAPTER THREE
Quantitative Demand Analysis

CHAPTER FOUR
The Theory of Individual Behaviour

CHAPTER FIVE
The Production Process and Costs

CHAPTER SIX
The Organization of the Firm

CHAPTER SEVEN
The Nature of Industry

CHAPTER EIGHT
Managing in Competitive, Monopolistic, and Monopolistically Competitive Markets

CHAPTER NINE
Basic Oligopoly Models

CHAPTER TEN
Game Theory: Inside Oligopoly

CHAPTER ELEVEN
Pricing Strategies for Firms with Market Power

CHAPTER TWELVE
The Economics of Information

CHAPTER THIRTEEN
Advanced Topics in Business Strategy

CHAPTER FOURTEEN
A Manager's Guide to Government in the Marketplace

Preface to the First Canadian Edition

As soon as I got my hands on the earlier U.S. edition of Michael Baye's *Managerial Economics and Business Strategy*, it was clear to me that it was the best textbook for the undergraduate and the MBA managerial economics courses I have been teaching at the Schulich School of business.

While the book is easily recognizable as Professor Baye's, I have made changes that increase its relevance to Canadian students. Some of these changes reflect important differences between the Canadian and U.S. economies. For example, the Canadian economy is much more open than the U.S. economy, and this fact is explicitly recognized in the open-economy applications of theory and policy, as well as in a more global approach in the application boxes (Inside Business) on topics including price cycles in retail gasoline markets in Canada and the United States, the international pricing positioning of Canadian Wheat Board, no-fault insurance in British Columbia, the Employment Insurance (EI), market-clearing prices in the world crude oil market, the softwood lumber dispute with the United States, airline mergers in Canada, the drug price differentiation in the global market, the Kyoto protocol, etc., throughout this edition. Other changes reflect important institutional differences between the two countries, including the structure of the antitrust laws, the nature of competition policy, and in general the role of government in the marketplace with regard to market failure—for example, environmental issues, discussed in Chapter 14. Finally, while this Canadian edition focuses on issues and includes examples that are more familiar and relevant to a Canadian audience, an attempt has been made to keep the evidence from the U.S. economy intact in order to make possible a comparison between the two countries.

What's New in the First Canadian Edition?

In addition to updating the book, I have refined its coverage and pedagogy with input from a panel of reviewers. Several topics appear in this edition that were missing from the U.S. edition, including the application of demand and supply in the open economy, and the incidence of sales taxes (Chapter 2), the attribute analysis of consumer choice (Chapter 4), and the utility analysis of risks (Chapter 12). I have also expanded on several existing topics, including oligopolies' strategic behaviour such as threats, commitments and credibility, and trigger strategies and price wars (Chapter 10), and risk pooling and insurance (Chapter 12). Furthermore, the algebraic solution to oligopolistic models has been extended to all models in order to enable the reader to compare them from the perspective of efficiency. Other, minor changes include inclusion of a section on the cost-benefit analysis (Chapter 14) as well as a new section to compare the Canadian public health system with the U.S.'s mixed system of private-public health from the perspective of moral hazards and adverse selection (Chapter 12). Almost all the Headline and most of the Inside Business features have been rewritten using Canadian examples. One deletion has been the discussion of isoprofit curves (from Chapter 9), which most users of the previous editions had found too complex for its marginal contribution.

Key Features

The first Canadian edition maintains all of the key features of the U.S. editions that enhance students' learning experiences and make it easier to teach from this book.

Headlines

Each chapter begins with a *Headline* based on a real-world economic problem—a problem that students should be able to address after completing the chapter. These headlines are essentially handpicked "mini-cases" designed to motivate students to learn the material in the chapter. Each headline is answered under *Answering the Headline* at the end of the relevant chapter—when the student is better prepared to deal with the complications of real-world problems. Reviewers as well as users of previous editions praise the headlines not only because they motivate students to learn the material in the chapter, but because the answers at the end of each chapter help students learn how to use economics to make business decisions.

Head line

Conditional and Unconditional Grants: Federal Contributions Associated with the Canada Health Act

In the November 2002 report from his Commission on the Future of Health Care in Canada, Mr. Romanow proposed the creation of a National Health Council to act as an auditor-general of medical care, in part because the provinces and Ottawa had proved themselves incapable of sharing health-care responsibilities. Eight months later, in their Charlottetown conference, Canada's premiers gave the council only qualified support.

money from the federal government in the form of unconditional grants, arguing that they knew best how to spend it. The federal government was reluctant to give the money without guarantees that the provinces would spend the money on designated services such as education and health care.

As an arbitrator, whom would you have agreed with? As background, you might find it useful to first discuss the old method of cost sharing between the

ANSWERING THE Head line

The Canada Health Act sets the criteria and conditions with respect to insured health services and extended health care services that must be met by provincial/ territorial health care insurance plans before a full cash contribution can be made by the federal government to each province or territory.

- *Conditional grants.* Conditional grants are a method of sharing costs between a smaller government and a larger government—the municipal vis-à-vis the provincial, or the provincial vis-à-vis the federal government. In effect, government conditional (direct) grants have the effect of making smaller governments more uniform and reducing the effects of intergovernmental competition. Grants can be used to fund an entire project, or to fund a portion of a project, the remainder of the funding being put forth by the lower-level government.

  Since the federal government began contributing to provincial and territorial health insurance programs in 1958, the arrangements for these contributions have evolved. Prior to 1977, the federal government *cost-shared* hospital and physician services with the provinces and territories

Demonstration Problems

The best way to learn economics is to practise solving economic problems. So, in addition to the *Headlines*, each chapter contains many *Demonstration Problems* sprinkled throughout the text, along with detailed answers. This provides students with a mechanism to verify that they have mastered the material, and reduces the cost to students and instructors of having to meet during office hours to discuss answers to problems.

Demonstration PROBLEM 2–3

Your research department estimates that the supply function for television sets is given by

$$Q_x^s = 2000 + 3P_x - 4P_r - P_w$$

where P_x is the price of TV sets, P_r represents the price of a computer monitor, and P_w is the price of an input used to make televisions. Suppose TVs are sold for \$400 per unit, computer monitors are sold for \$100 per unit, and the price of an input is \$2000. How many television sets are produced?

Answer

To find out how many television sets are produced, we insert the given values of prices into the supply function to get

$$Q_x^s = 2000 + 3(400) - 4(100) - 1(2000)$$

Inside Business Applications

Each chapter contains boxed material (called *Inside Business*) to illustrate how theories explained in the text relate to a host of different business situations. We have tried to strike a balance between applications drawn from the current economic literature and the popular press.

Inside BUSINESS

2–3 Market-Clearing Prices in the World Crude Oil Market

The Organization of Petroleum Exporting Countries (OPEC) rose to international prominence during 1970s as its member countries took control of their domestic petroleum industries and acquired a major say in the pricing of crude oil on world markets. Two developments have characterized the market for crude oil in the past two decades. First, after the two drastic oil price increases of 1973 and 1979, and a significant oil price decrease in 1986, the world economy has witnessed a period of reasonable tranquility. Second, though OPEC's objective since its inception has been to coordinate and unify petroleum policies among its member countries in order to secure a larger market share, this has gradually given way to a growing awareness of the need to shift its focus to market

estimate the world demand and also non-OPEC supply in each period. In reality, due to estimation errors caused by unforeseen factors, such as wars, climate changes, and production anomalies by non-OPEC producers, the art of gapology (residual supplying) may be less than perfect; see column (e).

The first half of 1998 brought a very sharp drop of 2.1 m b/d (2.1 million barrels of oil per day, or 2.8 percent) in demand. However, this downward trend in demand, which can be traced back to the Asian crisis of September 1997, was not balanced by a decrease in the world (OPEC and non-OPEC) supply of oil. This inevitably gave rise to a drastic fall in price of crude oil of 19.2 percent which lasted until the end of the year; see

Calculus and Non-Calculus Alternatives

Users can easily include or exclude calculus-based material without losing content or continuity. That's because the basic principles and formulas needed to solve a particular class of economic problems (e.g., $MR = MC$) are first stated without appealing to the notation of calculus. Immediately following each stated principle or formula is a clearly marked *Calculus Alternative*. Each of these calculus alternatives states the preceding principle or formula in calculus notation, and explains the relation between the calculus-based and the non-calculus-based formula. More detailed calculus derivations are relegated to *Appendixes*. Thus, the book is designed for use by instructors who want to integrate calculus into managerial economics, and by those who do not require students to use calculus.

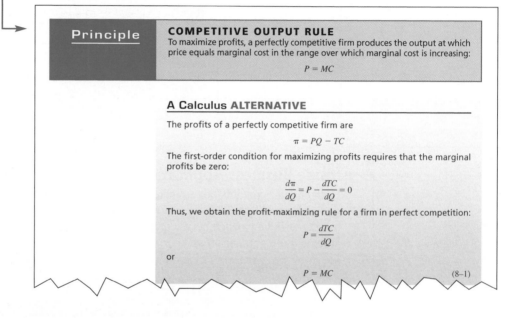

Principle

COMPETITIVE OUTPUT RULE
To maximize profits, a perfectly competitive firm produces the output at which price equals marginal cost in the range over which marginal cost is increasing:

$$P = MC$$

A Calculus ALTERNATIVE

The profits of a perfectly competitive firm are

$$\pi = PQ - TC$$

The first-order condition for maximizing profits requires that the marginal profits be zero:

$$\frac{d\pi}{dQ} = P - \frac{dTC}{dQ} = 0$$

Thus, we obtain the profit-maximizing rule for a firm in perfect competition:

$$P = \frac{dTC}{dQ}$$

or

$$P = MC \qquad (8-1)$$

Key Terms and Marginal Definitions

Each chapter ends with a list of key terms and concepts. These provide an easy way for professors to glean material covered in each chapter, and for students to check their mastery of terminology. In addition, marginal definitions are provided throughout the text, a full Glossary is provided at the end of the book, and a searchable Glossary is provided on the Baye Online Learning Centre.

End-of-Chapter Problems

The Canadian edition contains two types of problems. Highly structured but nonetheless challenging *Conceptual and Computational Questions* stress fundamentals. These are followed by *Problems and Applications* which are far less structured and, like real-world decision environments, may contain more information than is actually needed to solve the problem. Many of these applied problems are based on actual business events. Answers to selected problems are presented at the end of the book; detailed answers to all problems are available to instructors in the Instructor's Manual available on the Instructor's CD in Microsoft Word format.

Conceptual and Computational Questions

1. The X-Corporation produces a good (called X) that is a normal good. Its competitor, Y-Corp., makes a substitute good that it markets under the name Y. Good Y is an inferior good.
   a. How will the demand for good X change if consumer incomes increase?
   b. How will the demand for good Y change if consumer incomes decrease?
   c. How will the demand for good X change if the price of good Y decreases?
   d. Is good Y a lower-quality product than good X? Explain.
2. Good X is produced in a competitive market using input A. Explain what would happen to the supply of good X in each of the following situations:
   a. The price of input A increases.
   b. An excise tax of $1 is imposed on good X.
   c. An ad valorem tax of 5 percent is imposed on good X.
   d. A technological change reduces the cost of producing additional units of good Y.
3. Suppose the supply function for product X is given by $Q = 50 + 0.5P - 5P$.

Problems and Applications

9. You are the manager of a midsized company that assembles personal computers. You purchase most components—such as random access memory (RAM)—in a competitive market. Based on your marketing research, consumers earning over $75 000 purchase 1.3 times more RAM than consumers with lower incomes. One morning, you pick up a copy of *The Globe and Mail* and read an article indicating that a new technological breakthrough will permit manufacturers to produce RAM at a lower unit cost. On the basis of this information, what can you expect to happen to the price you pay for random access memory? Would your answer change if, in addition to this technological breakthrough, the article indicated that consumer incomes are expected to grow over the next two years as the economy pulls out of recession? Explain.
10. You are the manager of a firm that produces and markets a generic type of soft drink in a competitive market. In addition to the large number of generic products in your market, you also compete against major brands such as Coca-Cola and Pepsi.

Flexibility

Instructors of managerial economics have genuinely heterogeneous textbook needs. Reviewers praise the book for its flexibility, and assure us that sections or even entire chapters can be excluded without losing continuity.

Technology Solutions

Online Learning Centre

More and more students are studying online. That is why we offer an Online Learning Centre (OLC) that follows *Managerial Economics and Business Strategy* chapter by chapter. You don't have to build or maintain anything and it's ready to go the moment you and your students type in the URL:

www.mcgrawhill.ca/college/baye

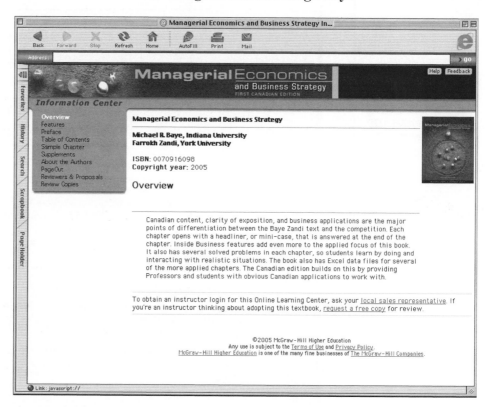

As your students study, they can refer to the OLC website for such benefits as:

- Chapter outline
- Chapter summary
- Searchable glossary and key terms
- Economics on the web

- Access to Σ-STAT & CANSIM database
- Business Week
- Econ Graph Kit
- Excel spreadsheet

Remember, the *Managerial Economics and Business Strategy* OLC content is flexible enough to use with any course management platform currently available. If your department or school is already using a platform, we can help. For information on our course management services, contact your *i*-Learning Sales Specialist or see "Superior Service" on page xxvi.

Superior Service

Superior Service

Service takes on a whole new meaning with McGraw-Hill Ryerson and *Managerial Economics and Business Strategy*. More than just bringing you the textbook, we have consistently raised the bar in terms of innovation and educational research—both in economics and in education in general. These investments in learning and the education community have helped us to understand the needs of students and educators across the country, and allowed us to foster the growth of truly innovative, integrated learning.

Integrated Learning

Your Integrated Learning Sales Specialist is a McGraw-Hill Ryerson representative who has the experience, product knowledge, training, and support to help you assess and integrate any of our products, technology, and services into your course for optimum teaching and learning performance. Whether it's helping your students improve their grades, or putting your entire course online, your *i*-Learning Sales Specialist is there to help you do it. Contact your *i*-Learning Sales Specialist today to learn how to maximize all of McGraw-Hill Ryerson's resources!

*i*Services

McGraw-Hill Ryerson offers a unique *i*Service package designed for Canadian faculty. Our mission is to equip providers of higher education with superior tools and resources required for excellence in teaching. For additional information, visit **www.mcgrawhill.ca/he/i-services**.

Teaching, Technology & Learning Conference Series

The educational environment has changed tremendously in recent years, and McGraw-Hill Ryerson continues to be committed to helping you acquire the skills you need to succeed in this new milieu. Our innovative Teaching, Technology & Learning Conference Series brings faculty together from across Canada with 3M Teaching Excellence award winners to share teaching and learning best practices in a collaborative and stimulating environment. Preconference workshops on general topics, such as teaching large classes and technology integration, will also be offered. We will also work with you at your own institution to customize workshops that best suit the needs of your faculty.

Research Reports into Mobile Learning and Student Success

These landmark reports, undertaken in conjunction with academic and private sector advisory boards, are the result of research studies into the challenges professors face in helping students succeed and the opportunities that new technology presents to impact teaching and learning.

Supplements

Managerial Economics and Business Strategy offers adopters the most comprehensive and easily accessible supplements in the market.

For the Student

Study Guide
In addition to the numerous problems and answers contained in the textbook, an updated *Study Guide* (ISBN 007-095576-X), prepared by Dr. V. Nallainayagam of Mount Royal College, is available to enhance student performance.

Student CD-ROM
Each new text includes a Learning CD that contains files to help students get hands-on experience at making economic decisions. The CD includes data needed for various regression problems, spreadsheet versions of key tables in the book to enable students to see how key economic concepts—such as marginal cost and profit maximization—can be implemented on standard spreadsheets, and spreadsheet macros that students can use to find the optimum price and quantity under a variety of market settings, including monopoly, Cournot oligopoly, and Stackelberg oligopoly.

Student Online Learning Centre
The Student Online Learning Centre (OLC), at **www.mcgrawhill.ca/college/baye**, offers Chapter Outline, Chapter Summary, a searchable glossary, Economics on the Web, Excel Spreadsheets, EconGraph Kit, access to Σ-STAT and the CANSIM II database, and other robust aids for student learning and exploration.

Σ-STAT is Statistics Canada's education resource that allows you to view socio-economic and demographic data in charts, graphs, and maps. Access to Σ-STAT and the CANSIM II database is made available to purchasers of *Managerial Economics and Business Strategy* from this website by special agreement between McGraw-Hill Ryerson and Statistics Canada. Please visit the Student OLC for additional information.

For the Instructor

Instructor's Online Learning Centre

The OLC includes a password-protected website for instructors; visit us at **www.mcgraw hill.ca/college/baye**. The site offers downloadable supplements and PageOut, the McGraw-Hill Ryerson course website development centre.

Instructor's CD-ROM
This CD-ROM includes the following Instructor's Supplements, which makes it easy for instructors to use the many supplements that make teaching managerial economics easy and fun:

- **Instructor's Manual** A thoroughly updated Instructor's Manual, prepared by Michael R. Baye, Patrick Scholten, and Farrokh Zandi, provides a summary of each chapter, a teaching outline for each chapter, and complete answers to all end-of-chapter problems.

- **Test Bank**   The Test Bank, prepared by Rashid Khan of McMaster University, and available in Microsoft Word, contains over 1000 multiple-choice questions and over 250 problems with detailed solutions.

- **PowerPoint Presentation**   The PowerPoint Presentation, prepared by Marc Prud'Homme of University of Ottawa, gives instructors the flexibility to integrate figures from the textbook. This package is available on the Instructor's CD or as a download from the Instructor's OLC.

- **Cases**   There are three new Canadian cases plus nine full-length U.S. cases available on the Instructor's CD-ROM or as a download from the Instructor's OLC. These cases contain rich detail about the market structure and conduct of firms in different industries. The Canadian cases include:

  1. *A case that investigates the relationship between increases in tuition fees and enrolment in postsecondary institutions in Canada.* This is an interesting study about the relationship between quantity demanded and price, and some of the other variables that influence demand.
  2. *A case that looks at the trend toward concentration in the Canadian banking sector.* This is a study highlighting the failure of government policy in promoting competition in a predominantly oligopoly market due to mergers and barriers to entry.
  3. *A case that outlines the perpetuation of monopoly power through the patent mechanism.* This is a study of the company AstraZeneca, manufacturer of the drug Losec.

  The U.S. cases concern Microsoft, Heinz, Visa, Staples, American Airlines, Sprint, and Kodak.

Course Management

PageOut

McGraw-Hill Ryerson's course management system, PageOut, is the easiest way to create a website for your economics course. There is no need for HTML coding, graphic design, or a thick how-to book. Just fill in a series of boxes in plain English and click on one of our professional designs. In no time, your course is online!

For the integrated instructor, we offer *Managerial Economics and Business Strategy* content for complete online courses. Whatever your needs, you can customize the *Managerial Economics and Business Strategy* Online Learning Centre content and author your own online course materials. It is entirely up to you. You can offer online discussion and message boards that will complement your office hours, and reduce the lines outside your door.

Content cartridges are also available for course management systems, such as **WebCT** and **Blackboard**. Ask your *i*-Learning Sales Specialist for details.

Acknowledgments

In addition to being deeply grateful to Michael Baye for giving me this opportunity to participate in this venture, I have also received some exceptional help in preparing this edition. I would like to acknowledge the comments offered by the reviewers that helped me shape up the initial proposal to adapt this book. In particular, I would like to thank the following reviewers for their extremely helpful comments and feedback:

Swati Basu, McGill University

Byron Eastman, Laurentian University

Rashid Khan, McMaster University

Saad Kiryakos, University of Ottawa

Joseph Kushner, Brock University

Allan Matadeen, Simon Fraser University

Richard Mueller, University of Lethbridge

William Strange, University of Toronto

James Vercammen, University of British Columbia

Without exception, their suggestions were thoughtful and relevant, and the book is much better because of them.

This book would not be nearly what it is without the care, attention, and most importantly the deep thought devoted to it by so many at McGraw Hill Ryerson. I would like to acknowledge the editorial, production, and marketing teams at McGraw-Hill Ryerson for their professionalism, advice, and encouragement throughout the process. Deserving of special mention in this regard are Ron Doleman, Economics Editor, for taking the initiative of involving me in this venture and for his continuous guidance and support; Maria Chu, who replaced Kamilah Reid as Developmental Editor seamlessly in early stages of this project, making sure I handed in my work (nearly) on time; Rodney Rawlings for showing that the practice of proofreading is indeed an art and that he is a wonderfully accomplished artist; Margaret Henderson, Senior Supervising Editor, who oversaw and coordinated the efforts of all three of us; and Dr. V. Nallainayagam of Mount Royal College, technical checker, from whose contribution this edition has benefited plenty. All five made my work harder, so that readers of this book would have an easier time.

Finally, I would like to thank my two research assistants Sadat Reza, currently a Ph.D. student in economics at York University, and Daniel Kennedy, former IMBA student here at Schulich School of Business, to whom I am deeply grateful for their invaluable assistance.

Farrokh Zandi

The Fundamentals of Managerial Economics

Headline

Stock Options to Align Management and Shareholder Interests: Their Values and Costs

Given the crisis in investor confidence these days, many business and investment pundits have publicly advocated the abolition of executive stock options, citing horror stories about wildly excessive option grants. Because options require no up-front cash from executives, the argument goes, there is no cash downside for the recipient. In some cases, CEOs have been almost free to write their own ticket, causing too many options to be granted to produce a given targeted net present value. There has long existed a rough rule of thumb for options that the net present value of an option grant, when allocated to each year of its term, should rarely if ever exceed the salary of the recipient.

This rule has, of course, been widely ignored, often flagrantly.

Others argue that the problem lies not in the principle but in the practice. They call for reforms that include limiting and controlling, by the board, the value of options granted, and granting them only in circumstances where corporate performance has been demonstrably superior.

What is the rationale for corporations' granting stock options? Are there any costs to CEOs of a failed stock option? If so, how are the costs measured?

Source: Adapted from *Canadian Business*, September 9, 2002.

Introduction

Many students taking managerial economics ask, "Why should I study economics? Will it tell me what the stock market will do tomorrow? Will it tell me where to invest my money or how to get rich?" Unfortunately, managerial economics by itself is unlikely to provide definitive answers to such questions. Obtaining the answers would require an accurate crystal ball. Nevertheless, managerial economics is a valuable tool for analyzing business situations such as the ones raised in the headlines that open each chapter of this book.[1]

In fact, if you surf the Internet, browse a business publication such as *The Globe and Mail* or *The National Post,* or read a trade publication such as *Restaurant News* or *Supermarket Business,* you will find a host of stories that involve managerial economics. A recent search generated the following headlines:

"Airline Sued for Predatory Pricing"

"Microsoft Loses Battle—Or Did It?"

"Competition Bureau Blocks Mergers Between Banks"

"NASDAQ Firm Pays $30.6 Million to Settle Price-Fixing Case"

"Telecommunication Firm's Plan to Cut Rates Unlikely to Boost Calls Much"

"Cola Price Wars Continue"

"The Recession: Great News?"

"Free Software on the Internet"

Sadly, billions of dollars are lost every year because many existing managers fail to use basic tools from managerial economics to shape pricing and output decisions, optimize the production process and input mix, choose product quality, guide horizontal and vertical merger decisions, or optimally design internal and external incentives. And happily, if you learn a few basic principles from managerial economics, you will be poised to drive the inept managers out of their jobs! You will also understand why the latest recession was great news to some firms and why some software firms spend millions on software development but permit consumers to download it for free.

Not only is managerial economics valuable to managers of Fortune 500 companies; it is also valuable to managers of not-for-profit organizations. It is useful to the manager of a food bank who must decide the best means for distributing food to the needy. It is valuable to the coordinator of a shelter for the homeless whose goal is to help the largest possible number of homeless, given a very tight budget. In fact, managerial economics provides useful insights into every facet of the business and nonbusiness world in which we live—including household decision making.

Why is managerial economics so valuable to such a diverse group of decision makers? The answer to this question lies in the meaning of the term *managerial economics.*

The Manager

manager
A person who directs resources to achieve a stated goal.

A **manager** is a person who directs resources to achieve a stated goal. This definition includes all individuals who (1) direct the efforts of others, including those who delegate tasks within an organization such as a firm, a family, or a club; (2) purchase

---

[1]Each chapter concludes with the solution to that chapter's opening Headline. After you read each chapter, you should attempt to solve the opening Headline on your own and then compare your solution to that presented at the end of the chapter.

inputs to be used in the production of goods and services such as the output of a firm, food for the needy, or shelter for the homeless; or (3) are in charge of making other decisions, such as product price or quality.

A manager generally has responsibility for his or her own actions as well as for the actions of individuals, machines, and other inputs under his or her control. This control may involve responsibilities for the resources of a multinational corporation or for those of a single household. In each instance, however, a manager must direct resources and the behaviour of individuals for the purpose of accomplishing some task. While much of this book assumes the manager's task is to maximize the profits of the firm that employs the manager, the underlying principles are valid for virtually any decision process.

Economics

economics
The science of making decisions in the situation of scarce resources.

The primary focus of this book is on the second word in *managerial economics*. **Economics** is the science of making decisions in the situation of scarce resources. *Resources* are simply anything used to produce a good or service or, more generally, to achieve a goal. Decisions are important because scarcity implies that by making one choice, you give up another. A computer firm that spends more resources on advertising has fewer resources to invest in research and development. A food bank that spends more on soup has less to spend on fruit. Economic decisions thus involve the allocation of scarce resources, and a manager's task is to allocate resources so as to best meet his or her goals.

One of the best ways to comprehend the pervasive nature of scarcity is to imagine that a genie has appeared and offered to grant you three wishes. If resources were not scarce, you would tell the genie you have absolutely nothing to wish for; you already have everything you want. Surely, as you begin this course, you recognize that time is one of the scarcest resources of all. Your primary decision problem is to allocate a scarce resource—time—to achieve a goal—presumably earning an A in this course.

Managerial Economics Defined

managerial economics
The study of how to direct scarce resources in the way that most efficiently achieves a managerial goal.

Managerial economics, therefore, is the study of how to direct scarce resources in the way that most efficiently achieves a managerial goal. It is a very broad discipline in that it describes methods useful for directing everything from the resources of a household to maximize household welfare to the resources of a firm to maximize profits.

To understand the nature of decisions that confront managers of firms, imagine that you are the manager of a Canadian Business Tech100 company that makes computers. You must make a host of decisions to succeed as a manager: Should you purchase components such as disk drives and chips from other manufacturers or produce them within your own firm? Should you specialize in making one type of computer or produce several different types? How many computers should you produce, and at what price should you sell them? How many employees should you hire, and how should you compensate them? How can you ensure that employees work hard and produce quality products? How will the actions of rival computer firms affect your decisions?

The key to making sound decisions is to know what information is needed to make an informed decision and then to collect and process the data. If you work for a large firm, your legal department can provide data about the legal ramifications of alternative decisions; your accounting department can provide tax advice and basic cost data; your marketing department can provide you with data on the characteristics of the market for your product; and your firm's financial analysts can provide summary data for alternative methods of obtaining financial capital. Ultimately, however, the manager must integrate all of this information, process it, and arrive at a decision. The remainder of this book will show you how to perform this important managerial function by using six principles that effective management comprises.

The Economics of Effective Management

The nature of sound managerial decisions varies depending on the underlying goals of the manager. Since this course is designed primarily for managers of firms, this book focuses on managerial decisions as they relate to maximizing profits or, more generally, the value of the firm. Before embarking on this special use of managerial economics, we provide an overview of the basic principles of effective management. In particular, an effective manager must (1) identify goals and constraints; (2) recognize the nature and importance of profits; (3) understand incentives; (4) understand markets; (5) recognize the time value of money; and (6) use marginal analysis.

Identify Goals and Constraints

The first step in making sound decisions is to have well-defined *goals* because achieving different goals entails making different decisions. If your goal is to maximize your grade in this course rather than maximize your overall grade-point average, your study habits will differ accordingly. Similarly, if the goal of a food bank is to distribute food to needy people in rural areas, its decisions and optimal distribution network will differ from those it would use to distribute food to needy inner-city residents. Notice that in both instances, the decision maker faces *constraints* that affect the ability to achieve a goal. The 24-hour day affects your ability to earn an A in this course; a budget affects the ability of the food bank to distribute food to the needy. Constraints are an artifact of scarcity.

Different units within a firm may be given different goals; those in a firm's marketing department might be instructed to use their resources to maximize sales or market share, while those in the firm's financial group might focus on earnings growth or risk-reduction strategies. Later in this book we will see how the firm's overall goal—maximizing profits—can be achieved by giving each unit within the firm an incentive to achieve potentially different goals.

Unfortunately, constraints make it difficult for managers to achieve goals such as maximizing profits or increasing market share. These constraints include such things as the available technology and the prices of inputs used in production. The goal of maximizing profits requires the manager to decide the optimal price to charge for a product, how much to produce, which technology to use, how much of each input to use, how to react to decisions made by competitors, and so on. This book provides tools for answering these types of questions.

Recognize the Nature and Importance of Profits

The overall goal of most firms is to maximize profits or the firm's value, and the remainder of this book will detail strategies managers can use to achieve this goal. Before we provide these details, let us examine the nature and importance of profits in a free-market economy.

Economic Versus Accounting Profits

When most people hear the word *profit,* they think of accounting profits. *Accounting profit* is the total amount of money taken in from sales (total revenue, or price times quantity sold) minus the dollar cost of producing goods or services. Accounting profits are what show up on the firm's income statement and are typically reported to the manager by the firm's accounting department.

A more general way to define profits is in terms of what economists refer to as economic profits. **Economic profits** are the difference between the total revenue and the total opportunity cost of producing the firm's goods or services. The **opportunity cost** of using a resource includes both the *explicit* (or *accounting*) *cost* of the resource and the *implicit cost* of giving up the next-best alternative use of the resource. The opportunity cost of producing a good or service generally is higher than accounting costs because it includes both the dollar value of costs (explicit, or accounting, costs) and any implicit costs.

Implicit costs are very hard to measure and therefore are often overlooked by managers. Effective managers, however, continually seek out data from other sources to identify and quantify implicit costs. Managers of large firms can use sources within the company, including the firm's finance, marketing, and/or legal departments, to obtain data about the implicit costs of decisions. In other instances managers must collect data on their own. For example, what does it cost you to read this book? The price you paid the bookstore for this book is an explicit (or accounting) cost, while the implicit cost is the value of what you are giving up by reading the book. You could be studying some other subject or watching TV, and each of these alternatives has some value to you. The "best" of these alternatives is your implicit cost of reading this book; you are giving up this alternative to read the book. Similarly, the opportunity cost of going to school is much higher than the cost of tuition and books; it also includes the amount of money you would earn had you decided to work rather than go to school.

In the business world, the opportunity cost of opening a restaurant is the next best alternative use of the resources used to establish the restaurant—say, opening a hairstyling salon. Again, these resources include not only the explicit financial resources needed to open the business but any implicit costs as well. Suppose you own a building in Vancouver that you use to run a small pizzeria. Food supplies are your only accounting costs. At the end of the year, your accountant informs you that these costs were $20 000 and that your revenues were $100 000. Thus, your accounting profits are $80 000.

However, these accounting profits overstate your economic profits, because the costs include only accounting costs. First, the costs do not include the time you spent running the business. Had you not run the business, you could have worked for someone else, and this fact reflects an economic cost not accounted for in accounting profits. To be concrete, suppose you could have worked for someone else for $30 000. Your opportunity cost of time would have been $30 000 for the year. Thus, $30 000 of your accounting profits are not profits at all but one of the implicit costs of running the pizzeria.

Second, accounting costs do not account for the fact that, had you not run the pizzeria, you could have rented the building to someone else. If the rental value of the building is $100 000 per year, you gave up this amount to run your own business. Thus, the costs of running the pizzeria include not only the costs of supplies ($20 000) but also the $30 000 you could have earned in some other business *and* the $100 000 you could have earned in renting the building to someone else. The economic cost of running the pizzeria is $150 000—the amount you gave up to run your business. Considering the revenue of $100 000, you actually lost $50 000 by running the pizzeria.

Throughout this book, when we speak of costs, we mean economic costs. Economic costs are opportunity costs and include not only the explicit (accounting) costs but also the implicit costs of the resources used in production.

economic profits
The difference between total revenue and total opportunity cost.

opportunity cost
The cost of the explicit and implicit resources that are forgone when a decision is made.

economic profits vs. opportunity cost examples

Inside BUSINESS

1–1 Profit and Principles: The Oil and Gas Industry Is Rethinking How It Does Business

It's an image engrained in the popular psyche by the 1980s prime-time soap *Dallas*. Big, bad oil company, led by ruthless J. R. Ewing, is interested only in maximizing profits—the environment and corporate responsibility be damned. Nor was J. R. ever accused of being innovative, unless it was about cheating one of his hapless business partners. But that image, says Shell Canada Ltd. president and CEO Linda Cook, is as dated as the TV series. "I think the industry has evolved quite a bit in the past 20 or 25 years," says Cook, 45, a Kansas native who became the first woman to head a major Canadian petroleum company this past summer. "Certainly, profits continue to be important, but we also need principles. We have to take into account not just economics, but the environmental and social implications of all that we do."

What Cook is talking about are things like community consultation, pollution reduction, and, yes, getting innovative about developing both hydrocarbons and other energy sources such as solar, wind, and hydrogen fuel cell power. According to the latest long-range forecast by Shell's parent, Royal Dutch/Shell, by 2050 oil and gas will supply about 50 percent of global energy needs with one-third coming from renewable sources and the rest from coal and nuclear energy. The lesson Cook takes from this is twofold. First, it's simply prudent for oil and

gas companies to get into the alternative energy game as Royal Dutch/Shell is doing by spending more than $500 million between 2000 and 2005 on fostering renewables. Second, it's essential to continue to find and produce new oil and gas deposits.

For Shell Canada, the most obvious example of the latter is the company's majority interest in the massive Athabasca Oil Sands Project near Fort McMurray, Alberta. When that fully comes on stream, it will produce 155 000 barrels a day of bitumen—or about 10 percent of Canada's oil needs. And as Shell expands its operations, it's also looking at new ways to develop the resource cleanly and efficiently. Shell researchers were recently recognized at the Alberta Science and Technology Awards for their work on a groundbreaking treatment process that allows the company to make more than 100 barrels of synthetic crude oil for every 100 barrels of standard bitumen—without producing coke (carbon) as a byproduct.

According to Cook, such measures not only cut costs, but also enhance a company's reputation. "Changing public expectations are raising the bar for what corporations do," she says. "People are telling us it is not just about making money."

Source: Maclean's, December 1, 2003.

The Role of Profits

A common misconception is that the firm's goal of maximizing profits is necessarily bad for society. Individuals who want to maximize profits often are considered self-interested, a quality that many people view as undesirable. However, consider Adam Smith's classic line from *The Wealth of Nations:* "It is not out of the benevolence of the butcher, the brewer, or the baker, that we expect our dinner, but from their regard to their own interest."[2]

Smith is saying that by pursuing its self-interest—the goal of maximizing profits—a firm ultimately meets the needs of society. If you cannot make a living as a rock singer, it is probably because society does not appreciate your singing; society would more highly value your talents in some other employment. If you break five dishes whenever you clean up after dinner, your talents are perhaps better suited for balancing the chequebook or mowing the lawn. Similarly, the profits of businesses signal where society's scarce resources are best allocated. When firms in a given industry earn economic profits, the opportunity cost to resource holders outside the industry increases. Owners of other resources soon recognize that, by continuing to operate their existing businesses, they are giving up profits. This induces new firms to enter the markets in which economic profits are available. As more firms enter the industry, the market price falls, and economic profits decline.

[2]Adam Smith, *An Inquiry into the Causes of the Wealth of Nations,* ed. Edwin Cannan (Chicago: University of Chicago Press, 1976).

Inside BUSINESS

1-2   Profits and the Computer Industry

The computer industry is one of the most dynamic industries in the world. Over the past two decades, many new firms entered the industry, and less-efficient firms left. The role of profits in the computer industry is to guide the use of resources used in manufacturing computers.

When profits in a given industry are higher than in other industries, we would expect more firms to enter that industry. When losses are recorded, some firms will likely leave the industry.

In the 1980s and 1990s small, medium-size, and large firms in the computer industry earned positive profits. According to economic theory, we would expect to see new firms enter the market to reap some of those profits. This is precisely what happened: over the past two

decades the number of firms selling personal computers has more than doubled. As a result of new entry and heightened competition, the overall profitability of firms in the industry has declined.

Thus, profits are a motivating factor in moving resources in and out of an industry. If we look at the advances in computer technology during the past decade, we see enormous improvement. In that short span of time, the speed of computers more than tripled, and storage capacity grew by more than a factor of 4. Profits therefore signalled productive resources into and out of the computer industry and helped generate great advances in technology. The ultimate result was better products at lower prices.

Thus, profits signal the owners of resources where the resources are most highly valued by society. By moving scarce resources toward the production of goods most valued by society, the total welfare of society is improved. As Adam Smith first noted, this phenomenon is due not to benevolence on the part of the firms' managers but to the self-interested goal of maximizing the firms' profits.

Principle	**PROFITS ARE A SIGNAL** Profits signal to resource holders where resources are most highly valued by society.

Understand Incentives

In our discussion of the role of profits, we emphasized that profits signal the holders of resources when to enter and exit particular industries. In effect, changes in profits provide an incentive to resource holders to alter their use of resources. Within a firm, *incentives* affect how resources are used and how hard workers work. To succeed as a manager, you must have a clear grasp of the role of incentives within an organization such as a firm and how to construct incentives to induce maximal effort from those you manage. Chapter 6 is devoted to this special aspect of managerial decision making, but it is useful here to provide a synopsis of how to construct proper incentives.

The first step in constructing incentives within a firm is to distinguish between the world, or the business place, as it is and the way you wish it were. Many professionals and owners of small establishments have difficulties because they do not fully comprehend the importance of the role incentives play in guiding the decisions of others.

A friend of mine—Mr. Hakim—opened a restaurant and hired a manager to run the business so he could spend time doing the things he enjoys. Recently, I asked him how his business was doing, and he reported that he had been losing money ever since the restaurant opened. When asked whether he thought the manager was doing a good job, he said, "For the $75 000 salary I pay the manager each year, the manager *should* be doing a good job."

Mr. Hakim believes the manager "should be doing a good job." This is the way he wishes the world was. But in the real world, individuals often are motivated by self-interest. This is not to say that people never act out of kindness or charity, but rather that human nature is such that people naturally tend to look after their own self-interest. Had Mr. Hakim taken a managerial economics course, he would know how to provide the manager with an incentive to do what is in Mr. Hakim's best interest. The key is to design a mechanism such that if the manager does what is in his or her *own* interest, he or she will indirectly do what is best for Mr. Hakim.

Since Mr. Hakim is not physically present at the restaurant to watch over the manager, he has no way of knowing what the manager is up to. Indeed, his unwillingness to spend time at the restaurant is what induced him to hire the manager in the first place. What type of incentive has he created by paying the manager $75 000 per year? The manager receives $75 000 per year regardless of whether he puts in 12-hour or 2-hour days. The manager receives no reward for working hard and incurs no penalty if he fails to make sound managerial decisions. The manager receives the same $75 000 regardless of the restaurant's profitability.

Fortunately, most business owners understand the problem just described. The owners of large corporations are shareholders, and most never set foot on company ground. How do they provide incentives for chief executive officers (CEOs) to be effective managers? Very simply, they provide them with "incentive plans" in the form of bonuses that are in direct proportion to the firm's profitability. If the firm does well, the CEO receives a large bonus. If the firm does poorly, the CEO receives no bonus and risks being fired by the stockholders. These types of incentives are also present at lower levels within firms. Some individuals earn commissions according to the revenue they generate for the firm's owner. If they put forth little effort, they receive little pay; if they put forth much effort and hence generate many sales, they receive a generous commission.

The thrust of managerial economics is to provide you with a broad array of skills that enable you to make sound economic decisions and to structure appropriate incentives within your organization. We will begin under the assumption that everyone with whom you come into contact is self-interested, that is, driven only by his or her own self-interest. In such a case, understanding incentives is a must. Of course, this is a worst-case scenario; more likely, some of your business contacts will not be so selfishly inclined. If you are so lucky, your job will be all the easier.

Understand Markets

In studying microeconomics in general, and managerial economics in particular, it is important to bear in mind that there are two sides to every transaction in a market: for every buyer of a good there is a corresponding seller. The final outcome of the market process, then, depends on the relative power of buyers and sellers in the marketplace. The power, or bargaining position, of consumers and producers in the market is limited by three sources of rivalry that exist in economic transactions: consumer–producer rivalry, consumer–consumer rivalry, and producer–producer rivalry. Each form of rivalry serves as a disciplining device to guide the market process, and each affects different markets to a different extent. Thus, your ability as a manager to meet performance objectives will depend on the extent to which your product is affected by these sources of rivalry.

Consumer–Producer Rivalry

Consumer–producer rivalry occurs because of the competing interests of consumers and producers. Consumers attempt to negotiate or locate low prices, while producers attempt to negotiate high prices. In a very loose sense, consumers attempt to "rip off" producers, and producers attempt to "rip off" consumers. Of course, there are limits to the ability of these parties to achieve their goals. If a consumer offers a price that is too low, the pro-

InsideBUSINESS

1-3 The Five Forces Model: The Link Between Strategic Management and Managerial Economics

Managerial economics provides tools that complement techniques learned in other business courses. For instance, courses in strategic management are designed to provide you with tools—like the Five Forces Model[1]—that help you see the big picture and frame questions that shape corporate strategy. Managerial economics provides additional tools that will help you refine the big picture and sort out the details required to implement your strategy.

The table here highlights the link between the Five Forces Model and managerial economics. As you can see,

the model suggests that the price you can charge for your product will depend on the nature of substitutes that exist for your product, the power you have over customers, and likely responses by your rivals. Managerial economics helps you quantify these effects, enabling you to figure out a specific price to charge in order to maximize profits or revenues.

[1]Michael Porter, *Competitive Strategy: Techniques for Analyzing Industries and Competitiors* (New York: Free Press, 1980).

Five Forces	General Question	Economic Tools Needed	Relevant Chapters
Substitutes	Do other firms produce substitutes for our product?	Demand elasticities, consumer preferences, consumer demand, regression analysis, product differentiation, consumer search	2–4, 8, 12
Customers	How much power do we have over consumers, and how does this affect our pricing and output decisions?	Demand elasticities, competition, monopoly, monopolistic competition, pricing strategies, reputation, regulation	3, 4, 8, 10, 11, 13, 14
Rivalry	How are rival firms likely to respond to our strategies?	Concentration, oligopoly, game theory, commitment, reputation, collusion, antitrust	7–11, 13, 14
Suppliers	From whom should we acquire inputs? How much and at what price?	Markets, productivity analysis, cost analysis, vertical integration, contracts, antitrust, auctions	2, 5–7, 12–14
New entrants	Is our position sustainable, or is entry into our market likely?	Economies of scale, entry barriers, entry deterrence, contestable markets, patents, product differentiation, commitment, government policy	5, 8–10, 13, 14

ducer will refuse to sell the product to the consumer. Similarly, if the producer asks a price that exceeds the consumer's valuation of a good, the consumer will refuse to purchase the good. These two forces provide a natural check and balance on the market process even in markets in which the product is offered by a single firm (a monopolist).

A classic example of consumer–producer rivalry is the transaction between the buyer of a new automobile and an automobile dealer. The consumer comes to the dealership with an idea of how much she is willing and able to pay for a new car. Of course, she wants to pay as little as possible, but she knows the dealer will not give her a car for free. If the highest price the consumer is willing and able to pay is less than the minimum price the dealer is willing and able to accept, no trade will take place. A car sale will result only when there is an overlap between the two prices.

In the case of the car dealership, the first offer is usually made by the car dealer in the form of a sticker price. Since the dealer wants to get as much money from the customer as possible, this first offer will be relatively high, but not so high as to scare off the customer. The customer, in turn, makes an initial offer for the car that is less than the amount she is actually willing and able to pay, but the offered price will not be so low that it scares off the dealer. After the initial offers have been made, the competition begins. Since neither party knows the most or the least the other is willing

InsideBUSINESS

1-4 Battle of the Giants—Sam's Club Is Taking on Costco in Canada and Giving Loblaw Food for Thought: A Case of Industry Rivalry and Threat of New Entrants

When shopping in a warehouse-club store, there's something about human nature that compels the average person to think that a 4.5-kilogram Toblerone chocolate bar or a can of tuna so big it could double as a wheel rim for a tire is a must-have item. Where else but a warehouse club can you pick up a 2.26-kilogram package of mixed fresh raw vegetables for $13.97, a $7890 diamond ring, and a big-screen TV for $3794 all in one trip? Call it the wow factor, when the novelty of stocking up on food and household staples combines with the serendipitous pleasure of finding a good deal on everything from patio furniture to computers. "We want people to feel excited when they come here, to think there's something different here every day," says Mario Pilozzi, president and CEO of Wal-Mart Canada, which opened four Sam's Club warehouse locations in the Toronto area on Oct. 30. It's the start of what he says will be a national chain of club stores. "Market research tells us there is great opportunity here."

Sure, warehouse clubs were originally designed with small-business customers in mind—the Toblerone bar (which sells for $59.97) is reportedly a popular door prize, and the 1.8-kilogram can of tuna (at a cost of $6.88) is meant more for restaurants or food kiosks than for making family lunches. But Canadian consumers—especially those who enjoy the trappings of a middle-class life—have come to enjoy cruising warehouse-club aisles, picking up large-format sizes of grocery and non-grocery products along with deals on one-time-only (what Pilozzi calls "treasure chest") items that change almost daily. Typically, shoppers head off to a club store, which charges an annual membership fee of between $40 and $50, with the intention of buying a few essentials at bargain prices. But often, they end up coming home with a couple of hundred dollars' worth of stuff they never knew they needed. The popularity of the concept is one reason why Costco Wholesale Canada—the country's only warehouse-club chain until the recent arrival of Sam's Club—brings in an estimated $8 billion in sales annually through its 62 stores.

It's no surprise, then, that Wal-Mart, the world's biggest and most successful retailer, would want to get in on the warehouse-club action in Canada, especially since Costco, a division of Costco Wholesale Corp. of Issaquah, Wash., has had the field to itself for years. But other than saying the chain will be national, and that two more outlets will open next year in London and Cambridge, Ont., Pilozzi won't divulge how many Sam's Clubs he expects to launch in Canada. Retail watchers have speculated the number could be as high as 50, with as many as 15 next year alone. Industry estimates are that the first Sam's Clubs—named after Wal-Mart founder Sam Walton—could do up to $2 million in business a week, or about $100 million a year.

However, David Schroeder, of Dominion Bond Rating Service in Toronto, says that on a sales-per-square-foot basis, Sam's Club stores in the United States do only about half the business of Costco outlets, which makes Costco's return on capital better than its rival's. "The management at Costco in the U.S. has been there for a long time, and they haven't messed with a successful strategy," Schroeder says. On the other hand, he adds, no one should underestimate Wal-Mart's ability to work on a retail strategy until they get it right.

Of course, the opening of Sam's Club in Canada has both retail watchers and the media trying to divine what Wal-Mart's latest venture means—especially whether it is a precursor to the arrival of Wal-Mart Supercenters, huge grocery stores with a low-price strategy that has dramatically changed the retail food industry in the United States. "The first four [Sam's Club] stores will be seen by some as signalling a coming food-industry apocalypse," CIBC World Markets analyst Perry Caicco says in a recent report. In reality, however, the impact of Sam's Club on the Canadian grocery sector will be minimal, says Caicco, and the new banner "does not in any way foreshadow the advent of Wal-Mart Supercenters in Canada." In fact, Caicco argues that the arrival of Sam's Club in Canada is proof that the giant grocery stores

and able to pay, the parties never know how close they got in the final transaction. However, one thing is certain: the buyer will try to get the lowest price possible, and the seller will try to get the highest price possible.

Consumer–Consumer Rivalry

A second source of rivalry that guides the market process occurs among consumers. *Consumer–consumer rivalry* reduces the negotiating power of consumers in the marketplace. It arises because of the economic doctrine of scarcity. When limited quantities of won't come here. "The Canadian grocery industry is strong, discount-oriented … and populated by large stores full of tremendous perishables and strong private-label programs," he says. "Wal-Mart Supercenters in this market would struggle."

Still, with Costco having slowed down its rate of growth in Canada in recent years, Caicco says the domestic warehouse-club industry is "understored," and that Wal-Mart recognizes a great opportunity to bring its Sam's Club banner here. While Schroeder says Costco had perhaps become "a bit complacent" in the absence of a direct competitor, the head of Costco in Canada, Louise Wendling, says that the chain is ready to grow again: she foresees about 10 new locations opening over the next couple of years. "We've always said we had a lot of room to grow in Canada," she says, pointing out in particular the potential to expand in the West and in Quebec.

Despite all the projected warehouse-club growth by Sam's Club and Costco, Caicco suggests the combined impact on the grocery industry would be minimal—a 0.66% grab of the Canadian consumer (non-business) food market by the end of 2005. A "worst-case" scenario would be a 1.53% grab of consumer food-market share by 2009, says Caicco, based on an estimate that the total number of warehouse-club stores would increase to 38 Sam's Clubs and 77 Costco outlets. But there would also be a gradual slowing in the rate of growth, with the two warehouse banners eventually starting to cannibalize from each other.

As for whether Sam's Club is a harbinger of Wal-Mart Supercenters in Canada, not everyone agrees with Caicco's assessment. Richard Talbot, a Toronto-based retail consultant, argues the launch of Sam's Clubs has expanded the amount of perishable items that Wal-Mart deals with—enhancing its ability to distribute grocery items beyond the "pantry" non-perishable goods and limited selection of fresh items it now sells in its original Wal-Mart stores. "Sam's Club is introducing the fresh and frozen stuff, so it's a relatively short leap to

Supercenters," says Talbot. He sees Wal-Mart's giant grocery stores beginning to roll out over the next 12 months. For his part, Pilozzi says there are currently no plans to open Supercenters in Canada, but adds he's not ruling anything out.

Whatever Wal-Mart does, Talbot says Canada's biggest grocer, Loblaw Cos. Ltd., is taking no chance. It is staking out a defensive strategy on both the grocery and non-grocery side of the business. One clear example is its decision to expand its own successful megastore banner, the Real Canadian Superstore, eastward from its strong base in provinces west of Ontario. Loblaw, which has 62 Real Canadian Superstores out west, recently opened three in Ontario and will open two more there by the end of November. The company plans to open at least a half dozen Superstores a year for several years. Such megastores offer not only a huge number of grocery items at discount prices, but they also sell everything from clothing to electronics, and typically have a gas bar and photo-finishing service. The stores also have a lower pay scale for workers on the non-grocery side, after successfully negotiating wage and scheduling concessions from their unions in Ontario. The launch of the Real Canadian Superstore banner in Ontario "demonstrates how aggressively Loblaw is prepared to attack the discount grocery segment," says analyst James Durran of National Bank Financial.

Loblaw spokesman Geoff Wilson insists that the company is simply doing its own thing, and sees a good opportunity to boost sales of non-grocery offerings. But Talbot says Loblaw is a shrewd retailer that "does everything with Wal-Mart in mind," and adds that while Sam's Club may not be a direct competitor, its arrival is just another reminder to stay alert. "Loblaw operates as if, when they wake up in the morning, Wal-Mart Supercenters have already arrived," says Talbot. "So if they ever do, they'll be ready."

Source: Canadian Business, November 24, 2003.

goods are available, consumers will compete with one another for the right to purchase the available goods. Consumers who are willing to pay the highest prices for the scarce goods will outbid other consumers for the right to consume the goods. Once again, this source of rivalry is present even in markets in which a single firm is selling a product.

A good example of consumer–consumer rivalry is an auction, a topic we will examine in detail in Chapter 12. The seller of the good attempts to get as many people as possible to bid on the item to initiate consumer–consumer rivalry. In Canada most auctions are ascending in nature. The auctioneer asks for a bid and, after receiving an opening bid, asks for someone to improve on that bid. Each potential consumer wants to buy the product for sale at the lowest possible price. However, each knows that if she or he offers some price that is lower than what others are willing and able to pay for the good, someone else will offer a higher price. At the end of the auction, the person who is willing and able to pay the highest price will get the item. But no matter what that price is, you can rest assured the actual buyer would have preferred to pay a lower price.

Producer–Producer Rivalry

A third source of rivalry in the marketplace is *producer–producer rivalry.* Unlike the other forms of rivalry, this disciplining device functions only when multiple sellers of a product compete in the marketplace. Given that customers are scarce, producers compete with one another for the right to service the customers available. Those firms that offer the best-quality product at the lowest price earn the right to serve the customers.

Pizza restaurants provide an excellent example of producer–producer rivalry. Each producer of pizza would prefer to be the only seller in town and be able to sell pizzas at a much higher price. But because there are many producers, the price of a pizza is relatively low. If only one store existed, the price of a pizza might be $20 or more. In fact, the first pizza parlors charged very high prices. Since there were economic profits to be made in the market for pizza, more companies opened restaurants. To attract customers, they offered a product similar to the pizza the existing restaurants offered, but at a lower price. The competition among producers of pizza is so strong that in most towns, two pizzas can be purchased for under $10. With producer–producer rivalry, each firm wants to sell its product for as much as possible, but the intense competition among sellers results in a much lower price.

Government and the Market

When agents on either side of the market find themselves disadvantaged in the market process, they frequently attempt to induce government to intervene on their behalf. For example, the market for electricity in most provinces is characterized by a sole provincial supplier of electricity, and thus there is no producer–producer rivalry. Consumer groups may initiate action by a public utility commission to limit the power of utilities in setting prices. Similarly, producers may lobby for government assistance to place them in a better bargaining position relative to consumers and foreign producers. Thus, in modern economies government also plays a role in disciplining the market process. Chapter 14 explores how government affects managerial decisions.

Recognize the Time Value of Money

The timing of many decisions involves a gap between the time when the costs of a project are borne and the time when the benefits of the project are received. In these instances it is important to recognize that $1 today is worth more than $1 received in the future. The reason is simple: the opportunity cost of receiving the $1 in the future is the forgone interest that could be earned were $1 received today. This opportunity cost reflects the *time value of money.* To properly account for the timing of receipts and expenditures, the manager must understand present value analysis.

present value (PV)
The amount that would have to be invested today at the prevailing interest rate to generate the given future value.

Present Value Analysis

The **present value (PV)** of an amount received in the future is the amount that would have to be invested today at the prevailing interest rate to generate the given future value. For example, suppose someone offered you $1.10 one year from today. What is the value today (the present value) of $1 to be received one year from today? Notice that if you could invest $1 today at a guaranteed interest rate of 10 percent, one year from now $1 would be worth $1 \times 1.1 = $1.10. In other words, over the course of one year, your $1 would earn $0.10 in interest. Thus, when the interest rate is 10 percent, the present value of receiving $1.10 one year in the future is $1.

A more general formula follows:

Formula (Present Value). The present value (PV) of a future value (FV) received n years in the future is

$$PV = \frac{FV_n}{(1 + i)^n} \tag{1–1}$$

where i is the guaranteed (risk-free) rate of interest.

For example, the present value of $100 in 10 years if the interest rate is at 7 percent is $50.76, since

$$PV = \frac{\$100}{(1 + 0.07)^{10}} = \frac{\$100}{1.97} = \$50.76$$

This essentially means that if you invested $50.76 today at a 7 percent interest rate, in 10 years your investment would be worth $100.

Notice that the interest rate appears in the denominator of the expression in Equation 1–1. This means that the higher the interest rate, the lower the present value of a future amount, and conversely. The present value of a future payment reflects the difference between the *future value (FV)* and the *opportunity cost of waiting (OCW)*: $PV = FV - OCW$. Intuitively, the higher the interest rate, the higher the opportunity cost of waiting to receive a future amount and thus the lower the present value of the future amount. For example, if the interest rate is zero, the opportunity cost of waiting is zero, and the present value and the future value coincide. This is consistent with Equation 1–1, since $PV = FV$ when the interest rate is zero.

The basic idea of the present value of a future amount can be extended to a series of future payments. For example, if you are promised FV_1 one year in the future, FV_2 two years in the future, and so on for n years, the present value of this sum of future payments is

$$PV = \frac{FV_1}{(1 + i)^1} + \frac{FV_2}{(1 + i)^2} + \frac{FV_3}{(1 + i)^3} + \ldots + \frac{FV_n}{(1 + i)^n}$$

Formula (Present Value of a Stream). When the interest rate is i, the present value of a stream of future payments of $FV_1, FV_2, \ldots, FV_n$ is

$$PV = \sum_{t=1}^{n} \frac{FV_t}{(1 + i)^t} \tag{1–2}$$

net present value (NPV)
The present value of the income stream generated by a project minus the current cost of the project.

Given the present value of the income stream that arises from a project, one can easily compute the net present value of the project. The **net present value (NPV)** of a project is simply the present value (PV) of the income stream generated by the project minus the current cost (C_0) of the project: $NPV = PV - C_0$. If the net present value of a project is positive, then the project is profitable because the present value of the earnings from the project exceed the current cost of the project. On the other hand, a manager should reject a project that has a negative net present value, since the cost of such a project exceeds the present value of the income stream that project generates.

Formula (Net Present Value). Suppose that by sinking C_0 dollars into a project today, a firm will generate income of FV_1 one year in the future, FV_2 two years in the future, and so on for n years. If the interest rate is i, the net present value of the project is

$$NPV = \frac{FV_1}{(1 + i)^1} + \frac{FV_2}{(1 + i)^2} + \frac{FV_3}{(1 + i)^3} + \ldots + \frac{FV_n}{(1 + i)^n} - C_0$$

Demonstration PROBLEM 1–1

The manager of Automated Products is contemplating the purchase of a new machine that will cost $300 000 and has a useful life of five years. The machine will yield (year-end) cost reductions to Automated Products of $50 000 in year 1, $60 000 in year 2, $75 000 in year 3, and $90 000 in years 4 and 5. What is the present value of the cost savings of the machine if the interest rate is 8 percent? Should the manager purchase the machine?

Answer

By spending $300 000 today on a new machine, the firm will reduce costs by $365 000 over five years. However, the present value of the cost savings is only

$$PV = \frac{50\,000}{1.08} + \frac{60\,000}{1.08^2} + \frac{75\,000}{1.08^3} + \frac{90\,000}{1.08^4} + \frac{90\,000}{1.08^5} = \$284\,679$$

Consequently, the net present value of the new machine is

$$NPV = PV - C_0 = \$284\,679 - \$300\,000 = -\$15\,321$$

Since the net present value of the machine is negative, the manager should not purchase the machine. In other words, the manager could earn more by investing the $300 000 at 8 percent than by spending the money on the cost-saving technology.

Present Value of Indefinitely Lived Assets

Some decisions generate cash flows that continue indefinitely. For instance, consider an asset that generates a cash flow of CF_0 today, CF_1 one year from today, CF_2 two years from today, and so on for an indefinite period of time. If the interest rate is i, the value of the asset is given by the present value of these cash flows:

$$PV_{Asset} = CF_0 + \frac{CF_1}{(1 + i)} + \frac{CF_2}{(1 + i)^2} + \frac{CF_3}{(1 + i)^3} + \ldots$$

While this formula contains terms that continue indefinitely, for certain patterns of future cash flows one can readily compute the present value of the asset. For instance, suppose that the current cash flow is zero ($CF_0 = 0$) and that all future cash flows are identical ($CF_1 = CF_2 = \ldots$). In this case the asset generates a perpetual stream of identical cash flows at the end of each period. If each of these future cash flows is CF, the value of the asset is the present value of the perpetuity:

$$PV_{Perpetuity} = \frac{CF}{(1+i)} + \frac{CF}{(1+i)^2} + \frac{CF}{(1+i)^3} + \dots$$

$$= \frac{CF}{i}$$

Examples of such an asset include perpetual bonds and preferred stocks. Each of these assets pays the owner a fixed amount at the end of each period, indefinitely. According to the above formula, the value of a perpetual bond that pays the owner $100 at the end of each year when the interest rate is fixed at 5 percent is given by

$$PV_{Perpetual\ bond} = \frac{CF}{i} = \frac{\$100}{0.05} = \$2000 \tag{1-3}$$

Present value analysis is also useful in determining the value of a firm, since the value of a firm is the present value of the stream of profits (cash flows) generated by the firm's physical, human, and intangible assets. In particular, if π_0 is the firm's current level of profits, then π_1 is next year's profit, and so on. Therefore, the value of the firm is:

$$PV_{Firm} = \pi_0 + \frac{\pi_1}{(1+i)} + \frac{\pi_2}{(1+i)^2} + \frac{\pi_3}{(1+i)^3} + \dots$$

In other words, the value of the firm today is the present value of its current and future profits. To the extent that the firm is a "going concern" that lives on forever even after its founder dies, firm ownership represents a claim to assets with an indefinite profit stream.

Notice that the *value of a firm* takes into account the long-term impact of managerial decisions on profits. When economists say that the goal of the firm is to maximize profits, it should be understood to mean that the firm's goal is to maximize its value, which is the present value of current and future profits.

Principle	**PROFIT MAXIMIZATION** Maximizing profits means maximizing the value of the firm, which is the present value of current and future profits.

While it is beyond the scope of this book to present all of the tools that Bay Street analysts use to estimate the value of firms, it is possible to gain insight into the issues involved by making a few simplifying assumptions. Suppose a firm's current profits are π_0, and that these profits have not yet been paid out to stockholders as dividends. Imagine that these profits are expected to grow at a constant rate of g percent each year, and that profit growth is less than the interest rate ($g < i$). In this case, profits one year from today will be $(1 + g)\pi_0$, profits two years from today will be $(1 + g)^2\pi_0$, and so on. The value of the firm, under these assumptions, is

$$PV_{Firm} = \pi_0 + \frac{\pi_0(1+g)}{(1+i)} + \frac{\pi_0(1+g)^2}{(1+i)^2} + \frac{\pi_0(1+g)^3}{(1+i)^3} + \dots$$

$$= \pi_0\left(\frac{1+i}{i-g}\right) \tag{1-4}$$

For a given interest rate and growth rate of the firm, it follows that maximizing the lifetime value of the firm (long-term profits) is equivalent to maximizing the firm's current (short-term) profits of π_0.

You may wonder how this formula changes if current profits have already been paid out as dividends. In this case, the present value of the firm is the present value of future profits (since current profits have already been paid out). The value of the firm immediately after its current profits have been paid out as dividends (called the *ex-dividend date*) may be obtained by simply subtracting π_0 from the above equation:

$$PV_{Firm}^{Ex\text{-}dividend} = PV_{Firm} - \pi_0$$

This may be simplified to yield the following formula:

$$PV_{Firm}^{Ex\text{-}dividend} = \pi_0\left(\frac{1+g}{i-g}\right)$$

Thus, so long as the interest rate and growth rate are constant, the strategy of maximizing current profits also maximizes the value of the firm on the ex-dividend date.

Principle

MAXIMIZING SHORT-TERM PROFITS MAY MAXIMIZE LONG-TERM PROFITS

If the growth rate in profits is less than the interest rate and both are constant, maximizing long-term profits is the same as maximizing current (short-term) profits.

Demonstration PROBLEM 1–2

Suppose the interest rate is 10 percent and the firm is expected to grow at a rate of 5 percent for the foreseeable future. The firm's current profits are $100 million.
(a) What is the value of the firm (the present value of its current and future earnings)?
(b) What is the value of the firm immediately after it pays a dividend equal to its current profits?

Answer
(a) The value of the firm is

$$PV_{Firm} = \pi_0 + \frac{\pi_0(1+g)}{(1+i)} + \frac{\pi_0(1+g)^2}{(1+i)^2} + \frac{\pi_0(1+g)^3}{(1+i)^3} + \ldots$$

$$= \pi_0\left(\frac{1+i}{i-g}\right)$$

$$= \$100\left(\frac{1+0.1}{0.1-0.05}\right) = (\$100)(22) = \$2200 \text{ million}$$

(b) The value of the firm on the ex-dividend date is this amount ($2200 million) less the current profits paid out as dividends ($100 million), or $2100 million. Alternatively, this may be calculated as

$$PV_{Firm}^{Ex\text{-}dividend} = \pi_0\left(\frac{1+g}{i-g}\right)$$

$$= (\$100)\left(\frac{1+0.05}{0.1-0.05}\right) = (\$100)(21) = \$2100 \text{ million}$$

Inside BUSINESS

Recently, a major airline offered a one-year membership in its Air Club for $125; alternatively, one could purchase a three-year membership for $300. Many managers and executives join air clubs because they offer a quiet place to work or relax while on the road; thus, productivity is enhanced.

Let's assume you wish to join the club for three years. Should you pay the up-front $300 fee for a three-year membership or pay $125 per year for three years for total payments of $375? For simplicity, let's suppose the airline will not change the annual fee of $125 over the next three years.

On the surface it appears that you save $75 by paying for three years in advance. But this approach ignores the time value of money. Is paying for all three years in advance profitable when you take the time value of money into account?

The present value of the cost of membership if you pay for three years in advance is $300, since all of that money is paid today. If you pay annually, you pay $125 today, $125 one year from today, and $125 two years from today. Given an interest rate of 5 percent, the present value of these payments is

$$PV = \$125 + \frac{\$125}{1.05} + \frac{\$125}{(1.05)^2}$$

or

$$PV = 125 + 119.05 + 113.38$$
$$= \$357.43$$

Thus, in present value terms, you save $57.43 if you pay for three years in advance. If you wish to join for three years and expect annual fees to either remain constant or rise over the next three years, it is better to pay in advance. Given the current interest rate, the airline is offering a good deal, but the present value of the savings is $57.43, not $75.

While the notion of the present value of a firm is very general, the simplified formula presented above is based on the assumption that the growth rate of the firm's profits is constant. In reality, however, the investment and marketing strategies of the firm will affect its growth rate. Moreover, the strategies used by competitors generally will affect the growth rate of the firm. In such instances, there is no substitute for using the general present value formula and understanding the concepts developed in later chapters in this book.

Use Marginal Analysis

Marginal analysis is one of the most important managerial tools—a tool we will use repeatedly throughout this text in alternative contexts. Simply put, *marginal analysis* states that optimal managerial decisions involve comparing the marginal (or incremental) benefits of a decision with the marginal (or incremental) costs. For example, the optimal amount of studying for this course is determined by comparing (1) the improvement in your grade that will result from an additional hour of studying and (2) the additional costs of studying an additional hour. So long as the benefits of studying an additional hour exceed the costs of studying an additional hour, it is profitable to continue to study. However, once an additional hour of studying adds more to costs than it does to benefits, you should stop studying.

More generally, let $TR(Q)$ denote the total revenue derived from Q units of some variable that is within the manager's control. This is a very general idea: $TR(Q)$ may be the revenue a firm generates from producing Q units of output; it may be the benefits associated with distributing Q units of food to the needy; or, in the context of our previous example, it may represent the benefits derived by studying Q hours for an exam. Let $TC(Q)$ represent the total costs of the corresponding level of Q. Depending on the nature of the decision problem, $TC(Q)$ may be the total cost to a firm of producing Q units of output, the total cost to a food bank of providing Q units of food to the needy, or the total cost to you of studying Q hours for an exam.

Discrete Decisions

We first consider the situation where the managerial control variable is discrete. In this instance, the manager faces a situation like that summarized in columns 1 through 3 in Table 1–1. Notice that the manager cannot use fractional units of Q; only integer values are possible. This reflects the discrete nature of the problem. In the context of a production decision, Q may be the number of litres of soft drink produced. The manager must decide how many litres of soft drink to produce (0, 1, 2, and so on), but cannot choose to produce fractional units (for example, half a litre). Column 2 of Table 1–1 provides hypothetical data for total revenue; column 3 gives hypothetical data for total costs.

Suppose the objective of the manager is to maximize the net profits (or profits)

$$\pi(Q) = TR(Q) - TC(Q)$$

which represent the premium of total revenue over total costs of using Q units of the managerial control variable, Q. The profits—$\pi(Q)$—for our hypothetical example are given in column 4 of Table 1–1. Notice that the profits in column 4 are maximized when profits equal 200, which occurs when 5 units of Q are chosen by the manager.[3]

To illustrate the importance of marginal analysis in maximizing profits, it is useful to define a few terms. **Marginal revenue** refers to the additional revenue that arises by using an additional unit of the managerial control variable. For example, the marginal revenue of the first unit of Q is 90, since the first unit of Q increases total

marginal revenue
The change in total revenue arising from a change in the managerial control variable, Q.

TABLE 1–1	Determining the Optimal Level of a Control Variable: The Discrete Case					
(1) Control Variable Q	(2) Total Revenue $TR(Q)$	(3) Total Costs $TC(Q)$	(4) Profit $\pi(Q)$	(5) Marginal Revenue $MR(Q)$	(6) Marginal Cost $MC(Q)$	(7) Marginal Profit $M\pi(Q)$
Given	Given	Given	(2) − (3)	Δ(2)	Δ(3)	Δ(4) or (5) − (6)
0	0	0	0	—	—	—
1	90	10	80	90	10	80
2	170	30	140	80	20	60
3	240	60	180	70	30	40
4	300	100	200	60	40	20
5	350	150	200	50	50	0
6	390	210	180	40	60	−20
7	420	280	140	30	70	−40
8	440	360	80	20	80	−60
9	450	450	0	10	90	−80
10	450	550	−100	0	100	−100

---

[3]Actually, net profits are equal to 200 for either 4 or 5 units of Q. This is due to the discrete nature of the data in the table, which restricts Q to be selected in one-unit increments. In the next section, we show that when Q can be selected in arbitrarily small increments (for example, when the firm can produce fractional litres of soft drink), net profits are maximized at a single level of Q. At this level of Q, marginal profits are equal to zero, which corresponds to 5 units of Q in Table 1–1.

revenue from 0 to 90. The marginal revenue of the second unit of Q is 80, since increasing Q from 1 to 2 increases total revenue from 90 to 170. The marginal revenue of each unit of Q—$MR(Q)$—is presented in column 5 of Table 1–1.

marginal cost
The change in total costs arising from a change in the managerial control variable, Q.

Marginal cost, on the other hand, is the additional cost incurred by using an additional unit of the managerial control variable. Marginal costs—$MC(Q)$—are given in column 6 of Table 1–1. For example, the marginal cost of the first unit of Q is 10, since the first unit of Q increases total costs from 0 to 10. Similarly, the marginal cost of the second unit of Q is 20, since increasing Q from 1 to 2 increases total costs by 20 (costs rise from 10 to 30).

marginal profits
The change in net profits that arises from a one-unit change in Q.

Finally, the **marginal profits** of Q—$M\pi(Q)$—are the change in net profits that arises from a one-unit change in Q. For example, by increasing Q from 0 to 1, net benefits rise from 0 to 80 in column 4 of Table 1–1, and thus the marginal net profit of the first unit of Q is 80. By increasing Q from 1 to 2, net profits increase from 80 to 140, so the marginal profits due to the second unit of Q is 60. Column 7 of Table 1–1 presents marginal profits for our hypothetical example. Notice that marginal profits may also be obtained as the difference between marginal revenue and marginal costs:

$$M\pi(Q) = MR(Q) - MC(Q)$$

Inspection of Table 1–1 reveals a remarkable pattern in the columns. Notice that by using 5 units of Q, the manager ensures that profits are maximized. At the profit-maximizing level of Q (5 units), the marginal profits of Q are zero. Furthermore, at the profit-maximizing level of Q (5 units), marginal revenue equals marginal costs (both are equal to 50 in this example). There is an important reason why $MR = MC$ at the level of Q that maximizes profits: so long as marginal revenue exceeds marginal costs, an increase in Q adds more to total revenue than it does to total costs. In this instance, it is profitable for the manager to increase the use of the managerial control variable. Expressed differently, when marginal revenue exceeds marginal costs, the profits of increasing the use of Q are positive; by using more Q, profits increase. For example, consider the use of 1 unit of Q in Table 1–1. By increasing Q to 2 units, total revenue increases by 80 and total costs increase by only 20. Increasing the use of Q from 1 to 2 units is profitable, because it adds more to total revenue than it does to total costs.

Principle

MARGINAL PRINCIPLE
To maximize profits, the manager should increase the managerial control variable to the point where marginal revenue equals marginal costs. This level of the managerial control variable corresponds to the level at which marginal profits are zero; nothing more can be gained by further changes in that variable.

Notice in Table 1–1 that while 5 units of Q maximizes profits, it does not maximize total revenue. In fact, total revenue is maximized at 10 units of Q, where marginal revenue is zero. The reason the profit-maximizing level of Q is less than the level of Q that maximizes total revenue is that there are costs associated with achieving more total revenue. The goal of maximizing profits takes costs into account, while the goal of maximizing total revenue does not. In the context of a firm, maximizing total revenue is equivalent to maximizing revenues without regard for costs. In the context of studying for an exam, maximizing total revenue requires studying until you maximize your grade, regardless of how much it costs you to study.

Continuous Decisions

The basic principles for making decisions when the control variable is discrete also apply to the case of a continuous control variable. The basic relationships in Table 1–1 are depicted graphically in Figure 1–1. The top panel of the figure presents the total revenue and total costs of using different levels of Q under the assumption that Q is infinitely divisible (instead of allowing the firm to produce soft drinks only in one-litre containers as in Table 1–1, it can now produce fractional units). The middle panel presents the profits, $TR(Q) - TC(Q)$, and represents the vertical difference between TR and TC in the top panel. Notice that profits are maximized at the point where the difference between $TR(Q)$ and $TC(Q)$ is the greatest in the top panel. Furthermore, the slope of $TR(Q)$ is $\Delta TR/\Delta Q$, or marginal revenue, and the slope of $TC(Q)$ is $\Delta TC/\Delta Q$, or marginal cost. The slopes of the total revenue curve and the total cost curve are equal when profits are maximized. This is just another way of saying that when profits are maximized, $MR = MC$. Furthermore, the total revenue is maximized at the point where $TR(Q)$ is at its maximum.

Principle	**MARGINAL VALUE CURVES ARE THE SLOPES OF TOTAL VALUE CURVES**
	When the control variable is infinitely divisible, the slope of a total value curve at a given point is the marginal value at that point. In particular, the slope of the total revenue curve at a given Q is the marginal revenue of that level of Q. The slope of the total cost curve at a given Q is the marginal cost of that level of Q. The slope of the profits curve at a given Q is the marginal profit of that level of Q.

A Calculus ALTERNATIVE

Since the slope of a function is the derivative of that function, the preceding principle means that the derivative of a given function is the marginal value of that function. For example,

$$MR = \frac{dTR(Q)}{dQ}$$

$$MC = \frac{dTC(Q)}{dQ}$$

$$M\pi = \frac{d(\pi)}{dQ}$$

The bottom panel of Figure 1–1 depicts the marginal revenue, marginal costs, and marginal profits. At the level of Q where the marginal revenue curve intersects the marginal cost curve, marginal profits are zero. That level of Q maximizes profits. Note that the total revenue is maximized where $MR = 0$.

FIGURE 1–1 Determining the Optimal Level of a Control Variable: The Continuous Case

The optimum level of output, where marginal profit ($M\pi$) is maximized, is shown in all three panels. Panel (a) does this by setting $MR = MC$, or where the gap between revenue and costs—$TR(Q) - TC(Q)$—is at its maximum. Panel (b) shows the same level of output, by depicting the maximum point of the $TR(Q) - TC(Q)$, where the slope of the curve is zero. Panel (c) shows the optimal level of output by setting $M\pi = 0$. The level of output where total revenue is maximized is shown in panels (a) and (c). In panel (a), this happens where $TR(Q)$ is at its maximum, and in panel (c) where $MR = 0$.

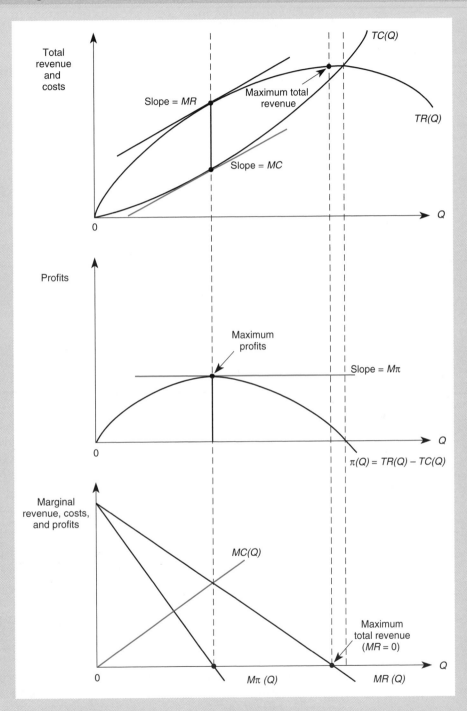

Demonstration PROBLEM 1–3

An engineering firm recently conducted a study to determine its revenue and cost structure. The results of the study are as follows:

$$TR(Y) = 300Y - 6Y^2$$

$$TC(Y) = 4Y^2$$

so that $MR = 300 - 12Y$ and $MC = 8Y$. The manager has been asked to determine the maximum level of profits and the level of Y that will yield that result.

Answer

Equating MR and MC yields $300 - 12Y = 8Y$. Solving this equation for Y reveals that the optimal level of Y is $Y^* = 15$. Plugging $Y^* = 15$ into the profit relation yields the maximum level of profits:

$$\pi = 300(15) - (6)(15^2) - (4)(15^2) = 2250$$

Incremental Decisions

Sometimes managers are faced with proposals that require a simple "thumbs up" or "thumbs down" decision. Marginal analysis is the appropriate tool to use for such decisions; the manager should adopt a project if the additional revenues that will be earned if the project is adopted exceed the additional costs required to implement the project. In the case of yes-or-no decisions, the additional revenues derived from a decision are called **incremental revenues**. The additional costs that stem from the decision are called **incremental costs**.

To illustrate, imagine that you are the CEO of Slick Drilling Inc.—a crude oil exploration and extraction company—and you must decide whether to drill for crude oil around Utikuma Lake in Alberta. You are relatively certain there are 10 000 barrels of crude oil at this location. An accountant working for you prepared the information in Table 1–2 to help you decide whether to adopt the new project.

incremental revenues
The additional revenues that stem from a yes-or-no decision.

incremental costs
The additional costs that stem from a yes-or-no decision.

TABLE 1–2	Incremental Costs and Revenues of the New Drilling Project		
	Current Situation	After New Drilling Project	Incremental Revenues and Costs
Total revenue	$1 740 400	$1 923 600	$183 200
Variable cost			
Drill augers	750 000	840 000	90 000
Temporary workers	500 000	575 000	75 000
Total variable cost	1 250 000	1 415 000	165 000
Direct fixed costs			
Depreciation—equipment	120 000	120 000	
Total direct fixed cost	120 000	120 000	0
Indirect fixed costs			
Supervisors' salaries	240 000	240 000	
Office supplies	30 000	30 000	
Total indirect fixed cost	270 000	270 000	0
Profit	$ 100 400	$ 118 600	$ 18 200

While the accountant supplied you with a lot of information in Table 1–2, the only data relevant for your decision are the incremental revenues and costs of adopting the new drilling project. In particular, notice that your direct and indirect fixed costs are the same regardless of whether you adopt the project and therefore are irrelevant to your decision. In contrast, note that your revenues increase by \$183 200 if you adopt the project. This change in revenues stemming from the adoption of the project represents your incremental revenues. To earn these additional revenues, however, you must spend an additional \$90 000 for drill augers and \$75 000 for additional temporary workers. The sum of these costs—\$165 000—represents the incremental cost of the new drilling project. Since your incremental revenues of \$183 200 exceed the incremental costs of \$165 000, you should give your "thumbs up" to the new project. Doing so adds \$18 200 to your bottom line.

Learning Managerial Economics

Before we continue our analysis of managerial economics, it is useful to provide some hints about how to study economics. Becoming proficient in economics is like learning to play music or ride a bicycle: the best way to learn is to practise, practise, and practise some more. Practising managerial economics means practising making decisions, and the best way to do this is to work and rework the problems presented in the text and at the end of each chapter. Before you can be effective at practising, however, you must understand the language of economics.

The terminology in economics has two purposes. First, the definitions and formulas economists use are needed for precision. Economics deals with very complex issues, and much confusion can be avoided by using the language economists have designed to break down complex issues into manageable components. Second, precise terminology helps practitioners of economics communicate more efficiently. It would be difficult to communicate if, like Dr. Seuss, each of us made words mean whatever we wanted them to mean. However, the terminology is not an end in itself but simply a tool that makes it easier to communicate and analyze different economic situations.

Understanding the definitions used in economics is like knowing the difference between a whole note and a quarter note in music. Without such an understanding, it would be very difficult for anyone other than an extremely gifted musician to learn to play an instrument or to communicate to another musician how to play a new song. Given an understanding of the language of music, anyone willing to take the time to practise can make beautiful music. The same is true of economics: Anyone willing to learn the language of economics and take the time to practise making decisions can learn to be an effective manager.

ANSWERING THE Headline

One characteristic of many large firms is the separation of ownership and control. In this case, the firm is run on a day-to-day basis by the managers, while the owners are not physically present to monitor the manager. How can the owner get the manager to do his or her job? A profit-sharing compensation scheme known as an *incentive contract* appears to provide a solution to this dilemma. Typically, CEOs receive stock options and bonuses directly related to profits. Share ownership provides both the upside potential for gain and the downside risk of loss that put management and shareholders in precisely the same position. However, it is also important to recognize that, contrary to conventional wisdom, the holder of a failed option does incur costs. First, there is the loss of the net present value of the option, as estimated at time of the grant—the amount that would have to be invested today at the prevailing interest rate to generate the given future value. There is also the opportunity cost lost by missing out on other, more secure forms of compensation, forgone by choosing or being asked to accept options.

Key Terms and Concepts

economic profits 5	marginal cost 19
economics 3	marginal revenue 18
incremental cost 22	marginal profit 19
incremental revenue 22	net present value (*NPV*) 13
manager 2	opportunity cost 5
managerial economics 3	present value (*PV*) 12

Conceptual and Computational Questions

1. Levi Strauss & Co. paid $46 532 for a 110-year-old pair of Levi's jeans—the oldest known pair of blue jeans—by outbidding several other bidders in an eBay Internet auction. Does this situation best represent producer–producer rivalry, consumer–consumer rivalry, or producer–consumer rivalry? Explain.

2. What is the maximum amount you would pay for an asset that generates an income of $150 000 at the end of each of five years if the opportunity cost of using funds is 9 percent?

3. Suppose that the total revenue and total cost from an activity are, respectively, given by the following equations: $TR(Q) = 150 + 28Q - 5Q^2$ and $TC(Q) = 100 + 8Q$. (*Note:* $MR(Q) = 28 - 10Q$ and $MC(Q) = 8$.)
   a. Write out the equation for the profits.
   b. What are the profits when $Q = 1$? $Q = 5$?
   c. Write out the equation for the marginal profits.
   d. What are the marginal profits when $Q = 1$? $Q = 5$?
   e. What level of Q maximizes profits?
   f. At the value of Q that maximizes profits, what is the value of marginal profit?
   g. What level of Q maximizes total revenue?
   h. At the value of Q that maximizes total revenue, what is the value of marginal revenue?

4. A firm's current profits are $550 000. These profits are expected to grow indefinitely at a constant annual rate of 5 percent. If the firm's opportunity cost of funds is 8 percent, determine the value of the firm
   a. The instant before it pays out current profits as dividends
   b. The instant after it pays out current profits as dividends

5. What is the value of a preferred stock that pays a perpetual dividend of $75 at the end of each year when the interest rate is 4 percent?

6. Complete the following table and answer these questions:
   a. At what level of the control variable are net profits maximized?
   b. What is the relation between marginal revenue and marginal cost at this level of the control variable?

Control Variable Q	Total Revenue TR(Q)	Total Cost TC(Q)	Profits π(Q)	Marginal Revenue MR(Q)	Marginal Cost MC(Q)	Marginal Profit Mπ(Q)
100	1200	950		210	40	
101	1400				50	
102	1590				60	
103	1770				70	
104	1940				80	
105	2100				90	
106	2250				100	
107	2390				110	
108	2520				120	
109	2640				130	
110	2750				140	

7. It is estimated that over 10 000 students will apply to the top 10 MBA programs in Canada this year.
   a. Using the concept of net present value and opportunity cost, explain when it is rational for an individual to pursue an MBA degree.
   b. What would you expect to happen to the number of applicants if the starting salaries of managers with MBA degrees remained constant but salaries of managers without such degrees increased by 15 percent? Why?

8. Jaynet spends $20 000 per year on painting supplies and storage space. She recently received two job offers from a famous marketing firm—one for $100 000 per year and the other for $90 000. However, she turned both jobs down to continue a painting career. If Jaynet sells 20 paintings per year at a price of $10 000 each
   a. What are her accounting profits?
   b. What are her economic profits?

Problems and Applications

9. You've recently learned that the company where you work is being sold for $275 000. The company's income statement indicates current profits of $10 000, which have yet to be paid out as dividends. Assuming the company will remain a "going concern" into the infinite future and that the interest rate will remain constant at 10 percent, at what constant rate does the owner believe that profits will grow? Does this seem reasonable?

10. You are in the market for a new refrigerator for your company's lounge, and you have narrowed the search down to two models. The energy-efficient model sells for $500 and will save you $25 at the end of each of the next five years in electricity costs. The standard model has features similar to the energy-efficient model but provides no future saving in electricity costs. It is priced at only $400. Assuming your opportunity cost of funds is 5 percent, which refrigerator should you purchase?

11. You are the human resources manager for a famous retailer, and you are trying to convince the president of the company to change the structure of employee compensation. Currently, the company's retail sales staff is paid a flat hourly wage of $18 per hour for each eight-hour shift worked. You propose a new pay structure whereby each salesperson in a store would be compensated $8 per hour, plus five-tenths of 1 percent of that store's daily profits. Assume that, when run efficiently, each

store's maximum daily profits are $40 000. Outline the arguments that support your proposed plan.

12. Tara is considering leaving her current job, which pays $56 000 per year, to start a new company that manufactures a line of special pens for personal digital assistants. Based on market research, she can sell about 160 000 units during the first year at a price of $20 per unit. With annual overhead costs and operating expenses amounting to $3 160 000, Tara expects a profit margin of 25 percent. This margin is 6 percent larger than that of her largest competitor, Pens, Inc.

    a. If Tara decides to embark on her new venture, what will her accounting costs be during the first year of operation? Her implicit costs? Her opportunity costs?

    b. Suppose that Tara's estimated selling price is lower than originally projected during the first year. How much revenue would she need in order to earn positive accounting profits? Positive economic profits?

13. Approximately 1 million Canadians are addicted to drugs and alcohol. The federal government estimates that these addicts cost the Canadian economy $30 billion in medical expenses and lost productivity. Despite the enormous potential market, many biotech companies have shied away from funding research and development (R&D) initiatives to find a cure for drug and alcohol addiction. Your firm—DrugAbuse Sciences (DAS)—is a notable exception. It has spent $17 million to date working on a cure, but is now at a crossroads. It can either abandon its program or invest another $3 million today. Unfortunately, the firm's opportunity cost of funds is 7 percent and it will take another five years before final approval from Health Canada is achieved and the product is actually sold. Expected (year-end) profits from selling the drug are presented in the table here. Should DAS continue with its plan to bring the drug to market, or should it abandon the project? Explain.

Year-End Profit Projections

Year 1	Year 2	Year 3	Year 4	Year 5	Year 6	Year 7	Year 8	Year 9
$0	$0	$0	$0	$15 000 000	$16 500 000	$18 150 000	$19 965 000	$21 961 500

14. As a marketing manager for one of the world's largest automakers, you are responsible for the advertising campaign for a new energy-efficient sports utility vehicle. Your support team has prepared the following table, which summarizes the (year-end) profitability, estimated number of vehicles sold, and average estimated selling price for alternative levels of advertising. The accounting department projects that the next-best use for the funds used in the advertising campaign is an investment returning 10 percent. In light of the staggering cost of advertising (which accounts for the lower projected profits in years 1 and 2 for the high and moderate advertising intensities), the team leader recommends a low advertising intensity in order to maximize the value of the firm. Do you agree? Explain.

Profitability by Advertising Intensity

	Profits (in millions)			Units Sold (in thousands)			Average Selling Price		
	Year 1	Year 2	Year 3	Year 1	Year 2	Year 3	Year 1	Year 2	Year 3
Advertising intensity									
High	$15	$ 90	$270	10	60	120	$24 000	$25 500	$26 000
Moderate	30	75	150	5	12.5	25	24 500	24 750	25 000
Low	70	105	126	4	6	7.2	24 800	24 850	24 900

15. The head of the accounting department at a major software manufacturer has asked you to put together a pro forma statement of the company's value under several possible growth scenarios and the assumption that the company's many divisions will remain a single entity forever. The manager is concerned that, despite the fact that the firm's competitors are comparatively small, collectively their annual revenue growth has exceeded 50 percent over each of the last 5 years. She has requested that the value projections be based on the firm's current profits of $2.5 billion (which have yet to be paid out to stockholders) and the average interest rate over the past 20 years (8 percent) in each of the following profit growth scenarios:
    a. Profits grow at an annual rate of 10 percent. (This one is tricky.)
    b. Profits grow at an annual rate of 3 percent.
    c. Profits grow at an annual rate of 0 percent.
    d. Profits decline at an annual rate of 3 percent.

16. You are the manager in charge of global operations at BankGlobal, a large commercial bank that operates in a number of countries around the world. You must decide whether to launch a new advertising campaign in the Canadian market. Your accounting department has provided the statement that follows, which summarizes the financial impact of the advertising campaign on Canadian operations. In addition, you recently received a call from a colleague in charge of foreign operations, and she indicated that her unit would lose $6 million if the Canadian advertising campaign were launched. Your goal is to maximize BankGlobal's value. Should you launch the new campaign? Explain.

Financial Impact on Canadian Operations

	Pre-advertising Campaign	Post-advertising Campaign
Total revenues	$20 540 100	$30 347 800
Variable cost		
TV airtime	6 100 000	9 045 700
Ad development labour	2 357 100	3 536 200
Total variable costs	8 457 100	12 581 900
Direct fixed cost		
Depreciation—computer equipment	1 500 000	1 500 000
Total direct fixed cost	1 500 000	1 500 000
Indirect fixed cost		
Managerial salaries	8 458 100	8 458 100
Office supplies	2 003 500	2 003 500
Total indirect fixed cost	$10 461 600	$10 461 600

APPENDIX: The Calculus of Maximizing Profits

This appendix provides a calculus-based derivation of the important rule that to maximize profits, a manager must equate marginal revenue and marginal costs.

Let $TR(Q)$ denote the benefits of using Q units of the managerial control variable, and let $T(Q)$ denote the corresponding costs. The profits are $\pi(Q) = TR(Q) - TC(Q)$. The objective is to choose Q so as to maximize

$$\pi(Q) = TR(Q) - TC(Q)$$

The first-order condition for a maximum is

$$\frac{d\pi}{dQ} = \frac{dTR}{dQ} - \frac{dTC}{dQ} = 0$$

But

$$\frac{dTR}{dQ} = MR$$

is nothing more than marginal revenue, while

$$\frac{dTC}{dQ} = MC$$

is simply marginal costs. Thus, the first-order condition for a maximum implies that

$$\frac{dTR}{dQ} = \frac{dTC}{dQ}$$

or $MR = MC$.

The second-order condition requires that the function $\pi(Q)$ be concave in Q or, in mathematical terms, that the second derivative of the profit function be negative:

$$\frac{d^2\pi}{dQ^2} = \frac{d^2TR}{dQ^2} - \frac{d^2TC}{dQ^2} < 0$$

Notice that $d^2TR/dQ^2 = d(MR)/dQ$, while $d^2TC/dQ^2 = d(MC)/dQ$. Thus, the second-order condition may be rewritten as

$$\frac{d^2\pi}{dQ^2} = \frac{d(MR)}{dQ} - \frac{d(MC)}{dQ} < 0$$

In other words, the slope of the marginal revenue curve must be less than the slope of the marginal cost curve.

Demonstration PROBLEM 1–4

Suppose $TR(Q) = 10Q - 2Q^2$ and $TC(Q) = 2 + Q^2$. What value of the managerial control variable, Q, maximizes profits?

Answer
Net benefits are

$$\pi(Q) = TR(Q) - TC(Q) = 10Q - 2Q^2 - 2 - Q^2$$

Taking the derivative of $\pi(Q)$ and setting it equal to zero gives

$$\frac{d\pi}{dQ} = 10 - 4Q - 2Q = 0$$

Solving for Q gives $Q = 10/6$. To verify that this is indeed a maximum, we must check that the second derivative of $\pi(Q)$ is negative:

$$\frac{d^2\pi}{dQ^2} = -4 - 2 = -6 < 0$$

Therefore, $Q = 10/6$ is indeed a maximum.

Market Forces:
Demand and Supply

Headline

Sam Robbins, owner and CEO of PC Solutions, arrived at the office and glanced at the front page of the daily financial paper waiting on his desk. One of the articles contained statements from executives of two of South Korea's largest semiconductor manufacturers—Samsung Electronic Company and Hyundai Electronics—indicating that they would suspend all their memory chip production for one week. The article went on to say that LG Semicon—another large semiconductor manufacturer—is likely to follow suit. Collectively, these three chip manufacturers produce about 30 percent of the world's basic semiconductor chips.

PC Solutions is a small but growing company that assembles PCs and sells them in the highly competitive market for "clones." PC Solutions experienced 100 percent growth last year and is in the process of interviewing recent graduates in an attempt to double its work force.

After reading the article, Sam picked up the phone and called a few of his business contacts to verify for himself the information contained in the paper. Satisfied that the information was correct, he called the director of personnel, Jane Remak. What do you think they discussed?

Introduction

The purpose of this chapter is to enable managers to analyze scenarios such as the one posed in the opening Headline. The chapter describes supply and demand, which are the driving forces behind a market economy such as that in Canada.

The model of supply and demand constitutes one of the most important managerial tools because it assists the manager in predicting changes in product and input prices. For those who have taken a principles-level course in economics, some parts of this chapter will be a review. However, make sure you have complete mastery of the tools of supply and demand. The rest of this book will assume you have a thorough working knowledge of the material in this chapter.

Demand

Suppose a clothing manufacturer desires information about the impact of its pricing decisions on the demand for its jeans in a small foreign market. To obtain this information, it might engage in market research to determine how many pairs of jeans consumers would purchase each year at alternative prices. The numbers from such a market survey would look something like those in Table 2–1. The market research reveals that if jeans were priced at $10 per pair, 60 000 pairs of jeans would be sold per year; at $30 per pair, 20 000 pairs of jeans would be sold annually.

Notice that the only differences between the rows in Table 2–1 are in the price of jeans and the quantity of jeans sold. Everything else that might influence buyer decisions, such as consumer income, advertising, and the prices of other goods such as shirts, is held constant. In effect, the market survey does not ask consumers how much they would buy at alternative levels of income or advertising; it simply seeks to determine how much would be purchased at alternative prices. The market research reveals that, holding all other things constant, the quantity of jeans consumers are willing and able to purchase goes down as the price rises. This fundamental economic principle is known as the *law of demand*: Price and quantity demanded are inversely related. That is, as the price of a good rises (falls) and all other things remain constant, the quantity demanded of the good falls (rises).

market demand curve
A curve indicating the total quantity of a good all consumers are willing and able to purchase at each possible price, holding the prices of related goods, income, advertising, and other variables constant.

Figure 2–1 plots the data in Table 2–1. The straight line, called the **market demand curve**, interpolates the quantities consumers would be willing and able to purchase at prices not explicitly dealt with in the market research. Notice that the line is downward-sloping, which reflects the law of demand, and that all other factors that influence demand are held constant at each point on the line.

TABLE 2–1	The Demand Schedule for Jeans in a Small Foreign Market			
Price of Jeans	Quantity of Jeans Sold	Average Consumer Income	Advertising Expenditure	Average Price of Shirts
5	70 000	25 000	50 000	20
10	60 000	25 000	50 000	20
15	50 000	25 000	50 000	20
20	40 000	25 000	50 000	20
25	30 000	25 000	50 000	20
30	20 000	25 000	50 000	20
35	10 000	25 000	50 000	20
40	0	25 000	50 000	20

FIGURE 2-1 The Demand Curve

The demand curve shows the relationship between the quantity demanded of jeans and its price. Keeping all else constant, as the price of jeans increases the quantity demanded decreases.

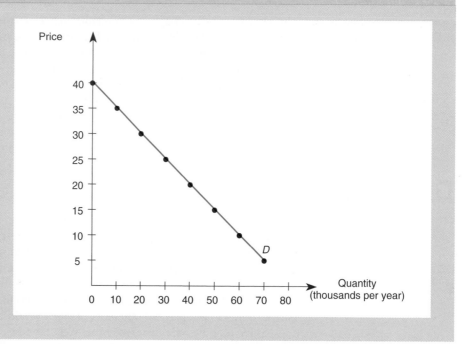

Demand Shifters

Economists recognize that variables other than the price of a good influence demand. For example, the number of pairs of jeans individuals are willing and financially able to buy also depends on the price of shirts, consumer income, advertising expenditures, and so on. Variables other than the price of a good that influence demand are known as *demand shifters*.

When we graph the demand curve for good X, we hold everything but the price of X constant. A representative demand curve is given by D^0 in Figure 2–2, which is assumed to be linear for convenience. The movement along a demand curve, such as the movement from A to B, is called a **change in quantity demanded**. Whenever advertising, income, or the price of related goods changes, it leads to a **change in demand**; the position of the entire demand curve shifts. A rightward shift in the demand curve is called an *increase in demand,* since more of the good is demanded at each price. A leftward shift in the demand curve is called a *decrease in demand.*

Now that we understand the general distinction between a shift in a demand curve and a movement along a demand curve, it is useful to explain how five demand shifters—consumer income, prices of related goods, advertising and consumer tastes, population, and consumer expectations—affect demand.

change in quantity demanded
Changes in the price of a good lead to a change in the quantity demanded of that good. This corresponds to a movement along a given demand curve.

change in demand
Changes in variables other than the price of a good, such as income or the price of another good, lead to a change in demand. This corresponds to a shift of the entire demand curve.

Income

Because income affects the ability of consumers to purchase a good, changes in income affect how much consumers will buy at any price. In graphical terms, a change in income shifts the entire demand curve. Whether an increase in income shifts the demand curve to the right or to the left depends on the nature of consumer consumption patterns. Accordingly, economists distinguish between two types of goods: normal and inferior goods.

FIGURE 2–2 Changes in Demand

The movement from point A to point B along D^0 reflects an increase in quantity demanded in response to a drop in the price of jeans. When factors other than the price change, the whole demand relation changes. Assuming a normal good, an increase in income causes a shift to the right in the demand from D^0 to D^1, whereas a decrease in income causes a shift to the left in the demand curve to D^2.

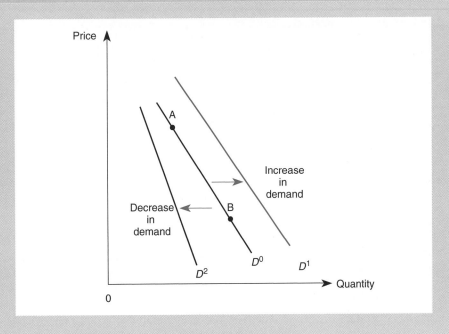

normal good
A good for which an increase (decrease) in income leads to an increase (decrease) in the demand for that good.

inferior good
A good for which an increase (decrease) in income leads to a decrease (increase) in the demand for that good.

A good whose demand increases (shifts to the right) when consumer incomes rise is called a **normal good**. Normal goods may include goods such as steak, airline travel, and designer jeans: as income goes up, consumers typically buy more of these goods at any given price. Conversely, when consumers suffer a decline in income, the demand for a normal good will decrease (shift to the left).

In some instances, an increase in income reduces the demand for a good. Economists refer to such a good as an **inferior good**. Bologna, bus travel, and "generic" jeans are possible examples of inferior goods. As income goes up, consumers typically consume less of these goods at each price. It is important to point out that by calling such goods *inferior,* we do not imply that they are of poor quality; we use this term simply to define products that consumers purchase less of when their incomes rise, and purchase more of when their incomes fall.

Prices of Related Goods

Changes in the prices of related goods generally shift the demand curve for a good. For example, if the price of a Coke increases, most consumers will begin to substitute Pepsi, because the relative price of Coke is higher than before. As more and more consumers substitute Pepsi for Coke, the quantity of Pepsi demanded at each price will tend to increase. In effect, an increase in the price of Coke increases the demand for Pepsi. This is illustrated by a shift in the demand for Pepsi to the right. Goods that interact in this way are known as **substitutes**.

substitutes
Goods for which an increase (decrease) in the price of one good leads to an increase (decrease) in the demand for the other good.

Many pairs of goods readily come to mind when we think of substitutes: chicken and beef, cars and trucks, raincoats and umbrellas. Such pairs of goods are substitutes for most consumers. However, substitutes need not serve the same function; for example, automobiles and housing might be substitutes. Goods are substitutes when an increase in the price of one good increases the demand for the other good.

InsideBUSINESS

2-1 Asahi Breweries Ltd. and the Asian Recession

During the late 1990s, recession-plagued Japan saw many business failures. Even businesses that traditionally do well during economic downturns, such as the beer brewing industry, were hit hard. Analysts blame the downturn in the beer market on two factors: (1) Japanese incomes (GDP) declined significantly as a result of the recession and (2) Japan's government imposed a beer tax in an effort to raise revenue.

As a result of these events, top Japanese breweries such as Kirin Brewery Company, Ltd. and Sapporo Breweries Ltd. experienced a sharp decline in domestic beer sales. Meanwhile, their competitor—Asahi Breweries Ltd.—touted double-digit growth and increased its market share. Asahi attributes its growth in sales to its superior sales network and strong marketing campaign for its best-selling beer, Asahi Super Dry.

While part of Asahi's growth and success is attributable to the company's sales force and marketing activities—both create greater consumer awareness—this does not fully explain why Asahi has done especially well during the recent Asian recession. One possibility is that Asahi beer is an inferior good. This does not mean that Asahi beer is "skunky" or of low quality; indeed, its Super Dry is the beer of choice for many Japanese beer drinkers. The term *inferior good* simply means that when Japanese incomes decline due to a recession, the demand for Asahi beer increases.

Sources: Annual reports for Asahi Breweries Ltd., Sapporo Breweries Ltd., and Kirin Brewery Company, Ltd.

---

complements
Goods for which an increase (decrease) in the price of one good leads to a decrease (increase) in the demand for the other good.

Not all goods are substitutes; in fact, an increase in the price of a good such as computer software may lead consumers to purchase fewer computers at each price. Goods that interact in this manner are called **complements**. Beer and pretzels are another example of complementary goods. If the price of beer increased, most beer drinkers would decrease their consumption of pretzels. Notice that when good X is a complement to good Y, a reduction in the price of Y actually increases (shifts to the right) the demand for good X. More of good X is purchased at each price due to the reduction in the price of the complement, good Y.

Advertising and Consumer Tastes

Another variable that is held constant when drawing a given demand curve is the level of advertising. An increase in advertising shifts the demand curve to the right, from D^1 to D^2, as in Figure 2–3. Notice that the impact of advertising on demand can be interpreted in two ways. Under the initial demand curve, D^1, consumers would buy 50 000 units of high-style clothing per month when the price is $40. After the advertising, the demand curve shifts to D^2, and consumers will now buy 60 000 units of the good when the price is $40. Alternatively, when demand is D^1, consumers will pay a price of $40 when 50 000 units are available. Advertising shifts the demand curve to D^2, so consumers will pay a higher price—$50—for 50 000 units.

Why does advertising shift demand to the right? Advertising often provides consumers with information about the existence or quality of a product, which in turn induces more consumers to buy the product. These types of advertising messages are known as *informative advertising*.

Advertising can also influence demand by altering the underlying tastes of consumers. For example, advertising that promotes the latest fad in clothing may increase the demand for a specific fashion item by making consumers perceive it as "the" thing to buy. These types of advertising messages are known as *persuasive advertising*.

Population

The market demand for a product is also influenced by changes in the size and composition of the population. Generally, as the population rises, more and more individ-

FIGURE 2-3   Advertising and the Demand for Clothing

An increase in advertising causes the demand for clothing to increase. This is reflected by a shift in the demand curve from D^1 to D^2, since at the each level of price the consumer now purchases more clothing.

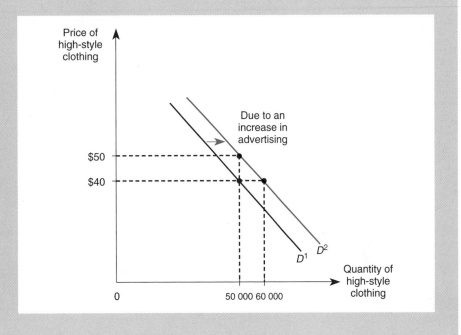

uals wish to buy a given product, and this has the effect of shifting the demand curve to the right. Over the twentieth century, the demand curve for food products shifted to the right considerably with the increasing population.

It is important to note that changes in the composition of the population can also affect the demand for a product. To the extent that middle-aged consumers desire different types of products than retirees, an increase in the number of consumers in the 30-to-40-year-old age bracket will increase the demand for products like real estate. Similarly, as a greater proportion of the population ages, the demand for medical services will tend to increase.

Consumer Expectations

Changes in *consumer expectations* arising from, say, an expected change in income due to a weaker job market or an expected price change, also can change the position of the demand curve for a product. For example, if consumers suddenly expect the price of automobiles to be significantly higher next year, the demand for automobiles today will increase. In effect, buying a car today is a substitute for buying a car next year. If consumers expect future prices to be higher, they will substitute current purchases for future purchases. This type of consumer behaviour is often referred to as *stockpiling*, and it generally occurs when products are durable in nature. The current demand for a perishable product such as bananas is generally not affected by expectations of higher future prices.

Other Factors

In concluding our list of demand shifters, we simply note that any variable that affects the willingness or ability of consumers to purchase a particular good is a potential demand shifter. Health scares affect the demand for cigarettes. The birth of a baby affects the demand for diapers.

The Demand Function

By now you should understand the factors that affect demand and how to use graphs to illustrate those influences. The final step in our analysis of the demand side of the market is to show that all the factors that influence demand may be summarized in what economists refer to as a **demand function**.

demand function
A function that describes how much of a good will be purchased at alternative prices of that good and related goods, alternative income levels, and alternative values of other variables affecting demand.

The demand function for good X describes how much X will be purchased at alternative prices of X and related goods, alternative levels of income, and alternative values of other variables that affect demand. Formally, let Q_x^d represent the quantity demanded of good X, P_x the price of good X, P_y the price of a related good, M income, and H the value of any other variable that affects demand, such as the level of advertising, the size of the population, or consumer expectations. Then the demand function for good X may be written as

$$Q_x^d = f(P_x, P_y, M, H) \qquad (2\text{–}1)$$

Thus, the demand function explicitly recognizes that the quantity of a good consumed depends on its price and on demand shifters. Different products will have demand functions of different forms. One very simple but useful form is the linear representation of the demand function: demand is *linear* if Q_x^d is a linear function of prices, income, and other variables that influence demand. The following equation is an example of a **linear demand function**:

linear demand function
A representation of the demand function in which the demand for a given good is a linear function of prices, income levels, and other variables influencing demand.

$$Q_x^d = \alpha_0 + \alpha_x P_x + \alpha_y P_y + \alpha_M M + \alpha_H H \qquad (2\text{–}2)$$

The α_is are fixed numbers that are typically provided to the manager by the firm's research department or an economic consultant. (Chapter 3 provides an overview of the statistical techniques used to obtain these numbers.)

By the law of demand, an increase in P_x leads to a decrease in the quantity demanded of good X. This means that $\alpha_x < 0$. The sign of α_y will be positive or negative depending on whether goods X and Y are substitutes or complements. If α_y is a positive number, an increase in the price of good Y will lead to an increase in the consumption of good X; therefore, good X is a substitute for good Y. If α_y is a negative number, an increase in the price of good Y will lead to a decrease in the consumption of good X; hence, good X is a complement to good Y. The sign of α_M also can be positive or negative depending on whether X is a normal or an inferior good. If α_M is a positive number, an increase in income (M) will lead to an increase in the consumption of good X, and good X is a normal good. If α_M is a negative number, an increase in income will lead to a decrease in the consumption of good X, and good X is an inferior good.

o If α_y is a negative number

Demonstration PROBLEM 2–1

An economic consultant for X Corp. recently provided the firm's marketing manager with this estimate of the demand function for the firm's product:

$$Q_x^d = 12\,000 - 3P_x + 4P_y - 1M + 2A_x$$

where Q_x^d represents the amount consumed of good X, P_x is the price of good X, P_y is the price of good Y, M is income, and A_x represents the amount of advertising spent on good X. Suppose good X sells for $200 per unit, good Y sells for $15 per unit, the company utilizes 2000 units of advertising, and consumer income is

$10 000. How much of good X do consumers purchase? Are goods X and Y substitutes or complements? Is good X a normal or an inferior good?

Answer

To find out how much of good X consumers will purchase, we substitute the given values of prices, income, and advertising into the linear demand equation to get

$$Q_x^d = 12\ 000 - 3(200) + 4(15) - 1(10\ 000) + 2(2000)$$

Adding up the numbers, we find that the total consumption of X is 5460 units. Since the coefficient of P_y in the demand equation is $4 > 0$, we know that a $1 increase in the price of good Y will increase the consumption of good X by 4 units. Thus, goods X and Y are substitutes. Since the coefficient of M in the demand equation is $-1 < 0$, we know that a $1 increase in income will decrease the consumption of good X by 1 unit. Thus, good X is an inferior good.

The information summarized in a demand function can be used to graph a demand curve. Since a demand curve is the relation between price and quantity, a representative demand curve holds everything but price constant. This means one may obtain the formula for a demand curve by inserting given values of the demand shifters into the demand function, but leaving P_x in the equation to allow for various values. If we do this for the demand function in Demonstration Problem 2–1 (where $P_y = \$15$, $M = \$10\ 000$, and $A_x = 2000$), we get

$$Q_x^d = 12\ 000 - 3P_x + 4(15) - 1(10\ 000) + 2(2000)$$

which simplifies to

$$Q_x^d = 6060 - 3P_x$$

Because we usually graph this relation with the price of the good on the vertical axis, it is useful to represent Equation 2–1 with price on the left-hand side and everything else on the right-hand side. This relation is called an *inverse demand function*. For this example, the inverse demand function is

$$P_x = 2020 - (1/3)Q_x^d$$

It reveals how much consumers are willing and able to pay for each additional unit of good X. This demand curve is graphed in Figure 2–4.

Consumer Surplus

We now show how a manager can use the demand curve to ascertain the value a consumer or group of consumers receives from a product. The concepts developed in this section are particularly useful in marketing and other disciplines that emphasize strategies such as *value pricing* and *price discrimination*.

By the law of demand, the amount a consumer is willing to pay for an additional unit of a good falls as more of the good is consumed. For instance, imagine that the demand curve in Figure 2–5(a) represents your demand for water immediately after participating in a 10K run. Initially, you are willing to pay a very high price—in this case, $5 per litre—for the first drop of water. As you consume more water, the amount

FIGURE 2-4 Graphing the Inverse Demand Function

The inverse demand function reveals how much consumers are willing to pay for each additional unit of good X. The negative slope $(-1/3)$ reflects the inverse relationship between the price and quantity demanded. Thus consumers are willing to pay a 1/3 of a dollar less for each additional unit of X. In other words, all else being equal, in order to induce consumers to buy one more unit of X, the price must be reduced by 1/3 of a dollar.

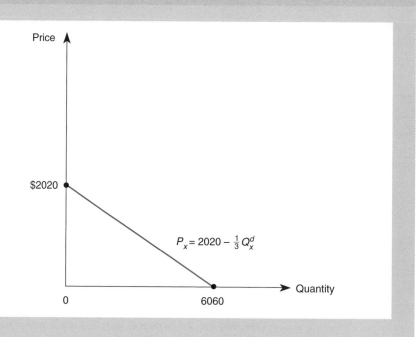

$$P_x = 2020 - \tfrac{1}{3} Q_x^d$$

FIGURE 2-5 Consumer Surplus

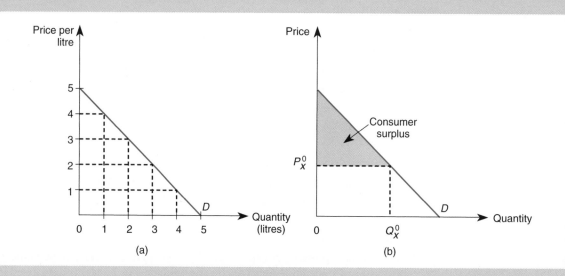

(a)

(b)

(a) A consumer is willing to pay a higher amount for the first units. As the number of units purchased increases, say from 1 to 4, she is willing to pay less for each additional unit. She pays $4 for the first unit and $3, $2, and $1 dollar for the subsequent units. Thus, by buying 4 units at $1, instead of buying each unit individually, the consumer receives more in value than she actually pays.

(b) The shaded triangle represents the consumer surplus associated with purchasing Q_x^0 units at a price of P_x^0 per unit.

you are willing to pay for an additional drop declines from $5 to $4.99 and so on as you move down the demand curve. Notice that after you have consumed an entire litre of water, you are willing to pay only $4 per litre for another drop. Once you have enjoyed 2 litres of water, you are willing to pay only $3 per litre for another drop.

To find your total value (or benefit) of 2 litres of water, we simply add up the maximum amount you were willing to pay for each of these drops of water between 0 and 2 litres. This amount corresponds to the area underneath the demand curve in Figure 2–5(a) up to the quantity of 2 litres. Since the area of this region is $8, the total value you receive from 2 litres of water is $8.

Fortunately, you don't have to pay different prices for the different drops of water you consume. Instead, you face a per-unit price of, say, $3 per litre and get to buy as many drops (or even litres) as you want at that price. Given the demand curve in Figure 2–5(a), when the price is $3 you will choose to purchase 2 litres of water. In this case, your total out-of-pocket expense for the 2 litres of water is $6. Since you value 2 litres of water at $8 and only have to pay $6 for it, you are getting $2 in value over and above the amount you have to pay for water. This "extra" value is known as **consumer surplus**—the value consumers get from a good but do not have to pay for. This concept is important to managers because it tells how much extra money consumers would be willing to pay for a given amount of a purchased product.

More generally, consumer surplus is the area above the price paid for a good but below the demand curve. For instance, the shaded triangle in Figure 2–5(b) illustrates the consumer surplus of a consumer who buys Q_x^0 units at a price of P_x^0. To see why, recall that each point on the demand curve indicates the value to the consumer of another unit of the good. The difference between each price on the demand curve and the price P_x^0 paid represents surplus (the value the consumer receives but does not have to pay for). When we add up the "surpluses" received for each unit between 0 and Q_x^0 (this sum equals the shaded region), we obtain the consumer surplus associated with purchasing Q_x^0 units at a price of P_x^0 each.

The notion of consumer surplus can be used by managers to determine the total amount consumers would be willing to pay for a package of goods. While this will be discussed in detail in Chapter 11 where we examine pricing strategies, we illustrate the basic idea in the following problem.

consumer surplus
The value consumers get from a good but do not have to pay for.

Demonstration PROBLEM 2–2

A typical consumer's demand for the Happy Beverage Company's product looks like that in Figure 2–5(a). If the firm charges a price of $2 per litre, how much revenue will the firm earn and how much consumer surplus will the typical consumer enjoy? What is the most a consumer would be willing to pay for a bottle containing exactly 3 litres of the firm's beverage?

Answer

At a price of $2 per litre, a typical consumer will purchase 3 litres of the beverage. Thus, the firm's revenue is $6 and the consumer surplus is $4.50 (the area of the consumer surplus triangle is one-half the base times the height, or $0.5(3)(\$5 - \$2) = \$4.50$). The total value of 3 litres of the firm's beverage to a typical consumer is thus $6 + $4.50, or $10.50. This is also the maximum amount a consumer would be willing to pay for a bottle containing exactly 3 litres of the firm's beverage. Expressed differently, if the firm sold the product in 3-litre bottles rather than in smaller units, it could sell each bottle for $10.50 to earn higher revenues and extract all consumer surplus.

Supply

market supply curve
A curve indicating the total quantity of a good that all producers in a competitive market would produce at each price, holding input prices, technology, and other variables affecting supply constant.

change in quantity supplied
Changes in the price of a good lead to a change in the quantity supplied of that good. This corresponds to a movement along a given supply curve.

change in supply
Changes in variables other than the price of a good, such as input prices or technological advances, lead to a change in supply. This corresponds to a shift of the entire supply curve.

In the previous section we focused on demand, which represents half of the forces that determine the price in a market. The other determinant is market supply. In a competitive market there are many producers, each producing a similar product. The **market supply curve** summarizes the total quantity all producers are willing and able to produce at alternative prices, holding other factors that affect supply constant.

While the market supply of a good generally depends on many things, when we graph a supply curve, we hold everything but the price of the good constant. The movement along a supply curve, such as the one from A to B in Figure 2–6, is called a **change in quantity supplied**. The fact that the market supply curve slopes upward reflects the *law of supply*: As the price of a good rises (falls) and other things remain constant, the quantity supplied of the good rises (falls). Producers are willing to produce more output when the price is high than when it is low.

Supply Shifters

Variables that affect the position of the supply curve are called *supply shifters,* and include the prices of inputs, the level of technology, the number of firms in the market, taxes, the weather, and producer expectations. Whenever one or more of these variables changes, the position of the entire supply curve shifts. Such a shift is known as a **change in supply**. The shift from S^0 to S^2 in Figure 2–6 is called an *increase in supply* since producers sell more output at each given price. The shift from S^0 to S^1 in Figure 2–6 represents a *decrease in supply* since producers sell less of the product at each price.

FIGURE 2-6 Changes in Supply

The supply curve S^0 shows the relationship between quantity supplied and the price of the good, everything else remaining the same. Changes in variables other than the price of the good (such as changes in technology) lead to a change in supply. As technology advances, it will be cheaper to produce each additional unit of output, and therefore the supply curve shifts from S^0 to S^2.

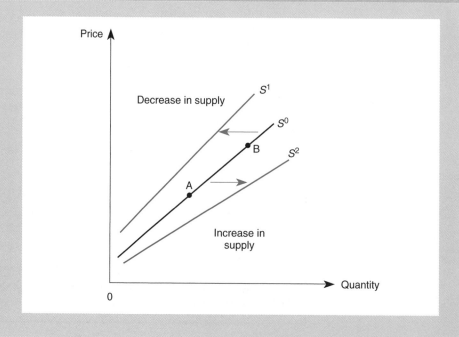

Inside BUSINESS

2-2 NAFTA and the Supply Curve

This past decade, a historic trade agreement between Canada, the United States, and Mexico went into force in 1995. This agreement, called the North American Free Trade Agreement (NAFTA), has provisions that are designed to reduce the cost of producing goods both at home and abroad and thus increase the North American supply of goods and services. Key provisions of NAFTA are:

- Phaseout of most tariffs and nontariff barriers in industrial products over 10 years, including textiles and apparel that have substantial regional content
- Phaseout of tariffs and most nontariff barriers in agricultural products over 15 years

- Investment rules ensuring national treatment, eliminating most performance requirements in all sectors, and reducing barriers to investment in the Mexican petrochemicals and financial services sectors
- Liberalization of financial, land transportation, and telecommunications services markets
- A dispute resolution mechanism
- Protection of intellectual property rights
- Funds for environmental cleanup and community adjustment along the border

Source: Department of Foreign Affairs and International Trade, 1995.

Input Prices

The supply curve reveals how much producers are willing to produce at alternative prices. As production costs change, the willingness of producers to produce output at a given price changes. In particular, as the price of an input rises, producers are willing to produce less output at each given price. This decrease in supply is depicted as a leftward shift in the supply curve.

Technology or Government Regulations

Technological changes and changes in government regulations also can affect the position of the supply curve. Changes that make it possible to produce a given output at a lower cost, such as the ones highlighted in Inside Business 2–2, have the effect of increasing supply. Conversely, natural disasters that destroy existing technology and government regulations, such as emissions standards that have an adverse effect on businesses, shift the supply curve to the left.

Number of Firms

The number of firms in an industry affects the position of the supply curve. As additional firms enter an industry, more and more output is available at each given price. This is reflected by a rightward shift in the supply curve. Similarly, as firms leave an industry, fewer units are sold at each price, and the supply decreases (shifts to the left).

Substitutes in Production

Many firms have technologies that are readily adaptable to several different products. For example, Bombardier can convert its 50-seaters jet assembly plant into a 70-seaters one by altering its production facilities. When the demand for smaller jets and hence its price increases, Bombardier can convert some of its larger jet assembly lines to smaller ones to increase the quantity of smaller jets supplied. This has the effect of shifting the 70-seaters jet supply curve to the left.

Taxes

The position of the supply curve is also affected by taxes. An *excise tax* is a tax on each unit of output sold, where the tax revenue is collected from the supplier. For

FIGURE 2-7 A Per-Unit (Excise) Tax

An excise tax causes the supply curve to shift upward by the full amount of tax. Therefore, a $0.05 tax per litre of gasoline results in an upward shift in the supply curve by $0.05 from S^0 to (S^0 + $0.05), implying that producers will continue to supply the same quantity of output as long if they can charge $1.05 for a net price of $1.05 − $0.05 tax.

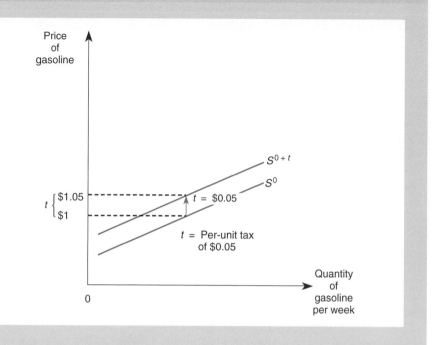

example, suppose the government levies a tax of $0.05 per litre on gasoline. Since each supplier must now pay the government $0.05 per litre for each litre of gasoline sold, each must receive an additional $0.05 per litre to be willing to supply the same quantity of gasoline as before the tax. An excise tax shifts the supply curve up by the amount of the tax, as in Figure 2–7. Note that at any given price, producers are willing to sell less gasoline after the tax than before. Thus, an excise tax has the effect of decreasing the supply of a good.

Another form of tax often used by a government agency is an ad valorem tax. *Ad valorem* literally means "according to the value." An *ad valorem tax* is a percentage tax; the GST is a well-known example. If the price of a good is $1 and a 10 percent ad valorem tax is attached to that good, the price after the tax is $1.10. Because an ad valorem tax is a percentage tax, it will be higher for high-priced items.

In Figure 2–8, S^0 represents the supply curve for backpacks before the inception of a 20 percent ad valorem tax. Notice that 1100 backpacks are offered for sale when the price of a backpack is $10 and 2450 backpacks are offered when the price is $20. Once the 20 percent tax is implemented, the price required to produce each unit goes up by 20 percent at any output level. Therefore, price will go up by $2 at a quantity of 1100 and by $4 at a quantity of 2450. An ad valorem tax will rotate the supply curve counterclockwise, and the new curve will shift farther away from the original curve as the price increases. This explains why S^1 is steeper than S^0 in Figure 2–8.

Producer Expectations
Producer expectations about future prices also affect the position of the supply curve. In effect, selling a unit of output today and selling a unit of output tomorrow are substitutes in production. If firms suddenly expect prices to be higher in the future and the product is not perishable, producers can hold back output today and sell it later at a higher price. This has the effect of shifting the current supply curve to the left.

FIGURE 2-8 An Ad Valorem Tax

An introduction of a 20 percent ad valorem tax increases by 20 percent the price required to induce producers to supply each unit. Thus, a backpack previously priced at $20 will cost $24. When the price of a backpack is only $10, the amount of tax that suppliers must pay increases the price of a good by only $2. Thus, the slope of the supply curve changes and supply rotates from S^0 to S^1.

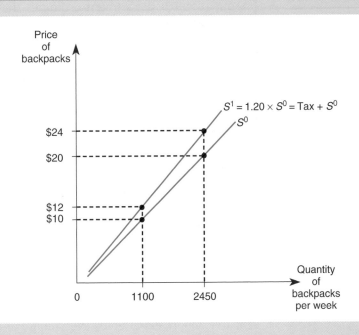

The Supply Function

You should now understand the difference between supply and quantity supplied and recognize the factors that influence the position of the supply curve. The final step in our analysis of supply is to show that all of the factors that influence the supply of a good can be summarized in a supply function.

supply function
A function that describes how much of a good will be produced at alternative prices of that good, alternative input prices, and alternative values of other variables affecting supply.

The **supply function** of a good describes how much of the good will be produced at alternative prices of the good, alternative prices of inputs, and alternative values of other variables that affect supply. Formally, let Q_x^s represent the quantity supplied of a good, P_x the price of the good, W the price of an input (such as the wage rate on labour), P_r the price of technologically related goods, and H the value of some other variable that affects supply (such as the existing technology, the number of firms in the market, taxes, or producer expectations). Then the supply function for good X may be written as

$$Q_x^s = f(P_x, P_r, W, H) \qquad (2\text{–}3)$$

Thus, the supply function explicitly recognizes that the quantity produced in a market depends not only on the price of the good but also on all of the factors that are potential supply shifters. While there are many different functional forms for different types of products, a particularly useful representation of a supply function is the linear relationship. Supply is *linear* if Q_x^s is a linear function of the variables that influence supply. The following equation is representative of a **linear supply function**:

linear supply function
A representation of the supply function in which the supply of a given good is a linear function of input prices and other variables affecting supply.

$$Q_x^s = \beta_0 + \beta_x P_x + \beta_r P_r + \beta_w W + \beta_H H \qquad (2\text{–}4)$$

The coefficients (the $\beta_i s$) represent given numbers that have been estimated by the firm's research department or an economic consultant.

Demonstration PROBLEM 2–3

Your research department estimates that the supply function for television sets is given by

$$Q_x^s = 2000 + 3P_x - 4P_r - P_w$$

where P_x is the price of TV sets, P_r represents the price of a computer monitor, and P_w is the price of an input used to make televisions. Suppose TVs are sold for $400 per unit, computer monitors are sold for $100 per unit, and the price of an input is $2000. How many television sets are produced?

Answer

To find out how many television sets are produced, we insert the given values of prices into the supply function to get

$$Q_x^s = 2000 + 3(400) - 4(100) - 1(2000)$$

Adding up the numbers, we find that the total quantity of television sets produced is 800.

The information summarized in a supply function can be used to graph a supply curve. Since a supply curve is the relationship between price and quantity, a representative supply curve holds everything but price constant. This means one may obtain the formula for a supply curve by inserting given values of the supply shifters into the supply function, but leaving P_x in the equation to allow for various values. If we do this for the supply function in Demonstration Problem 2–3 (where $P_r = \$100$ and $P_w = 2000$), we get

$$Q_x^s = 2000 + 3P_x - 4(100) - 1(2000)$$

which simplifies to

$$Q_x^s = 3P_x - 400$$

Since we usually graph this relation with the price of the good on the vertical axis, it is useful to represent Equation 2–2 with price on the left-hand side and everything else on the right-hand side. This is known as an *inverse supply function*. For this example, the inverse supply function is

$$P_x = 400/3 + (1/3)Q_x^s$$

which is the equation for the supply curve graphed in Figure 2–9. This curve reveals how much producers must receive to be willing to produce each additional unit of good X.

Producer Surplus

Just as consumers want price to be as low as possible, producers want price to be as high as possible. The supply curve reveals the amount producers will be willing to produce at a given price. Alternatively, it indicates the price firms would have to receive to be willing to produce an additional unit of a good. For example, the supply curve in Figure 2–9 indicates that a total of 800 units will be produced when the price

FIGURE 2-9 Producer Surplus

The shaded triangle represents the producer surplus. Producers are willing to supply for *less* than $400 per unit when the number of units is less than 800. Therefore, receiving exactly $400 per each unit when producers supply 800 units of good generates a producer surplus.

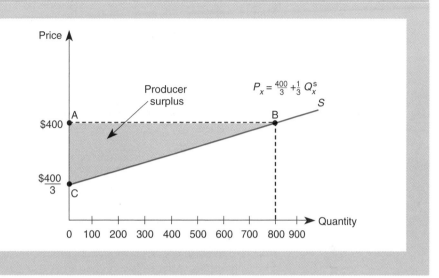

is $400. Alternatively, if 800 units are produced, producers will have to receive $400 to be induced to produce another unit of the good.

producer surplus
The amount producers receive in excess of the amount necessary to induce them to produce the good.

Producer surplus is the producer analogue to consumer surplus. It is the amount of money producers receive in excess of the amount necessary to induce them to produce the good. Note that producer surplus is also equal to revenue less variable cost. Put differently, producer surplus equals profits plus fixed costs. More specifically, note that producers are willing to sell each unit of output below 800 units at a price less than $400. But if the price is $400, producers receive an amount equal to $400 for each unit of output below 800, even though they would be willing to sell those individual units for a lower price.

Geometrically, producer surplus is the area above the supply curve but below the market price of the good. Thus, the shaded area in Figure 2–9 represents the surplus producers receive by selling 800 units at a price of $400—an amount above what would be required to produce each unit of the good. The shaded area, ABC, is the producer surplus when the price is $400. Mathematically, this area is one-half of 800 times $266.67, or $106 668.

Producer surplus can be a powerful tool for managers. For instance, suppose the manager of a major fast-food restaurant currently purchases 10 000 kilograms of ground beef each week from a supplier at a price of $1.25 per kilogram. The producer surplus the meat supplier earns by selling 10 000 kilograms at $1.25 per kilogram tells the restaurant manager the dollar amount that the supplier is receiving over and above what it would be willing to accept for meat. In other words, the meat supplier's producer surplus is the maximum amount the restaurant could save in meat costs by bargaining with the supplier over a package deal for 10 000 kilograms of meat. Chapters 6 and 10 will provide details about how managers can negotiate such a bargain.

Market Equilibrium

As we mentioned in the introduction to this chapter, the price in a competitive market is determined by the interactions of all buyers and sellers in the market. The concepts of market supply and market demand make this notion of interaction more precise: the price of a good in a competitive market is determined by the interaction of market supply and market demand for the good.

Since we will focus on the market for a single good, it is convenient to drop subscripts at this point and let P denote the price of this good and Q the quantity of the good. Figure 2–10 depicts the market supply and demand curves for such a good. To see how the competitive price is determined, let the price of the good be P^L. This price corresponds to point B on the market demand curve; consumers wish to purchase Q^1 units of the good. Similarly, the price of P^L corresponds to point A on the market supply curve; producers are willing to produce only Q^0 units at this price. Thus, when the price is P^L, there is a *shortage* of the good; that is, there is not enough of the good to satisfy all consumers willing to purchase it at that price.

In situations where a shortage exists, there is a natural tendency for the price to rise. As the price rises from P^L to P^e in Figure 2–10, producers have an incentive to expand output from Q^0 to Q^e. Similarly, as the price rises, consumers are willing to purchase less of the good. When the price rises to P^e, the quantity demanded is Q^e. At this price, just enough of the good is produced to satisfy all consumers willing and able to purchase at that price; quantity demanded equals quantity supplied.

Suppose the price is at a higher level—say, P^H. This price corresponds to point F on the market demand curve, indicating that consumers wish to purchase Q^0 units of the good. The price P^H corresponds to point G on the market supply curve; producers are willing to produce Q^1 units at this price. Thus, when the price is P^H, there is a *surplus* of the good; firms are producing more than they can sell at a price of P^H.

Whenever a surplus exists, there is a natural tendency for the price to fall to equate quantity supplied with quantity demanded. As the price falls from P^H to P^e, producers have an incentive to reduce quantity supplied to Q^e. Similarly, as the price falls, consumers are willing to purchase more of the good. When the price falls to P^e, the quantity demanded is Q^e; quantity demanded equals quantity supplied.

FIGURE 2–10 Market Equilibrium

In market equilibrium, quantity supplied equals quantity demanded, and equilibrium price P^e and quantity Q^e are established. When the price is at P^H (above the market-clearing level) there will be a surplus (*FG*), and when the price is at P^L (below the market-clearing level) there will be a shortage (*AB*). The surplus results in a decrease in the price, whereas the shortage gives rise to an increase in the price toward the market-clearing (equilibrium) level.

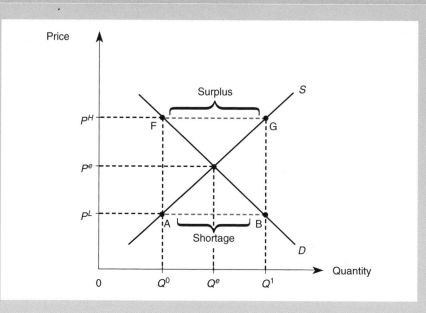

Thus, the interaction of supply and demand ultimately determines a competitive price, P^e, such that there is neither a shortage nor a surplus of the good. This price is called the *equilibrium price* and the corresponding quantity, Q^e, is called the *equilibrium quantity* for the competitive market. Once this price and quantity are realized, the market forces of supply and demand are balanced; there is no tendency for prices either to rise or to fall.

Principle	**COMPETITIVE MARKET EQUILIBRIUM** Equilibrium in a competitive market is determined by the intersection of the market demand and supply curves. The equilibrium price is the price that equates quantity demanded with quantity supplied. Mathematically, if $Q^d(P)$ and $Q^s(P)$ represent the quantity demanded and supplied when the price is P, the equilibrium price, P^e, is the price such that $$Q^d(P^e) = Q^s(P^e)$$ The equilibrium quantity is simply $Q^d(P^e)$ or, equivalently, $Q^s(P^e)$.

Demonstration PROBLEM 2–4

Imagine that you are an advisor to the Minister of the Department of Foreign Affairs and International Trade. The Russian government plans to privatize an industry, and you have been asked to help the committee determine the market price and quantity that would prevail in the Russian market if competitive forces were allowed to equilibrate the market. The best estimates of the market demand and supply for the Russian good (in Canadian dollar equivalent prices) are given by $Q^d = 10 - 2P$ and $Q^s = 2 + 2P$, respectively. Determine the competitive equilibrium price and quantity.

Answer

Competitive equilibrium is determined by the intersection of the market demand and supply curves. Mathematically, this simply means that $Q^d = Q^s$. Equating demand and supply yields

$$10 - 2P = 2 + 2P$$

or

$$8 = 4P$$

Solving this equation for P yields the equilibrium price, $P^e = 2$. To determine the equilibrium quantity, we simply plug this price into either the demand or the supply function (since, in equilibrium, quantity supplied equals quantity demanded). For example, using the supply function, we find that

$$Q^e = 2 + 2(2) = 6$$

Comparative Statics

You now understand how equilibrium is determined in a competitive. Next, we show how managers can use supply and demand to analyze the impact of changes in market conditions on the competitive equilibrium price and quantity. The study of the

Inside BUSINESS

2-3 Market-Clearing Prices in the World Crude Oil Market

The Organization of Petroleum Exporting Countries (OPEC) rose to international prominence during 1970s as its member countries took control of their domestic petroleum industries and acquired a major say in the pricing of crude oil on world markets. Two developments have characterized the market for crude oil in the past two decades. First, after the two drastic oil price increases of 1973 and 1979, and a significant oil price decrease in 1986, the world economy has witnessed a period of reasonable tranquility. Second, though OPEC's objective since its inception has been to coordinate and unify petroleum policies among its member countries in order to secure a larger market share, this has gradually given way to a growing awareness of the need to shift its focus to market stability with reasonable prices.

In the past decade or two, OPEC, with its production pegged at about 40 percent of the world supply, has been unofficially playing such a stabilizing role in the world crude oil market. For instance, when in 1998 the market witnessed a very sharp drop in world demand of around 4.52 percent and a collapse in the price of oil, OPEC members implemented a series of production cuts to balance the market. And when the demand was rising sharply in 2000 giving rise to renewed price increases, OPEC countries implemented a series of production increases that resulted in a more balanced market. In fact, since that year, OPEC has adhered to a new price targeting policy, introduced in 2000 and known as the "price band mechanism," that attempts to keep the crude oil price within the range of $22 to $28.

Table 2–2 shows the adjustments of world oil price, as represented by the West-Texas Intermediate (WTI), in response to the forces of demand and supply.

OPEC can be viewed as a residual (monopolist) supplier who steps into the market to fill the existing gap, (a) − (b), by setting production at a level that will influence the world price in a favourable and consistent fashion. Closing this gap, however, requires that OPEC first estimate the world demand and also non-OPEC supply in each period. In reality, due to estimation errors caused by unforeseen factors, such as wars, climate changes, and production anomalies by non-OPEC producers, the art of gapology (residual supplying) may be less than perfect; see column (e).

The first half of 1998 brought a very sharp drop of 2.1 m b/d (2.1 million barrels of oil per day, or 2.8 percent) in demand. However, this downward trend in demand, which can be traced back to the Asian crisis of September 1997, was not balanced by a decrease in the world (OPEC and non-OPEC) supply of oil. This inevitably gave rise to a drastic fall in price of crude oil of 19.2 percent, which lasted until the end of the year (see Table 2–2). The 1988 cumulative positive balance (surplus) of nearly 6 m b/d proved to be too large for the price of oil to hold steady.

The year 1999 witnessed a trend reversal in demand. The strong upward trend, especially in the last quarter, was only met by the suppliers' partial response. In fact, OPEC's production was down by 2.3 m b/d, from 28.3 m b/d in 1Q98 (the first quarter of 1998) to 26 m b/d in 4Q99. With world demand at 76.4 m b/d, up by 2.2 m b/d from 1Q98, and non-OPEC supply up by only a tiny 0.2 m b/d, the market positive balance (surplus) of the previous year turned into a negative balance (a deficit of −2.2 m b/d).

OPEC's subsequent responses to changing market conditions can be characterized as stabilizing. In 2000, in response to the increased world supply, OPEC implemented a series of production increases that resulted in a more balanced market. This included the new price band mechanism mentioned above, which aimed to keep the crude oil price within $22–$28. The target price was attained by the first quarter of 2001.

OPEC continued to be vigilant through 2001 and 2002, and took swift and consistent actions to stabilize the price; nonetheless, the events of September 11 and other circumstances that had already slowed down the

movement from one equilibrium to another is known as *comparative static analysis*. Throughout this analysis, we assume that no legal restraints (discussed later in this chapter) are in effect and that the price system is free to work to allocate goods among consumers.

Changes in Demand

Suppose that *The Globe and Mail* reports that consumer incomes are expected to rise by about 3.0 percent over the next year, and the number of individuals over 25 years of age will reach an all-time high by the end of the year. We can use our supply and

TABLE 2–2	World Market for Crude Oil, 1998–2002: Oil Supply/Demand Balance (quarterly data, millions of barrels a day)					
	(a) World Demand	(b) Non-OPEC Supply[a]	(c) Difference (a) − (b)	(d) OPEC Production[b]	(e) Balance (c) − (d)	World Price (WTI)
2002						
4Q	78.4	52.21	26.19	26.09	−0.1	$28.18
3Q	76.4	51.25	25.15	25.47	0.32	$28.33
2Q	74.69	51.67	23.02	24.61	1.59	$26.27
1Q	76.7	51.32	25.38	25.15	−0.23	$21.61
2001						
4Q	76.4	50.5	25.9	26.3	0.4	$20.40
3Q	75.7	49.9	25.8	27.2	1.4	$26.60
2Q	74.6	49.2	25.4	27.1	1.7	$27.88
1Q	76.6	49.5	27.1	28.1	1	$28.81
2000						
Q	78	49.2	28.8	28.8	0	$31.98
3Q	75.6	48.5	27.1	28.7	1.6	$31.66
2Q	74.1	48.4	25.7	27.9	2.2	$28.79
1Q	75.6	48.8	26.8	26.5	−0.3	$28.73
1999						
4Q	76.4	48.2	28.2	26	−2.2	$24.54
3Q	73.6	47.3	26.3	26.3	0	$21.73
2Q	72.6	46.8	25.8	26.2	0.4	$17.66
1Q	75.8	47.5	28.3	27.6	−0.09	$13.05
1998						
4Q	74.8	47.2	27.6	27.3	−0.03	$12.87
3Q	72.9	46.4	26.5	27.3	0.8	$14.13
2Q	72.1	47.3	24.8	28.1	3.3	$14.66
1Q	74.2	48	26.2	28.3	2.1	$15.93

[a]Non-OPEC supply includes supply by OECD, North America, Western Europe, Pacific, developing countries, former Soviet Union, other Europe, China.
[b]Eleven OPEC nations: Venezuela, Algeria, Libya, Nigeria, Iran, Iraq, Kuwait, Qatar, Saudi Arabia, United Arab Emirates, Indonesia.
Source: Adapted from Statistics Canada, "Industrial Organization and Concentration in Manufacturing, Mining, and Logging Industries," Catalogue 31-514, 1980.

wheels of the world economy caused an anomalous (and yet substantial) drop in oil prices in Q401. In 2002, the world demand rebounded to some extent; but with non-OPEC producers hiking their production, OPEC was forced to scale back its supply in order to keep the price within its target band.

demand apparatus to examine how these changes in market conditions will affect car rental agencies like Avis, Hertz, and Budget. It seems reasonable to presume that rental cars are normal goods: a rise in consumer incomes will most likely increase the demand for rental cars. The increased number of consumers aged 25 and older will also increase demand, since those who rent cars must be at least 25 years old.

We illustrate the ultimate effect of this increase in the demand for rental cars in Figure 2–11. The initial equilibrium in the market for rental cars is at point A, where demand curve D^0 intersects the market supply curve, S. The changes reported in *The Globe and Mail* suggest that the demand for rental cars will increase over the next year, from D^0 to some curve like D^1. The equilibrium moves to point B,

FIGURE 2–11 Effect of a Change in Demand for Rental Cars

An increase in demand resulting from an increase in income causes the demand curve to shift from D^0 to D^1 and the equilibrium to move from point A to point B. At B, equilibrium price has risen from $30 to $36 and equilibrium quantity from 10 000 to 10 400 rentals per day.

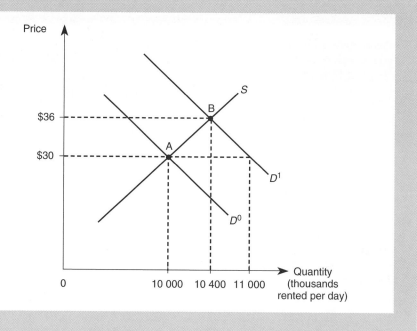

where car rental companies rent more cars and charge a higher price than before the demand increase.

The reason for the rise in rental car prices is as follows. The growing number of consumers aged 25 or older, coupled with the rise in consumer incomes, increases the demand for rental cars. At the old price of $25 per day, there are only 10 000 cars available. This is less than the 11 000 cars that customers want to rent at that price. Car rental companies thus find it in their interest to raise their prices and to increase their quantity supplied of rental cars until ultimately enough cars are available at the new equilibrium price of $36 to exactly equal the quantity demanded at this higher price.

Demonstration PROBLEM 2–5

The manager of a fleet of cars currently rents them out at the market price of $36 per day, with renters paying for their own gasoline and oil. In a front-page newspaper article, the manager learns that economists expect gasoline prices to rise dramatically over the next year, due to increased tensions in the Middle East. What should she expect to happen to the price of rental cars and to the number of cars her company rents?

Answer

Since gasoline and rental cars are complements, the increase in gasoline prices will decrease the demand for rental cars. To see the impact on the market price and quantity of rental cars, let D^1 in Figure 2–11 represent the initial demand for rental cars, so that the initial equilibrium is at point B. An increase in the price of gasoline will shift the demand curve for rental cars to the left (to D^0), resulting in a new equilibrium at point A. Thus, she should expect the price of rental cars to fall, and expect to rent out fewer cars over the next year.

Inside BUSINESS

2-4 Changes in the Supply and Demand for DVD Players

Prior to 1999, only a handful of manufacturers produced DVD (digital versatile disk or digital video disk) players. As a result, the price of DVD players hovered around $1000. Happily for consumers, 1999 was touted as the year of the DVD: entry by more than 20 manufacturers pushed the price of DVD players down from the stratosphere and into the budgets of millions of households that were willing to pay about $200 per machine. The number of DVD players sold is expected to continue increasing into 2004, thanks to the increasing number of movie titles released on DVD and available at rental outlets such as Blockbuster and Hollywood Videos.

Figure 2–12 illustrates the changing market for DVD players. In 1998 the market was in equilibrium at point A, where the equilibrium price of DVD players was about $1000. Due to the dramatic increase in the number of manufacturers of DVD players, the supply of DVD play-

ers increased (shifted rightward) to $S^{Current}$, resulting in a new equilibrium at point B. As a result of this increase in supply, the price of DVD players declined dramatically.

By the year 2005, many economists predict that the demand for DVD players will increase. In particular, the increase in the supply of movies released on DVD and stocked at major outlets will dramatically lower the price of renting or buying such movies. These lower prices for DVD movies (a *complement* to DVD players) will shift the demand for DVD players rightward to D^{2005}, resulting in a new equilibrium at point C. Notice that the predicted increase in demand will lead to even more DVD players being purchased, but the resulting impact on price is expected to be small compared to the sharp decline in DVD player prices that occurred during 1999. Accordingly, the predicted 2004 price of DVD players is closer to $200.

FIGURE 2-12 Market for DVD Players

Between 1998 and 2004, the increase in the number of manufacturers of DVD players caused the supply curve to shift to the right, driving down the price, as reflected by the movement from A to B. Furthermore, by 2005, the decrease in the price of DVD movies (a complement to DVD) is expected to cause the demand curve for DVD to shift to the right, a movement from B to C.

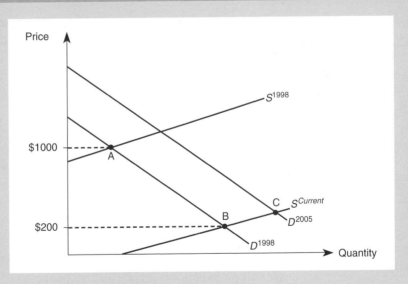

Changes in Supply

We can also use our supply and demand framework to predict how changes in one or more supply shifters will affect the equilibrium price and quantity of goods or services. For instance, consider a bill before Parliament that would increase the payroll tax paid by all employers, small and large alike. How would this bill affect the prices charged for goods at retailing outlets?

FIGURE 2–13 Effect of a Change in Supply

An increase in payroll taxes increases the cost of production. This causes the supply curve to shift up and to the left from S^0 to S^1, giving rise to an increase in the price to P^1 and a decrease in quantity of output sold to Q^1, point B.

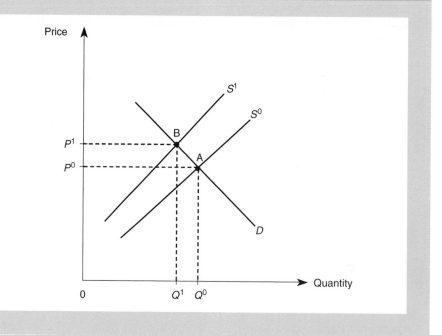

The increased payroll tax, which can reflect an increase in the CPP (Canada Pension Plan) premium, in the EI (Employment Insurance) premium, or in the health tax, or in a combination of them, would increase the cost to retailers and other firms of hiring workers. While firms might lower wages to some extent to offset the new cost, the net effect would be to raise the total cost to the firm of hiring workers. These higher labour costs, in turn, would decrease the supply of retail goods. The final result of the legislation would be to increase the prices charged by retailing outlets and to reduce the quantity of goods sold there.

We can see this more clearly in Figure 2–13. The market is initially in equilibrium at point A, where demand curve D intersects the market supply curve, S^0. Higher input prices decrease supply from S^0 to S^1, and the new competitive equilibrium moves to point B. In this instance, the market price rises from P^0 to P^1, and the equilibrium quantity decreases from Q^0 to Q^1.

Simultaneous Shifts in Supply and Demand

Managers in both the private and the public sector sometimes encounter events that lead to simultaneous shifts in demand and supply. A tragic example occurred in the late 1990s when an earthquake hit Kobe, Japan. The earthquake did considerable damage to Japan's sake wine industry, and the nation's supply of sake decreased as a result. Unfortunately, the stress caused by the earthquake led many to increase their demand for sake and other alcoholic beverages. We can use the tools of this chapter to examine how these simultaneous changes in supply and demand affected the equilibrium price and quantity of sake.

In Figure 2–14, the market is initially in equilibrium at point A, where demand curve D^0 intersects market supply curve S^0. Since the earthquake led to a simultaneous decrease in supply and increase in demand for sake, suppose supply decreases from S^0 to S^1 and demand increases from D^0 to D^1. In this instance, a new competitive

---

FIGURE 2–14 A Simultaneous Increase in Demand and Decrease in Supply Raises the Equilibrium Price

An earthquake that simultaneously increases demand for sake to D^1 and decreases supply to S^1 will drive both the price and the quantity higher, point B. If, however, it causes the supply curve to decrease to S^2 instead of S^1, the price will increase while quantity sold will decrease, C.

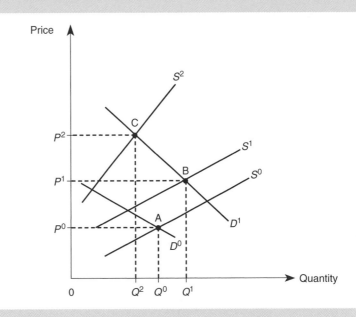

---

equilibrium occurs at point B; the price of sake increases from P^0 to P^1, and the quantity consumed increases from Q^0 to Q^1.

As the curves are drawn in Figure 2–14, the effect of the decrease in supply and increase in demand was to increase both the price and the quantity. But what if instead of shifting from S^0 to S^1, the supply curve shifted much farther to the left to S^2 so that it intersected the new demand curve at point C instead of B? In this instance, price would still be higher than the initial equilibrium price, P^0. But the resulting quantity would be lower than the initial equilibrium (point C implies a lower quantity than point A). Thus, we have seen that when demand increases and supply decreases, the market price rises, but the market quantity may rise or fall depending on the relative magnitude of the shifts.

When using supply and demand analysis to predict the effects of simultaneous changes in demand and supply, you must be careful that the predictions are not artifacts of how far you have shifted the curves. As shown in Table 2–3, simultaneous changes in demand and supply generally lead to ambiguities regarding whether the equilibrium price or quantity will rise or fall. A valuable exercise is to draw various simultaneous shifts in supply and demand to verify the results summarized in Table 2–3.

TABLE 2–3 Equilibrium Price and Quantity: The Impact of Simultaneous Shifts in Demand and Supply

Nature of the Change	Increase in Demand	Decrease in Demand
Increase in supply	Price: Ambiguous Quantity: Increases	Price: Decreases Quantity: Ambiguous
Decrease in supply	Price: Increases Quantity: Ambiguous	Price: Ambiguous Quantity: Decreases

FIGURE 2–15 A Simultaneous Increase in Demand and Supply Raises the Equilibrium Quantity

While a simultaneous increase in demand—due to the increased funding—and an increase in supply—due to the tax cut—unambiguously increases quantity of output sold, its impact on the price depends on the relative magnitude by which these two curves shift. Given the shift in demand, D^0 to D^1, the price level rises, point C, for a small increase in supply (S^1); it decreases, point F, for a large increase in supply (S^3); and it stays unchanged when supply increases to S^2, point F.

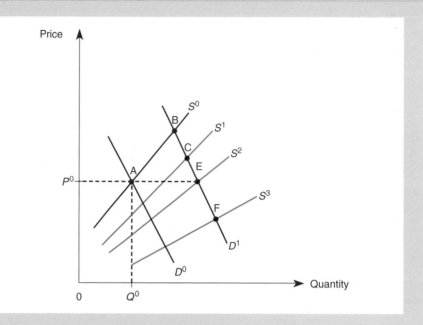

Demonstration PROBLEM 2–6

Suppose you are the manager of a chain of computer stores. For obvious reasons you have been closely following developments in the computer industry, and have just learned that the federal government has passed through Parliament a two-prong program designed to further enhance the Canadian computer industry's position in the global economy. The legislation provides increased funding for computer education in primary and secondary schools, as well as tax breaks for firms that develop software. As a result of this legislation, what do you predict will happen to the equilibrium price and quantity of software?

Answer

The equilibrium quantity certainly will increase, but the market price may rise, remain the same, or fall, depending on the relative changes in demand and supply. To see this, note that the increased funding for computer education at primary and secondary schools will lead to an increase in the demand for software, since it is a normal good. The reduction in taxes on software manufacturers will lead to an increase in the supply of software. To examine the impact of these simultaneous changes, suppose the initial equilibrium is at point A in Figure 2–15, where demand curve D^0 and supply curve S^0 intersect. Suppose demand increases to D^1. If supply increases a small amount to S^1, the resulting equilibrium (point C) implies a higher price and quantity. If supply increases by the same amount as demand to S^2, the resulting equilibrium (point E) implies no change in price but a higher quantity. If supply increases by much more than the increase in demand to S^3, the resulting equilibrium (point F) implies a lower price and greater quantity. In all cases, the equilibrium quantity increases. But the effect on the market price depends on the relative magnitudes of the increases in demand and supply.

Effect of Government Interventions

The previous section showed how prices and quantities are determined in a free market. In some instances, government places limits on how much prices are allowed to rise or fall, and these restrictions can affect the market equilibrium. In this section, we examine the impact of several forms of government intervention.

Price Ceilings

One basic implication of the economic doctrine of scarcity is that there are not enough goods to satisfy the desires of all consumers at a price of zero. As a consequence, some method must be used to determine who gets to consume goods and who does not. People who do not get to consume goods are essentially discriminated against. One way to determine who gets a good and who does not is to allocate the goods according to hair colour: if you have red hair, you get the good; if you don't have red hair, you don't get the good.

The price system uses price to determine who gets a good and who does not. The price system allocates goods to consumers who are willing and able to pay the most for the goods. If the competitive equilibrium price of a pair of jeans is $40, consumers willing and able to pay $40 will purchase the good; consumers unwilling or unable to pay that much for a pair of jeans will not buy the good.

It is important to keep in mind that it is not the price system that is "unfair" if one cannot afford to pay the market price for a good; rather, it is unfair that we live in a world of scarcity. Any method of allocating goods will seem unfair to someone, because there are not enough resources to satisfy everyone's wants. For example, if jeans were allocated to people on the basis of hair colour instead of the price system, you would think this allocation rule was unfair unless you were born with the "right" hair colour.

Often individuals who are discriminated against by the price system attempt to persuade the government to intervene in the market by requiring producers to sell the good at a lower price. This is only natural, for if we were unable to own a house because we had the wrong hair colour, we most certainly would attempt to get the government to pass a law allowing people with our hair colour to own a house. But then there would be too few houses to go around, and some other means would have to be used to allocate houses to people.

Suppose that, for whatever reason, the government views the equilibrium price of P^e in Figure 2–16 as "too high" and passes a law prohibiting firms from charging prices above P^c. Such a price is called a **price ceiling**.

Do not be confused by the fact that the price ceiling is below the initial equilibrium price; the term *ceiling* refers to that price being the highest permissible price in the market. It does not refer to a price set above the equilibrium price. In fact, if a ceiling were imposed above the equilibrium price, it would have no effect; the equilibrium price would be below the maximum legal price.

Given the regulated price of P^c, quantity demanded exceeds quantity supplied by the distance from A to B in Figure 2–16; there is a shortage of $Q^d - Q^s$ units. The reason for the shortage is twofold. First, producers are willing to produce less at the lower price, so the available quantity is reduced from Q^e to Q^s. Second, consumers wish to purchase more at the lower price; thus, quantity demanded increases from Q^e to Q^d. The result is that there is not enough of the good to satisfy all consumers willing and able to purchase it at the price ceiling.

How, then, are the goods to be allocated now that it is no longer legal to ration them on the basis of price? In most instances, goods are rationed on the basis of "first

price ceiling
The maximum legal price that can be charged in a market.

FIGURE 2-16 A Price Ceiling

The price ceiling of P^c, set above equilibrium value, results in an increase in quantity demanded and a decrease in quantity supplied, giving rise to an excess demand situation, AB. Since only Q^s units of the good are available, consumers would be willing to pay P^F for each unit (full economic price), point F on the demand curve. The difference, $P^F - P^c$, reflects the price per unit consumers are willing to pay extra to purchase the good. The shaded area reflects the loss of both consumer and producer surplus.

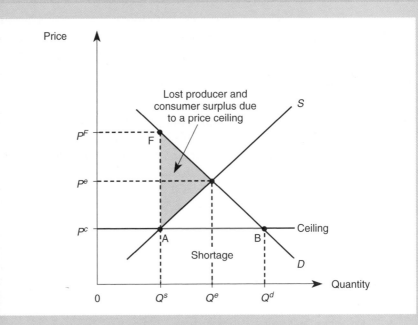

come, first served." As a consequence, price ceilings typically result in long lines such as those created in the 1970s due to price ceilings on gasoline. Thus, price ceilings discriminate against people who have a high opportunity cost of time and do not like to wait in lines. If a consumer has to wait in line two hours to buy 40 litres of gasoline and his or her time is worth $5 per hour, it costs the consumer $2 \times \$5 = \$10$ to wait in line. Since 40 litres of gasoline are purchased, this amounts to spending $0.25 per litre waiting in line to purchase the good. Another example is freezing the university tuition fees in the face of a rising number of applications. In this case, there would be an excess demand for university enrolment and grades would have to be used to ration the limited number of spaces, that is, to determine who gets accepted and who not.

This basic idea can be depicted graphically. Under the price ceiling of P^c, only Q^s units of the good are available. Since this quantity corresponds to point F on the demand curve in Figure 2–16, we see that consumers are willing to pay P^F for another unit of the good. By law, however, they cannot pay the firm more than P^c. The difference, $P^F - P^c$, reflects the price per unit consumers are willing to pay by waiting in line. The **full economic price** paid by a consumer (P^F) is thus the amount paid to the firm (P^c), plus the implicit amount paid by waiting in line ($P^F - P^c$). The latter price is paid not in dollars but through opportunity cost and thus is termed the *nonpecuniary price*.

full economic price
The dollar amount paid to a firm under a price ceiling, plus the nonpecuniary price.

$$
\underset{\substack{\text{Full} \\ \text{economic} \\ \text{price}}}{P^F} = \underset{\substack{\text{Dollar} \\ \text{price}}}{P^c} + \underset{\substack{\text{Nonpecuniary} \\ \text{price}}}{(P^F - P^c)}
$$

As Figure 2–16 shows, P^F is greater than the initial equilibrium price, P^e. When opportunity costs are taken into account, the full economic price paid for a good is actually higher after the ceiling is imposed. The shaded area in the figure reflects the producer and consumer surplus that is lost when output is reduced to Q^s.

Demonstration PROBLEM 2–7

On the basis of your answer to the Department of Foreign Affairs and International Trade (Demonstration Problem 2–4), one of the senators raises a concern that the free-market price might be too high for the typical Russian citizen to pay. Accordingly, she asks you to explain what would happen if the Russian government privatized the market, but then set a ceiling price at the Russian equivalent of $1.50. How do you answer? Assume that the market demand and supply curves (in Canadian dollar equivalent prices) are still given by

$$Q^d = 10 - 2P \text{ and } Q^s = 2 + 2P$$

Answer

Since the price ceiling is below the equilibrium price of $2, a shortage will result. More specifically, when the price ceiling is $1.50, quantity demanded is

$$Q^d = 10 - 2(1.50) = 7$$

and quantity supplied is

$$Q^s = 2 + 2(1.50) = 5$$

Thus, there is a shortage of $7 - 5 = 2$ units.

To determine the full economic price, we simply determine the maximum price consumers are willing to pay for the five units produced. To do this, we first set quantity equal to 5 in the demand formula:

$$5 = 10 - 2P^F$$

or

$$2P^F = 5$$

Next, we solve this equation for P^F to obtain the full economic price, $P^F = \$2.50$. Thus, consumers pay a full economic price of $2.50 per unit; $1.50 of this price is in money, and $1 represents the nonpecuniary price of the good.

From the preceding analysis, one might wonder why the government would ever impose price ceilings. One answer might be that politicians do not understand the basics of supply and demand. This is probably not the answer, however.

The answer lies in who benefits from and who is harmed by ceilings. When lines develop due to a shortage caused by a price ceiling, people with high opportunity costs are hurt, while people with low opportunity costs may actually benefit. For example, if you have nothing better to do than wait in line, you will benefit from the lower dollar price; your nonpecuniary price is close to zero. On the other hand, if you have a high opportunity cost of time because your time is valuable to you, you are made worse off by the ceiling. If a particular politician's constituents tend to have a lower-than-average opportunity cost, that politician naturally will attempt to invoke a price ceiling.

Sometimes when shortages are created by a ceiling, goods are not allocated on the basis of lines. Producers may discriminate against consumers on the basis of other factors, including whether or not consumers are regular customers. During the gasoline shortage of the 1970s, many gas stations sold gas only to customers who regularly used the stations. In California during the late 1990s, price ceilings were imposed on the fees that banks charged nondepositors for using their automatic teller machines (ATMs). The banks responded by refusing to let nondepositors use their ATM machines. In other situations, such as ceilings on loan interest rates, banks may allocate money only to consumers who are relatively well-to-do.

The key point is that in the presence of a shortage created by a ceiling, managers must use some method other than price to allocate the goods. Depending on which method is used, some consumers will benefit and others will be worse off.

Price Floors

price floor
The minimum legal price that can be charged in a market.

In contrast to the case of a price ceiling, sometimes the equilibrium competitive price may be considered too low for producers. In these instances, individuals may lobby for the government to legislate a minimum legal price for a good. Such a price is called a **price floor**. Perhaps the best-known price floors are minimum wages, the lowest legal wages that can be paid to workers, and farm price supports—subsidies.

If the equilibrium price is above the price floor, the price floor has no effect on the market. But if the price floor is set above the competitive equilibrium level, such as P^f in Figure 2–17, there is an effect. Specifically, when the price floor is set at P^f, quantity supplied is Q^s and quantity demanded is Q^d. In this instance, more is produced than consumers are willing to purchase at that price, and a surplus develops. In the context of the labour market, there are more people looking for work than there are jobs to go around at that wage, and unemployment results. In the context of a

---

FIGURE 2-17 A Price Floor

When a price floor is introduced above the equilibrium level at P^f, supplied exceeds demanded by $Q^s - Q^d$. Since the producers are prevented from lowering the price, a surplus results, FG. Consumers end up paying a higher price P^f and purchasing fewer units Q^d. The total cost of this support policy is represented by the shaded area, $(Q^s - Q^d)P^f$.

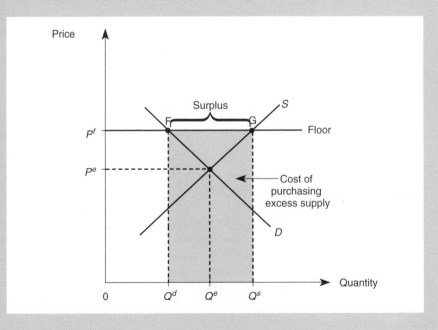

product market, the surplus translates into unsold inventories. In a free market, price would fall to alleviate the unemployment or excess inventories, but the price floor prevents this mechanism from working. Buyers end up paying a higher price and purchasing fewer units.

What happens to the unsold inventories? Sometimes the government agrees to purchase the surplus. This is the case with price floors on many agricultural products, such as cheese. Under a price floor, the quantity of unsold products is given by the distance from G to F in Figure 2–17, or $Q^s - Q^d$. If the government purchases this surplus at the price floor, the total cost to the government is $P^f (Q^s - Q^d)$. Since the area of a rectangle is its base times its height, the cost to the government of buying the surplus is given by the shaded area FGQ^sQ^d in Figure 2–17.

Demonstration PROBLEM 2–8

One of the Assistant Deputy Ministers of Foreign Affairs and International Trade has studied your analysis of Russian privatization (Demonstration Problems 2–4 and 2–7), but is worried that the free-market price might be too low to enable producers to earn a fair rate of return on their investment. He asks you to explain what would happen if the Russian government privatized the market, but agreed to purchase the good from suppliers at a floor price of $4. What do you tell the senator? Assume that the market demand and supply curves (in Canadian dollar equivalent prices) are still given by

$$Q^d = 10 - 2P \text{ and } Q^s = 2 + 2P$$

Answer

Since the price floor is above the equilibrium price of $2, the floor results in a surplus. More specifically, when the price is $4, quantity demanded is

$$Q^d = 10 - 2(4) = 2$$

and quantity supplied is

$$Q^s = 2 + 2(4) = 10$$

Thus, there is a surplus of $10 - 2 = 8$ units. Consumers pay a higher price ($4), and producers have unsold inventories of 8 units. However, the Russian government must purchase the amount consumers are unwilling to purchase at the price of $4. Thus, the cost to the Russian government of buying the surplus of 8 units is $4 \times 8 = \$32$.

Incidence of Taxes

incidence of tax
Where the burden of a tax falls.

The **incidence of tax** is basically who ends up paying a tax. When you buy products subject to sales taxes, you pay the price tag plus the tax. In some countries, sales taxes are pervasive and cover a large number of goods and services. In others, this is not the case. In some countries and tax jurisdictions, sales taxes are incorporated into the price tags, so you do not pay for taxes separately, whereas elsewhere the sales tax is added to the price. The important questions are:

1. How do we analyze the impact of sales taxes in the supply/demand framework?
2. What portion of the sales tax will consumers and producers end up paying? Will consumers end up paying all of it?

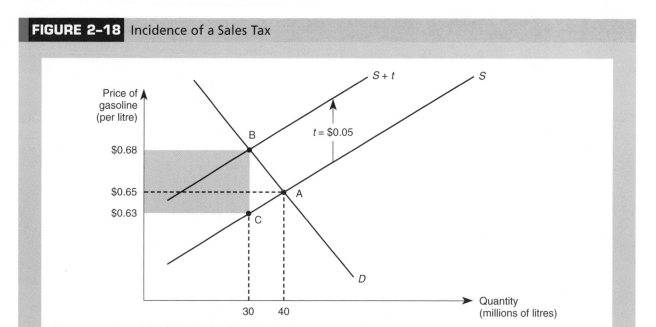

FIGURE 2-18 Incidence of a Sales Tax

When the sales tax is introduced, the equilibrium price paid by consumers rises to $0.68, while that received by sellers falls to $0.63.

Suppose the demand and supply curves before the tax are represented by D and S. The equilibrium price and the quantity before tax are $0.65 and 40 million litres per week. Suppose the government levies a sales tax on gasoline of $0.05 per litre ($T$/litre). What are the effects of this tax on quantity, and price paid by consumers and received by producers?

When the sales tax is introduced, the supply curve jumps up by the amount of the tax, $0.05, while leaving the position of the demand curve intact. As the overall price increases, however, quantity (of gas) demanded decreases—a movement along the demand curve from A to B. To see this logic, remember that the supply curve represents the quantities a firm is to offer at alternative prices. The supply curve (S), in Figure 2–18, reflects prices excluding taxes charged by the sellers. When the tax is levied, the price charged by the sellers must reflect the tax. Therefore, the supply curve shifts up to reflect a decrease in supply by the amount of tax ($0.05 on the vertical axis). Note that this is a parallel shift, since the amount of tax per litre is fixed and does not change with the volume of consumption. The tax-inclusive supply curve reflects the fact that sellers are willing to supply the same quantities only if they get paid $0.05 more than before per litre. The $0.05 added to the price is the sellers' new obligation to the government. Put differently, sellers are willing to sell as much gasoline as before at the same (net of the tax) prices.

At the new equilibrium, point B, the price has risen and the volume of transactions has fallen. However, the equilibrium price of $0.68 is the price paid by consumers. Note that the price does not rise by the full amount of $0.05 to consumers, even though the government has levied a $0.05 tax. In order to see this point more clearly, remember that the vertical distance between the two supply curves is $0.05, and that the demand curve is sloped. As a result of this slope, the degree to which the tax burden is passed on to the consumer is reflected by the slope of the curve, and not by a linear move up the Y-axis. Therefore, as long as the demand curve is not perfectly vertical, consumers will pay only a portion of the tax. The remainder is paid by sellers (suppliers) that are receiving $0.63 per litre (point C). In this example, consumers' share of the tax is $0.03 and producers' share is $0.02. The government collects its $0.05 regardless how the burden is shared. In fact, the government revenue from new taxation is equal to volume of gasoline sold after the imposition of tax (30 million litres) times $0.05 per litre ($1.5 million). That is equal to the area of the shaded rectangle in Figure 2–18.

Demonstration PROBLEM 2-9

The market for small toasters is characterized by the following supply and demand curves:

$$\text{Supply: } P = 2Q^s$$

and

$$\text{Demand: } P = 42 - Q^d$$

where P is the price of a toaster and Q^s and Q^d are quantity demanded and supplied, respectively. What are equilibrium values of price and quantity?

Now suppose the government levies a tax of $3 on each toaster sold, collected from sellers. What quantity of toasters will be sold in equilibrium? What per-unit price do buyers pay? What after-tax price do sellers now receive? How much money goes to the government? How is the burden of this excise tax shared between buyers and sellers?

Answer

Equilibrium values of Q and P are, respectively, 14 toasters and $28 per toaster. With the excise tax, the supply curve shifts up (in a parallel fashion) and the algebraic expression representing the supply curve changes to $P = 2Q^s + 3$. Therefore, the quantity falls to 13 units, the price (paid by buyers) rises to $29, and the after-tax price received by sellers falls to $26 (= $29 − $3 tax). The government revenue from taxation equals $39 (= $3 × 13). Buyers' share of the new tax is 1/3 × ($1), whereas sellers' share is 2/3 × ($2).

Government Intervention in an Open Economy

Every nation produces little or none of certain products. Any domestic consumption of these products must therefore be satisfied by imports from other countries. For example, many countries do not produce oil, whereas some both produce and export it. Oil is an example of a mineral that is also considered a commodity. In other words, it is standardized, easily gradable, and internationally tradable. There are numerous other examples of commodities such as gold, other precious metals, forest products such as lumber, and agricultural products. Of course, exports and imports are not limited to commodities. These days, the bulk of world trade is in manufactures and services.

It is believed that the markets for commodities around the world should command a single price. That is, the price of crude oil should be the same in the world markets irrespective of the market location. A single world price situation, however, requires that costs of buying and selling and transportation costs, such as brokerage fees, be insignificant. The concept of a single world price or *law of one price*, therefore, applies to commodities. The world price for a tradable commodity is the price determined by world demand and world supply. The law of one price does not apply to manufactures and services that are differentiated. Naturally, it does not apply to products that are internationally non-tradable, either.

How much influence a country may have on the world market depends on the relative importance (supply and demand) of that country in the world market. For example, Saudi Arabia is a major player in the market for oil, as is Canada in nickel, uranium, and wheat. These countries are known as "price makers" for these commodities, as they are able to influence the world price for these goods. To understand the effect of world prices on a country's imports and exports of a commodity, however, it is simplest to study the case of "price takers," countries whose import and export levels in no way affect the worldwide demand and supply. Assuming that the law of one price prevails in this case, producers and consumers in the small economy face a world price they cannot influence by their own actions, a price treated as a given. This implies that in a small importing nation, consumers can buy whatever amount of the product they choose at that price; the world price does not change according to the volume of the nation's purchase. In other terms, a horizontal world supply curve prevails.

Similarly, in a small exporting nation producers can sell whatever amount of the product they choose at the world price; the world price does not change with the volume of the nation's sale. A horizontal world demand curve prevails.

To determine the pattern of trade for a nation, we first show the domestic demand and supply curves for some product, say oil. The intersection of these two curves tells us what the price and quantity would be if there were no foreign trade. Now compare this no-trade price with the world price of that product. If the world price is lower, the actual domestic price will fall below the no-trade price, there will be an excess demand for the product, and the shortage of domestic supply will be imported from abroad. Conversely, if the world price is higher, the actual price in the nation will exceed the no-trade price, there will be an excess of domestic supply over domestic demand, and the surplus production will be exported for sale abroad.

Imports

Figure 2–19 shows the case of an importing nation. Suppose the importing market is the market for oil. D^S and S^S are the small nation's demand and supply curves respectively, and D^W and S^W are the world demand and supply curves in the oil market. Facing the world price level, P^W, which is below the domestic price, P^S, the nation's consumers will demand more, Q^D, and its producers will produce less, Q^S. The resulting excess demand (shortage) for oil, $Q^S Q^D$, will be imported from abroad, as shown in panel (b).

The net gains and losses from free trade can be examined as follows. Clearly, not everyone benefits from free trade. Since free trade forces the domestic price of imports down, domestic consumers are better off and domestic producers worse off. Consumers' gains are measured by the increased consumer surplus, $(B + D)$, whereas sellers' losses are captured by the reduced producer surplus, B. Total surplus therefore rises by the net amount of D, indicating that trade raises the economic well-being of the country as a whole.

Tariff Policies

A **tariff** is a tax on imports or exports. An **import tariff**, which can be in the form of either a percentage or dollars per unit, raises the price of imports above the world

tariff
A tax on imports or exports.

import tariff
A tax on imports in the form of either a percentage or dollars per unit.

[Handwritten margin notes:]
- If $P_{WORLD} < P_{domestic}$, $P_{DOMESTIC}$ will fall below the no trade price creating excess demand, and causing domestic country to import good.
- If $P_{world} > P_{domestic}$ there will be excess domestic supply, causing the domestic country to export the good.

FIGURE 2-19 International Trade in an Importing Country

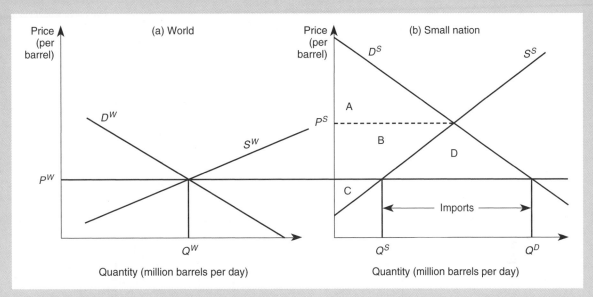

Being a price taker, the small country treats the world price of oil, P^W (intersection between the world demand and world supply of oil), as a given. At this price, its production level is Q^S and its consumption level is Q^D. The resulting gap, $Q^D - Q^S$, is imported.

price and hence reduces the quantity of imports. This moves the market closer to the pre-trade equilibrium point—the intersection of S^S and D^S in Figure 2–20. At this new tariff-ridden price, $P^W + T$, domestic consumption drops to $Q^{D'}$; domestic production increases to $Q^{S'}$, and $(Q^{D'} - Q^{S'})$ is imported. As a result, consumers lose, producers gain, and the government also gains by the amount of tariff revenue. The loss to consumers is equal to $(B' + E' + F' + G')$, producers' gain is equal to the area B', and the government revenue from the tariff is equal to the area F'. Therefore, the net effect of the tariff is a loss—a deadweight loss—equal to the sum of the areas $(E' + G')$. The area (triangle) E' represents the loss due to reduced consumption whereas the area (triangle) G' represents the efficiency loss due to increased production.

Demonstration PROBLEM 2-10

Suppose a small country's market for T-shirts is characterized by the following demand and supply expressions.

$$\text{Demand: } P = 4.5 - 0.05Q^d$$

and

$$\text{Supply: } P = 0.1Q^s$$

Assume that the world price of the standardized T-shirts is $1/unit. What are the pre-trade equilibrium values of the quantity and price in this small

FIGURE 2–20 The Effects of a Tariff

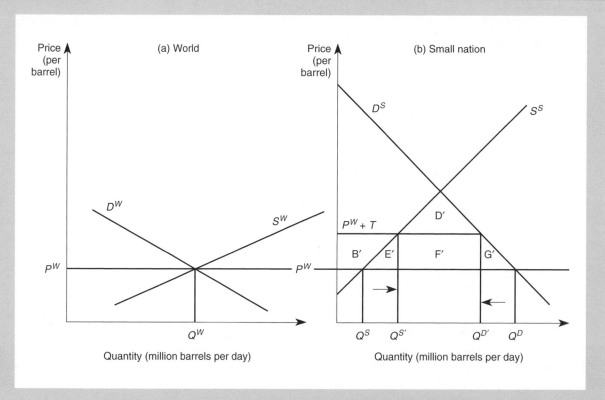

Imposition of tariff causes the domestic (tariff-ridden) price of oil to increase by T (tariff per unit). Domestic consumption decreases to $Q^{D'}$ and domestic production increases to $Q^{S'}$ and imports drop to $Q^{D'} - Q^{S'}$. Consumer surplus decreases by $B' + E' + F' + G'$, whereas producer surplus increases by B'. The government revenue from the tariff equals the area F (Imports $\times$ \$$T$). The net effect is a loss equal to the area of E' and G'.

country? With free trade, how many T-shirts are consumed and produced domestically, how many T-shirts are imported, and how much is paid?

Suppose now that the government imposes a per-unit tariff of \$1 on imports of T-shirts. What are the tariff-ridden levels of domestic consumption, domestic production, and imports of T-shirts? What is the magnitude of the deadweight loss?

Answer

In the absence of trade, the equilibrium value of the price and quantity are \$3 and 30 units, respectively. With free trade, at the world price of \$1, the quantity of T-shirts bought domestically increases to 70, while the level of domestic production decreases to 10. The volume of imports equals 60 T-shirts. With a tariff of \$1/unit, domestic price of T-shirts increases from \$1 to \$2/unit. Consumption, therefore, drops to 50 units, while production increases to 20 units. Imports drop to 30, and the deadweight loss due to the tariff equals to the sum of the area of the two triangles (not shown here): the loss associated with consumption, ½[\$1 $\times$ (20 − 10)], plus the loss associated with production, ½[\$1 $\times$ (70 − 50)], for a total of \$15.

ANSWERING THE Headline

Now that we have developed a formal apparatus for understanding how markets work, we will return to the story that opened this chapter.

Sam recognized that a cut in chip production will ultimately lead to higher chip prices. Since chips are a key input in the production of PCs, an increase in the price of chips would increase production costs and in turn lead to a decrease in the market supply of PCs, as indicated by the change in supply from S^0 to S^1 in Figure 2–21. Notice that total quantity of PCs sold in the market falls as the equilibrium moves from point A to point B. In light of this anticipated decline in PC sales, Sam and Jane discussed the wisdom of going ahead with their plan to double PC Solutions' work force at this time.

FIGURE 2–21 Rising Chip Prices Decrease the Supply of PCs

The rising chip prices shift the supply curve from S^0 to S^1 and the equilibrium point shifts from point A to point B. Given the demand curve D, the new equilibrium quantity of PCs will be lower and the price higher.

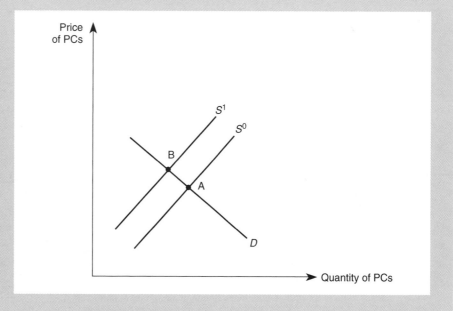

Summary

This chapter provided an overview of supply and demand and the interaction of these forces. We covered applications of demand, supply, comparative statics, price ceilings, and price floors. By reading this chapter and working through the demonstration problems presented, you should have a basic understanding of how to analyze the workings of a competitive market.

The model of supply and demand is just a starting point for this book. Throughout the remainder of the book, we assume you have a thorough understanding of the concepts presented in this chapter. In the next chapter, we will present the concepts of elasticity and show how to use them in making managerial decisions. We will also present some additional quantitative tools to help managers make better decisions.

Key Terms and Concepts

Conceptual and Computational Questions

1. The X-Corporation produces a good (called X) that is a normal good. Its competitor, Y-Corp., makes a substitute good that it markets under the name Y. Good Y is an inferior good.
   a. How will the demand for good X change if consumer incomes increase?
   b. How will the demand for good Y change if consumer incomes decrease?
   c. How will the demand for good X change if the price of good Y decreases?
   d. Is good Y a lower-quality product than good X? Explain.

2. Good X is produced in a competitive market using input A. Explain what would happen to the supply of good X in each of the following situations:
   a. The price of input A increases.
   b. An excise tax of $1 is imposed on good X.
   c. An ad valorem tax of 5 percent is imposed on good X.
   d. A technological change reduces the cost of producing additional units of good Y.

3. Suppose the supply function for product X is given by $Q_x^s = 50 + 0.5P_x - 5P_z$.
   a. How much of product X is produced when $P_x = \$500$ and $P_z = \$30$?
   b. How much of product X is produced when $P_x = \$50$ and $P_z = \$30$?
   c. Suppose $P_z = \$30$. Determine the supply function and inverse supply function for good X. Graph the inverse supply function.

4. The demand for good X is given by

$$Q_x^d = 1200 - \frac{1}{2}P_x + \frac{1}{4}P_y - 8P_z + \frac{1}{10}M$$

   Research shows that the prices of related goods are given by $P_y = \$5900$ and $P_z = \$90$, while the average income of individuals consuming this product is $M = \$55\,000$.
   a. Indicate whether goods Y and Z are substitutes or complements for good X.
   b. Is X an inferior or a normal good?
   c. How many units of good X will be purchased when $P_x = \$4910$?
   d. Determine the demand function and inverse demand function for good X. Graph the demand curve for good X.

5. The demand curve for product X is given by $Q_x^d = 460 - 4P_x$.
   a. Find the inverse demand curve.

  b. How much consumer surplus do consumers receive when $P_x = \$35$?

  c. How much consumer surplus do consumers receive when $P_x = \$25$?

  d. In general, what happens to the level of consumer surplus as the price of a good falls?

6. Suppose demand and supply are given by $Q^d = 50 - P$ and $Q^s = \dfrac{1}{2}P - 10$.

  a. What are the equilibrium quantity and price in this market?

  b. Determine the quantity demanded, the quantity supplied, and the magnitude of the surplus if a price floor of $42 is imposed in this market.

  c. Determine the quantity demanded, the quantity supplied, and the magnitude of the shortage if a price ceiling of $30 is imposed in this market. Also, determine the full economic price paid by consumers.

7. Use the graph shown here to answer these questions.

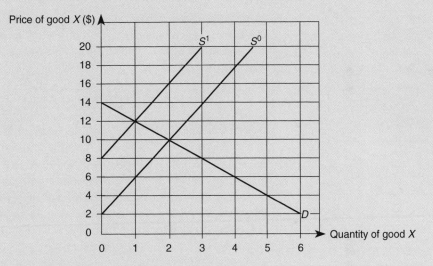

  a. Suppose demand is D and supply is S^0. If a price ceiling of $6 is imposed, what are the resulting shortage and full economic price?

  b. Suppose demand is D and supply is S^0. If a price floor of $12 is imposed, what is the resulting surplus? What is the cost to the government of purchasing any and all unsold units?

  c. Suppose demand is D and supply is S^0, so that the equilibrium price is $10. If an excise tax of $6 is imposed on this product, what happens to the equilibrium price paid by consumers? The price received by producers? The number of units sold?

  d. Calculate the level of consumer and producer surplus when demand and supply are given by D and S^0, respectively.

  e. Suppose demand is D and supply is S^0. Would a price ceiling of $2 benefit any consumers? Explain.

8. Suppose demand and supply are given by

$$Q^d_x = 7 - \frac{1}{2}P_x \quad \text{and} \quad Q^s_x = \frac{1}{4}P_x - \frac{1}{2}$$

  a. Determine the equilibrium price and quantity. Show the equilibrium graphically.

  b. Suppose a $6 excise tax is imposed on the good. Determine the new equilibrium price and quantity.

  c. How much tax revenue does the government earn with the $6 tax?

Problems and Applications

9. You are the manager of a midsized company that assembles personal computers. You purchase most components—such as random access memory (RAM)—in a competitive market. Based on your marketing research, consumers earning over $75 000 purchase 1.3 times more RAM than consumers with lower incomes. One morning, you pick up a copy of *The Globe and Mail* and read an article indicating that a new technological breakthrough will permit manufacturers to produce RAM at a lower unit cost. On the basis of this information, what can you expect to happen to the price you pay for random access memory? Would your answer change if, in addition to this technological breakthrough, the article indicated that consumer incomes are expected to grow over the next two years as the economy pulls out of recession? Explain.

10. You are the manager of a firm that produces and markets a generic type of soft drink in a competitive market. In addition to the large number of generic products in your market, you also compete against major brands such as Coca-Cola and Pepsi. Suppose that, due to the successful lobbying efforts of sugar producers in Canada, the federal government is going to levy a $0.50 per kilogram tariff on all imported raw sugar—the primary input for your product. In addition, Coke and Pepsi plan to launch an aggressive advertising campaign designed to persuade consumers that their branded products are superior to generic soft drinks. How will these events impact the equilibrium price and quantity of generic soft drinks?

11. Some have argued that higher cigarette prices do not deter smoking. While there are many arguments both for and against this view, some find the following argument to be the most persuasive of all: "The laws of supply and demand indicate that higher prices are ineffective in reducing smoking. In particular, higher cigarette prices will reduce the demand for cigarettes. This reduction in demand will push the equilibrium price back down to its original level. Since the equilibrium price will remain unchanged, smokers will consume the same number of cigarettes." Do you agree or disagree with this view? Explain.

12. You are the manager of an organization in Canada that distributes blood to hospitals in all provinces and territories. A recent report indicates that nearly 50 Canadians contract HIV each year through blood transfusions. Although every pint of blood donated in Canada undergoes a series of different tests, existing screening methods can detect only the antibodies produced by the body's immune system—not foreign agents in the blood. Since it takes weeks or even months for these antibodies to build up in the blood, newly infected HIV donors can pass along the virus through blood that has passed existing screening tests. Happily, researchers have developed a series of new tests aimed at detecting and removing infections from donated blood before it is used in transfusions. The obvious benefit of these tests is the reduced incidence of infection through blood transfusions. The report indicates that the current price of decontaminated blood is $80 per pint. However, if the new screening methods are adopted, the demand and supply for decontaminated blood will change to $Q^d = 175 - P$ and $Q^s = 2P - 200$. What price do you expect to prevail if the new screening methods are adopted? How many units of blood will be used in Canada? What is the level of consumer and producer surplus? Illustrate your findings in a graph.

13. As a result of increased tensions in the Middle East, oil production is down by 1.21 million barrels per day—a 5 percent reduction in the world's supply of crude oil. Explain the likely impact of this event on the market for gasoline and the market for small cars.

14. You are an assistant to a senator who chairs an ad hoc committee on reforming taxes on telecommunication services. On the basis of your research, Bell Canada has spent over $15 million on related paperwork and compliance costs. Moreover, depending on the locale, telecom taxes can amount to as much as 25 percent of a consumer's phone bill. These high tax rates on telecom services have become quite controversial, due to the fact that the deregulation of the telecom industry has led to a highly competitive market. Your best estimates indicate that, using current tax rates, the monthly market demand for telecommunication services is given by $Q^d = 250 - 5P$ and the market supply (including taxes) is $Q^s = 4P - 110$ (both in millions), where P is the monthly price of telecommunication services. The senator is considering tax reform that would dramatically cut tax rates, leading to a supply function under the new tax policy of $Q^s = 4.171P - 110$. How much money would a typical consumer save each month as a result of the proposed legislation?

15. XYZ Dry Foods Distributors specializes in the wholesale distribution of dry goods, such as rice and dry beans. The firm's manager is concerned about an article he read in the morning's *National Post* indicating that the incomes of individuals in the lowest income bracket are expected to increase by 10 percent over the next year. While the manager is pleased to see this group of individuals doing well, he is concerned about the impact this will have on XYZ Dry Foods. What do you think is likely to happen to the price of the products XYZ Dry Foods sells? Why?

16. Suppose the federal government is considering introduction of legislation to eliminate or reduce the surcharges that banks impose on noncustomers who make $10 million in withdrawals from other banks' ATM machines. On average, noncustomers earn a wage of $20 per hour and pay ATM fees of $1.50 per transaction. It is estimated that banks would be willing to maintain services for 4 million transactions at $0.75 per transaction, while noncustomers would attempt to conduct 16 million transactions at that price. Estimates suggest that, for every gap of 1 million between the desired and available transactions, a typical consumer will have to spend an extra minute travelling to another machine to withdraw cash. Using this information, construct a graph to carefully illustrate the impact of legislation that would put a $0.75 cap on the fees banks can charge for noncustomer transactions.

17. Rapel Valley in Chile is renowned for its ability to produce high-quality wine at a fraction of the cost of many other vineyards around the world. Rapel Valley produces over 20 million bottles of wine annually, of which 500 000 are exported to Canada. Each bottle entering Canada is subject to a $0.50 per bottle excise tax, which generates about $250 000 in tax revenues. Strong La Niña weather patterns have caused unusually cold temperatures, devastating many of the wine producers in that region of Chile. How will La Niña affect the price of Chilean wine? Assuming La Niña does not impact Canada's wine-producing regions, how will La Niña impact the market for domestic wines?

18. Assume that domestic supply and the demand curve for oil are represented by the following equations:

$$Q^s = 14 + 0.25P$$

$$Q^d = 19 - 0.25P$$

Furthermore, assume that the supply curve for foreign oil is represented by $P^W = \$5$ per barrel.

   a. If the domestic economy were to rely entirely on domestic oil production and also to ban flow of foreign oil, what would be domestic price and quantity of production and consumption of oil?

b. Is foreign oil cheaper to produce than domestic oil? If the domestic economy were to remove its ban on imported oil, what would be the level of domestic production and consumption of oil? How much oil would be imported?
c. Now assume that the domestic government decides to levy a 25 percent tariff on imported oil. Find the new level of domestic production, consumption, and volume of imported oil.

Quantitative Demand Analysis

Head<u>line</u>

Leonard Asper's Elasticity

At a conference call on September 17, 2001, Leonard Asper, CEO of CanWest Global Communications Corp. and new owner of the [*National*] *Post*, was announcing the Aspers' convergence strategy to downsize operations and reduce their corporate debt. This involved laying off about 130 employees, including roughly 60 editorial staff. At the time of the layoffs, the media and entertainment conglomerate carried $3.9 billion in debt, most of which was the result of the largest transaction in the history of Canadian media when the Aspers bought the Southam chain of newspapers and the *National Post* for $3.2 billion. In addition to these job cuts, CanWest announced cutting several sections of the *Post* and bulk sales, suspending its semiannual dividend payout, and selling television stations in order to get out of debt.

After his brief speech, analysts were allowed to ask questions. Responding to publisher's comment that he expected no significant decline in readership, Tim Casey, an analyst at BMO Nesbitt Burns, countered, "So let me get this straight: you're going to reduce the size of the paper so it covers less sports, less arts. You're not going to give away as many papers—in fact, you're not going to give away any—and you're going to raise the price. And you don't expect readership to go down?" Clearly flustered, Leonard Asper replied, "If you offer somebody something for free, of course they're going to take it for free." He argued that a price hike wouldn't deter readers, even if they're paying more money for a thinner paper. "It's like the proverbial cup of coffee that has gone from 60¢ to $3," said Asper. "We believe there's some price elasticity in newspapers."

Was Leonard Asper's response convincing? What could he mean by saying "there is some price elasticity"?

Source: Adapted from *Canadian Business*, October 15, 2001.

Introduction

In Chapter 2 we saw that the demand for a firm's product (Q_x^d) depends on its price (P_x), the prices of substitutes or complements (P_y), consumer incomes (M), and other variables (H) such as advertising, the size of the population, or consumer expectations:

$$Q_x^d = f(P_x, P_y, M, H) \qquad (3\text{--}1)$$

Up until now, our analysis of the impact of changes in prices and income on consumer demand has been qualitative rather than quantitative; that is, we have indicated only the directions of the changes and said little about their magnitude. The first half of this chapter remedies this by showing how a manager can use elasticities of demand to quantify the impact of changing market conditions on the firm's sales.

The second half of the chapter describes regression analysis, which is the technique economists use to estimate the parameters of demand functions. The primary focus is on how a manager can use managerial economics to evaluate information available in the library or provided by the firm's research department. Accordingly, we will explain how to interpret regression results and how managers can use regression tools contained in spreadsheet programs like Excel to actually estimate simple demand relationships.

The Elasticity Concept

Suppose some variable, such as the price of a product, increased by 10 percent. What would happen to the quantity demanded of the good? From the analysis in Chapter 2 and the law of demand, we know that the quantity demanded would fall. It would be useful for a manager to know whether the quantity demanded would fall by 5 percent, 10 percent, or some other amount.

The primary tool used to determine the magnitude of such a change is elasticity analysis. Indeed, the most important concept introduced in this chapter is elasticity. Elasticity is a very general concept. An **elasticity** measures the responsiveness of one variable to changes in another variable. For example, the elasticity of your grade with respect to studying, denoted $E_{G, S}$, is the percentage change in your grade ($\%\Delta G$) that will result from a given percentage change in the time you spend studying ($\%\Delta S$). In other words,

elasticity
A measure of the responsiveness of one variable to changes in another variable; the percentage change in one variable that arises due to a given percentage change in another variable.

$$E_{G, S} = \frac{\%\Delta G}{\%\Delta S}$$

Since $\%\Delta G = \Delta G/G$ and $\%\Delta S = \Delta S/S$, we may also write this as $E_{G, S} = (\Delta G/\Delta S)(S/G)$. Notice that $\Delta G/\Delta S$ represents the slope of the functional relation between G and S; it tells the change in G that results from a given change in S. By multiplying this by S/G, we convert each of these changes into percentages, which means that the elasticity measure does not depend on the units in which we measure the variables G and S.

A Calculus ALTERNATIVE

If the variable G depends on S according to the functional relationship $G = f(S)$, the elasticity of G with respect to S may be found using calculus:

$$E_{G, S} = \frac{dG}{dS} \frac{S}{G}$$

Two aspects of an elasticity are important: (1) whether it is positive or negative and (2) whether it is greater than 1 or less than 1 in absolute value. The sign of the elasticity determines the relationship between G and S. If the elasticity is positive, an increase in S leads to an increase in G. If the elasticity is negative, an increase in S leads to a decrease in G.

Whether the absolute value of the elasticity is greater or less than 1 determines how responsive G is to changes in S. If the absolute value of the elasticity is greater than 1, the numerator is larger than the denominator in the elasticity formula, and we know that a small percentage change in S will lead to a relatively large percentage change in G. If the absolute value of the elasticity is less than 1, the numerator is smaller than the denominator in the elasticity formula. In this instance, a given percentage change in S will lead to a relatively small percentage change in G. It is useful to keep these points in mind as we define some specific elasticities.

Own Price Elasticity of Demand

own price elasticity
A measure of the responsiveness of the quantity demanded of a good to a change in the price of that good; the percentage change in quantity demanded divided by the percentage change in the price of the good.

We begin with a very important elasticity concept: the **own price elasticity** of demand, which measures the responsiveness of quantity demanded to a change in price. Later in this section we will see that this measure can be used by managers to determine the quantitative impact of price hikes or cuts on the firm's sales and revenues. The own price elasticity of demand for good X, denoted E_{Q_x, P_x}, is defined as

$$E_{Q_x, P_x} = \frac{\% \Delta Q_x^d}{\% \Delta P_x} \tag{3–2}$$

If the own price elasticity of demand for a product is -2, for instance, we know that a 10 percent increase in the product's price leads to a 20 percent decline in the quantity demanded of the good, since $-20\%/10\% = -2$.

A Calculus ALTERNATIVE

The own price elasticity of demand for a good with a demand function $Q_x^d = f(P_x, P_y, M, H)$ may be found using calculus:

$$E_{Q_x, P_x} = \frac{\partial Q_x^d}{\partial P_x} \frac{P_x}{Q_x}$$

Recall that two aspects of an elasticity are important: (1) its sign and (2) whether it is greater or less than 1 in absolute value. By the law of demand, there is an inverse relation between price and quantity demanded; thus, the own price elasticity of demand is a negative number. The absolute value of the own price elasticity of demand can be greater or less than 1 depending on several factors that we will discuss next. However, it is useful to introduce some terminology to aid in this discussion.

First, demand is said to be **elastic** if the absolute value of the own price elasticity is greater than 1:

elastic demand
Demand is elastic if the absolute value of the own price elasticity is greater than 1.

$$|E_{Q_x, P_x}| > 1$$

inelastic demand
Demand is inelastic if the absolute value of the own price elasticity is less than 1.

Second, demand is said to be **inelastic** if the absolute value of the own price elasticity is less than 1:

$$|E_{Q_x, P_x}| < 1$$

unit-elastic demand
Demand is unit-elastic if the absolute value of the own price elasticity is equal to 1.

Finally, demand is said to be **unit-elastic** if the absolute value of the own price elasticity is equal to 1:

$$|E_{Q_x, P_x}| = 1$$

Conceptually, the quantity consumed of a good is relatively responsive to a change in the price of the good when demand is elastic and relatively unresponsive to changes in price when demand is inelastic. This means that price increases will reduce consumption very little when demand is inelastic. However, when demand is elastic, a price increase will reduce consumption considerably.

Elasticity and Total Revenue

Table 3–1 shows the hypothetical prices and quantities demanded of software, the own price elasticity, and the total revenue ($TR = P_x Q_x$) for the linear demand function, $Q_x^d = 80 - 2P_x$. Notice that the absolute value of the own price elasticity gets larger as price increases. In particular, the slope of this linear demand function is constant ($\Delta Q_x^d / \Delta P_x = -2$), which implies that $E_{Q_x, P_x} = (\Delta Q_x^d / \Delta P_x)(P_x / Q_x)$ increases in absolute value as P_x increases. Thus, the own price elasticity of demand varies along a linear demand curve.

When the absolute value of the own price elasticity is less than 1 (points A through D in Table 3–1), an increase in price increases total revenue. For example, an increase in price from $5 to $10 per unit increases total revenue by $250. Notice that for these two prices, the corresponding elasticity of demand is less than 1 in absolute value.

When the absolute value of own price elasticity is greater than 1 (points F through I in Table 3–1), an increase in price leads to a reduction in total revenue. For example, when the price increases from $25 (where the own price elasticity is −1.67) to $30 (where the own price elasticity is −3), we see that total revenue decreases by $150. The price-quantity combination that maximizes total revenue in Table 3–1 is at point E, where the own price elasticity equals −1.

The demand curve corresponding to the data in Table 3–1 is presented in the top panel of Figure 3–1, while the total revenue associated with each price-quantity combination on the demand curve is graphed in the lower panel. As we move up the demand curve from point A to point I, demand becomes increasingly elastic. At point E, where demand is unit-elastic, total revenue is maximized. At points to the northwest of E, demand is elastic and total revenue decreases as price increases. At points to the southeast of E, demand is inelastic and total revenue increases when price

	Price of Software (P_x)	Quantity of Software Sold (Q_x)	Own Price Elasticity (E_{Q_x, P_x})	Total Revenue ($P_x Q_x$)
A	$ 0	80	0.00	$ 0
B	5	70	−0.14	350
C	10	60	−0.33	600
D	15	50	−0.60	750
E	20	40	−1.00	800
F	25	30	−1.67	750
G	30	20	−3.00	600
H	35	10	−7.00	350
I	40	0	−∞	0

TABLE 3–1 Total Revenue and Elasticity ($Q_x^d = 80 - 2P_x$)

increases. This relationship among the changes in price, elasticity, and total revenue is called the *total revenue test*.

Principle	**TOTAL REVENUE TEST**
	If demand is elastic, an increase (decrease) in price will lead to a decrease (increase) in total revenue. If demand is inelastic, an increase (decrease) in price will lead to an increase (decrease) in total revenue. Finally, total revenue is maximized at the point where demand is unit-elastic, at which point a change in *P* yields no change in total revenue.

Managers pursuing the "Cut price and make it up in volume" strategy are, in effect, using the total revenue test. To see this, suppose the research department of a chain of discount stores estimates that the own price elasticity of demand for products sold at its outlets is −1.7. If the company cuts prices by 5 percent, will sales increase

FIGURE 3–1 Demand, Elasticity, and Total Revenue

A movement from point A to point I indicates an increase in elasticity. When demand is elastic, between points I to E, a decrease in price results in an increase in total revenue from $0 to $800. When demand is inelastic, between points E to A, a decrease in price results in a decrease in total revenue from $800 to $0. When demand is unit-elastic, at point E, total revenue is maximized at $800.

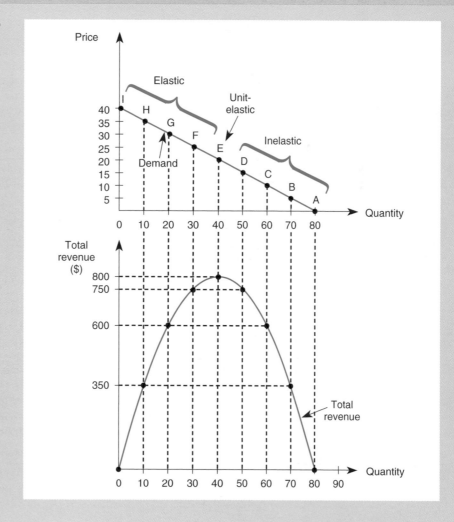

Inside BUSINESS

3-1 Calculating and Using the Arc Elasticity: An Application to Intra-city Passenger Travel

The text shows how managers can use the price elasticity of demand to analyze the impact of a price change on a good's sales volume. While in many instances managers can obtain estimates of elasticities from the library or the firm's research staff, sometimes managers are confronted with situations where elasticity estimates are not readily available. Fortunately, all is not lost in these instances, thanks to a concept called the *arc elasticity of demand*.

To be specific, suppose a manager has data that show when the price of a good was P_1, consumers purchased Q_1 units of the good. When the price changed to P_2, Q_2 units were purchased. Other things equal, these data can be used to approximate the price elasticity of demand for the good by using the arc elasticity formula:

$$E_{Q_x, P_x}^{Arc} = \frac{\Delta Q_x^d}{\Delta P_x} \times \frac{Average\ P}{Average\ Q}$$

In the formula, the average Q is

$$(Q_1 + Q_2)/2$$

and the average P is

$$(P_1 + P_2)/2$$

In order to see that this formula can be used to compute an elasticity from real-world data, consider the table from

Toronto's new toll highway (407 ETR Express Route) website indicating ridership on this highway. The figures represent the vehicle-kilometres travelled during a month.[1]

Since its inauguration six years ago, the Express Route's toll rates have increased five times, the dates for which are highlighted in Table 3–2. For purposes of calculation, however, we have focused on the period immediately before and after the first toll rate increase, September 27, 1999.

There are several justifications for this choice. First, the data exhibit seasonality patterns in most part of the year. While ridership tends to increase steadily between February and August of every year, the period between October and February is characterized by a downward trend. Therefore, it is likely that the impact on demand (ridership) of the toll rate changes in these periods—May 2000, January 2001, January 2002, and February 2003—are masked or dominated by the seasonality trend displayed by the data. On the other hand, that is not the case for the period of September to October, during which ridership exhibits either a stable or an upward trend, not a downward trend. The year 1999 is the only year in which ridership defies its seasonal trend during the September-October period and falls instead of rising.

Second, the period of September to October of 1999 is short enough that the influence of other factors can be confidently ignored. Third, the structure of toll rates,

TABLE 3-2	New Toll Highway Ridership, Vehicle-Kilometres Travelled During a Month				
	1999	**2000**	**2001**	**2002**	**2003**
January	80 494 161	96 781 942	108 896 286	128 859 358	132 002 894
February	82 662 503	98 690 468	101 081 669	121 859 739	121 117 558
March	94 282 901	109 342 334	113 496 837	131 658 058	133 661 213
April	96 805 554	106 898 035	111 941 117	142 770 822	135 421 468
May	104 610 518	123 177 366	128 627 276	156 948 270	153 183 944
June	117 173 179	130 547 113	132 236 874	161 433 595	
July	119 788 381	127 810 679	141 228 838	171 030 239	
August	121 995 562	140 102 030	167 215 191	172 755 171	
September	121 736 299	130 278 109	149 077 720	162 215 632	
October	118 568 132	130 296 551	161 920 898	168 246 182	
November	114 423 098	122 392 517	155 257 975	152 715 635	
December	130 344 093	105 060 804	129 800 318	135 638 884	

Note: The highlighted boxes show the dates that toll rates increased: September 27, 1999, May 1, 2000, January 1, 2001, January 1, 2002, and February 1, 2003.

which at times has been characterized by three categories (periods)—daytime peak hours, daytime off-peak hours, and night periods—and sometimes by two, was least disturbed by the toll rate change of 1999 than by the other rate changes.

Immediately before the price change, the highway toll for daytime off-peak period (9:30 a.m. to 4:00 p.m. and 7:00 p.m. to 11:00 p.m. on weekdays, and 5:30 a.m. to 11:00 p.m. on Saturdays, Sundays, and holidays), was $0.07 per kilometre for light (under five tonnes) vehicles. The corresponding quantity (ridership) for month of September 1999 was 121 736 299 VKT (vehicle kilometres travelled). Thus,

$$P_1 = \$0.07/km$$

and

$$Q_1 = 121\ 736\ 299$$

represent one point on the demand curve (for intra-city highway travel).

In October, the toll rate rose to $0.08 per kilometre for light vehicles during daytime off-peak hours[2] while the quantity dropped to 118 568 132 VKT, constituting the second point on the demand curve.

On the basis of these two points on the demand curve, we may approximate the price elasticity of demand for a fully electronic toll expressway in Toronto by using the arc elasticity formula:

$$E^{Arc}_{Q_x, P_x} = \frac{(Q_2 - Q_1)(P_1 + P_2)/2}{(P_2 - P_1)(Q_1 + Q_2)/2}$$

$$\frac{(118\ 568\ 132 - 121\ 736\ 299)}{(8 - 7)} \times$$

$$\frac{(8 + 7)/2}{(118\ 568\ 132 + 121\ 736\ 299)/2}$$

$$= -0.197$$

Note that arc elasticity is designed to provide a summary measure of price elasticity over the range of prices between $0.07 and $0.08.

Highway Toll Changes: Toll Rate During Daytime Off-Peak Period

September 1999	October 1999
$0.07	$0.08

The own price elasticity of demand is less than 1 in absolute value (inelastic), so by the total revenue test we know that the increase in the toll rate over the period resulted in higher total expenditures on travelling.

It is important to point out that the arc elasticity technique described here only approximates the true elasticity of demand. The accuracy of the approximation depends crucially on the assumption that the demand curve did not shift between September and October 1999. Judging by the observed upward pattern between September and October in subsequent years, however, one can confidently argue that the calculated figure (-0.197) understates the true price elasticity. The percentage drop in the quantity demanded would have been larger than 2.64% had the upward seasonal trend been removed.

Nonetheless, this low elasticity is an interesting result given that the calculation was done for a toll increase during off-peak hours, travelling during which is conceptually regarded as a luxury in relation to travelling during peak hours, which is a necessity.

Monthly Ridership: Vehicle Kilometres Travelled

September 1999	October 1999
121 736 299	118 568 132

1. See Table 3–2.
2. While the toll rates during other two remaining travel periods, daytime peak-hours and nightly period, remained unchanged, the daytime off-peak rate changes were not limited to light vehicles. For heavy single-unit vehicles, the toll rate was up by $0.02 from $0.14, and for heavy multiple unit vehicles the rate was up by $0.03 from $0.21. Nonetheless, these two categories of vehicles were disregarded given that more than 90 percent of this highway traffic belongs to light vehicles.

Source: 407 ETR (Express Toll Route) website, Toronto <www.407etr.com>, accessed June 2003.

enough to increase revenues due to the increased sales volume? We can answer this question by setting $-1.7 = E_{Q_x, P_x}$ and $-5 = \%\Delta P_x$ in the formula for the own price elasticity of demand:

$$-1.7 = \frac{\%\Delta Q_x^d}{-5}$$

Solving this equation for $\%\Delta Q_x^d$ yields $\%\Delta Q_x^d = 8.5$. In other words, the quantity of goods sold will rise by 8.5 percent if store prices are reduced by 5 percent. Since the percentage increase in quantity demanded is greater than the percentage decline in prices ($|E_{Q_x, P_x}| > 1$), the price cut will actually raise the firm's sales revenues. Expressed differently, since demand is elastic, a price cut results in a greater than proportional increase in sales, and thus increases the firm's total revenues.

perfectly elastic demand
Demand is perfectly elastic if the own price elasticity is infinite in absolute value. In this case the demand curve is horizontal.

In extreme cases the demand for a good may be perfectly elastic or perfectly inelastic. Demand is **perfectly elastic** if the own price elasticity of demand is infinite in absolute value. Demand is **perfectly inelastic** if the own price elasticity of demand is zero.

When demand is perfectly elastic, a manager who raises price even slightly will find that none of the good is purchased. In this instance the demand curve is horizontal, as illustrated in Figure 3–2(a). In contrast, when demand is perfectly inelastic, consumers do not respond at all to changes in price. In this case the demand curve is vertical, as shown in Figure 3–2(b).

perfectly inelastic demand
Demand is perfectly inelastic if the own price elasticity is zero. In this case the demand curve is vertical.

Usually, however, demand is neither perfectly elastic nor perfectly inelastic. In these instances knowledge of the particular value of an elasticity can be useful for a manager. Large firms, the government, and universities commonly hire economists or

FIGURE 3–2 Perfectly Elastic and Inelastic Demand

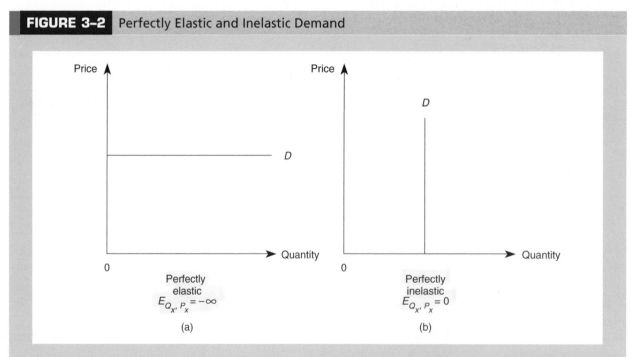

(a) The demand curve in part (a) represents a good with a perfect elasticity of demand.
(b) The demand curve in part (b) represents a good that has a zero price elasticity of demand or is perfectly inelastic.

statisticians to estimate the demand for products. The manager's job is to know how to interpret and use such estimates.

Factors Affecting the Own Price Elasticity

Now that you understand what the own price elasticity is and how it can be used to assess the impact of price changes on sales volume and revenues, we will discuss three factors that affect the magnitude of the own price elasticity of a good: available substitutes, time, and expenditure share.

Available Substitutes

One key determinant of the elasticity of demand for a good is the number of close substitutes for that good. Intuitively, the more substitutes available for the good, the more elastic the demand for it. In these circumstances, a price increase leads consumers to substitute toward another product, thus reducing considerably the quantity demanded of the good. When there are few close substitutes for a good, demand tends to be relatively inelastic. This is because consumers cannot readily switch to a close substitute when the price increases. Note that demand may be inelastic if perfect substitutes are available but inconvenient to access (for example, milk at a corner store).

A key implication of the effect of the number of close substitutes on the elasticity of demand is that the demand for broadly defined commodities tends to be more inelastic than the demand for specific commodities. For example, the demand for food (a broad commodity) is more inelastic than the demand for beef. Short of starvation, there are no close substitutes for food, and thus the quantity demanded of food is much less sensitive to price changes than is a particular type of food, such as beef. When the price of beef increases, consumers can substitute toward other types of food, including chicken, pork, and fish. Thus, the demand for beef is more elastic than the demand for food.

Table 3–3 shows own price elasticities from several market studies in Canada. These studies reveal that broader categories of goods have more inelastic demand

TABLE 3-3 Selected Own Price Elasticities	
Market	**Own Price Elasticities**
Meat and fish	
Red meat	−0.69[a]
White meat	−0.93[a]
Fresh fish	−0.91[a]
Canned fish	−7.14[b]
Fresh salmon	(−8.33 to −14.28)[c]
Air transportation	
Leisure, short-distance	−1.52[d]
Business, short-distance	−0.73[d]
Wine	
Domestic wine	−0.61[e]
Imported wine	−1.27[e]
Domestic and imported wine combined	−0.53[e]

[a]K. G. Salvanes and D. J. DeVoretz, "Household Demand for Fish and Meat Products: Separability and Demographic Effect," *Marine Resource Economics* 12, 1997.
[b]D. J. DeVoretz, "An Econometric Demand Model for Canadian Salmon," *Canadian Journal of Agricultural Economics* 30, 1982.
[c]M. Kabir, and N. B. Ridler, "The Demand for Atlantic Salmon in Canada," *Canadian Journal of Agricultural Economics* 32, 1984.
[d]D. Gillen, W. G. Morrison, and C. Stewart, *Air Travel Demand Elasticities: Concepts, Issues and Measurement* (Ottawa: Department of Finance, 2003).
[e]M. Adrian, and B. S. Ferguson, "Demand for Domestic and Imported Alcohol in Canada," *Applied Economics* 19, 1987.

than more specifically defined categories. The own price elasticity of fish and of white and red meat are inelastic, whereas the elasticity of more specific food items such as canned fish and salmon are significantly elastic. These findings are consistent with our expectations, because there are many substitutes for canned fish and salmon but few for fish or meat as a whole.

Furthermore, when the demand for wine is considered, the reported estimate of the own price elasticity for the most broadly defined group (domestic and imported wine combined) is more inelastic than demand for either domestic or imported wine. This is consistent with the notion that different brands within a category, such as domestic and imported wine, are more closely substitutable than categories themselves, such as beer and wine.

Table 3–3 also reveals that necessities have more inelastic demand than luxuries. As expected, the demand for business (short-distance) air travel is inelastic, whereas the demand for leisure (short-distance) air travel is elastic. There are a larger number of substitutes for the latter than the former.

Similarly, when we reconsider the wine example, we find the demand for imported wine to be more inelastic than the demand for domestic wine. This is consistent with the notion that between an imported and domestic wine the former is more likely to be deemed a luxury than the latter.

Time

Demand tends to be more inelastic in the short term than in the long term. The more time consumers have to react to a price change, the more elastic the demand for the good. Conceptually, time allows the consumer to seek out available substitutes. For example, if a consumer has 30 minutes to catch a flight, he or she is much less sensitive to the price charged for a taxi ride to the airport than would be the case if the flight were several hours later. Given enough time, the consumer can seek alternative modes of transportation such as a bus, a friend's car, or even on foot. But in the short term, the consumer does not have time to seek out the available substitutes, and demand for taxi rides is more inelastic.

Table 3–4 provides short-term and long-term own price elasticities for a variety of meat and dairy products, and also fuel, wine, and cocoa. As expected, all the short-

TABLE 3–4	Selected Short- and Long-Term Own Price Elasticities	
Market	**Short-Term Own Price Elasticities**	**Long-Term Own Price Elasticity**
Beef	−0.32	−0.44[a]
Pork	−0.21	−0.29[a]
Chicken	−0.51	−0.26[a]
Eggs	−0.24	−0.35[a]
Milk	−0.49	−0.98[a]
Butter	−0.62	−0.74[a]
Cheese	−0.07	−0.40[a]
Ice cream	−0.26	−1.03[a]
Fuel	−0.20	−0.40[b]
Wine	−0.50	−1.56[c]
Cocoa	−0.18	−0.28[d]

[a]D. Gordon and T. Hazledine, "Modelling Farm-Retail Price Linkage for Eight Agricultural Commodities," Agriculture and Agri-Food Canada, Technical Report # 1/96, 1996.

[b]J. Lawson, "Transport CO_2 Emission Trends in Canada and the Potential for Mitigation," Transport Canada, 1999.

[c]J. A. Johnson and E. H. Oksanen, "Estimation of Demand for Alcoholic Beverages in Canada," *Review of Economics and Statistics* 59, 1977.

[d]International Cocoa Organization (ICCO), "The World Cocoa Market: An Analysis of Recent Trends and of Prospects," *R. Dand International Cocoa Trade*, 2nd ed. (Cambridge, UK: Woodhead Publishing, 1999).

Inside BUSINESS

3-2 Inelastic Demand for Prescription Drugs

Many people perceive the demand for prescription drugs and other pharmaceutical products to be perfectly inelastic. After all, a patient needing an expensive cardiovascular drug might die in the absence of treatment. Moreover, in many instances the cost of medication is paid by an insurance company and not by the patient. These two factors do tend to make the demand for many pharmaceutical products relatively inelastic. However, since surgery and lifestyle changes are substitutes for many lifesaving drugs, economic theory predicts that the demand for such products is unlikely to be perfectly inelastic.

The table here summarizes results from two recent studies that confirm this prediction: the demand for pharmaceutical products is inelastic, but not perfectly so. For instance, the own price elasticity of demand for anti-ulcer drugs is −0.7, while the own price elasticity of demand for cardiovascular drugs is slightly more inelastic at −0.4. Consequently, a 10 percent increase in the price of anti-ulcer drugs reduces their use by 7 percent. A 10 percent increase in the price of cardiovascular

drugs results in only a 4 percent reduction in quantity demanded.

The own price elasticities of demand reported here are based on the industry demand for each type of drug in the United States. The demand for particular brands within each industry is even more responsive to price changes.

Type of Drug	Own Price Elasticity
Cardiovascular	−0.4
Anti-infective	−0.9
Psychotherapeutic	−0.3
Anti-ulcer	−0.7

Sources: M. Baye, R. Maness, and S. Wiggins, "Demand Systems and the True Subindex of the Cost of Living for Pharmaceuticals," *Applied Economics* 29, 1997, pp. 1179–89; and E. Berndt, L. Bui, D. Reiley, and G. Urban, "Information, Marketing, and Pricing in the U.S. Anti-ulcer Drug Market," *American Economic Review* 85(2), May 1995, pp. 100–05.

term elasticities (except for chicken) are less (in absolute value) than the corresponding long-term elasticities. In the short term, all the own price elasticities are less than 1 in absolute value. The absolute values of the long-term own price elasticities are also less than 1, except for ice cream and wine.

Expenditure Share

Goods that make up a relatively small share of consumers' budgets tend to be more inelastic than goods for which consumers spend a sizable portion of their incomes. In the extreme case, where a consumer spends her or his entire budget on a good, the consumer must decrease consumption when the price rises. In essence, there is nothing to give up but the good itself. When a good makes up only a small portion of the budget, the consumer can reduce the consumption of other goods when the price of the good increases. For example, most consumers spend very little on salt; a small increase in the price of salt would reduce quantity demanded very little, since salt constitutes a small fraction of consumers' total budgets.

Would you expect the own price elasticity of demand for meat and fish to be more or less than that for air transportation? Since meat and fish are a much greater necessity than transportation (after all, most people cannot live without them), one should expect the demand for them to be more inelastic than the demand for air transportation. This is confirmed by Table 3–3.

Marginal Revenue and the Own Price Elasticity of Demand

We learned in Chapter 1 that *marginal revenue (MR)* is the change in total revenue arising from the sale of one additional unit of output, and that to maximize profits a firm should produce where marginal revenue equals marginal cost. We will explore profit-maximizing output and pricing decisions in detail later in this book, but it is

FIGURE 3–3 Demand and Marginal Revenue

Thus, marginal revenue for the first unit is *MR*, while marginal revenue for the third unit is zero. Note that for both units the price exceeds marginal revenue. Hence, the marginal revenue curve is located below the demand curve for a good. Marginal revenue is positive in the elastic portion of the curve, between units 0 to 2; it equals zero at the unit-elastic point, at 3 units; and it is negative when demand is inelastic, between units 4 to 6.

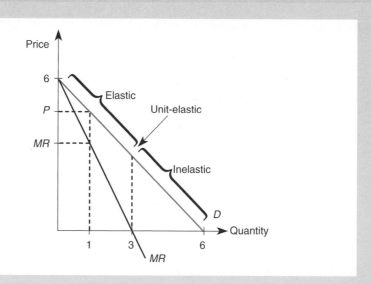

useful at this point to show how a firm's marginal revenue is linked to the own price elasticity of demand for the firm's product.

The line labelled *MR* in Figure 3–3 is the marginal revenue associated with each price-output pair on the demand curve. Notice that for a linear demand curve, the marginal revenue schedule lies exactly halfway between the demand curve and the vertical axis. Furthermore, marginal revenue is less than the price for each unit sold.[1]

Why is marginal revenue less than the price charged for the good? To induce consumers to purchase more of a good, a firm must lower its price. When the firm charges the same price for each unit sold, this lower price is received not only on the last unit sold, but also on those units that could have been sold at a higher price had the firm not lowered its price. To be concrete, suppose consumers purchase 1 unit of output at a price of $5 per unit, for total expenditures (revenues to producers) of $5 × 1 = $5. Consumers will purchase an additional unit of the good only if the price falls, say from $5 to $4 per unit. Now the firm receives $4 on the first unit sold, and $4 on the second unit sold. In effect, the firm loses $1 in revenue because the first unit now brings $4 instead of $5. Total revenue rises from $5 to $8 as output is increased by one unit, so marginal revenue is $8 − $5 = $3, which is less than price.

Notice in our example that by decreasing price from $5 to $4, quantity demanded increased from 1 unit to 2 units, and total revenues increased from $5 to $8. By the total revenue test, this means that demand is elastic over this range. In contrast, had the price reduction increased quantity demanded but decreased total revenues, demand would be inelastic over the range and marginal revenue would be negative. In fact, the more inelastic the demand for a product, the greater the decline in revenue that results from the increased quantity demanded brought on by a price cut.

---

[1]If the demand curve is given by $P = A - BQ$, then total revenue ($TR = P \times Q$) is given by $TR = AQ - BQ^2$ and marginal revenue (MR) is given by $A - 2BQ$.

The general relationship between marginal revenue and the elasticity of demand, which is formally derived in Chapter 8, is as follows:

$$MR = P\left[\frac{1 + E}{E}\right]$$

In this formula, which simplifies notation by dropping subscripts, P is the price of the good and E is the own price elasticity of demand for the good. Notice that when $-\infty < E < -1$, demand is elastic, and the formula implies that MR is positive. When $E = -1$, demand is unit-elastic, and marginal revenue is zero. As we learned in Chapter 1, the point where marginal revenue is zero corresponds to the output at which total revenue is maximized. Finally, when $-1 < E < 0$, demand is inelastic, and marginal revenue is negative. These general results are consistent with what you saw earlier in Table 3–1 for the case of linear demand.

Cross-Price Elasticity

cross-price elasticity
A measure of the responsiveness of the demand for a good to changes in the price of a related good; the percentage change in the quantity demanded of one good divided by the percentage change in the price of a related good.

Another important elasticity is the **cross-price elasticity** of demand, which reveals the responsiveness of the demand for a good to changes in the price of a related good. This elasticity helps managers ascertain how much its demand will rise or fall due to a change in the price of another firm's product. The cross-price elasticity of demand between goods X and Y, denoted E_{Q_x, P_y}, is mathematically defined as

$$E_{Q_x, P_y} = \frac{\% \Delta Q_x^d}{\% \Delta P_y} \tag{3–3}$$

For instance, if the cross-price elasticity of demand between Corel WordPerfect and Microsoft Word word processing software is 3, a 10 percent hike in the price of Word will increase the demand for WordPerfect by 30 percent, since $30\%/10\% = 3$. This increase in demand for WordPerfect occurs because consumers substitute away from Word and toward WordPerfect, due to the price increase.

A Calculus ALTERNATIVE

When the demand function is $Q_x^d = f(P_x, P_y, M, H)$, the cross-price elasticity of demand between goods X and Y may be found using calculus:

$$E_{Q_x, P_y} = \frac{\partial Q_x^d}{\partial P_y} \frac{P_y}{Q_x}$$

More generally, whenever goods X and Y are substitutes, an increase in the price of Y leads to an increase in the demand for X. Thus, $E_{Q_x, P_y} > 0$ whenever goods X and Y are substitutes. When goods X and Y are complements, an increase in the price of Y leads to a decrease in the demand for X. Thus, $E_{Q_x, P_y} < 0$ whenever goods X and Y are complements.

Table 3–5 provides some representative cross-price elasticities. As expected, the three pairs of products coffee and tea, electricity and natural gas, and margarine and butter have positive cross-price elasticity, implying that the products in each pair are substitutes for each other. More importantly, these data provide a quantitative

TABLE 3–5	Selected Cross-Price Elasticities
Market	**Cross-Price Elasticities**
Coffee and tea	0.15[a]
Electricity and natural gas	0.50[a]
Margarine and butter	1.53[a]
Cigarette and beer	−0.099[b]
Rail and truck modes*	0.144[c]
Rail and ship modes*	0.147[c]

[a]"Other Elasticities," PowerPoint presentation, Drake University, 2003, available <www.drake.edu>.
[b]Jonathan Gruber, Anindya Sen, Mark Stabile, "Estimating Price Elasticities When There Is Smuggling," NBER, Working Paper #8962, 2002.
[c]T. Oum, "Derived Demand for Freight Transport and Inter-Modal Competition in Canada," *Journal of Transport Economics and Policy* 13(2), 1979, pp. 149–168.
*For grain shipment on the Great Lakes and St. Lawrence Seaway.

measure of the impact of a change in the price of one product on another product. For instance, electricity and natural gas have a cross-price elasticity of 0.5. This means that if the price of electricity is increased by 10 percent, the demand for natural gas will increase by 5 percent.

It is interesting to note that the cross-price elasticity for cigarette and beer is negative, indicating complementarity between these two products. If the price of cigarette increases by 10 percent, the demand for beer decreases by 0.99 percent.

The cross-price elasticity of demand by mode (rail and truck or rail and ship) for grain is reported in the last two rows; as you would expect, these elasticities are positive, implying that alternative means of transportation are substitutes for each other. If the price of truck transport increases by 10 percent, the demand for rail transport increases by 1.44 percent; if the price of ship transport increases by 10 percent, the demand for rail transport increases by 1.47 percent.

Demonstration PROBLEM 3–1

You have just opened a new grocery store. Every item you carry is generic (generic bread, generic chicken, etc.). You recently read an article in *The National Post* reporting that the price of recreation is expected to increase by 15 percent. How will this affect your store's sales of generic food products?

Answer

Table 3–5 reveals that the cross-price elasticity of demand for coffee and tea is 0.15. If we insert the given information into the formula for the cross-price elasticity, we get

$$0.15 = \frac{\% \Delta Q_x^d}{15}$$

Solving this equation for $\% \Delta Q_x^d$, we get

$$\% \Delta Q_x^d = 2.25$$

Thus, coffee and tea are substitutes. If the price of recreation increases by 15 percent, you can expect the demand for generic food products to increase by 2.25 percent.

Cross-price elasticities play an important role in the pricing decisions of firms that sell multiple products. Indeed, many fast-food restaurants offer hamburgers for under $1 because their managers realize that hamburgers and sodas are complements: when consumers buy a hamburger, a soda typically accompanies the purchase. Thus, by lowering the price of burgers, a restaurant affects its revenues from both burger sales and soda sales. The precise impact on these revenues depends on the own price and cross-price elasticities of demand.

Specifically, we know from the total revenue test that a reduction in the price of hamburgers will increase (decrease) revenues from hamburger sales when the own price elasticity of demand for hamburgers is elastic (inelastic). In addition, since hamburgers and sodas are complements, reducing the price of hamburgers increases the quantity demanded of sodas, thus increasing soda revenues. The magnitude of the increase in soda revenues will depend on the magnitude of the cross-price elasticity of demand between burgers and soda.

More generally, suppose a firm's revenues are derived from the sales of two products, X and Y. We may express the firm's revenues as $R = R_x + R_y$, where $R_x = P_x Q_x$ denotes revenues from the sale of product X and $R_y = P_y Q_y$ represents revenues from product Y. The impact of a given percentage change in the price of product X ($\%\Delta P_x = \Delta P_x / P_x$) on the total revenues of the firm are given by:

$$\Delta R = [R_x(1 + E_{Q_x, P_x}) + R_y E_{Q_y, P_x}] \times \%\Delta P_x$$

To illustrate how to use this formula, suppose a restaurant earns $4000 per week in revenues from hamburger sales (product X) and $2000 per week from soda sales (product Y). Thus, $R_x = 4000 and $R_y = 2000. If the own price elasticity of demand for burgers is $E_{Q_x, P_x} = -1.5$ and the cross-price elasticity of demand between sodas and hamburgers is $E_{Q_y, P_x} = -4.0$, what would happen to the firm's total revenues if it reduced the price of hamburgers by 10 percent? Plugging these numbers into the above formula reveals

$$\Delta R = [\$4000(1 - 1.5) + \$2000(-4.0)](-10\%)$$
$$= \$200 + \$800$$
$$= \$1000$$

income elasticity
A measure of the responsiveness of the demand for a good to changes in consumer income; the percentage change in quantity demanded divided by the percentage change in income.

In other words, lowering the price of hamburgers 10 percent increases total revenues by $1000. Notice that $200 of this increase comes from increased burger revenues (the demand for burgers is elastic, so the reduction in the price of burgers increases hamburger revenues) and $800 of the increase is from additional soda sales (sales increase by 40 percent, resulting in additional revenues of $800 from soft drink sales). Note that cross-price impacts should always be considered when analyzing the revenue impact of a price change.

Income Elasticity

Income elasticity is a measure of the responsiveness of consumer demand to changes in income. Mathematically, the income elasticity of demand, denoted $E_{Q_x, M}$, is defined as

$$E_{Q_x, M} = \frac{\%\Delta Q_x^d}{\%\Delta M} \tag{3-4}$$

Inside BUSINESS

3-3 Using Alcohol Price Policies to Reduce Drunk Driving in Canada

A number of studies have attempted to model the relationship between alcohol consumption and economic factors, such as price and income, using elasticities. In general, studies in Canada have shown that the price elasticities of alcohol depend on a number of factors, including the type of alcoholic beverage, the time frame (short- or long-term), etc.

Earlier studies by Johnson and Oksanen[1] and Johnson and Oksanen[2] found that the consumption of alcoholic beverages (wine and spirits) was price elastic both in the short term and in the long term, whereas other beverages were price inelastic. For wine, the price elasticity in the short term ranged between −0.5 and −1.70, and for the long term it was −1.59. For spirits, the short-run price elasticity ranged between −0.91 and −1.36, and for the long term it was found to be −1.301. For beer, the price elasticity was −0.22 in the short term and −0.29 in the long term.

Adrian and Ferguson (1987)[3] found that the consumption of imported wine was price elastic, whereas other alcoholic beverages were price inelastic. The consumption of imported alcohol was more elastic than domestic alcohol for all types of alcoholic beverages; −0.37, −0.61, and −0.05 for domestic beer, wine, and spirits respectively; and −0.84, −1.27, and −0.96 for imported beer, wine, and spirits respectively.

A more recent paper by Adrian, Ferguson, and Her[4] studies this relationship in the context of the effect of "the price of alcohol on drunk driving." This study investigates three links: (1) the link between the price of alcohol and consumption of alcohol, (2) the link between consumption of alcohol and alcohol-involved traffic crashes and offences, and (3) the link between price of alcohol and drunk driving. Employing the time series as well as cross-section data for Ontario from 1972 to 1990, authors reported (1) a positive and significant relationship between alcohol consumption and alcohol-involved traffic accidents and crashes, and (2), in their rate of change, a negative and significant relation between alcohol price and alcohol-involved accidents and offences.

Offences = f (constant, income, young males, alcohol price)

Dependent Variable	Independent Variables	Coefficient	t-Statistic*
Offences	Constant	329.8	1.36
	Income	−0.009	−1.97
	Young males	33.5	3.45
	Alcohol price	−97.1	−4.00
R-square = 0.898			

*Statisticians use a t-test to determine statistically how large the coefficient of each independent variable (income, young males, alcohol price) must be in order for that variable to have a statistically significant impact on the dependent variable (offences). A simple rule of thumb to test for confidence in regression coefficient is for t-statistics to exceed 2. If so, we can be 95 percent confident that the estimated coefficient is significantly different from zero and that there is a statistically significant relationship between the variables.

A Calculus ALTERNATIVE

The income elasticity for a good with a demand function $Q_x^d = f(P_x, P_y, M, H)$ may be found using calculus:

$$E_{Q_x, M} = \frac{\partial Q_x^d}{\partial M} \frac{M}{Q_x}$$

When good X is a normal good, an increase in income leads to an increase in the consumption of X. Thus, $E_{Q_x, M} > 0$ when X is a normal good. When X is an inferior good, an increase in income leads to a decrease in the consumption of X. Thus, $E_{Q_x, M} < 0$ when X is an inferior good.

These results were further supported by a more sophisticated method of estimation—multiple regression techniques. Using these techniques (discussed later in this chapter), which allowed investigators to control for the effect of extraneous factors such as income, proportion of young males in population, changes in legal drinking age, etc., the authors were able to confirm a negative and significant relationship between price and the accidents and price and offences. While the impact on accidents and offences was examined in two separate equations in the original study, due to the overwhelming similarities between them only one of the estimated equations is reported here.

In this equation, the price of alcoholic beverages has a significant negative impact on alcohol-involved traffic offences. Income has a negative effect, and young males a positive and significant effect. An increase in income tends to increase consumption of alcohol, which in turn tends to increase the probability of being involved in accidents and committing driving offences. The magnitude of the effect of changes in the price of alcohol on reduction of drunk driving was estimated using a measure of elasticity. While the elasticity of alcohol-related motor vehicle accidents with respect to the price of alcohol was found to be relatively elastic (-1.2), the alcohol-related traffic offence was relatively price inelastic (-0.5).

These results suggest the conclusion that alcohol tax and pricing policies can be used to reduce the extent of drunk driving. Therefore, the question arises whether the government has been effective in the fight against drunk driving by raising the price of alcohol.

In Canada, taxes make up a considerable amount of the price of alcoholic beverages. In province of Ontario, the government's share, for the year this study was conducted, was over 60 percent in the price of a bottle of wine and 83 percent for spirits. Furthermore, alcohol tax revenues constituted an important component, up to 4 percent, of all government revenues in Canada. However, there are two caveats in this discussion. One, as indicated above, different alcoholic beverages have different price elasticities. Therefore, the effect of increasing the price of alcoholic beverages is not uniform. When price elasticity is low, consumption drops little; when it is high, consumption drops greatly. Furthermore, increasing the price of one type of beverage may induce consumers to switch to another. Two, price changes reflect changes in government alcohol tax revenue. If the drop in consumption caused by a tax-induced increase in the price is more than the increase in the price itself—elastic demand—the government revenue may be reduced. As is evidenced by higher costs of alcoholic beverages and the occurrence of black markets and smuggling, it would appear that, as with cigarettes, the Canadian government has actively used the price (tax) as an effective tool to achieve the delicate balance between revenue and consumption compared to other jurisdictions.

[1]James A. Johnson and Ernest H. Oksanen, "Socio-economic Determinants of the Consumption of Alcoholic Beverages," *Applied Economics* 6(4), 1974, pp. 293–301.
[2]James A. Johnson and Ernest H. Oksanen, "Estimation of Demand for Alcoholic Beverages in Canada from Pooled Time Series and Cross Sections," *The Review of Economics & Statistics* 59(1), 1977, pp. 113–18.
[3]M. Adrian and B. S. Ferguson, "Demand for Domestic and Imported Alcohol in Canada," *Applied Economics* 19(4), 1987, pp. 531–40.
[4]M. Adrian, B. S. Ferguson, and M. Her, "Can Alcohol Price Policies Be Used to Reduce Drunk Driving? Evidence from Canada," *Substance Use & Misuse* 36(13), December 2001, pp. 1923–57.

Table 3–6 presents some estimates of income elasticities for various products. The income elasticity for cocoa, 0.21, and for food, 0.45, in the first and second rows give us two pieces of information about the relationship between income and the demand for these items. First, since these income elasticities are positive, we know that cocoa and food in general are normal goods. Second, since their income elasticities are less than 1, we know that expenditures on these items grow less than income. When income declines, expenditures on cocoa and food decrease less rapidly than income.

The third row of Table 3–6 reveals that tobacco is an inferior good since its income elasticity is negative. According to this finding, consumption of tobacco will decrease by 0.50 percent for every 1 percent rise in consumer income.

In the fourth and fifth rows, the income elasticities of domestic and imported beer are reported. Notice that while both these figures are positive, domestic (Canadian)

TABLE 3–6	Selected Income Elasticities
Market	**Own Price Elasticities**
Cocoa	0.21[a]
Food	0.45[b]
Tobacco	−0.5[b]
Beer:	
Domestic	0.23[c]
Imported	1.54[c]
Services	1.75[d]

[a]International Cocoa Organization (ICCO), "The World Cocoa Market: An Analysis of Recent Trends and of Prospects," *R. Dand International Cocoa Trade*, 2nd ed. (Cambridge, UK: Woodhead Publishing, 1999).
[b]Cameron Gavin, "Consumer Choice and Market Demand," PowerPoint presentation, Oxford University, 2002, available <www.nuf.ox.ac.uk>.
[c]M. Adrian, B. S. Ferguson, "The Influence of Income on the Consumption of Alcohol in Ontario: A Cross-Section Study," in A. Carmi and S. Schneider, eds., *Drugs and Alcohol* (Medico-Legal Library Series) (Berlin: Springer-Verlag, 1986), pp. 151–157.
[d]"Other Elasticities," PowerPoint presentation, Drake University, 2003, available <www.drake.edu>.

beer, with an income elasticity of less than 1, is a normal good, whereas the imported beer, with an income elasticity of greater than 1, is a luxury (superior) good.

Finally, in the last row, the income elasticity of services, 1.75, indicates that not only is the relationship between income and demand for services positive, but also it is greater than 1. We therefore know that expenditures on services grow more than income—they are highly income elastic.

Demonstration PROBLEM 3–2

Your firm's research department has estimated the income elasticity of demand for nonfed ground beef to be −1.94. You have just read in *The Globe and Mail* that due to an upturn in the economy, consumer incomes are expected to rise by 10 percent over the next three years. As a manager of a meat processing plant, how will this forecast affect your purchases of nonfed cattle?

Answer

Set $E_{Q_x, M} = -1.94$ and $\%\Delta M = 10$ in the formula for the income elasticity of demand to obtain

$$-1.94 = \frac{\%\Delta Q_x^d}{10}$$

Solving this equation for $\%\Delta Q_x^d$ yields −19.4. Since nonfed ground beef has an income elasticity of −1.94 and consumer income is expected to rise by 10 percent, you can expect to sell 19.4 percent less nonfed ground beef over the next three years. Therefore, you should decrease your purchases of nonfed cattle by 19.4 percent, unless something else changes.

Other Elasticities

Given the general notion of an elasticity, it is not difficult to conceptualize how the impact of changes in other variables, such as advertising, may be analyzed in elastic-

TABLE 3–7 Selected Advertising Elasticities	
Market	**Advertising Elasticities**
Fluid milk	0.022
Butter	0.103
Cheese	0.035

Source: A. Tielu, "A Quantitative Analysis of Advertising Fluid Milk in Ontario," M.Sc. thesis, Department of Agricultural Economics and Business, University of Guelph, 1987.

ity terms. For example, the *own advertising elasticity* of demand for good X defines the percentage change in the consumption of X that results from a given percentage change in advertising spent on X. The *cross-advertising elasticity* between goods X and Y would measure the percentage change in the consumption of X that results from a given percentage change in advertising directed toward Y.

Table 3–7 shows estimates of the advertising elasticities for some dairy products. All elasticities are positive and less than 1. The fact that they are positive reveals, as you might expect, that increases in advertising lead to an increase in the demand for these products; that is, if dairy manufacturers increase their advertising, they can expect to sell more dairy products at any given price. Butter, at 0.103, seems to be more elastic than cheese and milk. This suggests that consumers are more sensitive to the information content of butter advertisements. Accordingly, a 10 percent increase in advertising on butter results an increase in demand for butter of 1.03 percent. The results also suggest that a 10 percent increase in advertising of cheese and milk will increase the demand for these products by 0.35 and 0.22 percent, respectively.

To illustrate how estimates such as these can be used by managers, imagine that you have just been hired by the Department of Tourism to help direct the tourist trade in Canada. Your boss knows you recently took a course in managerial economics and asks you how much she should increase advertising to increase the demand for recreation in Canada by 15 percent.

From Table 3–7, we know that $E_{Q_x, A_x} = 0.25$. Plugging this and $\%\Delta Q_x^d = 15$ into the general formula for the elasticity of Q_x^d with respect to A_x yields

$$0.25 = \frac{\%\Delta Q_x^d}{\%\Delta A_x} = \frac{15}{\%\Delta A_x}$$

Solving this equation for the percentage change in advertising shows that advertising must increase by a hefty 60 percent to increase the demand for recreation by 15 percent.

Obtaining Elasticities from Demand Functions

Now that you understand what elasticities are and how to use them to make managerial decisions, we will examine how to calculate elasticities from demand functions. First, we will consider elasticities based on linear demand functions. Then we will see how to calculate elasticities from particular nonlinear demand functions.

Elasticities for Linear Demand Functions

Given an estimate of a linear demand function, it is quite easy to calculate the various elasticities of demand.

Formula: Elasticities for Linear Demand. If the demand function is linear and given by

$$Q_x^d = \alpha_0 + \alpha_x P_x + \alpha_y P_y + \alpha_M M + \alpha_H H$$

the elasticities are

own price elasticity: $\quad E_{Q_x, P_x} = \alpha_x \dfrac{P_x}{Q_x}$ (3–5)

cross-price elasticity: $\quad E_{Q_x, P_y} = \alpha_y \dfrac{P_y}{Q_x}$ (3–6)

income elasticity: $\quad E_{Q_x, M} = \alpha_M \dfrac{M}{Q_x}$ (3–7)

A Calculus ALTERNATIVE

The elasticities for a linear demand curve may be found using calculus. Specifically,

$$E_{Q_x, P_x} = \frac{\partial Q_x^d}{\partial P_x} \frac{P_x}{Q_x} = \alpha_x \frac{P_x}{Q_x}$$

and similarly for the cross-price and income elasticities.

Thus, for a linear demand curve, the elasticity of demand with respect to a given variable is simply the coefficient of the variable multiplied by the ratio of the variable to the quantity demanded. For instance, the own price elasticity of demand is simply the coefficient of P_x (which is α_x in the demand function) multiplied by the ratio of the price of X to the quantity consumed of X.

As discussed earlier, for a linear demand curve, the value of an elasticity depends on the particular price and quantity at which it is calculated. This means that the own price elasticity is not the same as the slope of the demand curve. In fact, for a linear demand function, demand is elastic at high prices and inelastic at lower prices. To see this, note that when $P_x = 0$, $|E_{Q_x, P_x}| = \left| \alpha_x \dfrac{0}{Q_x} \right| = 0 < 1$. In other words, for prices near zero, demand is inelastic. On the other hand, when prices rise, Q_x decreases and the absolute value of the elasticity increases.

Demonstration PROBLEM 3–3

The daily demand for Invigorated PED shoes is estimated to be

$$Q_x^d = 100 - 3P_x + 4P_y - 0.01M + 2A_x$$

where A_x represents the amount of advertising spent on shoes (X), P_x is the price of good X, P_y is the price of good Y, and M is average income. Suppose good X sells at $25 a pair, good Y sells at $35, the company utilizes 50 units of advertising, and average consumer income is $20 000. Calculate and interpret the own price, cross-price, and income elasticity of demand.

Answer

To calculate the own price elasticity for linear demand, we use the formula

$$E_{Q_x, P_x} = \alpha_x \frac{P_x}{Q_x}$$

Here $\alpha_x = -3$, and $P_x = 25$. The only other information we need to calculate the elasticity is the quantity consumed of X. To find Q_x, we substitute the given values of prices, income, and advertising into the demand equation to get

$$Q_x^d = 100 - 3(25) + 4(35) - 0.01(20\,000) + 2(50) = 65 \text{ units}$$

Hence the own price elasticity of demand is given by

$$E_{Q_x, P_x} = -3\left(\frac{25}{65}\right) = -1.15$$

If Invigorated PED raises shoe prices, the percentage decline in the quantity demanded of its shoes will be greater in absolute value than the percentage rise in price. Consequently, demand is elastic: total revenues will fall if it raises shoe prices.

Similarly, the cross-price elasticity of demand is

$$E_{Q_x, P_y} = 4\left(\frac{35}{65}\right) = 2.15$$

Since this is positive, good Y is a substitute for Invigorated PED shoes. The income elasticity of demand for Invigorated PED's shoes is

$$E_{Q_x, M} = -0.01\left(\frac{20\,000}{65}\right) = -3.08$$

Invigorated PED's shoes are inferior goods, since this is a negative number.

Elasticities for Nonlinear Demand Functions

Managers frequently encounter situations where a product's demand is not a linear function of prices, income, advertising, and other demand shifters. In this section we demonstrate that the tools we developed can easily be adapted to these more complex environments.

Suppose the demand function is not a linear function but instead is given by

$$Q_x^d = cP_x^{\beta_x}P_y^{\beta_y}M^{\beta_M}H^{\beta_H}$$

where c is a constant. In this case, the quantity demanded of good X is not a linear function of prices and income but a nonlinear function. If we take the natural logarithm of this equation, we obtain an expression that is linear in the logarithms of the variables:[2]

$$\ln Q_x^d = \beta_0 + \beta_x \ln P_x + \beta_y \ln P_y + \beta_M \ln M + \beta_H \ln H \qquad (3–8)$$

log-linear demand
Demand is log-linear if the logarithm of demand is a linear function of the logarithms of prices, income, and other variables.

where $\beta_0 = \ln(c)$ and the β_i's are derived real numbers. This relation is called a **log-linear demand** function.

As in the case of linear demand, the sign of the coefficient of P_y determines whether goods X and Y are substitutes or complements, whereas the sign of the coefficient of M determines whether X is a normal or an inferior good. For example, if β_y is a positive number, an increase in the price of good Y will lead to an increase in the consumption of good X; in this instance, X and Y are substitutes. If β_y is a negative number, an increase in the price of good Y will lead to a decrease in the consumption of good X; in this instance, goods X and Y are complements.

Similarly, if β_M is a positive number, an increase in income leads to an increase in the consumption of good X, and X is a normal good. If β_M is a negative number, an increase in income leads to a decrease in the consumption of good X, and X is an inferior good.

Formula: Elasticities for Log-Linear Demand. When the demand function for good X is log-linear and given by

$$\ln Q_x^d = \beta_0 + \beta_x \ln P_x + \beta_y \ln P_y + \beta_M \ln M + \beta_H \ln H$$

the elasticities are

own price elasticity: $\quad E_{Q_x, P_x} = \beta_x$
cross-price elasticity: $\quad E_{Q_x, P_y} = \beta_y$
income elasticity: $\quad E_{Q_x, M} = \beta_M$

A Calculus ALTERNATIVE

The above result may also be derived using calculus. Taking the antilogarithm of the equation for log-linear demand gives

$$Q_x^d = cP_x^{\beta_x}P_y^{\beta_y}M^{\beta_M}H^{\beta_H}$$

where c is a constant. Using the calculus formula for an elasticity yields

$$E_{Q_x, P_x} = \frac{\partial Q_x^d}{\partial P_x}\left(\frac{P_x}{Q_x}\right) = \beta_x cP_x^{\beta_x-1}P_y^{\beta_y}M^{\beta_M}H^{\beta_H}\left(\frac{P_x}{cP_x^{\beta_x}P_y^{\beta_y}M^{\beta_M}H^{\beta_H}}\right) = \beta_x$$

and similarly for the cross-price and income elasticities.

Notice that when demand is log-linear, the elasticity with respect to a given variable is simply the coefficient of the corresponding logarithm. The own price elasticity of demand is the coefficient of $\ln(P_x)$, and in fact, the coefficient of *any* other logarithm on the right-hand side of the log-linear demand relation tells us the elasticity of demand with respect to that demand shifter. Since all of these coefficients are constants, none of the elasticities depend on the value of variables like prices, income, or advertising.

---

[2]Here, "ln" denotes the *natural logarithm*. In some spreadsheet software (such as Excel), this function is denoted LN.

TABLE 3-8	The Log-Linear Demand for Breakfast Cereal

$\ln(Q_c) = -7.256 - 1.647 \ln(P_c) + 1.071 \ln(M) + 0.146 \ln(A)$

Q_c = per capita consumption of breakfast cereal
P_c = price of cereal
M = per capita income
A = a measure of advertising by the top four cereal firms

Source: Adapted from Michael R. Baye, *The Economic Effects of Proposed Regulation of TV Advertising Directed at Children: A Theoretical and Empirical Analysis,* senior honours thesis, Texas A&M University, 1980.

Table 3–8 shows the results of a statistical study that found the demand for breakfast cereal to be log-linear. Since this is a log-linear demand relation, we know that the coefficients may be interpreted as elasticities.

The study summarized in Table 3–8 focused primarily on the effect of advertising on the demand for breakfast cereal. Other factors affecting the demand for cereal include its price and the average (per capita) income of consumers. Surprisingly, the study found that the price of milk was not an important determinant of the demand for breakfast cereal.

In Table 3–8, the coefficient of the logarithm of price is -1.647. This shows that the demand for cereal is elastic and downward-sloping. Furthermore, a decrease of 10 percent in the price of cereal will increase the quantity of cereal demanded by 16.47 percent, and therefore raise the sales revenues of cereal manufacturers. The coefficient of the logarithm of income is $+1.071$, indicating that cereal is a normal good. A 10 percent increase in consumers' per capita income would result in a 10.7 percent increase in cereal demand. The coefficient of the logarithm of advertising is positive, indicating that an increase in cereal advertising will increase cereal demand. However, notice that the advertising elasticity is relatively small. A 10 percent increase in cereal advertising increases the demand for cereal by only 1.46 percent. Apparently, cereal advertising does not induce consumers to eat cereal for lunch and dinner.

As a final check of your ability to utilize elasticities, try to work the following problem.

Demonstration PROBLEM 3-4

An analyst for a major apparel company estimates that the demand for its raincoats is given by

$$\ln Q_x^d = 10 - 1.2 \ln P_x + 3 \ln R - 2 \ln A_y$$

where R denotes the daily amount of rainfall and A_y represents the level of advertising on good Y. What would be the impact on demand of a 10 percent increase in the daily amount of rainfall? What would be the impact of a 10 percent reduction in the amount of advertising directed toward good Y? Can you think of a good that might be good Y in this example?

Answer

We know that for log-linear demand functions, the coefficient of the logarithm of a variable gives the elasticity of demand with respect to that variable. Thus, the elasticity of demand for raincoats with respect to rainfall is

$$E_{Q_x, R} = \beta_R = 3$$

Furthermore,

$$E_{Q_x, R} = \beta_R = \frac{\% \Delta Q_x^d}{\% \Delta R}$$

Hence,

$$3 = \frac{\% \Delta Q_x^d}{10}$$

Solving this equation yields $\% \Delta Q_x^d = 30$. In other words, the 10 percent increase in rainfall will lead to a 30 percent increase in the demand for raincoats.

To examine the impact on the demand for raincoats of a 10 percent reduction in advertising spent on good Y, again note that for log-linear demand functions, each coefficient gives the elasticity of demand with respect to that variable. Thus, the elasticity of demand for raincoats with respect to advertising directed toward good Y is

$$E_{Q_x, A_y} = \beta_{A_y} = -2$$

Furthermore,

$$E_{Q_x, A_y} = \beta_{A_y} = \frac{\% \Delta Q_x^d}{\% \Delta A_y}$$

Hence,

$$-2 = \frac{\% \Delta Q_x^d}{-10}$$

Solving this equation yields $\% \Delta Q_x^d = 20$. In other words, the 10 percent reduction in advertising directed toward good Y leads to a 20 percent increase in the demand for raincoats. Perhaps good Y is umbrellas, for one would expect the demand for raincoats to increase whenever fewer umbrella advertisements are made.

Regression Analysis*

The preceding analysis assumes the manager knows the demand for the firm's product. We pointed out several studies that provide explicit estimates of demand elasticities and functional forms for demand functions. As a manager, you may obtain estimates of demand and elasticity from published studies available in the library or from a consultant hired to estimate the demand function on the basis of the specifics of your product. Or you might enter data into a spreadsheet program and click the regression toolbar to obtain an estimated demand function, along with some regression diagnostics. Regardless of how the manager obtains the estimates, it is useful to have a general understanding of how demand functions are estimated and what the various diagnostic statistics that accompany the reported output mean. This entails knowledge of a branch of economics called econometrics.

Econometrics is simply the statistical analysis of economic phenomena. It is far beyond the scope of this book to teach you how to estimate demand functions, but it is possible to convey the basic ideas econometricians use to obtain such information.

---

*This section is optional.

FIGURE 3–4   The Regression Line

The linear regression line is an approximation of the expected or average relation between Y and X. In this case, the regression slope, given by b, is negative, reflecting the inverse relationship between X and Y. Since the regression is an approximation, there is always some discrepancy, denoted by $\hat{e}$, between the actual data and the line.

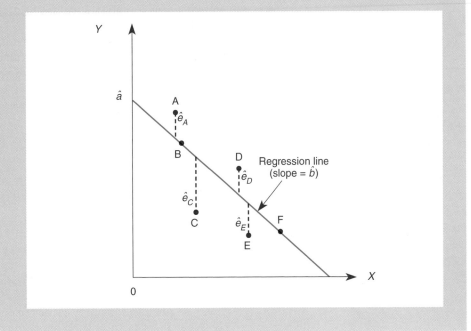

Your primary job as a manager is to use the information to make decisions similar to the examples provided in previous sections of this chapter.

Let us briefly examine the basic ideas underlying the estimation of the demand for a product. Suppose there is some underlying data on the relation between a dependent variable, Y, and some explanatory variable, X. Suppose that when the values of X and Y are plotted, they appear as points A, B, C, D, E, and F in Figure 3–4. Clearly, the points do not lie on a straight line, or even a smooth curve (try alternative ways of connecting the dots if you are not convinced).

The job of the econometrician is to find a smooth curve or line that does a "good" job of approximating the points. For example, suppose the econometrician believes that, on average, there is a linear relation between Y and X, but there is also some random variation in the relationship. Mathematically, this would imply that the true relationship between Y and X is

$$Y = a + bX + e$$

where a and b are unknown parameters and e is a random variable (an error term) that has a zero mean. Because the parameters that determine the expected relation between Y and X are unknown, the econometrician must find out the values of the parameters a and b.

Note that for any line drawn through the points, there will be some discrepancy between the actual points and the line. For example, consider the line in Figure 3–4, which does a reasonable job of fitting the data. If a manager used the line to approximate the true relation, there would be some discrepancy between the actual data and the line. For example, points A and D actually lie above the line, while points C and E lie below it. The deviations between the actual points and the line are given by the distance of the dashed lines in Figure 3–4, namely $\hat{e}_A$, $\hat{e}_C$, $\hat{e}_D$, and $\hat{e}_E$. Since the line represents the expected, or average, relation between Y and X, these deviations are analogous to the deviations from the mean used to calculate the variance of a random variable.

The econometrician uses a regression software package to find the values of a and b that minimize the sum of the squared deviations between the actual points and the line. In essence, the *regression line* is the line that minimizes the squared deviations between the line (the expected relation) and the actual data points. These values of a and b, frequently denoted $\hat{a}$ and $\hat{b}$, are called *parameter estimates,* and the corresponding line is called the **least squares regression**.

least squares regression
The line that minimizes the sum of squared deviations between the line and the actual data points.

The least squares regression line for the equation

$$Y = a + bX + e$$

is given by

$$Y = \hat{a} + \hat{b}X$$

The parameter estimates, $\hat{a}$ and $\hat{b}$, represent the values of a and b that result in the smallest *sum of squared errors* between a line and the actual data.

Spreadsheet software packages, such as Excel or Lotus, make it easy to use regression analysis to estimate demand functions. To illustrate, suppose a television manufacturer has data on the price and quantity of TVs sold last month at 10 outlets in Halifax. Here we use price and quantity as our explanatory and dependent variables, respectively. When the data are entered into a spreadsheet, it looks like the first 11 rows in Table 3–9. A few clicks of the mouse and the spreadsheet calculates the average price and quantity reported in row 12. Furthermore, by clicking the regression toolbar, the regression output reported in rows 16 through 33 is produced. Cell 32-B shows that the intercept of the estimated demand function for TVs is 1631.47, and cell 33-B shows that the estimated coefficient of price is -2.60. Thus, the linear demand function for TVs that minimizes the sum of squared errors between the actual data points and the line through the points is[3]

$$Q = 1631.47 - 2.60 \, P$$

Notice that the spreadsheet program also produces detailed information about the regression and the estimated coefficients as a by-product of the regression. In the following discussion, these statistics enable the manager to test for the statistical significance of the estimated coefficients and to assess the performance of the overall regression.

Evaluating the Statistical Significance of Estimated Coefficients

Rows 30 through 33 of the regression output in Table 3–9 provide information about the precision with which the parameters of the demand function are estimated. The coefficients reported in cells 32-B and 33-B are merely the parameter estimates—estimates of the true, unknown coefficients. Given different data generated from the same true demand relation, different estimates of the true coefficients would be obtained. The *standard error* of each estimated coefficient is a measure of how much each estimated coefficient would vary in regressions based on the same underlying

---

[3]Note that this example is merely a simple exposition and is not meant as a rigorous test of regression analysis.

TABLE 3-9 Using a Spreadsheet to Perform a Regression

	A	B	C	D	E	F	G
1	Observation	Quantity	Price				
2	1	180	475				
3	2	590	400				
4	3	430	450				
5	4	250	550				
6	5	275	575				
7	6	720	375				
8	7	660	375				
9	8	490	450				
10	9	700	400				
11	10	210	500				
12	Average	450.50	455.00				
13							
14							
15							
16	*Regression Statistics*						
17							
18	Multiple *R*	0.87					
19	*R*-square	0.75					
20	Adjusted *R*-square	0.72					
21	Standard error	112.22					
22	Observations	10.00					
23							
24	*Analysis of Variance*						
25		*df*	*Sum of Squares*	*Mean Square*	*F*	*Significance F*	
26	Regression	1.00	301 470.89	301 470.89	23.94	0.0012	
27	Residual	8.00	100 751.61	12 593.95			
28	Total	9.00	402 222.50				
29							
30		*Coefficients*	*Standard Error*	*t-Statistic*	*P-Value*	*Lower 95%*	*Upper 95%*
31							
32	Intercept	1631.47	243.97	6.69	0.0002	1068.87	2194.07
33	Price	−2.60	0.53	−4.89	0.0012	−3.82	−1.37

true demand relation, but with different observations. The smaller the standard error of an estimated coefficient, the smaller the variation in the estimate given data from different outlets (different samples of data).

The least squares parameter estimates are unbiased estimators of the true demand parameters whenever the errors (the e_i's) in the true demand relation have a zero mean. If, in addition, the e_i's are independently and identically distributed normal random variables (*iid normal* random variables for short), the reported standard errors of the estimated coefficients can be used to construct confidence intervals and to perform significance tests. These techniques are discussed below.

Confidence Intervals

Given a parameter estimate, its standard error, and the *iid normal* assumption, the firm manager can construct upper and lower bounds on the true value of the estimated coefficient by constructing a 95 percent confidence interval. A useful rule of thumb is presented in the principle below, but fortunately regression packages compute precise confidence intervals for each coefficient estimated in a regression. For instance, the last two cells in the final row of Table 3–9 indicate that the upper and lower bounds of the 95 percent confidence interval for the coefficient of price are -3.82 and -1.37. The parameter estimate for the price coefficient, -2.60, lies in the middle of these bounds. Thus, we know that the best estimate of the price coefficient is -2.60, and we are 95 percent confident that the true value lies between -3.82 and -1.37.

Principle	**RULE OF THUMB FOR A 95 PERCENT CONFIDENCE INTERVAL**
	If the parameter estimates of a regression equation are $\hat{a}$ and $\hat{b}$, the 95 percent confidence intervals for the true values of a and b can be approximated by $$\hat{a} \pm 2\sigma_{\hat{a}}$$ and $$\hat{b} \pm 2\sigma_{\hat{b}}$$ where $\sigma_{\hat{a}}$ and $\sigma_{\hat{b}}$ are the standard errors of $\hat{a}$, and $\hat{b}$, respectively.

The *t*-Statistic

t-statistic
The ratio of the value of a parameter estimate to the standard error of the parameter estimate.

The **t-statistic** of a parameter estimate is the ratio of the value of the parameter estimate to its standard error. For example, if the parameter estimates are $\hat{a}$ and $\hat{b}$ and the corresponding standard errors are $\sigma_{\hat{a}}$ and $\sigma_{\hat{b}}$, the *t*-statistic for $\hat{a}$ is

$$t_{\hat{a}} = \frac{\hat{a}}{\sigma_{\hat{a}}}$$

and the *t*-statistic for $\hat{b}$ is

$$t_{\hat{b}} = \frac{\hat{b}}{\sigma_{\hat{b}}}$$

When the *t*-statistic for a parameter estimate is large in absolute value, then you can be confident that the true parameter is not zero. The reason for this is that, when the absolute value of the *t*-statistic is large, the standard error of the parameter estimate is small relative to the absolute value of the parameter estimate. Thus, one can be more confident that, given a different sample of data drawn from the true model, the new parameter estimate will be in the same ballpark.

A useful rule of thumb is that if the absolute value of a *t*-statistic is greater than or equal to 2, then the corresponding parameter estimate is statistically different from zero. Regression packages report *P-values,* which are a much more precise measure of statistical significance. For instance, in cell 33-E of Table 3–9 we see that the *P*-value for the estimated coefficient of price is 0.0012. This means that there is only a 12 in 10 000 chance that the true coefficient of price is actually 0. Notice that the lower the *P*-value for an estimated coefficient, the more confident you are in the estimate.

Usually, *P*-values of 0.05 or lower are considered low enough for a researcher to be confident that the estimated coefficient is statistically significant. If the *P*-value is 0.05, we say that the estimated coefficient is statistically significant at the 5 percent level. Notice that the *P*-value reported in Table 3–9 for the coefficient of price implies that it is statistically significant at the 0.12 percent level: the estimated coefficient is highly significant. It is important to note that, like confidence intervals, reported *P*-values presume that the errors in the true regression equation are *iid normal*.

Principle	**A RULE OF THUMB FOR USING *t*-STATISTICS** When the absolute value of the *t*-statistic is greater than 2, the manager can be 95 percent confident that the true value of the underlying parameter in the regression is not zero.

Evaluating the Overall Fit of the Regression Line

In addition to evaluating the statistical significance of one or more coefficients, one can also measure the precision with which the overall regression line fits the data. Two yardsticks frequently used to measure the overall fit of the regression line—the *R*-square and the *F*-statistic—are discussed next.

The *R*-Square

Rows 18 through 20 of Table 3–9 provide diagnostics that indicate how well the regression line explains the sample of observations of the dependent variable (in the example, quantity is the dependent variable and price is the explanatory variable). The *R-square* (also called the *coefficient of determination*) tells the fraction of the total variation in the dependent variable that is explained by the regression. It is computed as the ratio of the sum of squared errors from the regression ($SS_{Regression}$) to the total sum of squared errors (SS_{Total}):

$$R^2 = \frac{Explained\ Variation}{Total\ Variation} = \frac{SS_{Regression}}{SS_{Total}}$$

For instance, in cell 26-C of Table 3–9 we see that the sum of squared errors from the regression is 301470.89, while cell 28-C reveals that the total sum of squared errors is 402222.50. Thus, the *R*-square is 0.75 (= 301470.89/402222.50). This means that the estimated demand equation (the regression line) explains 75 percent of the total variation in TV sales across the sample of 10 outlets. Most spreadsheet regression packages automatically calculate the *R*-square, as seen in cell 19-B of Table 3–9.[4]

The value of an *R*-square ranges from 0 and 1:

$$0 \leq R^2 \leq 1$$

The closer the *R*-square is to 1, the "better" the overall fit of the estimated regression equation to the actual data. Unfortunately, there is no simple cutoff that can be used to determine whether an *R*-square is close enough to 1 to indicate a "good" fit. With time series data, *R*-squares are often in excess of 0.9; with cross-sectional data, 0.5

---

[4]The square root of the *R*-square, called the multiple *R*, is also reported by most spreadsheet regression programs. It is given in cell 18-B of Table 3–9.

might be considered a reasonably good fit. Thus, a major drawback of the R-square is that it is a subjective measure of goodness of fit.

Another problem with the R-square is that it cannot decrease when additional explanatory variables are included in the regression. Thus, if we included income, advertising, and other explanatory variables in our regression, but held other things constant, we would almost surely get a higher R-square. Eventually, when the number of estimated coefficients increased to the number of observations, we would end up with an R-square of 1. Sometimes, the R-square is very close to 1 merely because the number of observations is small relative to the number of estimated parameters. This situation is undesirable from a statistical viewpoint, because it can provide a very misleading indicator of the goodness of fit of the regression line. For this reason, many researchers use the adjusted R-square reported in cell 20-B of Table 3–9 as a measure of goodness of fit.

The *adjusted R-square* is given by

$$\bar{R}^2 = 1 - (1 - R^2)\frac{(n-1)}{(n-k)}$$

where n is the total number of observations and k is the number of estimated coefficients. In performing a regression, the number of parameters to be estimated cannot exceed the number of observations. The difference, $n - k$, represents the *residual degrees of freedom* after conducting the regression. Notice that the adjusted R-square "penalizes" the researcher for performing a regression with only a few degrees of freedom (that is, estimating numerous coefficients from relatively few observations). In fact, the penalty can be so high that, in some instances, the adjusted R-square is actually negative.

In our example, cell 22-B in Table 3–9 shows us that $n = 10$. Cells 32-B and 33-B indicate that we estimated 2 parameters, so $k = 2$. With 8 residual degrees of freedom, the adjusted R-square of our regression is $1 - (1 - 0.75)(9/8) = 0.72$. This number is reported in cell 20-B. For these data, there is little difference between the R-square and the adjusted R-square, so it does not appear that the "high" R-square is a result of an excessive number of estimated coefficients relative to the sample size.

The F-Statistic

While the R-square and adjusted R-square of a regression both provide a gauge of the overall fit of a regression, we noted that there is no universal rule for determining how "high" they must be to indicate a good fit. An alternative measure of goodness of fit, called the *F-statistic,* does not suffer from this shortcoming. The F-statistic provides a measure of the total variation explained by the regression relative to the total unexplained variation. The greater the F-statistic, the better the overall fit of the regression line through the actual data. In our example, the F-statistic is reported as 23.94 in cell 26-E of Table 3–9.

The primary advantage of the F-statistic stems from the fact that its statistical properties are known. Thus, one can objectively determine the statistical significance of any reported F value. The significance value for our regression, 0.0012, is reported in cell 26-F of Table 3–9. This low number means that there is only a 0.12 percent chance that the estimated regression model fit the data purely by accident.

As with P-values, the lower the significance value of the F-statistic, the more confident you can be of the overall fit of the regression equation. Regressions that have F-statistics with significance values of 5 percent or less are generally considered significant. Based on the significance value reported in cell 26-F of Table 3–9, our regression is significant at the 0.12 percent level. The regression is therefore highly significant.

FIGURE 3–5 Log-Linear Regression Line

This log-linear regression line is an approximation of the average relation between the price and the quantity. As the price and quantity are not linearly related, the demand function takes the form of a curve.

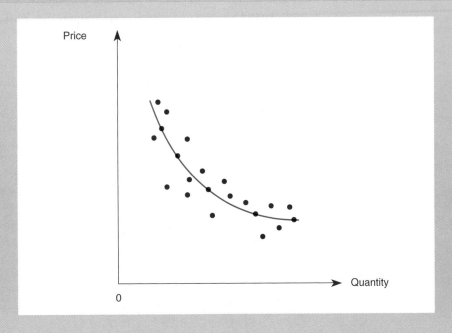

Nonlinear and Multiple Regressions

The techniques described above to estimate a linear demand function with a single explanatory variable can also be used to estimate nonlinear demand functions. These same tools can be used to estimate demand functions in which the quantity demanded depends on several explanatory variables, such as prices, income, advertising, and so on. These issues are discussed below.

Nonlinear Regressions

Sometimes, a plot of the data will reveal nonlinearities in the data, as seen in Figure 3–5. Here, it appears that price and quantity are not linearly related: the demand function is a curve. The log-linear demand curve we examined earlier in this chapter has such a curved shape.

To estimate a log-linear demand function, the econometrician takes the natural logarithm of prices and quantities before executing the regression routine that minimizes the sum of squared errors (e):

$$\ln Q = \beta_0 + \beta_P \ln P + e$$

In other words, by using a spreadsheet to compute $Q' = \ln Q$ and $P' = \ln P$, this demand specification can be viewed equivalently as

$$Q' = \beta_0 + \beta_P P' + e$$

which is linear in Q' and P'. Therefore, one can use procedures identical to those described earlier and regress the transformed Q' on P' to obtain parameter estimates. Recall that the resulting parameter estimate for β_P in this case is the own price elasticity of demand, since this is a log-linear demand function.

Multiple Regressions

In general, the demand for a good will depend not only on the good's price, but also on demand shifters. Regression techniques can also be used to perform multiple regressions—regressions of a dependent variable on multiple explanatory variables. For the case of a linear demand relation, one might specify the demand function as

$$Q_x^d = \alpha_0 + \alpha_x P_x + \alpha_y P_y + \alpha_M M + \alpha_H H + e$$

where the α's are the parameters to be estimated, P_y, M, and H are demand shifters, and e is the random error term that has a zero mean. Alternatively, a log-linear specification might be appropriate if the quantity demanded is not linearly related to the explanatory variables:

$$\ln Q_x^d = \beta_0 + \beta_x \ln P_x + \beta_y \ln P_y + \beta_M \ln M + \beta_H \ln H + e$$

Provided the number of observations is greater than the number of parameters to be estimated, one can use standard regression packages included in spreadsheet programs to find the values of the parameters that minimize the sum of squared errors of the regression. The R-square, F-statistic, t-statistics, and confidence intervals for multiple regressions have the same use and interpretations described earlier for the case of a simple regression with one explanatory variable. The following Demonstration Problem illustrates this fact.

Demonstration PROBLEM 3–5

FCI owns 10 apartment buildings in a small university town, which it rents exclusively to students. Each apartment building contains 100 rental units, but the owner is having cash flow problems due to an average vacancy rate of nearly 50 percent. The apartments in each building have comparable floor plans, but some buildings are closer to campus than others. The owner of FCI has data from last year on the number of apartments rented, the rental price (in dollars), and the amount spent on advertising (in hundreds of dollars) at each of the 10 apartments. These data, along with the distance (in kilometres) from each apartment building to campus, are presented in rows 1 through 11 of Table 3–10. The owner regressed the quantity demanded of apartments on price, advertising, and distance. The results of the regression are reported in rows 16 through 35 of Table 3–10. What is the estimated demand function for FCI's rental units? If FCI raised rents at one complex by $100, what would you expect to happen to the number of units rented? If FCI raised rents at an average apartment building, what would happen to FCI's total revenues? What inferences should be drawn from this analysis?

Answer

Letting P, A, and D represent price, advertising, and distance from campus, the estimated coefficients imply the following demand for rental units at an apartment building:

$$Q_x^d = 135.15 - 0.14P + 0.54A - 5.78D$$

Since the coefficient of price is -0.14, a $100 increase in price reduces the quantity demanded at an apartment building by 14 units. The own price elasticity of demand for FCI's rental units, calculated at the average price and quantity, is $(-0.14)(420/53.10) = -1.11$. Since demand is elastic, raising the rent at an average apartment building would decrease not only the number of units rented, but total revenues as well.

TABLE 3–10 Input and Output from a Multiple Regression

	A	B	C	D	E	F	G
1	Observation	Quantity	Price	Advertising	Distance		
2	1	28	250	11	12		
3	2	69	400	24	6		
4	3	43	450	15	5		
5	4	32	550	31	7		
6	5	42	575	34	4		
7	6	72	375	22	2		
8	7	66	375	12	5		
9	8	49	450	24	7		
10	9	70	400	22	4		
11	10	60	375	10	5		
12	Average	53.10	420.00	20.50	5.70		
13							
14							
15							
16	*Regression Statistics*						
17							
18	Multiple *R*	0.89					
19	*R*-square	0.79					
20	Adjusted *R*-square	0.69					
21	Standard error	9.18					
22	Observations	10.00					
23							
24	*Analysis of Variance*						
25		*df*	*Sum of Squares*	*Mean Square*	*F*	*Significance F*	
26	Regression	3.00	1920.99	640.33	7.59	0.0182	
27	Residual	6.00	505.91	84.32			
28	Total	9.00	2426.90				
29							
30		*Coefficients*	*Standard Error*	*t-Statistic*	*P-Value*	*Lower 95%*	*Upper 95%*
31							
32	Intercept	135.15	20.65	6.54	0.0006	84.61	185.68
33	Price	−0.14	0.06	−2.41	0.0500	−0.29	0.00
34	Advertising	0.54	0.64	0.85	0.4296	−1.02	2.09
35	Distance	−5.78	1.26	−4.61	0.0037	−8.86	−2.71

The *R*-square of 0.79 indicates that the regression explains 79 percent of the variation in the quantity of apartments rented across the 10 buildings. The *F*-statistic suggests that the regression is significant at the 1.82 percent level, so the manager can be reasonably confident that the good fit of the equation is not due to chance. Notice that all of the estimated parameters are statistically significant at the 5 percent level, except for the coefficient of advertising. Thus, it does not appear that advertising has a statistically significant effect on the demand for the rental units.

Distance from campus appears to be a very significant determinant of the demand for apartments. The *t*-statistic for this coefficient is in excess of 4 in absolute value, and the *P*-value is 0.37 percent. On the basis of the lower and upper bound of its confidence interval, the owner can be 95 percent confident that for every mile an apartment is away from campus, FCI loses between 2.71 and 8.86 renters.

Since FCI can't relocate its apartments closer to campus, and advertising does not have a statistically significant impact on units rented, it would appear that all FCI can do to reduce its cash flow problems is to lower rents at those apartment buildings where demand is elastic.

ANSWERING THE Headline

At the beginning of the chapter we asked two questions. First, whether the strategy of the new owner of *The National Post*, CanWest Global Communications Corp., as spelled out by its CEO Leonard Asper, made any economic sense. In his remarks to an audience of analysts and journalists, he stated that CanWest expected no drop in the readership of the *Post*, despite reducing the size of the paper, reducing advertising through the number of papers given away, and at the same time raising the price. This case illustrates the theory of price elasticity and why managers need to be aware of the environment that their products are in as well as how the demand for their products relates to those of others.

In the vacuum of theory, if CanWest raised the price of its newspaper, price elasticity theory dictates that demand for the paper would fall. This results from the consumer recognizing that they would get more value from the *Post*'s competition, for example, *The Globe and Mail* and other daily papers. Arguing that a price hike wouldn't deter readers, even if they're paying more money for a thinner paper, implies that the new owner perceived no substitutes for its paper; a case of a perfectly inelastic demand curve (zero price elasticity). Clearly, this assumption was not shared by Asper's audience, who saw this strategy as a recipe for a sharp drop in the readership, given the number of substitutes. Furthermore, it appears that Mr. Asper confused a change in relative price with a change across the board. If he meant that the *Post* was to be marketed as a higher-quality paper in comparison to others, analogously to gourmet coffee versus ordinary coffee, he failed to spell out how the quality of his paper was to be enhanced. If, on the other hand, he was referring to a general increase in the price of all papers, he was not being factual.

The second question was: What did Mr. Asper mean by "We believe there's some price elasticity in newspapers"? By stating this, it appears, Mr. Asper was contradicting himself. To be consistent, he should have instead said "We believe there is no price elasticity in newspapers." Acknowledging that there is price elasticity, implies that a price hike would in fact result in a drop in the readership, something that he did not seem prepared to concede.

Summary

In this chapter we covered quantitative aspects of demand analysis, including the own price elasticity, income elasticity, and cross-price elasticity of demand. We examined functional forms for demand functions, including linear and log-linear specifications, and discussed the regression procedures used to estimate demand relationships. Armed with these tools, a manager can predict not only the direction of changes in demand but how far demand will move when one of the determinants of demand

Visit the Web site @**www.mcgrawhill.ca/college/baye**

changes. Knowing the concepts of elasticity and the use of *t*-statistics and confidence intervals is extremely important when making decisions about how much inventory to hold, how many employees to schedule, and how many units of a product to produce when different determinants of demand change.

In this chapter, we saw that increasing price does not always increase revenues. If the absolute value of own price elasticity is greater than 1, an increase in price will decrease total revenue. We also covered the magnitude of changes caused by a change in the price of a substitute or a complement.

Finally, we introduced the concepts of regression and confidence intervals. By utilizing the elasticities based on an estimated demand function and constructing a confidence interval, a manager can be 95 percent certain about the amount by which demand will move when a variable like income or advertising changes.

Key Terms and Concepts

cross-price elasticity 83
elastic demand 73
elasticity 72
income elasticity 85
inelastic demand 73
least squares regression 96

log-linear demand 92
own price elasticity of demand 73
perfectly elastic demand 78
perfectly inelastic demand 78
t-statistic 98
unit-elastic demand 74

Conceptual and Computational Questions

1. Answer the following questions based on the accompanying diagram.
   a. How much would the firm's revenue change if it lowered price from $12 to $10? Is demand elastic or inelastic in this range?
   b. How much would the firm's revenue change if it lowered price from $4 to $2? Is demand elastic or inelastic in this range?
   c. What price maximizes the firm's total revenues? What is the elasticity of demand at this point on the demand curve?

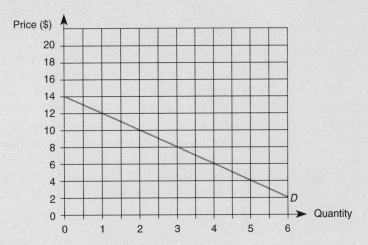

2. The demand curve for a product is given by $Q_x^d = 1000 - 2P_x + 0.02P_z$, where $P_z = \$400$.

a. What is the own price elasticity of demand when $P_x = \$154$? Is demand elastic or inelastic at this price? What would happen to the firm's revenue if it decided to charge a price below $154?

b. What is the own price elasticity of demand when $P_x = \$354$? Is demand elastic or inelastic at this price? What would happen to the firm's revenue if it decided to charge a price above $354?

c. What is the cross-price elasticity of demand between good X and good Z when $P_x = \$154$? Are goods X and Z substitutes or complements?

3. Suppose the demand function for a firm's product is given by

$$\ln Q_x^d = 3 - 0.5 \ln P_x - 2.5 \ln P_y + \ln M + 2 \ln A$$

where
$P_x = \$10$,
$P_y = \$4$,
$M = \$20\ 000$, and
$A = \$250$.

a. Determine the own price elasticity of demand, and state whether demand is elastic, inelastic, or unit-elastic.

b. Determine the cross-price elasticity of demand between good X and good Y, and state whether these two goods are substitutes or complements.

c. Determine the income elasticity of demand, and state whether good X is a normal or inferior good.

d. Determine the own advertising elasticity of demand.

4. Suppose the own price elasticity of demand for good X is -2, its income elasticity is 3, its advertising elasticity is 4, and the cross-price elasticity of demand between it and good Y is -6. Determine how much the consumption of this good will change if

a. The price of good X increases by 5 percent

b. The price of good Y increases by 10 percent

c. Advertising decreases by 2 percent

d. Income falls by 3 percent

5. Suppose the cross-price elasticity of demand between goods X and Y is -5. How much would the price of good Y have to change in order to increase the consumption of good X by 50 percent?

6. You are the manager of a firm that receives revenues of $30 000 per year from product X and $70 000 per year from product Y. The own price elasticity of demand for product X is -2.5, and the cross-price elasticity of demand between product Y and X is 1.1. How much will your firm's total revenues (revenues from both products) change if you increase the price of good X by 1 percent?

7. An econometrician from your firm used a linear demand specification to estimate the demand for its product and sent you a hard copy of the results. Unfortunately, some entries are missing because the toner was low in her printer. Use the information presented below to find the missing values labelled 1 through 7 (round your answer to the nearest hundredth). Then answer the accompanying questions.

a. Using these estimates, write an equation that summarizes the demand for the firm's product.

b. Which regression coefficients are statistically significant at the 5 percent level?

c. Comment on how well the regression line fits the data.

	A	B	C	D	E	F	G
1	SUMMARY OUTPUT						
2							
3	*Regression Statistics*						
4	Multiple *R*	0.62					
5	*R*-square	'1'					
6	Adjusted *R*-square	'2'					
7	Standard error	190.90					
8	Observations	100.00					
9							
10	*Analysis of Variance*						
11		*Degrees of Freedom*	*Sum of Squares*	*Mean Square*	*F*	*Significance F*	
12	Regression	2.00	'3'	1 111 508.88	30.50	0.00	
13	Residual	97.00	3 535 019.49	36 443.50			
14	Total	'4'	5 758 037.26				
15							
16		*Coefficients*	*Standard Error*	*t-Statistic*	*P-Value*	*Lower 95%*	*Upper 95%*
17	Intercept	187.15	'5'	0.35	0.73	−880.56	1254.86
18	Price of *X*	−4.32	0.69	'6'	0.00	−5.69	−2.96
19	Income	'7'	0.02	4.47	0.00	0.05	0.14

8. Suppose the true inverse demand relation for good X is $P = a + bQ + e$, and you estimated the parameters to be $\hat{a} = 10$, $\hat{b} = -2.5$, $\sigma_{\hat{a}} = 1$, and $\sigma_{\hat{b}} = 0.5$. Find the approximate 95 percent confidence interval for the true values of a and b.

Problems and Applications

9. Revenue at Palm Inc. was $1.4 billion for the nine months ending March 2, 2001, up 97 percent over revenues for the same period of fiscal year 2000. Management attributes the increase in revenues to a 137 percent increase in personal digital assistant (PDA) shipments, despite a 17 percent drop in the average blended selling price of Palm's line of PDAs. Given this information, is it surprising that Palm's revenue increased when it decreased the average selling price of its PDAs? Explain.

10. You are the manager of a firm that sells a leading brand of alkaline batteries. The Chapter 3 folder of the CD that accompanies this textbook contains a file named Q10.xls with data on the demand for your product. Specifically, the file contains data on the natural logarithm of your quantity sold, price, and the average income of consumers in various regions around the world. Use this information to perform a log-linear regression, and then determine the likely impact of a 3 percent decline in global income on the overall demand for your product.

11. For the first time in two years, Big G (the cereal division of General Mills) raised cereal prices by 2 percent during its 2001 fiscal year. If, as a result of this price

increase, the volume of all cereal sold by Big G dropped by 3 percent, what can you infer about the own price elasticity demand for Big G cereal? Can you predict whether revenues on sales of its Lucky Charms brand increased or decreased? Explain.

12. Fiscal year 2000 was prosperous for the Starbucks Coffee Company. Revenues increased 9 percent, excluding the 1035 new retail outlets that were opened. Suppose management attributes this revenue growth to a 5 percent increase in the quantity of coffee purchased. If Starbucks' marketing department estimates the income elasticity of demand for its coffee to be 1.75, how will looming fears of a recession (expected to decrease consumers' incomes by 4 percent over the next year) impact the quantity of coffee Starbucks expects to sell?

13. You are a manager at the Chevrolet division of General Motors. If your marketing department estimates that the semiannual demand for the Chevy Tahoe is $Q = 100\,000 - 1.25P$, what price should you charge in order to maximize revenues from sales of the Tahoe?

14. You are a manager in charge of monitoring cash flow at Kodak. Traditional photography equipment makes up 80 percent of Kodak's revenues, which grow about 2 percent annually. You recently received a preliminary report that suggests consumers take three times more digital photographs than photos with traditional film, and that the cross-price elasticity of demand between digital and disposable cameras is -0.2. Over the last several years, Kodak has invested over $5 billion to develop and begin producing digital cameras. In 2000, Kodak earned about $400 million from sales of digital cameras and about $600 million from sales of disposable cameras. If the own price elasticity of demand for disposable cameras is -2.5, how will a 1 percent decrease in the price of disposable cameras affect Kodak's overall revenues from both disposable and digital camera sales?

15. As newly appointed "Energy Czar," your goal is to reduce the total demand for residential heating fuel in your state. You must choose one of three legislative proposals designed to accomplish this goal: (*a*) a tax that would effectively increase the price of residential heating fuel by $2; (*b*) a subsidy that would effectively reduce the price of natural gas by $1; or (*c*) a tax that would effectively increase the price of electricity (produced by hydroelectric facilities) by $5. To assist you in your decision, an economist in your office has estimated the demand for residential heating fuel using a linear demand specification. The regression results are presented below. In view of this information, which proposal would you favour? Explain.

16. As the owner of Barney's Broilers—a fast-food chain—you see an increase in the demand for broiled chicken as consumers become more health-conscious and reduce their consumption of beef and fried foods. As a result, you believe it is necessary to purchase another oven to meet the increased demand. To finance the oven you go to the bank seeking a loan. The loan officer tells you that your revenues of $750 000 are insufficient to support additional debt. To qualify for the loan, Barney's Broilers' revenue would need to be $50 000 higher. In developing a strategy to generate the additional revenue, you collect data on the price (in cents) per kilogram you charge customers and the related quantity of chicken consumed per year in kilograms. This information is contained in the file called Q16.xls in the Chapter 3 folder of the CD that accompanies this textbook. Use these data and a log-linear demand specification to obtain least squares estimates of the demand for broiled chicken. Write an equation that summarizes the demand for broiled chicken, and then determine the percentage price increase or decrease that is needed in order to boost revenues by $50 000.

	A	B	C	D	E	F	G
1	**SUMMARY OUTPUT**						
2							
3	*Regression Statistics*						
4	Multiple *R*	0.76					
5	*R*-square	0.57					
6	Adjusted *R*-square	0.49					
7	Standard error	47.13					
8	Observations	25					
9							
10	*Analysis of Variance*						
11		*Degrees of Freedom*	*Sum of Squares*	*Mean Square*	*F*	*Significance* F	
12	Regression	4	60 936.56	15 234.14	6.86	.03	
13	Residual	20	44 431.27	2 221.56			
14	Total	24	105 367.84				
15							
16		*Coefficients*	*Standard Error*	*t-Statistic*	*P-Value*	*Lower 95%*	*Upper 95%*
17	Intercept	136.96	43.46	3.15	0.01	50.60	223.32
18	Price of residential heating fuel	−91.69	29.09	−3.15	0.01	−149.49	−33.89
19	Price of natural gas	43.88	9.17	4.79	0.00	25.66	62.10
20	Price of electricity	−11.92	8.35	−1.43	0.17	−28.51	4.67
21	Income	−0.050	0.3500	−0.14	0.90	−0.75	0.65

The Theory of Individual Behaviour

Head line

Conditional and Unconditional Grants: Federal Contributions Associated with the Canada Health Act

In the November 2002 report from his Commission on the Future of Health Care in Canada, Mr. Romanow proposed the creation of a National Health Council to act as an auditor-general of medical care, in part because the provinces and Ottawa had proved themselves incapable of sharing health-care responsibilities. Eight months later, in their Charlottetown conference, Canada's premiers gave the council only qualified support. The provinces were demanding more money from the federal government in the form of unconditional grants, arguing that they knew best how to spend it. The federal government was reluctant to give the money without guarantees that the provinces would spend the money on designated services such as education and health care.

As an arbitrator, whom would you have agreed with? As background, you might find it useful to first discuss the old method of cost sharing between the provinces and the federal government.

Introduction

In Chapter 2, we developed the supply and demand model to analyze economic questions concerning markets, open and closed. In Chapter 3, we considered the major factors likely to influence the total demand and sales revenue for a product; furthermore, the concept of elasticity—a means of measuring and summarizing the direction and magnitude of the influence each variable has on the total demand for a particular product—was discussed in that chapter. However, the concept of market demand and its associated ideas cannot be used to answer questions concerning individuals.

This chapter develops tools that help a manager understand the behaviour of individuals, such as consumers and workers, and the impact of alternative incentives on their decisions. This is not as simple as you might think. Human beings use complicated thought processes to make decisions, and the human brain is capable of processing vast quantities of information. At this very moment your heart is pumping blood throughout your body, your lungs are providing oxygen and expelling carbon dioxide, and your eyes are scanning this page while your brain processes the information on it. The human brain can do what even supercomputers and sophisticated "artificial intelligence" technology are incapable of doing.

Despite the complexities of human thought processes, managers need a model that explains how individuals behave in the marketplace and in the work environment. Of course, attempts to model individual behaviour cannot capture the full range of real-world behaviour. Life would be simpler for managers of firms if the behaviour of individuals were not so complicated. On the other hand, the rewards for being a manager of a firm would be much lower. If you achieve an understanding of individual behaviour, you will gain a marketable skill that will help you to succeed in the business world.

Our model of behaviour will necessarily be an abstraction of the way individuals really make decisions. We must begin with a simple model that focuses on essentials instead of dwelling on behavioural features that would do little to enhance our understanding. Keep these thoughts in mind as we begin our study of an economic model of consumer behaviour.

Consumer Behaviour

Now that you recognize that any theory about individual behaviour must be an abstraction of reality, we may begin to develop a model to help us understand how consumers will respond to the alternative choices that confront them. A *consumer* is an individual who purchases goods and services from firms for the purpose of consumption. As a manager of a firm, you are interested not only in who consumes the good but in who purchases it. A six-month-old baby consumes goods but is not responsible for purchase decisions. If you are employed by a manufacturer of baby food, it is the parent's behaviour you must understand, not the baby's.

In characterizing consumer behaviour, there are two important but distinct factors to consider: consumer opportunities and consumer preferences. *Consumer opportunities* represent the possible goods and services consumers can afford to consume. *Consumer preferences* determine which of these goods will be consumed. The distinction is very important: while I can afford (and thus have the opportunity to consume) one kilogram of beef liver a week, my preferences are such that I would be unlikely to choose to consume beef liver at all. Keeping this distinction in mind, let us begin by modelling consumer preferences.

In today's global economy literally millions of goods are offered for sale. However, to focus on the essential aspects of individual behaviour and to keep things manageable, we will assume that only two goods exist in the economy. This assumption is made purely to simplify our analysis: all of the conclusions that we draw from this two-good setting remain valid when there are many goods. We will let X represent the quantity of one good and Y the quantity of the other good. By using this notation to represent the two goods, we have a very general model in the sense that X and Y can be any two goods rather than restricted to, say, beef and pork.

Assume a consumer is able to order his or her preferences for alternative bundles or combinations of goods from best to worst. We will let $>$ denote this ordering and write $A > B$ whenever the consumer prefers bundle A to bundle B. If the consumer views the two bundles as equally satisfying, we will say she or he is indifferent between bundles A and B and use $A \sim B$ as shorthand notation. If $A > B$, then, if given a choice between bundle A and bundle B, the consumer will choose bundle A. If $A \sim B$, the consumer, given a choice between bundle A and bundle B, will not care which bundle he or she gets. The preference ordering is assumed to satisfy four basic properties: completeness, more is better, diminishing marginal rate of substitution, and transitivity. Let us examine these properties and their implications in more detail.

Property 4–1: Completeness. For any two bundles—say, A and B—either $A > B$, $B > A$, or $A \sim B$.

By assuming that preferences are *complete*, we assume the consumer is capable of expressing a preference for, or indifference among, all bundles. If preferences were not complete, there might be cases where a consumer would claim not to know whether he or she preferred bundle A to B, preferred B to A, or was indifferent between the two bundles. If the consumer cannot express her or his own preference for or indifference among goods, the manager can hardly predict that individual's consumption patterns with reasonable accuracy.

Property 4–2: More Is Better. If bundle A has at least as much of every good as bundle B and more of some good, bundle A is preferred to bundle B.

If *more is better,* the consumer views the products under consideration as "goods" instead of "bads." Graphically, this implies that as we move in the northeast direction in Figure 4–1, we move to bundles that the consumer views as being better than bundles to the southwest. For example, in Figure 4–1 bundle A is preferred to bundle D because it has the same amount of good X and more of good Y. Bundle C is also preferred to bundle D, because it has more of both goods. Similarly, bundle B is preferred to bundle D.

While the assumption that more is better provides important information about consumer preferences, it does not help us determine a consumer's preference for all possible bundles. For example, note in Figure 4–1 that the "more is better" property does not reveal whether bundle B is preferred to bundle A or bundle A is preferred to bundle B. To be able to make such comparisons, we will need to make some additional assumptions.

indifference curve
A curve that defines the combinations of two or more goods that give a consumer the same level of satisfaction.

An **indifference curve** defines the combinations of goods X and Y that give the consumer the same level of satisfaction; that is, the consumer is indifferent between any combination of goods along an indifference curve. A typical indifference curve is depicted in Figure 4–1. By definition, all combinations of X and Y located on the indifference curve provide the consumer with the same level of satisfaction. For example, if you asked the consumer "Which would you prefer—bundle A, bundle B, or bundle C?" the consumer would reply "I don't care," because bundles A, B, and C

| **FIGURE 4–1** | The Indifference Curve |

All the points on the indifference curve represent bundles of goods *X* and *Y*, generating the same level of satisfaction to consumer. Thus, the consumer is indifferent between the bundles. All points that lie below the curve generate less satisfaction to consumer. Bundle *D* is inferior to bundle *A* where a person can consume more units of *Y* and same number of units of *X*. The rate at which a consumer is willing to substitute one good for another changes along the curve; this slope is also known as the *marginal rate of substitution*.

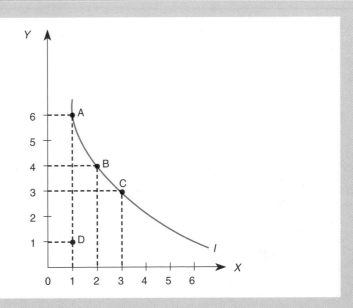

all lie on the same indifference curve. In other words, the consumer is indifferent among the three bundles.

The shape of the indifference curve depends on the consumer's preferences. Different consumers generally will have indifference curves of different shapes. One important way to summarize information about a consumer's preferences is in terms of the marginal rate of substitution. The **marginal rate of substitution (*MRS*)** is the absolute value of the slope of an indifference curve. The marginal rate of substitution between two goods is the rate at which a consumer is willing to substitute one good for the other and still maintain the same level of satisfaction.[1]

marginal rate of substitution (*MRS*)
The rate at which a consumer is willing to substitute one good for another good and still maintain the same level of satisfaction.

The concept of the marginal rate of substitution is actually quite simple. In Figure 4–1, the consumer is indifferent between bundles *A* and *B*. In moving from *A* to *B*, the consumer gains 1 unit of good *X*. To remain on the same indifference curve, she or he gives up 2 units of good *Y*. Thus, in moving from point A to point B, the marginal rate of substitution between goods *X* and *Y* is 2.

The careful reader will note that the marginal rate of substitution associated with moving from A to B in Figure 4–1 differs from the rate at which the consumer is willing to substitute between the two goods in moving from B to C. In particular, in moving from B to C, the consumer gains 1 unit of good *X*. But now he or she is willing to give up only 1 unit of good *Y* to get the additional unit of *X*. The reason is that this indifference curve satisfies the property of *diminishing marginal rate of substitution*.

---

[1]When two goods are perfect substitutes, the *MRS* is a constant, that is, indifference curves are straight lines. However, when two goods are perfect complements, consumers would want to consume them in fixed proportions. Indifference curves, in this case, are L-shaped, and the *MRS* = 0.

FIGURE 4–2 A Family of Indifference Curves

A family of indifference curves describes a person's preferences. Every bundle on an indifference curve III is preferred to those on curve II, and every bundle on an indifference curve II is preferred to those on curve I. Thus, curves farther from the origin indicate a higher level of satisfaction.

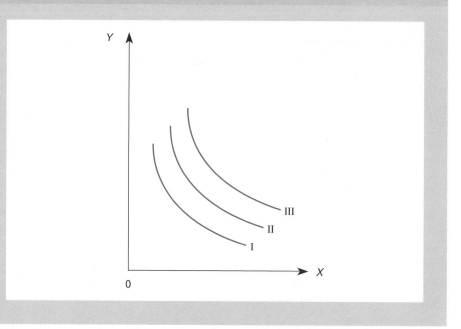

Property 4–3: Diminishing Marginal Rate of Substitution. As a consumer obtains more of good X, the rate at which he or she is willing to substitute good X for good Y decreases.

This assumption implies that indifference curves are convex from the origin; that is, they look like the indifference curve in Figure 4–1. To see how the locations of various indifference curves can be used to illustrate different levels of consumer satisfaction, we must make an additional assumption: that preferences are *transitive*.

Property 4–4: Transitivity. For any three bundles, A, B, and C, if $A \succ B$ and $B \succ C$, then $A \succ C$. Similarly, if $A \sim B$ and $B \sim C$, then $A \sim C$.

The assumption of transitive preferences, together with the "more is better" assumption, implies that indifference curves do not intersect one another. It also eliminates the possibility that the consumer is caught in a perpetual cycle in which she or he never makes a choice.

To see this, suppose Billy's preferences are such that he prefers jelly beans to licorice, licorice to chocolate, and chocolate to jelly beans. He asks the clerk to fill a bag with jelly beans, because he prefers jelly beans to licorice. When the clerk hands him a bagful of jelly beans, Billy tells her he likes chocolate even more than jelly beans. When the clerk hands him a bagful of chocolate, he tells her he likes licorice even more than chocolate. When the clerk hands him a bagful of licorice, Billy tells her he likes jelly beans even more than licorice. The clerk puts back the licorice and hands Billy a bagful of jelly beans. Now Billy is right back where he started! He is unable to choose the "best" kind of candy because his preferences for kinds of candy are not transitive.

The implications of these four properties are conveniently summarized in Figure 4–2, which depicts three indifference curves. Every bundle on indifference curve III is preferred to those on curve II, and every bundle on indifference curve II is preferred to those on curve I. The three indifference curves are convex and do not cross.

Curves farther from the origin imply higher levels of satisfaction than curves closer to the origin.

Constraints

In making decisions, individuals face *constraints*. There are legal constraints, time constraints, physical constraints, and, of course, budget constraints. To maintain our focus on the essentials of managerial economics without delving into issues beyond the scope of this course, we will examine the role prices and income play in constraining consumer behaviour.

The Budget Constraint

Simply stated, the *budget constraint* restricts consumer behaviour by forcing the consumer to select a bundle of goods that is affordable. If a consumer has only $30 in his or her pocket when reaching the checkout line in the supermarket, the total value of the goods the consumer presents to the cashier cannot exceed $30.

To demonstrate how the presence of a budget constraint restricts the consumer's choice, we need some additional shorthand notation. Let M represent the consumer's income, which can be any amount. By using M instead of a particular value of income, we gain generality in that the theory is valid for a consumer with any income level. We will let P_x and P_y represent the prices of goods X and Y, respectively. Given this notation, the opportunity set (also called the **budget set**) may be expressed mathematically as

budget set
The bundles of goods a consumer can afford.

$$P_xX + P_yY \leq M \qquad (4\text{--}1)$$

In words, the budget set defines the combinations of goods X and Y that are affordable for the consumer: the consumer's expenditures on good X, plus her or his expenditures on good Y, do not exceed the consumer's income. Note that if the consumer spends his or her entire income on the two goods, this equation holds with equality. This relation is called the **budget line**:

budget line
The bundles of goods that exhaust a consumer's income.

$$P_xX + P_yY = M$$

In other words, the budget line defines all the combinations of goods X and Y that exactly exhaust the consumer's income.

It is useful to manipulate the equation for the budget line to obtain an alternative expression for the budget constraint in slope-intercept form. If we multiply both sides of the budget line by $1/P_y$, we get

$$\frac{P_x}{P_y}X + Y = \frac{M}{P_y}$$

Solving for Y yields

$$Y = \frac{M}{P_y} - \frac{P_x}{P_y}X$$

Note that Y is a linear function of X with a vertical intercept of M/P_y and a slope of $-P_x/P_y$.

Inside BUSINESS

4-1 Indifference Curves and Risk Preferences

Have you ever wondered why some individuals choose to undertake risky prospects, such as skydiving and investing in risky financial assets, while others choose safer activities? Indifference curve analysis provides an answer to this question.

The table here presents the five-year average annual returns and quality ratings of three investment options offered by T. Rowe Price, a major no-load mutual fund. A mutual fund is an investment company that invests in a portfolio of financial assets (the assets listed in the table are portfolios of municipal bonds, which are debt obligations issued by municipal governments). *No-load* simply means that investors do not pay a fee to purchase or sell shares in the fund.

Selected Five-Year Average Annual Returns and Quality Ratings of Three T. Rowe Price Mutual Funds

	Fund Name	Five-Year Average Annual Return	Safety
A	Tax-free Short-intermediate	5.05%	Higher
B	Summit municipal Intermediate	5.95%	Moderate
C	Summit municipal Income	6.74%	Lower

Source: T. Rowe Price website, November 1, 2001.

The three options are tax-free investments with varying degrees of risk. With tax-free investments, the interest income received is exempt from federal income taxes. This makes these investments attractive to individuals in high tax brackets.

Fund A is the safest investment, but it offers the lowest reward; fund B is of medium safety, with a moderate reward; and fund C is the least safe, but it carries the highest reward. Points A, B, and C in Figure 4-3 characterize these three investment options.[1]

Investors view safety and the level of the return on an investment as "goods"; investments with higher returns and higher levels of safety are preferred to investments with lower returns and lower levels of safety. Investors are willing to substitute between the level of return and the level of safety. Given the three options, from an investor's viewpoint, there is a tradeoff between a higher reward (return) and the level of safety of the investment.

The relatively steep indifference curves drawn in panel (a) of Figure 4-3 describe an investor who has a high marginal rate of substitution between return and safety; she or he must receive a large return to be induced to give up a small amount of safety. The relatively flat indifference curves drawn in panel (b) indicate an investor with a low marginal rate of substitution between return and safety. This individual is willing to give up a lot of safety to get a slightly higher return. An investor with indifference curves such as those in panel (a) finds investment option A most attractive, because it is associated with the highest indifference curve. In contrast, an investor with indifference curves such as those in panel (b) achieves the highest indifference curve with investment option C. Both types of investors are rational, but one investor is willing to give up some additional financial return for more safety.

[1]The safety–return diagram is more conventionally demonstrated in terms of the risk–return diagram in which indifference curves would be downward-sloping instead.

The consumer's budget constraint is graphed in Figure 4-4. The shaded area represents the consumer's budget set, or opportunity set. In particular, any combination of goods X and Y within the shaded area, such as point G, represents an affordable combination of X and Y. Any point above the shaded area, such as point H, represents a bundle of goods that is unaffordable.

The upper boundary of the budget set in Figure 4-4 is the budget line. If a consumer spent her or his entire income on good X, the expenditures on good X would exactly equal the consumer's income:

$$P_x X = M$$

FIGURE 4-3 Risk Preferences

The three curves represent the three investment alternatives that differ in reward for a specific investor. The steep slopes of the curves in panel (a) imply that an investor's marginal rate of substitution between return and safety is high. An investor must receive a large return in order to be induced to give up a small amount of safety. Therefore, she prefers point A, which lies at the highest indifference curve, with low return of 2.89 percent but a high level of security.

The relatively flat slopes of the indifference curves in panel (b) indicate a second investor's willingness to give up a lot of safety in order to obtain a slightly higher return. Thus, the investor's marginal rate of substitution between return and safety is low and he maximizes his satisfaction at point C, with a high return of 7.29 percent but low safety.

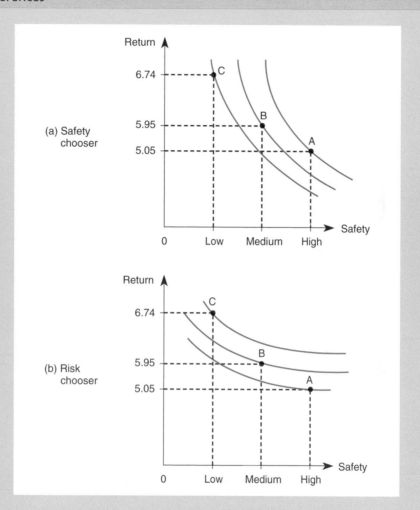

By manipulating this equation, we see that the maximum affordable quantity of good X consumed is

$$X = \frac{M}{P_x}$$

This is why the horizontal intercept of the budget line is

$$\frac{M}{P_x}$$

FIGURE 4–4 The Budget Set

The budget line is a boundary between affordable and unaffordable consumption choices. Any point above the shaded area, an area referred to as the consumer's *budget set*, represents a bundle of goods that is unaffordable to that consumer. Point G, within the budget line boundary, is affordable; point H is not. Any point on the budget line represents a maximized use of the budget, and maximized satisfaction.

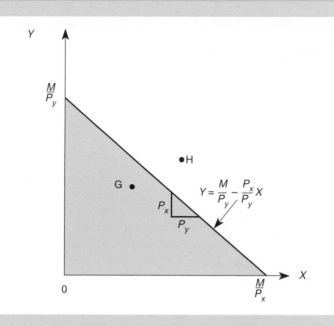

Similarly, if the consumer spent his or her entire income on good Y, expenditures on Y would exactly equal income:

$$P_yY = M$$

Consequently, the maximum quantity of good Y that is affordable is

$$Y = \frac{M}{P_y}$$

market rate of substitution
The rate at which one good may be traded for another in the market; the slope of the budget line.

The slope of the budget line is given by $-P_x/P_y$ and represents the **market rate of substitution** between goods X and Y. To obtain a better understanding of the market rate of substitution between goods X and Y, consider Figure 4–5, which presents a budget line for a consumer who has $10 in income and faces a price of $1 for good X and a price of $2 for good Y. If we substitute these values of P_x, P_y, and M into the formula for the budget line, we observe that the vertical intercept of the budget line (the maximum amount of good Y that is affordable) is $M/P_y = 10/2 = 5$. The horizontal intercept is $M/P_x = 10/1 = 10$ and represents the maximum amount of good X that can be purchased. The slope of the budget line is $-P_x/P_y = -(1/2)$.

The reason the slope of the budget line represents the market rate of substitution between the two goods is as follows. Suppose a consumer purchased bundle A in Figure 4–5, which represents the situation where the consumer purchases 3 units of good Y and 4 units of good X. If the consumer purchased bundle B instead of bundle A, she would gain one additional unit of good Y. But to afford this, she must give up 2 units $(4 - 2 = 2)$ of good X. For every unit of good Y the consumer purchases, she must give up 2 units of good X in order to be able to afford the additional unit of good

FIGURE 4–5 The Budget Line

The budget line reflects the tradeoff between buying more units of X and Y. Thus, in order to obtain two more units of X, the consumer must sacrifice one unit of Y.

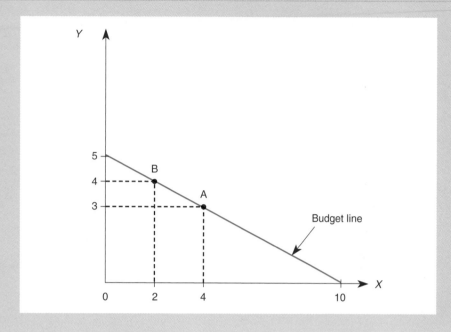

Y. Thus the market rate of substitution is $\Delta Y/\Delta X = (4 - 3)/(2 - 4) = -1/2$, which is the slope of the budget line.

Changes in Income

The consumer's opportunity set depends on market prices and the consumer's income. As these parameters change, so will the consumer's opportunities. Let us now examine the effects on the opportunity set of changes in income by assuming prices remain constant.

Suppose the consumer's initial income in Figure 4–6 is M^0. What happens if M^0 increases to M^1 while prices remain unchanged? Recall that the slope of the budget line is given by $-P_x/P_y$. Under the assumption that prices remain unchanged, the increase in income will not affect the slope of the budget line. However, the vertical and horizontal intercepts of the budget line both increase as the consumer's income increases, because more of each good can be purchased at the higher income. Thus, when income increases from M^0 to M^1, the budget line shifts to the right in a parallel fashion. This reflects an increase in the consumer's opportunity set, because more goods are affordable after the increase in income than before. Similarly, if income decreases to M^2 from M^0, the budget line shifts toward the origin and the slope of the budget line remains unchanged.

Changes in Prices

Now suppose the consumer's income remains fixed at M, but the price of good X decreases to $P_x^1 < P_x^0$. Furthermore, suppose the price of good Y remains unchanged. Since the slope of the budget line is given by $-P_x/P_y$, the reduction in the price of good X changes the slope, making it flatter than before. Since the maximum amount

FIGURE 4–6 Changes in Income Shrink or Expand Opportunities

As the consumer's income level rises, the budget line shifts to the right, because now he can buy more of both X and Y. As long as the relative prices for goods X and Y remain unchanged, the slope of the budget line will not change.

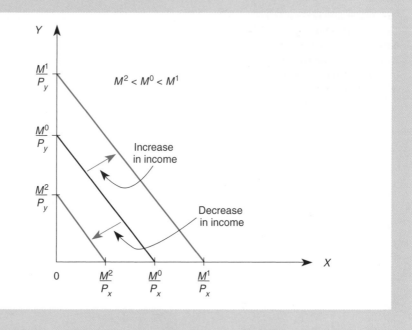

of good Y that can be purchased is M/P_y, a reduction in the price of good X does not change the Y intercept of the budget line. But the maximum amount of good X that can be purchased at the lower price (the X intercept of the budget line) is M/P_x^1, which is greater than M/P_x^0. Thus, the ultimate effect of a reduction in the price of good X is to rotate the budget line counterclockwise, as in Figure 4–7.

Similarly, an increase in the price of good X leads to a clockwise rotation of the budget line, as the next Demonstration Problem indicates.

Demonstration PROBLEM 4–1

A consumer has initial income of $100 and faces prices of $P_x = \$1$ and $P_y = \$5$. Graph the budget line, and show how it changes when the price of good X increases to $P_x^1 = \$5$.

Answer

Initially, if the consumer spends his entire income on good X, he can purchase $M/P_x = 100/1 = 100$ units of X. This is the horizontal intercept of the initial budget line in Figure 4–8. If the consumer spends his entire income on good Y, he can purchase $M/P_y = 100/5 = 20$ units of Y. This is the vertical intercept of the initial budget line. The slope of the initial budget line is $-P_x/P_y = -1/5$.

When the price of good X increases to 5, the maximum amount of X the consumer can purchase is reduced to $M/P_x = 100/5 = 20$ units of X. This is the horizontal intercept of the new budget line in Figure 4–8. If the consumer spends his entire income on good Y, he can purchase $M/P_y = 100/5 = 20$ units of Y. Thus, the vertical intercept of the budget line remains unchanged; the slope changes to $-P_x^1/P_y = -5/5 = -1$.

FIGURE 4–7 A Decrease in the Price of Good X

Whenever the relative price of good X or good Y changes, the slope of the budget line changes as well. As the price of good X declines from P^0 to P^1, the maximum amount of good X that can be purchased becomes larger. This leads to a *counterclockwise* rotation of the budget line.

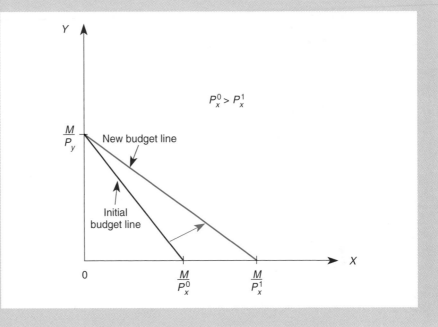

FIGURE 4–8 An Increase in the Price of Good X

An increase in the price of good X from $1 to $5 leads to a *clockwise* rotation of the budget line.

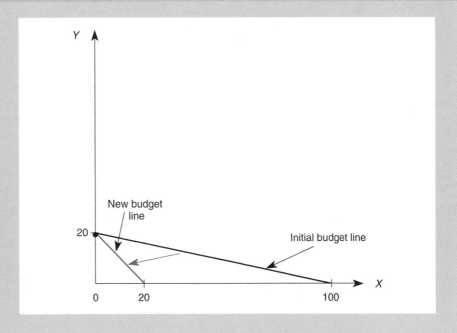

FIGURE 4–9 Consumer Equilibrium

Consumer equilibrium occurs at the point of tangency (that is, equal slopes) between the indifference curve and the budget line. Notice that the only point of tangency is point C, where curve III crosses the budget line. Points A and B, crossing the budget lines with the curves I and II, are both affordable, yet are suboptimal as they do not offer as much satisfaction as point C. Point C, the equilibrium, represents the point at which the consumer has no incentive to change to a different affordable bundle. Point D is preferable to point C, yet is unaffordable as it lies beyond the budget line.

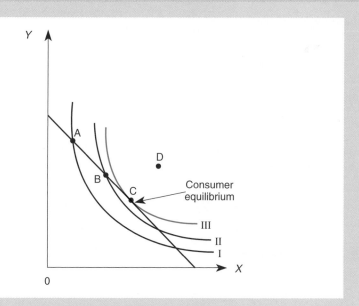

Consumer Equilibrium

The objective of the consumer is to choose the consumption bundle that maximizes his or her utility, or satisfaction. If there was no scarcity, the "more is better" property would imply that the consumer would want to consume bundles that contained infinite amounts of goods. However, one implication of scarcity is that the consumer must select a bundle that lies inside the budget set, that is, an affordable bundle. Let us combine our theory of consumer preferences with our analysis of constraints to see how the consumer goes about selecting the best affordable bundle.

Consider a bundle such as A in Figure 4–9. This combination of goods X and Y lies on the budget line, so the cost of bundle A completely exhausts the consumer's income. Given the income and prices corresponding to the budget line, can the consumer do better—that is, can the consumer achieve a higher indifference curve? Clearly, if the consumer consumed bundle B instead of bundle A, she or he would be better off since the indifference curve through B lies above the one through A. Moreover, bundle B lies on the budget line and thus is affordable. In short, it is inefficient for the consumer to consume bundle A because bundle B both is affordable and yields a higher level of well-being.

consumer equilibrium
The equilibrium consumption bundle—the affordable bundle that yields the greatest satisfaction to the consumer.

Is bundle B optimal? The answer is no. Bundle B exhausts the consumer's budget, but there is another affordable bundle that is even better: bundle C. Note that there are bundles, such as D, that the consumer prefers more than bundle C, but those bundles are not affordable. Thus, we say bundle C represents the **consumer equilibrium** choice. The term *equilibrium* refers to the fact that the consumer has no incentive to change to a different affordable bundle once this point is reached.

An important property of consumer equilibrium is that at the equilibrium consumption bundle, the slope of the indifference curve is equal to the slope of the budget line. Recalling that the absolute value of the slope of the indifference curve is called the *marginal rate of substitution* and the slope of the budget line is given by $-P_x/P_y$, we see that at a point of consumer equilibrium,

$$MRS = \frac{P_x}{P_y}$$

(4–2)

If this condition did not hold, the personal rate at which the consumer is willing to substitute between goods X and Y would differ from the market rate at which he or she is able to substitute between the goods. For example, at point A in Figure 4–9, the slope of the indifference curve is steeper than the slope of the budget line. This means the consumer is willing to give up more of good Y to get an additional unit of good X than she or he actually has to give up, based on market prices. Consequently, it is in the consumer's interest to consume less of good Y and more of good X. This substitution continues until ultimately the consumer is at a point such as C in Figure 4–9, where the *MRS* is equal to the ratio of prices.

Comparative Statics

Price Changes and Consumer Behaviour

A change in the price of a good will lead to a change in the equilibrium consumption bundle. To see this, recall that a reduction in the price of good X leads to a counter-clockwise rotation of the budget line. Thus, if the consumer initially is at equilibrium at point A in Figure 4–10, when the price of good X falls to P_x^1, his or her opportunity set expands. Given this new opportunity set, the consumer can achieve a higher level of satisfaction. This is illustrated as a movement to the new equilibrium point, B, in Figure 4–10.

Precisely where the new equilibrium point lies along the new budget line after a price change depends on consumer preferences. Accordingly, it is useful to recall the definitions of substitutes and complements that were introduced in Chapter 2.

First, goods X and Y are called *substitutes* if an increase (decrease) in the price of X leads to an increase (decrease) in the consumption of Y. Most consumers would view Coke and Pepsi as substitutes. If the price of Pepsi increased, most people would tend to consume more Coke. If goods X and Y are substitutes, a reduction in the price of X would lead the consumer to move from point A in Figure 4–10 to a point such as B, where less of Y is consumed than at point A.

Second, goods X and Y are called *complements* if an increase (decrease) in the price of good X leads to a decrease (increase) in the consumption of good Y. Beer and pretzels are an example of complementary goods. If the price of beer increased, most beer drinkers would decrease their consumption of pretzels. When goods X and Y are complements, a reduction in the price of X would lead the consumer to move from point A in Figure 4–11 to a point such as B, where more of Y is consumed than before.

From a managerial perspective, the key thing to note is that changes in prices affect the market rate at which a consumer can substitute among various goods. Therefore, changes in prices will change the behaviour of consumers. Price changes might occur because of updated pricing strategies within your own firm. Or they might arise because of price changes made by rivals or firms in other industries.

FIGURE 4–10 Change in Consumer Equilibrium Due to a Decrease in the Price of Good X (Note that good Y is a substitute for X)

A decrease in the price of good X from P^0 to P^1 leads to a counterclockwise rotation of the budget line, which expands consumer's opportunity set. Consequently, the consumer is able to achieve a higher level of satisfaction at point B. In this example, as goods X and Y are *substitutes* for one another, the reduction in price of X leads to a *reduction* in consumption of Y.

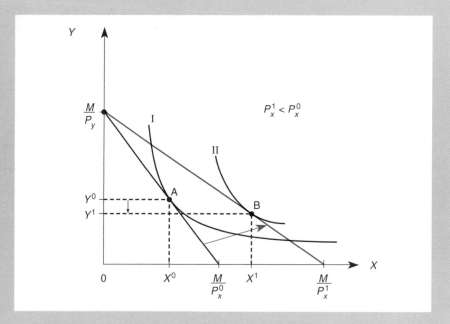

FIGURE 4–11 When the Price of Good X Falls, the Consumption of Complementary Good Y Rises

When the price of good X falls, the consumption of *complementary* good Y rises from Y^1 to Y^2.

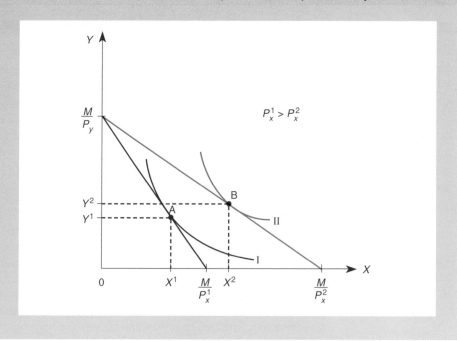

Ultimately, price changes alter consumer incentives to buy different goods, thereby changing the mix of goods they purchase in equilibrium. The primary advantage of indifference curve analysis is that it allows a manager to see how price changes affect the mix of goods that consumers purchase in equilibrium. As we will see below, indifference curve analysis also allows us to see how changes in *income* affect the mix of goods purchased by consumers.

Income Changes and Consumer Behaviour

A change in income also will lead to a change in the consumption patterns of consumers. The reason is that changes in income either expand or contract the consumer's budget constraint, and the consumer therefore finds it optimal to choose a new equilibrium bundle. For example, assume the consumer initially is at equilibrium at point A in Figure 4–12. Now suppose the consumer's income increases to M^1 so that his or her budget line shifts out. Clearly the consumer can now achieve a higher level of satisfaction than before. This particular consumer finds it in her or his interest to choose bundle *B* in Figure 4–12, where the indifference curve through point B is tangent to the new budget line.

As in the case of a price change, the exact location of the new equilibrium point will depend on consumer preferences. Let us now review our definitions of normal and inferior goods.

Recall that good *X* is a *normal good* if an increase (decrease) in income leads to an increase (decrease) in the consumption of good *X*. Normal goods include goods such as steak, airline travel, and designer jeans. As income goes up, consumers typically buy more of these goods. Note in Figure 4–12 that the consumption of both

---

FIGURE 4–12 An Increase in Income Increases the Consumption of Normal Goods

An increase in income increases the consumption of normal goods. Thus the consumption of both *X* and *Y* increases. The indifference curve shifts out simultaneously, retaining its slope.

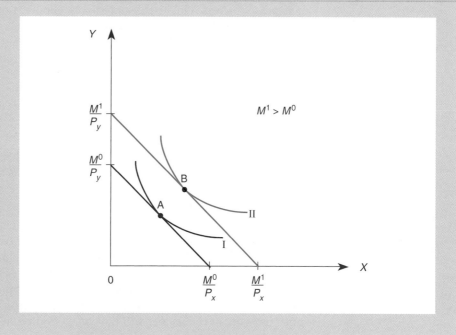

FIGURE 4–13 An Increase in Income Decreases the Equilibrium Consumption of Good *X*—an Inferior Good

An increase in income shifts the opportunity set further to the right, enabling the consumer to purchase more units of both good *X* and good *Y*. However, the demand for inferior good *X* declines as income rises. Therefore a consumer prefers point B to point A, as he is able to achieve a higher indifference curve at point B, where he consumes less units of inferior good *X* and more units of normal good *Y*.

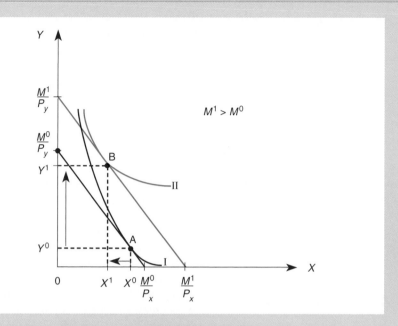

goods *X* and *Y* increased due to the increase in consumer income. Thus, the consumer views *X* and *Y* as normal goods.

Recall that good *X* is an *inferior good* if an increase (decrease) in income leads to a decrease (increase) in the consumption of good *X*. Bologna, bus travel, and generic jeans are examples of inferior goods. As income goes up, consumers typically consume less of these goods and services. It is important to repeat that by calling the goods *inferior,* we do not imply that they are of poor quality; it is simply a term used to define products consumers purchase less of when their incomes rise.

Figure 4–13 depicts the effect of an increase in income for the case when good *X* is an inferior good. When income increases, the consumer moves from point A to point B to maximize his or her satisfaction given the higher income. Since at point B the consumer consumes more of good *Y* than at point A, we know that good *Y* is a normal good. However, note that at point B less of good *X* is consumed than at point A, so we know this consumer views *X* as an inferior good.

Substitution and Income Effects

We can combine our analysis of price and income changes to gain a better understanding of the effect of a price change on consumer behaviour. Suppose a consumer initially is in equilibrium at point A in Figure 4–14, along the budget line connecting points F and G. Suppose the price of good *X* increases so that the budget line rotates clockwise and becomes the budget line connecting points F and H. There are two things to notice about this change. First, since the budget set is smaller due to the price increase, the consumer will be worse off after the price increase. A lower "real income" will be achieved, as a lower indifference curve is all that can be reached after the price increase. Second, the increase in the price of good *X* leads to a budget line

FIGURE 4–14 An Increase in the Price of Good X Leads to a Substitution Effect (A to B) and an Income Effect (B to C)

An increase in the price of X creates an income effect and a substitution effect. The substitution effect $X^0 - X^m$ is reflected in the move from A to B; the increase in the relative price of X causes the shift, while real income remains constant. Thus the consumer moves along her indifference curve to consume more units of Y. The income effect $X^m - X^1$, which is reflected in the move from point B to point C, keeps relative prices constant but decreases the purchasing power or an opportunity set of the consumer. As a result of the higher prices, indifference curve I becomes unreachable, and the consumer moves to a lower indifference curve II.

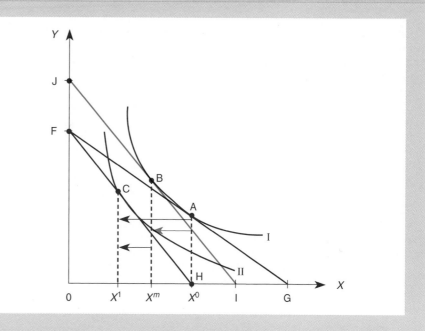

with a steeper slope, reflecting a higher market rate of substitution between the two goods. These two factors lead the consumer to move from the initial consumer equilibrium (point A) to a new equilibrium (point C) in Figure 4–14.

It is useful to isolate the two effects of a price change to see how each effect individually alters consumer choice. In particular, ignore for the moment the fact that the price increase leads to a lower indifference curve. Suppose that after the price increase, the consumer is given enough income to achieve the budget line connecting points J and I in Figure 4–14. This budget line has the same slope as budget line FH, but it implies a higher income than budget line FH. Given this budget line, the consumer will achieve equilibrium at point B, where less of good X is consumed than in the initial situation, point A. The movement from A to B is called the **substitution effect**; it reflects how a consumer will react to a different market rate of substitution. The substitution effect is the difference $X^0 - X^m$ in Figure 4–14. Importantly, the movement from A to B leaves the consumer on the same indifference curve, so the reduction in the consumption of good X implied by that movement reflects the higher market rate of substitution, not the reduced "real income," of the consumer.

The consumer does not actually face budget line JI when the price increases but instead faces budget line FH. Let us now take back the income we gave to the consumer to compensate for the price increase. When this income is taken back, the budget line shifts from JI to FH. This shift in the budget line reflects only a reduction in income; the slopes of budget lines JI and FH are identical. Thus, the movement from B to C is called the **income effect**. The income effect is the difference $X^m - X^1$

substitution effect
The movement along a given indifference curve that results from a change in the relative prices of goods, holding real income constant.

income effect
The movement from one indifference curve to another that results from the change in real income caused by a price change.

InsideBUSINESS

4-2 Price Changes and Inventory Management for Multiproduct Firms

One of the more important decisions a manager must make is how much inventory to have on hand. Too little inventory means an insufficient quantity of products to meet the demand of consumers, in which case your customers may defect to another store. The opportunity cost of inventory is the forgone interest that could be earned on the money tied up in inventory. In performing inventory management, an effective manager recognizes the relationship that exists among products in the store and the impact of a change in the price of one product on the required inventories of other products. In the late 1990s, the price of personal computers declined dramatically. This not only increased the quantity demanded of computers but dramatically increased the demand for computer software, which is a complementary good. This result has obvious implications for inventory management.

A more subtle aspect of a reduction in the price of computers is its impact on the demand for, and optimal inventories of, substitute goods. If a store sells many products, and some of the products are substitutes for computers, a reduction in the price of computers will lead to a reduction in the sales of these other goods. When the price of computers is reduced, the consumption of computers increases as a direct consequence of the price reduction. However, note that the consumption of substitutes like calculators will decrease as a result of the reduction in the price of computers. If the manager does not understand the impact of a price reduction on the consumption of substitute goods, he or she will face a buildup of inventories of calculators when the price of computers decreases.

It is important to emphasize that we have not described the optimal pricing policy for firms that sell multiple products (we will do this in a later chapter). We have pointed out that managers of firms that sell multiple products must think carefully about all of the implications of a price change.

in Figure 4–14; it reflects the fact that when price increases, the consumer's "real income" falls. Since good X is a normal good in Figure 4–14, the reduction in income leads to a further reduction in the consumption of X.

The total effect of a price increase thus is composed of substitution and income effects. The substitution effect reflects a movement along an indifference curve, thus isolating the effect of a relative price change on consumption. The income effect results from a parallel shift in the budget line; thus, it isolates the effect of reduced "real income" on consumption and is represented by the movement from B to C. The total effect of a price increase, which is what we observe in the marketplace, is the movement from A to C. The total effect of a change in consumer behaviour results not only from the effect of a higher relative price of good X (the movement from A to B) but also from the reduced real income of the consumer (the movement from B to C).

Applications of Indifference Curve Analysis

Choices by Consumers

Buy One, Get One Free
A very popular sales technique at pizza restaurants is to offer the following deal:

> Buy one large pizza, get one large pizza free (limit one free pizza per customer).

It is tempting to conclude that this is simply a 50 percent reduction in the price of pizza so that the budget line rotates as it does for any price decrease. This conclusion is invalid, however. A price reduction decreases the price of each unit purchased. The type of deal summarized above reduces only the price of the second unit purchased (in fact, it reduces the price of the second large pizza to zero). The offer does not change the price of units below one pizza and above two pizzas.

Inside BUSINESS

4-3 Income Effects and the Business Cycle

An important consideration in running a firm is the impact of changes in prices on the demand for the firm's product. Suppose you are the manager of a firm that sells a product that is a normal good and are considering expanding your product line to include another good. There are several things you may wish to consider in making your decision. Since your product is a normal good, you will sell more of it when the economy is booming (consumer incomes are high) than when times are tough (incomes are low). Your product is a cyclical product, that is, sales vary directly with the economy. This information may be useful to you when considering alternative products to include in your store. If you expand your offerings to include more normal goods, you will continue to have an operation that sells more during an economic boom than during a recession. But if you include in your operation some inferior goods, the demand for these products will increase during bad economic times (when incomes are low) and perhaps

offset the demand for normal goods. This is not to say that the optimal mix of products involves a 50-50 mix of normal and inferior goods; indeed, the optimal mix will depend on your own risk preference. The analysis does suggest that running a gourmet food store will likely involve a higher level of risk than running a supermarket. In particular, gourmet shops sell almost exclusively normal goods, while supermarkets have a more "balanced portfolio" of normal and inferior goods. This explains why, during recessions, many gourmet shops go out of business while supermarkets do not.

It is also useful to know the magnitude of the income effect when designing a marketing campaign. If the product is a normal good, it is most likely in the firm's interest to target advertising campaigns toward individuals with higher incomes. These factors should be considered when determining which magazines and television shows are the best outlets for advertising messages.

The *buy one, get one free* deal is quite easy to analyze in our framework. In Figure 4–15, a consumer initially faces a budget line connecting points A and B and is in equilibrium at point C. Point C represents one-half of a large pizza (say, a small pizza), so the consumer decides it is best to buy a small pizza instead of a large one. Point D represents the point at which she buys one large pizza, but, as we can see, the consumer prefers bundle C to bundle D, since it lies on a higher indifference curve.

When the consumer is offered the "buy one, get one free" marketing scheme, her budget line becomes ADEF. The reason is as follows. If she buys less than one large pizza, she gets no deal, and her budget line to the left of one pizza remains as it was, namely AD. But if she buys one large pizza, she gets a second one free. In this instance, the budget line becomes DEF as soon as she buys one pizza. In other words, the price of pizza is zero for units between one and two large pizzas. This implies that the budget line for pizzas is horizontal between one and two units (recall that the slope of the budget line is $-(P_x/P_y)$, and for these units P_x is zero). If the consumer wants to consume more than two large pizzas, she must buy them at regular prices. But note that if she spent all of her income on pizza, she could buy one more than she could before (since one of the pizzas is free). Thus, for pizzas in excess of two units, the budget constraint is the line connecting points E and F. After the deal is offered, the opportunity set increases. In fact, bundle E is now an affordable bundle. Moreover, it is clear that bundle E is preferred to bundle C, and the consumer's optimal choice is to consume bundle E, as in Figure 4–15. The sales technique has induced the consumer to purchase more pizza than she would have otherwise.

Cash Gifts, In-Kind Gifts, and Gift Certificates

Along with death and taxes, lines in refund departments after Christmas appear to be an unpleasant but necessary aspect of life. To understand why, and to be able to pose a potential solution to the problem, consider the following story.

Inside BUSINESS

4–4 The "Deadweight Loss" of In-Kind Gifts

Gift-givers are resorting to gift certificates in droves. A recent survey showed that almost 34 percent of Christmas shoppers plan to give gift certificates. The total dollar value of these certificates amounts to a staggering $10 billion. Why are gift certificates such a popular medium of gift-giving?

Recently, an economist offered one explanation. Using data from a group of college students, the researcher estimated that between 10 and 30 percent of the monetary value of the typical in-kind gift is "lost." This loss stems from the discrepancy between the amount actually paid for the gift and how much the recipient values it. These data from the real world indicate that it is indeed difficult to pick a gift that exactly matches that recipient's preferences. For this reason, in-kind gifts create a "deadweight loss" that averages 10 to 30 percent of the amount spent on gifts.

As the text shows, one way of avoiding this deadweight loss is to give cash rather than an in-kind gift. Unfortunately, this creates a different type of loss when there is a stigma associated with giving cash: the gift is "discounted" because the recipient feels that little thought went into it. Gift certificates are a happy medium. Ideally, they are able to eliminate both the stigma associated with cash gifts and the deadweight loss that stems from giving a gift that doesn't exactly match the recipient's preferences.

Sources: "Harried Shoppers Turn to Gift Certificates," *The New York Times*, January 4, 1997; J. Waldfogel, "The Deadweight Loss of Christmas," *American Economic Review* 83(5), December 1993, pp. 1328–36.

One Christmas morning, a consumer named Sam is in equilibrium, consuming bundle A as in Figure 4–16. He opens a package and, to his surprise, it contains a fruitcake. He smiles and tells Aunt Sarah that he always wanted a fruitcake. Graphically, when Sam receives the gift his opportunity set expands to include point B in Figure 4–16. Note that bundle B is just like bundle A except that it has one more

---

FIGURE 4–15 A "Buy One, Get One Free" Pizza Deal

When the consumer is offered a "buy one, get one free" deal, the cost of a second pizza becomes zero ($P_x = 0$). Consequently, the slope (given by $-P_x/P_y$) of the budget line between point D and point E becomes zero as well, thus expanding the opportunity set. The new opportunity set ADEF includes bundle E, which is preferable to bundle C because it lies on a higher indifference curve.

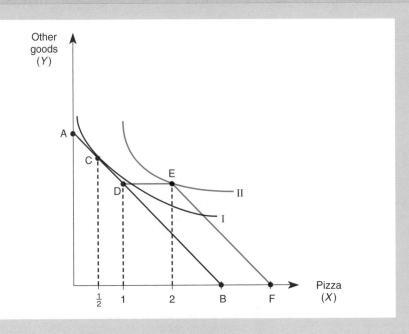

FIGURE 4–16 A Gift of One Fruitcake

A gift of a fruitcake moves Sam from point A to point B and to a more preferable indifference curve II, despite the fact that the budget line remains constant. With the gift Sam is able to consume one more unit of cake without sacrificing any units of Y.

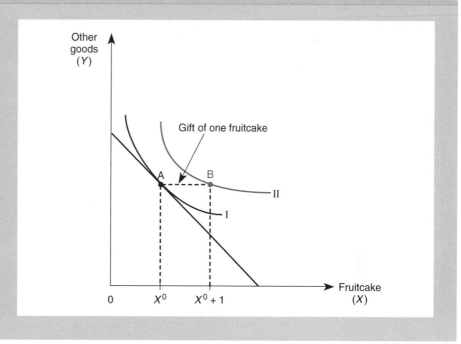

fruitcake than bundle *A*. Given this new opportunity set, Sam moves to the higher indifference curve through point *B* after receiving the gift.

While Sam likes fruitcake and is better off after receiving it, the gift is not what he would have purchased had Aunt Sarah given him the cash she spent on the fruitcake. For concreteness, suppose the cost of the fruitcake was $10. Had Sam been given $10 in cash, his budget line would have shifted out, parallel to the old budget line but through point *B*, as in Figure 4–17. To see why, note that when Sam gets additional income, prices are not changed, so the slope of the budget line is unchanged. Note also that if Sam used the money to buy one more fruitcake, he would exactly exhaust his income. Thus, the budget line after the cash gift must go through point *B*—and, given the cash gift, Sam would achieve a higher level of satisfaction at point *C* compared to the gift of a fruitcake (point *B*).

Thus, a cash gift generally is preferred to an in-kind gift of equal value, unless the in-kind gift is exactly what the consumer would have purchased personally. This explains why refund departments are so busy after the Christmas holidays; individuals exchange gifts for cash so that they can purchase bundles they prefer.

One way stores attempt to reduce the number of gifts returned is to sell gift certificates. To see why, suppose Sam received a gift certificate, good for $10 worth of merchandise at store X, which sells good *X*, instead of the $10 fruitcake. Further, suppose the certificate is not good at store Y, which sells good *Y*. By receiving a gift certificate, Sam cannot purchase any more of good *Y* than he could before he received the certificate. But if he spends all of his income on good *Y*, he can purchase $10 worth of good *X*, since he has a certificate worth $10 at store X. And if he spends all of his income on good *X*, he can purchase $10 more than he could before because of the gift certificate. In effect, the gift certificate is like money that is good only at store X.

FIGURE 4–17 A Cash Gift Yields Higher Utility Than an In-Kind Gift

A cash gift shifts the budget line to the right so that it passes through point B. As Sam does not have to buy an additional cake he can choose a more satisfying mix of products at point C, where Sam's utility is maximized. Thus a cash gift yields higher utility than an in-kind gift.

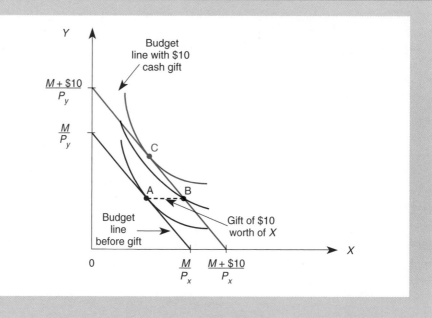

Graphically, the effect of receiving a gift certificate at store X is depicted in Figure 4–18. The straight black line is the budget line before Sam receives the gift certificate. When the $10 gift certificate is received, the budget constraint becomes the coloured one. In effect, the gift certificate allows the consumer up to $10 worth of good X without spending a dime of his own money.

FIGURE 4–18 A Gift Certificate Valid at Store X

A gift certificate expands an opportunity set farther to the right as it allows the consumer up to $10 worth of good X without spending a dime of his own money. If both goods are normal goods the consumer will move from point A to point C, consuming more of each good. Note that point C is preferable to point B, because it lies on a higher indifference curve. Thus the net increase in consumption of good X will rise by less than $10 from its original equilibrium level at point A.

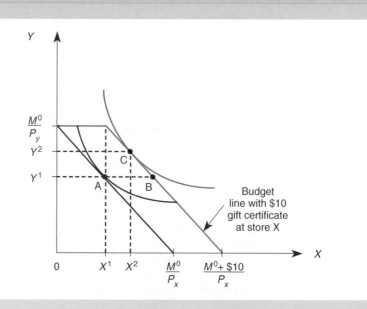

The effect of gift certificates on consumer behaviour depends, among other things, on whether good X is a normal or inferior good. To examine what happens to behaviour when a consumer receives a gift certificate, let us suppose a consumer initially is in equilibrium at point A in Figure 4–18, spending $10 on good X. What happens if the consumer is given a $10 gift certificate good only for items in store X? If both X and Y are normal goods, the consumer will desire to spend more on both goods as income increases. Thus, if both goods are normal goods, the consumer moves from A to C as in Figure 4–18. In this instance, the consumer reacts to the gift certificate just as she or he would have reacted to a cash gift of equal value.

Demonstration PROBLEM 4–2

How would the analysis of gift certificates just presented change if good X were an inferior good?

Answer

In this instance, a gift of $10 in cash would result in a movement from point A in Figure 4–19 to a point like D, since X is an inferior good. However, when a $10 gift certificate is received, bundle D is not affordable, and the best the consumer can do is consume bundle E. In other words, had the consumer been given cash, his or her budget line would have extended up along the dotted line, and point D would have been an affordable bundle. If given cash, the consumer would have purchased less of good X than she or he did with the gift certificate. Also, note that the consumer would have achieved a higher indifference curve with the cash than that achieved with the gift certificate. (An end-of-chapter problem asks you whether a gift certificate always leads to a lower indifference curve and higher sales than a cash gift when the good is inferior.)

FIGURE 4–19 Here, a Cash Gift Yields Higher Utility Than a Gift Certificate of Equal Dollar Value

When X is an inferior good and a cash equivalent of $10 is gifted, the consumer would normally prefer bundle D with less units of X and more units of Y. However, with the gift certificate a consumer cannot consume bundle D anymore, because it is outside the opportunity set. Therefore, she would move from point A to point E. Note that a gift certificate results in lower satisfaction than a cash gift.

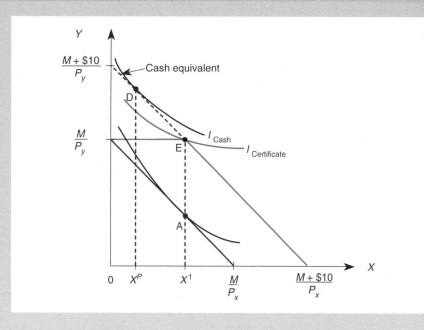

This analysis reveals two important benefits to a firm that sells gift certificates. First, as a manager you can reduce the strain on your refund department by offering gift certificates to customers looking for gifts. This is true for both normal and inferior goods. Second, if you sell an inferior good, offering to sell gift certificates to those looking for gifts may result in a greater quantity sold than if customers resorted to giving cash gifts. (This assumes you do not permit individuals to redeem gift certificates for cash.)

Choices by Workers and Managers

Until now, our analysis of indifference curves has focused on the decisions of consumers of goods and services. Managers and workers also are individuals and therefore have preferences among the alternatives that confront them. In this section, we will see that the indifference curve analysis developed earlier for consumers can easily be modified to analyze the behaviour of managers and other individuals employed by firms. In Chapter 6 we will show how these insights into the behaviour of workers and managers can be used to construct efficient employment contracts.

A Simplified Model of Income–Leisure Choice

Most workers view both leisure and income as goods and substitute between them at a diminishing rate along an indifference curve. Thus, a typical worker's indifference curve has the usual shape in Figure 4–20, where we measure the quantity of leisure consumed by an employee on the horizontal axis and worker income on the vertical axis. Note that while workers enjoy leisure, they also enjoy income.

To induce workers to give up leisure, firms must compensate them. Suppose a firm offers to pay a worker $10 for each hour of leisure the worker gives up (that is, spends working). In this instance, opportunities confronting the worker or manager are given by the straight line in Figure 4–20. If the worker chooses to work 24-hour days, he or she consumes no leisure but earns $10 × 24 = $240 per day, which is the vertical inter-

---

FIGURE 4–20 Labour–Leisure Choice

The worker attempts to reach a higher indifference curve until he gets to curve III that is tangent to the opportunity set at point E. Point E sets up an equilibrium amount of work hours.

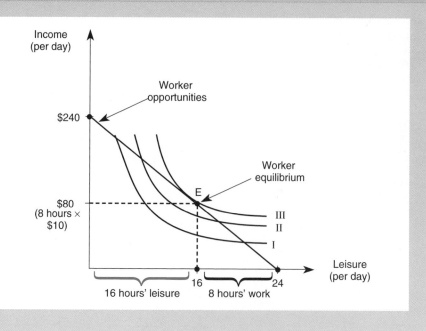

cept of the line. If the worker chooses not to work, he or she consumes 24 hours of leisure but earns no income. This is the horizontal intercept of the line in Figure 4–20.

Worker behaviour thus may be examined in much the same way we analyzed consumer behaviour. The worker attempts to achieve a higher indifference curve until he or she achieves one that is tangent to the opportunity set at point E in Figure 4–20. In this instance, the worker consumes 16 hours of leisure and works 8 hours to earn a total of $80 per day.

Demonstration PROBLEM 4–3

Suppose a worker is offered a wage of $5 per hour, plus a fixed payment of $40. What is the equation for the worker's opportunity set in a given 24-hour day? What are the maximum total earnings the worker can earn in a day? The minimum? What is the price to the worker of consuming an additional hour of leisure?

Answer
The total earnings (E) of a worker who consumes L hours of leisure in a 24-hour day is given by

$$E = \$40 + \$5(24 - L)$$

so the combinations of earnings (E) and leisure (L) satisfy

$$E = \$160 - \$5L$$

Thus, the most a worker can earn in a 24-hour day is $160 (by consuming no leisure); the least that can be earned is $40 (by not working at all). The price of a unit of leisure is $5, since the opportunity cost of an hour of leisure is one hour of work.

The Decisions of Managers

William Baumol[2] has argued that many managers derive satisfaction from the underlying output and profits of their firms. According to Baumol, higher profits and sales lead to a larger firm, and larger firms provide more "perks" like spacious offices, executive health clubs, corporate jets, and the like.

Suppose a manager's preferences are such that she or he views the "profits" and the "output" of the firm to be "goods" so that more of each is preferred to less. We are not suggesting that it is optimal for you, as a manager, to have these types of preferences, but there may be instances in which your preferences are so aligned. In many sales jobs, for example, individuals receive a bonus depending on the overall profitability of the firm. But the salesperson's ability to receive reimbursement for certain business-related expenses may depend on that individual's total output (for example, number of cars sold). In this instance, the individual may value both output and profits. Alternatively, perks such as a company plane, car, and so forth may be allocated to individuals based on the firm's output. In that case, managerial preferences may depend on the firm's profits as well as output.

Panels (a), (b), and (c) of Figure 4–21 show the relation between profits and the output of a firm on the curve labelled "firm's profits." This curve goes from the origin

---

[2]William J. Baumol, *Business Behavior, Value, and Growth*, rev. ed. (New York: Harcourt, Brace and World, 1967).

FIGURE 4-21 A Manager's Preferences Might Depend On:

(a) The manager attempts to reach a higher indifference curve in order to maximize her desire for more output and profit, until she reaches equilibrium on curve I_1 at point A. Note that, as both profit *and* output are seen as "goods," the manager's desire for greater output leads to suboptimal profit performance from the standpoint of the firm.

(b) In this case the manager's preferences depend solely on output. Therefore, indifference curves take the shape of vertical lines. Since the manager attempts to reach higher and higher indifference curves, she chooses an output of Q_0 at point B, because at that point her satisfaction is maximized. Note that equilibrium level of output does not maximize the firm's profits.

(c) If the manager is motivated solely by the profits of the firm, the manager's indifference curves take a shape of horizontal lines. The manager will chose point C, because at that point her satisfaction is maximized; the highest indifference curve is reached. Note that in this case the manager's decision maximizes the firm's profits as well, and therefore such an outcome is desirable for the firm.

(a) Profits and output

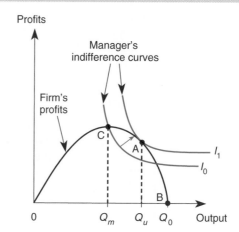

(b) Output only

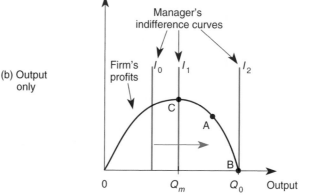

(c) Profits only

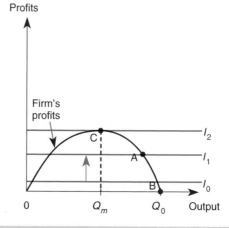

through points C, A, and B, and represents the profits of the firm as a function of output. When the firm sells no output, profits are zero. As the firm expands output, profits increase, reach a maximum at Q_m, and then begin to decline until, at point Q_0, they are again zero.

Given this relationship between output and profits, a manager who views output and profits as "goods" (the Baumol hypothesis) has indifference curves like those in Figure 4–21(a). She attempts to achieve higher and higher indifference curves until she eventually reaches equilibrium at point A. Note that this level of output, Q_u, is greater than the profit-maximizing level of output, Q_m. Thus, when the manager views both profits and output as "goods," she produces more than the profit-maximizing level of output.

In contrast, when the manager's preferences depend solely on output, the indifference curves look like those in Figure 4–21(b), which are vertical straight lines. One example of this situation occurs when the owner of a car dealership pays the manager based solely on the number of cars sold (the manager gets nothing if the company goes bankrupt). Since the manager does not care about profits, his or her indifference curves are vertical lines, and satisfaction increases as the lines move farther to the right. A manager with such preferences will attempt to obtain the indifference curves farther and farther to the right until indifference curve I_2 is reached. Point B represents equilibrium for this manager, where Q_0 units of output are produced. Again, in this instance the manager produces more than the profit-maximizing level of output.

Finally, suppose the manager cares solely about the profits of the firm. In this instance, the manager's indifference curves are horizontal straight lines as shown in Figure 4–21(c). The manager maximizes satisfaction at point C, where the indifference curve I_2 is as high as possible given the opportunity set. In this instance, profits are greater and output is lower than in the other two cases.

An important issue for the firm's owners is to induce managers to care solely about profits so that the result is the maximization of the underlying value of the firm, as in Figure 4–21(c). We will examine this issue in more detail in Chapter 6.

The Relationship Between Indifference Curve Analysis and Demand Curves

We have seen how the consumption patterns of an individual consumer depend on variables that include the prices of substitute goods, the prices of complementary goods, tastes (that is, the shape of indifference curves), and income. The indifference curve approach developed in this chapter, in fact, is the basis for the demand functions we studied in Chapters 2 and 3. We conclude by examining the link between indifference curve analysis and demand curves.

Individual Demand

To see where the demand curve for a normal good comes from, consider Figure 4–22(a). The consumer initially is in equilibrium at point A, where income is fixed at M and prices are P_x^0 and P_y. But when the price of good X falls to the lower level, indicated by P_x^1, the opportunity set expands and the consumer reaches a new equilibrium at point B. The important thing to notice is that the only change that caused the consumer to move from A to B was a change in the price of good X; income and the price of good Y are held constant in the diagram. When the price of good X is P_x^0, the consumer consumes X^0 units of good X; when the price falls to P_x^1, the consumption of X increases to X^1.

This relationship between the price of good X and the quantity consumed of good X is graphed in Figure 4–22(b) and is the individual consumer's demand curve for good X. This consumer's demand curve for good X indicates that, holding other things constant, when the price of good X is P_x^0, the consumer will purchase X^0 units of X; when the price of good X is P_x^1, the consumer will purchase X^1 units of X.

Market Demand

You will usually, in your role as a manager, be interested in determining the total demand by all consumers for your firm's product. This information is summarized in the market demand curve. The market demand curve is the horizontal summation of individual demand curves and indicates the total quantity all consumers in the market would purchase at each possible price.

FIGURE 4–22 Deriving an Individual's Demand Curve

A reduction in the price of a normal good X, from P^0 to P^1, holding income and price of Y fixed, will increase demand for normal good X (lower graph). This causes a counterclockwise rotation of the budget line, allowing the consumer to move to a higher indifference curve to choose bundle B, located on the higher indifference curve II. Thus the consumer will move to higher and higher indifference curves in order to maximize her satisfaction as the price for good X decreases.

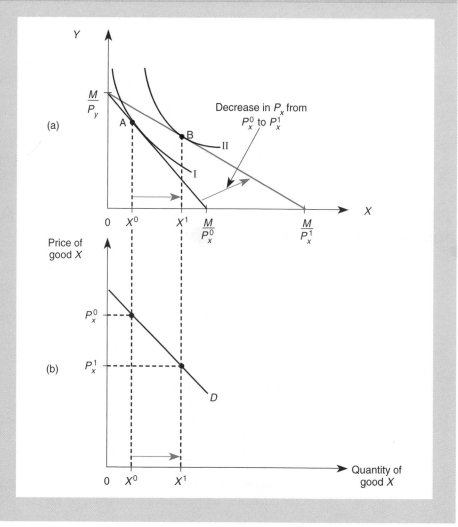

FIGURE 4-23 Deriving the Market Demand Curve

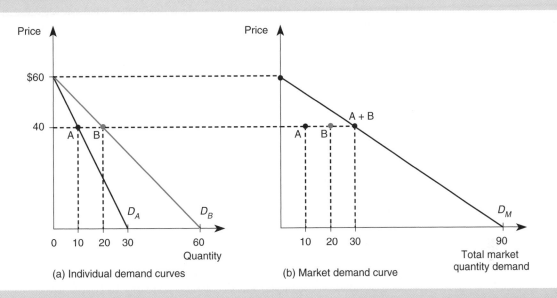

(a) Individual demand curves   (b) Market demand curve

The market demand curve is derived through a horizontal summation of individual demand curves D_A and D_B, and indicates the total quantity that consumers A and B would purchase at each price. As A is willing to purchase 10 units of good at a price of $40 and B is willing to purchase 20 units of good at a price of $40, together they will be willing to purchase 30 units at the price of $40.

This concept is illustrated graphically in Figures 4–23(a) and 4–23(b). The curves D_A and D_B represent the individual demand curves of two hypothetical consumers, Ms. A and Mr. B, respectively. When the price is $60, Ms. A buys 0 units and Mr. B buys 0 units. Thus, at the market level, 0 units are sold when the price is $60, and this is one point on the market demand curve (labelled D_M in Figure 4–23(b)). When the price is $40, Ms. A buys 10 units (point A) and Mr. B buys 20 units (point B). Thus, at the market level (Figure 4–23(b)), 30 units are sold when the price is $40, and this is another point (point A + B) on the market demand curve. When the price of good X is zero, Ms. A buys 30 units and Mr. B buys 60 units; thus, at the market level, 90 units are sold when the price is $0. If we repeat the analysis for all prices between $0 and $60, we get the curve labelled D_M in Figure 4–23(b).

Thus, the demand curves we studied in Chapters 2 and 3 are based on indifference curve analysis.

The Attribute Approach to Consumer Choice*

Our discussion of consumer behaviour so far has failed to explain why some customers opt to purchase brand A over brand B for the same general good or service. To analyze consumer choice criteria for competing brands, we can study the modern consumer theory known as *attribute analysis*.[3] The attribute model of consumer behaviour

---

*This section is optional.

[3]Kelvin Lancaster, "A New Approach to Consumer Demand," *Journal of Political Economy*, April 1966.

holds that consumers derive utility not from the products themselves but from the characteristics or attributes provided by the products. It is a product's characteristics, performance features, or attributes that create utility; thus, what causes a buyer to prefer one brand over another has to do with the different attributes of rival brands. For instance, what business travellers care about in their notebook computers are low weight, long battery life, and high computing power, rather than the logo on the case. There are tradeoffs between these good things; what differentiates one notebook from another is where in this **attribute space** or *characteristics space* they are located.

Therefore, the major contribution of attribute analysis is its ability to explain that a consumer's preference for brand A over brand B is rooted in the fact that the consumer attaches more utility or satisfaction to some attributes than to others. Thus, the approach greatly facilitates the explanation of consumer choice within groups of substitutes.

attribute space
Possible combinations of attributes that can be possessed by products, conceived as a graph in several dimensions.

Depicting Products in Attribute Space

For purposes of our graphical analysis here, consider the situation of buying a notebook computer assuming that a prospective buyer is familiar enough with its two most important attributes (other than price)—that is, low weight and high computing power. To demonstrate how a consumer might choose among products to maximize utility derived from the two attributes, suppose there are three notebook brands. After a careful evaluation, the buyer ranks each on a scale of 1 to 10, the lowest being 1 and the highest 10, and comes up with the information given in Table 4–1. Assume that each product supplies both attributes in some ratio.

In Figure 4–24, each notebook brand is shown in the "attribute space" as a ray drawn from the origin. Graphically, the slope of each ray is determined by the ratio of low weight to computing power, as listed in the last column in the table. If the buyer buys notebook A, she will travel out along the steepest ray, absorbing the two attributes in the ratio 2.25. The other notebook computers are indicated by the lower rays because these offer the two attributes at lower ratios.

What determines how far along each ray the buyer might go and how much of each product she might purchase depends on the her budget (budget constraint). In case of an indivisible purchase, such as purchase of an automobile or a notebook computer—the products, on the one hand, that are available only in discrete units and, on the other hand, the prices of which are large in relation to the consumer's income—the consumer is expected to stop at purchasing just one unit of the product: one automobile and one notebook computer. This, of course, assumes the buyer's budget is large enough to permit the purchase of any of the three brands despite the price differences.

efficiency frontier
The outer boundary of the attainable combinations of attributes in attribute space.

Following this logic, the **efficiency frontier**, which is the outer boundary of the attainable combinations of attributes, is obtained. This frontier, called "efficient"

TABLE 4–1	Attributes and Prices of Three Brands of Notebook Computers			
		Attribute Rating		
Notebook Brand	Notebook Price	Low Weight	High Computing Power	Ratio of Low Weight to High Computing Power
A	$2500	9	4	2.25
B	2800	7	6	1.16
C	3200	5	9	0.55

FIGURE 4–24 The Utility-Maximizing Attribute Combination

The slope of each ray is the ratio of low weight to high computing power, 2.25, 1.16, and 0.55, respectively for brands A, B, and C. The efficient frontier is represented by the kinked line ABC. The buyer maximizes utility by choosing the notebook brand with the attribute combination on the highest indifference curve attainable, *I**.

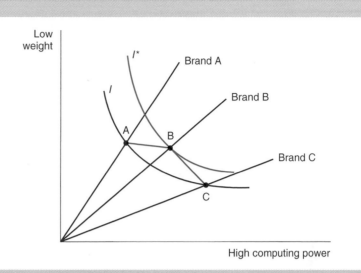

because only combinations on this frontier allow the consumer to maximize utility, consists of the points joining the limit points—points A, B, and C—on each product ray. Each is found by first dividing the buyer's income by the price of the respective product in order to determine the number of the units of the product, and then multiplying the outcome by the attribute content of each unit. The point depicted along each ray shows the maximum intake of the two attributes that can be obtained by consuming each notebook.[4]

Utility Maximization from Attributes

Just as consumers can express preference or indifference between combinations of products, they can express preference or indifference between combinations of attributes. At any particular combination of "light weight" and "high computing power," our buyer will be able to express a marginal rate of substitution between the two attributes: at any point, an extra unit of "low weight" will be worth giving up some amount of "high computing power." These evaluations produce a set of indifference curves expressing her tastes and preferences at each possible attribute combination. Since our buyer cannot mix brands but rather needs to choose one notebook brand or another, she must be content with the constrained point: A, B, or C, Figure 4–24. Of these options, point B allows her to attain the highest indifference curve, *I**.[5]

---

[4]If our example involved a product such as going to restaurants or going to the movies, more than "1 unit" might well be purchased over a short period of time. In this case, the distance on each that the buyer can travel is found by (1) dividing the consumer's allotted budget for the item by the price of each brand to arrive at how many units can be purchased and (2) calculating the total amounts of each attribute that can thus be obtained.

[5]If these products were mixable (see previous footnote) the consumer would maximize utility by mixing brands to attain the highest indifference curve tangent to a flat section of the efficiency frontier (AB or BC) to consume a combination of two goods (two restaurants or two movies), instead of touching one of the corners (points A, B, or C).

ANSWERING THE **Head**line

The Canada Health Act sets the criteria and conditions with respect to insured health services and extended health care services that must be met by provincial/territorial health care insurance plans before a full cash contribution can be made by the federal government to each province or territory.

- *Conditional grants.* Conditional grants are a method of sharing costs between a smaller government and a larger government—the municipal vis-à-vis the provincial, or the provincial vis-à-vis the federal government. In effect, government conditional (direct) grants have the effect of making smaller governments more uniform and reducing the effects of intergovernmental competition. Grants can be used to fund an entire project, or to fund a portion of a project, the remainder of the funding being put forth by the lower-level government.

    Since the federal government began contributing to provincial and territorial health insurance programs in 1958, the arrangements for these contributions have evolved. Prior to 1977, the federal government *cost-shared* hospital and physician services with the provinces and territories. Under the Hospital Insurance and Diagnostic Services Act, the federal government reimbursed the provinces and territories for approximately 50 percent of the costs of hospital insurance. Moreover, subsequently, under the Medical Care Act, enacted in 1968, the federal contribution in support of medical care was 50 percent of the average national per capita costs of the insured services multiplied by the number of insured persons in each province and territory.

- *Unconditional grants.* Unconditional grants are used to allow the revenue source of a higher-level government to finance activities of a lower-level government. For example, tax revenues are collected by the federal government and given to provincial and municipal governments to spend as they see fit.

In 1977, *cost-sharing* arrangements were replaced by Established Programs Financing. Unlike the previous cost-sharing arrangements, EPF was a *block-funding system*. Then, on April 1, 1996, the Canada Health and Social Transfer (CHST), a *single-block fund*, replaced the EPF and the Canada Assistance Plan (CAP); it continues to provide support through both cash and tax transfers for health and other social programs delivered by the provinces and territories.

Conditional grants are made for a specific purpose: to grant the contributing government more control over the way the money is spent. For example, the grant may specify how the money is to be used.

Suppose the federal government offers a conditional grant to the provinces to provide more health services, by introducing a program whereby for every $1 spent on health services the federal government provides a $0.50 subsidy. Let us assume that the subsidy program is not an open-ended system and is subject to a ceiling of $600. Initially the province's operating budget is assumed to be $1000 and the price of health services is $10. Accordingly, the initial budget line is represented by KJ, and the maximum number of health services attainable is 100 (see Figure 4–25).

Without a grant, the provinces are at point A and spend $400 on health services and $600 on all other subsidies, reaching the indifference curve I_2. With the subsidy (grant) of $600, the budget line pivots around point K to KL, giving the provinces the incentive to locate at point B on I_3. At point B, total spending on health services by the provinces as well as the federal government is $700 (70 × $10), of which one-third is paid by the federal government and two-thirds budgeted by the provinces. The amount of the conditional grant is therefore $233.34. If an unconditional lump-sum

FIGURE 4–25 A Conditional or an Unconditional Grant in the Health System?

Without a grant, point A, the province spends $400 on health services and $600 on everything else. A conditional grant causes the budget line KJ to rotate to KL. At the new equilibrium point, B, where the budget line is tangent to I_3, health spending has increased to $700 with one-third ($233.34) paid by the federal government and two-thirds by the provincial government. An unconditional grant (lump sum) of equal magnitude, however, causes the original budget line to shift to MN, where C is above B.

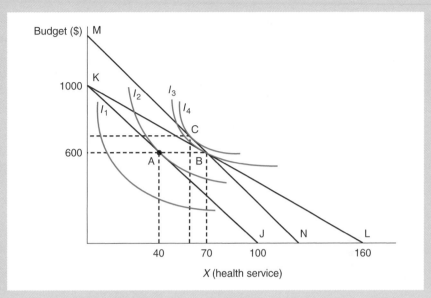

grant of equal magnitude ($233.34) were given instead, the provinces would be able to relocate to point C (I_4), the tangent between MN (drawn parallel to KJ and to go through point B) and I_4, which is higher than I_3. At this point, the provinces would end up spending less on the health services and more on other services.

Therefore, from the perspective of the provinces, an unconditional grant is considered superior to a conditional grant because it allows them to spend a fixed budget in a way that maximizes its utility. This argument is somewhat similar to that between a cash gift versus a gift certificate, in which the recipient is invariably in favour of the former than the latter. However, this view is neither shared by the taxpayers nor consistent with Romanow's recommendation for creation of a national health council, a milestone in the newly adopted national health program. Under (pre-Romanow) CHST's *single*-block funding formula, support was provided to each province and territory for health, education, and other social programs in one, big *unconditional* lump, giving them significant leeway in their budget allocation of social services. While this is clearly the reason why the provinces prefer more money with no strings attached, the absence of accountability gives rise to a greater need to reassure patients and taxpayers alike that the publicly funded health-care system is spending its money wisely.

Summary

In this chapter, we provided a basic model of individual behaviour that enables the manager to understand the impact of various managerial decisions on the actions of consumers and workers.

After reading and working through the Demonstration Problems in this chapter, you should understand what a budget constraint is and how it changes when prices or income change. You should also understand that when there is a change in the price of a good, consumers change their behaviour because there is a change in the ratio of prices (which leads to a substitution effect) and a change in real income (which leads to the income effect). The model of consumer behaviour also articulates the assumptions underlying the demand curve.

In equilibrium, consumers adjust their purchasing behaviour so that the ratio of prices they pay just equals their marginal rate of substitution. This information, along with observations of consumer behaviour, helps a manager determine when to use a "buy one, get one free" pricing strategy instead of a half-price offer. During holiday seasons, the same manager will have a sound basis for determining whether offering gift certificates is a wise strategy.

Effective managers also use the theory of consumer behaviour to direct the behaviour of employees. In this chapter, we examined the benefits to the firm of paying overtime wages; additional issues will be discussed in Chapter 6.

The attribute approach to consumer behaviour offers several valuable insights into consumer choice that are not so apparent in the product approach. For one, by allowing the entire range of substitutes available to the consumer to be depicted on the same graph, it is able to explain why a consumer buys one brand of a product in preference to the other brands. Furthermore, the attribute approach easily explains why a consumer will purchase combinations of substitute products.

In conclusion, remember that the models of individual behaviour developed in this chapter are basic tools for analyzing the behaviour of your customers and employees. By taking the time to become familiar with the models and working through the Demonstration and end-of-chapter Problems, you will be better equipped to make decisions that will maximize the value of your firm.

Key Terms and Concepts

attribute space 140
budget line 115
budget set 115
consumer equilibrium 122
efficiency frontier 140

income effect 127
indifference curve 112
marginal rate of substitution (*MRS*) 113
market rate of substitution 118
substitution effect 127

Conceptual and Computational Questions

1. A consumer has $400 to spend on goods X and Y. The market prices of these two goods are $P_x = \$10$ and $P_y = \$40$.
   a. What is the market rate of substitution between goods X and Y?
   b. Illustrate the consumer's opportunity set in a carefully labelled diagram.
   c. Show how the consumer's opportunity set changes if income increases by $400. How does the $400 increase in income alter the market rate of substitution between goods X and Y?

2. A consumer must divide $250 between the consumption of product X and product Y. The relevant market prices are $P_x = \$5$ and $P_y = \$10$.
   a. Write the equation for the consumer's budget line.
   b. Illustrate the consumer's opportunity set in a carefully labelled diagram.

    c. Show how the consumer's opportunity set changes when the price of good *X* increases to $10. How does this change alter the market rate of substitution between goods *X* and *Y?*

3. A consumer is in equilibrium at point A in the figure shown here. The price of good *X* is $5.

    a. What is the price of good *Y?*

    b. What is the consumer's income?

    c. At point A, how many units of good *X* does the consumer purchase?

    d. Suppose the budget line changes so that the consumer achieves a new equilibrium at point B. What change in the economic environment led to this new equilibrium? Is the consumer better off or worse off as a result of the price change?

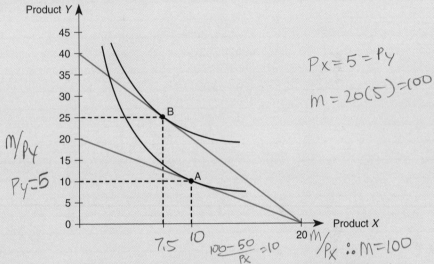

4. In the answer to Demonstration Problem 4–2 in the text, we showed a situation in which a gift certificate leads a consumer to purchase a greater quantity of an inferior good than he or she would consume if given a cash gift of equal value. Is this always the case? Explain.

5. Provide an intuitive explanation for why a "buy one, get one free" deal is not the same as a half-price sale.

6. In the figure shown next, a consumer is initially in equilibrium at point C. The consumer's income is $300, and the budget line through point C is given by $300 = $50X + $100Y. When the consumer is given a $50 gift certificate that is good only at store X, she moves to a new equilibrium at point D.

    a. Determine the prices of goods *X* and *Y*.

    b. How many units of product *Y* could be purchased at point A?

    c. How many units of product *X* could be purchased at point E?

    d. How many units of product *X* could be purchased at point B?

    e. How many units of product *X* could be purchased at point F?

    f. Assuming this consumer's preferences, rank bundles *A, B, C,* and *D* from most preferred to least preferred.

    g. Is product *X* a normal or an inferior good?

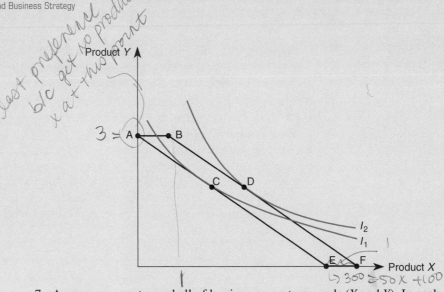

last preference b/c get to product x at this point

$3 = A$

$\llcorner$ 300 $\geq$ 50x +100

7. A consumer must spend all of her income on two goods (X and Y). In each of the following scenarios, indicate whether the equilibrium consumption of goods X and Y will increase or decrease. Assume good X is an inferior good and good Y is a normal good.
   a. Income doubles.
   b. Income quadruples and all prices double.
   c. Income and all prices quadruple.
   d. Income is halved and all prices double.

8. Determine which, if any, of Properties 4–1 through 4–4 are violated by the indifference curves shown in the diagram.

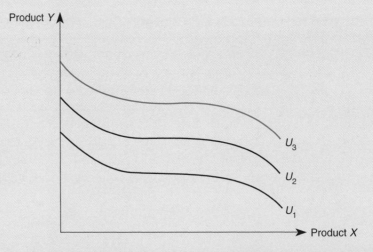

9. In the computer market, show graphically why three different consumers might choose three different computers in the simple case where they desire only two attributes, the hard drive capacity and speed.

Problems and Applications

10. It is common for supermarkets to carry both generic (store-label) and brand-name (producer-label) varieties of sugar and other products. Many consumers view these

products as perfect substitutes, meaning that consumers are always willing to substitute a constant proportion of the store brand for the producer brand. Consider a consumer who is always willing to substitute three kilograms of a generic store-brand sugar for two kilograms of a brand-name sugar. Do these preferences exhibit a diminishing marginal rate of substitution between store-brand and producer-brand sugar? Assume that this consumer has $10 of income to spend on sugar, and the price of store-brand sugar is $1 per kilogram and the price of producer-brand sugar is $2 per kilogram. How much of each type of sugar will be purchased? How would your answer change if the price of store-brand sugar was $2 per kilogram and the price of producer-brand sugar was $1 per kilogram?

11. A recent newspaper circular advertised the following special on Goodyear tires: "Buy three, get the fourth tire for free—limit one free tire per customer." If a consumer has $500 to spend on tires and other goods and each tire usually sells for $50, how does this deal impact the consumer's opportunity set?

12. Upscale hotels in Toronto recently cut their prices by 20 percent in an effort to bolster dwindling occupancy rates among business travellers. A survey performed by a major research organization indicated that businesses are wary of current economic conditions and are now resorting to electronic media, such as the Internet and the telephone, to transact business. Assume a company's budget permits it to spend $5000 per month on either business travel or electronic media to transact business. Graphically illustrate how a 20 percent decline in the price of business travel would impact this company's budget set if the price of business travel was initially $1000 per trip and the price of electronic media was $500 per hour. Suppose that, after the price of business travel drops, the company issues a report indicating that its marginal rate of substitution between electronic media and business travel is -1. Is the company allocating resources efficiently? Explain.

13. A recent study reports that over 60 percent of the Canadian population is covered by employer-sponsored dental insurance plans. Consider an employee who does not receive employer-based dental insurance and must divide her $700 per week in after-tax income between dental insurance and "other goods." Draw this worker's opportunity set if the price of dental insurance is $100 per week and the price of "other goods" is $100 per week. On the same graph, illustrate how the opportunity set would change if the employer agreed to give this employee $100 worth of dental insurance per week (under current tax laws, this form of compensation is nontaxable). Would this employee be better or worse off if, instead of the dental insurance, the employer gave her a $100 per week raise that was taxable at a rate of 25 percent? Explain.

14. An internal study at Mimeo Corporation—a manufacturer of low-end photocopiers—revealed that each of its workers assembles three photocopiers per hour and is paid $3 for each assembled copier. Although the company does not have the resources needed to supervise the workers, a full-time inspector verifies the quality of each unit produced before a worker is paid for his or her output. You have been asked by your superior to evaluate a new proposal designed to cut costs. Under the plan, workers would be paid a fixed wage of $8 per hour. Would you favour the plan? Explain.

15. Mega Wraps, a Canadian fast-food retailer known for its "wraps" (healthy sandwiches), offers a frequent-buyer program whereby a consumer receives a stamp every time she purchases one wrap for $5. After a consumer accrues 10 stamps, she receives one wrap free. This offer is an unlimited offer, valid throughout the

year. The manager knows her products are normal goods. Given this information, construct the budget set for a consumer who has $150 to spend on wraps and other goods throughout the year. Does Mega Wraps' frequent-buyer program have the same effect on the consumption of its wraps as would occur if it simply lowered the price of a wrap by 3 percent? Explain.

16. The average 15-year-old purchases 12 CDs and 15 cheese pizzas in a typical year. If cheese pizzas are inferior goods, would the average 15-year-old be indifferent between receiving a $30 gift certificate at a local music store and $30 in cash? Explain.

17. A common marketing tactic among many U.S. liquor stores is to offer their clientele quantity (or volume) discounts. For instance, the second-leading brand of wine exported from Chile sells in the United States for $8 per bottle if the consumer purchases up to eight bottles. The price of each additional bottle is only $4. If a consumer has $100 to divide between purchasing this brand of wine and other goods, graphically illustrate how this marketing tactic affects the consumer's budget set if the price of other goods is $1. Will a consumer ever purchase exactly eight bottles of wine? Explain.

APPENDIX: A Calculus Approach to Individual Behaviour

The Utility Function

Suppose the preferences of a consumer are represented by a utility function $U(X,Y)$. Let $A = (X^A, Y^A)$ be the bundle with X^A units of good X and Y^A units of good Y, and let $B = (X^B, Y^B)$ be a different bundle of the two goods. If bundle A is preferred to bundle B, then $U(A) > U(B)$; the consumer receives a higher utility level from bundle A than from bundle B. Similarly, if $U(B) > U(A)$, the consumer views bundle B as "better" than bundle A. Finally, if $U(A) = U(B)$, the consumer views the two bundles to be equally satisfying; she or he is indifferent between bundles A and B.

Utility Maximization

Given prices of P_x and P_y and a level of income M, the consumer attempts to maximize utility subject to the budget constraint. Formally, this problem can be solved by forming the Lagrangian

$$\mathcal{L} \equiv U(X,Y) + \lambda(M - P_x X - P_y Y)$$

where λ is the Lagrange multiplier. The first-order conditions for this problem are

$$\frac{\partial \mathcal{L}}{\partial X} = \frac{\partial U}{\partial X} - \lambda P_x = 0 \qquad \text{(A–1)}$$

$$\frac{\partial \mathcal{L}}{\partial Y} = \frac{\partial U}{\partial Y} - \lambda P_y = 0 \qquad \text{(A–2)}$$

$$\frac{\partial \mathcal{L}}{\partial \lambda} = M - P_x X - P_y Y = 0$$

Equations A–1 and A–2 imply that

$$\frac{\partial U/\partial X}{\partial U/\partial Y} = \frac{P_x}{P_y} \qquad (A\text{–}3)$$

or in economic terms, the ratio of the marginal utilities equals the ratio of prices.

The Marginal Rate of Substitution

Along an indifference curve, utility is constant:

$$U(X,Y) = \text{Constant}$$

Taking the total derivative of this relation yields

$$\frac{\partial U}{\partial X} dX + \frac{\partial U}{\partial Y} dY = 0$$

Solving for dY/dX along an indifference curve yields

$$\left.\frac{dY}{dX}\right|_{\text{Utility constant}} = -\frac{\partial U/\partial X}{\partial U/\partial Y}$$

Thus, the slope of an indifference curve is

$$-\frac{\partial U/\partial X}{\partial U/\partial Y}$$

The absolute value of the slope of an indifference curve is the marginal rate of substitution (MRS). Thus,

$$MRS = \frac{\partial U/\partial X}{\partial U/\partial Y} \qquad (A\text{–}4)$$

The $MRS = P_x/P_y$ Rule

Substitution of Equation A–4 into A–3 reveals that to maximize utility, a consumer equates

$$MRS = \frac{P_x}{P_y}$$

CHAPTER 5

The Production Process and Costs

Headline

In an effort to save its shrinking rank and file, the United Auto Workers (UAW) began a two-month-long strike against General Motors. At issue was GM's desire to eliminate its "pegged rate" pay system and cut its North American work force by about 40 000 jobs over four years. GM's pegged rate pay system allows plant workers who meet a daily quota in five or six hours to either go home for the day or collect overtime pay for the remaining portion of the day—a system that GM says creates great inefficiencies in production. GM believes that eliminating its pegged rate pay system and some workers will make its operations more efficient and raise workers' productivity. However, the UAW is fighting tooth and nail on both issues to keep its declining membership from further shrinking.

To support their position, GM officials cited lagging efficiency measures and high wages relative to other automakers. Workers at Ford produced an average of 33.2 vehicles per year and were paid wages that averaged $43 per hour. In contrast, GM workers produced an average of 27.9 vehicles per year and received $45 per hour.

Do these figures justify GM's proposed actions? Why or why not?

Sources: Jay Palmer, "Reviving GM," *Barron's Online,* June 22, 1998; and Paul Ingrassia, "A Long Road to Good Labor Relations at GM," *The Wall Street Journal Interactive Edition,* June 30, 1998.

Introduction

In this chapter we will develop tools to help managers answer complex questions such as those posed in the opening Headline. Our analysis will show how managers can determine which inputs and how much of each input to use to produce output efficiently. The material in this chapter will serve as the foundation for later chapters, which describe in more detail pricing and output techniques for managers interested in maximizing profits.

The Production Function

We will begin by describing the technology available for producing output. Technology summarizes the feasible means of converting raw inputs, such as steel, labour, and machinery, into an output such as an automobile. The technology effectively summarizes engineering know-how. Managerial decisions, such as those concerning expenditures on research and development, can affect the available technology. In this chapter, we will see how a manager can exploit an existing technology to its greatest potential. In subsequent chapters, we will analyze the decision to improve a technology.

To begin our analysis, let us consider a production process that utilizes two inputs, *capital* and *labour,* to produce output. We will let K denote the quantity of capital, L the quantity of labour, and Q the level of output produced in the production process. Although we call the inputs capital and labour, the general ideas presented here are valid for any two inputs. However, most production processes involve machines of some sort (referred to by economists as *capital*) and people (*labour*), and this terminology will serve to solidify the basic ideas.

The technology available for converting capital and labour into output is summarized in the production function. The **production function** is an engineering relation that defines the maximum amount of output that can be produced with a given set of inputs. Mathematically, the production function is denoted as

production function
A function that defines the maximum amount of output that can be produced with a given set of inputs.

$$Q = F(K, L) \tag{5–1}$$

that is, the maximum amount of output that can be produced with K units of capital and L units of labour.

Short-Run Versus Long-Run Decisions

As a manager, your job is to use the available production function efficiently; this effectively means that you must determine how much of each input to use to produce output. In the short run, some factors of production are **fixed**, and this limits your choices in making input decisions. For example, it takes several years for Ford to build an assembly line. The level of capital is generally fixed in the short run. However, in the short run Ford can adjust its use of inputs such as labour and steel; such inputs are called **variable** factors of production.

fixed *and* variable factors of production
Fixed factors are the inputs the manager cannot adjust in the short run. Variable factors are the inputs a manager can adjust to alter production.

The *short run* is defined as the time frame in which at least one factor of production is fixed. To illustrate, suppose capital and labour are the only two inputs in production and that the level of capital is fixed in the short run. In this case the only short-run input decision to be made by a manager is how much labour to utilize. The short-run production function is essentially only a function of labour, since capital is

Inside BUSINESS

5-1   Where Does Technology Come From?

In this chapter, we simply assume that the manager knows the underlying technology available for producing goods. How do managers acquire information about technology? The answer varies considerably across firms and industries. The accompanying table reports the results of a survey of 650 executives in 130 industries. They were asked to rate how they obtain technical knowledge of new technologies developed by competitors. The responses varied considerably among executives, and there were also systematic differences in responses depending on whether the technical knowledge pertained to a process innovation or a product innovation. A *process innovation* is simply a new method for producing a given good, while a *product innovation* is the creation of a new product.

INDEPENDENT R&D

As the table here shows, the most important means of acquiring product and process innovations is independent research and development (R&D). This essentially involves engineers employed by the firm who devise new production processes or products. Most large firms have a research and development department that is charged with engineering aspects of product and process innovations.

LICENSING TECHNOLOGY

The firm that was originally responsible for developing the technology and thus owns the rights to the technology often sells the production function to another firm for a licensing fee. The fee may be fixed, in which case the cost of acquiring the technology is a fixed cost of production. The fee may involve payments based on how much output is produced. In this instance, the cost of the technology is a variable cost of production.

PUBLICATIONS OR TECHNICAL MEETINGS

Trade publications and meetings provide a forum for the dissemination of information about production processes.

REVERSE ENGINEERING

As the term suggests, this involves working backward: taking a product produced by a competitor and devising a method of producing a similar product. The typical result is a product that differs slightly from the existing product and involves a slightly different production function from that used by the original developer.

HIRING EMPLOYEES OF INNOVATING FIRMS

Former employees of other firms often have information about the production process.

Methods of Acquiring Technology (ranked from most important to least important)

Method of Acquisition	Rank	
	Process Innovations	Product Innovations
Independent R&D	1	1
Licensing technology	2	3
Publications/technical meetings	3	5
Reverse engineering	4	2
Hiring employees of innovating firms	5	4
Patent disclosures	6	6
Conversations with employees of innovating firm	7	7

Source: Adapted from Richard C. Levin, "Appropriability, R&D Spending, and Technological Performance," *American Economic Review* 78, May 1988, pp. 424–28.

PATENT DISCLOSURES

A *patent* gives the holder the exclusive rights to an invention for a specified period of time—17 to 20 years in most countries. However, to obtain a patent an inventor must file detailed information about the invention, which becomes public information. Virtually anyone can look at the information filed, including competitors. In many instances, this information can enable a competitor to "clone" the product in a way that does not infringe on the patent. Interestingly, while a patent is pending, this information is not publicly available. For this reason, stretching out the time in which a patent is pending often provides more protection for an inventor than actually acquiring the patent.

CONVERSATIONS WITH EMPLOYEES OF INNOVATING FIRMS

Despite the obvious benefits of keeping trade secrets "secret," employees inadvertently relay information about the production process to competitors. This is especially common in industries where firms are concentrated in the same geographic region and employees from different firms intermingle in nonbusiness settings.

fixed rather than variable. If K^* is the fixed level of capital, the short-run production function may be written as

$$Q = f(L) = F(K^*, L)$$

Columns 1, 2, and 4 in Table 5–1 give values of the components of a short-run production function where capital is fixed at $K^* = 2$. For this production function, 5 units of labour are needed to produce 1100 units of output. Given the available technology and the fixed level of capital, if the manager wishes to produce 1952 units of output, 8 units of labour must be utilized. In the short run, more labour is needed to produce more output, because increasing capital is not possible.

The *long run* is defined as the horizon over which all factors of production are variable, while technology is fixed. If it takes Ford three years to acquire additional capital machines, the long run for Ford's management is three years, and the short run is less than three years.

Measures of Productivity

An important component of managerial decision making is the determination of the productivity of inputs used in the production process. As we will see, these measures are useful for evaluating the effectiveness of a production process and for making input decisions that maximize profits. The three most important measures of productivity are total product, average product, and marginal product.

Total Product

total product
The maximum level of output that can be produced with a given amount of inputs.

Total product (*TP*) is simply the maximum level of output that can be produced with a given amount of inputs. For example, the total product of the production process described in Table 5–1 when 5 units of labour are employed is 1100. Since the production function defines the maximum amount of output that can be produced with a given level of inputs, this is the amount that would be produced if the 5 units of

TABLE 5–1	The Production Function				
(1)	(2)	(3)	(4)	(5)	(6)
K^*	L	ΔL	Q	$\dfrac{\Delta Q}{\Delta L} = MP_L$	$\dfrac{Q}{L} = AP_L$
Fixed Input (Capital) [Given]	Variable Input (Labour) [Given]	Change in Labour [$\Delta(2)$]	Output [Given]	Marginal Product of Labour [$\Delta(4)/\Delta(2)$]	Average Product of Labour [$(4)/(2)$]
2	0	—	0	—	—
2	1	1	76	76	76
2	2	1	248	172	124
2	3	1	492	244	164
2	4	1	784	292	196
2	5	1	1100	316	220
2	6	1	1416	316	236
2	7	1	1708	292	244
2	8	1	1952	244	244
2	9	1	2124	172	236
2	10	1	2200	76	220
2	11	1	2156	−44	196

labour put forth maximal effort. Of course, if workers did not put forth maximal effort, output would be lower. Five workers who drink coffee all day cannot produce any output, at least given this production function.

Average Product

average product (AP)
A measure of the output produced per unit of input.

In many instances, managerial decision makers are interested in the average productivity of an input. For example, a manager may wish to know, on average, how much each worker contributes to the total output of the firm. This information is summarized in the economic concept of average product. The **average product (AP)** of an input is defined as total product divided by the quantity used of the input. In particular, the average product of labour (AP_L) is

$$AP_L = \frac{Q}{L}$$

and the average product of capital (AP_K) is

$$AP_K = \frac{Q}{K}$$

Thus, average product is a measure of the output produced per unit of input. In Table 5–1, for example, 5 workers can produce 1100 units of output; this amounts to 220 units of output per worker.

Marginal Product

marginal product
The change in total output attributable to the last unit of an input.

The **marginal product (MP)** of an input is the change in total output attributable to the last unit of an input. The marginal product of capital (MP_K) therefore is the change in total output divided by the change in capital:

$$MP_K = \frac{\Delta Q}{\Delta K}$$

The marginal product of labour (MP_L) is the change in total output divided by the change in labour:

$$MP_L = \frac{\Delta Q}{\Delta L}$$

For example, in Table 5–1 the second unit of labour increases output by 172 units, so the marginal product of the second unit of labour is 172.

Table 5–1 illustrates an important characteristic of the marginal product of an input. Notice that as the units of labour are increased from 0 to 5 in column 2, the marginal product of labour increases in column 5. This helps explain why assembly lines are used in so many production processes: by using several workers, each performing potentially different tasks, a manager can avoid inefficiencies associated with stopping one task and starting another. But note in Table 5–1 that after 5 units of labour, the marginal product of each additional unit of labour declines and eventually becomes negative. A negative marginal product means that the last unit of the input actually *reduced* the total product. This is consistent with common sense. If a manager continued to expand the number of workers on an assembly line, he or she would

FIGURE 5–1 | Increasing, Decreasing, and Negative Marginal Returns

The total product (*TP*), average product (*AP*$_L$), and marginal product (*MP*$_L$) curves often have the shapes shown above. The total product curve in range 1 shows the total product steadily rising, first at an increasing rate and then at a decreasing rate. This causes both the average and the marginal product curves to rise at first and then to decline. The point of diminishing average productivity is when 7 units of labour are employed ($MP_L = AP_L$). Range 2 starts from this point and extends up to the point where the total product begins declining into range 3.

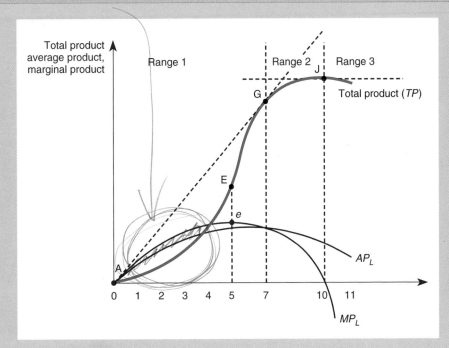

wrong diagram! (handwritten)

increasing marginal returns
Range of input usage over which marginal product increases.

decreasing (diminishing) marginal returns
Range of input usage over which marginal product declines.

negative marginal returns
Range of input usage over which marginal product is negative.

eventually reach a point where workers were packed like sardines along the line, getting in one another's way and resulting in less output than before.

Figure 5–1 shows graphically the relationship among total product, marginal product, and average product. The first thing to notice is that as the use of labour increases between points A and E, the slope of the total product curve increases (becomes steeper); thus, marginal product increases over this range. The range over which marginal product increases is known as the range of **increasing marginal returns**.

In Figure 5–1, we see that marginal product reaches its maximum at point *e*, where 5 units of labour are employed. As the usage of labour increases from the 5th through the 10th unit, total output increases, but at a decreasing rate. This is why marginal product declines between 5 and 10 units of labour but is still positive. The range over which marginal product is positive but declining is known as the range of **decreasing** or **diminishing marginal returns** to the variable input.

In Figure 5–1, marginal product becomes negative when more than 10 units of labour are employed. After a point, using additional units of input actually reduces total product, which is what it means for marginal product to be negative. The range over which marginal product is negative is known as the range of **negative marginal returns**.

The relationship between marginal product and total product, exhibited in Figure 5–1, can be summarized as follows.

As long as the MP_L curve is rising, the total product curve increases at an increasing rate and is convex to the horizontal axis. The quantity of input L at which the TP curve changes its curvature corresponds precisely to the point at which the MP_L curve peaks. This occurs at approximately 5 units of input, as shown by point E, also known as the inflection point. Note that marginal product is the slope of *TP* curve. When the total-product curve reaches point J, its maximum, MP_L (the slope of the line tangent to the *TP* curve) is zero. Beyond this point, the marginal product is negative and the total product declines.

AP_L is initially subject to the law of increasing returns, reaching a maximum at approximately 7 units of labour, also shown by point G. Beyond that, it becomes subject to the law of diminishing returns. Note that average product is the slope of the line that connects the point of origin to a point on the *TP* curve. To sum up: the average product increases as variable input increases as long as the marginal product exceeds the average product. When the marginal product is less than the average product, the average product decreases as variable input increases. When the average product is at a maximum, the average product and marginal product are equal.

Figure 5–1 also illustrates the three ranges of a typical production function:

- *Range 1*. This range extends from zero input of the variable factor to the level of input where the average product, which is also represented by the line that connects the origin to a point on the total product curve, 0G, is at a maximum. In this range, the fixed factors are excessive relative to the variable input. Consequently, output can be increased by increasing the variable input relative to the fixed input. Put differently, the rational producer would not produce in this range of production because this corresponds to negative marginal return to the other factor of production—that is, capital. For example, if a large department store were understaffed with salespersons, sales could be increased by hiring more salespersons, labour (the variable input), relative to floor space and fixtures (the fixed input). Throughout stage 1, marginal product is greater than the average product.
- *Range 2*. This range extends from the end of range 1 (the point where the marginal product and the average product are equal, G, the maximum point of the average product) to the point where the marginal product is zero and the total product is at a maximum, point J in Figure 5–1. Range 2 is a range in which the rational producer will produce; this is a range in which relatively good balance has been achieved between the variable and fixed inputs.
- *Range 3*. In this range, in which input is greater than 10 units, the variable-input factor is excessive relative to the fixed factors, the marginal product is negative, and the total product is falling. It is completely irrational to produce in this range.

Principle

PHASES OF MARGINAL RETURNS
As the usage of an input increases, marginal product initially increases (increasing marginal returns), then begins to decline (decreasing marginal returns), and eventually becomes negative (negative marginal returns).

In studying for an exam, you have very likely experienced various phases of marginal returns. The first few hours spent studying increase your grade much more than the last few hours. For example, suppose you will make a 0 if you do not study but will make a 75 if you study 10 hours. The marginal product of the first 10 hours thus is 75 points. If it takes 20 hours of studying to score 100 on the exam, the marginal product of the second 10 hours is only 25 points. Thus, the marginal improvement in your grade diminishes as you spend additional hours studying. If you have ever "pulled an all-nighter" and ended up sleeping through an exam or performing poorly due to a lack of sleep, you studied in the range of negative marginal returns. Clearly, neither students nor firms should ever employ resources in this range.

The Role of the Manager in the Production Process

The manager's role in guiding the production process described earlier is twofold:
(1) to ensure that the firm operates on the production function and (2) to ensure that
the firm uses the correct level of inputs. These two aspects ensure that the firm operates at the right point on the production function. These two aspects of production
efficiency are discussed next.

Produce on the Production Function

The first managerial role is relatively simple to explain, but it is one of the most difficult for a manager to perform. The production function describes the maximum possible output that can be produced with given inputs. For the case of labour, this means
that workers must be putting forth maximal effort. To ensure that workers are in fact
working at full potential, the manager must institute an incentive structure that
induces them to put forth the desired level of effort. For example, the manager of a
restaurant must institute an incentive scheme that ensures that food servers do a good
job waiting on tables. Most restaurants pay workers low wages but allow them to collect tips, which effectively provides the workers with an incentive to perform on the
job. More generally, many firms institute profit-sharing plans to provide workers with
an incentive to produce on the production function. A more detailed discussion of this
role of the manager is presented in Chapter 6.

Use the Right Level of Inputs

The second role of the manager is to ensure that the firm operates at the right point on
the production function. For a restaurant manager, this means hiring the "correct"
number of servers. To see how this may be accomplished, let us assume that the output produced by a firm can be sold in a market at a price of $3. Furthermore, assume
each unit of labour costs $400. How many units of labour should the manager hire to
maximize profits? To answer this question, we must first determine the benefit of hiring an additional worker. Each worker increases the firm's output by his or her marginal product, and this increase in output can be sold in the market at a price of $3.
Thus, the benefit to the firm from each unit of labour is $3 \times MP_L$. This number is
called the **value marginal product** of labour. The value marginal product of an input
thus is the value of the output produced by the last unit of that input. For example, if
each unit of output can be sold at a price of P, the value marginal product of labour is

value marginal product
The value of the output produced by the last unit of an input.

$$VMP_L = P \times MP_L \qquad (5\text{–}2)$$

and the value marginal product of capital is

$$VMP_K = P \times MP_K \qquad (5\text{–}3)$$

In our example, the cost to the firm of an additional unit of labour is $400. As
Table 5–2 shows, the first unit of labour generates $VMP_L = \$228$ and the VMP_L of the
second unit is $516. If the manager were to look only at the first unit of labour and its
corresponding VMP_L, no labour would be hired. However, careful inspection of the
table shows that the second worker will add $116 in value above her or his cost. If the
first worker is not hired, the second will not be hired.

In fact, each worker between 2 and 9 produces additional output whose value
exceeds the cost of hiring the worker. It is profitable to hire units of labour so long as
the VMP_L is greater than $400. Notice that the VMP_L of the 10th unit of labour is
$228, which is less than the cost of the 10th unit of labour. It would not pay for the

TABLE 5–2	The Value Marginal Product of Labour			
(1)	(2)	(3)	(4)	(5)
L	P	$\frac{\Delta Q}{\Delta L} = MP_L$	$VMP_L = P \times MP_L$	w
Variable Input (Labour) [Given]	Price of Output [Given]	Marginal Product of Labour [Column 5 of Table 5–1]	Value Marginal Product of Labour [(2) × (3)]	Unit Cost of Labour [Given]
0	$3	—	—	$400
1	3	76	$228	400
2	3	172	516	400
3	3	244	732	400
4	3	292	876	400
5	3	316	948	400
6	3	316	948	400
7	3	292	876	400
8	3	244	732	400
9	3	172	516	400
10	3	76	228	400
11	3	−44	−132	400

firm to hire this unit of labour, because the cost of hiring it would exceed the benefits. The same is true for additional units of labour. Thus, given the data in Table 5–2, the manager should hire 9 workers to maximize profits.

Principle

PROFIT-MAXIMIZING INPUT USAGE
To maximize profits, a manager should use inputs at levels at which the marginal benefit equals the marginal cost. More specifically, when the cost of each additional unit of labour is w, the manager should continue to employ labour up to the point where $VMP_L = w$ in the range of diminishing marginal product.

The *profit-maximizing input usage* rule defines the demand for an input by a profit-maximizing firm. For example, in Figure 5–2 the value marginal product of labour is graphed as a function of the quantity of labour utilized. When the wage rate is w^0, the profit-maximizing quantity of labour is that quantity such that $VMP_L = w^0$ in the range of diminishing marginal returns. In the figure, we see that the profit-maximizing quantity of labour is L_0 units. Note that the optimal quantity of labour, L_0, is obtained in terms of profit maximization—not output maximization, which would have occurred where $VMP_L = 0$ (the horizontal intercept).

The downward-sloping portion of the VMP_L curve defines demand for labour by a profit-maximizing firm. Thus, an important property of the demand for an input is that it slopes downward because of the law of diminishing marginal returns. Since the marginal product of an input declines as more of that input is used, the value of the marginal product also declines as more of the input is used. Since the demand for an input is the value marginal product of the input in the range of diminishing marginal returns, the demand for an input slopes downward. In effect, each additional unit of an input adds less profits than the previous unit. Profit-maximizing firms thus are willing to pay less for each additional unit of an input.

FIGURE 5-2   The Demand for Labour

When the wage rate is w^0, the profit-maximizing quantity of labour is that quantity such that $VMP_L = w^0$ in the range of diminishing marginal returns. Profit-maximizing quantity of labour is L_0 units. The downward-sloping portion of the VMP_L curve represents the demand for labour by a profit-maximizing firm. The demand for labour (or any input) slopes downward because of the law of diminishing marginal returns.

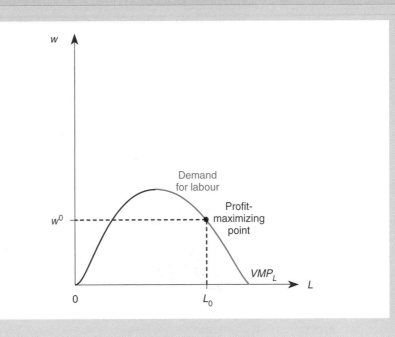

Algebraic Forms of Production Functions

Up until now, we have relied on tables and graphs to illustrate the concepts underlying production. The underlying notion of a production function can be expressed mathematically, and in fact it is possible to use statistical techniques like those discussed in Chapter 3 to estimate a particular functional form for a production function. In this section, we highlight some more commonly encountered algebraic forms of production functions. We begin with the most simple production function: a linear function of the inputs.

linear production function
A production function that assumes a perfect linear relationship between all inputs and total output.

The **linear production function** is

$$Q = F(K, L) = aK + bL$$

where a and b are constants. With a linear production function, inputs are perfect substitutes. There is a perfect linear relationship between all the inputs and total output. For instance, suppose it takes workers at a plant 4 hours to produce what a machine can make in 1 hour. In this case the production function is linear with $a = 4$ and $b = 1$:

$$Q = F(K, L) = 4K + L$$

Leontief (fixed-proportions) production function
A production function that assumes that inputs are used in fixed proportions.

This is the mathematical way of stating that capital is always 4 times as productive as labour. Furthermore, since $F(5, 2) = 4(5) + 1(2) = 22$, we know that 5 units of capital and 2 units of labour will produce 22 units of output.

Another important technology is the Leontief production function. The **Leontief production function** is given by

$$Q = F(K, L) = \min\{bK, cL\}$$

where b and c are constants. The Leontief production function is also called the *fixed-proportions production function,* because it implies that inputs are used in fixed proportions. To see this, suppose the production function for a word processing firm is Leontief, with $b = c = 1$; think of K as the number of keyboards and L as the number of keyboarders. The production function then implies that one keyboarder and one keyboard can produce one paper per hour, two keyboarders and two keyboards can produce two papers per hour, and so forth. But how many papers can one keyboarder and five keyboards produce per hour? The answer is only one paper. Additional keyboards are useful only to the extent that additional keyboarders are available to use them. In other words, keyboards and keyboarders must be used in the fixed proportion of one keyboarder for every keyboard.

Demonstration PROBLEM 5–1

The engineers at Morris Industries obtained the following estimate of the firm's production function:

$$Q = F(K, L) = \min\{3K, 4L\}$$

How much output is produced when 2 units of labour and 5 units of capital are employed?

Answer

We simply calculate $F(5, 2)$. But $F(5, 2) = \min\{3(5), 4(2)\} = \min\{15, 8\}$. Since the minimum of the numbers "15" and "8" is 8, we know that 5 units of capital and 2 units of labour produce 8 units of output.

A production function that lies between the extremes of the linear production function and the Leontief production function is the Cobb-Douglas production function. The **Cobb-Douglas production function** is given by

Cobb-Douglas production function
A production function that assumes some degree of substitutability among inputs.

$$Q = F(K, L) = K^a L^b$$

where a and b are constants.

Unlike in the case of the linear production function, the relationship between output and inputs is not linear. Unlike in the Leontief production function, inputs need not be used in fixed proportions. The Cobb-Douglas production function assumes some degree of substitutability between the inputs, albeit not perfect substitutability.

Algebraic Measures of Productivity

Given an algebraic form of a production function, we may calculate various measures of productivity. For example, we learned that the average product of an input is the output produced divided by the number of units used of the input. This concept can easily be extended to production processes that use more than one input.

To be concrete, suppose a consultant provides you with the following estimate of your firm's Cobb-Douglas production function:

$$Q = F(K, L) = K^{1/2} L^{1/2}$$

What is the average product of labour when 4 units of labour and 9 units of capital are employed? Since $F(9, 4) = 9^{1/2} 4^{1/2} = (3)(2) = 6$, we know that 9 units of capital and

4 units of labour produce 6 units of output. Thus, the average product of 4 units of labour is $AP_L = 6/4 = 1.5$ units.

Notice that when output is produced with both capital and labour, the average product of labour will depend not only on how many units of labour are used but also on how much capital is used. Since total output (Q) is affected by the levels of both inputs, the corresponding measure of average product depends on both capital and labour. Likewise, the average product of capital depends not only on the level of capital but also on the level of labour used to produce Q.

Recall that the marginal product of an input is the change in output that results from a given change in the input. When the production function is linear, the marginal product of an input has a very simple representation, as the following formula reveals.

Formula: Marginal Product for a Linear Production Function. If the production function is linear and given by

$$Q = F(K, L) = aK + bL$$

then

$$MP_K = a$$

and

$$MP_L = b$$

A Calculus ALTERNATIVE

The marginal product of an input is the derivative of the production function with respect to the input. Thus, the marginal product of labour is

$$MP_L = \frac{\partial Q}{\partial L}$$

and the marginal product of capital is

$$MP_K = \frac{\partial Q}{\partial K}$$

For the case of the linear production function, $Q = aK + bL$, so

$$MP_K = \frac{\partial Q}{\partial K} = a \quad \text{and} \quad MP_L = \frac{\partial Q}{\partial L} = b$$

Thus, for a linear production function, the marginal product of an input is simply the coefficient of the input in the production function. This implies that the marginal product of an input is independent of the quantity of the input used whenever the production function is linear; linear production functions do not obey the law of diminishing marginal product.

In contrast to the linear case, the marginal product of an input for a Cobb-Douglas production function does depend on the amount of the input used, as the following formula reveals.

Formula: *Marginal Product for a Cobb-Douglas Production Function.* If the production function is Cobb-Douglas and given by

$$Q = F(K, L) = K^a L^b$$

then

$$MP_L = bK^a L^{b-1}$$

and

$$MP_K = aK^{a-1} L^b$$

A Calculus ALTERNATIVE

The marginal product of an input is the derivative of the production function with respect to the input. Taking the derivative of the Cobb-Douglas production function yields

$$MP_K = \frac{\partial Q}{\partial K} = aK^{a-1} L^b$$

and

$$MP_L = \frac{\partial Q}{\partial L} = bK^a L^{b-1}$$

which correspond to the equations above.

Recall that the profit-maximizing use of an input occurs at the point where the value marginal product of an input equals the price of the input. As the next problem illustrates, we can apply the same principle to algebraic functional forms of production functions to attain the profit-maximizing use of an input.

Demonstration PROBLEM 5-2

A firm produces output that can be sold at a price of $10. The production function is given by

$$Q = F(K, L) = K^{1/2} L^{1/2}$$

If capital is fixed at 1 unit in the short run, how much labour should the firm employ to maximize profits if the wage rate is $2?

Answer

We simply set the value marginal product of labour equal to the wage rate and solve for L. Since the production function is Cobb-Douglas, we know that $MP_L = bK^a L^{b-1}$. Here $a = 1/2$, $b = 1/2$, and $K = 1$. Hence, $MP_L = 0.5L^{1/2-1}$. Now, since $P = \$10$, we know that $VMP_L = P \times MP_L = 5L^{-1/2}$. Setting this equal to the wage, which is $2, we get $5L^{-1/2} = 2$. If we square both sides of this equation, we get $25/L = 4$. Thus the profit-maximizing quantity of labour is $L = 25/4 = 6.25$ units.

Isoquants

Our next task is to examine the optimal choice of capital and labour in the long run, when both inputs are free to vary. In the presence of multiple variables of production, there exist various combinations of inputs that enable the manager to produce the same level of output. For example, an automobile assembly line can produce 1000 cars per hour by using 10 workers and 1 robot. It can also produce 1000 cars by using only 2 workers and 3 robots. To minimize the costs of producing 1000 cars, the manager must determine the efficient combination of inputs to use to produce them. The basic tool for understanding how alternative inputs can be used to produce output is an isoquant. An **isoquant** defines the combinations of inputs (K and L) that yield the producer the same level of output; that is, any combination of capital and labour along an isoquant produces the same level of output.

isoquant
Defines the combinations of inputs that yield the same level of output.

Figure 5–3 depicts a typical set of isoquants. Because input bundles A and B both lie on the same isoquant, each will produce the same level of output, namely Q_0 units. Input mix A implies a more capital-intensive plant than does input mix B. As more of both inputs are used, a higher isoquant is obtained. Thus as we move in the northeast direction in the figure, each new isoquant is associated with higher and higher levels of output.

Notice that the isoquants in Figure 5–3 are convex. The reason isoquants are typically drawn with a convex shape is that inputs such as capital and labour are not perfectly substitutable. In Figure 5–3, for example, if we start at point A and begin substituting labour for capital, it takes increasing amounts of labour to replace each unit of capital that is taken away. The rate at which labour and capital can substitute for each other is called the **marginal rate of technical substitution (*MRTS*)**. The *MRTS* of capital and labour is the absolute value of the slope of the isoquant and is simply the ratio of the marginal products:

marginal rate of technical substitution (*MRTS*)
The rate at which a producer can substitute between two inputs and maintain the same level of output.

$$MRTS_{KL} = \frac{MP_L}{MP_K}$$

(5–4)

FIGURE 5–3 A Family of Isoquants

An isoquant map shows a set of isoquants, one for each level of output. Each corresponds to a specific level of output and shows factor combinations that are technologically efficient methods of producing that output. Increasing output is shown by moving from Q_0 to Q_1 to Q_2 in a "northeast" direction.

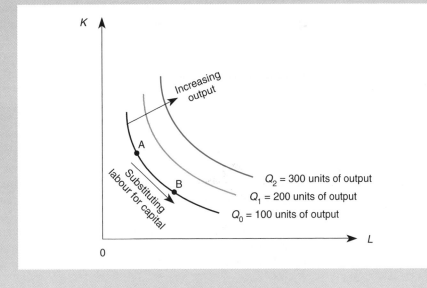

FIGURE 5-4 Linear Isoquants

A linear production function implies a linear isoquant. This is because inputs are perfect substitutes for each other and the rate at which the producer can substitute between the inputs is independent of the level of input usage.

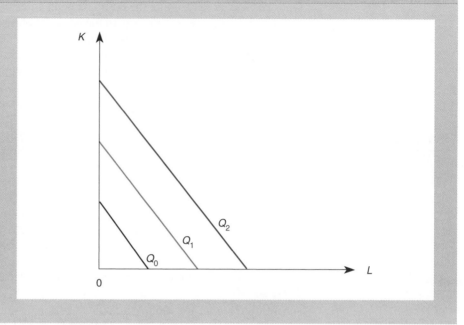

Different production functions will imply different marginal rates of technical substitution. For example, the linear production function implies isoquants that are *linear,* as in Figure 5–4. This is because the inputs are perfect substitutes for each other and the rate at which the producer can substitute between the inputs is independent of the level of input usage. Specifically, for the linear production function $Q = aK + bL$, the marginal rate of technical substitution is b/a, since $MP_L = b$ and $MP_K = a$. This is independent of the level of inputs utilized.

The Leontief production function, on the other hand, implies isoquants that are *L-shaped,* as in Figure 5–5. In this case, inputs must be used in fixed proportions; the manager cannot substitute between capital and labour and maintain the same level of output. For the Leontief production function there is no *MRTS*, because there is no substitution among inputs along an isoquant.

For most production relations, the isoquants lie somewhere between the perfect-substitute and fixed-proportions cases. In these instances, the inputs are substitutable for one another, but not perfectly, and the rate at which a manager can substitute between inputs will change along an isoquant. For instance, by moving from point A to point B in Figure 5–6, the manager substitutes 1 unit of capital for 1 unit of labour and still produces 100 units of output. But in moving from point C to point D, the manager would have to substitute 3 units of capital for 1 unit of labour to produce 100 units of output. Thus, the production function satisfies the **law of diminishing marginal rate of technical substitution**: as a producer uses less of an input, increasingly more of the other input must be employed to produce the same level of output. It can be shown that the Cobb-Douglas production function implies isoquants that have a diminishing marginal rate of technical substitution. Whenever an isoquant exhibits a diminishing marginal rate of technical substitution, the corresponding isoquants are convex from the origin; that is, they look like the isoquants in Figure 5–6.

law of diminishing marginal rate of technical substitution
A property of a production function stating that as less of one input is used, increasing amounts of another input must be employed to produce the same level of output.

FIGURE 5-5 Leontief Isoquants

Unlike the perfect substitute case in Figure 5–4, Figure 5–5 shows the case of perfect complements. In a Leontief production function, inputs must be used in fixed proportions. One cannot substitute between capital and labour and maintain the same level of output, and there is no *MRTS* as a result.

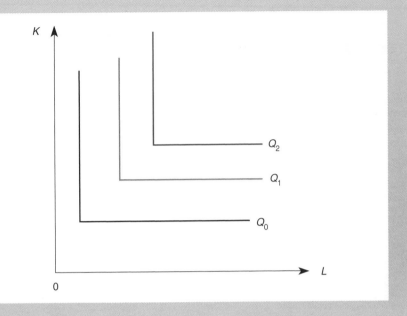

FIGURE 5-6 The Marginal Rate of Technical Substitution

This graph shows some of the methods available to produce 100 units of output. Combination D uses 9 units of capital (*K*) and 1 unit of labour (*L*). As you move down the graph, labour is substituted for capital in such a way as to keep output constant. At point A, 3 units of *K* are being used and 4 units of *L* to produce 100 units of output. Note that as we move "southeast" along the graph, the absolute value of the rate of technical substitution declines.

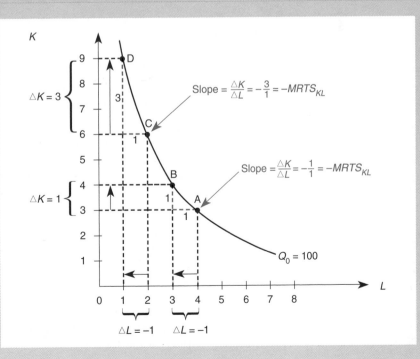

Isocosts

Isoquants describe the combinations of inputs that produce a given level of output. Notice that there exist different combinations of capital and labour that end up costing the firm the same amount. The combinations of inputs that will cost the firm the same amount make up an **isocost line**.

isocost line
A line that represents the combinations of inputs that will cost the producer the same amount of money.

The relation for an isocost line is graphed in Figure 5–7(a). To understand this concept, suppose the firm spends exactly C on inputs. Then the cost of labour plus the cost of capital exactly equals C:

$$wL + rK = C \qquad (5-1)$$

where w is the wage rate (the price of labour) and r is the rental rate (the price of capital). This equation represents the formula for an isocost line.

We may obtain a more convenient expression for the slope and intercept of an isocost line as follows. We multiply both sides of Equation 5–1 by $1/r$ and get

$$\frac{w}{r}L + K = \frac{C}{r}$$

or

$$K = \frac{C}{r} - \frac{w}{r}L$$

Thus, along an isocost line, K is a linear function of L with a vertical intercept of C/r and a slope of $-w/r$.

Note that if the producer wishes to use more of both inputs, more money must be spent. Thus, isocosts associated with higher costs lie above those with lower costs. When input prices are constant, the isocost lines will be parallel to one another. Figure 5–7(b) illustrates the isocost lines for cost levels C^0 and C^1, where $C^0 < C^1$.

Similarly, changes in input prices affect the position of the isocost line. An increase in the price of labour makes the isocost curve steeper, while an increase in the price of capital makes it flatter. For instance, Figure 5–7(c) reveals that the isocost line rotates clockwise when the wage rate increases from w^0 to w^1.

Principle	**CHANGES IN ISOCOSTS** For given input prices, isocosts farther from the origin are associated with higher costs. Changes in input prices change the slopes of isocost lines.

Cost Minimization

The isocosts and isoquants just defined may be used to determine the input usage that minimizes production costs. If there were no scarcity, the producer would not care about production costs. But because scarcity is an economic reality, producers are interested in *cost minimization*—that is, producing output at the lowest possible cost. After all, to maximize profits, the firm must first produce its output in the least-cost manner. Even not-for-profit organizations can achieve their objectives by providing a given level of service at the lowest possible cost. Let us piece together the tools developed thus far to see how to choose the optimal mix of capital and labour.

FIGURE 5-7 Isocosts

(a) This line shows alternative factor combinations that can be purchased for a given outlay. The equation of the line is $K = (C/r) - (W/r)L$.

(b) The $C^0/r(C^0/w)$ line represents all combinations of the two factors that the firm could buy for C^0. The line $C^1/r(C^1/w)$ represents a higher cost associated with a greater quantity of inputs when input prices are kept constant.

(c) A rise in the price of L from w^0 to w^1 (with the price of K being held constant) pivots the C/r line inward as shown. Any output previously produced for C/w^0 will cost more at the new prices if it uses any labour.

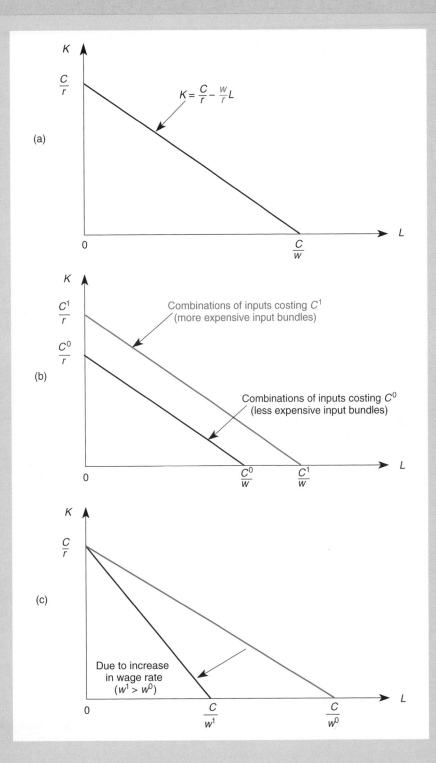

Inside BUSINESS

5-2 A Cobb-Douglas Production Function for Water Desalination

One worldwide area of concern today is the availability of fresh water. Because of this issue, the production of fresh water through the process of desalination of salt water has become a viable area of research. The Middle East is a leader in this form of fresh-water extraction, but desalination is becoming a growing industry along the west coast of the United States.

Recently three economists used statistical and econometric techniques to estimate the production function for a water desalination plant. The results of the study suggest that the production function is Cobb-Douglas and is given by

$$Q = F^{0.6}H^{0.4}$$

where Q is cubic metres of desalted water produced per day, F represents factors of production (an aggregation of evaporating pumps, maintenance of those pumps, and labour), and H is the per diem level of heat, which is used in the evaporation process. According to the authors of the study,

The technical inputs of water desalination can be classified into two groups: those for which the cost per unit of desalted water is increasing when the technical index of the number of effects is increasing, and those for which this cost is

decreasing under the same circumstances. This classification permits us to express production of desalted water as a function of two aggregates of inputs, corresponding to the above substitutional groups. Thus a production function is extracted for the general case of full-load annual operation of the desalination plant.

Since the estimated production function is Cobb-Douglas, we can apply our formulas for the marginal products of a Cobb-Douglas production function to obtain an algebraic expression for the marginal product of heat in the production of fresh water,

$$MP_H = 0.4F^{0.6}H^{-0.6}$$

and for the marginal product of other factors of production,

$$MP_F = 0.6F^{-0.4}H^{0.4}$$

These equations reveal that the production of fresh water obeys the law of diminishing marginal returns.

Source: N. Zagouras, Y. Caouris, and E. Kantsos, "Production and Cost Functions of Water Low-Temperature Solar Desalination," *Applied Economics* 21, September 1989, pp. 1177–90.

Consider an input bundle such as that at point A in Figure 5–8. This combination of L and K lies on the isoquant labelled Q_0 and thus produces Q_0 units of output. It also lies on the isocost line through point A. Thus, if the producer uses input mix A, he or she will produce Q_0 units of output at a total cost of C^1. Is this the cost-minimizing way to produce the given level of output? Clearly not, for by using input mix B instead of A, the producer could produce the same amount of output at a lower cost, namely C^2. In short, it is inefficient for the producer to use input mix A, because input mix B produces the same output and lies on a lower isocost line.

At the cost-minimizing input mix, the slope of the isoquant is equal to the slope of the isocost line. Recalling that the absolute value of the slope of the isoquant reflects the marginal rate of technical substitution and that the slope of the isocost line is given by $-w/r$, we see that at the cost-minimizing input mix,

$$MRTS_{KL} = w/r \tag{5–5}$$

If this condition did not hold, the technical rate at which the producer could substitute between L and K would differ from the market rate at which she or he could substitute between the inputs. For example, at point A in Figure 5–8, the slope of the isoquant is steeper than the slope of the isocost line. Consequently, capital is "too expensive"; the producer finds it in his or her interest to use less capital and more labour to produce the given level of output. This substitution continues until ulti-

FIGURE 5-8 Input Mix B Minimizes the Cost of Producing 100 Units of Output

At point B, 100 units are being produced and the cost is the C^2 line. At point A, the cost of producing 100 units of output is $C^1 > C^2$. Moving along the isoquant in any direction from point B increases costs. Thus, the least-cost methods of production are represented by points of tangency between isoquant and isocost lines.

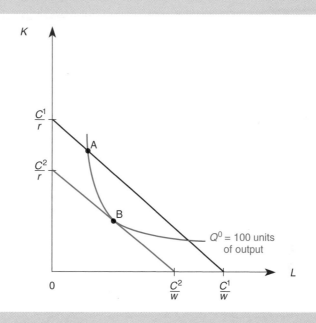

mately the producer is at a point such as B, where the *MRTS* is equal to the ratio of input prices. The condition for the cost-minimizing use of inputs also can be stated in terms of marginal products.

Principle

COST-MINIMIZING INPUT RULE
To minimize the cost of producing a given level of output, the marginal product per dollar spent should be equal for all inputs:

$$\frac{MP_L}{w} = \frac{MP_K}{r}$$

Equivalently, to minimize the cost of production, a firm should employ inputs such that the marginal rate of technical substitution is equal to the ratio of input prices:

$$\frac{MP_L}{MP_K} = \frac{w}{r}$$

Recall that we obtained a similar condition at the solution to a consumer's utility-maximization problem in Chapter 4.

To see why this condition must hold to be able to minimize the cost of producing a given level of output, suppose $MP_L/w > MP_K/r$. Then, on a last-dollar-spent basis, labour is a better deal than capital, and the firm should use less capital and more labour to minimize costs. In particular, if the firm reduced its expenditures on capital by \$1, it could produce the same level of output if it increased its expenditures on labour by less than \$1. Thus, by substituting away from capital and toward labour, the firm could reduce its costs while producing the same level of output. This substitution clearly would continue until the marginal product per dollar spent on capital exactly equalled the marginal product per dollar spent on labour.

Demonstration PROBLEM 5-3

Temporary Services uses 4 word processors and 2 typewriters to produce reports. The marginal product of a typewriter is 50 pages per day, and the marginal product of a word processor is 500 pages per day. The rental price of a typewriter is $1 per day, whereas the rental price of a word processor is $50 per day. Is Temporary Services utilizing typewriters and word processors in a cost-minimizing manner?

Answer

Let MP_T be the marginal product of a typewriter and MP_W be the marginal product of a word processor. If we let P_W and P_T be the rental prices of a word processor and a typewriter, respectively, cost minimization requires that

$$\frac{MP_T}{P_T} = \frac{MP_W}{P_W}$$

Substituting in the appropriate values, we see that

$$\frac{50}{1} = \frac{MP_T}{P_T} > \frac{MP_W}{P_W} = \frac{500}{50}$$

Thus, the marginal product per dollar spent on typewriters exceeds the marginal product per dollar spent on word processors. Word processors are 10 times more productive than typewriters, but 50 times more expensive. The firm clearly is not minimizing costs, and thus should use fewer word processors and more typewriters.

Optimal Input Substitution

A change in the price of an input will lead to a change in the cost-minimizing input bundle. To see this, suppose the initial isocost line in Figure 5–9 is FG and the producer is cost-minimizing at input mix A, producing Q_0 units of output. Now suppose that the wage rate increases so that if the firm spent the same amount on inputs, its isocost line would rotate clockwise to FH in Figure 5–9. Clearly, if the firm spends the amount it spent prior to the increase in the wage rate, it cannot produce the same level of output.

Given the new slope of the isocost line, which reflects a higher relative price of labour, the cost-minimizing way to maintain the output implied by the initial isoquant is at point B, where isocost line IJ is tangent to the isoquant. Due to the increase in the price of labour relative to capital, the producer substitutes away from labour and toward capital and adopts a more capital-intensive mode of production. This suggests the following important result:

Principle	**OPTIMAL INPUT SUBSTITUTION** To minimize the cost of producing a given level of output, the firm should use less of an input and more of other inputs when that input's price rises.

FIGURE 5-9 Substituting Capital for Labour, Due to Increase in the Wage Rate

The initial cost line is FG with cost-minimizing at input mix A. As a result of an increase in the wage rate, this line pivots to FH. Given this new slope (reflecting a higher cost of L), the cost-minimizing way to maintain the output implied by the isoquant is at point B, where isocost line IJ is tangent to the isoquant. At point B, the producer substitutes away from labour toward capital as a result of the increase in wages.

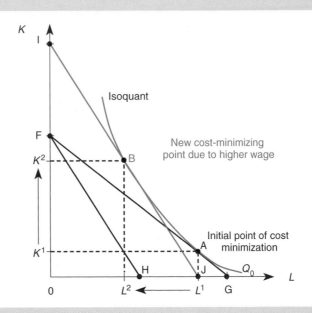

Isoquant

New cost-minimizing point due to higher wage

Initial point of cost minimization

Figure 5–10 shows the isocost line (AB) and isoquant for a firm that produces rugs using computers and labour. The initial point of cost minimization is at point M, where the manager has chosen to use 40 units of capital (computers) and 80 units of labour when the wage rate is $w = \$20$ and the rental rate of computers (capital) is $r^0 = \$20$. This implies that at point M, total costs are $TC^0 = (\$20 \times 40) + (\$20 \times 80) = \$2400$. Notice also at point M that the *MRTS* equals the ratio of the wage to the rental rate.

Now assume that due to a decrease in the supply of silicon chips, the rental rate of capital increases to $r^1 = \$40$. What will the manager do to minimize costs? Since the price of capital has increased, the isocost line will rotate counterclockwise from AB to DB. To produce the same amount of output, the manager will have to spend more than $C^0 = \$2400$. The additional expenditures will shift the isocost line out to EF in Figure 5–10. The new point of cost minimization is at point N, where the firm now employs more labour (120 units) and less capital (10 units) to minimize the production costs of rugs. Costs are now $C^1 = (\$40 \times 10) + (\$20 \times 120) = \$2800$, which are higher than C^0.

The Cost Function

Now that we understand how a manager can use information about the production function to minimize the cost of producing a given level of output, it is useful to examine a very simple way to summarize the information contained in the production function.

For given input prices, different isoquants will entail different production costs, even allowing for optimal substitution between capital and labour. Each isoquant corresponds to a different level of output, and the isocost line tangent to higher isoquants

FIGURE 5–10 Substituting Labour for Computers, Due to Higher Computer Prices

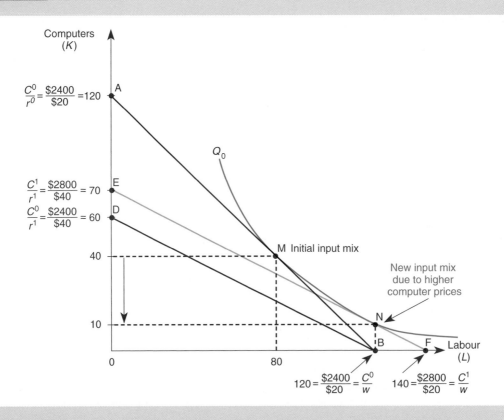

The initial cost line is AB with cost-minimizing at input mix M. As a result of an increase in the rental rate of capital, this line pivots to DB. Given this new slope (reflecting a higher cost of K), the cost-minimizing way to maintain the output implied by the isoquant is at point N, where isocost line EF is tangent to the isoquants. At this point, labour has been substituted for capital as a result of the increase in the rental rate of capital.

will imply higher costs of production, even assuming the firm uses the cost-minimizing input mix. Since the cost of production increases as higher isoquants are reached, it is useful to let $C(Q)$ denote the cost to the firm of producing isoquant Q in the cost-minimizing fashion. The function, C, is called the *cost function*.

The cost function is extremely valuable because, as we will see in later chapters, it provides essential information a manager needs to determine the profit-maximizing level of output. In addition, the cost function summarizes information about the production process. The cost function thus reduces the amount of information the manager has to process to make optimal output decisions.

fixed costs
Costs that do not change with changes in output; include the costs of fixed inputs used in production.

variable costs
Costs that change with changes in output; include the costs of inputs that vary with output.

Short-Run Costs

Recall that the short run is defined as the period over which the amounts of some inputs are fixed. In the short run, the manager is free to alter the use of variable inputs but is "stuck" with existing levels of fixed inputs. Because inputs are costly whether fixed or variable, the total cost of producing output in the short run consists of (1) the cost of fixed inputs and (2) the cost of variable inputs. These two components of

Inside BUSINESS

5-3 Fringe Benefits and Input Substitution in Canada and the United States

Some of the most important personal consumption items that individuals receive are closely tied to work and are provided or financed by employers either voluntarily or by government mandate. These benefits include retirement income, health care, unemployment insurance, workers' compensation, etc. Employers' costs for total benefits as they stand now represent one-third of total labour cost in most industrialized countries.

Given these figures, it is not surprising that there has been a great deal of interest among economists and other analysts in the role that benefits play in labour markets. Research suggests that social insurance programs financed by employer contributions tend to raise labour cost and thereby reduce employment. The assumption that benefits represent quasi-fixed costs is common in studies of the effect of benefits on decisions of employers and employees. To the extent that this is true, the structure of employee compensation packages may influence employers' demand for full and part-time workers. In fact, the evidence from the United States[1] shows that benefits are found to limit the employment opportunity. This is found to be especially true for health care benefits—a true quasi-fixed cost to employers—for which the average per-hour cost is greater for part-time workers than for full-time workers.[2]

To illustrate this, consider a company that hires computer programmers and secretaries. Suppose the annual wage bill of a computer programmer is $30 000 and that of a secretary is $15 000. The company is considering offering a family health care plan worth $3600 annually to its employees. Ignoring the cost of health care plan, the relative price of a secretary to a computer programmer is $15 000/$30 000 = 0.5. But when the cost of the health care plan is added in, the relative price of a secretary increases to a little over 0.55 ($18 600/$33 600) of that of a computer programmer. Isoquant and isocost analysis suggests that firms should substitute away from now higher-priced secretaries, to minimize costs.

The study for the United States mentioned above found that industries offering more generous health care plans employed significantly fewer bookkeepers, keypunch operators, receptionists, secretaries, clerk typists, janitors, and food service workers than industries with lower health care costs. Furthermore, industries with higher levels of fringe benefits hired more part-time workers than industries with lower fringe-benefit levels, since the U.S. tax department, the IRS, does not require firms to offer pension, health care, and many other fringe benefits to part-time workers.

It is important to note, however, that there are substantial differences between the employee benefit systems of Canada and of the United States, the most striking being the health care systems. In Canada, health care is provided through a system of provincial and territorial plans funded by the federal government out of general revenues, whereas in the United States it is provided through a mixed private/public system financed largely by employer contributions and payroll taxes. Because the Canadian health plans are funded out of general revenue, they are not perceived as an employer cost as in the United States.[3] In the light of this, the argument that health care benefits constitute a quasi-fixed cost to employers and thereby limit employment opportunities of low-income workers does not apply to Canada.

[1]Frank Scott, Mark Berger, and Dan Black, "Effects of Fringe benefits on Labour Market Segmentation," *Industrial and Labour Relations Review* 42, January 1989.

[2]Michael K. Lettau and Thomas C. Buchmueller, "Comparing Benefit Costs for Full- and Part-Time Workers," *Monthly Labor Review*, March 1999.

[3]William T. Alpert and Stephen A. Woodbury, eds., *Employee Benefits and Labour Markets in Canada and the United States* (Kalamazoo, MI: W. E. Upjohn Institute for Employment Research, 2000), available <www.upjohninst.org/publications/ch1/alpert-woodbury.pdf>, accessed June 18, 2004.

short-run cost function
A function that defines the minimum possible cost of producing each output level when variable factors are employed in the cost-minimizing fashion.

short-run total cost are called fixed costs and variable costs, respectively. **Fixed costs**, denoted *FC*, are costs that do not vary with output. Fixed costs include the costs of fixed inputs used in production. **Variable costs**, denoted $VC(Q)$, are costs that change when output is changed. Variable costs include the costs of inputs that vary with output.

Since all costs fall into one or the other category, the sum of fixed and variable costs is the firm's short-run cost function. In the presence of fixed factors of production, the **short-run cost function** summarizes the minimum possible cost of producing each level of output when variable factors are being used in the cost-minimizing way.

TABLE 5-3 The Cost Function

(1) K Fixed Input [Given]	(2) L Variable Input [Given]	(3) Q Output [Given]	(4) FC Fixed Cost [$1000 × (1)]	(5) VC Variable Cost [$400 × (2)]	(6) TC Total Cost [(4) + (5)]
2	0	0	$2000	$ 0	$2000
2	1	76	2000	400	2400
2	2	248	2000	800	2800
2	3	492	2000	1200	3200
2	4	784	2000	1600	3600
2	5	1100	2000	2000	4000
2	6	1416	2000	2400	4400
2	7	1708	2000	2800	4800
2	8	1952	2000	3200	5200
2	9	2124	2000	3600	5600
2	10	2200	2000	4000	6000
2	11	2156	2000	4400	6400

Table 5–3 illustrates the costs of producing with the technology used in Table 5–1. Notice that the first three columns make up a short-run production function, because they summarize the maximum amount of output that can be produced with two units of the fixed factor (capital) and alternative units of the variable factor (labour). Assuming capital costs $1000 per unit and labour costs $400 per unit, we can calculate the fixed and variable costs of production, which are summarized in columns 4 and 5 of Table 5–3. Notice that irrespective of the amount of output produced, the cost of the capital equipment is $1000 × 2 = $2000. Thus, every entry in column 4 contains this number, illustrating the principle that fixed costs do not vary with output.

To produce more output, more of the variable factor must be employed. For example, to produce 1100 units of output, 5 units of labour are needed; to produce 1708 units of output, 7 units of labour are required. Since labour is the only variable input in this simple example, the variable cost of producing 1100 units of output is the cost of 5 units of labour, or $400 × 5 = $2000. Similarly, the variable cost of producing 1708 units of output is $400 × 7 = $2800. Total costs, summarized in the last column of Table 5–3, are simply the sum of fixed costs (column 4) and variable costs (column 5) at each level of output.

Figure 5–11 illustrates graphically the relations between total costs (TC), variable costs (VC), and fixed costs (FC). Because fixed costs do not change with output, they are constant for all output levels and must be paid even if zero units of output are produced. Variable costs, on the other hand, are zero if no output is produced but increase as output increases above zero. Total cost is the sum of fixed costs and variable costs. Thus, the distance between the TC and VC curves in Figure 5–11 is simply fixed costs.

Average and Marginal Costs

One common misconception about costs is that large firms have lower costs than smaller firms because they produce larger quantities of output. One fundamental implication of scarcity is that to produce more output, more must be spent. What indi-

FIGURE 5–11 The Relationships Between Costs

Fixed costs (*FC*) do not vary with output. Variable costs (*VC*) and total costs (*TC*)(*TC = VC + FC*) rise with output, first at a decreasing rate and then at an increasing rate.

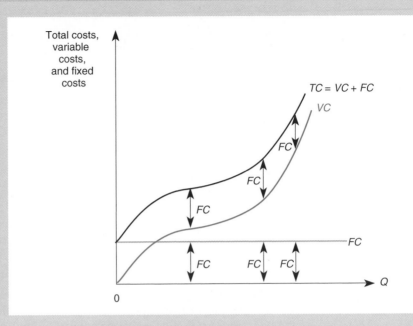

viduals most likely have in mind when they consider the advantages of producing large quantities of output is that the overhead is spread out over a larger level of output. This idea is intricately related to the economic concept of average fixed cost. **Average fixed cost (*AFC*)** is defined as fixed costs (*FC*) divided by the number of units of output:

average fixed cost (*AFC*)
Fixed costs divided by the number of units of output.

$$AFC = \frac{FC}{Q}$$

Since fixed costs do not vary with output, as more and more output is produced, the fixed costs are allocated over a greater quantity of output. As a consequence, average fixed costs decline continuously as output is expanded. This principle is revealed in column 5 of Table 5–4, where we see that average fixed costs decline as total output increases.

Average variable cost provides a measure of variable costs on a per-unit basis. **Average variable cost (AVC)** is defined as variable cost (*VC*) divided by the number of units of output:

average variable cost (*AVC*)
Variable costs divided by the number of units of output.

$$AVC = \frac{VC(Q)}{Q}$$

Column 6 of Table 5–4 provides the average variable cost for the production function in our example. Notice that as output increases, average variable cost initially declines, reaches a minimum between 1708 and 1952 units of output, and then begins to increase.

TABLE 5-4 Derivation of Average Costs

(1) Q Output [Given]	(2) FC Fixed Cost [Given]	(3) VC Variable Cost [Given]	(4) TC Total Cost [(2) + (3)]	(5) AFC Average Fixed Cost [(2)/(1)]	(6) AVC Average Variable Cost [(3)/(1)]	(7) ATC Average Total Cost [(4)/(1)]
0	$2000	$ 0	$2000	—	—	—
76	2000	400	2400	$26.32	$5.26	$31.58
248	2000	800	2800	8.06	3.23	11.29
492	2000	1200	3200	4.07	2.44	6.50
784	2000	1600	3600	2.55	2.04	4.59
1100	2000	2000	4000	1.82	1.82	3.64
1416	2000	2400	4400	1.41	1.69	3.11
1708	2000	2800	4800	1.17	1.64	2.81
1952	2000	3200	5200	1.02	1.64	2.66
2124	2000	3600	5600	0.94	1.69	2.64
2200	2000	4000	6000	0.91	1.82	2.73

Average total cost is analogous to average variable cost, except that it provides a measure of *total* costs on a per-unit basis. *Average total cost (ATC)* is defined as total cost (*TC*), or *TC(Q)*, divided by the number of units of output:

$$ATC = \frac{TC}{Q} = \frac{TC(Q)}{Q}$$

Column 7 of Table 5–4 provides the average total cost of various outputs in our example. Notice that average total cost declines as output expands to 2124 units and then begins to rise. Furthermore, note that average total cost is the sum of average fixed costs and average variable costs (the sum of columns 5 and 6) in Table 5–4.

The most important cost concept is marginal (or incremental) cost. Conceptually, **marginal cost (MC)** is the cost of producing an additional unit of output, that is, the change in cost attributable to the last unit of output:

marginal (incremental) cost (MC)
The cost of producing an additional unit of output.

$$MC = \frac{\Delta TC}{\Delta Q}$$

To understand this important concept, consider Table 5–5, which summarizes the short-run cost function with which we have been working. Marginal cost, depicted in column 7, is calculated as the change in costs arising from a given change in output. For example, increasing output from 248 to 492 units ($\Delta Q = 244$) increases costs from 2800 to 3200 ($\Delta TC = \$400$). Thus, the marginal cost of 492 units of output is $\Delta TC/\Delta Q = 400/244 = \$1.64$.

When only one input is variable, the marginal cost is the price of that input divided by its marginal product:

$$VC = wL$$

where w is, as before, the wage rate and L the amount of labour required to produce Q (holding capital, K, constant), hence:

TABLE 5–5	Derivation of Marginal Cost					
(1) Q [Given]	(2) ΔQ [Δ(1)]	(3) VC [Given]	(4) ΔVC [Δ(3)]	(5) TC [Given]	(6) ΔTC [Δ(5)]	(7) MC [(6)/(2) or (4)/2)]
0	—	0	—	2000	—	—
76	76	400	400	2400	400	400/76 = 5.26
248	172	800	400	2800	400	400/172 = 2.33
492	244	1200	400	3200	400	400/244 = 1.64
784	292	1600	400	3600	400	400/292 = 1.37
1100	316	2000	400	4000	400	400/316 = 1.27
1416	316	2400	400	4400	400	400/316 = 1.27
1708	292	2800	400	4800	400	400/292 = 1.37
1952	244	3200	400	5200	400	400/244 = 1.64
2124	172	3600	400	5600	400	400/172 = 2.33
2200	76	4000	400	6000	400	400/76 = 5.26

$$MC = \frac{\Delta TC}{\Delta Q} = \frac{\Delta VC}{\Delta Q} = \frac{w\Delta L}{\Delta Q} = \frac{w}{\Delta Q/\Delta L} = \frac{w}{MP_L} \tag{5–6}$$

Remember that marginal product increases initially, reaches a maximum, and then decreases. As the above relationship holds, marginal cost is the reciprocal of marginal product times the input's price (wage rate); it decreases as marginal product increases and increases when marginal product is decreasing.

Similarly, the average variable cost is the price of the variable input divided by its average product:

$$AVC = \frac{VC}{Q} = \frac{wL}{Q} = \frac{w}{Q/L} = \frac{w}{AP_L} \tag{5–7}$$

Therefore, the short-run average cost curves are the mirror image of the short-run average product curve.

Relations Between Costs

Figure 5–12 graphically depicts average total, average variable, average fixed, and marginal costs under the assumption that output is infinitely divisible (the firm is not restricted to producing only the outputs listed in Tables 5–4 and 5–5 but can produce any outputs). The shapes of the curves indicate the relation between the marginal and average costs presented in those tables. These relations between the cost curves, also depicted in Figure 5–12, are very important. The first thing to notice is that the marginal cost curve intersects the *ATC* and *AVC* curves at their minimum points. This implies that when marginal cost is below an average cost curve, average cost is declining, and when marginal cost is above average cost, average cost is rising.

There is a simple explanation for this relationship between the various cost curves. Again consider your grade in this course. If your grade on an exam is below your average grade, the new grade lowers your average grade. If the grade you score on an exam is above your average grade, the new grade increases your average. In essence, the new grade is the marginal contribution to your total grade. When the marginal is above the average, the average increases; when the marginal is below the average, the average decreases. The same principle applies to marginal and average costs, and this is why the curves in Figure 5–12 look the way they do.

FIGURE 5-12 The Relationships Between Average and Marginal Costs

Average fixed costs (AFC) declines as output increases. Average variable costs (AVC) and average total cost (ATC) fall and then rise as output increases. Marginal cost (MC) does the same, intersecting ATC and AVC at their minimum points.

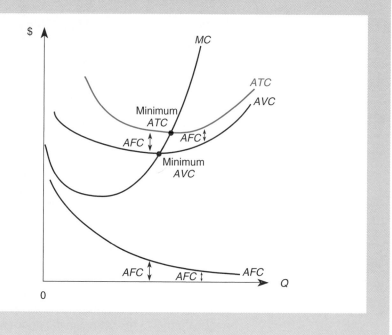

The second thing to notice in Figure 5–12 is that the *ATC* and *AVC* curves get closer together as output increases. This is because the only difference in *ATC* and *AVC* is *AFC*. To see why, note that total costs consist of variable costs and fixed costs:

$$TC = VC + FC$$

If we divide both sides of this equation by total output (Q), we get

$$\frac{TC}{Q} = \frac{VC}{Q} + \frac{FC}{Q}$$

But $TC/Q = ATC$, $VC/Q = AVC$, and $FC/Q = AFC$. Thus,

$$ATC = AVC + AFC$$

The difference between average total costs and average variable costs is $ATC - AVC = AFC$. Since average fixed costs decline as output is expanded, as in Figure 5–12, this difference between average total and average variable costs diminishes as fixed costs are spread over increasing levels of output.

Fixed and Sunk Costs

sunk cost
A cost that is forever lost after it has been paid.

We now make an important distinction between fixed costs and sunk costs. Recall that a fixed cost is a cost that does not change when output changes. A related concept, called **sunk cost**, is a cost that is lost forever once it has been paid. To be concrete, imagine that you are the manager of a coal company and have just paid $10 000 to lease a railcar for one month. This expense reflects a fixed cost to your firm—the cost is $10 000 regardless of whether you use the railcar to transport 10 tonnes or 10 000 tonnes of coal. How much of this $10 000 is a sunk cost depends on the terms of your lease. If the lease does not permit you to recoup any of the $10 000 once it has been paid, the entire $10 000 is a sunk cost—you have already incurred the cost, and there is nothing you can do to change it. If the lease states that you will be refunded $6000 in the event you do not need the railcar, then only $4000 of the $10 000 in fixed costs is a sunk cost. Sunk costs are thus the amount of these fixed costs that cannot be recouped.

Since sunk costs are lost forever once they have been paid, they are irrelevant to decision making. To illustrate, suppose you paid a nonrefundable amount of $10 000 to lease a railcar for one month, but immediately after signing the lease you realize that you do not need it—the demand for coal is significantly lower than you expected. A farmer approaches you and offers to sublease the railcar from you for $2000. If the terms of your lease permit you to sublease the railcar, should you accept the farmer's offer?

You might reason that the answer is no; after all, your firm would appear to lose $8000 by subleasing a $10 000 railcar for a measly $2000. *This reasoning is wrong.* Your lease payment is nonrefundable, which means that the $10 000 is an unavoidable cost that has already been lost. Since there is nothing you can do to eliminate this $10 000 cost, the only relevant issue is whether you can do something to enhance your inflow of cash. In this case your optimal decision is to sublease the railcar because doing so provides you with $2000 in revenues that you would not get otherwise. Notice that, while sunk costs are irrelevant in making your decision, they do affect your calculation of total profits. If you do not sublease the railcar, you lose $10 000; if you sublease it, you lose only $8000.

Principle	**IRRELEVANCE OF SUNK COSTS** A decision maker should ignore sunk costs to maximize profits or minimize losses.

Demonstration PROBLEM 5–4

ACME Coal paid $5000 to lease a railcar from the Reading Railroad. Under the terms of the lease, $1000 of this payment is refundable if the railcar is returned within two days of signing the lease.

1. Upon signing the lease and paying $5000, how large are ACME's fixed costs? Its sunk costs?
2. One day after signing the lease, ACME realizes that it has no use for the railcar. A farmer has a bumper crop of corn and has offered to sublease the railcar from ACME at a price of $4500. Should ACME accept the farmer's offer?

Answer

1. ACME's fixed costs are $5000. For the first two days, its sunk costs are $4000 (this is the amount that cannot be recouped). After two days, the entire $5000 becomes a sunk cost.
2. Yes, ACME should sublease the railcar. Note that ACME's total loss is $500 if it accepts the farmer's offer. If it does not, its losses will equal $4000 (assuming it returns the railcar by the end of the next business day).

Algebraic Forms of Cost Functions

In practice, cost functions may take many forms, but the cubic cost function is frequently encountered and closely approximates any cost function. The **cubic cost function** is given by

$$TC = f + aQ + bQ^2 + cQ^3$$

where a, b, c, and f are constants. Note that f represents fixed costs.

Given an algebraic form of the cubic cost function, we may directly calculate the marginal cost function.

Formula: Marginal Cost for Cubic Costs. For a cubic cost function,

$$TC = f + aQ + bQ^2 + cQ^3$$

the marginal cost function is

$$MC = a + 2bQ + 3cQ^2$$

A Calculus ALTERNATIVE

Marginal cost is simply the derivative of the cost function with respect to output:

$$MC = \frac{dTC}{dQ}$$

For example, the derivative of the cubic cost function with respect to Q is

$$\frac{dTC}{dQ} = a + 2bQ + 3cQ^2$$

which is the formula for marginal cost given above.

Demonstration PROBLEM 5–5

The cost function for Managerial Enterprises is given by $TC = 20 + 3Q^2$. What are the marginal cost, average fixed cost, average variable cost, and average total cost of producing 10 units of output?

Answer

Using the formula for marginal cost (here $a = c = 0$), we know that $MC = 6Q$. Thus, the marginal cost of producing the 10th unit of output is $60.

To find the various average costs, we must first calculate total costs. The total cost of producing 10 units of output is

$$TC(10) = 20 + 3(10)^2 = \$320$$

Fixed costs are those costs that do not vary with output; thus fixed costs are $20. Variable costs are the costs that vary with output, namely $VC = 3Q^2$. Thus, $VC(10) = 3(10)^2 = \$300$. It follows that the average fixed cost of producing 10 units is $2, the average variable cost is $30, and the average total cost is $32.

FIGURE 5–13 Optimal Plant Size and Long-Run Average Cost

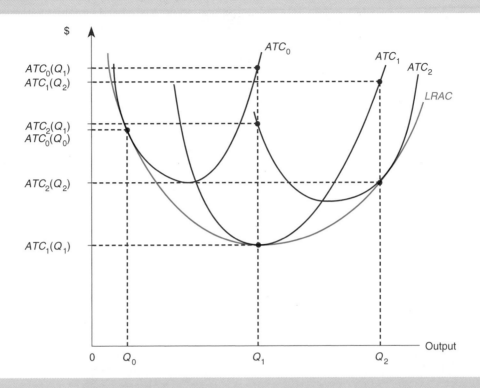

At Q_1, for example, the *ATC* would be $ATC_0(Q_1)$ in the short run, since fixed factors are not allowed to change. In the long run, the firm can adjust the fixed factors and could produce on curve ATC_1 and have an *ATC* of $ATC_1(Q_1)$. Each short-run curve shows how costs vary if output varies, with the fixed factor being held constant at the level optimal for the output at the point of tangency. The *LRAC* defines the minimum average cost of producing alternative levels of output, allowing for optimal selection of all variables of production.

Long-Run Costs

In the long run all costs are variable, because the manager is free to adjust the levels of all inputs. In Figure 5–13, the short-run average cost curve ATC_0 is drawn under the assumption that there are some fixed factors of production. The average total cost of producing output level Q_0, given the fixed factors of production, is $ATC_0(Q_0)$. In the short run, if the firm increases output to Q_1, it cannot adjust the fixed factors, and thus average costs rise to $ATC_0(Q_1)$. In the long run, however, the firm can adjust the fixed factors. Let ATC_1 be the average cost curve after the firm adjusts the fixed factor in the optimal manner. Now the firm can produce Q_1 with average cost curve ATC_1. If the firm produced Q_1 with average cost curve ATC_0, its average costs would be $ATC_0(Q_1)$. By adjusting the fixed factors in a way that optimizes the scale of operation, the firm economizes in production and can produce Q_1 units of output at a lower average cost, $ATC_1(Q_1)$. Notice that the curve labelled ATC_1 is itself a short-run average cost curve, based on the new levels of fixed inputs that have been selected to minimize the cost of producing Q_1. If the firm wishes to further expand output—say, to Q_2—it would follow curve ATC_1 in the short run to $ATC_1(Q_2)$ until it again changed its fixed factors to incur lower average costs of producing Q_2 units of output, namely $ATC_2(Q_2)$.

long-run average cost curve
A curve that defines the minimum average cost of producing alternative levels of output, allowing for optimal selection of both fixed and variable factors of production.

The **long-run average cost curve**, denoted *LRAC* in Figure 5–13, defines the minimum average cost of producing alternative levels of output, allowing for optimal selection of all variables of production (both fixed and variable factors). The long-run average cost curve is the lower envelope of all the short-run average cost curves. This means that the long-run average cost curve lies below every point on the short-run average cost curves, except that it equals each short-run average cost curve at the points where the short-run curve uses fixed factors optimally. In essence, we may think of each short-run average cost curve in Figure 5–13 as the average cost of producing in a plant of fixed size. Different short-run average cost curves are associated with different plant sizes. In the long run, the firm's manager is free to choose the optimal plant size for producing the desired level of output, and this determines the long-run average cost of producing that output level.

Demonstration PROBLEM 5–6

Consider the three short-run average cost curves in Figure 5–14. Each curve is associated with a different-size plant. Which plant can produce 5 units of output most efficiently? Which can produce 10 units most efficiently?

Answer

The smallest plant in Figure 5–14 is ATC_S, the largest plant is ATC_L, and the medium-size plant is ATC_M. If the firm wished to produce 5 units of output, it would choose the medium-size plant. The average cost would be at level A,

---

FIGURE 5–14 A Medium-Sized Plant Produces Five Units at Lowest Cost

The three average cost curves, ATC_S, ATC_M, and ATC_L, are associated with three different plant sizes, where ATC_S is the smallest and ATC_L is the largest plant.

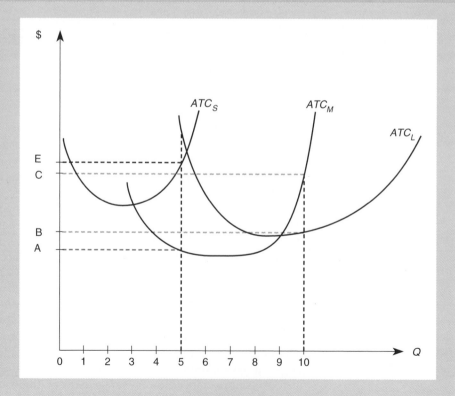

which entails the lowest possible cost for producing 5 units. If this company chose to produce 10 units, it would choose the largest plant. The average total cost would be at level B, which is the least-cost way of producing 10 units of output.

economies of scale
Exist whenever long-run average costs decline as output is increased.

diseconomies of scale
Exist when long-run average costs rise as output is increased.

constant returns to scale
Exist when long-run average costs remain constant as output is increased.

Economies of Scale

Notice that the long-run average cost curve in Figure 5–15(a) is U-shaped. This implies that initially an expansion of output allows the firm to produce at lower long-run average cost, as is shown for outputs between 0 and Q^*. This condition is known as **economies of scale**. When there are economies of scale, increasing the size of the operation decreases the minimum average cost. After a point, such as Q^* in Figure 5–15(a), further increases in output lead to an increase in average costs. This condition is known as **diseconomies of scale**. Sometimes the technology in an industry allows a firm to produce different levels of output at the same minimum average cost, as in Figure 5–15(b). This condition is called **constant returns to scale**.

FIGURE 5–15 Economies of Scale

(a) An initial expansion of output allows the firm to produce at a lower long-run average cost (from 0 to Q^*) (economies of scale). Beyond Q^*, further increases in output lead to an increase in average costs (diseconomies of scale). Within the close proximity of Q^* (the flat portion of the *LRAC*), increases in output lead to no change in long-run average cost.
(b) Constant returns to scale can result from a specific technology possessed by an industry that allows a firm to produce different levels of output at the same minimum average cost.

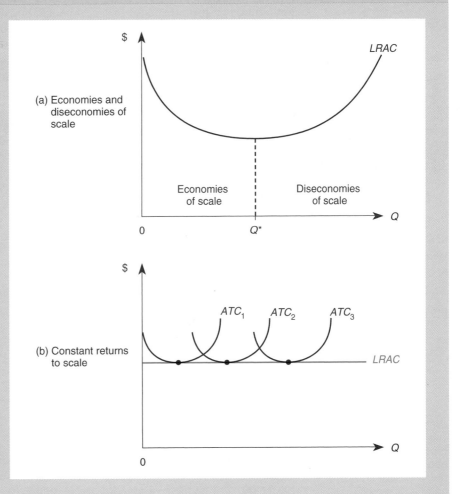

A Reminder: Economic Costs Versus Accounting Costs

In concluding this section, it is important to recall the difference between economic costs and accounting costs. Accounting costs are the costs most often associated with the costs of producing. For example, accounting costs include direct payments to labour and capital to produce output. Accounting costs are the costs that appear on the income statements of firms.

These costs are not the only costs of producing a good, however. The firm could use the same resources to produce some other good. By choosing to produce one good, producers give up the opportunity for producing some other good. Thus, the costs of production include not only the accounting costs but also the opportunities forgone by producing a given product.

Multiple-Output Cost Functions

Up until now, our analysis of the production process has focused on situations where the firm produces a single output. There are also numerous examples of firms that produce multiple outputs. General Motors produces both cars and trucks (and many varieties of each); IBM produces many different types of computers and printers. While our analysis for the case of a firm that produces a single output also applies to a multiproduct firm, the latter raises some additional issues. This section will highlight these concepts.

In this section, we will assume that the cost function for a multiproduct firm is given by $TC(Q_1, Q_2)$, where Q_1 is the number of units produced of product 1 and Q_2 is the number of units produced of product 2. The **multiproduct cost function** thus defines the cost of producing Q_1 units of product 1 and Q_2 units of product 2 assuming all inputs are used efficiently.

Notice that the multiproduct cost function has the same basic interpretation as a single-output cost function. Unlike with a single-product cost function, however, the costs of production depend on how much of each type of output is produced. This gives rise to what economists call economies of scope and cost complementarities, discussed next.

multiproduct cost function
A function that defines the cost of producing given levels of two or more types of outputs assuming all inputs are used efficiently.

Economies of Scope

Economies of scope exist when the total cost of producing Q_1 and Q_2 together is less than the total cost of producing Q_1 and Q_2 separately, that is, when

$$TC(Q_1, 0) + TC(0, Q_2) > TC(Q_1, Q_2) \tag{5-8}$$

In a restaurant, for example, to produce given quantities of steak and chicken dinners, it generally is cheaper to produce both products in the same restaurant than to have two restaurants, one that sells only chicken and one that sells only steak. The reason is, of course, that producing the dinners separately would require duplication of many common factors of production, such as ovens, refrigerators, tables, the building, and so forth.

economies of scope
When the total cost of producing two types of outputs together is less than the total cost of producing each type of output separately.

Cost Complementarity

Cost complementarity exists in a multiproduct cost function when the marginal cost of producing one output is reduced when the output of another product is increased. Let $TC(Q_1, Q_2)$ be the cost function for a multiproduct firm, and let $MC_1(Q_1, Q_2)$ be

cost complementarity
The marginal cost of producing one type of output decreasing when the output of another good is increased.

the marginal cost of producing the first output. The cost function exhibits cost complementarity if

$$\frac{\Delta MC_1(Q_1, Q_2)}{\Delta Q_2} < 0 \qquad (5\text{--}9)$$

that is, if an increase in the output of product 2 decreases the marginal cost of producing product 1.

Economies of scope and cost complementarities are so close in meaning that it is useful to try to define both with an example. By definition, economies of scope arise in situations wherein it is cheaper to produce two types of outputs together than to produce each output separately. Arguably, cost complementarities can cause this to occur. Cost complementarities, after all, refer to an instance in which the marginal cost of one service decreases when the output of another good is increased—so it is cheaper to produce them together and economies of scope are created. For example, soap production relies on fat as a primary ingredient. The production process results in residuals that can, with a little additional effort, be turned into glycerin for resale. It is cheaper to produce glycerin as a byproduct of the soap-making process (cost complementarities) than it is to product the two separately (economies of scope having been achieved).

The concepts of economies of scope and cost complementarity can also be examined within the context of an algebraic functional form for a multiproduct cost function. For example, suppose the multiproduct cost function is quadratic:

$$TC(Q_1, Q_2) = f + aQ_1Q_2 + (Q_1)^2 + (Q_2)^2$$

For this cost function,

$$MC_1 = aQ_2 + 2Q_1$$

Notice that when $a < 0$, an increase in Q_2 reduces the marginal cost of producing product 1. Thus, if $a < 0$, this cost function exhibits cost complementarity. If $a > 0$, there are no cost complementarities.

Formula: Quadratic Multiproduct Cost Function. The multiproduct cost function

$$TC(Q_1, Q_2) = f + aQ_1Q_2 + (Q_1)^2 + (Q_2)^2$$

has corresponding marginal cost functions,

$$MC_1(Q_1, Q_2) = aQ_2 + 2Q_1$$

and

$$MC_2(Q_1, Q_2) = aQ_1 + 2Q_2$$

To examine whether economies of scope exist for a quadratic multiproduct cost function, recall that there are economies of scope if

$$TC(Q_1, 0) + TC(0, Q_2) > TC(Q_1, Q_2)$$

or, rearranging,

$$TC(Q_1, 0) + TC(0, Q_2) - TC(Q_1, Q_2) > 0$$

This condition may be rewritten as

$$f + (Q_1)^2 + f + (Q_2)^2 - [f + aQ_1Q_2 + (Q_1)^2 + (Q_2)^2] > 0$$

which may be simplified to

$$f - aQ_1Q_2 > 0$$

Thus, economies of scope are realized in producing output levels Q_1 and Q_2 if $f > aQ_1Q_2$.

Summary of the Properties of the Quadratic Multiproduct Cost Function. The multiproduct cost function $TC(Q_1, Q_2) = f + aQ_1Q_2 + (Q_1)^2 + (Q_2)^2$

1. Exhibits cost complementarity whenever $a < 0$.
2. Exhibits economies of scope[1] whenever $f - aQ_1Q_2 > 0$.

Demonstration PROBLEM 5–7

Suppose the cost function of firm A, which produces two goods, is given by

$$TC = 100 - 0.5Q_1Q_2 + (Q_1)^2 + (Q_2)^2$$

The firm wishes to produce 5 units of good 1 and 4 units of good 2.

1. Do cost complementarities exist? Do economies of scope exist?
2. Firm A is considering selling the subsidiary that produces good 2 to firm B, in which case it will produce only good 1. What will happen to firm A's costs if it continues to produce 5 units of good 1?

Answer

1. For this cost function, $a = -1/2 < 0$, so indeed there are cost complementarities. To check for economies of scope, we must determine whether $f - aQ_1Q_2 > 0$. This is clearly true, since $a < 0$ in this problem. Thus, economies of scope exist in producing 5 units of good 1 and 4 units of good 2.
2. To determine what will happen to firm A's costs if it sells the subsidiary that produces good 2 to firm B, we must calculate costs under the alternative scenarios. By selling the subsidiary, firm A will reduce its production of good 2 from 4 to 0 units; since there are cost complementarities, this will increase the marginal cost of producing good 1. Notice that the total costs to firm A of producing the 5 units of good 1 fall from

$$TC(5, 4) = 100 - 10 + 25 + 16 = 131$$

---

[1]Note that while the concept of complementarity is independent of economics of scope, a further examination reveals their underlying interrelationship. We know that in order for scope economies to be present, $f - aQ_1Q_2 > 0$. However, since production, Q_1 and Q_2, cannot be negative and fixed costs are normally positive, this condition will be reduced to a (with $a < 0$), which is the same as that for cost complementarity.

to

$$TC(5, 0) = 100 + 25 = 125$$

But the costs to firm B of producing 4 units of good 2 will be

$$TC(0, 4) = 100 + 16 = 116$$

Firm A's costs will fall by only \$6 when it stops producing good 2, and the costs to firm B of producing 4 units of good 2 will be \$116. The combined costs to the two firms of producing the output originally produced by a single firm will be \$110 more than the cost of producing by a single firm.

The preceding problem illustrates some important aspects of mergers and sales of subsidiaries. First, when there are economies of scope, two firms producing distinct outputs could merge into a single firm and enjoy a reduction in costs. Second, selling off an unprofitable subsidiary could lead to only minor reductions in costs. In effect, when economies of scope exist, it is difficult to "allocate costs" across product lines.

ANSWERING THE Headline

The numbers reported in the opening headline indicate that Ford's hourly workers produce an average of 33.2 vehicles per year, whereas GM employees produce an average of only 27.9 vehicles per year. Notice that these numbers represent the average product of GM and Ford workers and imply that for every 1000 cars produced, GM employs about 36 workers while Ford employs about 30. Since GM pays its workers a higher hourly wage (\$45) than Ford (\$43), these numbers suggest that GM is not producing in the cost-minimizing manner. To minimize costs, GM needs to use less labour and more capital.

More formally, assume that Ford and GM produce automobiles by using capital and labour. Further assume that the two firms have similar technologies and pay similar rates for the capital machines used in production. Under these assumptions, the higher wage paid by GM implies that it has a steeper isocost line than Ford; thus GM should use more capital and less labour to minimize the costs of producing a given number of automobiles (that is, to achieve a given isoquant). In other words, the higher wage faced by GM calls for it to substitute capital for labour to minimize production costs; to produce a given number of automobiles, GM should employ fewer workers than Ford. Since the figures indicate that GM is actually using more workers than Ford for each 1000 automobiles produced, GM needs to reduce its use of labour and increase its use of capital to minimize costs. This is precisely what GM attempted to do through its negotiations with the union.

Summary

In this chapter, we introduced the production and cost functions, which summarize important information about converting inputs into outputs sold by a firm. For firms that use several inputs to produce output, isocosts and isoquants provide a convenient way to determine the optimal input mix.

We broke down the cost function into average total cost, average fixed cost, average variable cost, and marginal cost. These concepts help build a foundation for understanding the profit-maximizing input and output decisions that will be covered in greater detail in later chapters.

Given a desired level of output, isoquants and isocosts provide the information needed to determine the cost-minimizing level of inputs. The cost-minimizing level of inputs is determined by the point at which the ratio of input prices equals the ratio of marginal products for the various inputs.

Finally, we showed how economies of scale, economies of scope, and cost complementaries influence the level and mix of outputs produced by single- and multi-product firms. In the next chapter we will look at the acquisition of inputs. We will see how managers can use spot markets, contracts, or vertical integration to efficiently obtain the inputs needed to produce their desired mix of outputs.

Key Terms and Concepts

average fixed cost (*AFC*) 175
average product (*AP*) 154
average variable cost (*AVC*) 175
Cobb-Douglas production function 160
constant returns to scale 183
cost complementarity 184
cubic cost function 180
decreasing (diminishing) marginal
 returns 155
diseconomies of scale 183
economies of scale 183
economies of scope 184
fixed costs 172
fixed factors of production 151
increasing marginal returns 155
isocost line 166
isoquant 163
law of diminishing marginal rate of
 technical substitution 164

Leontief (fixed-proportions) production
 function 159
linear production function 159
long-run average cost curve 182
marginal (incremental) cost (*MC*) 176
marginal product (*MP*) 154
marginal rate of technical substitution
 (*MRTS*) 163
multiproduct cost function 184
negative marginal returns 155
production function 151
short-run cost function 173
sunk cost 178
total product (*TP*) 153
value marginal product 157
variable costs 172
variable factors of production 151

Conceptual and Computational Questions

1. A firm can manufacture a product according to the production function

$$Q = F(K, L) = K^{3/4}L^{1/4}$$

a. Calculate the average product of labour, AP_L, when the level of capital is fixed at 16 units and the firm uses 16 units of labour. How does the average product of labour change when the firm uses 81 units of labour?

b. Find an expression for the marginal product of labour, MP_L, when the amount of capital is fixed at 16 units. Then, illustrate that the marginal product of labour depends on the amount of labour hired by calculating the marginal product of labour for 16 and 81 units of labour.

c. Suppose capital is fixed at 16 units. If the firm can sell its output at a price of $100 per unit and can hire labour at $25 per unit, how many units of labour should the firm hire in order to maximize profits?

2. A firm's product sells for $2 per unit in a highly competitive market. The firm produces output using capital (which it rents at $75 per hour) and labour (which is paid a wage of $15 per hour under a contract for 20 hours of labour services). Complete the following table and use that information to answer the questions that follow.

K	L	Q	MP_K	AP_K	AP_L	VMP_K
0	20	0				
1	20	50				
2	20	150				
3	20	300				
4	20	400				
5	20	450				
6	20	475				
7	20	475				
8	20	450				
9	20	400				
10	20	300				
11	20	150				

 a. Identity the fixed and variable inputs.
 b. What are the firm's fixed costs?
 c. What is the variable cost of producing 475 units of output?
 d. How many units of the variable input should be used to maximize profits?
 e. What are the maximum profits this firm can earn?
 f. Over what range of the variable input usage do increasing marginal returns exist?
 g. Over what range of the variable input usage do decreasing marginal returns exist?
 h. Over what range of input usage do negative marginal returns exist?

3. Explain the difference between the law of diminishing marginal returns and the law of diminishing marginal rate of technical substitution.

4. An economist estimated that the cost function of a single-product firm is

$$TC(Q) = 50 + 25Q + 30Q^2 + 5Q^3$$

 Using this information, determine:
 a. The fixed cost of producing 10 units of output.
 b. The variable cost of producing 10 units of output.
 c. The total cost of producing 10 units of output.
 d. The average fixed cost of producing 10 units of output.
 e. The average variable cost of producing 10 units of output.
 f. The average total cost of producing 10 units of output.
 g. The marginal cost of producing 10 units of output.

5. A manager hires labour and rents capital equipment in a very competitive market. Currently the wage rate is $6 per hour and capital is rented at $12 per hour. If the marginal product of labour is 50 units of output per hour and the marginal product of capital is 75 units of output per hour, is the firm using the cost-minimizing combination of labour and capital? If not, should the firm increase or decrease the amount of capital used in its production process?

6. A firm's fixed costs for 0 units of output and its average total cost of producing different output levels are summarized in the table below. Complete the table to find the fixed cost, variable cost, total cost, average fixed cost, average variable cost, and marginal cost at all relevant levels of output.

Q	FC	VC	TC	AFC	AVC	ATC	MC
0	$10 000					—	
100						$200	
200						125	
300						133 1/3	
400						150	
500						200	
600						250	

7. A multiproduct firm's cost function was recently estimated as

$$TC(Q_1, Q_2) = 75 - 0.25Q_1Q_2 + 0.1Q_1^2 + 0.2Q_2^2$$

   a. Are there economies of scope in producing 10 units of product 1 and 10 units of product 2?
   b. Are there cost complementarities in producing products 1 and 2?
   c. Suppose the division selling product 2 is floundering and another company has made an offer to buy the exclusive rights to produce product 2. How would the sale of the rights to produce product 2 change the firm's marginal cost of producing product 1?

8. Explain the difference between fixed costs, sunk costs, and variable costs. Provide an example that illustrates that these costs are, in general, different.

Problems and Applications

9. In an effort to stop the migration of several automobile manufacturing facilities from the southern Ontario area, the Ontario government is considering passing a statute that would give investment tax credits to auto manufacturers. Effectively, this would reduce auto manufacturers' costs of using capital and high-tech equipment in their production processes. On the evening of the vote, union officials representing auto workers voiced serious objections to this statute. Outline the basis of the argument most likely used by union officials. (*Hint:* Consider the impact that the statute would have on auto manufacturers' capital-to-labour ratio.) As a representative for one of the automakers, how would you counter the union officials' argument?

10. You were recently hired to replace the manager of the Roller Division at a major conveyor-manufacturing firm, despite the manager's strong external sales record. Roller manufacturing is relatively simple, requiring only labour and a machine that cuts and crimps rollers. As you begin reviewing the company's production information, you learn that labour is paid $8 per hour and the last worker hired produced 100 rollers per hour. The company rents roller cutters and crimping machines for $16 per hour, and the marginal product of capital is 100 rollers per hour. What do you think the previous manager could have done to keep his job?

11. You are a manager for Dorel—a major manufacturer of office furniture. You recently hired an economist to work with engineering and operations experts to estimate the production function for a particular line of office chairs. The report from these experts indicates that the relevant production function is

$$Q = 2(K)^{1/2}(L)^{1/2}$$

where K represents capital equipment and L is labour. Your company has already spent a total of $10 000 on the 4 units of capital equipment it owns. Due to current economic conditions, the company does not have the flexibility needed to acquire additional equipment. If workers at the firm are paid a competitive wage of $100 and chairs can be sold for $200 each, what is your profit-maximizing level of output and labour usage? What is your maximum profit?

12. In 2003, Bombardier Aerospace recorded orders for 1319 CRJ Series Regional jet planes and delivered 1046 planes. To maintain its output, this division of Bombardier Inc. combines efforts of capital and more than 7000 workers. Suppose the Brazilian company Embraer-Empresa Brasileira de Aeronáutica S.A. enjoys a similar number of aircraft, but labour costs (including fringe benefits) are higher in Canada than in Brazil. Would you expect workers at Embraer to have the same marginal product as workers at Bombardier? Explain carefully.

13. You are a manager at the Donnelly Corporation—a mirror and window supplier to the major automakers. Recently, you conducted a study of the production process for your DirectBond single-side encapsulated window (a product that was first introduced on Chrysler minivans). The results from the study are summarized in the table below, and are based on the 5 units of capital currently available at your plant. Workers are paid $50 per unit, per-unit capital costs are $10, and your encapsulated windows sell for $5 each. Given this information, optimize your human resource and production decisions. Do you anticipate earning a profit or a loss? Explain carefully.

Labour	Output
0	0
1	10
2	30
3	60
4	80
5	90
6	95
7	95
8	90
9	80
10	60
11	30

14. The World of Videos operates a retail store that rents VCR and DVD videos. For each of the last 10 years, World of Videos has consistently earned profits exceeding $25 000 per year. The store is located on prime real estate in a college town. World of Videos pays $2000 per month in rent for its building, but it uses only 50 percent of the square footage rented for video rental purposes. The other portion of rented space is essentially vacant. Noticing that World of Videos only occupies a portion of the building, a real estate agent told the owner of World of Videos that she could add $1200 per month to her firm's profits by renting out the unused portion of the store. While the prospect of adding an additional $1200 to World of Videos' bottom line was enticing, the owner was also contemplating using the additional space to rent video games. What is the opportunity cost of using the unused portion of the building for video game rentals?

15. A local restaurateur who had been running a profitable business for many years recently purchased a three-way liquor licence, which gives the owner the legal right to sell beer, wine, and spirits in her restaurant. The cost of obtaining the licence was about $75 000, since only 300 such licences are issued by the province. While the licence is transferable, only $65 000 is refundable if the owner chooses not to use the licence. After selling alcoholic beverages for about one year, the restaurateur

came to the realization that she was losing dinner customers and that her profitable restaurant was turning into a noisy, unprofitable bar. Subsequently, she spent about $6000 placing advertisements in various newspapers and restaurant magazines across the province offering to sell the licence for $70 000. After a long wait, she finally received one offer to purchase her licence for $66 000. What is your opinion of the restaurateur's decisions? Would you recommend that she accept the $66 000 offer?

16. In the wake of the energy crisis in California a few years ago, many electric generating facilities across the nation are reassessing their projections of future demand and capacity for electricity in their respective markets. As a manager at Alberta Power Company, you are in charge of determining the optimal size of two electricity generating facilities. The figure below illustrates the short-run average total cost curves associated with different facility sizes. Demand projections indicate that 210 megawatts must be produced at your Cavalier power station, and 90 megawatts at your Balzac power station. Determine the optimal facility size (S, M, or L) for these two regions, and indicate whether there will be economies of scale, diseconomies of scale, or constant returns to scale if the facilities are built optimally.

Average Total Cost for Various Plant Sizes

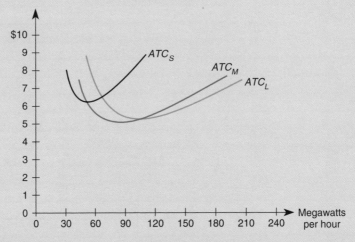

17. The A-1 Corporation supplies airplane manufacturers with preformed sheet-metal panels that are used on the exterior of aircraft. Manufacturing these panels requires only five sheet-metal-forming machines, which cost $300 each, and workers. These workers can be hired on an as-needed basis in the labour market at $7000 each. Given the simplicity of the manufacturing process, the preformed sheet-metal panel market is highly competitive. Therefore, the market price for one of A-1's panels is $50. Based on the production data in the following table, how many workers should A-1 hire to maximize its profits?

Sheet-Metal-Forming Machines	Workers	Number of Panels Produced
5	0	0
5	1	600
5	2	1000
5	3	1290
5	4	1480
5	5	1600
5	6	1680

APPENDIX: The Calculus of Production and Costs

The Profit-Maximizing Usage of Inputs

In this section we use calculus to show that the profit-maximizing level of an input is the level at which the value marginal product of the input equals the input's price. Let P denote the price of the output, Q, which is produced with the production function $F(K, L)$. The profits of the firm are

$$\pi = PQ - wL - rK$$

PQ is the revenue of the firm, and wL and rK are labour costs and capital costs, respectively. Since $Q = F(K, L)$, the objective of the manager is to choose K and L so as to maximize

$$\pi = PF(K, L) - wL - rK$$

The first-order condition for maximizing this function requires that we set the first derivatives equal to zero:

$$\frac{\partial \pi}{\partial K} = P \frac{\partial F(K, L)}{\partial K} - r = 0$$

and

$$\frac{\partial \pi}{\partial L} = P \frac{\partial F(K, L)}{\partial L} - w = 0$$

But since

$$\partial F(K, L)/\partial L = MP_L$$

and

$$\partial F(K, L)/\partial K = MP_K$$

this implies that to maximize profits, $P \times MP_L = w$ and $P \times MP_K = r$; that is, each input must be used up to the point where its value marginal product equals its price.

The Slope of an Isoquant

In this section, we use calculus to show that the slope of an isoquant is the negative of the ratio of the marginal products of two inputs.

Let the production function be $Q = F(K, L)$. If we take the total derivative of this relation, we have

$$dQ = \frac{\partial F(K, L)}{\partial K} dK + \frac{\partial F(K, L)}{\partial L} dL$$

Since output does not change along an isoquant, then $dQ = 0$. Thus,

$$0 = \frac{\partial F(K, L)}{\partial K} dK + \frac{\partial F(K, L)}{\partial L} dL$$

Solving this relation for dK/dL yields

$$\frac{dK}{dL} = -\frac{\partial F(K, L)/\partial L}{\partial F(K, L)/\partial K}$$

Since

$$\partial F(K, L)/\partial L = MP_L$$

and

$$\partial F(K, L)/\partial K = MP_K$$

we have shown that the slope of an isoquant (dK/dL) is

$$\frac{dK}{dL} = -\frac{MP_L}{MP_K}$$

The Optimal Mix of Inputs

In this section, we use calculus to show that to minimize the cost of production, or to maximize profit, the manager chooses inputs such that the slope of the isocost line equals the *MRTS*.

To choose K and L so as to minimize

$$wL + rK \text{ subject to } F(K, L) = Q$$

we form the Lagrangian

$$H = wL + rK + \mu[Q - F(K, L)]$$

where μ is the Lagrange multiplier. The first-order conditions for a maximum are

$$\frac{\partial H}{\partial L} = w - \mu \frac{\partial F(K, L)}{\partial L} = 0 \qquad \text{(A–1)}$$

$$\frac{\partial H}{\partial K} = r - \mu \frac{\partial F(K, L)}{\partial K} = 0 \qquad \text{(A–2)}$$

and

$$\frac{\partial H}{\partial \mu} = Q - F(K, L) = 0 \qquad \text{(A–3)}$$

Taking the ratio of Equations A–1 and A–2 gives us

$$\frac{w}{r} = \frac{\partial F(K, L)/\partial L}{\partial F(K, L)/\partial K} \qquad \text{(A–4)}$$

which is

$$\frac{w}{r} = \frac{MP_L}{MP_K} = MRTS \qquad \text{(A–5)}$$

In essence, the profit-maximizing of output choice implies the cost-minimizing of input choice. Put differently, profit-maximization implies cost minimization. In the derivation shown above, the view is one of the firm's choosing output and then choosing input quantities to minimizing total costs. Alternatively, the firm might be viewed as choosing inputs to maximize profits. In either case, the input combination the firm selects to minimize its costs happens to be the very same one that maximizes profits. Rearranging the last equation:

$$\frac{MP_K}{r} = \frac{MP_L}{w} \qquad \text{(A–6)}$$

This condition suggests that the additional output the firm gets from every additional dollar spent on capital (MP_K/r) equals the additional output the firm gets from every dollar spent on labour (MP_L/w).

The Relation Between Average and Marginal Costs

Finally, we will use calculus to show that the relation between average and marginal costs in the diagrams in this chapter is indeed correct. If TC is the cost function (the analysis that follows is valid for both variable and total costs, so we do not distinguish between them here), average cost is $ATC = TC/Q$. The change in average cost due to a change in output is simply the derivative of average cost with respect to output. Taking the derivative of ATC with respect to Q and using the quotient rule, we see that

$$\frac{dATC}{dQ} = \frac{Q(dTC/dQ) - TC}{Q^2} = \frac{1}{Q}[MC - ATC] \qquad \text{(A–7)}$$

since $dTC/dQ = MC$. Thus, when $MC < ATC$, average cost declines as output increases. When $MC > ATC$, average cost rises as output increases. Finally, when $MC = ATC$, average cost is at its minimum.

Head<u>line</u>

**Incentives
at Saturn:
Will a New
Kind of Car
Company
Continue
to Roll?**

When General Motors first introduced its Saturn division to compete with the makers of small Japanese cars, Saturn's workers opted for unique contract terms. Under these contract terms, workers were paid a base salary that was, on average, 12 percent less than their GM counterparts. However, this "risk-and-reward pay system" allowed workers to earn bonuses based on achieving certain targets, such as production, quality, waste reduction, and training. In the early years, Saturn's program was popular as workers earned, on average, $4000 more than other GM workers once bonuses were factored in.

More recently, however, Saturn's sales have slipped and workers have received fewer bonuses. This has prompted some workers to call for a referendum to scrap the risk-and-reward system in favour of a standard GM-UAW contract that would protect worker incomes.

If you were a manager at Saturn, how would you defend the risk-and-reward pay system to the doubtful employees?

Sources: "UAW Votes on 'The Saturn Way' of Paying Workers in Tennessee," *The Wall Street Journal Interactive Edition*, March 10, 1998; Dave Phillips, "Saturn UAW Retains Labor Pact," *The Detroit News*, March 12, 1998.

Introduction

In Chapter 5 we saw how a manager can select the mix of inputs that minimizes the cost of production. However, our analysis in that chapter left unresolved two important questions. First, what is the optimal way to acquire this efficient mix of inputs? Second, how can the owners of a firm ensure that workers put forth the maximum effort consistent with their capabilities? In this chapter, we address these two issues.[1]

Figure 6–1 illustrates why it is important to resolve these two questions. The cost function defines the minimum possible cost of producing each level of output. Point A corresponds to the situation where a firm has costs in excess of the minimum costs necessary to produce a given level of output. At point A, 10 units of output are being produced for a total cost of $100. Notice that this cost is greater than $80, which is the minimum cost necessary to produce 10 units of output. Even if the firm has the right mix of inputs, if it did not obtain them efficiently, or if workers are not expending the maximum effort consistent with their capabilities, the firm's costs will be higher than the minimum possible costs.

In this chapter we consider techniques a firm can use to ensure that it is operating on the cost function (point B in Figure 6–1) and not above it (point A). We begin by discussing three methods managers can use to obtain inputs needed in production: spot exchange, contracts, and vertical integration. To minimize costs, a firm must not only use all inputs efficiently (the $MRTS_{KL} = w/r$ rule discussed in the previous chapter); it must use the least-cost method of obtaining the inputs. We will explain when

---

FIGURE 6–1 Producing at Minimum Cost

At point B, this firm is producing 10 units of output at the minimum cost of $80. Even with the right mix of inputs, if they were not obtained efficiently or if workers are not expending the maximum effort consistent with their capabilities, a situation like A can arise where the firm's costs are higher than the minimum possible costs.

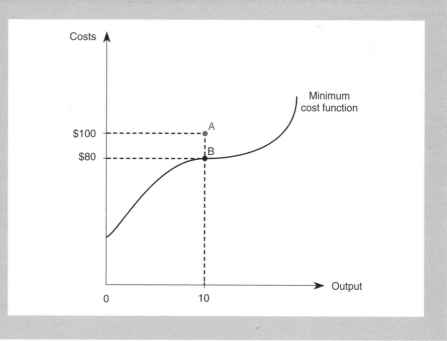

---

[1]Other questions that remain include how much output to produce and how to price the product. These important questions will be answered in the remaining chapters of this book.

it is optimal to acquire inputs (1) via spot exchange, (2) by writing contracts with input suppliers, or (3) by producing the inputs within the firm (vertical integration). Thus, the first part of this chapter provides managers with the information needed to acquire a given set of inputs in the optimal manner.

The second part of the chapter examines how a firm can ensure that labour inputs, including both managers and workers, put forth the maximum effort consistent with their capabilities. This is an important consideration, because conflicts of interest often arise among workers, managers, and the firm's owners. For example, the manager may wish to spend the firm's resources on plush office carpeting or corporate jets, while the owners prefer that the funds be invested to increase profits, which accrue to them by virtue of their status as owners. Or workers may wish to spend most of their day gossiping in the lunchroom instead of working. When employees and owners have conflicting interests, a *principal-agent* problem is said to exist. We will see how manager and worker compensation plans can be constructed to ensure that all employees put forth their highest levels of effort.

Methods of Procuring Inputs

A manager can use several approaches to obtain the inputs needed to produce a final product. Consider the manager of a car rental company. One input needed to produce output (rental cars) is automobile servicing (tuneups, oil changes, lube jobs, and the like). The manager has three options: (1) simply take the cars to a firm that services automobiles and pay the market price for the services; (2) sign a contract with a firm that services automobiles and, when service is needed, pay the price negotiated in the contract for that particular service; or (3) create within the firm a division that services automobiles. Each of these methods of servicing automobiles generally will imply different cost functions for producing car rental services. The manager's job is to choose the method that minimizes costs. Before we examine how to determine the best method of acquiring a given type of input, it is useful to provide a broad overview of these three methods of acquiring inputs.

Purchase the Inputs Using Spot Exchange

spot exchange
An informal relationship between a buyer and seller in which neither party is obligated to adhere to specific terms for exchange.

One method of acquiring inputs is to use spot exchange. **Spot exchange** occurs when the buyer and seller of an input meet, exchange, and then go their separate ways. If the manager of a car rental company simply takes a car to one of many firms that provide automobile servicing and pays for the services, the manager has used spot exchange to obtain automobile servicing. With the spot exchange, buyers and sellers essentially are "anonymous"; the parties may make an exchange without even knowing each other's names, and there is no formal (legal) relationship between buyer and seller.

A key advantage of acquiring inputs with spot exchange is that the firm gets to specialize in doing what it does best: converting the inputs into output. The input manufacturer specializes in what it does best: producing inputs. Spot exchange often is used when inputs are "standardized." In that case, one simply purchases the desired input from one of many suppliers that will sell the input.

Acquire Inputs Under a Contract

contract
A formal relationship between a buyer and seller that obligates the buyer and seller to exchange at terms specified in a legal document.

A **contract** is a legal document that creates an extended relationship between a particular buyer and seller of an input. It specifies the terms under which they agree to exchange over a given time horizon, say, three years. For example, the manager of a car rental firm might choose to formalize her relationship with a particular firm that services automobiles by signing a contract. Such a contract specifies the range of services covered, the price of each service, and the hours during which the cars will be serviced. As long as the service requirements for the automobiles are understood beforehand, the parties can address all the important issues in the written contract. However, if the number of services needed during the term of the contract is very large, or if some types of unanticipated breakdowns occur, the contract may be incomplete. A contract is incomplete if, for example, a car needs a new transmission and the contract does not specify the price at which the servicing firm will provide this service. Of course, this opens the door to a dispute between the two parties regarding the price of the service needed but not spelled out in the contract.

By acquiring inputs with contracts, the purchasing firm enjoys the benefits of specializing in what it does best, because the other firm actually produces the inputs the purchasing firm needs. This method of obtaining inputs works well when it is relatively easy to write a contract that describes the characteristics of the inputs needed. One key disadvantage of contracts is that they are costly to write; it takes time, and often legal fees, to draw up a contract that specifies precisely the obligations of both parties. Also, it can be extremely difficult to cover all of the contingencies that could occur in the future. Thus, in complex contracting environments, contracts will necessarily be incomplete.

Produce the Inputs Internally

Finally, a manager may choose to produce the inputs needed for production within the firm. In this situation the manager of the car rental company dispenses with outside service firms entirely. She sets up a facility to service the automobile fleet with her own employees as service personnel. The firm thus bypasses the service market completely and does the work itself. When a firm shuns other suppliers and chooses to produce an input internally, it has engaged in **vertical integration**.

vertical integration
A situation where a firm produces the inputs required to make its final product.

With vertical integration, however, a firm loses the gains in specialization it would realize were the inputs purchased from an independent supplier. Moreover, the firm now has to manage the production of inputs as well as the production of the final product produced with those inputs. This leads to the bureaucratic costs associated with a larger organization. On the other hand, by producing the inputs it needs internally, the firm no longer has to rely on other firms to provide the desired inputs.

Demonstration PROBLEM 6–1

Determine whether the following transactions involve spot exchange, a contract, or vertical integration:

1. Clone 1 PC is legally obligated to purchase 300 computer chips each year for the next three years from AMI. The price paid in the first year is $200 per chip, and the price rises during the second and third years by the same percentage by which the wholesale price index rises during those years.
2. Clone 2 PC purchased 300 computer chips from a firm that ran an advertisement in the back of a computer magazine.
3. Clone 3 PC manufactures its own motherboards and computer chips for its personal computers.

Answer

1. Clone 1 PC is using a contract to purchase its computer chips.
2. Clone 2 PC used spot exchange to acquire its chips.
3. Clone 3 PC uses vertical integration to obtain its chips and motherboards.

Transaction Costs

transaction costs
Costs associated with acquiring an input that are in excess of the amount paid to the input supplier.

When a firm acquires an input, it may incur costs that are in excess of the actual amount paid to the input supplier. These costs are known as **transaction costs** and play a crucial role in the determination of optimal input procurement.

The transaction costs of acquiring an input are the costs of locating a seller of the input, negotiating a price at which the input will be purchased, and putting the input to use. Transaction costs include:

1. The cost of searching for a supplier willing to sell a given input.
2. The costs of negotiating a price at which the input will be purchased. These costs may be in terms of the opportunity cost of time, legal fees, and so forth.
3. Other investments and expenditures required to facilitate exchange.

Many transaction costs are obvious. For example, if an input supplier charges a price of $10 per unit but requires you to furnish your own trucks and drivers to pick up the input, the transaction costs to your firm include the cost of the trucks and the personnel needed to "deliver" the input to your plant. Clearly, the relevant price of the input to your firm includes not only the $10 per unit but also the transaction costs of getting the input to your plant.

Some important transaction costs, however, are less obvious. To understand these "hidden" transaction costs, we must distinguish between transaction costs that are specific to a particular trading relationship and those that are general in nature. The key to this distinction is the notion of a specialized investment. A **specialized investment** is simply an investment in a particular exchange that cannot be recovered in another trading relationship. For example, suppose that to ascertain the quality of bolts, it is necessary to spend $100 on a machine that tests the bolts' strength. If the machine is useful only for testing a particular manufacturer's bolts and the investment in the machine is a sunk (and therefore nonrecoverable) cost, it is a specialized investment. In contrast, if the machine can be resold at its purchase price or used to test the quality of bolts produced by other firms, it does not represent a specialized investment.

specialized investment
An expenditure that must be made to allow two parties to exchange but has little or no value in any alternative use.

relationship-specific exchange
A type of exchange that occurs when the parties to a transaction have made specialized investments.

When specialized investments are required to facilitate an exchange, the resulting relationship between the parties is known as a **relationship-specific exchange**. The distinguishing feature of relationship-specific exchange is that the two parties are "tied together" because of the specific investments made to facilitate exchange between them. As we will see, this feature often creates transaction costs due to the sunk nature of the specific investments.

Types of Specialized Investments

Before we examine how specialized investments affect transaction costs and the optimal method of acquiring inputs, it is important to recognize that specialized investments occur in many forms. Common examples of different types of specialized investments are provided next.

Site Specificity

Site specificity occurs when the buyer and the seller of an input must locate their plants close to each other to be able to engage in exchange. For example, electric power plants often locate close to a particular coal mine to minimize the transportation costs of obtaining coal; the output (electricity) is less expensive to ship than the input (coal). The cost of building the two plants close to each other represents a specialized investment that would have little value if the parties were not involved in exchange.

Physical-Asset Specificity

Physical-asset specificity refers to a situation where the capital equipment needed to produce an input is designed to meet the needs of a particular buyer and cannot be readily adapted to produce inputs needed by other buyers. For example, if producing a lawn mower engine requires a special machine that is useful only for producing engines for a particular buyer, the machine is a specific physical asset for producing the engines.

Dedicated Assets

Dedicated assets are general investments made by a firm that allow it to exchange with a particular buyer. For example, suppose a computer manufacturer opens a new assembly line to enable it to produce enough computers for a large government purchaser. If opening the new assembly line is profitable only if the government actually purchases the firm's computers, the investment represents a dedicated asset.

Human Capital

A fourth type of specialized investment is *human capital*. In many employment relationships, workers must learn specific skills to work for a particular firm. If these skills are not useful or transferable to other employers, they represent a specialized investment.

Implications of Specialized Investments

Now that you have a broad understanding of specialized investments and relationship-specific exchange, we will consider how the presence of specialized investments can affect the transaction costs of acquiring inputs. Specialized investments increase transaction costs because they lead to (1) costly bargaining, (2) underinvestment, and (3) opportunism.

Costly Bargaining

In situations where transaction costs are low and the desired input is of uniform quality and sold by many firms, the price of the input is determined by the forces of supply and demand. When specialized investments are not required to facilitate exchange, very little time is expended negotiating a price. The scenario differs, however, if specialized investments are required to obtain the input.

Specialized investments imply that only a few parties are prepared for a trading relationship. There is no other supplier capable of providing the desired input at a moment's notice; obtaining the input the buyer needs requires making a specialized investment before the input becomes available. Consequently, there generally is no "market price" for the input; the two parties in the relationship-specific exchange bargain with each other over a price at which the input will be bought and sold. The bargaining process generally is costly, as each side employs negotiators to obtain a more favourable price. The parties may also behave strategically to enhance their bargaining positions. For example, the buyer may refuse to accept delivery to force the seller to accept a lower price. Ultimatums may be given. The supplier may reduce the quality of the input and the buyer may complain about the input's quality through company attorneys. All of these factors generate transaction costs as the two firms negotiate a price for the input.

Underinvestment

When specialized investments are required to facilitate exchange, the level of the specialized investment often is lower than the optimal level. To see this, suppose the specialized investment is human capital. To work for a particular firm, a worker must first invest his own time in learning how to perform some task. If the worker perceives that he may not work at the firm for very long (due to being laid off or accepting another job), he will not invest as heavily in learning the task as he otherwise would. For example, if you plan to transfer to another university at the end of the semester, you will not invest very heavily in learning how to use the library facilities at your present university. The investment in learning about the library facilities is an investment in human capital specific to your present university and will have little value at another university with a completely different library setup.

Similar problems exist with other types of specialized investments. For example, if an input supplier must invest in a specific machine to produce an input used by a particular buyer (physical-asset specificity), the supplier may invest in a cheaper machine that produces an input of inferior quality. This is because the supplier recognizes that the machine will not be useful if the buyer decides to purchase from another firm, in which case the supplier will be "stuck" with an expensive machine it cannot use. Thus, specialized investments may be lower than optimal, resulting in higher transaction costs because the input produced is of inferior quality.

Opportunism and the "Hold-Up Problem"

When a specialized investment must be made to acquire an input, the buyer or seller may attempt to capitalize on the "sunk" nature of the investment by engaging in *opportunism*. To be concrete, suppose the buyer of an input must make a specific investment of $10, say the cost of verifying the quality of a particular supplier's input. The manager knows there are many firms willing to sell the input at a price of $100, so she goes to one of them at random and spends $10 inspecting the input. Once she has paid this $10, the supplier attempts to take advantage of the specialized investment and behave in an opportunistic manner: it attempts to "hold up" the manager by asking for a price of $109—$9 more than the price charged by all other suppliers. Since the manager has already spent $10 inspecting this firm's input, she is better off paying the $109 than spending an additional $10 inspecting another supplier's input. After all, even if the other supplier did not engage in opportunistic behaviour, it would cost the firm $10 + $100 = $110 to inspect and purchase another supplier's input. This is the "hold-up problem": once a firm makes a specialized investment, the other party may attempt to "rob" it of its investment by taking advantage of the investment's sunk nature. This behaviour, of course, would make firms reluctant to engage in relationship-specific investments in the first place unless they can structure contracts to mitigate the hold-up problem.

In many instances, both sides in a trading relationship are required to make specialized investments, in which case both parties may engage in opportunism. For example, suppose an automaker needs crankshafts as an input for making engines. The crankshafts are a specialized input designed for use by that particular automobile manufacturer and require an investment by the producer in highly specialized capital equipment to produce them. If the crankshaft manufacturer does not sell the crankshafts to the automaker, the automaker's investment in continuing production of the engine will be effectively worthless. Similarly, if the automobile manufacturer does not buy the crankshafts, the supplier's investment in the capital equipment is likely to be wasted as well, since the equipment is not designed to serve the needs of other automobile makers. The investments made by both parties have tied them together in

InsideBUSINESS

6-1   The Cost of Using an Inefficient Method of Procuring Inputs

A recent study by Scott Masten, James Meehan, and Edward Snyder not only quantifies the transaction costs of acquiring inputs but points up the high cost to managers of using an inappropriate method to acquire an input.

Based on the procurement decisions of a naval construction firm, the study reveals that transaction costs account for roughly 14 percent of the total costs of ship construction. Thus, transaction costs are an important component of costs; managers must consider them when they make decisions.

What is the cost of not carefully considering transaction costs when deciding which method to use to acquire an input? The authors of the study report that mistaken integration—that is, producing internally a component that should have been purchased from another firm—increased transaction costs by an average of 70 percent. Subcontracting work that would have been more efficiently performed within the firm, on the other hand, raised transaction costs by almost 300 percent. The potential cost savings to a firm that chooses the best method of acquiring inputs are thus substantial.

Source: Scott Masten, James Meehan, and Edward Snyder, "The Costs of Organization," *Journal of Law, Economics and Organization* 7, Spring 1991, pp. 1–25.

relationship-specific exchange, giving each firm a potential incentive to engage in opportunistic behaviour. Once the supplier has invested in the equipment to make crankshafts, the automaker may attempt to capitalize on the sunk nature of the investment by asking for a lower price. On the other hand, once the automaker reaches the stage of production where it must have crankshafts to finish the cars, the crankshaft supplier may ask for a higher price to capitalize on the sunk investment made by the automaker. The result is that the two parties spend considerable time negotiating over precisely how much will be paid for the crankshafts, thus increasing the transaction costs of acquiring the input.

Optimal Input Procurement

Now we will examine how the manager should acquire inputs in such a way as to minimize costs. The cost-minimizing method will depend on the extent to which there is relationship-specific exchange.

Spot Exchange

The most straightforward way for a firm to obtain inputs for a production process is to use spot exchange. If there are no transaction costs and there are many buyers and sellers in the input market, the market price (say, p^*) is determined by the intersection of the supply and demand curves for the input. The manager can easily obtain the input from a supplier chosen at random by paying a price of p^* per unit of input. If any supplier attempted to charge a price greater than p^*, the manager could simply decline and purchase the input from another supplier at a price of p^*.

Why, then, would a manager ever wish to bear the expense of drafting a contract or have the firm expend resources to integrate vertically and manufacture the inputs itself? The reason is that in the presence of specialized investments, spot exchange does not insulate a buyer from opportunism, and the parties may end up spending considerable time bargaining over the price and incur substantial costs if negotiations break down. These problems will occur each time the buyer attempts to obtain additional units of the input. Also, as we noted earlier, the input purchased may be of inferior quality due to underinvestment in specialized investments needed to facilitate the exchange.

Demonstration PROBLEM 6–2

Jiffyburger, a fast-food outlet, sells approximately 8000 one-hundred-gram hamburgers in a given week. To meet that demand, Jiffyburger needs 800 kilograms of ground beef delivered to its premises every Monday morning by 8:00 a.m. sharp.

1. As the manager of a Jiffyburger franchise, what problems would you anticipate if you acquired ground beef using spot exchange?
2. As the manager of a firm that sells ground beef, what problems would you anticipate if you were to supply meat to Jiffyburger through spot exchange?

Answer

1. While ground beef for hamburgers is a relatively standardized product, the delivery of one tonne of meat to a particular store involves specialized investments (in the form of dedicated assets) on the part of both Jiffyburger and the supplier. In particular, Jiffyburger would face a hold-up problem if the supplier showed up at 8:00 a.m. and threatened not to unload the meat unless Jiffyburger paid it "ransom"; it would be difficult to find another supplier that could supply the desired quantity of meat on such short notice. The supplier may even attempt to unload meat of inferior quality. Thus, Jiffyburger is not protected from opportunism, bargaining, and underinvestment in quality when it uses spot exchange to acquire such a large quantity of ground beef.

2. By showing up at Jiffyburger at 8:00 a.m. with one tonne of meat, the supplier makes a specific investment in selling to Jiffyburger. Consequently, the supplier also is subject to a potential hold-up problem. Suppose Jiffyburger behaves opportunistically by asking 10 other suppliers to show up with a tonne of meat at 8 a.m. too. Since each supplier would rather unload its meat at a low price than let it spoil, Jiffyburger can bargain with the suppliers to get a great deal on the meat. In this case, each supplier risks selling meat at a low price or not at all, since it is not protected from opportunism by using spot exchange.

When the acquisition of an input requires substantial specialized investments, spot exchange is likely to result in high transaction costs due to opportunism, bargaining costs, and underinvestment. Clearly, managers must consider alternatives to spot exchange when inputs require substantial specialized investments.

Contracts

Given the prospect of the hold-up problem and a need to bargain over price each time an input is to be purchased, an alternative strategy is to acquire an input from a particular supplier under an appropriately structured contract. While a contract often requires substantial upfront expenditures in terms of negotiations, attorneys' fees, and the like, it offers several advantages. First, a contract can specify prices of the input before the parties make specialized investments. This feature reduces the magnitude of costly opportunism down the road. For example, if the managers in Demonstration Problem 6–2 had written a contract that specified a price and a quantity of ground beef before the specialized investments were made, they would not have been subject to the hold-up problem. Both parties would have been legally obligated to honour the contracted price and quantity.

Second, by guaranteeing an acceptable price for both parties for an extended time horizon, a contract reduces the incentive for either the buyer or the seller to skimp on the specialized investments required for the exchange. For example, a worker who has a contract that guarantees employment with a particular firm for three years will have a greater incentive to invest in human capital specific to that firm. Similarly, if the firm knows the worker will be around for three years, it will be willing to invest in more training for the worker.

Demonstration PROBLEM 6–3

In the real world, virtually all purchases involve some type of specialized investment. For instance, by driving to a particular supermarket, you invest time (and gasoline) that is valuable to you only if you purchase groceries at that supermarket. Why, then, don't consumers sign contracts with supermarkets to prevent the supermarkets from engaging in opportunism once they are inside the store?

Answer

The cost of driving to another supermarket if you are "held up" is relatively low: the cashier may be able to extract an extra few cents on a can of beans, but not much more. Thus, when specialized investments involve only small sums of money, the potential cost of being held up is very low compared to the cost of writing a contract to protect against such opportunism. It doesn't make sense to pay an attorney $200 to write a contract that would potentially save you only a few cents. Moreover, when only a small gain can be realized by engaging in opportunistic behaviour, the supermarket will likely not find it in its interest to hold up customers. If a supermarket attempts to take advantage of a customer's minuscule specialized investment, the customer can threaten to tell others not to ever shop at that store. In this instance, the extra few cents extracted from the customer would not be worth the lost future business. In essence, there is an implicit agreement between the two parties—not an agreement that is enforceable in a court of law, but one that is enforceable by consumers' future actions. Thus, when the gains from opportunistic behaviour are small compared to the costs of writing contracts, formal contracts will not emerge. However, when the gains from opportunism are sufficiently large, formal contracts are needed to prevent opportunistic behaviour.

Once the decision is made to use a contract to acquire an input, how long should the contract last? The "optimal" contract length reflects a fundamental economic tradeoff between the marginal costs and marginal benefits of extending the length of a contract. The marginal cost (MC) of extending contract length increases as contracts become longer, as illustrated in Figure 6–2. This is because as a contract gets longer, more time and money must be spent writing into the contract a larger number of increasingly hypothetical contingencies (for example, "If an Ice Age begins, the price will be . . ."). It may be easy to specify a mutually acceptable price for a contract that is to be executed tomorrow, but with a 10-year agreement it is difficult (and expensive) to write clauses that include contingencies and prices for each year of the contract. Furthermore, the longer the contract, the more locked in the buyer is to a particular seller and the greater the likelihood that some other supplier can provide the input at a lower cost in the future. In other words, the longer the contract, the less flexibility the firm has in choosing an input supplier. For these reasons, the marginal cost of contract length in Figure 6–2 is upward-sloping.

The marginal benefit (MB) of extending a contract for another year is the avoided transaction costs of opportunism and bargaining. These benefits may vary with the length of the contract, but for simplicity we have drawn a flat MB curve in Figure 6–2. The optimal contract length, L^*, is the point at which the marginal costs and marginal benefits of longer contracts are equal.

FIGURE 6–2 Optimal Contract Length

The *MC* of a contract length is upward-sloping since the longer the contract, (a) the more money and time must be spent writing a contract that can deal with a larger number of possible contingencies and (b) the less flexibility the firm has in choosing an input supplier. For simplicity, the *MB* line is horizontal and represents the marginal benefit of extending a contract for another year (that is, avoiding transaction costs of opportunism and bargaining). The optimal length is where *MC* and *MB* cross at *L** and *MC* = *MB*.

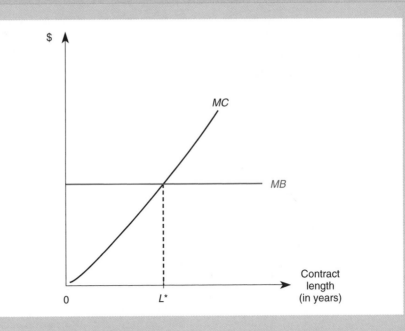

The optimal contract length will increase when the level of specialized investment required to facilitate an exchange increases. To see this, note that as specialized investments become more important, the parties face higher transaction costs once the contract expires. Since these costs can be avoided by writing longer contracts, higher levels of specialized investments increase the marginal benefit of writing longer contracts from MB^0 to MB^1 in Figure 6–3. The result is an increase in the length of the optimal contract from L_0 to L_1.

The optimal contract length also depends on factors that affect the marginal cost of writing longer contracts. As an input becomes more standardized and the future economic environment becomes more certain, the marginal cost of writing longer contracts in Figure 6–4 decreases from MC^0 to MC^1. This decrease in the complexity of the contracting environment leads to longer optimal contracts (from L_0 to L_1). In contrast, as the input becomes more complex and the future economic environment becomes more uncertain, contracts must be made more detailed. This increase in the complexity of the contracting environment increases the marginal cost of writing longer contracts from MC^0 to MC^2 in Figure 6–4. Optimal contracts, in this case, will be shorter in duration.

As the contract length shortens due to the complexity of the contracting environment, firms must continually write new contracts as existing ones expire. Considerable resources are spent on attorneys' fees and bargaining over contract terms, and because of the complex contracting environment it is not efficient to write longer contracts to reduce these costs. Faced with such a prospect, a manager may wish to use yet another method to procure a necessary input: have the firm integrate vertically and make the input itself.

FIGURE 6–3 Specialized Investments and Contract Length

MB^0 shifts up to MB^1 due to a greater need for specialized investments. Transaction costs can be avoided with longer contracts; therefore, the MB of writing longer contracts shifts up. The increase in the length of the contract is seen by the shift from L_0 to L_1.

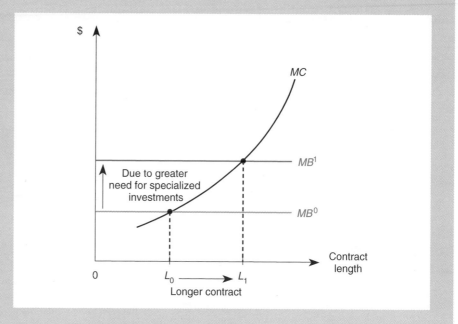

FIGURE 6–4 Contracting Environment and Contract Length

As an input becomes more standardized and the future economic environment becomes more certain, the MC of writing longer contracts decreases from MC^0 to MC^1. This increases the length of the contract from L_0 to L_1. Conversely, as an input becomes more complex and the future economic environment becomes more uncertain, the MC of writing longer contracts moves from MC^0 to MC^2, causing contracts to be shorter in duration.

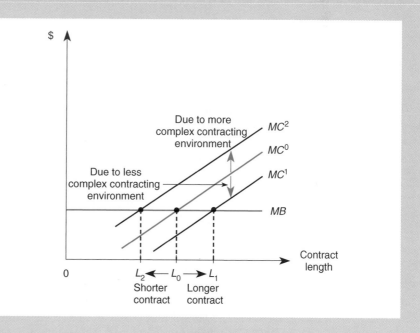

InsideBUSINESS

6-2 Factors Affecting the Length of Coal and Natural-Gas Contracts

Two studies have examined how specialized investments and the contracting environment affect the length of contracts. Paul Joskow studied the effect of specialized investments on the length of contracts between coal mines and electric utilities. As the importance of specialized investments increases, transaction costs due to opportunism and bargaining rise, and longer contracts are desirable. Joskow found that site specificity (the need for the utilities to locate close to the coal mine) increased the length of the contracts by an average of 12 years. Joskow also found that the degree of physical-asset specificity affected contract length. Since each generation facility uses equipment designed to burn a specific type of coal, plants designed to burn low-energy, low-sulfur western coal were tightly tied to their suppliers because there were few transportation alternatives. Plants designed to use high-energy, high-sulfur eastern coal, on the other hand, could purchase from numerous sources. Because physical-asset specificity is more pronounced in transactions involving western coal, the average contract for western coal was 11 years longer than contracts for eastern coal.

Keith Crocker and Scott Masten examined how changes in the contracting environment affected the length of contracts between owners of natural-gas wells and owners of natural-gas pipelines. Historically, these contracts were long in duration due to the specialized investments involved in laying pipes and drilling wells. During the early 1970s, however, two factors affected the cost of writing contracts. First, price controls placed on natural-gas sales by the government induced pipelines to try to compensate well owners in nonprice terms of the contracts, such as agreeing to accept delivery of the gas when they preferred not to. These nonprice agreements made contracts less efficient and increased the costs of being bound by a contract. The result was that price controls reduced contract length by an average of 14 years. Second, the increased uncertainty in the natural-gas market caused by the Arab oil embargo raised the cost of writing contracts and reduced contract length by an additional three years.

Sources: Paul Joskow, "Contract Duration and Relationship-Specific Investments: Empirical Evidence from Coal Markets," *American Economic Review* 77, March 1987, pp. 168–85; Keith Crocker and Scott Masten, "Mitigating Contractual Hazards: Unilateral Options and Contract Length," *Rand Journal of Economics* 19, Autumn 1988, pp. 327–43.

Vertical Integration

When specialized investments generate transaction costs (due to opportunism, bargaining costs, or underinvestment), and when the product being purchased is extremely complex or the economic environment is plagued by uncertainty, complete contracts will be extremely costly or even impossible to write. The only choice left is for the firm to set up a facility to produce the input internally. This process is referred to as *vertical integration* because it entails the firm moving farther up the production stream toward increasingly basic inputs. For example, most automobile manufacturers make their own fenders from sheet steel and plastics, having vertically integrated up the production stream from automobile assembly to the fabrication of body parts.

The advantage of vertical integration is that the firm "skips the middleman" by producing its own inputs. This reduces opportunism by uniting previously distinct firms into divisions of a single, integrated firm. While this strategy might seem desirable in general, because it mitigates transaction costs by eliminating the market, this approach has some disadvantages as well. Managers must replace the discipline of the market with an internal regulatory mechanism, a formidable task to anyone familiar with the failure of central planning often encountered in nonmarket economies. In addition, the firm must bear the cost of setting up production facilities for producing a product that, at best, may be tangentially related to the firm's main line of business; the firm no longer specializes in doing what it does best. Because of these difficulties, vertical integration should be viewed as a last resort, undertaken only when spot exchange or contracts have failed.

Inside BUSINESS

6-3 Vertical Integration and Competition in Canada's Television Industry

Government regulations often have unintended consequences. This is true for competition levels in Canada. Consider the ramifications of the government's regulations on vertical integration in the television industry for Alliance Atlantis.

The Canadian Radio-television and Telecommunications Commission's directive on vertical integration is fairly simple: eight hours of Canadian "priority" programming during "peak" viewing hours must be aired per week. Seventy-five percent of this content must be purchased from "independent" production houses not affiliated with Canadian television companies. Thus, the opportunity for such stations as CTV and Global to produce their own material is limited to 25 percent of what they air—a situation hardly conducive to cost-effective vertical integration.

However, this situation is very lucrative for Alliance Atlantis. As Canada's largest vertically integrated entertainment company, with independent production house operations and cable television shows, it has the widest assortment of content to sell to both CTV and Global, as well as other Canadian stations. Additionally, Alliance owns such "specialty" or cable television stations as Food Network Canada, Showcase, Life Network, and National Geographic Channel, on which it airs a steady stream of Alliance-produced material.

In theory, vertical integration can produce market failures because it stifles creative competition. When networks commission programs from non-affiliated producers, they create a competitive market that allows networks to select the best shows. Conversely, when a TV network is affiliated with a producer, it can find itself captive to a quasi-monopoly market driven by the nonoptimal logic of self-dealing. The upshot is that the current regulations governing vertical integration tend to hamper the ability of general-access channels such as CTV and Global, given their limited air time, to produce shows whose costs compete with those faced by Alliance Atlantis.

Source: Adapted from: Matthew Fraser, "The Benefits and Threats of Vertical Integration: TV Producer Alliance Atlantis Faces Both," *National Post*, August 7, 2001, available <209.47 .161.50/articles/NationalPost/np010807-2.htm>, accessed June 19, 2004; additional material at allianceatlantis.com.

The Economic Tradeoff

The cost-minimizing method of acquiring an input depends on the characteristics of the input. Whether a manager chooses spot exchange or an alternative method such as a contract or vertical integration depends on the importance of the specialized investments that lead to relationship-specific exchange. The basic questions involved are illustrated in Figure 6–5.

When the desired input does not involve specialized investments, the firm can use spot exchange to obtain the input without concern for opportunism and bargaining costs. By purchasing the input from a supplier, the firm can specialize in doing what it does best rather than spending money writing contracts or engaging in vertical integration.

When substantial specialized investments are required to facilitate exchange, managers should think twice about using spot exchange to purchase inputs. Specialized investments lead to opportunism, bargaining costs, and underinvestment, and these transaction costs of using spot exchange often can be reduced by using some other method to acquire an input. When the contracting environment is simple and the cost of writing a contract is less than the transaction costs associated with spot exchange, it is optimal to acquire the input through a contract. In this case, the optimal contract length is determined by the intersection of the marginal cost and marginal benefits of writing a longer contract, as we illustrated previously in Figure 6–2.

Finally, when substantial specialized investments are required and the desired input has complex characteristics that are difficult to specify in a contract, or when it is very costly to write into the contract all of the clauses needed to protect the parties

FIGURE 6-5 Optimal Procurement of Inputs

When the desired input does not involve specialized investments, the firm can use spot exchange to obtain the input. When substantial specialized investments are required to facilitate exchange, and the contracting environment is simple, it is optimal to acquire the input through a contract. Alternatively, if the desired input has complex characteristics difficult to specify in a contract, a firm should integrate vertically to minimize the cost of acquiring inputs needed for production.

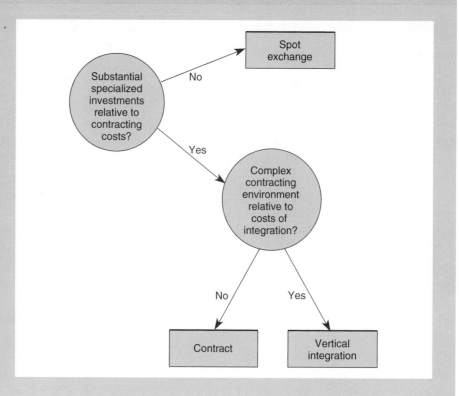

from changes in future conditions, the manager should integrate vertically to minimize the cost of acquiring inputs needed for production—provided the costs of integration are not too high. In this instance, the firm produces the input internally. The firm no longer specializes in doing what it does best, but the elimination of opportunism, bargaining, and underinvestment more than makes up for lack of specialization.

Demonstration PROBLEM 6–4

Big Bird Air is legally obligated to purchase 50 jet engines from ERUS at the end of two years at a price of $200 000 per engine. Confident that it is protected from opportunism with this contract, Big Bird begins making aircraft bodies designed to fit ERUS's engines. Due to unforeseen events in the aerospace industry, in the second year of the contract ERUS is on the brink of bankruptcy. It tells Big Bird that unless it increases the engine price to $300 000, it will go bankrupt.

1. What should the manager of Big Bird Air do?
2. How could this problem have been avoided?
3. Did the manager of Big Bird Air use the wrong method of acquiring inputs?

Answer

1. Big Bird is experiencing a hold-up problem because of an incomplete contract; the contract did not specify what would happen if ERUS went belly up. ERUS claims it

will go bankrupt if Big Bird does not pay a price of $300 000 for the engines, in which case Big Bird will lose its specialized investment in aircraft bodies. The manager should verify that ERUS is indeed on the brink of bankruptcy. If not, Big Bird can take ERUS to court if ERUS does not honour the contract price. If ERUS is on the verge of bankruptcy, the manager should determine how much it would cost to obtain engines from another supplier versus making them within the firm. Once the manager knows the cost of each alternative, Big Bird may wish to bargain with ERUS over how much more it will pay for the engines. This could be risky, however; the lower the price negotiated, the greater the chance ERUS will go bankrupt. New clauses must be put into the contract to protect Big Bird against ERUS' bankruptcy. The manager should especially guard against attempts by ERUS to reduce the quality of the engines in an attempt to save money. In any event, Big Bird should not spend more money drawing up a new contract and paying for ERUS' engines than it would cost to obtain them from the best alternative source.

2. This problem illustrates that when contracts are incomplete, unanticipated events can occur that lead to costly bargaining and opportunism. The problem could have been avoided had Big Bird written clauses into the contract that protected it against ERUS' going bankrupt. If this was not possible, it could have vertically integrated and produced its own engines.

3. Big Bird's manager did not necessarily choose the wrong method of acquiring engines. If it was not possible (or would have been extremely costly) to write into the initial contract protection against ERUS' going bankrupt, and if the costs of vertically integrating would exceed the likely costs of opportunism due to an incomplete contract, the manager made the correct decision at the time. Sometimes bad things happen even when managers make good decisions. If this was not the case, either a more complete contract should have been written or Big Bird should have decided to make its own engines.

Managerial Compensation and the Principal-Agent Problem

You now know the principal factors in selecting the best method of acquiring inputs. Our remaining task in this chapter is to explain how to compensate labour inputs to ensure that they put forth their "best" effort. After completing this section you will better understand why restaurants rely on tips to compensate employees, why secretaries usually are paid an hourly wage, and even why textbook authors are paid royalties. We will begin, however, by examining managerial compensation.

One characteristic of many large firms is the separation of ownership and control: the owners of the firm often are distantly located stockholders, and the firm is run on a day-to-day basis by a manager. The fact that the firm's owners are not physically present to monitor the manager creates a fundamental incentive problem. Suppose the owners pay the manager a salary of $50 000 per year to manage the firm. Since the owners cannot monitor the manager's effort, if the firm has lost $1 million by year's end, they will not know whether the fault lies with the manager or with bad luck. Uncertainty regarding whether low profits are due to low demand or to low effort by the manager makes it difficult for the owners to determine precisely why profits are low. Even if the fault lies with the manager—perhaps he or she never showed up at the plant but instead took an extended fishing trip—the manager can claim it was just a "bad year." The manager might say, "You should be very glad you hired me as your manager. Had I not worked 18-hour days, your company would have lost twice the amount it did. I was lucky to keep our loss to its current level, but I am confident things will improve next year when our new product line hits the

InsideBUSINESS

6-4 The Evolution of Input Decisions in the Automobile Industry

An interesting account of a firm moving from spot exchange to a long-term contractual relationship and finally to vertical integration is provided by the General Motors–Fisher Body relationship, which has been extensively documented by Benjamin Klein. In the early part of the century, car bodies were primarily open, wooden structures built by craftspeople with fairly general skills. Thus specialized investments were relatively unimportant, and General Motors bought the bodies for its cars using spot exchange.

As the automobile industry developed, it became apparent that closed metal bodies would be a superior method of manufacturing cars. This finding, however, introduced a high degree of physical-asset specificity because it required investment in very specialized machines to stamp out the body parts. To constrain opportunism, General Motors and Fisher Body signed a 10-year contract that set the price of the car bodies and obligated General Motors to purchase all of its closed metal car bodies from Fisher Body.

Initially this agreement worked well enough to permit the parties to make the necessary specialized investments. But as time went on, it became clear that the original agreement was not nearly complete, leaving numerous opportunities for the parties to engage in opportunism. For example, the pricing formula contained in the contract permitted Fisher Body to receive a 17.6 percent profit on labour and transportation costs. This encouraged Fisher to produce with inefficient labour-intensive technologies in remotely located plants and pass on the costs of inefficiency to General Motors.

In retrospect, it appears that both General Motors and Fisher Body underestimated the difficulty of writing a contract to govern their relationship. Rather than spend time and money writing a more detailed contract, the problem was solved in 1926 when General Motors vertically integrated by purchasing Fisher Body.

Source: Benjamin Klein, "Vertical Integration as Organizational Ownership: The Fisher Body–General Motors Relationship Revisited," *Journal of Law, Economics and Organization* 4, Spring 1988, pp. 199–213. For an alternative view suggesting that the merger was motivated out of a desire to improve coordination of production and inventories, to assure GM of adequate supplies of auto bodies, and to provide GM with access to the executive talents of the Fisher brothers, see Ramon Casadesus-Masanell and Daniel F. Spulber, "The Fable of Fisher Body," *Journal of Law and Economics* 43, April 2000, pp. 67–104.

market." Since the owners are not present at the firm, they will not know the true reason for the low profits.

By creating a firm, an owner enjoys the benefits of reduced transaction costs. But when ownership is separated from control, the *principal-agent problem* emerges. This is because there are asymmetries of information due to either hidden information (*moral hazard*) or hidden actions (*adverse selection*) and the preferences of the agent are not identical to those of the principal. These concepts are explored extensively in Chapter 12. If the owner is not present to monitor the manager, how can she get the manager to do what is in her best interest?

The essence of the problem is that the manager likes to earn income, but he also likes to consume leisure. Clearly, if the manager spent every waking hour on the job, he would be unable to consume any leisure. But the less time he spends on the job, the more time he has for ball games, fishing trips, and other activities that he values. The job description indicates that the manager is supposed to spend eight hours per day on the job. The important question, from the owner's point of view, is how much leisure (*shirking*) the manager will consume while on the job. Shirking may take the form of excessive coffee breaks, long lunch hours, leaving work early, or, in the extreme case, not showing up on the job at all. Note that while the manager enjoys shirking, the owner wants the manager to work hard to enhance profits.

When the manager is offered a fixed salary of $50 000 and the owner is not physically present at the workplace, he will receive the same $50 000 regardless of

	TABLE 6-1	Managerial Earnings and Firm Profits Under a Fixed Salary		
Manager's Earnings	**Hours Worked by Manager**	**Hours Shirked by Manager**	**Profits of Firm**
$50 000	8	0	$3 000 000
50 000	7	1	2 950 000
50 000	6	2	2 800 000
50 000	5	3	2 500 000
50 000	4	4	2 000 000
50 000	3	5	1 800 000
50 000	2	6	1 300 000
50 000	1	7	700 000
50 000	0	8	0

whether he works a full eight hours (hence, doesn't shirk) or spends the entire day at home (shirks eight hours). This situation is illustrated in Table 6–1. From the point of view of the owner, the fixed salary does not give the manager a strong incentive to monitor the other employees, and this has an adverse effect on the firm's profits. For example, as Table 6–1 shows, if the manager spends the entire day on the job monitoring the other employees (that is, making sure that they put out maximum effort), shirking is zero and the firm's profits are $3 million. If the manager spends the entire day shirking, profits are zero. If the manager shirks two hours and thus works six hours, the firm's profits are $2.8 million. Since the fixed salary of $50 000 provides the manager with the same income regardless of his effort level, he has a strong incentive to shirk eight hours. In this case the profits of the firm are zero but the manager still earns $50 000.

How can the owner of the firm get the manager to spend time monitoring the production process? You might think if she paid the manager a higher salary, the manager would work harder. But this will not work when the owner cannot observe the manager's effort; the employment contract is such that there is absolutely no cost to the manager of shirking. Many managers would prefer to earn money without having to work for it, and such a contract allows this manager to do just that.

Suppose the owner of the firm offers the manager the following *incentive contract:* the manager is to receive 10 percent of profits (gross of managerial compensation) earned by the firm. Table 6–2 summarizes the implications of such a contract. Note that if the manager spends eight hours shirking, profits are zero and the manager

	TABLE 6-2	Managerial Earnings and Firm Profits with Profit Sharing		
Hours Worked by Manager	**Hours Shirked by Manager**	**Gross Profits for Firm (π)**	**Manager's Share of Profits (0.10 × π)**
8	0	$3 000 000	$300 000
7	1	2 950 000	295 000
6	2	2 800 000	280 000
5	3	2 500 000	250 000
4	4	2 000 000	200 000
3	5	1 800 000	180 000
2	6	1 300 000	130 000
1	7	700 000	70 000
0	8	0	0

Inside BUSINESS

6–5 The Principal-Agent Problem: The Case of Enron

In 2001, Enron, the United States' seventh-largest corporation in terms of revenue, declared bankruptcy owing more than $5 billion and lacking the ability to pay the interest on that debt.

Enron was an energy trading company. It bought electricity, oil, natural gas, gasoline, and other energy sources from producers, with the intent of reselling it to industrial companies and utilities. It made money by "buying low and selling high." It did this rather well for several years during the 1990s. Later it started getting into sideline businesses such as the buying and selling of bandwidth for the Internet.

"Buying low and selling high" is always good business practice, but it is hard to sustain because economic profit always induces entry (that is, new competition) especially when there are few barriers. Enron had few competitors in this industry in the early 1990s, but when other companies saw that profits were achievable in this arena, they jumped in. With no barriers against getting into the arena, Dynegy Inc., Reliant Energy, El Paso Energy, Duke Energy North American, and Calpine Corp. joined the competition, and they raided Enron for valued employees who knew the game. Had this been the end of the story, there would not have been much of one. It would have been the typical "company has idea, milks it for as long as it can, and then settles in for a run of normal profits."

What happened with Enron was that its management wanted to keep things going and its executives were paid almost exclusively in stock and stock options. One of the classic problems in corporate capitalism is called the principal-agent problem, a problem that occurs when the owners of the company (the shareholders) are motivated by long-term profitability for the company and the managers are motivated by monetary gain for themselves. When chief executive officers (CEOs) are paid high salaries they may avoid potentially lucrative business avenues that might be accompanied by some level of risk. The problem is that the agent, in this case the CEO, is not making decisions consistent with the principals', in this case the stockholders', wishes. The primary concern in this example of the principal-agent problem is that salaried CEOs will avoid risking their jobs and will err on the side of caution.

For years it has been taken on faith that the best way for stockholders to get the CEO to do their bidding was to tie the CEO's compensation to stock performance. One version of this has the CEO paid only in stock. Thus, when stock prices are low the CEO is paid less than when the stock price is high.

An extreme version of this scheme is in place when management is paid in stock options. Stock options are authorizations that allow those who hold them to buy a specific number of shares of stock at the price stated on the option. They are enormously valuable when the stock price is above the option price but have no value when the underlying stock price is below the option price. Enron's

earns nothing. But if the manager does not shirk at all, the firm earns $3 million in gross profits and the manager receives compensation equal to 10 percent of those profits: $300 000.

Exactly what the manager does under the profit-sharing compensation scheme depends on his preferences for leisure and money. But one thing is clear: if the manager wants to earn income, he cannot shirk the entire day. The manager faces a trade-off: he can consume more leisure on the job, but at a cost of lower compensation. For example, suppose the manager has carefully evaluated the tradeoff between leisure on the job and income in Table 6–2 and wishes to earn $250 000. He can achieve this by working five hours instead of shirking all day. What is the impact of the profit-sharing plan on the owner of the firm? The manager has decided to work five hours to earn $250 000 in compensation. The five hours of managerial effort generate $2.5 million in gross profits for the firm. Thus, by making managerial compensation dependent on performance, the gross profits for the owner rise from zero (under the fixed-salary arrangement) to $2.5 million. Note that even after deducting the manager's compensation, the owner ends up with a hefty $2 500 000 − $250 000 = $2.25 million in profits. The performance bonus has increased not only the manager's earnings, but the owner's net profits.

compensation package for its managers were a combination of stocks and options.

Enron's management compensation was thus tied to stock performance, and in the eyes of Enron shareholders, this was good. It unfortunately also put management in the position that if it could deceive the markets into thinking it was doing better than it actually was, management might enrich itself. This is not new. It is the primary reason accounting firms exist. They are supposed to guard against such deception by going over corporate financial statements to certify to the public that when a company says it earned $1 billion, it actually did.

Enron's deception took the form of high debt (off the books) and gambles. Enron created several subsidiaries, named, for whatever reason, for *Star Wars* characters, and it saddled each with millions in debt. Each subsidiary had a high-risk, high-return niche market. None of this would be interesting except for the fact that the debt of these firms was secured by assets of the larger corporation. That in turn would not be interesting except that this debt was deceptively noted in Enron financial statements. Enron would state that it was owed money by other companies; it would report this as an asset but would not mention that it was also a debt. Even more troubling was that the smaller subsidiaries would borrow from banks to pay Enron the interest, thus raising Enron's reported profits. In the final analysis, Enron was overstating its profits by $1.2 billion and its assets by even more.

When the whole thing collapsed in the fall of 2001, there were two fatally wounded companies: Enron and its accounting firm Arthur Andersen. Andersen had certified Enron's books to be accurate when they demonstrably were not. It had participated in the creation of the subsidiaries and had gone along with the attempt to cover things up by issuing a reminder to employees working on the Enron account to shred "unneeded" documents. Though this "reminder" was technically a simple restatement of company policy, everyone at Andersen who worked on the Enron case knew that it meant to shred the evidence. Why would an accounting firm participate in such fraud? It again boils down to the principal-agent problem. The lead accountant in any firm wants to please his or her clients. The clients pay the firms millions in fees per year for which the lead accountants are handsomely rewarded. The principal, the accounting firm, must trust the action of its agent, the lead accountant. Their interests are sometimes at odds because the accounting firm is worthless without a reputation for honesty. That reputation was effectively sold by the lead accountant without Andersen's knowledge or consent. The upshot of all this is that Andersen may well be destroyed by the actions of its lead accountant in the Enron case.

Source: James Surowiecki, "Shredders Through the Ages," The Financial Page, *The New Yorker*, February 2002.

Forces That Discipline Managers

Incentive Contracts

Typically the chief executive officer of a corporation receives stock options and other bonuses directly related to profits. It may be tempting to argue that a CEO who earns over $1 million per year is receiving excessive compensation. What is important, however, is *how* the executive earns the $1 million. If the earnings are due largely to a performance bonus, it could be a big mistake to reduce the executive's compensation. This point is important, because the media often imply that it is unfair to heavily reward CEOs of major corporations. Remember, however, that performance-based rewards benefit stockholders as well as CEOs, and reducing such rewards may result in declining profits for the firm.

Demonstration PROBLEM 6-5

You are attending the annual stockholders' meeting of PIC Company. A fellow shareholder points out that the manager of PIC earned $100 000 last year, while the manager of a rival firm, CUP Enterprises, earned only $50 000. A motion is made to lower the salary of PIC's manager. Given only this information, what should you do?

Answer

There is not enough information to make an informed decision about the appropriate way to vote; you should ask for additional information. If none is forthcoming, you should move to table the motion until shareholders can obtain additional information about such things as the profits and sales of the two firms, how much of each manager's earnings is due to profit sharing and performance bonuses, and the like. Explain to the other shareholders that the optimal contract will reward the manager for high profits; if PIC's manager's high earnings are due to a huge performance bonus paid because of high profits, eliminating the bonus would not be prudent. On the other hand, if CUP's manager has generated larger profits for that firm than your manager has for PIC, you may wish to adjust your manager's contract to reflect incentives similar to those of the rival firm or even attempt to hire CUP's manager to work for PIC.

External Incentives

The preceding analysis focused on factors within the firm that provide the manager with an incentive to maximize profits. In addition, forces outside the firm often provide managers with an incentive to maximize profits.

Reputation

Managers have increased job mobility when they can demonstrate to other firms that they have the managerial skills needed to maximize profits. It is costly to be an effective manager; many hours must be spent supervising workers and planning production outlays. These costs represent an investment by the manager in a reputation for being an excellent manager. In the long run, this reputation can be sold at a premium in the market for managers, where other firms compete for the right to hire the best managers. Thus, even when the employment contract does not explicitly include a performance bonus, a manager may choose to do a good job of running the firm if he or she wishes to work for another firm at some future date.

Takeovers

Another external force that provides managers with an incentive to maximize profits is the threat of a takeover. If a manager is not operating the firm in a profit-maximizing manner, investors will attempt to buy the firm and replace management with new managers who will. By installing a better manager, the firm's profits will rise and the value of the firm's stock will increase. Thus, one cost to a manager of doing a poor job of running the firm is the increased likelihood of a takeover. To avoid paying this cost, managers will work harder than they otherwise would, even if they are paid only a fixed salary.

The Manager-Worker Principal-Agent Problem

When we introduced the principal-agent problem, the owner of the firm was viewed as having different objectives from the manager. There is nothing special about the owner-manager relationship that gives rise to the principal-agent problem; indeed, there is a similar problem between the manager and the employees she or he supervises.

To see this, suppose the manager is being paid a fraction of profits and thus has an incentive to increase the firm's profits. The manager cannot be in several places at

InsideBUSINESS

6-6 Compensation in Fast-Food Restaurants

About 30 percent of firms in the fast-food industry are owned by the company, and 70 percent are franchised to owner-operators. The owner-operator's income is entirely derived from the profitability of the individual store. Typically the franchising parent requires the owner-operator to be in residence. The franchise owner receives profits, less a franchise fee, as remuneration.

In contrast, the manager of a company-owned store is usually paid a flat fee for managing a restaurant. This leads the manager to have less incentive to lower employee costs and other operating expenses. The manager whose income is not tied to profits also has less incentive to ensure high sales. Given that the income of a franchise manager is directly tied to profits whereas the income of the manager of the company-owned store is not, we would expect profits to be lower in company-owned stores. Company-owned stores also would face higher employee wages and less effective supervision of employees.

Alan B. Kruger provides some interesting insights into the relationship between employees and managers in the fast-food industry. As the table here shows, employees subjectively rate managers in company-owned stores as less effective than those in franchise-owned stores. Company-owned crew workers and franchise crew members earn roughly the same hourly wages; thus, the positive evaluations of franchise managers would not appear to be due to differentials in pay.

Historically, profitability is higher in franchised stores than in the company-owned stores. A 1967 survey showed that stores changing from franchise ownership to company ownership experienced a drop in profitability from 9.5 percent to 1.8 percent. It is clear why so many fast-food chains franchise their restaurants. Franchising mitigates the principal-agent problem by making managers' compensation dependent on profitability; thus, more profits are made than would otherwise be the case.

Employee Evaluation of Supervision in Company-Owned and Franchised Restaurants

Employee Evaluation of Manager	Proportion of Employees Agreeing (standard deviations in parentheses)	
	Company-Owned	Franchise-Owned
Manager provides adequate supervision to workers	0.326 (0.010)	0.452 (0.014)
Assistant manager provides adequate supervision to workers	0.332 (0.010)	0.405 (0.013)
Supervisor provides adequate supervision to workers	0.360 (0.011)	0.468 (0.014)

Source: Data based on Alan B. Kruger, "Ownership, Agency, and Wages: An Examination of Franchising in the Fast-Food Industry," *Quarterly Journal of Economics* 106, February 1991, pp. 75–102.

---

the same time and thus cannot monitor every worker even if he or she wanted to. The workers, on the other hand, would just as soon gossip and drink coffee as work. How can the manager (the principal) induce the workers (the agents) not to shirk?

Solutions to the Manager-Worker Principal-Agent Problem

profit sharing
Mechanism used to enhance workers' efforts that involves tying compensation to the underlying profitability of the firm.

Profit Sharing

One mechanism the manager can use to enhance workers' efforts is **profit sharing**—making the workers' compensation dependent on the underlying profitability of the firm. By offering workers compensation that is tied to underlying profitability, an incentive is provided for workers to put forth more effort.

revenue sharing
Mechanism used to enhance workers' efforts that involves linking compensation to the underlying revenues of the firm.

Revenue Sharing

Another mechanism for inducing greater effort by workers is **revenue sharing**—linking compensation to the underlying revenues of the firm. Examples of this type of incentive scheme include tips and sales commissions. Food servers usually receive a

InsideBUSINESS

6-7 Paying for Performance

A recent study by Edward Lazear on the employment practices of the Safelite Glass Corporation documents the importance of properly structuring incentives. The company's average output per worker increased by almost 50 percent when it changed compensation from an hourly wage to a piece-rate system. Moreover, the average worker's pay increased by about 10 percent under piece-rate compensation. By more closely aligning the incentives of workers and the firm, both the firm and its employees benefited from the change.

Pay-for-performance contracts are most effective in environments where a worker's responsibilities are clearly identified and each worker's output is objectively measured. They are least effective when the measurement of individual effort is garbled or when it is not possible to write a contract to control important aspects of worker behaviour. For instance, the usual benefits of pay-for-performance are mitigated when the production process requires a team of workers. In this case, workers may "shirk" in anticipation of being able to "piggyback" on other employees' hard work (this behaviour is called "free riding" in the economics literature). Likewise, when contracts are incomplete, high-powered contracts may lead to dysfunctional behaviour. For example, workers may focus exclusively on those aspects of their jobs where performance is rewarded.

For these reasons, the optimality and prevalence of high-powered incentive schemes like piece-rate systems vary across different types of occupations. As the table here shows, piece-rate pay is more common in occupations where output is clearly measurable and quality is relatively unimportant (such as farm labour). It is much less common when quality is important or difficult to objectively measure.

The Percentage of Young Workers Paid a Piece Rate in Selected Occupations

Occupation	Percentage Paid a Piece Rate
Farm labour	16.7
Craftsmen	3.6
Clerical	1.3
Managers	0.9

Sources: Edward P. Lazear, "Performance Pay and Productivity," *American Economic Review*, December 2000, pp. 1346–61; Canice Prendergast, "The Provision of Incentives in Firms," *Journal of Economic Literature*, March 1999, pp. 7–63.

very low wage, plus tips. Tips are simply a commission paid by the person being served. If the server does a terrible job, the tip is low; if the server does an excellent job, the tip usually is higher. Similarly, car salespeople and insurance agents usually receive a percentage of the sales they generate. The idea behind all of these compensation schemes is that it is difficult, if not impossible, for the manager to monitor these people's efforts, and there is uncertainty regarding what final sales will be. By making these workers' incomes dependent on their performance, the manager gives workers an incentive to work harder than they otherwise would. By working harder, they benefit both the firm and themselves.

Revenue sharing is particularly effective when worker productivity is related to revenues rather than costs. For example, a restaurant manager can design a contract whereby servers get some fraction of a tip; the tip is presumed to be an increasing function of the servers' quality (productivity). The manager of a sales firm can provide incentives to employees by paying them a percentage of the sales they generate.

One problem with revenue-based incentive schemes is that they do not provide an incentive for workers to minimize costs. For example, a food server may attempt to collect a big tip by offering the customer larger portions, free drinks, and the like, which will enhance the tip at the expense of the restaurant's costs.

Piece Rates

An alternative compensation method is to pay workers based on a *piece rate* rather than on a fixed hourly wage. For example, by paying a typist a fixed amount per page typed, the payment to the typist depends on the output produced. To earn more money, the typist must type more pages during a given time period.

A potential problem with paying workers based on a piece rate is that effort must be expended in quality control; otherwise, workers may attempt to produce quantity at the expense of quality. One advantage of revenue or profit sharing is that it reduces the incentive to produce low-quality products. Lower quality reduces sales, thus reducing compensation to those receiving revenue- or profit-sharing incentives.

Demonstration PROBLEM 6–6

Your boss, who has just earned an MBA, has finished reading Chapter 6 of a noted economics textbook. She asks you why the firm pays its secretaries an hourly wage instead of piece rates or a percentage of the firm's profits. How do you answer her?

Answer

Incentive contracts such as piece rates and profit sharing are designed to solve principal-agent problems when effort is not observable. There is little need to provide "incentive contracts" to secretaries given the presence of bosses in the workplace. In particular, it is very easy to monitor the secretaries' effort; they usually are within the boss's eyesight, and there are numerous opportunities to observe the quality of their work (for example, letters for the boss's signature). Thus, there is no real separation between the "principal" (the boss) and the agent (the secretary); the secretary's "boss" knows when the secretary "messes up" and can fire him or her if performance is consistently low. In most instances, this provides secretaries with a stronger incentive to work hard than would paying them a fraction of the profits generated by the effort of all employees in the firm.

Paying secretaries piece rates would be an administrative nightmare; it would be extremely costly to keep track of all of the pages typed and tasks performed during the course of a week. Piece rates may also encourage secretaries to worry more about the quantity instead of the quality of the work done. All things considered, hourly wages are a reasonable way to compensate most secretaries—provided their bosses are given an incentive to monitor them.

Time Clocks and Spot Checks

Many firms use time clocks to assist managers in monitoring workers. However, time clocks are generally not useful in addressing the principal-agent problem. Time clocks essentially are designed to verify when an employee arrives and departs from the job. They do not monitor effort; rather, they simply measure presence at the workplace at the beginning and end of the workday.

A more useful mechanism for monitoring workers is for a manager to engage in spot checks of the workplace. In this case, the manager enters the workplace from time to time to monitor workers. Spot checks allow the manager to verify not only that workers are physically present but also that worker effort and the quality of the work are satisfactory.

The advantage of spot checks is that they reduce the cost of monitoring workers. With spot checks, the manager needn't be in several places at the same time. Because workers do not know when the manager will show up, they will put forth more effort than they would otherwise, since getting caught "goofing off" may lead to dismissal or a reduction in pay. Thus, to be effective, spot checks need to be random; that is, workers should not be able to predict when the manager will be monitoring the workplace.

A disadvantage of spot checks is that they must occur frequently enough to induce workers not to risk getting caught shirking and they must entail some penalty for workers caught shirking. Spot checks work, in effect, through threat. Performance bonuses, on the other hand, work through a promise of reward. These characteristics can have different psychological effects on workers.

ANSWERING THE Headline

The key to defending the risk-and-reward pay system is to communicate effectively that the incentives generated by an incentive-based contract create a win-win situation. The fact that managers cannot monitor every worker's actions creates a principal-agent problem, and the best way to boost productivity is to provide workers with an incentive to use their time productively. When the company does well because employees are working productively, then employees share in the prosperity. The current contract creates win-win relationships between workers, management, and shareholders. Saturn workers appear to understand this, as the referendum calling for a standard GM-UAW contractual relationship was defeated 4052 to 2120.

Summary

In this chapter, we examined the optimal institutional choice for input procurement and the principal-agent problem as it relates to managerial compensation and worker incentives. The manager must decide which inputs will be purchased from other firms and which inputs the firm will manufacture itself. Spot exchange generally is the most desirable alternative when there are many buyers and sellers and low transaction costs. It becomes less attractive when substantial specialized investments generate opportunism, resulting in transaction costs associated with using a market.

When market transaction costs are high, the manager may wish to purchase inputs from a specific supplier using a contract or, alternatively, forgo the market entirely and have the firm set up a subsidiary to produce the required input internally. In a fairly simple contracting environment, a contract may be the most effective solution. But as the contracting environment becomes more complex and uncertain, internal production through vertical integration becomes an attractive managerial strategy.

The chapter also demonstrated a solution to the principal-agent problem: Rewards must be constructed so as to induce the activities desired of workers. For example, if all a manager wants from a worker is for the worker to show up at the workplace, an hourly wage rate and a time clock form an excellent incentive scheme. If it is desirable to produce a high level of output with very little emphasis on quality, piece-rate pay schemes work well. However, if both quantity and quality of output are concerns, profit sharing is an excellent motivator.

Key Terms and Concepts

contract 198
profit sharing 217
relationship-specific exchange 200
revenue sharing 217

specialized investment 200
spot exchange 198
transaction costs 200
vertical integration 199

Conceptual and Computational Questions

1. Discuss the optimal method for procuring inputs that have well-defined and measurable quality specifications and require highly specialized investments. What are the primary advantages and disadvantages of acquiring inputs through this means? Give an example not used in the textbook that uses this method of procurement.

2. Discuss the optimal method for procuring a modest number of standardized inputs sold by many firms in the marketplace. What are the primary advantages and disadvantages of using this method to acquire inputs? Give an example not used in the textbook that uses this method of procurement.

3. Identify whether each of the following transactions involves spot exchange, contract, or vertical integration.
   a. Barnacle, Inc. has a legal obligation to purchase two tonnes of structural steel per week to manufacture conveyor frames.
   b. Petro-Canada uses the oil extracted from its wells to produce raw polypropylene, a type of plastic.
   c. Canadian Boat Lifts purchases generic AC motors from a local distributor.
   d. Green Park Construction—a home building contractor—purchases 50 kilograms of nails from the local Home Depot.

4. Explain why automobile manufacturers produce their own engines but purchase mirrors from independent suppliers.

5. Identify the type of specialized investment that is required in each of the following situations.
   a. You hire an employee to operate a machine that only your company uses.
   b. An aerosol canning company designs a filling line that can be used only for a particular firm's product.
   c. A company builds a manufacturing facility across the street from its primary buyer.

6. Describe how a manager who derives satisfaction from both income and shirking allocates a 10-hour day between these activities when paid an annual, fixed salary of $125 000. When this same manager is given an annual, fixed salary of $125 000 and 3 percent of the firm's profits—amounting to $150 000 per year—the manager chooses to work seven hours and shirks for three hours. Explain which of the compensation schemes the manager prefers.

7. Compare the advantages and disadvantages of using spot checks/hidden video cameras in the workplace and pay-for-performance pay schemes as means to influence worker performance.

8. Discuss the impact of the following factors on the optimal method of procuring an input.
   a. Benefits from specialization
   b. Bureaucracy costs
   c. Opportunism on either side of the transaction
   d. Specialized investments
   e. Unspecifiable events
   f. Bargaining costs

Problems and Applications

9. During the beginning of the twenty-first century, the growth in computer sales declined for the first time in almost two decades. As a result, PC makers

dramatically reduced their orders of computer chips from Intel and other vendors. Explain why computer manufacturers such as Dell are likely to write relatively short contracts for computer chips.

10. Country Donuts caters to its retirement population by selling over 10 000 donuts every week. To produce that many donuts weekly, Country Donut uses 1000 kilograms of flour, which must be delivered by 5:00 a.m. every Friday morning. How should the manager of Country Donut acquire flour? Explain.

11. Pension fund managers for the Province of Alberta control more than $45 billion in assets. The manager of one of these funds is compensated entirely on the basis of fund performance; he earned over $1.2 million last year. As a result, the fund is contemplating a proposal to cap the compensation of fund managers at $100 000. Provide an argument against the proposal.

12. Recently, spun-off Pitney Bowes Office Services Inc.—the fax and copier division of Pitney Bowes Inc.—signed a five-year, $25 million contract for IT services from CGI Group, a Canadian information technology company. If you were the manager of the Pitney Bowes division, how would you justify the long-term nature of your contract with CGI Group?

13. In the business section of a national daily paper, you read that a maker of company network equipment plans to offer its more than 1000 employees the opportunity to reprice their stock options. The company's announcement comes at a time when its stock price is down 90 percent, leaving many employees' stock options worthless. How do you think the company's CEO justified repricing the employees' stock options to the shareholders?

14. Suppose that GM is on the verge of signing a 15-year contract with TRW to supply airbags to the automobile manufacturer. The terms of the contract include providing GM with 85 percent of the airbags used in new automobiles. Just prior to signing the contract, a manager reads that one of TRW's competitors has introduced a comparable airbag using a new technology that reduces the cost by 30 percent. How would this information affect GM's optimal contract length with TRW?

15. ABC, a materials handling company, pays each of its salespersons a base salary plus a percentage of revenues generated. To reduce overhead, ABC has switched from giving each salesperson a company car to reimbursing them $0.35 for each business-related kilometre driven. Accounting records show that, on average, each salesperson drives 100 business-related kilometres per day, 240 days per year. Can you think of an alternative way to restructure the compensation of ABC's sales force that could potentially enhance profits? Explain.

16. Teletronics reported record profits of $100 000 last year and is on track to exceed those profits this year. Teletronics competes in a very competitive market where many of the firms are merging in an attempt to gain competitive advantages. Currently, the company's top manager is compensated with a fixed salary that does not include any performance bonuses. Explain why this manager might nonetheless have a strong incentive to maximize the firm's profits.

17. In 2008, a 10-year contract between a national manufacturer of airplanes and a distributor of raw aluminum will expire. The contract, valued at $300 million when initially signed, stemmed from the manufacturer's desire in the late 1990s to reduce production bottlenecks resulting from supply shortages. Recent declines in the demand for commercial aircraft have led some analysts to challenge the manufacturer's wisdom in signing such a long-term contract. Do you share this view? Explain.

APPENDIX: An Indifference Curve Approach to Managerial Incentives

The essence of the problem with compensation payments that are not tied to performance is depicted graphically in Figure 6–6. The manager views both leisure and income to be goods. Moreover, the manager is willing to substitute between leisure on the job (shirking) and income. This is why his indifference curve has the usual shape in Figure 6–6, where we measure the quantity of leisure consumed at the workplace on the horizontal axis and income on the vertical axis. Note that while the manager enjoys shirking, the owner does not want the manager to shirk.

When the manager is offered a fixed salary of $50 000, his opportunity set becomes the shaded area in Figure 6–6. The reason is simple: since the owner is not physically present at the workplace, the manager will receive the same $50 000 regardless of whether he works a full eight hours (and hence doesn't shirk) or spends the entire day at home (and shirks eight hours). If profits are low, the owner will not know whether this is due to poor managerial effort or simply bad luck. The manager can take advantage of the separation of ownership from control by pushing his indifference curve as far to the northeast as possible until he is in equilibrium at point A, where he shirks the entire day every day of the year but still collects the $50 000.

From the viewpoint of the firm's owner, the fixed salary has an adverse effect on profits because it does not provide the manager with an incentive to monitor other employees. To see this, suppose the profits of the firm are a simple linear function of the amount of shirking done by the manager during each eight-hour period. Such a relationship is graphed in Figure 6–7. The line through point C defines the level of firm profits, which depends on the manager's degree of shirking. For example, if the manager spends the entire day on the job monitoring other employees, shirking is

---

FIGURE 6-6 Impact of a Fixed Salary on Managerial Behaviour

The indifference curve shows a tradeoff between leisure on the job (shirking) and income. When offered a fixed salary of $50 000, the manager opportunity set becomes the shaded area, because whether he works a full eight hours a day with no shirking or shirks the entire day, he still collects $50 000. Point A is the manager's equilibrium point on the highest indifference curve.

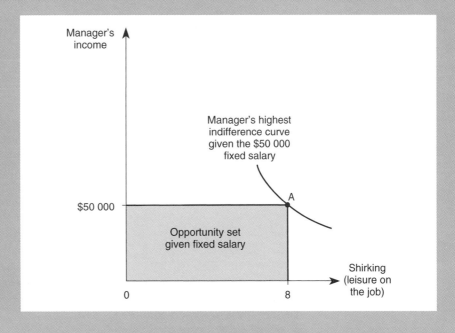

FIGURE 6–7 A Profit-Sharing Incentive Bonus

The solid line through point C defines the level of the firm's profits, which at one end (the vertical intercept) reaches its maximum level of $3 million, when the manager does not engage in shirking, and at the other end (the horizontal intrcept) is equal to zero, where the manager is engaged in all-day shirking. The coloured line through D defines the manager's bonus. Offered a 10 percent share of profits, the manager earns a bonus of $300 000 (the vertical intercept) if he works all day and generates a profit of $3 million for the total compensation of $350 000. At D, his bonus is $225 000 (10 percent of $2.2 million) plus salary, when he shirks for two hours each day, while he receives zero bonus when he shirks the entire day (the horizontal intercept).

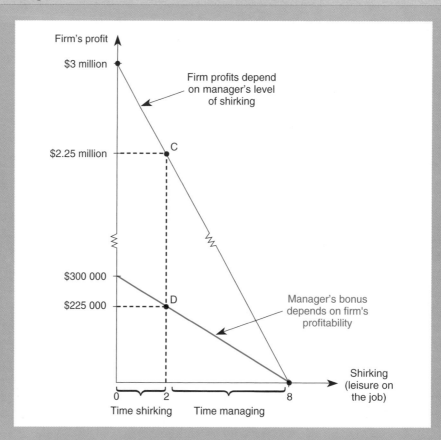

zero and firm profits are $3 million. If the manager spends the entire day shirking, profits are zero. If the manager shirks two hours and thus works six hours, the profits of the firm are $2.25 million. Since the fixed salary of $50 000 provides the manager with an incentive to shirk eight hours, the profits of the firm will be zero if it uses that compensation plan.

How can the owner get the manager to spend time monitoring the production process? You might think that if she paid the manager a bigger salary, the manager would work harder. But this is not correct; a larger salary would simply shift the vertical intercept of the opportunity set in Figure 6–6 above $50 000, but the equilibrium would still imply eight hours of shirking. In essence, the employment contract is such that there is absolutely no cost to the manager of shirking.

Suppose the owner offers the manager the following type of employment contract: a fixed salary of $50 000, plus a bonus of 10 percent of the profits. In this instance, if the manager spends eight hours shirking, profits are zero and the manager gets only $50 000. If the manager does not shirk at all, the firm earns $3 million in profits and the manager gets a bonus equal to 10 percent of those profits. In this instance, the bonus is $300 000. The bonus to the manager, as a function of his level of shirking, is depicted in Figure 6–7 as the line through point D. Note that when the manager shirks for two hours each day, the firm earns $2.25 million in gross profits and the manager's bonus is $225 000.

FIGURE 6–8 A Profit-Sharing Incentive Scheme Increases Managerial Effort

The line through AB represents the manager's total compensation. At A, associated with eight hours of shirking, the manager receives only the fixed salary of $50 000. At B, with two hours of shirking, the manager's income consists of $50 000 fixed salary plus 10 percent (of $2.2 million profits) in bonus for the total of $275 000. The vertical intercept represents the zero-shirking scenario, at which the manager earns up to $350 000. Clearly, from the perspective of both the firm and the manager, point B, on a higher indifference curve, is superior to point A.

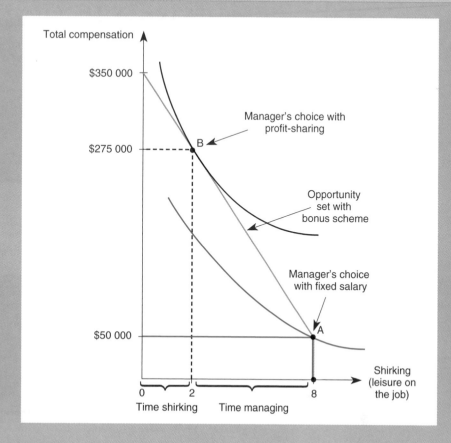

The effect of a salary-plus-bonus compensation plan on managerial behaviour is illustrated in Figure 6–8. The manager's opportunity set is now given by the line through points A and B. For example, if the manager shirks eight hours, profits are zero and he receives no bonus; therefore, his income is $50 000. If the manager does not shirk at all, a bonus of $300 000 is added to his fixed salary; thus, the manager can earn $350 000 if he does not shirk.

Exactly what the manager does under the salary-plus-bonus plan depends on his preferences. But as we see in Figure 6–8, this manager can attain a higher indifference curve by shirking less and moving from point A to point B. At point B, the manager earns $275 000 in income—$225 000 in the form of a bonus payment and $50 000 as a fixed salary. The manager clearly prefers this compensation scheme. Note also that the manager still shirks two hours each day, but this is considerably less than under the fixed-salary/no-bonus plan.

What is the impact of the bonus on the owner of the firm? In Figure 6–7, we see that when the manager shirks two hours each day, the firm earns $2.25 million in gross profits. Thus, the salary plus bonus increases the owner's gross profits from zero (under the fixed salary) to $2.25 million. The bonus has increased the welfare not only of the manager but also of the owner; profits, net of managerial compensation, are

$$\$2\ 250\ 000 - \$275\ 000 = \$1\ 975\ 000$$

Visit the Web site @ **www.mcgrawhill.ca/college/baye**

CHAPTER 7

The Nature of Industry

Headline

Canadian Bank Mergers Failure: Finance Minister Rejects Bank Merger Proposals

On December 14, 1998, then–Canadian Finance Minister Paul Martin rejected the proposed mergers of the Royal Bank with the Bank of Montreal and CIBC with the Toronto-Dominion Bank. The reasons for deciding against these mergers were no surprise. The Finance Minister concluded that the mergers were not in the public interest, as they would result in (a) too much concentration of economic power in Canada in the hands of too few financial institutions, (b) a reduction in competition in the Canadian financial services sector, and (c) a reduction in the Canadian government's flexibility to address future concerns. Now, five years later, Canada's Ministry of Finance has indicated that it will not consider any additional merger talks until September 2004 at the earliest.

Canada's financial services sector has been marked by mergers over the past decade, resulting in the "Big Five" banks. Although credit unions and smaller banks do operate within Canada, it is quite clear that the four banks listed above, and Scotiabank, have a dominant position in Canada's market. What could cause discussion of increased consolidation of the banking sector in Canada today? Would such consolidation be beneficial to Canada? How? Would it benefit Canadian customers?

Introduction

Managers of firms do not make decisions in a vacuum. Numerous factors affect decisions such as how much output to produce, what price to charge, how much to spend on research and development, advertising, and so on. Unfortunately, no single theory or methodology provides managers with the answers to these questions. The optimal pricing strategy for an automobile manufacturer generally will differ from that of a computer firm; the level of research and development will differ for food manufacturers and defence contractors. In this chapter we highlight important differences that exist among industries. In subsequent chapters, we will see why these differences arise and examine how they affect managerial decisions.

Much of the material in this chapter is factual and is intended to acquaint you with aspects of the "real world" that are relevant for managers. You will be exposed to statistics for numerous industries. Some of these statistics summarize how many firms exist in various industries; others indicate which firms and industries are the largest and which industries tend to charge the highest markups.

The numbers presented in this chapter will change over time; the largest firm today is unlikely to be the largest firm in 40 years. Consequently, the most important thing for you to grasp in this chapter is that industries differ substantially in nature; not all industries are created equal. Our task in the remaining chapters of this book is to determine what it is about firms and industries that gives rise to systematic differences in price-cost margins, advertising expenditures, and other managerial decision variables. This will be particularly valuable to you as a manager, since you do not know in which industry you will work during the next 40 years of your career. An effective manager is able to adapt to the nature of the industry in which his or her firm competes. As the nature of the industry changes, so will the manager's optimal decisions.

Market Structure

market structure
Factors that affect managerial decisions, including the number of firms competing in a market, the relative size of firms, technological and cost considerations, demand conditions, and the ease with which firms can enter or exit the industry.

Market structure refers to factors such as the number of firms that compete in a market, the relative size of the firms (concentration), technological and cost conditions, demand conditions, and the ease with which firms can enter or exit the industry. Different industries have different structures, and these structures affect the decisions the prudent manager will make. The following subsections provide an overview of the major structural variables that affect managerial decisions.

Firm Size

It will come as no surprise to you that some firms are larger than others. Consider Tables 7–1A and 7–1B, which list the sales of the largest firms in Canadian and the U.S. industries. Notice that there are considerable differences in the size of the largest firm in each industry. According to Table 7–1A, General Motors Canada is the largest firm in the motor industry and the largest in sales, with revenue of over $37 billion; while Zellers is the largest discount retailer, with sales of just over $4.5 billion. Also notice that while the largest Canadian firm ranked according to its sales revenue is in the auto industry, the largest U.S. firm, Exxon-Mobil, is in petroleum refining, as is reported in Table 7–1B. One important lesson for future managers is that some industries naturally give rise to larger firms than do other industries. A goal of the remaining chapters in this book is to explain why.

TABLE 7–1A The Largest Firms in Selected Canadian Industries		
Industry	Largest Company	Sales (millions of dollars), 2002
Motor vehicles and parts	GM Canada	$37 000
Aero-transportation	Bombardier	$23 799
Food	George Weston Ltd.	$27 464
Banking	Royal Bank of Canada	$23 234
Telecommunications	BCE Inc.	$19 809
Financial services	Sun Life Assurance Canada	$25 950
Petroleum refining	Imperial Oil	$15 821
Automotive components	Magna International	$13 044
Aluminum and packing	Alcan Inc.	$12 553
Discount retail	Zellers	$ 4 656
Construction	PCL Construction Group	$ 3 006
Wireless communications	Nortel	$10 621
Manufacturing services	Celestica	$ 8 289
Hydro generators and appliances	General Electric Canada	$ 3 379
Industrial chemicals	Dupont Canada	$ 2 484
Newsprint and uncoated groundwood papers	Abitibi Consolidated	$ 5 191
Gold mining	Barrick Gold	$ 2 108
Printing and media	Quebecor World	$ 6 242
Railway construction/development	Canadian National Railway Co.	$ 6 173

Sources: "The Top 1000: Canada's Power Book," *Globeinvestor*, available <www.globeinvestor.com/series/top1000/ 2003>; "Top 100 Hold the Line," *Canada's Corporate Innovation Leaders*, a Research Infosource Inc. supplement, available <www.researchinfosource.com/2003-analysis.pdf>; "Canada's Top 100 Corporate R&D Spenders List 2003," Research Infosource Inc., available <www.researchinfosource.com/2003-analysis.shtml>; *Canadian Business*, available <www.canadianbusiness.com/homepage/index.jsp>. All accessed July 4, 2004.

Industry Concentration

The data in Tables 7–1A and 7–1B reveal considerable variation in the size of the largest firm in various industries. Another factor that affects managerial decisions is the size distribution of firms within an industry. That is, are there many small firms within an industry or only a few large firms? This question is important because, as we will see in later chapters, the optimal decisions of a manager who faces little competition from other firms in the industry will differ from those of a manager who works in an industry in which there are many firms.

Some industries are dominated by a few large firms, while others are composed of many small firms. Before presenting concentration data for various Canadian and U.S. industries, we examine two measures that economists use to gauge the degree of concentration in an industry.

Measures of Industry Concentration

Concentration ratios measure how much of the total output in an industry is produced by the largest firms in that industry. The most common concentration ratio is the four-firm concentration ratio (C_4). The **four-firm concentration ratio** is the fraction of total industry sales produced by the four largest firms in the industry.

Let S_1, S_2, S_3, and S_4 denote the sales of the four largest firms in an industry, and let S_T denote the total sales of all firms in the industry. The four-firm concentration ratio is given by

four-firm concentration ratio
The fraction of total industry sales generated by the four largest firms in the industry.

$$C_4 = \frac{S_1 + S_2 + S_3 + S_4}{S_T} \qquad (7\text{–}1)$$

TABLE 7-1B The Largest Firms in Selected U.S. Industries

Industry	Largest Company	Sales (millions of dollars), 2001
Aerospace	Boeing	51 321
Apparel	Nike	8 995
Beverages	Coca-Cola	20 458
Building materials	Owens-Illinois	5 815
Chemicals	du Pont	29 202
Commercial banks	J. P. Morgan Chase	60 065
Computers, office equipment	IBM	88 396
Electronics, electrical equipment	Emerson Electric	15 545
Food production	IBP	16 950
Forest and paper products	International Paper	28 180
Furniture	Leggett & Platt	4 276
Industrial and farm equipment	Caterpillar	20 175
Metal products	Gillette	9 986
Metals	Alcoa	23 090
Mining, crude oil production	Occidental Petroleum	14 543
Motor vehicles and parts	General Motors	184 632
Petroleum refining	Exxon Mobil	210 392
Pharmaceuticals	Merck	40 363
Publishing and printing	Gannett	6 244
Rubber and plastic products	Goodyear Tire & Rubber	14 417
Scientific and photographic equipment	Minnesota Mining & Mfg. (3M)	16 724
Soaps, cosmetics	Procter & Gamble	39 951
Textiles	Mohawk Industries	3 256
Tobacco	Philip Morris	63 276
Toys, sporting goods	Mattel	5 590
Transportation equipment	Brunswick	4 507

Sources: Fortune 500 List, April 14, 2001; company 10-Ks; and author's calculations.

Equivalently, the four-firm concentration ratio is the sum of the market shares of the top four firms:

$$C_4 = w_1 + w_2 + w_3 + w_4$$

where

$$w_1 = S_1/S_T,$$
$$w_2 = S_2/S_T,$$
$$w_3 = S_3/S_T, \text{ and}$$
$$w_4 = S_4/S_T$$

When an industry is composed of a very large number of firms, each of which is very small, the four-firm concentration ratio is close to zero. When four or fewer firms produce all of an industry's output, the four-firm concentration ratio is 1. The closer the four-firm concentration ratio is to zero, the less concentrated is the industry; the closer the ratio is to 1, the more concentrated is the industry.

Demonstration PROBLEM 7-1

Suppose an industry is composed of six firms. Four firms have sales of $10 each, and two firms have sales of $5 each. What is the four-firm concentration ratio for this industry?

Answer

Total industry sales are $S_T = \$50$. The sales of the four largest firms are

$$S_1 + S_2 + S_3 + S_4 = \$40$$

Therefore, the four-firm concentration ratio is

$$C_4 = \frac{40}{50} = 0.80$$

This means that the four largest firms in the industry account for 80 percent of total industry output.

Four-firm concentration ratios that are close to 0 indicate markets in which there are many sellers, giving rise to much competition among producers for the right to sell to consumers. Industries with four-firm concentration ratios close to 1 indicate markets in which there is little competition among producers for sales to consumers.

Another measure of concentration is the **Herfindahl-Hirschman index (*HHI*)**, which is the sum of the squared market shares of firms in a given industry, multiplied by 10 000 to eliminate the need for decimals. By squaring the market shares before adding them up, the index weights firms with high market shares more heavily.

Suppose firm i's share of the total market output is $w_i = S_i/S_T$, where S_i is firm i's sales and S_T is total sales in the industry. Then the Herfindahl-Hirschman index is

$$HHI = 10\ 000\ \Sigma w_i^2 \tag{7–2}$$

The value of the Herfindahl-Hirschman index lies between 0 and 10 000. A value of 10 000 arises when a single firm (with a market share of $w_1 = 1$) exists in the industry. A value of zero results when there are numerous infinitesimally small firms.

Herfindahl-Hirschman index (*HHI*)
The sum of the squared market shares of firms in a given industry multiplied by 10 000.

Demonstration PROBLEM 7–2

Suppose an industry consists of three firms. Two firms have sales of $10 each, and one firm has sales of $30. What is the Herfindahl-Hirschman index for this industry? What is the four-firm concentration ratio?

Answer

Since total industry sales are $S_T = \$50$, the largest firm has a market share of $w_1 = 30/50$ and the other two firms have a market share of 10/50 each. Thus, the Herfindahl-Hirschman index for this industry is

$$HHI = 10\ 000\left[\left(\frac{30}{50}\right)^2 + \left(\frac{10}{50}\right)^2 + \left(\frac{10}{50}\right)^2\right] = 4400$$

The four-firm concentration ratio is 1, since the top three firms account for all industry sales.

The Concentration of Canadian and U.S. Industries

Now that you understand the algebra of industry concentration and Herfindahl-Hirschman indexes, we may use them to examine the concentration of representative industries within Canada and the United States. Tables 7–2A and B provide concen-

TABLE 7-2A Four-Firm Concentration Ratios and Herfindahl-Hirschman Indexes for Selected Canadian Manufacturing Industries

Industry	C_4	HHI (value shipped)
Breweries	99.00	3177
Asphalt roofing manufacturers	96.3	2458
Motor vehicle manufacturers	93.7	3865
Manufacturers of major appliances	77.0	1751
Gold, quartz mines	75.0	1874
Vegetable oil mills	70.9	1499
Wineries	72.0	1543
Uranium mines	(N/A)	2708
Shipbuilding and repair	56.4	1066
Jewellery and silverware industry	53.2	990
Men's clothing factories	20.6	225
Sawmills and planning mills	19.2	181
Signs and display manufacturers	15.9	141
Hardware, tool, and cutlery manufacturers	12.9	106
Furniture reupholstery and repair	8.1	45
Machine shops	6.4	42
Logging	1.4	219

Source: Adapted from "Industrial Organization and Concentration in the Manufacturing, Mining and Logging Industries," Statistics Canada, Catalogue 31-514, 1980.

TABLE 7-2B Four-Firm Concentration Ratios and Herfindahl-Hirschman Indexes for Selected U.S. Manufacturing Industries

Industry	C_4	HHI
Breakfast cereals	83	2446
Breweries	90	N/A
Cookies and crackers	60	1383
Distilleries	60	1076
Electronic computers	45	728
Fluid milk	21	205
Games and toys	43	564
Household refrigerators and home freezers	82	2025
Jewellery (excluding costume)	13	81
Luggage	52	1419
Men's and boys' clothing	42	846
Motor vehicles	82	2506
Pens and mechanical pencils	65	1375
Ready-mixed concrete	7	29
Semiconductors	34	414
Snack foods	63	2619
Soap and detergent	65	1618
Soft drinks	47	800
Tires	73	1814
Women's and girls' clothing	14	111
Wood containers and pallets	6	16

Source: Concentration Ratios in Manufacturing, U.S. Bureau of the Census, 1997.

tration ratios (in percentages) and Herfindahl-Hirschman indexes for selected Canadian and U.S. industries. Notice that there is considerable variation between industries in the degree of concentration. In Canada, as indicated in Table 7–2A, the top four breweries account for 99 percent of the total output of beer, suggesting considerable concentration. Similarly, the markets for motor vehicles, asphalt roofing, and major appliances also have high four-firm concentration ratios. In contrast, the four-firm concentration ratios for logging, machine shops, furniture reupholstery and repair, and hardware, tools, and cutlery are lower, suggesting greater competition between producers. For example, the four largest producers of logging account for only 1.4 percent of the total market.

Similarly, in the United States, as indicated by Table 7–2B, the beer and motor vehicles industries are considerably concentrated. The least concentrated industries, as portrayed by their four-firm concentration ratios, are ready-mixed concrete and wood containers and pallets.

On balance, the Herfindahl-Hirschman indexes reported in Tables 7–2A and 7–2B reveal a similar pattern: the industries with high four-firm concentration ratios tend to have higher Herfindahl-Hirschman indexes. There are exceptions, however. Notice that according to the four-firm concentration ratio, the asphalt roofing industry in Canada is more concentrated than the motor vehicles industry. However, the Herfindahl-Hirschman index for the motor vehicles industry is higher than that for the asphalt roofing industry. Why do the conclusions drawn from these two indexes differ?

First, the four-firm concentration indexes are based on the market shares of only the four largest firms in an industry, while the Herfindahl-Hirschman indexes are based on the market shares of all firms in an industry. In other words, the C_4 does not take into account the fifth-largest firm, whereas the Herfindahl-Hirschman index does. Second, the *HHI* is based on squared market shares, while the four-firm concentration ratio is not. Consequently, the Herfindahl-Hirschman index puts a greater weight on firms with large market shares than the four-firm concentration ratio. These two factors can lead to differences in the ranking of firms by the C_4 and the *HHI*.

Because the *HHI* puts greater weights on firms with larger market shares, it takes more account of the size distribution problem. Note that, in the case of equal-sized firms, the $HHI = (1/N)10\,000$, where N stands for the number of equal-sized firms in the industry. For example, for a two-firm situation with equal market shares, that is, $w_1 = w_2 = 1/2$, the *HHI* equals $1/2(10\,000)$, and for three equal-sized firms, where $w_1 = w_2 = w_3 = 1/3$, the *HHI* equals $1/3(10\,000)$. If the market share distribution is not uniform, $HHI > (1/N)10\,000$. For example, for the case where $w_1 = 1/2$; $w_2 = 1/4$; $w_3 = 1/4$, $HHI = 3000/8$. In this case, the industry is about as concentrated as one with 2.6 equal-sized firms. Furthermore, note that this index tends to grows with the increase in inequality between the firms in the industry.

Limitations of Concentration Measures

Statistics and other data should always be interpreted with caution, and the preceding measures of concentration are no exception. In concluding our discussion of industry concentration, it is important to point out three potential limitations of the numbers reported in Tables 7–2A and B.

Global Markets. The four-firm concentration and Herfindahl-Hirschman indexes reported in Tables 7–2A and B are based on a definition of the product market that includes foreign imports. That is, in calculating C_4 and *HHI*, Statistics Canada, unlike its American counterpart the Bureau of the Census, takes into account the penetration by foreign firms into Canadian markets. Excluding them would overstate the true level of concentration in industries in which a significant number of foreign producers serve the market.

For example, consider the four-firm concentration ratio for the brewery industry. On the basis of Table 7–2A, the top four Canadian firms account for 99 percent of industry sales. However, this figure ignores beer produced by the many well-known

InsideBUSINESS

7–1 North American Industry Classification System

NAICS (North American Industry Classification System) is the agreed-upon common framework for the production of comparable statistics that was developed by Statistics Canada, Mexico's Instituto Nacional de Estadística, Geografía e Informática (INEGI) and the Economic Classification Policy Committee (ECPC) of the Office of Management and Budget (OMB).

Created against the background of the North American Free Trade Agreement, it is designed to provide common definitions of the industrial structure of the three countries and a common statistical framework to facilitate the analysis of the three economies. NAICS is based on supply-side or production-oriented principles, to ensure that industrial data, classified to NAICS, is suitable for the analysis of production related issues such as industrial performance. This new system replaced Statistics Canada's Standard Industrial Classifications, which had been in place since 1948.

The economic transactors for which NAICS is designed are businesses (and other organizations) engaged in the production of goods and services. They include farms, incorporated and unincorporated business, and government business enterprises. They also include government institutions and agencies engaged in the production of marketed and non-marketed services, as well as organizations such as professional associations and unions and charitable or nonprofit organizations and the employees of households.

NAICS is a comprehensive system encompassing all economic activities. It has a hierarchical structure. At the highest level, it divides the economy into 20 sectors. At lower levels, it further distinguishes the different economic activities in which businesses are engaged.

The numbering system adopted is a six-digit code, of which the first five digits are used to describe the NAICS levels that will be used by the three countries to produce comparable data. The first two digits designate the sector, the third digit designates the subsector, the fourth digit designates the industry group, and the fifth digit designates industries. The sixth digit is used to designate national industries.

With some important exceptions, NAICS 2002 provides a set of standard five-digit industries that describe the industrial structure and composition of the Canadian, United States, and Mexican economies at selected levels of aggregation where agreement occurred among the three countries on a compatible classification. Below the agreed-upon level of compatibility, each country has added additional detailed six-digit industries as necessary, to meet national needs, provided that this additional detail aggregates to the NAICS level.

Exceptions to the rule of five-digit industry level are as follows:

NAICS Level

2-digit sector	Wholesale trade
	Retail trade
	Public administration
3-digit subsector	Waste management and remediation services
	Credit intermediation and related activities
	Utilities
4-digit industry group	Finance (except subsector 522) and insurance
	Real estate

NAICS with Canadian detail will be designated *NAICS Canada*, while Mexico and the United States will produce NAICS with their own six-digit detail, which they will publish as *SCIAN Mexico* and *NAICS United States*.

Comparability across the three countries is indicated by superscript abbreviations at the end of industry titles in the Classification Structure and Descriptions chapters of NAICS Canada 2002. A superscript "CAN" (CAN) indicates a Canadian industry, "Mex" (MEX) indicates Canadian and Mexican industries are comparable, and "US" (US) indicates Canadian and United States industries are comparable. When no superscript appears, the Canadian, Mexican, and United States industries are comparable.

NAICS Canada 2002 consists of 20 sectors, 103 subsectors, 328 industry groups, 728 industries, and 928 national industries. The structure and hierarchy of NAICS has been designed to allow for maximum data comparability across three countries whose economies differ in size and complexity, rather than to reflect the size or importance of industries in each country. Therefore, some Canadian industries that were at the three-digit level of the 1980 SIC can now be found at the five- and the six-digit level of NAICS Canada.

Interpreting NAICS Codes

NAICS	NAICS Code	Description
Sector	51	Information and cultural industries
Subsector	517	Telecommunications
Industry group	5172	Wireless telecommunications carrier, except satellite
Industry	51741	Satellite telecommunications
Canadian industry	517210	Beeper (radio pager) communications carriers

Inside BUSINESS

7-2 The Impact of Increasing the Size of the Market Through Trade Liberalization on Concentration

The period since the signing of the Canada–United States Free Trade Agreement at the beginning of 1988, and the later addition of Mexico to create the North American Free Trade Agreement (NAFTA), has been a time of rapid adjustment for most Canadian industries. Canada has a small, relatively open economy, and for the most part its agricultural producers, processors, and input providers face world prices and do not exercise market power on world markets. In this context, trade liberalization was seen as a force in promoting competitive behaviour. This is consistent with older theories of industrial organization, discussed in this chapter, that are structured around the Structure-Conduct-Performance paradigm.

A long-held belief in industrial economics is that extending the size of the market reduces concentration and diminishes the ability of firms to exercise market power. The idea is based on the notion that the larger the market, the greater the number of firms and hence the greater the likelihood of more competitive pricing. This belief has had particular application in the area of trade. Most trade models assume that open borders help discipline monopolistic behaviour in domestic markets. Specifically, the international trade models that have accounted for imperfect competition indicate that imperfect competition provides additional sources of gains from trade that result from the "pro-competitive" effect of trade: import competition increases the perceived elastic-

ity of demand for domestic firms, leading them to reduce their markups of price over marginal cost. In countries with small economies, such as Canada, the problem may be made worse by the fact that the size of the domestic market is such that only a small number of firms operate, often at less than the minimum efficient scale.

A paper by James Rude and Murray Fulton[1] examines the issues of whether larger markets result in greater concentration and whether greater concentration results in a greater exercise of market power. The focus of the study is the Canadian agribusiness sector over the period 1983–96. Here, we report the results on the first question. On the basis of the analysis, there is no consistent evidence that imports had a beneficial impact on competition in the Canadian market during that period; that is, little connection was found between larger markets and market concentration. The paper could identify only a few instances in which increased market size (as measured by trade liberalization in the form of CUSTA) lead to changes in concentration.

The table here examines the relationship between trade liberalization and market concentration in Canadian food and beverage processing. Concentration is measured by a Herfindahl-Hirschman index, which is equal to the sum of the squared market shares for all firms in the industry. The second and third columns of this table show the average *HHI* for the periods prior to CUSTA (1983–88) and after (1989–96).

breweries in Mexico, Canada, Europe, Australia, and Asia. The four-firm concentration ratio based on both domestic and imported beer would be lower.

National, Regional, and Local Markets. A second deficiency in the numbers reported in Tables 7–2A and B is that they are based on figures for the entire economy. In many industries, the relevant markets are local and may be composed of only a few firms. When the relevant markets are local, the use of national data tends to understate the actual level of concentration in the local markets.

For example, suppose that each of the provinces and territories had only one gasoline station. If all gasoline stations were the same size, each firm would have a market share of only 1/13. The four-firm concentration ratio, based on national data, would be 4/13, or 30 percent. This would suggest that the market for gasoline services is somewhat concentrated. However, it does a consumer in central Ontario little good to have gas stations in 12 other regions, since the relevant market for buying gasoline for this consumer is his or her local market. Thus, geographical differences between markets can lead to biases in concentration measures.

In summary, indexes of market structure based on national data tend to understate the degree of concentration when the relevant markets are local.

Food and Beverage Concentration (pre- and post-CUSTA)

Sector	Avg. Herfindahl-Hirschman Index	
	Pre-CUSTA	Post-CUSTA
Poultry products	0.0505	0.0670
Other dairy	0.0846	0.1161
Prepared flour mixes and cereals	0.1757	0.1036
Potato chips	0.2650	0.3416
Soft drinks	0.1214	0.1951
Brewery products	0.3047	0.4230
Vegetable oil	0.1586	0.3215
Canned and preserved fruit and vegetables	0.0598	0.0613
Frozen fruit and vegetables	0.1931	0.1654
Fluid milk	0.0772	0.0889
Flour	0.1842	0.1770
Biscuits	0.2431	0.2358
Bread and other bakery	0.0654	0.0790
Confections	0.1381	0.1319
Dry pasta	0.2467	0.2460
Malt	0.0409	0.0396
Distillery products	0.2366	0.2506
Winery	0.1350	0.1654
Meat and meat products	0.0593	0.0380
Feed	0.0242	0.0205

The *HHI* takes account of both the number of firms and their relative sizes. The reason why the index is used, rather than a CR-4 index, is because all of the industry's activities are accounted for rather than just those of just the four largest firms. As well, data on *HHI*s are frequently available when CR-4 ratios are withheld for reasons of confidentiality.

A number of conclusions can be drawn about concentration in the food and beverage industry from the data in the table. First, over half the sectors display no significant change, suggesting that trade liberalization has had little effect on industry structure, at least as measured by the *HHI*. Second, a number of the sectors that showed a statistically significant increase in concentration involved goods with little trade, either because the border is closed due to supply management (for example, poultry products and other dairy) or because the products are not extensively traded because of high product transportation costs (soft drinks), or because of product characteristics (taste) specific to Canada (potato chips and brewery products). Third, concentration fell in only two sectors, (1) meat and meat products and (2) feed.

[1]James Rude and Murray Fulton, "Concentration and Market Power in Canadian Agribusiness," in *Structural Change as a Source of Trade Disputes Under NAFTA*, eds. R.M.A. Loyns, K. Meilke, R. D. Knutson, and A. Yunez-Naude, proceedings of the Seventh Agricultural and Food Policy Systems Information Workshop, February 2001, Tucson, AZ.

Industry Definitions and Product Classes. We have already emphasized that the geographic definition of the relevant market (local or national) can lead to a bias in concentration ratios. Similarly, the definition of product classes used to define an industry also affects indexes.

Specifically, in constructing indexes of market structure, there is considerable aggregation across product classes. Consider the four-firm concentration ratio for logging, which is only 1.4 percent in Table 7–2A. This number may seem surprisingly low when one considers how a few major companies dominate the market for forestry and logging. However, the concentration ratio of 1.4 percent is based on a much more broadly defined notion of logging and forestry. In fact, the product classes used by Statistics Canada include many more branches of activities within this branch, including cutting timber, producing rough, round, hewn, or riven primary wood, felling, cutting, bucking, and producing wood chips in the forest on a fee or contract basis.

How does one determine which products belong in which industry? As a general rule, products that are close substitutes (have large, positive cross-price elasticities) are considered to belong to a given industry class. Indeed, one might view the above-mentioned soft drinks to be close substitutes for cola drinks, thus justifying their inclusion into the industry before calculating concentration ratios.

Technology

Industries also differ with regard to the technologies used to produce goods and services. Some industries are very labour-intensive, requiring much labour to produce goods and services. Other industries are very capital-intensive, requiring large investments in plant, equipment, and machines to be able to produce goods or services. These differences in technology give rise to differences in production techniques across industries. In the petroleum-refining industry, for example, firms utilize approximately one employee for each $1 million in sales. In contrast, the beverage industry utilizes roughly 17 workers for each $1 million in sales.

Technology is also important within a given industry. In some industries, firms have access to identical technologies and therefore have similar cost structures. In other industries, one or two firms have access to a technology that is not available to other firms. In these instances, the firms with superior technology will have an advantage over other firms. When this technological advantage is significant, the technologically superior firm (or firms) will completely dominate the industry. In the remaining chapters, we will see how such differences in technologies affect managerial decisions.

Demand and Market Conditions

Industries also differ with regard to the underlying demand and market conditions. In industries with relatively low demand, the market may be able to sustain only a few firms. In industries where demand is great, the market may require many firms to produce the quantity demanded. One of our tasks in the remaining chapters is to explain how the degree of market demand affects the decisions of managers.

The information accessible to consumers also tends to vary across markets. It is very easy for a consumer to find the lowest airfare on a flight from Toronto to Vancouver; all one has to do is call a travel agent or surf the Internet to obtain price quotes. In contrast, it is much more difficult for consumers to obtain information about the best deal on a used car. The consumer not only has to bargain with potential sellers over the price but also must attempt to ascertain the quality of the used car. As we will learn in subsequent chapters, the optimal decisions of managers will vary depending on the amount of information available in the market.

Finally, the elasticity of demand for products tends to vary from industry to industry. Moreover, the elasticity of demand for an individual firm's product generally will differ from the market elasticity of demand for the product. In some industries, there is a large discrepancy between an individual firm's elasticity of demand and the market elasticity. The reason for this can be easily explained.

In Chapter 3 we learned that the demand for a specific product depends on the number of close substitutes available for the product. As a consequence, the demand for a particular brand of product (for example, Seven Up) will be more elastic than the demand for the product group in general (soft drinks). In markets where there are no close substitutes for a given firm's product, the elasticity of demand for that product will coincide with the market elasticity of demand for the product group (since there is only one product in the market). In industries where many firms produce substitutes for a given firm's product, the demand for the individual firm's product will be more elastic than the overall industry demand.

One measure of the elasticity of industry demand for a product relative to that of an individual firm is the Rothschild index. The **Rothschild index** provides a measure of the sensitivity to price of the product group as a whole relative to the sensitivity of the quantity demanded of a single firm to a change in its price.

Rothschild index
A measure of the sensitivity to price of a product group as a whole relative to the sensitivity of the quantity demanded of a single firm to a change in its price.

The Rothschild index is given by

$$R = \frac{E_T}{E_F} \tag{7-3}$$

where E_T is the elasticity of demand for the total market and E_F is the elasticity of demand for the product of an individual firm.

The Rothschild index takes on a value between 0 and 1. When the index is 1, the individual firm faces a demand curve that has the same sensitivity to price as the market demand curve. In contrast, when the elasticity of demand for an individual firm's product is much greater (in absolute value) than the elasticity of the market demand, the Rothschild index is close to 0. In this instance, an individual firm's quantity demanded is more sensitive to a price increase than is the industry as a whole. In other words, when the Rothschild index is less than 1, a 10 percent increase in one firm's price will decrease that firm's quantity demanded by more than the total industry quantity would fall if all firms in the industry increased their prices by 10 percent. The Rothschild index therefore provides a measure of how price-sensitive an individual firm's demand is relative to the entire market. When an industry is composed of many firms, each producing similar products, the Rothschild index will be close to zero.

Table 7–3 provides estimates of the firm and market elasticities of demand and the Rothschild indexes for ten U.S. industries. The table reveals that firms in some industries are more sensitive to price increases than firms in other industries. Notice that the Rothschild indexes for tobacco and for chemicals are unity. This means that the representative firm in the industry faces a demand curve that has exactly the same elasticity of demand as the total industry demand. In contrast, the Rothschild index for food is 0.26, which means that the demand for an individual food producer's product is roughly four times more elastic than that of the industry as a whole. Firms in the food industry face a demand curve that is much more sensitive to price than the industry as a whole.

TABLE 7-3	Market and Representative Firm Demand Elasticities and Corresponding Rothschild Indexes for Selected U.S. Industries		
Industry	**Own Price Elasticity of Market Demand**	**Own Price Elasticity of Demand for Representative Firm's Product**	**Rothschild Index**
Food	−1.0	−3.8	0.26
Tobacco	−1.3	−1.3	1.00
Textiles	−1.5	−4.7	0.32
Apparel	−1.1	−4.1	0.27
Paper	−1.5	−1.7	0.88
Printing and publishing	−1.8	−3.2	0.56
Chemicals	−1.5	−1.5	1.00
Petroleum	−1.5	−1.7	0.88
Rubber	−1.8	−2.3	0.78
Leather	−1.2	−2.3	0.52

Source: Matthew D. Shapiro, "Measuring Market Power in U.S. Industry," National Bureau of Economic Research, Working Paper No. 2212, 1987.

Demonstration PROBLEM 7–3

The industry elasticity of demand for airline travel is −3, and the elasticity of demand for an individual carrier is −4. What is the Rothschild index for this industry?

Answer

The Rothschild index is

$$R = \frac{-3}{-4} = 0.75$$

Potential for Entry

The final structure variable we discuss in this chapter is the potential for entry into an industry. In some industries, it is relatively easy for new firms to enter the market; in others, it is more difficult. The optimal decisions by firms in an industry will depend on the ease with which new firms can enter the market.

Numerous factors can create a *barrier to entry*, making it difficult for other firms to enter an industry. One potential barrier to entry is the explicit cost of entering an industry, such as capital requirements. Another is patents, which give owners of patents the exclusive right to sell their products for a specified period of time. In this instance, the patent serves as a barrier to entry; other firms cannot readily produce the product produced by the patent holder.

Economies of scale also can create a barrier to entry. In some markets, only one or two firms exist because of economies of scale. If additional firms attempted to enter, they would be unable to generate the volume necessary to enjoy the reduced average costs associated with economies of scale. As we will learn in subsequent chapters, barriers to entry have important implications for the long-run profits a firm will earn in a market.

Conduct

In addition to structural differences across industries, the *conduct,* or behaviour, of firms also tends to differ across industries. Some industries charge higher markups than other industries. Some industries are more susceptible to mergers or takeovers than others. In addition, the amount spent on advertising and research and development tends to vary across industries. The following subsections describe important differences in conduct that exist across industries.

Pricing Behaviour

Firms in some industries charge higher markups than firms in other industries. To illustrate this fact, we introduce what economists refer to as the Lerner index. The **Lerner index** is given by

Lerner index
A measure of the difference between price and marginal cost as a fraction of the product's price.

$$L = \frac{P - MC}{P} \tag{7–4}$$

where P is price and MC is marginal cost. Thus, the Lerner index measures the difference between price and marginal cost as a fraction of the price of the product.

InsideBUSINESS

7-3 The Elasticity of Demand at the Firm and Market Levels

In general, the demand for an individual firm's product is more elastic than that for the industry as a whole. The exception is the case of monopoly where a single firm comprises the market (the demand for a monopolist's product is the same as the industry demand). How much more elastic is the demand for an individual firm's product compared to that for the market?

Table 7–4 provides an answer to this question. The second column gives the own price elasticity of the market demand for a given industry. This elasticity measures how responsive total industry quantity demanded is to an industrywide price increase. The third column provides the elasticity of demand for an individual firm's product. Thus, that column measures how responsive the quantity demanded of an individual firm's product is to a change in that firm's price.

Notice in Table 7–4 that the market elasticity of demand in the agriculture industry is −1.8. This means that a 1 percent increase in the industrywide price would lead to a 1.8 percent reduction in the total quantity demanded of agricultural products. In contrast, the elasticity of demand for a representative firm's product is −96.2. If an individual firm raised its price by 1 percent, the quantity demanded of the firm's product would fall by a whopping 96.2 percent. The demand for an individual agricultural firm's product is very elastic indeed, because there are numerous firms in the industry selling close substitutes. The more competition among producers in an industry, the more elastic the demand for an individual firm's product.

TABLE 7–4	Market and Representative Firm Demand Elasticities for Selected U.S. Industries	
Industry	**Own Price Elasticity of Market Demand**	**Own Price Elasticity of Demand for Representative Firm's Product**
Agriculture	−1.8	−96.2
Construction	−1.0	−5.2
Durable manufacturing	−1.4	−3.5
Nondurable manufacturing	−1.3	−3.4
Transportation	−1.0	−1.9
Communication and utilities	−1.2	−1.8
Wholesale trade	−1.5	−1.6
Retail trade	−1.2	−1.8
Finance	−0.1	−5.5
Services	−1.2	−26.4

Source: Matthew D. Shapiro, "Measuring Market Power in U.S. Industry," National Bureau of Economic Research, Working Paper No. 2212, 1987.

When a firm sets its price equal to the marginal cost of production, the Lerner index is zero; consumers pay a price for the product that exactly equals the cost to the firm of producing another unit of the good. When a firm charges a price that is higher than marginal cost, the Lerner index takes on a value greater than zero, with the maximum possible value being unity. The Lerner index therefore provides a measure of how much firms in an industry mark up their prices over marginal cost. The higher the Lerner index, the greater the firm's markup. In industries in which firms rigorously compete for consumer sales by attempting to charge the lowest price in the market, the Lerner index is close to zero. When firms do not rigorously compete for consumers through price competition, the Lerner index is closer to 1.

The Lerner index is related to the markup charged by a firm. In particular, we can rearrange the formula for the Lerner index to obtain

$$P = \left(\frac{1}{1 - L}\right)MC$$

In this equation, $1/(1 - L)$ is the markup factor. It defines the factor by which marginal cost is multiplied to obtain the price of the good. When the Lerner index is zero, the markup factor is 1, and thus the price is exactly equal to marginal cost. If the Lerner index is 1/2, the markup factor is 2. In this case, the price charged by a firm is two times the marginal cost of production.

Tables 7–5A and B provide estimates of the Lerner index and markup factor for several Canadian and U.S. industries, respectively. Notice that there are considerable differences across industries. In both countries, the industry with the largest numbers is tobacco. In Canada, its Lerner index is 39 percent, which means that for every dollar paid to the firm by consumers, $0.39 is markup; alternatively, the price is 1.64 times the actual marginal cost of production. In the United States, the Lerner index and the markup factor are even greater, 76 percent and 4.17 respectively.

The Lerner index and markup factor for clothing/apparel are much lower. In Canada, for every dollar, a clothing manufacturer receives a negative markup; alternatively, the price of clothing articles is 0.96 times (that is, less than) the actual marginal cost of production. In the United States, this index is 24 percent, while the price apparel product is only 1.32 times the actual marginal cost. Again, the message for managers is that the markup charged for a product will vary with the nature of the market in which the product is sold. An important goal in the remaining chapters of this book is to help managers determine the optimal markup for a product.

TABLE 7–5A Lerner Indexes and Markup Factors for Selected Canadian Industries, 1978–79			
Industry Group	**No. of Observations***	**Lerner Index**	**Markup Factor**
Food and beverage industries	9	0.069	1.074
Tobacco products industries	1	0.391	1.641
Rubber and plastic products	2	0.214	1.272
Textile industries	7	0.070	1.076
Clothing industries	6	−0.043	0.959
Printing and publishing	3	0.012	1.012
Machinery industries	3	0.089	1.098
Wood industries	6	0.091	1.100
Primary metal industries	7	0.113	1.127
Electrical product industries	6	0.156	1.185
Petroleum and coal products	2	0.192	1.238
Chemical products	7	0.027	1.028
Furniture and fixture industries	4	0.162	1.193
Transportation equipment	5	0.121	1.137

*The number of three-digit industries included in each major industry group.
Source: Aileen J. Thompson, "Import Competition and Market Power: Canadian Evidence," rev. of Carleton Economic Paper #99-14 and Statistics Canada Research Paper Series #139 (Washington, DC: Federal Trade Commission, January 2001), available <www.ftc.gov/be/workpapers/wp232.pdf>, accessed July 6, 2004.

TABLE 7–5B	Lerner Indexes and Markup Factors for Selected U.S. Industries	
Industry	**Lerner Index**	**Markup Factor**
Food	0.26	1.35
Tobacco	0.76	4.17
Textiles	0.21	1.27
Apparel	0.24	1.32
Paper	0.58	2.38
Printing and publishing	0.31	1.45
Chemicals	0.67	3.03
Petroleum	0.59	2.44
Rubber	0.43	1.75
Leather	0.43	1.75

Source: Michael R. Baye and Jae-Woo Lee, "Ranking Industries by Performance: A Synthesis," Texas A&M University, Working Paper No. 90-20, March 1990; Matthew D. Shapiro, "Measuring Market Power in U.S. Industry," National Bureau of Economic Research, Working Paper No. 2212, 1987.

Demonstration PROBLEM 7–4

A firm in the airline industry has a marginal cost of $200 and charges a price of $300. What are the Lerner index and markup factor?

Answer

The Lerner index is

$$L = \frac{P - MC}{P} = \frac{300 - 200}{300} = \frac{1}{3}$$

The markup factor is

$$\frac{1}{1 - L} = \frac{1}{1 - 1/3} = 1.5$$

Integration and Merger Activity

Integration and merger activity also differ across industries. *Integration* refers to the uniting of productive resources. Integration can occur through a merger, in which two or more existing firms "unite," or merge, into a single firm. Alternatively (and as discussed in Chapter 6), integration can occur during the formation of a firm. By its very nature, integration results in larger firms than would exist in the absence of integration.

Economists distinguish between three types of integration, or mergers: vertical, horizontal, and conglomerate.

Vertical Integration

Vertical integration refers to a situation where various stages in the production of a single product are carried out in a single firm. For instance, an automobile manufacturer that produces its own steel, uses the steel to make car bodies and engines, and finally sells an automobile is vertically integrated. This is in contrast to a firm that buys car bodies and engines from other firms and then assembles all the parts supplied by the different suppliers. A *vertical merger* is the integration of two or more firms that produce components for a single product. We learned in Chapter 6 that firms vertically integrate to reduce the transaction costs associated with acquiring inputs.

Horizontal Integration

Horizontal integration refers to the merging of the production of similar products into a single firm. For example, if two computer firms merged into a single firm, horizontal integration would occur. Horizontal integration involves the merging of two or more final products into a single firm, whereas vertical integration involves the merging of two or more phases of production into a single firm.

In contrast to vertical integration, which occurs because this strategy reduces transaction costs, the primary reasons firms engage in horizontal integration are (1) to enjoy the cost savings of economies of scale or scope and (2) to enhance their market power. In some instances, horizontal integration allows firms to enjoy economies of scale and scope, thus leading to cost savings in producing the good. As a general rule, these types of horizontal mergers are socially beneficial. On the other hand, a *horizontal merger,* by its very definition, reduces the number of firms that compete in the product market. This tends to increase both the four-firm concentration ratio and the Herfindahl-Hirschman index for the industry, which reflects an increase in the market power of firms in the industry. The social benefits of the reduced costs due to a horizontal merger must be weighed against the social costs associated with a more concentrated industry.

When the benefits of cost reductions are small relative to the gain in market power enjoyed by the horizontally integrated firm, the government—specifically the Competition Bureau in association with Canada's Department of Justice—may choose to block the merger. The Merger Enforcement Guidelines (MEG) in Canada are discussed in Inside Business 7–4. In Chapter 14, we will discuss these and other government means of reducing market power.

Conglomerate Mergers

Finally, a *conglomerate merger* involves the integration of different product lines into a single firm. For example, if a cigarette maker and a cookie manufacturer merged into a single firm, a conglomerate merger would result. A conglomerate merger is similar to a horizontal merger in that it involves the merging of final products into a single firm. It differs from a horizontal merger because the final products are not related.

Why do some firms find a conglomerate merger advantageous? The cyclical nature of the demand for many products is such that there are times when demand is high and periods in which demand is low. Conglomerate mergers can improve firms' cash flows—revenues derived from one product line can be used to generate working capital when the demand for another product is low. This can reduce the variability of firm earnings and thus enhance a firm's ability to obtain funds in the capital market.

Trends in Mergers, Takeovers, and Acquisitions

Merger activity varied considerably during the twentieth century. As previously noted, mergers can result from an attempt by firms to reduce transaction costs, reap the benefits of economies of scale and scope, increase market power, or gain better access to capital markets. Some mergers are "friendly" in that both firms desire to merge into a single firm. Others are "hostile," meaning that one of the firms does not desire the merger to take place.

In some instances, mergers or takeovers occur because it is perceived that the management of one of the firms is doing an inadequate job of managing the firm. In this instance, the benefit of the takeover is the increased profits that result from "cleaning house," that is, firing the incompetent managers. Many managers fear

Inside BUSINESS

7–4 Merger Enforcement Guidelines: Calculation of Market Shares and Concentration Levels in Canada

The Competition Act in Canada, administered by the Competition Bureau together with the Department of Justice, is designed to maintain and encourage competition by preventing individuals and corporations from engaging in various kinds of anticompetitive conduct.

In defining the nature of anticompetitive conduct, however, it may help to distinguish between merger and monopolization cases and to understand why mergers are a concern in competition law. "In monopolization (abuse of dominance) cases, the issue is usually retrospective, i.e. whether the firm has exercised market power. The question is whether the firm has charged a price that exceeds the competitive price. In merger review, the concern is prospective. A merger should not be permitted if it creates or enhances market power, the ability of a single seller or group of sellers acting collectively to profitably increase and maintain prices above competitive levels. The analysis typically involves a comparison of the pre-merger price and industry structure with the likely post-merger environment."[1]

A prevention or lessening of competition can only result from a merger where the parties to the merger are, or would likely be, able to exercise a greater degree of market power, unilaterally or interdependently with others, than if the merger did not proceed.

A merger can lessen competition in two different ways. First, it may enable the merged entity to unilaterally raise price in any part of the relevant market. Second, it may bring about a price increase as a result of increased scope for interdependent behaviour in the market. Competition can also be prevented when a merger will inhibit the development of greater rivalry in a market already characterized by interdependent behaviour. This can occur, for example, as a result of the acquisition of a future entrant or of an increasingly vigorous incumbent in a highly stable market.

The first stage in the Bureau's review of a merger involves identifying the relevant market or markets in which the merging parties operate. A relevant market is defined as *the smallest group of products (which includes those of the merging firms) and the smallest geographic area such that a sole supplier of these products could profitably maintain a small but significant, non-transitory price increase greater than would prevail absent the merger*. In merger analysis, relevant markets are defined by reference to actual and potential sources of competition that constrain the exercise of market power. As a general principle, it cannot be assumed that the products of merging parties are in the same relevant market, even when there appears to be some overlap in the products they sell and in the geographic areas where they operate.

The next step is to calculate market shares and concentration levels. Mergers generally will not be challenged on the basis of concerns relating to the unilateral exercise of market power if the post-merger market share of the merged entity would be less than 35 percent. Similarly, mergers generally will not be challenged on the basis of concerns relating to the interdependent exercise of market power if the share of the market accounted for by the largest four firms (C_4) in the market post-merger would be less than 65 percent. However, even if the C_4 market share exceeds 65 percent, the Bureau will not challenge a merger on the basis of concerns relating to the interdependent exercise of market power if the merged entity's market share would be less than 10 percent. These thresholds merely serve to distinguish mergers unlikely to have anticompetitive consequences from those that require further analysis of various qualitative assessment criteria such as those highlighted in section 93 of the Competition Act.

Nonetheless, the competitive implications of a merger cannot be assessed solely on the basis of industry concentration or the market shares of the participants. In all cases, an assessment of market shares and concentration is only the starting point of analysis. The Competition Act requires that a whole range of other "qualitative" factors be considered: the extent of effective foreign competition; the possibility of a failing business; the availability of acceptable product substitutes; the existence of any trade, regulatory, or other barriers to entry; the extent of effective competition remaining in the market; whether the merger is likely to result in the removal of a vigorous and effective competitor; the nature and extent of innovation; and any other relevant factor.

It is important to note that market shares are calculated both for firms that currently produce output in the relevant market and for firms that can potentially participate in the relevant market through a supply response.

In contrast, in the United States, the merger guidelines primarily focus on Herfindahl-Hirschman Index (*HHI*). Accordingly, the U.S. Justice Department views industries with *HHI* in excess of 1800 to be " highly concentrated" and may attempt to block a horizontal merger if it will increase the *HHI* index by more than 100. However, similarly to the current practice in Canada, mergers in industries that have high *HHI* when there is evidence of significant foreign competition, an emerging new technology, or increased efficiency may be permitted. Industries with *HHI* below 1000 after a merger are generally considered "unconcentrated" by the authorities, and horizontal mergers are usually allowed. In cases in which the *HHI* is between 1000 and 1800, the Department relies on other factors, such as economies of scale and ease of entry into an industry, in determining whether to block a horizontal merger.

[1]Larry Schwartz, "The Hypothetical Monopolist Model: An Exposition" (Ottawa: Competition Tribunal, Competition Bureau).

InsideBUSINESS

7-5 The Language of Corporate Takeovers

Crown jewel. The most valued asset held by an acquisition target; divestiture of this asset is frequently a sufficient defense to dissuade takeover.

Fair price amendment. Requires super-majority approval of non-uniform, or two-tier, takeover bids not approved by the board of directors; can be avoided by a uniform bid for less than all outstanding shares (subject to prorationing under federal law if the offer is oversubscribed).

Going private. The purchase of publicly owned stock of a company by the existing or another competing management group; the company is delisted and public trading in the stock ceases.

Golden parachutes. The provisions in the employment contracts of top-level managers that provide for severance pay or other compensation should they lose their job as a result of a takeover.

Greenmail. The premium paid by a targeted company to a raider in exchange for his shares of the targeted company.

Leveraged buyout. The purchase of publicly owned stock of a company by the existing management with a portion of the purchase price financed by outside investors; the company is delisted and public trading in the stock ceases.

Lockup defense. Gives a friendly party (see *white knight*) the right to purchase assets of the firm, in particular the *crown jewel*, thus dissuading a takeover attempt.

Maiden. A term sometimes used to refer to the company at which the takeover is directed (target).

Poison pill. Gives stockholders other than those involved in a hostile takeover the right to purchase securities at a very favorable price in the event of a takeover.

Proxy contest. The solicitation of stockholder votes generally for the purpose of electing a slate of directors in competition with the current directors.

Raider. The person(s) or corporation attempting the takeover.

Shark repellents. Anti-takeover corporate charter amendments such as staggered terms for directors, a super-majority requirement for approving merger, or a mandate that bidders pay the same price for all shares in a buyout.

Standstill agreement. A contract in which a raider or firm agrees to limit its holdings in the target firm and not attempt a takeover.

Stripper. A successful raider who, once the target is acquired, sells off some of the assets of the target company.

Target. The company at which the takeover attempt is directed.

Targeted repurchase. A repurchase of common stock from an individual holder or a tender repurchase that excludes an individual holder; the former is the most frequent form of greenmail, while the latter is a common defensive tactic.

Tender offer. An offer made directly to shareholders to buy some or all of their shares for a specified price during a specified time.

Two-tier offer. A takeover offer that provides a cash price for sufficient shares to obtain control of the corporation, then a lower noncash (securities) price for the remaining shares.

White knight. A merger partner solicited by the management of a target who offers an alternative merger plan to that offered by the raider which protects the target company from the attempted takeover.

Source: Reprinted from Mack Ott and G. J. Santoni, "Mergers and Takeovers—The Value of Predators' Information," Federal Reserve Bank of St. Louis *Review,* December 1985, pp. 16–28.

mergers and acquisitions because they are uncertain about the impact of a merger on their position.

While conglomerate mergers were fashionable during the 1960s and 1970s, mergers in the 1980s, 1990s, and early 2000s tended to be horizontal in nature. Merger activity slowed considerably during the early 1990s, but since then has steadily increased. In 1997, for instance, nearly 4000 mergers were filed—more than twice the number in 1992. Between 1997 and 2001 the dollar value of mergers again more than doubled, thanks in part to the AOL–Time Warner and Exxon-Mobil

Inside BUSINESS

7-6 Recent Mergers in Various Canadian Industries

Pacifica Paper Inc. On March 26, 2001, Norske Skog Canada and Pacifica Papers announced that Norske Skog had agreed to acquire Pacifica for approximately C$961 million in cash, stock and assumed debt. The newly formed company is a significant player in the North American newsprint, uncoated groundwood papers, and telephone directory markets.

Mackenzie Financial. On January 29, 2001, after an extensive search and three serious bids, Mackenzie and Investors Group announced an agreement whereby Investors Group would acquire Mackenzie for C$30 per share.

JDS Uniphase Corporation. On February 14, 2001, JDS Uniphase Corporation completed its previously announced acquisition of SDL Inc. At C$21.8 billion, the deal ranks as one of the larger completed technology deals.

CanWest Global Communications Corporation. On July 31, 2000, CanWest Global Communications Corp. announced it would buy most of Hollinger's Canadian newspaper for approximately C$3.5 billion in cash, stock and debt. CanWest also obtained a 50 percent interest in Hollinger's *National Post* at the time of the transaction.

Amvescap Plc (AIM Canada). On May 9, 2000, Amvescap Plc, the world's second-largest publicly traded fund manager by assets, agreed to acquire Trimark Financial Corporation for C$2.7 billion in cash, stock, and debt to boost its share of Canada's C$410 billion mutual fund market. Combining Trimark, Canada's sixth-largest mutual fund company, with Amvescap's existing Canadian operations (AIM Canada) moved Amvescap Plc to the number two spot in the Canadian market.

BCE Inc. On February 15, 2000, BCE Inc. offered to buy the 77 percent of Teleglobe Inc. it didn't already own for C$9.8 billion in stock to expand its international telephone network for electronic commerce and data services. Teleglobe shareholders were to receive BCE shares with a value of C$48.41 for each Teleglobe common share.

On June 19, 2000, BCE Inc. cut the value of its offer to purchase Teleglobe to C$6.5 billion, or C$32.67 per common share. The transaction was completed November 1, 2000 with Teleglobe shareholders receiving 0.907 of a BCE common share and ($0.10 cash per Teleglobe share).

Abitibi-Consolidated. On February 11, 2000, Abitibi-Consolidated, the world's largest newsprint manufacturer, agreed to buy Donohue Inc. for C$7.1 billion to create a company with one-third of the North American newsprint

market. The new company also became the fifth-largest lumber producer in North America. Abitibi paid C$11 in cash C$31 in stock for each Donohue share, with the assumption of C$1.3 billion in debt.

Newcourt Credit Group Inc. On March 9, 1999, Newcourt Credit Group Inc. and The CIT Group agreed to merge in a transaction valued at C$6.3 billion. Newcourt shareholders were to receive 0.92 shares of CIT shares per Newcourt share. After failing to meet an earnings test, Newcourt agreed to a revised exchange ratio of 0.70 CIT shares per Newcourt share.

JDS FITEL Inc. On January 28, 1999, JDS FITEL Inc. ("JDS") and Uniphase Corporation ("Uniphase") agreed to a merger of equals transaction. The deal ranked as the second-largest M&A transaction involving a Canadian technology company to date.

Battle Mountain Gold. The merger of Battle Mountain Gold Company with a wholly-owned subsidiary of Newmont Mining Corp. was completed on January 10, 2001. Under the merger agreement, each of Battle Mountain's exchangeable shares was exchanged for 0.105 of a share of Newmont common stock. In addition, each of Battle Mountain's convertible preferred shares was exchanged for one share of Newmont convertible preferred shares with substantially identical terms and conditions.

Canadian Oil Sands Trust. On March 8, 2001, Athabasca Oil Sands Trust and Canadian Oil Sands Trust announced that they had entered into an agreement in principle to merge. The transaction closed on July 10, 2001. Each unitholder of Athabasca Oil Sands received one unit of Canadian Oil Sands in exchange for each unit of Canadian Oil Sands held. Athabasca Oil Sands unitholders also received a special cash distribution of C$0.50 per unit. The combined trust had a market capitalization of C$2 billion and a 21.74 percent ownership interest in the Syncrude Joint Venture, the world's largest oil sands mining project.

TD Securities. On January 17, 2001, after having received all necessary regulatory approvals, TD Bank Financial Group announced that TD Securities had completed its acquisition of Newcrest Capital Inc. The transaction, which was initially announced on November 7, 2000, combined the strengths of Newcrest, as Canada's leading independent investment banking and institutional equities firm, with the global capabilities of TD Securities, the wholesale side of TD Bank Financial Group.

mergers. Thus, we see that over the past several decades there has been considerable variation in the type and level of merger activity.

Research and Development

Earlier we noted that firms and industries differ with respect to the underlying technologies used to produce goods and services. One way firms gain a technological advantage is by engaging in research and development (R&D) and then obtaining a patent for the technology developed through the R&D. Tables 7–6A and B provide R&D spending as a percentage of sales for selected firms in Canada and the United States. Notice the variation in R&D spending across industries. According to Table 7–6A, in the telecommunication industry in Canada, for example, Nortel reinvested almost 20 percent of its sales revenue in R&D, whereas in mining and metals Alcan reinvested only 0.92 percent of its sales revenue in R&D. In the United States, Table 7–6B, the highest figure relates to the pharmaceutical industry, in which Bristol-Myers Squibb reinvested 10.6 percent of its sales revenue in R&D, whereas in the food industry Kellogg reinvested only 1.7 percent of its sales revenue in R&D.

The message is clear for manager: the optimal amount to spend on R&D will depend on the characteristics of the industry in which the firm operates. One goal

TABLE 7–6A	R&D, Advertising, and Profits as a Percentage of Sales for Selected Canadian Firms			
Company (2002 figures used)	Industry	R&D as % of Sales	Advertising as % of Sales	Profits as % of Sales
Nortel Networks	Telecommunications	20.59	17.88	2.84
Magna International	Automotive	4.27	6.01	4.27
Bombardier	Aerospace	1.20	N/A	−2.60
Pfizer Canada	Pharmaceuticals	15.99	33.50	28.19
IBM Canada	Software/computer services	6.16	20.03	8.99
Alcan	Mining and metals	0.92	4.60	2.98

Sources: 2002 annual reports of the companies.

TABLE 7–6B	R&D, Advertising, and Profits as a Percentage of Sales for Selected U.S. Firms			
Company	Industry	R&D as Percentage of Sales	Advertising as Percentage of Sales	Profits as Percentage of Sales
AT&T	Telecommunications	0.6	3.0	7.1
Bristol-Myers Squibb	Pharmaceuticals	10.6	9.2	25.9
Ford	Motor vehicles and parts	2.1	4.8	2.5
Gillette	Metal products	1.9	6.5	4.2
Goodyear Tire & Rubber	Rubber and plastic products	2.9	1.7	0.3
Kellogg	Food	1.7	8.7	8.5
Procter & Gamble	Soaps and cosmetics	4.8	9.2	8.6

Source: 2000 annual reports of the companies; author's calculations.

in the remaining chapters of this book is to examine the major determinants of R&D spending.

Advertising

As Tables 7–6A and B reveal, there is also considerable variation across firms in the level of advertising utilized. In Canada, firms in pharmaceutical industry, such as Pfizer, spend about 33 percent of their sales revenue on advertising (see Table 7–6A). In contrast, firms in the mining and metals industry, such as Alcan, spend less than 5 percent of their sales revenue on advertising. In the United States, the highest percentage of advertising to sales revenue is shown in the pharmaceuticals and the soaps and cosmetics industry, 9.2 percent as indicated in Table 7–6B; the lowest is shown in rubber and plastic products, 1.7 percent.

Performance

Performance refers to the profits and social welfare that result in a given industry. It is important for future managers to recognize that profits and social welfare vary considerably across industries.

Profits

Tables 7–6A and B highlight differences in profits across firms in different industries. Ford generated more sales than any other firm on the list, yet its profits as a percentage of sales are among the lowest listed. One task in the next several chapters is to examine why "big" firms do not always earn big profits. As a manager, it would be a mistake to believe that just because your firm is large, it will automatically earn profits.

Social Welfare

Dansby-Willig (DW) performance index
Ranks industries according to how much social welfare would improve if the output in an industry were increased by a small amount.

Another gauge of industry performance is the amount of consumer and producer surplus generated in a market. While this type of performance is difficult to measure, R. E. Dansby and R. D. Willig have proposed a useful index. The **Dansby-Willig (DW) performance index** measures how much social welfare (defined as the sum of consumer and producer surplus) would improve if firms in an industry expanded output in a socially efficient manner. If the Dansby-Willig index for an industry is zero, there are no gains to be obtained by inducing firms in the industry to alter their outputs; consumer and producer surplus are maximized given industry demand and cost conditions. When the index is greater than zero, social welfare would improve if industry output was expanded.

This index, which measures the magnitude of the change in social benefits (gross social gains), is sensitive to the underlying industry structure and reduces to standard market concentration and monopoly power indexes such as the four-firm concentration ratio, the *HHI*, and the Lerner index given familiar sets of assumptions on firm behaviour. The Dansby-Willig index thus allows one to rank industries according to how much social welfare would rise if the industry altered its output. Industries with large index values have poorer performance than industries with lower values. In Table 7–7, for instance, we see that the chemical industry has the highest DW index. This suggests that a slight change in output in the chemical industry would increase social welfare more than would a slight change in the output in any of the other industries. The textile industry has the lowest DW index, which reveals the best performance.

TABLE 7–7	Dansby-Willig Performance Indexes for Selected U.S. Industries
Industry	**Dansby-Willig Index**
Food	0.51
Textiles	0.38
Apparel	0.47
Paper	0.63
Printing and publishing	0.56
Chemicals	0.67
Petroleum	0.63
Rubber	0.49
Leather	0.60

Source: Michael R. Baye and Jae-Woo Lee, "Ranking Industries by Performance: A Synthesis," Texas A&M Working Paper No. 90–20, March 1990.

Demonstration PROBLEM 7–5

Suppose you are the manager of a firm in the textile industry. You have just learned that the government has placed the textile industry at the top of its list of industries it plans to regulate and intends to force the industry to expand output and lower the price of textile products. How should you respond?

Answer

You should point out to government's counsel that the textile industry in Canada has one of the lowest Lerner index out of the 14 major industries listed in Table 7–5A only $0.07 of each $1 paid by consumers is markup. The efficient way for government to improve social welfare is to alter output in the other industries first.

The Structure-Conduct-Performance Paradigm

You now have a broad overview of the structure, conduct, and performance of U.S. industry. The *structure* of an industry refers to factors such as technology, concentration, and market conditions. *Conduct* refers to how individual firms behave in the market; it involves pricing decisions, advertising decisions, and decisions to invest in research and development, among other factors. *Performance* refers to the resulting profits and social welfare that arise in the market. The *structure-conduct-performance paradigm* views these three aspects of industry as being integrally related.

The Causal View

The *causal view* of industry asserts that market structure "causes" firms to behave in a certain way. In turn, this behaviour, or conduct, "causes" resources to be allocated in certain ways, leading to either "good" or "poor" market performance. To better understand the causal view, consider a highly concentrated industry in which only a few firms compete for the right to sell products to consumers. According to the causal view, this structure gives firms market power, enabling them to charge high prices for their products. The behaviour (charging high prices) is caused by market structure (the presence of few competitors). The high prices, in turn, "cause" high profits and poor performance (low social welfare). Thus, according to the causal view, a concentrated market "causes" high prices and poor performance.

The Feedback Critique

Today most economists recognize that the causal view provides, at best, an incomplete view of the relations between structure, conduct, and performance. According to the *feedback critique,* there is no one-way causal link among structure, conduct, and performance. The conduct of firms can affect market structure; market performance can affect conduct as well as market structure. To illustrate the feedback critique, let us apply it to the previous analysis, which stated that concentration causes high prices and poor performance.

According to the feedback critique, the conduct of firms in an industry may itself lead to a concentrated market. If the (few) existing firms are charging low prices and earning low economic profits, there will be no incentive for additional firms to enter the market. If this is the case, it could actually be low prices that "cause" the presence of few firms in the industry. In summary, then, it is a simplification of reality to assert that concentrated markets cause high prices. Indeed, the pricing behaviour of firms can affect the number of firms. As we will see in subsequent chapters, low prices and good performance can occur even if only one or two firms are operating in an industry. A detailed explanation of this possibility will have to wait until we develop models for various market structures.

Overview of the Remainder of the Book

In the remaining chapters of this book, we examine the optimal managerial conduct under a variety of market structures. To have some terminology that will enable us to distinguish between various types of market structures, it is useful to introduce the four basic models we will use to accomplish this goal. Recognize, however, that our discussion of these four models provides only an overview; indeed, entire chapters will be devoted to making managerial decisions in each of these situations.

Perfect Competition

In markets characterized by *perfect competition,* there are many firms, each of which is small relative to the entire market. The firms have access to the same technologies and produce similar products, so no firm has any real advantage over other firms in the industry. Firms in perfectly competitive markets do not have market power; that is, no individual firm has a perceptible impact on the market price, quantity, or quality of the product produced in the market. In perfectly competitive markets, both concentration ratios and Rothschild indexes tend to be close to zero. We will study perfectly competitive markets in detail in the next chapter.

Monopoly

A *monopoly* is a firm that is the sole producer of a good or service in the relevant market. For instance, most local utility companies are the sole providers of electricity, natural gas, and local telephone services in a given city. Some towns have a single gasoline station or movie theatre that serves the entire local market. All of these constitute local monopolies.

When there is a single provider of a good or service in a market, there is a tendency for the seller to capitalize on the monopoly position by restricting output and charging

Inside BUSINESS

7-7 The Evolution of Market Structure in the Computer Industry

Industries can change dramatically over time. During the course of its evolution, a given industry may go through phases that include monopoly, oligopoly, monopolistic competition, and perfect competition. For this reason, it is important to understand how to make decisions in all four environments, even if you "know" you will work for a monopoly when you graduate. The following description of the evolution in the computer industry should convince you of this fact.

In the 1960s, a few large firms produced mainframe computers for universities, scientific think tanks, and large business applications. Each computer was designed almost exclusively for a specific user, and its cost often was over $100 000. Because each computer kept its own standards, a customer whose computer needed repair was forced to go to the original manufacturer or write off the original purchase. This allowed the few companies that produced computers to act as virtual monopolists once they had a customer base. The early computer firms enjoyed high profit margins, some as high as 50 to 60 percent. These large profits induced several new firms to enter the computer market.

With entry came innovation in technology that reduced the size of mainframes, lowered the cost of production, and, because of increased competition, reduced the price to the customer. This influx of new competitors and products brought the market for computers into an oligopolistic-type structure. As a result, each firm became acutely aware of competitors and their actions. However, each firm held on to the specialized hardware and software for each user. Because of the specialized nature of the smaller machines, customers were still subject to their original purchases when it came to upgrades. However, since the price of the original machines was lower in the new environment, it was less costly to write off the original purchase and shift from one company to another. Of course, suppliers recognized this fact, which led to more vigorous competition. In the 1970s, the combination of

lower prices and more competition decreased the returns in the market to 20 to 40 percent for the industry.

The 1980s brought the personal computer into many medium-size businesses that previously could not afford a computer. Along with the PC came workstations and minicomputers. Although profit margins had dropped in the 1970s, they were still high enough in the 1980s to entice new entry. The computer market of the 1980s was moving toward monopolistic competition, with a few large firms and many small firms, each producing slightly different styles of computers. Computers became affordable to many households and smaller businesses. As more firms entered the market, profit margins dropped drastically and copycat firms began opening the systems; thus, many parts became interchangeable between machines. Economic profits still were being earned, but profit margins had dropped to around 10 to 20 percent.

During the 1990s, computer makers attempted to maintain margins by differentiating their products. This tactic was of limited success, as the open systems of the 1990s led to standardized technology at virtually all levels of the computer industry. By early 2000, many components of PCs had become "commodities" that were bought and sold in markets resembling those with perfect competition. As a consequence, there were few dimensions other than price for PC makers to use in differentiating their products. This heightened price competition in the early 2000s significantly reduced the profits of computer manufacturers, including key players such as Dell and Gateway. As of 2002, this strain on profits has begun to translate into exit and consolidation within the industry. Further changes in industry structure are almost certain over the next decade. The computer industry thus provides an enlightening look at the dynamics of industry.

Sources: Simon Forge, "Why the Computer Industry Is Restructuring Now," *Futures* 23, November 1991, pp. 960–77; annual reports of the companies.

a price above marginal cost. Because there are no other firms in the market, consumers cannot switch to another producer in the face of higher prices. Consequently, consumers either buy some of the product at the higher price or go without it. In monopolistic markets, there is extreme concentration and the Rothschild index is unity.

Monopolistic Competition

In a market characterized by *monopolistic competition,* there are many firms and consumers, just as in perfect competition. Thus, concentration measures are close to zero. Unlike in perfect competition, however, each firm produces a product that is slightly different from the products produced by other firms; Rothschild indexes are greater than zero. Those who manage restaurants in a city containing numerous food establishments operate in a monopolistically competitive industry.

A firm in a monopolistically competitive market has some control over the price charged for the product. By raising the price, some consumers will remain loyal to the firm due to a preference for the particular characteristics of its product. But some consumers will switch to other brands. For this reason, firms in monopolistically competitive industries often spend considerable sums on advertising in an attempt to convince consumers that their brands are "better" than other brands. This reduces the number of customers who switch to other brands when a firm raises the price for its product.

Oligopoly

In an *oligopolistic* market, a few large firms tend to dominate the market. Firms in highly concentrated industries such as the airline, automobile, and aerospace industries operate in an oligopolistic market.

When one firm in an oligopolistic market changes its price or marketing strategy, not only its own profits but the profits of the other firms in the industry are affected. Consequently, when one firm in an oligopoly changes its conduct, other firms in the industry have an incentive to react to the change by altering their own conduct. Thus, the distinguishing feature of an oligopolistic market is *mutual interdependence* among firms in the industry.

The interdependence of profits in an oligopoly gives rise to strategic interaction among firms. For example, suppose the manager of an oligopoly is considering increasing the price charged for the firm's product. To determine the impact of the price increase on profits, the manager must consider how rival firms in the industry will respond to the price increase. Thus, the strategic plans of one firm in an oligopoly depend on how that firm expects other firms in the industry to respond to the plans, if they are adopted. For this reason, it is very difficult to manage a firm that operates in an oligopoly. Because large rewards are paid to managers who know how to operate in oligopolistic markets, we will devote two chapters to an analysis of managerial decisions in such markets.

ANSWERING THE Headline

The headline discussed the failed bank mergers of 1998, and indicated that the Ministry of Finance could not entertain additional merger talks until, at the earliest, the end of September 2004. One of Canada's senators argued that "both sides present strong and closely reasoned arguments."[1] Among these arguments for such mergers were that the mergers would provide for economies of scale necessary to be competitive globally. Arguments against included all of the concerns from the 1998 decision, including the concentration of economic power and decreased levels of financial services.

It is instructive to realize that, while a March 2003 House Committee report indicated that it was in favour of bank mergers, it did so with a few concerns. It

---

[1]E. Leo Kolber, "A Case for Bank Mergers: Keeping Canada Competitive in a Global Financial Services Industry," *Policy Options*, March 2003, available <www.irpp.org/po/archive/mar03/kolber.pdf>, accessed July 6, 2004.

wanted to ensure that job losses would be minimal, and that service to rural and small communities would not be interrupted. Additionally, the report indicated that any merger would have to make it easier for small- and medium-sized enterprises to access capital.[2]

These findings were similar to those in 1998, which were influenced by two independent reviews: the Competition Bureau's assessment and the review by the Office of Superintendent of Financial Institutions (OSFI). The Competition Bureau concluded that the proposed bank mergers would likely lead to a substantial lessening or prevention of competition, while OSFI noted that if one of the merged banks were to run into trouble, the policy options for government would be severely reduced.

Nevertheless, the argument that mergers would improve global competitiveness bears consideration. Although Canada's major banks are, for the most part, Canada-centric, the fact remains that major financial transactions are global in nature. Canada's banks are sizable, but by comparison to Citigroup, the largest bank in the world, they are financial lightweights. Canada's competitive edge as a nation rests, partly, on the strength of its financial system, so mergers to strengthen this pillar may be welcome. The trick will be to ensure that they don't strengthen Canada beyond its borders, while weakening it within.

Summary

This chapter reveals that different industries have different market structures and require different types of managerial decisions. The structure of an industry, and therefore the job of the manager, is dependent on the number of firms in the industry, the structure of demand and costs, the availability of information, and the behaviour of other firms in the industry.

The four-firm concentration ratio is one measure of market structure. If the ratio equals one, the industry is a monopoly or oligopoly; if it is zero, the industry is competitive. Another measure of market structure is the Herfindahl-Hirschman index (*HHI*), which can range from 10 000 for a monopoly to zero for a perfectly competitive industry. Of course, these indexes must be used in conjunction with other information, including whether the market is local and whether the firm competes with foreign firms.

Other summary statistics include the Lerner index, the Rothschild index, and the Dansby-Willig index. These indexes provide a manager information about industry cost and demand conditions. For instance, the greater the Lerner index in an industry, the greater the ability of a firm in the industry to charge a high markup on its product. The information needed to construct these indexes can be obtained from sources listed in the resource list provided in the appendix to this chapter.

The data presented in this chapter reveal industrywide differences in activities such as advertising and research and development. The remainder of the book will explain why these differences exist and the optimal managerial decisions for alternative market structures. The next chapter begins with a study of managerial decisions under perfect competition, monopoly, and monopolistic competition.

[2]"Manley Says No Bank Mergers Before September 2004," CBC News site, December 4, 2003 <www.cbc.ca/stories/2003/06/23/manley_0306223>, accessed July 6, 2004.

Key Terms and Concepts

Dansby-Willig (DW) performance
    index 247
four-firm concentration ratio 228
Herfindahl-Hirschman index (*HHI*) 230

Lerner index 238
market structure 227
Rothschild index 236

Conceptual and Computational Questions

1. Ten firms compete in a market to sell product X. The total sales of all firms selling the product are \$1 million. Ranking the firms' sales from highest to lowest, we find the top four firms' sales to be \$175 000, \$150 000, \$125 000, and \$100 000, respectively. Calculate the four-firm concentration ratio in the market for product X.

2. An industry consists of three firms with sales amounting of \$200 000, \$500 000, and \$400 000.
   a. Calculate the Herfindahl-Hirschman index *(HHI).*
   b. Calculate the four-firm concentration ratio (C_4).
   c. On the basis of Canada's Merger Enforcement Guidelines (MEGs) described in the text, do you think the Competition Bureau would block a horizontal merger between two firms with sales of \$200 000 and \$400 000? How would your answer change if the U.S. merger guidelines were applied? Explain.

3. Suppose the own price elasticity of market demand for retail gasoline is -0.9, the Rothschild index is 0.6, and a typical gasoline retailer enjoys sales of \$1.2 million annually. What is the price elasticity of demand for a representative gasoline retailer's product?

4. A firm has \$1 million in sales, a Lerner index of 0.65, and a marginal cost of \$35, and competes against 1000 other firms in its relevant market.
   a. What price does this firm charge its customers?
   b. By what factor does this firm mark up its price over marginal cost?
   c. Do you think this firm enjoys much market power? Explain.

5. Evaluate the following statement: "Managers should specialize by acquiring only the tools needed to operate in a particular market structure. That is, managers should specialize in managing either a perfectly competitive, monopoly, monopolistically competitive, or oligopoly firm."

6. Under what conditions might the Competition Bureau approve a merger between two companies that operate in an industry with a pre-merger total market share of less than 35 percent?

7. Based only on the knowledge that the pre-merger market share of two firms proposing to merge was 20 percent each, an economist working for the Competition Bureau was able to determine that, if approved, the post-merger *HHI* would increase by 800. How was the economist able to draw this conclusion without knowledge of the other firms' market shares? From this information, can you devise a general rule explaining how the Herfindahl-Hirschman index is affected when exactly two firms in the market merge? (*Hint:* Compare $a^2 + b^2$ with $(a + b)^2$.)

8. Consider a firm that operates in a market that competes aggressively in prices. Due to the high fixed cost of obtaining the technology associated with entering this market, only a limited number of other firms exist. Furthermore, over 70 percent of the products sold in this market are protected by patents for the next eight years. Does this industry conform to an economist's definition of a perfectly competitive market?

Problems and Applications

9. You work at a firm on Bay Street that specializes in mergers, and you are the team leader in charge of getting approval for a merger between two major beer manufacturers in Canada. While Table 7–2A in the text indicates that the four-firm concentration ratio for the breweries operating in Canada is 99 percent, your team has put together a report suggesting that the merger does not present competition concerns even though the two firms each enjoy a 15 percent share of the Canadian market. Provide an outline of your report.

10. Forey, Inc. competes against many other firms in a highly competitive industry. Over the last decade, several firms have entered this industry and, as a consequence, Forey is earning a return on investment that roughly equals the interest rate. Furthermore, the four-firm concentration ratio and the Herfindahl-Hirschman index are both quite small, but the Rothschild index is significantly greater than zero. On the basis of this information, which market structure best characterizes the industry in which Forey competes? Explain.

11. Firms like Pizza Pizza, Domino's, and Pizza Hut sell pizza and other products that are differentiated in nature. While numerous pizza chains exist in most locations, the differentiated nature of these firms' products permits them to charge prices above marginal cost. Given these observations, is the pizza industry most likely a monopoly, perfectly competitive, monopolistically competitive, or an oligopoly industry? Use the causal view of structure, conduct, and performance to explain the role of differentiation in the market for pizza. Then apply the feedback critique to the role of differentiation in the industry.

12. Which of the following would most likely to be scrutinized under the Competition Bureau's guidelines for horizontal mergers?
    a. Mackenzie and Investors Group announce an agreement whereby Investors Group would acquire Mackenzie.
    b. CanWest Global Communications Corp. announces it will buy most of Hollinger's Canadian newspapers.
    c. Air Canada acquires Canadian Airlines International.
    d. A merger is proposed between the Bank of Montreal and the Royal Bank.

13. Nationwide Bank has approached Hometown Bank with a proposal to merge. The following table lists the sales of the top nine banks in the area. Use this information to calculate the four-firm concentration ratio and Herfindahl-Hirschman index. In view of the Competition Bureau's merger guidelines described in the text, do you think the proposed merger is likely to be blocked?

Bank Name	2001 Sales (in millions)
MegaBank	$900
City Bank	850
Nationwide Bank	735
Atlantic Savings	555
Provincial Bank	345
Metropolitan Bank	340
Canadian Bank	265
Hometown Bank	120
Urban Bank	90

14. In November 2000, Trilogy Retail Enterprises L.P., in a hostile takeover attempt, announced an offer to acquire a majority share of Chapters Inc., with the purpose of merging Chapters with Indigo Books & Music Ltd. In February 2001, Trilogy was successful in this bid. The market was highly concentrated. Chapters was the dominant book retailer in Canada, owning 76 book superstores, the World's Biggest Bookstore in Toronto, and 231 mall-based bookstores. Indigo was the only other significant owner of book superstores in Canada. The Competition Bureau's initial review determined that the proposed transaction would be problematic for both consumers and publishers, and might substantially lessen or prevent competition in both upstream and downstream markets. On the basis of this information, do you think the Bureau would have unconditionally approved the merger? Under what circumstances would the Bureau consider this merger?

15. Use the estimated elasticities in Table 7–4 to calculate the Rothschild index for each industry. On the basis of these calculations, which industry most closely resembles perfect competition? Which industry most closely resembles monopoly?

16. In 2000, Pfizer and Warner-Lambert agreed to a $90 billion merger, creating one of the world's largest pharmaceutical companies. As Tables 7–6A and B illustrate, pharmaceutical companies tend to spend a greater percentage of sales on R&D activities than many other industries. The government encourages these R&D activities by granting companies patents for drugs approved by Health Canada. For instance, Pfizer spent large sums of money developing its popular cholesterol-lowering drug, Liptor, which is currently protected under a patent. Liptor sells for about $3 per pill. Calculate the Lerner index if the marginal cost of producing Liptor is $0.30 per pill. Does the Lerner index make sense in this situation? Explain.

17. Many MBAs who ventured into the dot-com world of the late 1990s found themselves unemployed by 2001 as many firms in that industry ceased to exist. However, during their tenure with these companies, these managers gained valuable skills in how to operate within a highly competitive environment. On the basis of the numbers in Table 7–3 in this chapter, which industries represent the best match for these managers' expertise? Looking at the industries listed in Table 7–3, what factors give rise to the varying levels of market power?

APPENDIX: Data Sources for Managers

Financial Websites for Canadian Businesses

A number of websites are available to all managers that outline and discuss economic trends and news stories that may be of interest to managers in Canada. Canada's two major newspapers, *The Globe and Mail* and *National Post*, have comprehensive, constantly updated news stories and well-informed columnists, as well as links to financial sections. *The Globe and Mail* has a dedicated financial site <www.globeinvestor.com> that acts as a combined source of the latest news and individual company information for firms listed on the Toronto Stock Exchange (TSX). *National Post* has a similar site <www.nationalpost.com/financialpost/index.html>. First-time users of these sites should be aware that some of the online financial reporting is exclusive to the sites, and cannot be found in the individual newspapers' print versions. *The Globe and Mail*'s magazine Report on Business is also available online <www.robmagazine.com>.

The Bank of Canada Website

For a comprehensive picture of how Canada's monetary policy is implemented, the Bank of Canada's website <www.bankofcanada.ca> is excellent. It contains news reports relating to the Bank's actions (for example, what the effects of changes in indirect taxes on CPI are), press releases from the Bank and speeches by the Bank's Governor, and access to comprehensive coverage of interest rates, inflation, monetary policy, and a host of other Bank of Canada–related issues.

Government of Canada Websites

The Government of Canada has a host of websites that relate to the economy as a whole, individual components of the economy, small businesses, economics, strategy, and human resources development. An excellent place for managers to go for a wide variety of business-related information is the Strategis Canada site <strategis.ic.gc.ca>. With information on everything from bankruptcy to mergers and competition to patents, it provides a plethora of information useful in making decisions. Statistics Canada <www.statscan.ca> is a portal to a wide variety of information on everything from population size to individual industry sales data in Canada. It should be noted that access to many of these documents is on a fee-for-service basis, but the items can be accessed without charge if your academic institution's library has access to Statistics Canada's electronic journal service.

Websites of Canada's Top Financial Institutions

Each of Canada's leading banks has information and analysis on the economy available online and, depending on the site, significant industries. The sites offer description and analysis of key economic indicators, market trends, and economic forecasts. RBC Financial Group, for example, have an online *Economic Digest* that discusses current trends and analysis, news forecasts, financial markets, global markets, and U.S. leading indicators. The Bank of Montreal offers BMO Economics that offers data releases, regular publications, outlook publications, industry analysis, and special reports. Which site provides the best information will be a matter of individual preference, since all leading financial institutions provide comprehensive, interesting, and solid analysis and discussion.

Canadian Economic Think Tanks

Canada, like the United States, has institutions that specialize in reviewing and analyzing both micro and macro issues in the Canadian economy, and reporting on them. Many of these institutions are widely respected, and figure prominently in news media. Institutes such as the Toronto-based C. D. Howe Institute <www.cdhowe.org>, the Vancouver-based Fraser Institute <www.fraserinstitute.ca>, the Canadian Centre for Policy Alternatives <www.policyalternatives.ca>, and the Atlantic Institute for Maritime Studies <www.aims.ca> have online access to many publications touching on local, regional, and national issues relevant to the economy. Some of these publications may be available only through subscription, but there are abstracts for most studies available.

International/Global Perspectives

Managers interested in contextualizing their knowledge are encouraged to seek publications with an international perspective. Two of the best are the magazine *The Economist* <www.theeconomist.com> and *Financial Times* <www.ft.com>. These offer only limited access to nonsubscribers online, but even this limited offering reveals the quality and depth of analysis provided. Managers are encouraged to review these two publications if they are interested in a non–North American view of their industries and nations.

The Wall Street Journal

The Wall Street Journal is a daily business newspaper that is a highly useful information source for managers. It contains general information about trends in the economy, recent mergers and acquisitions, and government regulations. Its economic news coverage is international in scope, featuring 130 overseas journalists. A section called "Marketplace" provides insights into strategies used by firms to enhance sales and market penetration. The "Economy" page, located in the first section, contains stories regarding macroeconomics, inflation trends, unemployment, and Federal Reserve policy. Another economics-related element of *The Wall Street Journal* is the Performance Graph, which on many days provides a graph of a major economic gauge. There is also an online version of *The Wall Street Journal* (wsj.com) that contains a 30-day research archive with articles from the *Journal, Barron's,* and Dow Jones newswires.

Business Week, Fortune, and Forbes

Business Week, Fortune, and *Forbes* are business magazines that contain detailed information about individual firms in various industries. Numerous "special issues" are published that provide information about firms' profits and sales, changes in profits and sales by industry, and compensation paid to top executives at major U.S. firms. Featured in *Business Week* (www.businessweek.com) are sections called "Economic Viewpoint" and "Economic Trends" as well as articles focusing on government regulation and labour and management issues. Both *Fortune* (www.fortune.com) and *Forbes* (www.forbes.com) contain extensive "Market" sections in their magazines.

Economic Journals

Numerous economic journals provide estimates of elasticities of demand for various goods and services. *Review of Economics and Statistics* traditionally publishes regression results for problems of interest to managers, including demand and cost functions. Each issue contains estimates of elasticities of some underlying economic relationship. The previous 19 issues, from February 1997 to August 2001, are available within the Catchword website (www.catchword.co.uk). *Applied Economics* also publishes empirical studies of demand and costs. *The Journal of Human Resources* publishes studies of labour demand and supply. Each issue since 1990 can be found at *The Journal of Human Resources'* website (www.ssc.wisc.edu/jhr). *The Journal of Economic Perspectives,* which is a journal of the American Economic Association, publishes descriptive articles that provide managers with an overview of specific economic issues. For instance, recent issues have focused on such topics as horizontal mergers and e-commerce. The journal strives to provide economic analysis of public policy issues and to integrate ideas across different fields of thinking; it can be found on the American Economic Association's website (www.aeaweb.org/jep/). *The Journal of Economics and Management Strategy* specializes in articles that are of particular interest to managers. This journal also is accessible through the Catchword website (www.catchword.co.uk).

Headline

In June 2002, McDonald's launched the "Lighter Choices Menu," a new, uniquely Canadian menu category full of products with significant reductions of calories or fat—and most often both—compared with other menu products. McDonald's is one of the world's largest food service retailers, serving over 43 million customers every day. More than 85 percent of McDonald's restaurants around the world are owned and operated by independent franchisees.

McDonald's Lighter Choices Menu is an innovative plan to offer Canadian customers more choice, more variety, and more great taste with items including the McVeggie Burger, the Whole Wheat Chicken McGrill with BBQ Sauce, the Fruit 'n Yogurt Parfait, Chicken Fajitas, Mandarin California Greens Salad, Chicken Caesar Salad, Side Garden Salad, Warm Crispy Chicken Oriental Salad, and Warm Chicken Oriental Salad.

The company worked with a leading Canadian nutritionist and some of Canada's leading companies in the development of the menu category. For example, McDonald's partnered with Yves Veggie Cuisine, North America's biggest maker of meat alternatives, to develop the exclusive McVeggie Burger, with Danone to develop the Fruit 'n Yogurt Parfait, and Hellmann's to provide the wide selection of salad dressings offered under the Lighter Choices banner.

Do you think the new launch will have a sustainable impact on the company's bottom line? Explain.

Introduction

In the previous chapter, we examined the nature of industries and saw that industries differ with respect to their underlying structures, conduct, and performances. In this chapter, we characterize the optimal price, output, and advertising decisions of managers operating in environments of (1) perfect competition, (2) monopoly, and (3) monopolistic competition. We will analyze oligopoly decisions in Chapters 9 and 10 and examine more sophisticated pricing strategies in Chapter 11. With an understanding of the concepts presented in these chapters, you will be prepared to manage a firm that operates in virtually any environment.

Because this is the beginning of our analysis of output decisions of managers operating in an industry, it is logical to start with the most simple case: a situation in which managerial decisions have no perceptible impact on the market price. Thus, in the first section of this chapter we will analyze output decisions of managers operating in perfectly competitive markets. In subsequent sections, we will examine output decisions by firms that have market power: monopoly and monopolistic competition. The analysis in this chapter will serve as a building block for the analyses in the remainder of the book.

Perfect Competition

perfectly competitive market
A market in which (1) there are many buyers and sellers; (2) each firm produces a homogeneous product; (3) buyers and sellers have perfect information; (4) there are no transaction costs; and (5) there is free entry and exit.

We begin our analysis by examining the output decisions of managers operating in perfectly competitive markets. The key conditions for a **perfectly competitive market** are as follows:

1. There are many buyers and sellers in the market, each of which is "small" relative to the market.
2. Each firm in the market produces a homogeneous (identical) product.
3. Buyers and sellers have perfect information.
4. There are no transaction costs.
5. There is free entry into and exit from the market.

Taken together, the first four assumptions imply that no single firm can influence the price of the product. The fact that there are many small firms, each selling an identical product, means that consumers view the products of all firms in the market as perfect substitutes. Because there is perfect information, consumers know the quality and price of each firm's product. There are no transaction costs (such as the cost of travelling to a store); if one firm charged a slightly higher price than the other firms, consumers would not shop at that firm but instead would purchase from a firm charging a lower price. Thus, in a perfectly competitive market all firms charge the same price for the good, and this price is determined by the interaction of all buyers and sellers in the market.

The assumption of *free entry* and *exit* simply implies that additional firms can enter the market if economic profits are being earned, and firms are free to leave the market if they are sustaining losses. As we will show later in this chapter, this assumption implies that in the long run, firms operating in a perfectly competitive market earn zero economic profits.

One classic example of a perfectly competitive market is agriculture. There are many farmers and ranchers, and each is so small relative to the market that he or she has no perceptible impact on the prices of corn, wheat, pork, or beef. Agricultural products tend to be homogeneous; there is little difference between corn produced by farmer Jones and corn produced by farmer Smith. The retail mail-order market for computer software and computer memory chips also is close to perfect competition. A quick look at the back of a computer magazine reveals that there are hundreds of mail-order computer product retailers, each selling identical brands of software packages and memory chips and charging the same price for a given product. The reason there is so little price variation is that if one mail-order firm charged a higher price than a competitor, consumers would purchase from another retailer.

Demand at the Market and Firm Levels

No single firm operating in a perfectly competitive market exerts any influence on price; price is determined by the interaction of all buyers and sellers in the market. The firm manager must charge this "market price" or consumers will purchase from a firm charging a lower price. Before we characterize the profit-maximizing output decisions of managers operating in perfectly competitive markets, it is important to explain more precisely the relation between the market demand for a product and the demand for a product produced by an individual perfectly competitive firm.

In a competitive market, price is determined by the intersection of the market supply and demand curves. Because the market supply and demand curves depend on all buyers and sellers, the market price is outside the control of a single perfectly competitive firm. In other words, because the individual firm is "small" relative to the market, it has no perceptible influence on the market price.

Figure 8–1 illustrates the distinction between the market demand curve and the **firm demand curve** that faces a perfectly competitive firm. The left-hand panel depicts the market, where the equilibrium price, P^e, is determined by the intersection of the market supply and demand curves. From the individual firm's point of view, the firm can sell as much as it wishes at a price of P^e; thus, the demand curve facing an individual perfectly competitive firm is given by the horizontal line in the right-hand panel, labelled D^f. The fact that the individual firm's demand curve is perfectly

firm demand curve
The demand curve for an individual firm's product; in a perfectly competitive market, it is simply the market price.

FIGURE 8–1 Demand at the Market and Firm Levels Under Perfect Competition

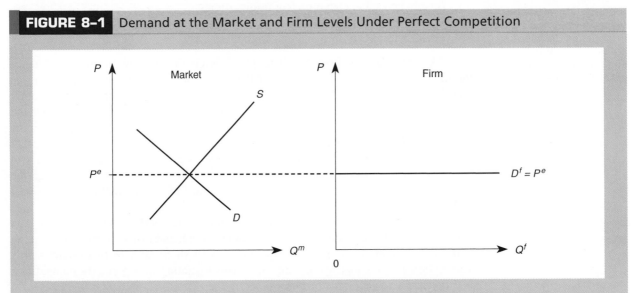

While the industry's demand curve is negatively sloped, the firm's demand curve is horizontal. The individual firm in a perfectly competitive market takes the market price as given. The firm's horizontal demand curve is the result of the quantity scale representing a very small part of the industry's demand curve. The firm's output variation has only a tiny percentage effect on industry output.

elastic reflects the fact that if the firm charged a price even slightly above the market price, it would sell nothing. Thus, in a perfectly competitive market, the demand curve for an individual firm's product is simply the market price.

Since the demand curve for an individual perfectly competitive firm's product is perfectly elastic, the pricing decision of the individual firm is trivial: charge the price that every other firm in the industry charges. All that remains is to determine how much output should be produced to maximize profits.

Short-Run Output Decisions

Recall that the short run is the period of time in which there are some fixed factors of production. For example, suppose a building is leased at a cost of $10 000 for a one-year period. In the short run (for one year) these costs are fixed, and they are paid regardless of whether the firm produces 0 or 1 million units of output. In the long run (after the lease is up), this cost is variable; the firm can decide whether or not to renew the lease. To maximize profits in the short run, the manager must take as given the fixed inputs (and thus the fixed costs) and determine how much output to produce given the variable inputs that are within his or her control. The next subsection characterizes the profit-maximizing output decision of the manager of a perfectly competitive firm.

Maximizing Profits

marginal revenue (*MR*)
The change in revenue attributable to the last unit of output; for a competitive firm, *MR* is the market price.

Under perfect competition, the demand for an individual firm's product is the market price of output, which we denote *P*. If we let *Q* represent the output of the firm, the total revenue to the firm of producing *Q* units is $TR = PQ$. Since each unit of output can be sold at the market price of *P*, each unit adds exactly *P* dollars to revenues. As Figure 8–2 illustrates, there is a linear relation between revenues and the output of a competitive firm. **Marginal revenue (*MR*)** is the change in revenue attributable to

---

FIGURE 8–2 Revenue, Costs, and Profits for a Perfectly Competitive Firm

The firm chooses the output for which the gap between the total revenue (*TR*) and the total cost (*TC*) curves is the largest. At each output, the vertical distance between the *TR* and *TC* curves shows how much *TR* exceeds *TC*. In this figure, the gap is largest at output *Q**, which is thus the profit-maximizing output.

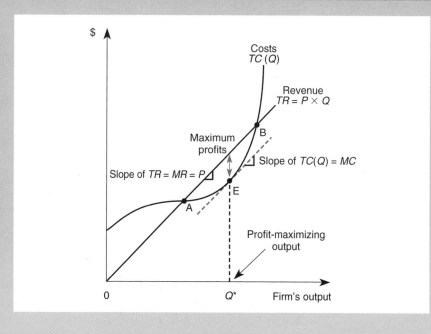

the last unit of output. Geometrically, it is the slope of the revenue curve. Expressed in economic terms, the marginal revenue for a competitive firm is the market price.

A Calculus ALTERNATIVE

Marginal revenue is the derivative of the revenue function. If revenues are a function of output,

$$TR = TR(Q)$$

then

$$MR = \frac{dTR}{dTQ}$$

Principle

COMPETITIVE FIRM'S DEMAND

The demand curve for a competitive firm's product is a horizontal line at the market price. This price is the competitive firm's marginal revenue.

$$D^f = P = MR$$

A Calculus ALTERNATIVE

Marginal revenue is the derivative of the revenue function. For a perfectly competitive firm, revenue is

$$TR = PQ$$

where *P* is the market equilibrium price. Thus,

$$MR = \frac{dTR}{dQ} = P$$

The profits of a perfectly competitive firm are simply the difference between revenues and costs:

$$\pi = PQ - TC$$

Geometrically, profits are given by the vertical distance between the cost function, labelled *TC* (or *TC(Q)*) in Figure 8–2, and the revenue line. Note that for output levels to the left of point A, the cost curve lies above the revenue line, which implies that the firm would incur losses if it produced any output to the left of point A. The same is true of output levels to the right of point B.

For output levels between points A and B, the revenue line lies above the cost curve. This implies that these outputs generate positive levels of profit. The profit-maximizing level of output is the level at which the vertical distance between the revenue line and the cost curve is greatest. This is given by the output level Q^* in Figure 8–2.

There is a very important geometric property of the profit-maximizing level of output. As we see in Figure 8–2, the slope of the cost curve at the profit-maximizing level of output (point E) exactly equals the slope of the revenue line. Recall that the slope of the cost curve is marginal cost and the slope of the revenue line is marginal revenue. Therefore, the profit-maximizing output is the output at which marginal revenue equals marginal cost. Since marginal revenue is equal to the market price for a perfectly competitive firm, the manager must equate price with marginal cost to maximize profits.

An alternative way to express the competitive output rule is depicted in Figure 8–3, where standard average and marginal cost curves have been drawn. If the market price is given by P^e, this price intersects the marginal cost curve at an output of Q^*. Thus, Q^* represents the profit-maximizing level of output. For outputs below Q^*, price exceeds marginal cost. This implies that by expanding output, the firm can sell additional units at a price that exceeds the cost of producing the additional units. Thus, a profit-maximizing firm will not choose to produce output levels below Q^*. Similarly, output levels above Q^* correspond to the situation in which marginal cost exceeds price. In this instance, a reduction in output would reduce costs by more than it would reduce revenue. Thus, Q^* is the profit-maximizing level of output.

The shaded rectangle in Figure 8–3 represents the maximum profits of the firm. To see this, note that the area of the shaded rectangle is given by its base (Q^*) times the height $[P^e - ATC(Q^*)]$. Recall that $ATC(Q^*) = TC(Q^*)/Q^*$; that is, average total cost is total cost divided by output. The area of the shaded rectangle is

$$Q^* \left[P^e - \frac{TC(Q^*)}{Q^*} \right] = P^e Q^* - TC(Q^*)$$

which is the definition of profits. Intuitively, $[P^e - ATC(Q^*)]$ represents the profits per unit produced. When this is multiplied by the profit-maximizing level of output (Q^*), the result is the amount of total profits earned by the firm.

FIGURE 8–3 Profit Maximization Under Perfect Competition

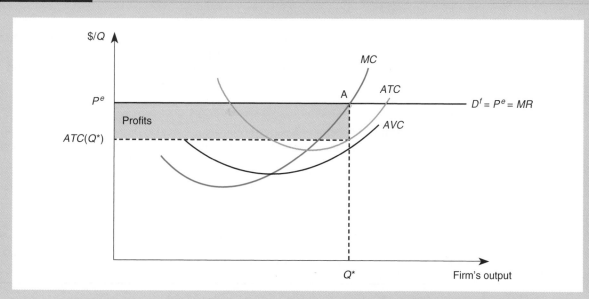

The firm's profits are maximized at point A, where the market price (P^e) crosses the marginal cost curve at an output of Q^*. The maximized profits represented by the shaded area equals profits per unit ($P^e - ATC(Q^*)$) times Q^*.

Principle	**COMPETITIVE OUTPUT RULE** To maximize profits, a perfectly competitive firm produces the output at which price equals marginal cost in the range over which marginal cost is increasing: $$P = MC$$

A Calculus ALTERNATIVE

The profits of a perfectly competitive firm are

$$\pi = PQ - TC$$

The first-order condition for maximizing profits requires that the marginal profits be zero:

$$\frac{d\pi}{dQ} = P - \frac{dTC}{dQ} = 0$$

Thus, we obtain the profit-maximizing rule for a firm in perfect competition:

$$P = \frac{dTC}{dQ}$$

or

$$P = MC \tag{8-1}$$

Demonstration PROBLEM 8-1

The cost function for a firm is given by

$$TC = 5 + Q^2$$

If the firm sells output in a perfectly competitive market and other firms in the industry sell output at a price of $20, what price should the manager of this firm put on the product? What level of output should be produced to maximize profits? How much profit will be earned?

Answer

Since the firm competes in a perfectly competitive market, it must charge the same price other firms charge; thus, the manager should price the product at $20. To find the profit-maximizing output, we must equate price with marginal cost. This firm's marginal costs are $MC = 2Q$. Equating this with price yields

$$20 = 2Q$$

so the profit-maximizing level of output is 10 units. The maximum profits are thus

$$\pi = (20)(10) - (5 + 10^2) = 200 - 5 - 100 = \$95$$

Minimizing Losses

In the previous section, we demonstrated the optimal level of output to maximize profits. In some instances, short-run losses are inevitable. Here we analyze procedures for minimizing losses in the short run. If losses are sustained in the long run, the best thing for the firm to do is exit the industry.

Short-Run Operating Losses. Consider first a situation where there are some fixed costs of production. Suppose the market price, P^e, lies below the average total cost curve but above the average variable cost curve, as in Figure 8–4. In this instance, if the firm produces the output Q^*, where $P^e = MC$, a loss of the shaded area will result. However, since the price exceeds the average variable cost, each unit sold generates more revenue than the cost per unit of the variable inputs. Thus, the firm should continue to produce in the short run, even though it is incurring losses.

Expressed differently, notice that the firm in Figure 8–4 has fixed costs that would have to be paid even if the firm decided to shut down its operation. Therefore, the firm would *not* earn zero economic profits if it shut down but would instead realize a loss equal to these fixed costs. Since the price in Figure 8–4 exceeds the average variable cost of producing Q^* units of output, the firm earns revenues on each unit sold that are more than enough to cover the variable cost of producing each unit. By producing Q^* units of output, the firm is able to put an amount of money into its cash drawer that exceeds the variable costs of producing these units and thus contributes toward the firm's payment of fixed costs. In short, while the firm in Figure 8–4 suffers a short-run loss by operating, this loss is less than the loss that would result if the firm completely shut down its operation.

The Decision to Shut Down. Now suppose the market price is so low that it lies below the average variable cost, as in Figure 8–5. If the firm produced Q^*, where $P^e = MC$ in the range of increasing marginal cost, it would incur a loss equal to the

FIGURE 8–4 Loss Minimization

Here, $P < ATC$ and the firm is suffering losses (given by the shaded area). Since $P > AVC$, in the short run it is worthwhile for the firm to keep producing, but it is not worthwhile for it to replace its capital equipment as it wears out.

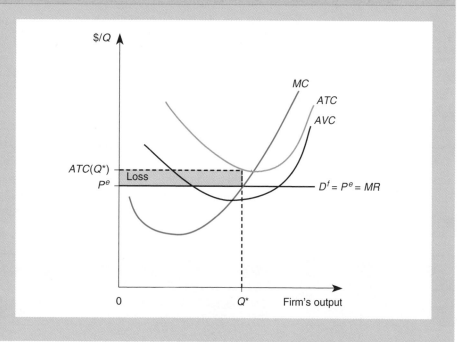

FIGURE 8–5 The Shut-Down Case

Here, *P* < *ATC* and the firm is suffering losses. In addition, *P* < *AVC*, which means the firm would shut down. The upper shaded area represents the loss that results from shutting down, the lower shaded area the loss if the firm continued to produce. The total loss is the sum of the two shaded areas.

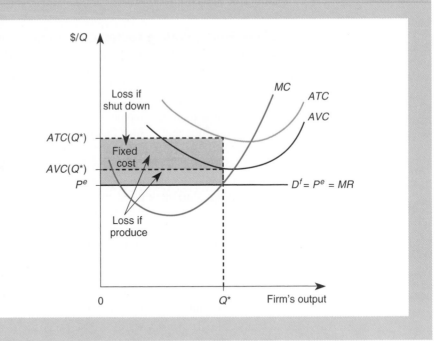

sum of the two shaded rectangles in Figure 8–5. In other words, for each unit sold, the firm would lose

$$ATC(Q^*) - P^e$$

When this per-unit loss is multiplied by Q^*, negative profits result that correspond to the sum of the two shaded rectangles in Figure 8–5.

Now suppose that instead of producing Q^* units of output this firm decided to shut down its operation. In this instance, its losses would equal its fixed costs, that is, those costs that must be paid even if no output is produced. Geometrically, fixed costs are represented by the top rectangle in Figure 8–5, since the area of this rectangle is

$$[ATC(Q^*) - AVC(Q^*)]Q^*$$

which equals fixed costs. Thus, when price is less than the average variable cost of production, the firm loses less by shutting down its operation (and producing zero units) than it does by producing Q^* units. To summarize, we have demonstrated the following principle:

Principle	**SHORT-RUN OUTPUT DECISION UNDER PERFECT COMPETITION**
	To maximize short-run profits, a perfectly competitive firm should produce in the range of increasing marginal cost where *P* = *MC*, provided that *P* ≥ *AVC*. If *P* < *AVC*, the firm should shut down its plant to minimize its losses.

Demonstration PROBLEM 8–2

Suppose the cost function for a firm is given by $TC = 100 + Q^2$. If the firm sells output in a perfectly competitive market and other firms in the industry sell output at a price of $10, what level of output should the firm produce to maximize profits or minimize losses? What will be the level of profits or losses if the firm makes the optimal decision?

Answer

First, note that there are fixed costs of 100 and variable costs of Q^2, so the question deals with a short-run scenario. If the firm produces a positive level of output, it will produce where price equals marginal cost. The firm's marginal costs are $MC = 2Q$. Equating this with price yields $10 = 2Q$, or $Q = 5$ units. The average variable cost of producing 5 units of output is $AVC = 5^2/5 = 25/5 = 5$. Since $P \geq AVC$, the firm should produce 5 units in the short run. By producing 5 units of output, the firm incurs a loss of

$$\pi = (10)(5) - (100 + 5^2) = 50 - 100 - 25 = -\$75$$

which is less than the loss of $100 (fixed costs) that would result if the firm shut down its plant in the short run.

The Short-Run Firm and Industry Supply Curves

Now that you understand how perfectly competitive firms determine their output, we will examine how to derive firm and industry short-run supply curves.

Recall that the profit-maximizing perfectly competitive firm produces the output at which price equals marginal cost. For example, when the price is given by P_0 as in Figure 8–6, the firm produces Q_0 units of output (the point where $P = MC$ in the

---

FIGURE 8–6 The Short-Run Supply Curve for a Competitive Firm

The supply curve of this price-taking firm, shown by the coloured line, is the same as its MC curve above the minimum point of the AVC. The firm will not produce when price falls below AVC (P_0) because it will not be able to cover even its variable cost.

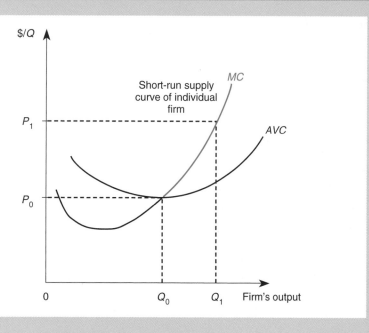

range of increasing marginal cost). When the price is P_1, the firm produces Q_1 units of output. For prices between P_0 and P_1, output is determined by the intersection of price and marginal cost.

When the price falls below the *AVC* curve, however, the firm produces zero units, because it does not cover the variable costs of production. Thus, to determine how much a perfectly competitive firm will produce at each price, we simply determine the output at which marginal cost equals that price. To ensure that the firm will produce a positive level of output, price must be above the average variable cost curve.

Principle	**THE FIRM'S SHORT-RUN SUPPLY CURVE**
	The short-run supply curve for a perfectly competitive firm is its marginal cost curve above the minimum point on the *AVC* curve, as illustrated in Figure 8–6.

The market (or industry) supply curve is closely related to the supply curve of individual firms in a perfectly competitive industry. Recall that the market supply curve reveals the total quantity that will be produced in the market at each possible price. Since the amount an individual firm will produce at a given price is determined by its marginal cost curve, the horizontal sum of the marginal costs of all firms determines how much total output will be produced at each price. More specifically, since each firm's supply curve is the firm's marginal cost curve above the minimum *AVC*, the market supply curve for a perfectly competitive industry is the horizontal sum of the individual marginal costs above their respective *AVC* curves.

Figure 8–7 illustrates the relation between an individual firm's supply curve (MC_i) and the market supply curve (S) for a perfectly competitive industry composed of 500 firms. When the price is $10, each firm produces zero units, and thus total

---

FIGURE 8–7 The Market Supply Curve

The market supply curve is the horizontal sum of the supply curves of each of the firms in the industry. The market supply curve (the coloured line) relates the price to the sum of the quantities produced by each firm. The black line is an individual firm's supply curve, which is also that firm's marginal cost curve above its *AVC* curve.

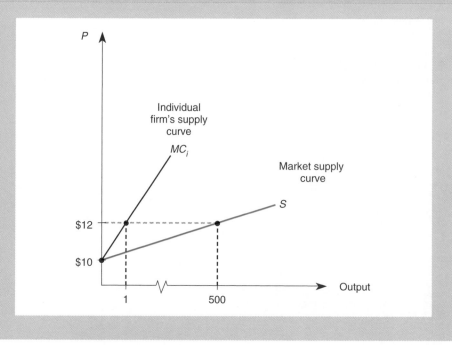

industry output also is zero. When the price is $12, each firm produces 1 unit, so the total output produced by all 500 firms is 500 units. Notice that the industry supply curve is flatter than the supply curve of an individual firm and that the more firms in the industry, the farther to the right is the market supply curve.

Long-Run Decisions

One important assumption underlying the theory of perfect competition is that of free entry and exit. If firms earn short-run economic profits, in the long run additional firms will enter the industry in an attempt to reap some of those profits. As more firms enter the industry, the industry supply curve shifts to the right. This is illustrated in Figure 8–8 as the shift from S^0 to S^1, which lowers the equilibrium market price from P^0 to P^1. This shifts down the demand curve for an individual firm's product, which in turn lowers its profits.

If firms in a competitive industry sustain short-run losses, in the long run they will exit the industry since they are not covering their opportunity costs. As firms exit the industry, the market supply curve decreases from S^0 in Figure 8–8 to S^2, thus increasing the market price from P^0 to P^2. This, in turn, shifts up the demand curve for an individual firm's product, which increases the profits of the firms remaining in the industry.

The process just described continues until ultimately the market price is such that all firms in the market earn zero economic profits. This is the case in Figure 8–9. At the price of P^e, each firm receives just enough to cover the average costs of production (AC is used because in the long run there is no distinction between fixed and

FIGURE 8–8 Entry and Exit: The Market and Firm's Demand

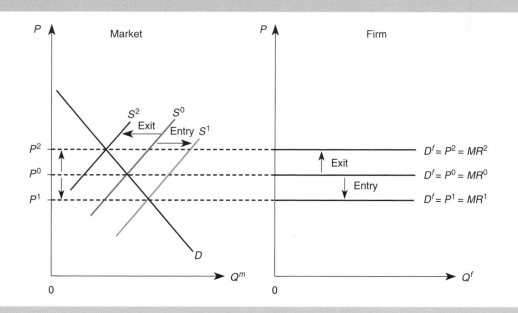

Starting from equilibrium price P^0, the presence of the short-run profits causes more firms to enter, shifting the supply curve to the right and so lowering the equilibrium price to P^1. Firms facing a short-run loss exit the industry, causing the supply curve to shift left and raise the equilibrium price, P^2.

FIGURE 8–9 Long-Run Competitive Equilibrium

In the long-run competitive equilibrium, each firm is operating at the minimum point on its AC curve. Each firm must be (a) maximizing short-run profits ($P = MC$), (b) earning profits of zero on its existing plant ($P = AC$), and (c) unable to increase its profits by altering the scale of its operations. These conditions are met at Q^* with the price P^e and on the minimum point on the ATC curve.

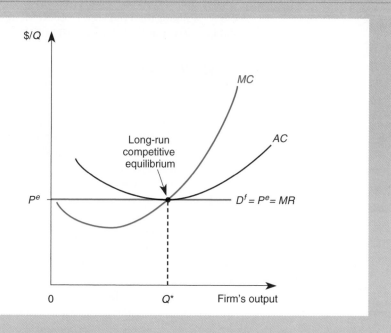

variable costs), and economic profits are zero. If economic profits were positive, entry would occur and the market price would fall until the demand curve for an individual firm's product was just tangent to the AC curve. If economic profits were negative, exit would occur, increasing the market price until the firm demand curve was tangent to the AC curve.

It should be noted that if it is costly for the firm in the industry to exit, the incentives to enter are reduced. Typically the exit cost is associated with sunk costs that cannot be recovered. For example, suppose that a firm in the market must have very specialized equipment that is difficult to resell. In this case, the firm may be hesitant to enter if the profit opportunities in the market are short-lived.

Principle	**LONG-RUN COMPETITIVE EQUILIBRIUM**

LONG-RUN COMPETITIVE EQUILIBRIUM
In the long run, perfectly competitive firms produce a level of output such that

1. $P = MC$
2. $P = $ minimum of AC (8–2)

These long-run properties of perfectly competitive markets have two important welfare implications. First, note that the market price is equal to the marginal cost of production. The market price reflects the value to society of an additional unit of output. This valuation is based on the preferences of all consumers in the market. Marginal cost reflects the cost to society of producing another unit of output. These costs represent the resources that would have to be taken from some other sector of the economy to produce more output in this industry.

To see why it is important, from a social perspective, that price equal marginal cost, suppose price exceeded marginal cost in equilibrium. This would imply that

Inside BUSINESS

8–1 Competition in the PC Component Market

Over the past decade the market for PC components has become increasingly competitive. As a result, many products sold in these markets (such as computer memory) are viewed as "commodities"—that is, products bought and sold in a competitive market. As a result, firms selling PC components have watched their profits erode over the past several years as more firms have entered the market to get a piece of the action.

Figure 8–10 shows the representative market supply and demand curves and a cost structure for an individual firm. S^1 in Figure 8–10(a) represents market supply for PC components a few years ago. With market supply of S^1, the equilibrium price is P_1 in panel (a). In panel (b), an individual firm chooses to produce q_1 units of output, resulting in profits of the area ABCE for each firm.

The profits earned by existing firms a few years ago induced other firms to enter the market. The increased entry shifts the market supply curve to the right, as shown by the

shift from S^1 to S^2 in Figure 8–10(a). This increase in supply reduces the equilibrium price to P_2. The new market equilibrium at point Z in Figure 8–10(a) illustrates that more PC components are now purchased—and at a lower price.

As the price falls to P_2, each individual firm decreases its output to q_2 in Figure 8–10(b) (since marginal cost now equals P_2 at point F). Each firm enjoys lower profits, which are now area EFGH in panel (b). Notice that enough new firms enter the market that the total market output in panel (a) increases, even though the output of each individual firm in panel (b) declines.

This description of the market for PC components explains the dramatic reductions in memory prices over the past few years, as well as the significant reductions in firm profits. In the long run, firms selling commodities do not have a sustainable advantage and will inevitably earn zero economic profits.

society would value another unit of output more than it would cost to produce another unit of output. If the industry produced an output such that price exceeded marginal cost, it would thus be inefficient; social welfare would be improved by expanding output. Since in a competitive industry price equals marginal cost, the industry produces the socially efficient level of output.

FIGURE 8–10 Entry Shrinks Profits

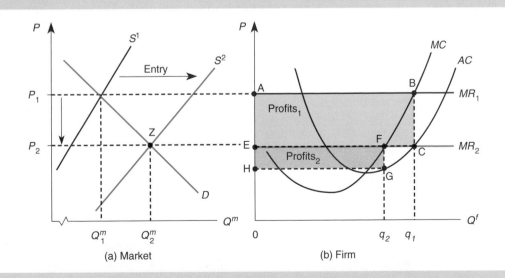

(a) Market

(b) Firm

Entrants cause the supply curve to shift right, causing profits to decrease as shown in the graph on the right. The lower equilibrium price causes the firm's quantity to decrease from q_1 to q_2. Profits shrink from the upper shaded region to the lower (marked Profits$_1$ and Profits$_2$, respectively).

The second thing to note about long-run competitive equilibrium is that price equals the minimum point on the average cost curve. This implies not only that firms are earning zero economic profits (that is, just covering their opportunity costs) but also that all economies of scale have been exhausted. There is no way to produce the output at a lower average cost of production.

It is important to remember the distinction we made in Chapters 1 and 5 between economic profits and accounting profits. The fact that a firm in a perfectly competitive industry earns zero economic profits in the long run does not mean that accounting profits are zero; rather, zero economic profits implies that accounting profits are just high enough to offset any implicit costs of production. The firm earns no more, and no less, than it could earn by using the resources in some other capacity. This is why firms continue to produce in the long run even though their economic profits are zero.

Monopoly

monopoly
A market structure in which a single firm serves an entire market for a good that has no close substitutes.

In the previous section we characterized the optimal output decisions of firms that are small relative to the total market. In this context, *small* means the firms have no control whatsoever over the prices they charge for the product. In this section, we will consider the opposite extreme: monopoly. **Monopoly** refers to a situation wherein a single firm serves an entire market for a good for which there are no close substitutes.

Monopoly Power

In determining whether a market is characterized by monopoly, it is important to specify the relevant market for the product. For example, utility companies are local monopolies in that only one utility offers service to a given neighbourhood. To be sure, there are almost as many utility companies as there are cities in the world, but the utilities do not directly compete against one another for customers. The substitutes for electric services in a given city are poor and, short of moving to a different city, consumers must pay the price for local utility services or go without electricity. It is in this sense that a utility company is a monopoly in the local market for utility services.

When one thinks of a monopoly, one usually envisions a very large firm. This needn't be the case, however; the relevant consideration is whether there are other firms selling close substitutes for the good in a given market. For example, a gas station located in a small town that is hundreds of kilometres from another gas station is a monopolist in that town. In a large town there typically are many gas stations, and the market for gasoline is not characterized by monopoly.

The fact that a firm is the sole seller of a good in a market clearly gives that firm greater market power than it would have if it competed against other firms for consumers. Since there is only one producer in the market, the market demand curve is the demand curve for the monopolist's product. This is in contrast to the case of perfect competition, where the demand curve for an individual firm is perfectly elastic. A monopolist does not have unlimited power, however.

Figure 8–11 depicts the demand curve for a monopolist. Since all consumers in the market demand the good from the monopolist, the market demand curve, D^M, is the same as the demand for the firm's product, D^f. In the absence of legal restrictions, the monopolist is free to charge any price for the product. But this does not mean the firm can sell as much as it wants to at that price. Given the price set by the monopolist, consumers decide how much to purchase. For example, if the monopolist sets the relatively low price of P^1, the quantity demanded by consumers is Q^1. The monopo-

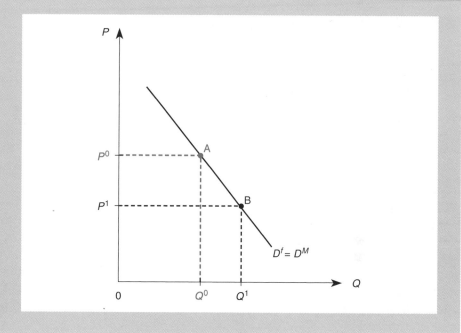

FIGURE 8–11 The Monopolist's Demand

A monopolist's demand curve is downward-sloping. Since all consumers in the market demand the good from the monopolist, the market demand curve, D^M, is the same as the demand for the firm's product, D^f.

list can set a higher price of P^0, but there will be a lower quantity demanded of Q^0 at that price.

In summary, the monopolist is restricted by consumers to choose only those price-quantity combinations along the market demand curve. The monopolist can choose a price or a quantity, but not both. The monopolist can sell higher quantities only by lowering the price. If the price is too high, consumers may choose to buy nothing at all.

Sources of Monopoly Power

The next issue we will address is how a firm obtains monopoly power, that is, why a monopolist has no competitors. There are four primary sources of monopoly power. One or more of these sources create a barrier to entry that prevents other firms from entering the market to compete against the monopolist.

Economies of Scale

economies of scale
Exist whenever average total costs decline as output increases.

diseconomies of scale
Exist whenever average total costs increase as output increases.

The first source of monopoly power we will discuss is technological in nature. First, however, it is useful to recall some important terminology. **Economies of scale** exist whenever average total costs decline as output increases. **Diseconomies of scale** exist whenever average total costs increase as output increases. For many technologies, there is a range over which economies of scale exist and a range over which diseconomies exist. For example, in Figure 8–12 there are economies of scale for output levels below Q^* (since ATC is declining in this range) and diseconomies of scale for output levels above Q^* (since ATC is increasing in this range).

Notice in Figure 8–12 that if the market were composed of a single firm that produced Q^M units, consumers would be willing to pay a price of P^M per unit for the Q^M

FIGURE 8–12 Economies of Scale and Minimum Prices

Points to the left of Q^* indicate the presence of economies of scale whereas points to the right of Q^* indicate diseconomies of scale. When one firm is producing Q^M units, consumers will pay P^M for it. Positive profits are earned at this point (since $P^M > ATC(Q^M)$. If two firms shared the market (each producing $Q^M/2$, the price would remain the same, but each would produce half as much at $ATC(Q^M/2)$ (economic loss). Thus, economies of scale can lead to a situation in which a single firm supplies the entire market to earn positive profits.

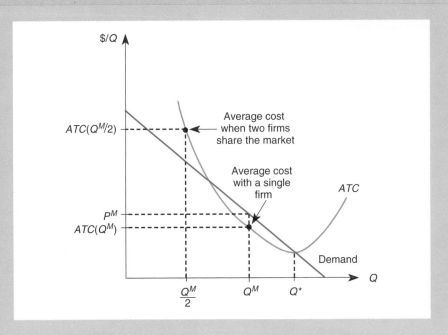

units. Since $P^M > ATC(Q^M)$, the firm sells the goods at a price that is higher than the average cost of production, and thus earns positive profits. Now suppose another firm entered the market and the two firms ended up sharing the market (each firm producing $Q^M/2$). The total quantity produced would be the same, and thus the price would remain at P^M. But with two firms, each producing only $Q^M/2$ units, each firm has an average total cost of $ATC(Q^M/2)$—a higher average total cost than when a single firm produced all of the output. Also notice in Figure 8–12 that each firm's average cost is greater than P^M, which is the price consumers are willing to pay for the total Q^M units produced in the market. Having two firms in the industry leads to losses, but a single firm can earn positive profits because it has higher volume and enjoys reduced average costs due to economies of scale. Thus, we see that economies of scale can lead to a situation where a single firm services the entire market for a good.

This analysis of economies of scale also reveals why it is so important to define the relevant market when determining whether or not a firm is a monopolist. As we noted earlier, a gas station may be a monopolist in a small town located hundreds of kilometres from another gas station, whereas a gas station situated in a large city is unlikely to be a monopolist. In terms of Figure 8–12, the demand for gasoline in a small town typically is low relative to Q^*, which gives rise to economies of scale in the relevant range (outputs below Q^*). In large cities the demand for gasoline is large relative to Q^*, which makes it possible for several gas stations to coexist in the market.

Natural Monopoly

A natural monopoly arises when the average cost of production declines throughout the relevant range of product demand, so that any level of demand can be met at lower average cost by a single firm rather than by two or more firms. Utilities, water, electric power, gas, etc. fall into this category. It is argued that the firms operating in the regulated sector are natural monopolies. According to Figure 8–12, a single producer is able to realize economies of scale unavailable to firms in the presence of competition. To put it differently, if an industry characterized by a declining average cost curve over the relevant range of market demand consisted of several competing firms, competitive forces would force weaker firms to gradually leave the industry until a single firm would emerge as a natural monopoly. Government regulation of monopolies is discussed in Chapter 14.

Economies of Scope

economies of scope
Exist when the total cost of producing two products within the same firm is lower than when the products are produced by separate firms.

Recall that **economies of scope** exist when the total cost of producing two products within the same firm is lower than when the products are produced by separate firms, that is, when it is cheaper to produce outputs Q_1 and Q_2 jointly.

In the presence of economies of scope, efficient production requires that a firm produce several products jointly. While multiproduct firms do not necessarily have more market power than firms producing a single product, economies of scope tend to encourage "larger" firms. In turn, this may provide greater access to capital markets, where working capital and funds for investment are obtained. To the extent that smaller firms have more difficulty obtaining funds than larger firms, the higher cost of capital may serve as a barrier to entry. In extreme cases, economies of scope can lead to monopoly power.

Cost Complementarity

cost complementarities
The marginal cost of producing one type of output decreasing when the output of another good is increased.

Cost complementarities exist in a multiproduct cost function when the marginal cost of producing one output is reduced when the output of another product is increased; that is, when an increase in the output of product 2 decreases the marginal cost of producing output 1.

Multiproduct firms that enjoy cost complementarities tend to have lower marginal costs than firms producing a single product. This gives multiproduct firms a cost advantage over single-product firms. Thus, in the presence of cost complementarities, firms must produce several products to be able to compete against the firm with lower marginal costs. To the extent that greater capital requirements exist for multiproduct firms than for single-product firms, this requirement can limit the ability of small firms to enter the market. In extreme cases, monopoly power can result.

Patents and Other Legal Barriers

The sources of monopoly power just described are technological in nature. In some instances, government may grant an individual or a firm a monopoly right. For example, a city may prevent another utility company from competing against the local utility company. The most common example is the monopoly power generated by the *patent* system.

The patent system gives the inventor of a new product the exclusive right to sell the product for a given period of time (see Inside Business 8–3). The rationale behind granting monopoly power to a new inventor is based on the following argument. Inventions take many years and considerable sums of money to develop. Once an invention becomes public information, in the absence of a patent system other firms might produce the product and compete against the individual or firm that developed it. Since these firms do not have to expend resources developing the product, they would make higher profits than the original developer. In the absence of a patent system, there would be a reduced incentive on the part of firms to develop new technologies and products.

InsideBUSINESS

8-2 Minimum Efficient Scale and Monopoly Power

How large does a firm need to be to be able to fully exploit all economies of scale? The answer depends on the size of total industry demand in a country as well as on the nature of the underlying technology used to produce the product. One study estimated the number of individual plants needed to fully exploit economies of scale in various markets. Economies of scale are fully exploited when the average cost curve at a given plant is at its minimum. Table 8–1 provides the results of that study for twelve industries and six nations.

Consider the numbers reported for the storage battery industry. In the United States, the size of the market is large enough to permit 53.5 firms to operate in the market, with each plant fully exploiting all economies of scale. In contrast, in Sweden it takes only 1.4 firms to exploit all economies of scale. (Since there cannot be fractional parts of firms, the relevant number of firms is the closest integer.) The storage battery industry in Sweden is a natural monopoly; costs are minimized when only one firm is in the market.

Two aspects of the numbers reported in Table 8–1 bear pointing out. First, there is considerable variation across industries in the number of firms needed to fully

exploit economies of scale. In some industries, the number of firms necessary to exploit economies of scale is small, giving rise to monopoly or oligopoly. In others, such as the shoe industry, the cost structure is compatible with a more competitive market structure.

Second, note that there is also considerable variation across countries in the number of efficiently sized plants that can be accommodated. In Sweden, for instance, the market for cigarettes is not large enough to accommodate even one efficiently sized firm. A firm producing cigarettes in Sweden would have to charge a higher price than firms in all other countries, since the other countries can accommodate one or more efficiently sized firms. This puts producers of cigarettes in Sweden at a disadvantage when competing against firms that ship cigarettes to Sweden. In the presence of such a disadvantage, the Swedish government may impose tariffs or trade restrictions on imports of cigarettes to "protect" Swedish producers. This would benefit the producers, but smokers would end up paying higher prices for cigarettes than they would in the presence of free trade. The same phenomenon has occurred in the refrigerator industry in Canada.

TABLE 8-1 Number of Efficient Plants Compatible with Domestic Consumption in Six Nations

	U.S.	Canada	U.K.	Sweden	France	Germany
Brewing	29.0	2.9	10.9	0.7	4.5	16.1
Cigarettes	15.2	1.3	3.3	0.3	1.6	2.8
Fabrics	451.7	17.4	57.0	10.4	56.9	52.1
Paints	69.8	6.3	9.8	2.0	6.6	8.4
Petroleum refining	51.6	6.0	8.6	2.5	7.7	9.9
Shoes	532.0	59.2	164.5	23.0	128.2	196.9
Glass bottles	65.5	7.2	11.1	1.7	6.6	7.9
Cement	59.0	6.6	16.5	3.5	21.7	28.8
Steel	38.9	2.6	6.5	1.5	5.5	10.1
Bearings	72.0	5.9	22.8	3.3	17.0	N/A
Refrigerators	7.1	0.7	1.2	0.5	1.7	2.8
Storage batteries	53.5	4.6	7.7	1.4	12.8	10.5

Source: F. M. Scherer, A. Beckenstein, E. Kaufer, and R. D. Murphy, with the assistance of Francine Bougeon-Maassen, *The Economics of Multi-Plant Operation: An International Comparison Study* (Cambridge, MA and London: Harvard University Press, 1975), p. 94. Reprinted by permission of the publishers. © 1975 by the President and Fellows of Harvard College.

Maximizing Profits

Now that you know what monopoly power is and the factors that lead to monopoly power, we will see how the manager of a monopoly may exploit this power to maximize profits. In particular, in this section we presume that the manager is in charge of a firm that is a monopoly. Our goal is to characterize the price and output decisions that maximize the monopolist's profits.

Marginal Revenue

Suppose the monopolist faces a demand curve for its product such as the one in Figure 8–13(a). In Chapter 3, we learned that a linear demand curve is elastic at high prices and inelastic at low prices. If the monopolist produces zero units of output, its revenues are zero. As output is increased above zero, demand is elastic and the increase in output (which implies a lower price) leads to an increase in total revenue, as shown in Figure 8–13(b). This follows from the total revenue test. As output is

---

FIGURE 8–13 Elasticity of Demand and Total Revenues

For a monopolist, *MR* is always less than price. When *TR* is rising, *MR* is greater than zero and elasticity is greater than one. When *TR* is falling, *MR* is less than zero and elasticity is less than one.

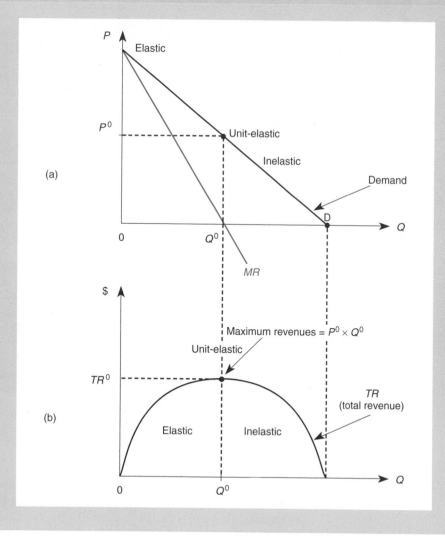

Inside BUSINESS

8–3 Patents, Copyright, and Trademark Protection

PATENT

A patent is a monopoly granted by the government, which affords the holder of the patent the exclusive right to manufacture, sell, or use an invention throughout Canada for a period of 20 years from the date of the application. It is a document protecting the rights of the inventor and a repository of useful technical information for the public.

A patent can be obtained in respect of any new invention, including art, processes, machines, a method of manufacturing, or a composition, or any new and useful improvement to these. The key is that there must be a new and inventive element to the device or process/composition. Patents cannot be issued to protect a scientific principle or theorem, although it is now possible to obtain patent protection for some forms of software and business processes.

The rights conferred by a Canadian patent extend throughout Canada, but not to foreign countries. You must apply for patent rights in other countries separately. Conversely, foreign patents do not protect an invention in Canada. In Canada, a patent is issued to the inventor who first files a patent application—not, as in the United States, to the first person to invent. A separate patent must be obtained in every country in which the owner wishes protection. By virtue of patent treaties, if an application is filed in Canada within one year of filing in the United States, the Canadian filing date is backdated to that of the United States.

There are three basic criteria for patentability: *novelty*, *utility*, and *ingenuity*. The invention must be new (first in the world), it must be useful (functional and operative), and it must show inventive ingenuity and not be obvious to someone skilled in that area.

COPYRIGHT

In Canada, copyright arises automatically upon creation of a work. It affords the owner of the copyright the sole right to produce, reproduce, or publish the work or any substantial part of it in any form. It applies to any original literary, dramatic, musical, or artistic work—for example books, manuals, brochures, paintings, drawings, maps, photographs, films, sound recordings, and computer programs. Copyright does not protect the ideas in these works, but it does protect the form in which they are expressed.

Generally, copyright protection lasts for 50 years following the death of the author. For sound recordings, photographs, and cinematographic works, the protection lasts for 50 years respectively after the time of the first fixation, after the original plate or negative was made, and after first publication.

TRADEMARK

A trademark is a word, a symbol, a design, or a combination of these features used to distinguish the wares or services of one person or organization from those of others in the marketplace. Trademarks come to represent not only actual wares and services, but also the reputation of the producer. As such, they are considered valuable intellectual property. A registered trademark can be protected through legal proceedings from misuse and imitation. There are three basic categories of trademarks: *Ordinary marks* are words or symbols (or a combination of them) that distinguish the wares or services of a specific firm or individual. *Certification marks* identify wares or services which meet a defined standard; they are owned by one person but licensed to others to identify wares or services. *Distinguishing guise* identifies the shaping of wares or their containers, or is a mode of wrapping or packaging wares.

UNITED STATES

The United States grants inventors three types of patent protection: utility, design, and plant patents. A "utility patent" protects the way an invention is used and works, while a "design patent" protects the way and invention looks. A "plant patent" protects an inventor who has discovered and asexually reproduced a distinct and new variety of plant (excluding tuber-propagated plants or plants found in an uncultivated state). Utility and plant patents provide 20 years of protection, while design patents last 14 years.

In the United States, patents and trademarks are administered through the U.S. Patent and Trademark Office, while the U.S. Copyright Office handles copyrights.

Canadian sources: Canadian Intellectual Property Office, Industry Canada <strategis.ic.gc.ca/sc_mrksv/cipo/patents/pat_gd _protect-e.html#section01>; *U.S. sources:* United States Patent and Trademark Office <www.uspto.gov>; United States Copyright Office <www.copyright.gov>. All accessed July 6, 2004.

---

increased beyond Q^0 into the inelastic region of demand, further increases in output actually decrease total revenue, until at point D the price is zero and revenues are again zero. This is depicted in Figure 8–13(b). Thus, total revenue is maximized at an output of Q^0 in Figure 8–13(b). This corresponds to the price of P^0 in Figure 8–13(a), where demand is unit-elastic.

The line labelled *MR* in Figure 8–13(a) is the marginal revenue schedule for the monopolist. Recall that marginal revenue is the change in total revenue attributable to the last unit of output; geometrically, it is the slope of the total revenue curve. As Figure 8–13(a) shows, the marginal revenue schedule for a monopolist lies below the demand curve; in fact, for a linear demand curve, the marginal revenue schedule lies exactly halfway between the demand curve and the vertical axis. This means that for a monopolist, marginal revenue is less than the price charged for the good.

There are two ways to understand why the marginal revenue schedule lies below the monopolist's demand curve. Consider first a geometric explanation. Marginal revenue is the slope of the total revenue curve, (*TR*), in Figure 8–13(b). As output increases from zero to Q^0, the slope of the total revenue curve decreases until it becomes zero at Q^0. Over this range, marginal revenue decreases until it reaches zero when output is Q^0. As output expands beyond Q^0, the slope of the total revenue curve becomes negative and gets increasingly negative as output continues to expand. This means that marginal revenue is negative for outputs in excess of Q^0.

Formula: Monopolist's Marginal Revenue. The marginal revenue of a monopolist is given by the formula

$$MR = P\left[\frac{1+E}{E}\right] \tag{8–3}$$

where E is the elasticity of demand for the monopolist's product and P is the price charged for the product.

A Calculus ALTERNATIVE

The monopolist's revenue is

$$TR = P \times Q$$

Taking the derivative with respect to Q yields

$$\frac{dTR}{dQ} = \frac{dP}{dQ}Q + P$$

$$= P\left[\left(\frac{dP}{dQ}\right)\left(\frac{Q}{P}\right) + 1\right]$$

$$= P\left[\frac{1}{E} + 1\right]$$

$$= P\left[\frac{1+E}{E}\right]$$

where E is the elasticity of demand. Since $dTR/dQ = MR$, this means that

$$MR = P\left[\frac{1+E}{E}\right]$$

Demonstration PROBLEM 8–3

Show that if demand is elastic (say $E = -2$), marginal revenue is positive but less than price. Show that if demand is unit-elastic ($E = -1$), marginal revenue is zero. Finally, show that if demand is inelastic (say $E = -0.5$), marginal revenue is negative.

Answer

Setting $E = -2$ in the marginal revenue formula yields

$$MR = P\left[\frac{1-2}{-2}\right] = \frac{-1}{-2}P$$

so $MR = 0.5P$. Thus, when demand is elastic, marginal revenue is positive but less than price (in this example, marginal revenue is one-half of the price).
    Setting $E = -1$ in the marginal revenue formula yields

$$MR = P\left[\frac{1-1}{-1}\right] = 0$$

so $MR = 0$. Thus, when demand is unit-elastic, marginal revenue is zero.
    Finally, setting $E = -0.5$ in the marginal revenue formula yields

$$MR = P\left[\frac{1-0.5}{-0.5}\right] = P\left[\frac{0.5}{-0.5}\right] = -P$$

so $MR = -P$. Thus, when demand is inelastic, marginal revenue is negative and less than price (in this example, marginal revenue is the negative of the price).

An alternative explanation for why marginal revenue is less than price for a monopolist is as follows. Suppose a monopolist sells one unit of output at a price of $4 per unit, for a total revenue of $4. What happens to revenue if the monopolist produces one more unit of output? Revenue increases by less than $4. To see why, note that the monopolist can sell one more unit of output only by lowering price, say, from $4 to $3 per unit. But the price reduction necessary to sell one more unit lowers the price received on the first unit from $4 to $3. The total revenue associated with two units of output thus is $6. The change in revenue due to producing one more unit is therefore $2, which is less than the price charged for the product.

    Since the price a monopolist can charge for the product depends on how much is produced, let $P(Q)$ represent the price per unit paid by consumers for Q units of output. This relation summarizes the same information as a demand curve, but because price is expressed as a function of quantity instead of the other way around, it is called an *inverse demand function*. The inverse demand function, denoted $P(Q)$, indicates the price per unit as a function of the firm's output. The most common inverse demand function is the linear inverse demand function. The *linear inverse demand function* is given by

$$P(Q) = a + bQ$$

where a is a number greater than zero and b is a number less than zero.
    In addition to the general formula for marginal revenue that is valid for all demand functions, it is useful to have the following formula for marginal revenue, which is valid for the special case of a linear inverse demand function.

Formula: MR for Linear Inverse Demand. For the linear inverse demand function, $P(Q) = a + bQ$, marginal revenue is given by

$$MR = a + 2bQ$$

A Calculus ALTERNATIVE

With a linear inverse demand function, the revenue function is
$$TR = (a + bQ)Q$$

Marginal revenue is

$$MR = \frac{dTR}{dQ} = a + 2bQ$$

Demonstration PROBLEM 8–4

Suppose the inverse demand function for a monopolist's product is given by

$$P = 10 - 2Q$$

What is the maximum price per unit a monopolist can charge to be able to sell 3 units? What is the marginal revenue associated with 3 units of output?

Answer

First, we set $Q = 3$ in the inverse demand function (here $a = 10$ and $b = -2$) to get

$$P = 10 - 2(3) = 4$$

Thus, the maximum price per unit the monopolist can charge to be able to sell 3 units is $4. To find marginal revenue when 3 units are produced, we set $Q = 3$ in the marginal revenue formula for linear inverse demand to get

$$MR = 10 - [(2)(2)(3)] = -2$$

Thus, the third unit sold reduced revenue by $2.

The Output Decision

Revenues are one determinant of profits; costs are the other. Since the revenue a monopolist receives from selling Q units is $TR = Q[P(Q)]$, the profits of a monopolist with a cost function of TC are

$$\pi = TR - TC$$

Typical revenue and cost functions are graphed in Figure 8–14(a). The vertical distance between the revenue and cost functions in panel (a) reflects the profits to the monopolist of alternative levels of output. Output levels below point A and above point B imply losses, since the cost curve lies above the revenue curve. For output levels between points A and B, the revenue function lies above the cost function, and profits are positive for those output levels.

Figure 8–14(b) depicts the profit function, which is the difference between *TR* and *TC* in panel (a). As Figure 8–14(a) shows, profits are greatest at an output of Q^M, where the vertical distance between the revenue and cost functions is the greatest. This corresponds to the maximum profit point in panel (b). A very important property of the profit-maximizing level of output (Q^M) is that the slope of the revenue function in panel (a) equals the slope of the cost function. In economic terms, marginal revenue equals marginal cost at an output of Q^M.

Principle	**MONOPOLY OUTPUT RULE** A profit-maximizing monopolist should produce the output, Q^M, such that marginal revenue equals marginal cost:

$$MR(Q^M) = MC(Q^M) \qquad (8\text{–}4)$$

FIGURE 8–14 Costs, Revenues, and Profits Under Monopoly

In (a), profits are greatest at Q^M, where the vertical distance between the revenue and cost functions is greatest. This corresponds to the maximum profit point in panel (b). Notice that the slopes of revenue and cost are equal in (a), which is $MR = MC$ in economic terms.

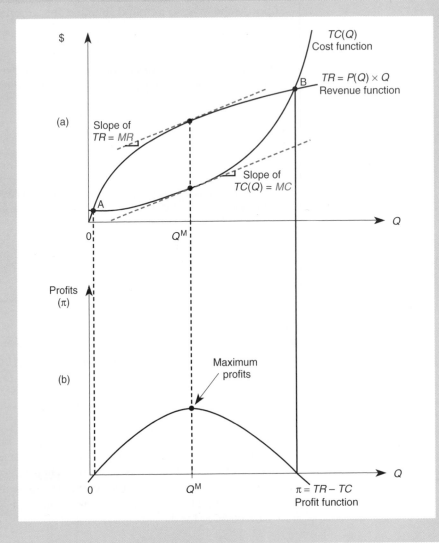

A Calculus ALTERNATIVE

The profits for a monopolist are

$$\pi = TR - TC$$

To maximize profits, marginal profits must be zero:

$$\frac{d\pi}{dQ} = \frac{dTR}{dQ} - \frac{dTC}{dQ} = 0$$

or

$$MR = MC$$

The economic intuition behind this important rule is as follows. If marginal revenue was greater than marginal cost, an increase in output would increase revenues more than it would increase costs. Thus, a profit-maximizing manager of a monopoly should continue to expand output when $MR > MC$. On the other hand, if marginal cost exceeded marginal revenue, a reduction in output would reduce costs by more than it would reduce revenue. A profit-maximizing manager thus is motivated to produce where marginal revenue equals marginal cost.

An alternative characterization of the profit-maximizing output decision of a monopoly is presented in Figure 8–15. The marginal revenue curve intersects the marginal cost curve when Q^M units are produced, so the profit-maximizing level of output is Q^M. The maximum price per unit that consumers are willing to pay for Q^M units is P^M, so the profit-maximizing price is P^M. Monopoly profits are given by the shaded rectangle in the figure, which is the base (Q^M) times the height $[P^M - ATC(Q^M)]$.

FIGURE 8–15 Profit Maximization Under Monopoly

The profit-maximizing output is Q^M, where $MR = MC$; price is P^M, which is above MC at that output. Positive profits are shown by the shaded area.

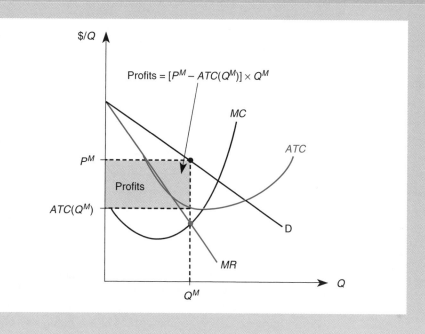

Principle	**MONOPOLY PRICING RULE**
	Given the level of output, Q^M, that maximizes profits, the monopoly price is the price on the demand curve corresponding to the Q^M units produced:

$$P^M = P(Q^M) \qquad\qquad (8\text{--}5)$$

Demonstration PROBLEM 8–5

Suppose the inverse demand function for a monopolist's product is given by

$$P = 100 - 2Q$$

and the cost function is given by

$$TC = 10 + 2Q$$

Determine the profit-maximizing price and quantity and the maximum profits.

Answer

Using the marginal revenue formula for linear inverse demand and the formula for marginal cost, we see that

$$MR = 100 - (2)(2)(Q) = 100 - 4Q$$
$$MC = 2$$

Next, we set $MR = MC$ to find the profit-maximizing level of output:

$$100 - 4Q = 2$$

or

$$4Q = 98$$

Solving for Q yields the profit-maximizing output of $Q^M = 24.5$ units. We find the profit-maximizing price by setting $Q = Q^M$ in the inverse demand function:

$$P = 100 - 2(24.5) = 51$$

Thus, the profit-maximizing price is $51 per unit. Finally, profits are given by the difference between revenues and costs:

$$\pi = P^M Q^M - TC(Q^M)$$
$$= (51)(24.5) - [10 + 2(24.5)]$$
$$= \$1190.50$$

When a firm controls its price in the market, we say it has market power. The important difference between a perfectly competitive firm and a monopoly, representing two market structures that are diagonally opposite to each other, is that a perfectly competitive firm has no market power because it produces at the point where price equals marginal cost, while a monopoly charges prices that exceed marginal cost. As defined in Chapter 7, a popular measure of market power, monopoly power in this case, is given by the Lerner index, $L = (P - MC)/P$, where $P = P^M$ and MC is marginal cost.

Ranging between zero and one—zero when price equals marginal cost and greater than zero for any industry that deviates from perfect competition—the Lerner index can be expressed in terms of price elasticity of demand. As discussed earlier, a key determinant of price elasticity is the availability of substitutes. Therefore, for a monopolist that faces little competition from outside and hence enjoys significant market power, the markup is high. The greater the Lerner index, the greater the firm's markup. In equilibrium, where $MR = MC$, Equation 7–4 can be arranged to obtain:

$$L = \frac{P - MC}{P} = -\frac{1}{E_{Q_x, P_x}}$$

(8–6)

Remember from Chapter 3 that E_{Q_x, P_x} is the price elasticity of the firm's demand curve. The smaller the number of substitutes, and the smaller the price elasticity, the higher the Lerner index.

The Absence of a Supply Curve

Recall that a supply curve determines how much will be produced at a given price. Since perfectly competitive firms determine how much output to produce on the basis of price ($P = MC$), supply curves exist in perfectly competitive markets. In contrast, a monopolist determines how much to produce on the basis of marginal revenue, which is less than price ($P > MR = MC$). As a consequence, there is no supply curve in markets served by a monopolist.

Multiplant Decisions

Up until this point, we have assumed that the monopolist produces output at a single location. In many instances, however, a monopolist has different plants at different locations. An important issue for the manager of such a *multiplant monopoly* is the determination of how much output to produce at each plant.

Suppose the monopolist produces output at two plants. The cost of producing Q_1 units at plant 1 is $TC_1(Q_1)$, and the cost of producing Q_2 units at plant 2 is $TC_2(Q_2)$. Further, suppose the outputs produced at the two plants are identical, so the price per unit consumers are willing to pay for the total output produced at the two plants is $P(Q)$, where

$$Q = Q_1 + Q_2$$

Profit maximization implies that the two-plant monopolist should produce output in each plant such that the marginal cost of producing in each plant equals the marginal revenue of total output.

Principle

MULTIPLANT OUTPUT RULE
Let $MR(Q)$ be the marginal revenue of producing a total of $Q = Q_1 + Q_2$ units of output. Suppose the marginal cost of producing Q_1 units of output in plant 1 is $MC_1(Q_1)$ and that of producing Q_2 units in plant 2 is $MC_2(Q_2)$. The profit-maximization rule for the two-plant monopolist is to allocate output among the two plants such that

$$MR(Q) = MC_1(Q_1)$$ (8–7)

$$MR(Q) = MC_2(Q_2)$$ (8–8)

A Calculus ALTERNATIVE

If profits are

$$\pi = TR(Q_1 + Q_2) - TC_1(Q_1) - TC_2(Q_2)$$

the first-order conditions for maximizing profits are

$$\frac{d\pi}{dQ_1} = \frac{TdR(Q_1 + Q_2)}{dQ_1} - \frac{TdC_1(Q_1)}{dQ_1} = 0$$

$$\frac{d\pi}{dQ_2} = \frac{TdR(Q_1 + Q_2)}{dQ_2} - \frac{TdC_2(Q_2)}{dQ_2} = 0$$

The economic intuition underlying the multiplant output rule is precisely the same as all of the profit-maximization principles. If the marginal revenue of producing output in a plant exceeds the marginal cost, the firm will add more to revenue than to cost by expanding output in the plant. As output is expanded, marginal revenue declines until it ultimately equals the marginal cost of producing in the plant.

The conditions for maximizing profits in a multiplant setting imply that

$$MC_1(Q_1) = MC_2(Q_2) \tag{8–9}$$

This too has a simple economic explanation. If the marginal cost of producing in plant 1 is lower than that of producing in plant 2, the monopolist might reduce costs by producing more output in plant 1 and less in plant 2. As more output is produced in plant 1, the marginal cost of producing in the plant increases until it ultimately equals the marginal cost of producing in plant 2.

Demonstration PROBLEM 8–6

Suppose the inverse demand for a monopolist's product is given by

$$P(Q) = 70 - 0.5Q$$

The monopolist can produce output in two plants. The marginal cost of producing in plant 1 is $MC_1 = 3Q_1$, and the marginal cost of producing in plant 2 is $MC_2 = Q_2$. How much output should be produced in each plant to maximize profits, and what price should be charged for the product?

Answer

To maximize profits, the firm should produce output in the two plants such that

$$MR(Q) = MC_1(Q_1)$$

$$MR(Q) = MC_2(Q_2)$$

In this instance, marginal revenue is given by

$$MR(Q) = 70 - Q$$

where $Q = Q_1 + Q_2$. Substituting these values into the formula for the multiplant output rule, we get

$$70 - (Q_1 + Q_2) = 3Q_1$$
$$70 - (Q_1 + Q_2) = Q_2$$

Thus, we have two equations and two unknowns, and we must solve for the two unknowns. The first equation implies that

$$Q_2 = 70 - 4Q_1$$

Substituting this into the second equation yields

$$70 - (Q_1 + 70 - 4Q_1) = 70 - 4Q_1$$

Solving this equation, we find that $Q_1 = 10$. Next, we substitute this value of Q_1 into the first equation:

$$70 - (10 + Q_2) = 3(10)$$

Solving this equation, we find that $Q_2 = 30$. Thus, the firm should produce 10 units in plant 1 and 30 units in plant 2 for a total output of $Q = 40$ units.

To find the profit-maximizing price, we must find the maximum price per unit that consumers will pay for 40 units of output. To do this, we set $Q = 40$ in the inverse demand function:

$$P = 70 - 0.5(40) = 50$$

Thus, the profit-maximizing price is $50.

Implications of Entry Barriers

Our analysis of monopoly reveals that a monopolist may earn positive economic profits. If a monopolist is earning positive economic profits, the presence of barriers to entry prevents other firms from entering the market to reap a portion of those profits. Thus, monopoly profits, if they exist, will continue over time so long as the firm maintains its monopoly power. It is important to note, however, that the presence of monopoly power does not imply positive profits; it depends solely on where the demand curve lies in relation to the average total cost curve. For example, the monopolist depicted in Figure 8–16 earns zero economic profits, because the optimal price exactly equals the average total cost of production. Moreover, in the short run a monopolist may even experience losses.

The monopoly power a monopolist enjoys often implies some social costs to society. Consider, for example, the monopolist's demand, marginal revenue, and marginal cost curves graphed in Figure 8–17. For simplicity, these curves are graphed as linear functions of output, and the position of the average cost curve is suppressed for now. The profit-maximizing monopolist produces Q^M units of output and charges a price of P^M.

The first thing to notice about monopoly is that price exceeds the marginal cost of production: $P^M > MC$. The price in a market reflects the value to society of another unit of output. Marginal cost reflects the cost to society of the resources needed to produce an additional unit of output. Since price exceeds marginal cost, the monopolist produces less output than is socially desirable. In effect, society would be willing to pay more for one more unit of output than it would cost to produce the unit. Yet the

FIGURE 8–16 A Monopolist Earning Zero Profits

A monopolist earning zero economic profits is depicted here. The *ATC* is tangent to the demand curve and is the same point that Q^M and P^M intersect. This means the monopolist is charging just enough to cover its opportunity costs.

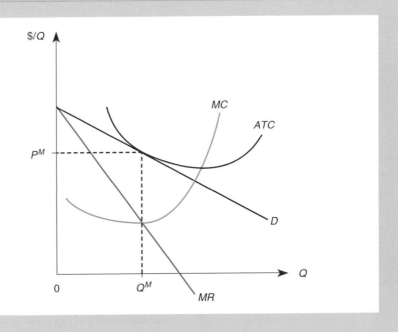

FIGURE 8–17 Deadweight Loss of Monopoly

Here the $P^M > MC$. Because of this, the monopolist produces less output than is socially desirable. The monopolist produces less output (Q^M rather than Q^C) and charges a higher price (P^M rather than P^C) than under perfect competition. This deadweight loss reflects the welfare loss to society due to the monopolist producing output below the competitive level.

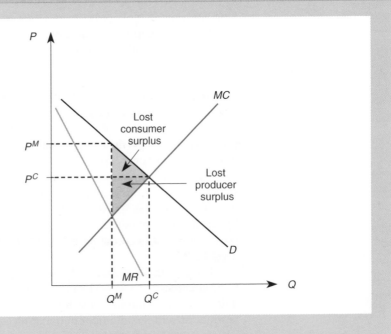

monopolist refuses to do so because it would reduce the firm's profits. This is because marginal revenue for a monopolist lies below the demand curve.

In contrast, given the same demand and cost conditions, a firm in a perfectly competitive industry would continue to produce output up to the point where price equals marginal cost; this corresponds to an industry output and price of Q^C and P^C under perfect competition. Thus, the monopolist produces less output and charges a higher price than would a perfectly competitive industry. The shaded area in Figure 8–17 corresponds to the lost consumer and producer surplus that arises under monopoly. This **deadweight loss** reflects the welfare loss to society due to the monopolist producing output below the competitive level.

deadweight loss of monopoly
The consumer and producer surplus that is lost due to the monopolist charging a price in excess of marginal cost.

So far, the discussion of monopoly has focused only on the efficiency effects. But the effects on distribution of income must also be taken into account. Clearly, the monopolist benefits by obtaining all of the monopoly's profits, as represented by the rectangle to the left of the shaded area labelled "lost consumer surplus" in Figure 8–17. This above-normal profit, which is expected to continue into the long run in the absence of entry by new firms, is sometimes referred to as *monopoly rents*. This above-normal profit is indeed a transfer from consumers to the monopolist. This subject is further discussed in Chapter 14.

Monopolistic Competition

monopolistically competitive market
A market in which (1) there are many buyers and sellers; (2) each firm produces a differentiated product; and (3) there is free entry and exit.

A market structure that lies between the extremes of monopoly and perfect competition is *monopolistic competition*. A **monopolistically competitive market** exhibits some characteristics present in both perfect competition and monopoly.

Conditions for Monopolistic Competition

An industry is monopolistically competitive if

1. There are many buyers and sellers
2. Each firm in the industry produces a differentiated product
3. There is free entry into and exit from the industry

There are numerous industries in which firms produce products that are close substitutes, and the market for hamburgers is a prime example. Many fast-food restaurants produce hamburgers, but the hamburgers produced by one firm differ from those produced by other firms. Moreover, it is relatively easy for new firms to enter the market for hamburgers.

The key difference between the models of monopolistic competition and perfect competition is that in a market with monopolistic competition, each firm produces a product that differs slightly from other firms' products. The products are close, but not perfect, substitutes. For example, other things being equal, some consumers prefer McDonald's hamburgers, whereas others prefer to eat at Wendy's, Burger King, or one of the many other restaurants that serve hamburgers. As the price of a McDonald's hamburger increases, some consumers will substitute toward hamburgers produced by another firm. But some consumers may continue to eat at McDonald's even if the price is higher than at other restaurants. The fact that the products are not perfect substitutes in a monopolistically competitive industry thus implies that each firm faces a downward-sloping demand curve for its product. To sell more of its product, the firm must lower the price. In this sense, the demand curve facing a monopolistically competitive firm looks more like the demand for a monopolist's product than like the demand for a competitive firm's product.

There are two important differences between a monopolistically competitive market and a market serviced by a monopolist. First, while a monopolistically competitive firm faces a downward-sloping demand for its product, there are other firms in the industry that sell similar products, which makes the demand curve faced by a monopolistic competitor flatter (more price-elastic). Second, in a monopolistically competitive industry, there are no barriers to entry. As we will see later, this implies that firms will enter the market if existing firms earn positive economic profits.

Profit Maximization

The determination of the profit-maximizing price and output under monopolistic competition is precisely the same as for a firm operating under monopoly. To see this, consider the demand curve for a monopolistically competitive firm presented in Figure 8–18. Since the demand curve slopes downward, the marginal revenue curve lies below it, just as under monopoly. To maximize profits, the monopolistically competitive firm produces where marginal revenue equals marginal cost. This output is given by Q^* in Figure 8–18. The profit-maximizing price is the maximum price consumers are willing to pay for Q^* units of the firm's output, namely P^*. The firm's profits are given by the shaded region.

Now that you understand that the basic principles of profit maximization are the same under monopolistic competition and monopoly, it is important to highlight one important difference in the interpretation of our analysis. The demand and marginal revenue curves used to determine the monopolistically competitive firm's profit-maximizing output and price are based not on the market demand for the product but on the demand for the individual firm's product. The demand curve facing a monopolist, in contrast, is the market demand curve.

FIGURE 8–18 Profit Maximization Under Monopolistic Competition

The rule for short-run profit maximization for a firm under monopolistic competition is similar to that of a monopoly. $MR = MC$ at Q^* and profits are shown by the shaded area. The price being charged is above the ATC, P^*, at that point, and therefore profits are positive.

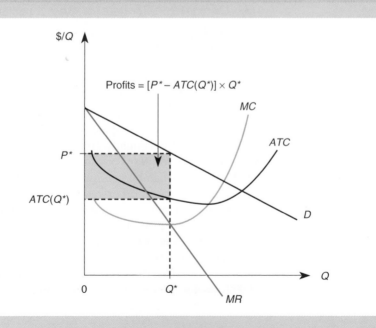

In fact, because the firms in a monopolistically competitive industry produce differentiated products, the notion of an industry or market demand curve is not well defined. To find market demand, one must add up the total quantities purchased from all firms in the market at each price. But in monopolistically competitive markets, each firm produces a product that differs from other firms' products. Adding up these different products would be like adding up apples and oranges.

Principle

PROFIT-MAXIMIZATION RULE FOR MONOPOLISTIC COMPETITION

To maximize profits, a monopolistically competitive firm produces where its marginal revenue equals marginal cost. The profit-maximizing price is the maximum price per unit that consumers are willing to pay for the profit-maximizing level of output. In other words, the profit-maximizing output, Q^*, is such that

$$MR(Q^*) = MC(Q^*) \tag{8-10}$$

and the profit-maximizing price is

$$P^* = P(Q^*) \tag{8-11}$$

Demonstration PROBLEM 8–7

Suppose the inverse demand function for a monopolistically competitive firm's product is given by

$$P = 100 - 2Q$$

and the cost function is given by

$$TC = 5 + 2Q$$

Determine the profit-maximizing price and quantity and the maximum profits.

Answer

Using the marginal revenue formula for linear inverse demand and the formula for marginal cost, we see that

$$MR = 100 - (2)(2)(Q) = 100 - 4Q$$
$$MC = 2$$

Next, we set $MR = MC$ to find the profit-maximizing level of output:

$$100 - 4Q = 2$$

or

$$4Q = 98$$

Solving for Q yields the profit-maximizing output of $Q^* = 24.5$ units. The profit-maximizing price is found by setting $Q = Q^*$ in the inverse demand function:

$$P^* = 100 - 2 \times 24.5 = 51$$

Thus, the profit-maximizing price is $51 per unit. Finally, profits are given by the difference between revenues and costs:

$$\pi = P^*Q^* - TC(Q^*)$$
$$= (51)(24.5) - [5 + 2(24.5)]$$
$$= \$1195.50$$

Long-Run Equilibrium

Because there is free entry into monopolistically competitive markets, if firms earn short-run profits in a monopolistically competitive industry, additional firms will enter the industry in the long run to capture some of those profits. Similarly, if existing firms incur losses, in the long run some firms will exit the industry.

To explain the impact of entry and exit in monopolistically competitive markets, suppose a monopolistically competitive firm is earning positive economic profits. The potential for profits induces other firms to enter the market and produce slight variations of the existing firm's product. As additional firms enter the market, some consumers who were buying the firm's product will begin to consume one of the new firms' products. Thus, one would expect the existing firms to lose a share of the market when new firms enter.

To make this notion more precise, suppose a monopolistically competitive firm that sells brand X faces an initial demand curve of D^0 in Figure 8–19. Since this demand curve lies above the *ATC* curve, the firm is earning positive economic profits. This, of course, lures more firms into the industry. As additional firms enter, the demand for this firm's product will decrease because some consumers will substitute

FIGURE 8–19 Effect of Entry on a Monopolistically Competitive Firm's Demand

The effect of entry on a monopolistically competitive firm's demand is to cause it to shift to the left due to new firms selling other brands (substitute goods). This lowers the equilibrium price and quantity as both the demand curve and the *MR* curve rotate clockwise.

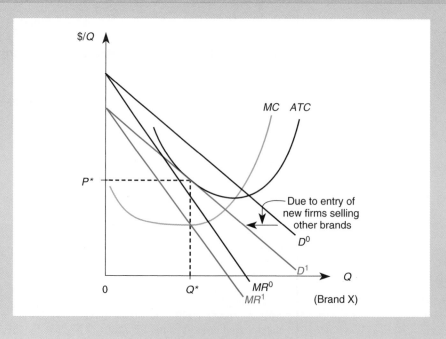

FIGURE 8-20 Long-Run Equilibrium Under Monopolistic Competition

In the long run, demand is tangent to the *ATC*. This is the position of each firm when the industry is in long-run equilibrium. Firms enter and exit the market until zero economic profits are obtained.

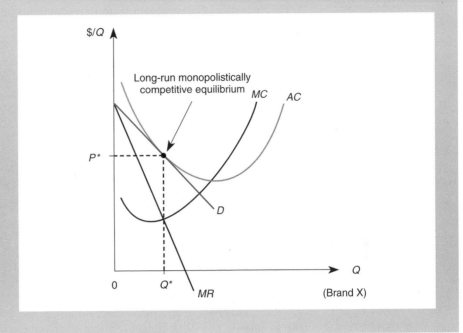

toward the new products offered by the entering firms. Entry continues until the demand curve decreases to D^1, where it is just tangent to the firm's average cost curve. At this point, firms in the industry are earning zero economic profits, and there is no incentive for additional firms to enter the industry.

The story is similar if firms in the industry initially are incurring losses. However, in this instance firms will exit the industry, and the demand for the products offered by the firms that remain will increase. This process leads to increased profits (or, more accurately, reduced losses) for the remaining firms. Ultimately, firms stop leaving the industry when the remaining firms earn zero economic profits.

Thus, the long-run equilibrium in a monopolistically competitive industry is characterized by the situation in Figure 8–20. Each firm earns zero economic profits but charges a price that exceeds the marginal cost of producing the good.

Principle	**THE LONG RUN AND MONOPOLISTIC COMPETITION**

THE LONG RUN AND MONOPOLISTIC COMPETITION
In the long run, monopolistically competitive firms produce a level of output such that

1. $P > MC$ (8–12)
2. $P = ATC >$ minimum of average costs

As in the case of monopoly, the fact that price exceeds marginal cost implies that monopolistically competitive firms produce less output than is socially desirable. In essence, consumers are willing to pay more for another unit than it would cost the firm to produce another unit; yet the firm will not produce more output because of its concern with profits.

Because price equals average costs, firms earn zero economic profits just as firms in perfectly competitive markets do. Even though the firms have some control over price, competition among them leads to a situation where no firm earns more than its opportunity cost of producing.

Finally, note that the price of output exceeds the minimum point on the average cost curve. This implies that firms do not take full advantage of economies of scale in production. In a sense there are too many firms in the industry to enable any individual firm to take full advantage of economies of scale in production. On the other hand, some argue that this is simply the cost to society of having product variety. If there were fewer firms, economies of scale could be fully exploited, but there would be less product variety in the market.

Implications of Product Differentiation

The key difference between perfect competition and monopolistic competition is the assumption that firms produce *differentiated products*. Since there are many products in a monopolistically competitive industry, the only reason firms have any control over their price is that consumers view the products as differentiated. The demand for a firm's product is less elastic when consumers view other firms' products as poor substitutes for it. The less elastic the demand for a firm's product, the greater the potential for earning profits.

For this reason, many firms in monopolistically competitive industries continually attempt to convince consumers that their products are better than those offered by other firms. A number of examples of such industries come readily to mind: fast-food restaurants, toothpaste, mouthwash, gasoline, aspirin, car wax—undoubtedly you can add other industries to the list. Each of these industries consists of many firms, and the different brands offered by firms in each industry are very close substitutes. In some instances, firms introduce several varieties of products; each soft-drink producer, for example, produces a variety of cola and noncola drinks.

Firms in monopolistically competitive industries employ two strategies to persuade consumers that their products are better than those offered by competitors. First, monopolistically competitive firms spend considerable amounts on advertising campaigns. Very typically, these campaigns involve **comparative advertising** designed to differentiate a given firm's brand from brands sold by competing firms. Comparative advertising is common in the fast-food industry, where firms such as McDonald's attempt to stimulate demand for their hamburgers by differentiating them from competing brands. To the extent that comparative advertising is effective, it may induce consumers to pay a premium for a particular brand. The additional value that a brand adds to the product is known as **brand equity**.

Second, firms in monopolistically competitive industries frequently introduce new products into the market to further differentiate their products from those of other firms. These include not only "new, improved" products, such as an "improved" version of laundry detergent, but completely different product lines. Monopolistically competitive firms may also attempt to create and advertise new products that fill special needs in the market. This strategy—called **niche marketing**—involves products or services targeted to a specific group of consumers. Through **green marketing**, for instance, firms create and advertise "environmentally friendly" products in an attempt to capture the segment of the market that is concerned with environmental issues. Examples of green marketing include package labels that prominently indicate a toy is made from recycled plastic or a particular brand of laundry detergent is biodegradable.

comparative advertising
A form of advertising in which a firm attempts to increase the demand for its brand by differentiating its product from competing brands.

brand equity
The additional value added to a product because of its brand.

niche marketing
A marketing strategy in which goods and services are tailored to meet the needs of a particular segment of the market.

green marketing
A form of niche marketing in which firms target products toward consumers who are concerned about environmental issues.

As the manager of a firm in a monopolistically competitive industry, it is important to remember that, in the long run, additional firms will enter the market if your firm earns short-run profits with its product. Thus, while you may make short-run profits by introducing a new product line, in the long run other firms will mimic your product and/or introduce new product lines, and your economic profits will decrease to zero.

Optimal Advertising Decisions

How much should a firm spend on advertising in order to maximize profits? The answer depends, in part, on the nature of the industry in which the firm operates. Firms that operate in perfectly competitive markets generally do not find it profitable to advertise, because consumers already have perfect information about the large number of substitutes that exist for any given firm's product. A wheat farmer who operates a small family farm, for instance, is unlikely to profit by spending family funds on an advertising campaign designed to increase the demand for the family's wheat. In contrast, firms that have market power—such as monopolists and monopolistically competitive firms—will generally find it profitable to spend a fraction of their revenues on advertising.

As with any economic decision, the optimal amount of advertising balances marginal benefits and marginal costs: to maximize these profits, managers should advertise up to the point where the incremental revenue from advertising equals the incremental cost. The incremental cost of advertising is simply the dollar cost of the resources needed to increase the level of advertising. These costs include fees paid for additional advertising space and the opportunity cost of the human resources needed to put together the advertising campaign. The incremental revenue is the extra revenue the firm gets as a result of the advertising campaign. These extra revenues depend on the number of additional units that will be sold as a result of an advertising campaign, and how much is earned on each of these units. Fortunately, a simple formula is available that permits managers to easily determine the optimal level of advertising.

Formula: The Profit-Maximizing Advertising-to-Sales Ratio. The profit-maximizing advertising-to-sales ratio (A/TR) is given by

$$\frac{A}{TR} = \frac{E_{Q,A}}{-E_{Q,P}} \qquad (8\text{--}13)$$

where $E_{Q,P}$ represents the own price elasticity of demand for the firm's product, $E_{Q,A}$ is the advertising elasticity of demand for the firm's product, A represents the firm's expenditures on advertising, and $TR = PQ$ denotes the dollar value of the firm's sales (that is, the firm's revenues).

A Calculus ALTERNATIVE

A firm's profits are revenues minus production costs and advertising expenditures. If we let A represent advertising expenditures, $Q = Q(P, A)$ denote the demand for the firm's product, and $TC(Q)$ denote production costs, firm profits are functions of P and A:

$$\pi(P, A) = Q(P, A)P - TC[Q(P, A)] - A$$

The first-order conditions for maximizing profits require

$$\frac{\partial \pi}{\partial P} = \frac{\partial Q}{\partial P}P + Q - \frac{\partial TC}{\partial Q}\frac{\partial Q}{\partial P} = 0$$

and

$$\frac{\partial \pi}{\partial A} = \frac{\partial Q}{\partial A}P - \frac{\partial TC}{\partial Q}\frac{\partial Q}{\partial A} - 1 = 0$$

Noting that $\partial C/\partial Q = MC$, $E_{Q,P} = (\partial Q/\partial P)(P/Q)$, and $E_{Q,A} = (\partial Q/\partial A)(A/Q)$, we may write the above equation as

$$\frac{P - MC}{P} = \frac{-1}{E_{Q,P}}$$

$$\frac{A}{TR} = \left(\frac{P - MC}{P}\right)E_{Q,A}$$

Combining these two equations yields the above formula, Equation 8–13.

Two aspects of this formula are worth noting. First, the more elastic the demand for a firm's product, the lower the optimal advertising-to-sales ratio. In the extreme case where $E_{Q,P} = -\infty$ (perfect competition), the formula indicates that the optimal advertising-to-sales ratio is zero. Second, the greater the advertising elasticity, the greater the optimal advertising-to-sales ratio. Firms that have market power (such as monopolists and monopolistically competitive firms) face a demand curve that is not perfectly elastic. As a consequence, these firms will generally find it optimal to engage in some degree of advertising. Exactly how much such firms should spend on advertising, however, depends on the quantitative impact of advertising on demand. The more sensitive demand is to advertising (that is, the greater the advertising elasticity), the greater the number of additional units sold because of a given increase in advertising expenditures, and thus the greater the optimal advertising-to-sales ratio.

Demonstration PROBLEM 8–8

Corpus Industries produces a product at constant marginal cost that it sells in a monopolistically competitive market. In an attempt to bolster profits, the manager hired an economist to estimate the demand for its product. She found that the demand for the firm's product is log-linear, with an own price elasticity of demand of -10 and an advertising elasticity of demand of 0.2. To maximize profits, what fraction of revenues should the firm spend on advertising?

Answer

To find the profit-maximizing advertising-to-sales ratio, we simply plug $E_{Q,P} = -10$ and $E_{Q,A} = 0.2$ into the formula for the optimal advertising-to-sales ratio:

$$\frac{A}{TR} = \frac{E_{Q,A}}{-E_{Q,P}} = \frac{0.2}{10} = 0.02$$

Thus, Corpus Industries' optimal advertising-to-sales ratio is 2 percent—to maximize profits, the firm should spend 2 percent of its revenues on advertising.

ANSWERING THE Headline

The McDonald's Lighter Choices Menu is unlikely to have a sustainable impact on the company's bottom line. As noted earlier in this chapter, the fast-food restaurant business has many features of monopolistic competition. Indeed, the owner of a typical McDonald's franchise competes not only against Burger King and Wendy's but against a host of other establishments such as KFC, Arby's, and Taco Bell. While each of these establishments offers quick meals at reasonable prices, the products offered are clearly differentiated. This gives these businesses some market power.

While a monopolistically competitive business like McDonald's might earn positive economic profits in the short run by introducing new products more quickly than its rivals, in the long run its competitors will attempt to mimic the strategies that are profitable. Thus, while the McDonald's Lighter Choices Menu might lead to short-run profits, in the long run other firms are likely to copy this strategy if it proves successful. This type of entry by rival firms would reduce the demand for meals at McDonald's and ultimately result in long-run economic profits of zero. A similar chain of events occurred in 1978 when McDonald's successfully launched its Egg McMuffin. Other fast-food restaurants eventually responded by launching their own breakfast items, which ultimately reduced McDonald's share of the breakfast market and its economic profits.

Summary

In this chapter, we examined managerial decisions in three market environments: perfect competition, monopoly, and monopolistic competition. Each of these market structures provides a manager with a different set of variables that can influence the firm's profits. A manager may need to pay particularly close attention to different decision parameters because different market structures allow control of only certain variables. Managers who recognize which variables are relevant for a particular industry will make more profits for their firms.

Managers in perfectly competitive markets should concentrate on producing the proper quantity and keeping costs low. Because perfectly competitive markets contain a very large number of firms that produce perfect substitutes, a manager in this market has no control over price. A manager in a monopoly, in contrast, needs to recognize the relation between price and quantity. By setting a quantity at which marginal cost equals marginal revenue, the manager of a monopoly will maximize profits. This is also true for the manager of a firm in a monopolistically competitive market, who also must evaluate the firm's product periodically to ensure that it is differentiated from other products in the market. In many instances, the manager of a monopolistically competitive firm will find it advantageous to slightly change the product from time to time to enhance product differentiation.

Key Terms and Concepts

brand equity 294
comparative advertising 294
cost complementarities 275
deadweight loss of monopoly
  289

diseconomies of scale 273
economies of scale 273
economies of scope 275
firm demand curve 260
green marketing 294

Visit the Web site @ **www.mcgrawhill.ca/college/baye**

Conceptual and Computational Questions

1. The graph here summarizes the demand and costs for a firm that operates in a perfectly competitive market.
   a. What level of output should this firm produce in the short run?
   b. What price should this firm charge in the short run?
   c. What is the firm's total cost at this level of output?
   d. What is the firm's total variable cost at this level of output?
   e. What is the firm's fixed cost at this level of output?
   f. What is the firm's profit if it produces this level of output?
   g. What is the firm's profit if it shuts down?
   h. In the long run, should this firm continue to operate or shut down?

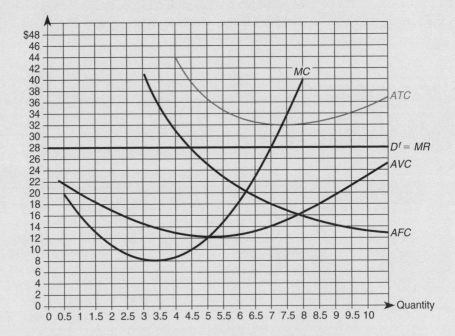

2. A firm sells its product in a perfectly competitive market where other firms charge a price of $80 per unit. The firm's total costs are $TC = 40 + 8Q + 2Q^2$.
   a. How much output should the firm produce in the short run?
   b. What price should the firm charge in the short run?
   c. What are the firm's short-run profits?
   d. What adjustments should be anticipated in the long run?

3. The following graph summarizes the demand and costs for a firm that operates in a monopolistically competitive market.
   a. What is the firm's optimal output?
   b. What is the firm's optimal price?
   c. What are the firm's maximum profits?
   d. What adjustments should the manager be anticipating?

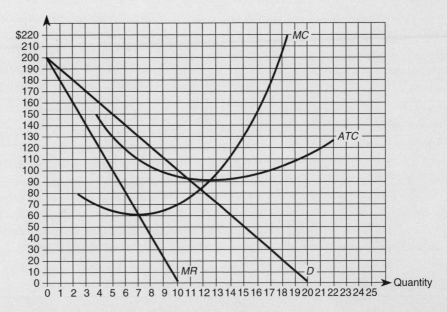

4. You are the manager of a monopoly, and your demand and cost functions are given by $P = 200 - 2Q$ and $TC = 2000 + 3Q^2$, respectively.
   a. What price-quantity combination maximizes your firm's profits?
   b. Calculate the maximum profits.
   c. Is demand elastic, inelastic, or unit-elastic at the profit-maximizing price-quantity combination?
   d. What price-quantity combination maximizes revenue?
   e. Calculate the maximum revenues.
   f. Is demand elastic, inelastic, or unit-elastic at the revenue-maximizing price-quantity combination?

5. You are the manager of a firm that produces a product according to the cost function $TC = 100 + 50q_i - 4q_i^2 + q_i^3$. Determine the short-run supply function if
   a. You operate a perfectly competitive business
   b. You operate a monopoly
   c. You operate a monopolistically competitive business

6. The following diagram shows the demand, marginal revenue, and marginal cost of a monopolist.

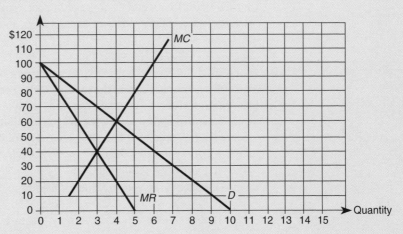

    a. Determine the profit-maximizing output and price.

    b. What price and output would prevail if this firm's product was sold by price-taking firms in a perfectly competitive market?

    c. Calculate the deadweight loss of this monopoly.

7. You are the manager of a monopolistically competitive firm, and your demand and cost functions are given by $Q = 20 - 2P$ and $TC = 104 - 14Q + Q^2$.

    a. Find the inverse demand function for your firm's product.

    b. Determine the profit-maximizing price and level of production.

    c. Calculate your firm's maximum profits.

    d. What long-run adjustments should you expect? Explain.

8. The elasticity of demand for a firm's product is -2 and its advertising elasticity of demand is 0.1.

    a. Determine the firm's optimal advertising-to-sales ratio.

    b. If the firm's revenues are \$50 000, what is its profit-maximizing level of advertising?

Problems and Applications

9. The CEO of a major automaker overheard one of its division managers make the following statement regarding the firm's production plans: "In order to maximize profits, it is essential that we operate at the minimum point of our average total cost curve." If you were the CEO of the automaker, would you praise or chastise the manager? Explain.

10. You are the manager of a small Canadian firm that sells nails in a competitive Canadian market. (The nails you sell are a standardized commodity; stores view your nails as identical to those available from hundreds of other firms.) You are concerned about two events you recently learned about through trade publications: (1) the overall market supply of nails will decrease by 2 percent, due to exit by foreign competitors; (2) due to a growing Canadian economy, the overall market demand for nails will increase by 2 percent. In the light of this information, should you plan to increase or decrease your production of nails? Explain.

11. When the first Pizza Hut opened its doors back in 1958, it offered consumers one style of pizza: its Original Thin Crust Pizza. Since its modest beginnings, Pizza Hut has established itself as the leader of the \$25 billion pizza industry. Today, Pizza Hut offers four styles of pizza in Canada: the Original Thin Crust Pizza, Pan Pizza, Stuffed Crust Pizza, and Oven Baked Pizza. Explain why Pizza Hut has expanded its offerings of pizza over the past five decades, and discuss the long-run profitability of such a strategy.

12. You are the manager of a small pharmaceutical company that received a patent on a new drug three years ago. Despite strong sales (\$125 million last year) and a low marginal cost of producing the product (\$0.25 per pill), your company has yet to show a profit from selling the drug. This is, in part, due to the fact that the company spent \$1.2 billion developing the drug and obtaining Health Canada approval. An economist has estimated that, at the current price of \$1.25 per pill, the own price elasticity of demand for the drug is -2.5. On the basis of this information, what can you do to boost profits? Explain.

13. Hydro-Québec is the sole provider of electricity in the province of Quebec and also a supplier of electricity to external markets. To meet the monthly demand for electricity in its markets, which is given by the inverse demand function $P = 1000 - 5Q$, the utility company has set up two generating facilities: Q_1 kilowatts are

produced at facility 1 and Q_2 kilowatts are produced at facility 2 (so $Q = Q_1 + Q_2$). The costs of producing electricity at each facility are given by $TC_1(Q_1) = 10\,050 + 5Q_1^2$ and $TC_2(Q_2) = 5000 + 2Q_2^2$, respectively. Determine the profit-maximizing amounts of electricity to produce at the two facilities, the optimal price, and the utility company's profits.

14. You are the manager of College Computers, a manufacturer of customized computers that meet the specifications required by the local university. Over 90 percent of your clientele consists of college students. College Computers is not the only firm that builds computers to meet this university's specifications; indeed, it competes with many manufacturers online and through traditional retail outlets. To attract its large student clientele, College Computers runs a weekly ad in the student paper advertising its "free service after the sale" policy in an attempt to differentiate itself from the competition. The weekly demand for computers produced by College Computers is given by $Q = 1000 - P$, and its weekly cost of producing computers is $TC = 2000 + Q^2$. If other firms in the industry sell PCs at $600, what price and quantity of computers should you produce to maximize your firm's profits? What long-run adjustments should you anticipate? Explain.

15. You are the general manager of a firm that manufactures personal computers. Due to a soft economy, demand for PCs has dropped 50 percent from the previous year. The sales manager of your company has identified only one potential client, who has received several quotes for 10 000 new PCs. According to the sales manager, the client is willing to pay $650 each for 10 000 new PCs. Your production line is currently idle, so you can easily produce the 10 000 units. The accounting department has provided you with the following information about the unit (or average) cost of producing three potential quantities of PCs:

	10 000 PCs	15 000 PCs	20 000 PCs
Materials (PC components)	$500	$500	$500
Depreciation	200	150	100
Labour	100	100	100
Total unit cost	$800	$750	$700

Based on this information, should you accept the offer to produce 10 000 PCs at $650 each? Explain.

16. You are a manager at Spacely Sprockets—a small firm that manufactures Type A and Type B bolts. The accounting and marketing departments have provided you with the following information about the per-unit costs and demand for Type A bolts:

Accounting Data for Type A Bolts		Marketing Data for Type A Bolts	
Item	Unit Cost	Quantity	Price
Materials and labour	$2.75	0	$10
Overhead	5.00	1	9
		2	8
Total cost per unit	$7.75	3	7
		4	6
		5	5

Materials and labour are obtained in a competitive market on an as-needed basis, and the reported costs per unit for materials and labour are constant over the relevant range of output. The reported unit overhead costs reflect the $10 spent last month on machines, divided by the projected output of 2 units that was planned when the machines were purchased. In addition to the above information, you know that the firm's assembly line can produce no more than 5 bolts. Since the firm also makes Type B bolts, this means that each Type A bolt produced reduces the number of Type B bolts that can be produced by one unit; the total number of Type A and B bolts produced cannot exceed 5 units. A call to a reputable source has revealed that unit costs for producing Type B bolts are identical to those for producing Type A bolts, and that Type B bolts can be sold at a constant price of $4.75 per unit. Determine your relevant marginal cost of producing Type A bolts and your profit-maximizing production of Type A bolts.

17. In a statement to Gillette's shareholders, Chairman and CEO James Kilts indicated that "Despite several new product launches, Gillette's advertising-to-sales declined dramatically . . . to 6.5 percent last year. Gillette's advertising spending, in fact, is one of the lowest in our peer group of consumer product companies." If the elasticity of demand for Gillette's consumer products is similar to that of other firms in its peer group (which averages −4.5), what is Gillette's advertising elasticity? Is Gillette's demand more or less responsive to advertising than other firms in its peer group? Explain.

APPENDIX 1: The Calculus of Profit Maximization ●

Perfect Competition

The profits of a perfectly competitive firm are

$$\pi = PQ - TC$$

The first-order conditions for maximizing profits require that marginal profits be zero:

$$\frac{d\pi}{dQ} = P - \frac{dTC}{dQ} = 0$$

Thus, we obtain the profit-maximizing rule for a firm in perfect competition:

$$P = \frac{dTC}{dQ}$$

or

$$P = MC$$

The second-order condition for maximizing profits requires that

$$\frac{d^2\pi}{dQ^2} = -\frac{d^2TC}{dQ^2} = -\frac{dMC}{dQ} < 0$$

This means that $d(MC)/dQ > 0$, or that marginal cost must be increasing in output.

Monopoly and Monopolistic Competition

$MR = MC$ Rule

The profits for a firm with market power are

$$\pi = TR - TC$$

where $TR = P(Q)Q$ is total revenue. To maximize profits, marginal profits must be zero:

$$\frac{d\pi}{dQ} = \frac{dTR}{dQ} - \frac{dTC}{dQ} = 0$$

or

$$MR = MC$$

The second-order condition requires that

$$\frac{d^2\pi}{dQ^2} = \frac{d^2TR}{dQ^2} - \frac{d^2TC}{dQ^2} < 0$$

which means that

$$\frac{dMR}{dQ} < \frac{dMC}{dQ}$$

But this simply means that the slope of the marginal revenue curve must be less than the slope of the marginal cost curve.

APPENDIX 2: The Algebra of Perfectly Competitive Supply Functions

This appendix shows how to obtain the short-run firm and industry supply functions from cost data. Suppose there are 500 firms in a perfectly competitive industry, with each firm having a cost function of

$$TC = 50 + 2q_i + 4q_i^2$$

The corresponding average total cost (ATC), average variable cost (AVC), and marginal cost (MC) functions are

$$ATC_i = \frac{50}{q_i} + 2 + 4q_i$$

$$AVC_i = 2 + 4q_i$$

and

$$MC_i = 2 + 8q_i$$

Recall that a firm's supply curve is the firm's marginal cost curve above the minimum of average variable cost. Since *AVC* is at its minimum where it equals marginal cost, to find the quantity where average variable cost equals marginal cost we must set the two functions equal to each other and solve for q_i. When we do this for the above equations, we find that the quantity at which marginal cost equals average variable cost is $q_i = 0$.

Next, we recognize that an individual firm maximizes profits by equating $P = MC_i$, so

$$P = 2 + 8q_i$$

Solving for q_i gives us the individual firm's supply function:

$$q_i = -\frac{2}{8} + \frac{1}{8}P$$

To find the supply curve for the industry, we simply sum the above equation over all 500 firms in the market:

$$Q = \sum_{i=1}^{500} q_i = 500\left(-\frac{2}{8} + \frac{1}{8}P\right) = -\frac{1000}{8} + \frac{500}{8}P$$

or

$$Q = -125 + 62.5P$$

Basic Oligopoly Models

CHAPTER

9

Headline

Beer Wars Brewing

Canada has long had two giants in its beer industry—Molson and Labatt. The two largest breweries in Canada have recently seen smaller firms such as Sleeman's and Moosehead encroach on their market share nationally, but arguably remain the powerhouses to be reckoned with in the industry. Their economies of scale, marketing budgets, and wide assortment of brands have virtually guaranteed them dominance in every province and territory across Canada.

That is, until Mountain Crest Liquors in Alberta opened for business. What this firm has done is move quickly to take advantage of a tax break that came about in 2002, one that allows the U.S. supplier of Mountain Crest's beer to qualify for the province's small brewers tax break. Under the small brewers legislation, small manufacturers are taxed at $0.40 per litre, in contrast with $0.98 per litre for the likes of Molson and Labatt, giving Mountain Crest a price advantage of more than $2 on a case of 12 cans or bottles of beer compared with their big competitors. By pricing

its products at a steep discount ($5.99 per six-pack for its Mountain Crest Classic Lager versus $8.99 for six Molson Canadian or Labatt Blue), the company has captured a sizable share of the provincial market with little or no advertising. Depending on which rival you speak to, Mountain Crest has achieved as much as a 4 percent penetration into Alberta's beer market in less than 18 months.

And they have done this with no advertising. The company's strategic use of the tax loophole, coupled with at-times-controversial packaging (resembling that of one of their big rivals), Mountain Crest has established itself as a player in an otherwise highly competitive market.

How sustainable is the firm's position given the oligopoly nature of this industry?

Source: Adapted from Paul Brent, "Mountain Crest Sparks Industry Hangover," *Financial Post*, July 21, 2003. Material reprinted with the express permission of National Post Company, a CanWest Partnership.

Introduction

Up until now, our analysis of markets has not considered the impact of strategic behaviour on managerial decision making. At one extreme, we examined profit maximization in perfectly competitive and monopolistically competitive markets. In these types of markets, there are so many firms competing with one another that no individual firm has any effect on other firms in the market. At the other extreme, we examined profit maximization in a monopolistic market. In this instance there is only one firm in the market, and strategic interactions among firms thus are irrelevant.

This chapter is the first of two chapters in which we examine managerial decisions in oligopolistic markets. Here we focus on basic output and pricing decisions in four specific types of oligopolies: Sweezy, Cournot, Stackelberg, and Bertrand. In the next chapter, we will develop a more general framework for analyzing other decisions, such as advertising, research and development, entry into an industry, and so forth. First, let us briefly review what is meant by the term *oligopoly*.

Conditions for Oligopoly

oligopoly
A market structure in which there are only a few firms, each of which is large relative to the total industry.

Oligopoly refers to a situation where there are relatively few large firms in an industry. No explicit number of firms is required for oligopoly, but the number usually is somewhere between two and ten. The products the firms offer may be either identical or differentiated. An oligopoly composed of only two firms is called a *duopoly*.

The market structure, as discussed in Chapter 7, also refers to other factors including the size of the firms (concentration). We also learned in that chapter that economic models link the structure of a market to the conduct and financial performance. The four-firm concentration ratios (C_4) and the Herfindahl-Hirschman index (HHI) are the two most popular measures of market structure. Of course, these indexes must be used in conjunction with other information in regard to circumstances surrounding the competitive interaction of firms in order to assess the nature of competition in an industry.

Oligopoly is perhaps the most interesting of all market structures; in fact, the next chapter is devoted entirely to the analysis of situations that arise under oligopoly. But from the viewpoint of the manager, a firm operating in an oligopoly setting is the most difficult to manage. The key reason is that there are few firms in an oligopolistic market and the manager must consider the likely impact of her or his decisions on the decisions of other firms in the industry. Moreover, the actions of other firms will have a profound impact on the manager's optimal decisions. It should be noted that due to the complexity of oligopoly, there is no single model that is relevant for all oligopolies.

The Role of Beliefs and Strategic Interaction

To gain an understanding of oligopoly interdependence, consider a situation where several firms selling differentiated products compete in an oligopoly. In determining what price and output to charge, the manager must consider the impact of his or her decisions on other firms in the industry. For example, if the price for the product is lowered, will other firms lower their prices or maintain their existing prices? If the price is increased, will other firms do likewise or maintain their current prices? The optimal decision of whether to raise or lower price will depend on how the manager believes other managers will respond. If other firms lower their prices when the firm

FIGURE 9–1 A Firm's Demand Depends on Actions of Rivals

At point B, price is P_0 and quantity is Q_0. Demand curve D_1 is based on the assumption that rivals will match any price change, while D_2 is based on the assumption that they will not match a price change. Demand is more inelastic when rivals follow suit than when they do not. For example, if price drops, a firm will sell more if rivals do not cut their prices (D_2) than it will if they lower their prices (D_1).

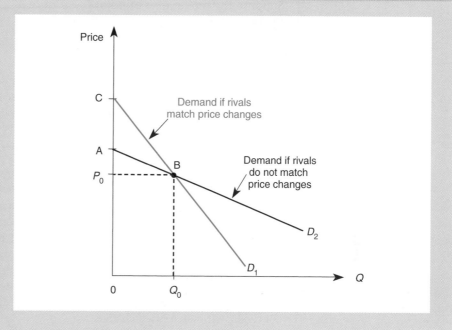

lowers its price, it will not sell as much as it would if the other firms maintained their existing prices.

As a point of reference, suppose the firm initially is at point B in Figure 9–1, charging a price of P_0. Demand curve D_1 is based on the assumption that rivals will match any price change, while D_2 is based on the assumption that they will not match a price change. Note that demand is more inelastic when rivals match a price change than when they do not. The reason for this is simple. For a given price reduction, a firm will sell more if rivals do not cut their prices (D_2) than it will if they lower their prices (D_1). In effect, a price reduction increases quantity demanded only slightly when rivals respond by lowering their prices. Similarly, for a given price increase, a firm will sell more when rivals also raise their prices (D_1) than it will when they maintain their existing prices (D_2).

Demonstration PROBLEM 9–1

Suppose the manager is at point B in Figure 9–1, charging a price of P_0. If the manager believes rivals will not match price reductions but will match price increases, what does the demand for the firm's product look like?

Answer

If rivals do not match price reductions, prices below P_0 will induce quantities demanded along curve D_2. If rivals do match price increases, prices above P_0 will generate quantities demanded along D_1. Thus, if the manager believes rivals will not match price reductions but will match price increases, the demand curve for the firm's product is given by CBD_2.

Demonstration PROBLEM 9-2

Suppose the manager is at point B in Figure 9–1, charging a price of P_0. If the manager believes rivals will match price reductions but will not match price increases, what does the demand for the firm's product look like?

Answer

If rivals match price reductions, prices below P_0 will induce quantities demanded along curve D_1. If rivals do match price increases, prices above P_0 will induce quantities demanded along D_2. Thus, if the manager believes rivals will match price reductions but will not match price increases, the demand curve for the firm's product is given by ABD_1.

The preceding analysis reveals that the demand for a firm's product in oligopoly depends critically on how rivals respond to the firm's pricing decisions. If rivals will match any price change, the demand curve for the firm's product is given by D_1. In this instance, the manager will maximize profits where the marginal revenue associated with demand curve D_1 equals marginal cost. If rivals will not match any price change, the demand curve for the firm's product is given by D_2. In this instance, the manager will maximize profits where the marginal revenue associated with demand curve D_2 equals marginal cost. In each case, the profit-maximizing role is the same as that under monopoly; the only difficulty for the firm manager is determining whether or not rivals will match price changes.

Profit Maximization in Four Oligopoly Settings

In the following subsections, we will examine profit maximization based on alternative assumptions regarding how rivals will respond to price or output changes. Each of the four models has different implications for the manager's optimal decisions, and these differences arise because of differences in the ways rivals respond to the firm's actions.

Sweezy Oligopoly

The Sweezy model is based on a very specific assumption regarding how other firms will respond to price increases and price cuts. An industry is characterized as a **Sweezy oligopoly** if

Sweezy oligopoly
An industry in which (1) there are few firms serving many consumers; (2) firms produce differentiated products; (3) each firm believes rivals will respond to a price reduction but will not follow a price increase; and (4) barriers to entry exist.

1. There are few firms in the market serving many consumers
2. The firms produce differentiated products
3. Each firm believes rivals will cut their prices in response to a price reduction but will not raise their prices in response to a price increase
4. Barriers to entry exist

Because the manager of a firm competing in a Sweezy oligopoly believes other firms will match any price decrease but not match price increases, the demand curve for the firm's product is given by ABD_1 in Figure 9–2. For prices above P_0, the relevant demand curve is D_2; thus, marginal revenue corresponds to this demand curve. For prices below P_0, the relevant demand curve is D_1, and marginal revenue corresponds to D_1. Thus, the marginal revenue curve (MR) the firm faces is initially the marginal revenue curve associated with D_2; at Q_0, it jumps down to the marginal revenue curve corresponding to D_1. In other words, the Sweezy oligopolist's marginal revenue curve, denoted MR, is ACEF in Figure 9–2.

FIGURE 9–2 Sweezy Oligopoly

This Sweezy oligopoly model shows an effective demand curve of ABD_1. This kinked demand curve (resulting from other firms matching price decreases, but not increases) results in an effective *MR* curve of ACEF. Notice the profit-maximizing level of output remains unchanged within the discontinuous range of *MC*, between C and E.

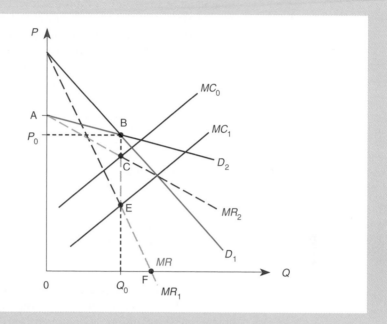

The profit-maximizing level of output occurs where marginal revenue equals marginal cost, and the profit-maximizing price is the maximum price consumers will pay for that level of output. For example, if marginal cost is given by MC_0 in Figure 9–2, marginal revenue equals marginal cost at point C. In this case the profit-maximizing output is Q_0 and the optimal price is P_0.

An important implication of the Sweezy model of oligopoly is that there will be a range (CE) over which changes in marginal cost do not affect the profit-maximizing level of output. This is in contrast to competitive, monopolistically competitive, and monopolistic firms, all of which increase output when marginal costs decline.

To see why firms competing in a Sweezy oligopoly may not increase output when marginal cost declines, suppose marginal cost decreases from MC_0 to MC_1 in Figure 9–2. Marginal revenue now equals marginal cost at point E, but the output corresponding to this point is still Q_0. Thus the firm continues to maximize profits by producing Q_0 units at a price of P_0.

In a Sweezy oligopoly, firms have an incentive not to change their pricing behaviour provided marginal costs remain in a given range. The reason for this stems purely from the assumption that rivals will match price cuts but not price increases. Firms in a Sweezy oligopoly do not want to change their prices because of the effect of price changes on the behaviour of other firms in the market.

The Sweezy model has been criticized because it offers no explanation of how the industry settles on the initial price P_0 that generates the kink in each firm's demand curve. Nonetheless, the Sweezy model does show us that strategic interactions among firms and a manager's beliefs about rivals' reactions can have a profound impact on pricing decisions. In practice, the initial price and a manager's beliefs may be based on a manager's experience with the pricing patterns of rivals in a given market. If your experience suggests that rivals will match price reductions but will not match price increases, the Sweezy model is probably the best tool to use in formulating your pricing decisions.

Cournot Oligopoly

Imagine that a few large oil producers must decide how much oil to pump out of the ground. The total amount of oil produced will certainly affect the market price of oil, but the underlying decision of each firm is not a pricing decision but rather the *quantity* of oil to produce. If each firm must determine its output level at the same time other firms determine their output levels, or more generally, if each firm expects its own output decision to have no impact on rivals' output decisions, then this scenario describes a Cournot oligopoly.

More formally, an industry is a **Cournot oligopoly** if

Cournot oligopoly
An industry in which
(1) there are few firms
serving many consumers;
(2) firms produce either
differentiated or
homogeneous products;
(3) each firm believes
rivals will hold their
output constant if it
changes its output; and
(4) barriers to entry exist.

1. There are few firms in the market serving many consumers
2. The firms produce either differentiated or homogeneous products
3. Each firm believes rivals will hold their output constant if it changes its output
4. Barriers to entry exist

Thus, in contrast to the Sweezy model of oligopoly, the Cournot model is relevant for decision making when managers make output decisions and believe that their decisions do not affect the output decisions of rival firms. Furthermore, the Cournot model applies to situations in which the products are either identical or differentiated.

Reaction Functions and Equilibrium

To highlight the implications of Cournot oligopoly, suppose there are only two firms competing in a Cournot duopoly: each firm must make an *output* decision, and each firm believes that its rival will hold output constant as it changes its own output. To determine its optimal output level, firm 1 will equate marginal revenue with marginal cost. Notice that since this is a duopoly, firm 1's marginal revenue is affected by firm 2's output level. In particular, the greater the output of firm 2, the lower the market price and thus the lower is firm 1's marginal revenue. This means that the profit-maximizing level of output for firm 1 depends on firm 2's output level: a greater output by firm 2 leads to a lower profit-maximizing output for firm 1. This relationship between firm 1's profit-maximizing output and firm 2's output is called a reaction function.

reaction function
A function that defines
the profit-maximizing
level of output for a firm
for given output levels
of another firm.

A **reaction function** defines the profit-maximizing level of output for a firm for given output levels of the other firm. More formally, the profit-maximizing level of output for firm 1 given that firm 2 produces Q_2 units of output is

$$Q_1 = r_1(Q_2)$$

Similarly, the profit-maximizing level of output for firm 2 given that firm 1 produces Q_1 units of output is given by

$$Q_2 = r_2(Q_1)$$

Cournot reaction functions for a duopoly are illustrated in Figure 9–3, where firm 1's output is measured on the horizontal axis and firm 2's output is measured on the vertical axis.

To understand why reaction functions are shaped as they are, let us highlight a few important points in the diagram. First, if firm 2 produced zero units of output, the profit-maximizing level of output for firm 1 would be Q_1^M, since this is the point on firm 1's reaction function (r_1) that corresponds to zero units of Q_2. This combination of outputs corresponds to the situation where only firm 1 is producing a positive level of output; thus, Q_1^M corresponds to the situation where firm 1 is a monopolist. If instead of producing zero units of output firm 2 produced Q_2^* units, the profit-maximizing

FIGURE 9–3 Cournot Reaction Functions

In a Cournot equilibrium, neither firm has an incentive to change its output given the output of the other firm (point E). This occurs as output levels move from point A to B to C to D, and then to E where the two reaction functions intersect.

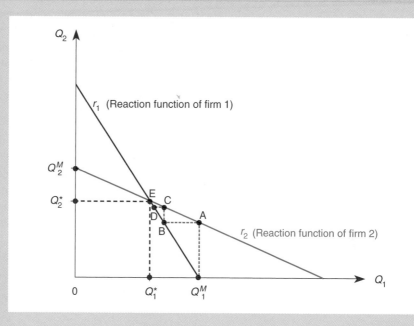

level of output for firm 1 would be Q_1^*, since this is the point on r_1 that corresponds to an output of Q_2^* by firm 2.

The reason the profit-maximizing level of output for firm 1 decreases as firm 2's output increases is as follows. The demand for firm 1's product depends on the output produced by other firms in the market. When firm 2 increases its level of output, the demand and marginal revenue for firm 1 decline. The profit-maximizing response by firm 1 is to reduce its level of output.

Demonstration PROBLEM 9–3

In Figure 9–3, what is the profit-maximizing level of output for firm 2 when firm 1 produces zero units of output? What is it when firm 1 produces Q_1^* units?

Answer

If firm 1 produces zero units of output, the profit-maximizing level of output for firm 2 will be Q_2^M, since this is the point on firm 2's reaction function that corresponds to zero units of Q_1. The output of Q_2^M corresponds to the situation where firm 2 is a monopolist. If firm 1 produces Q_1^* units, the profit-maximizing level of output for firm 2 will be Q_2^*, since this is the point on r_2 that corresponds to an output of Q_1^* by firm 1.

To examine equilibrium in a Cournot duopoly, suppose firm 1 produces Q_1^M units of output. Given this output, the profit-maximizing level of output for firm 2 will correspond to point A on r_2 in Figure 9–3. Given this positive level of output by firm 2, the profit-maximizing level of output for firm 1 will no longer be Q_1^M, but will correspond to point B on r_1. Given this reduced level of output by firm 1, point C will be the point on firm 2's reaction function that maximizes profits. Given this new output by firm 2, firm 1 will again reduce output to point D on its reaction function.

How long will these changes in output continue? Until point E in Figure 9–3 is reached. At point E, firm 1 produces Q_1^* and firm 2 produces Q_2^* units. Neither firm has an incentive to change its output given that it believes the other firm will hold its output constant at that level. Point E thus corresponds to the Cournot equilibrium. **Cournot equilibrium** is the situation where neither firm has an incentive to change its output given the output of the other firm. Graphically, this condition corresponds to the intersection of the reaction curves.

Cournot equilibrium
A situation in which neither firm has an incentive to change its output given the other firm's output.

Thus far, our analysis of Cournot oligopoly has been graphical rather than algebraic. However, given estimates of the demand and costs within a Cournot oligopoly, we can explicitly solve for the Cournot equilibrium. How do we do this? To maximize profits, a manager in a Cournot oligopoly produces where marginal revenue equals marginal cost. The calculation of marginal cost is straightforward; it is done just as in the other market structures we have analyzed. The calculation of marginal revenues is a little more subtle. Consider the following formula:

Formula: Marginal Revenue for Cournot Duopoly. If the (inverse) market demand in a homogeneous-product Cournot duopoly is

$$P = a - b(Q_1 + Q_2)$$

where a and b are positive constants, then the marginal revenues of firms 1 and 2 are

$$MR_1(Q_1, Q_2) = a - bQ_2 - 2bQ_1$$
$$MR_2(Q_1, Q_2) = a - bQ_1 - 2bQ_2$$

A Calculus ALTERNATIVE

Firm 1's revenues are

$$TR_1 = PQ_1 = [a - b(Q_1 + Q_2)]Q_1$$

Thus,

$$MR_1(Q_1, Q_2) = \frac{\partial TR_1}{\partial Q_1} = a - bQ_2 - 2bQ_1$$

A similar analysis yields the marginal revenue for firm 2.

Notice that the marginal revenue for each Cournot oligopolist depends not only on the firm's own output but also on the other firm's output. In particular, when firm 2 increases its output, firm 1's marginal revenue falls. This is because the increase in output by firm 2 lowers the market price, resulting in lower marginal revenue for firm 1.

Since each firm's marginal revenue depends on its own output *and* that of the rival, the output where a firm's marginal revenue equals marginal cost depends on the other firm's output level. If we equate firm 1's marginal revenue with its marginal cost and then solve for firm 1's output as a function of firm 2's output, we obtain an algebraic expression for firm 1's reaction function. Similarly, by equating firm 2's marginal revenue with marginal cost and performing some algebra, we obtain firm 2's reaction function. The results of these computations are summarized below.

Formula: Reaction Functions for Cournot Duopoly. For the linear (inverse) demand function

$$P = a - b(Q_1 + Q_2)$$

and cost functions,

$$TC_1(Q_1) = c_1 Q_1$$
$$TC_2(Q_2) = c_2 Q_2$$

the reaction functions are

$$Q_1 = r_1(Q_2) = \frac{a - c_1}{2b} - \frac{1}{2}Q_2 \qquad (9\text{--}1)$$

$$Q_2 = r_2(Q_1) = \frac{a - c_2}{2b} - \frac{1}{2}Q_1 \qquad (9\text{--}2)$$

A Calculus ALTERNATIVE

To maximize profits, firm 1 sets output such that

$$MR_1(Q_1, Q_2) = MC_1$$

For the linear (inverse) demand and cost functions, this means that

$$a - bQ_2 - 2bQ_1 = c_1$$

Solving this equation for Q_1 in terms of Q_2 yields

$$Q_1 = r_1(Q_2) = \frac{a - c_1}{2b} - \frac{1}{2}Q_2$$

The reaction function for firm 2 is computed similarly.
It turns out that the value of Q_1 and Q_2 that maximize each duopolist's profit is

$$Q_1 = \frac{a - 2c_1 + c_2}{3b} \qquad (9\text{--}3)$$

$$Q_2 = \frac{a - 2c_2 + c_1}{3b}$$

Note that if the two duapolists are identical in terms of their cost functions, $c_1 = c_2$, each will produce

$$Q_1 = Q_2 = \frac{a - c}{3b} \qquad (9\text{--}4)$$

and the industry output will be

$$Q_1 + Q_2 = 2\left(\frac{a - c}{3b}\right) = \frac{2}{3}\left(\frac{a - c}{b}\right) \qquad (9\text{--}5)$$

Demonstration PROBLEM 9–4

Suppose the inverse demand function for two Cournot duopolists is given by

$$P = 10 - (Q_1 + Q_2)$$

and their costs are zero.

1. What is each firm's marginal revenue?
2. What are the reaction functions for the two firms?
3. What are the Cournot equilibrium outputs?
4. What is the equilibrium price?

Answer

1. Using the formula for marginal revenue under Cournot duopoly, we find that

$$MR_1(Q_1, Q_2) = 10 - Q_2 - 2Q_1$$
$$MR_2(Q_1, Q_2) = 10 - Q_1 - 2Q_2$$

2. Similarly, the reaction functions are

$$Q_1 = r_1(Q_2) = \frac{10}{2} - \frac{1}{2}Q_2$$

$$= 5 - \frac{1}{2}Q_2$$

$$Q_2 = r_2(Q_1) = \frac{10}{2} - \frac{1}{2}Q_1$$

$$= 5 - \frac{1}{2}Q_1$$

3. To find the Cournot equilibrium, we must solve the two reaction functions for the two unknowns:

$$Q_1 = 5 - \frac{1}{2}Q_2$$

$$Q_2 = 5 - \frac{1}{2}Q_1$$

Inserting Q_2 into the first reaction function yields

$$Q_1 = 5 - \frac{1}{2}\left[5 - \frac{1}{2}Q_1\right]$$

Solving for Q_1 yields

$$Q_1 = \frac{10}{3}$$

To find Q_2, we plug $Q_1 = 10/3$ into firm 2's reaction function to get

$$Q_2 = 5 - \frac{1}{2}\left(\frac{10}{3}\right)$$

$$= \frac{10}{3}$$

Inside BUSINESS

9-1 Using Experiments to Understand Oligopoly Behaviour

It often is difficult to find data that allow one to test theory in its purest form. Therefore, social scientists often use experimental methods to test their theories. In the case of economics, using the laboratory as a place to test and develop theory is relatively new. The first experiments were run by E. Chamberlain in 1948. The next attempt at running economic experiments came in 1963 and was conducted by Fouraker and Siegel. Since 1960, several economists have taken up the tool of experimental economics to help determine how different environments and informational situations affect behaviour. Many experiments have been used to specifically address the different forms of oligopoly theories.

In experiments, subjects (usually students) are recruited to participate as economic agents. As such, they are participants in a decision-making process in which their decisions and the decisions of other people in the experiment determine the outcome of some market process. To induce the students to take the experiment seriously and to motivate behaviour, their decisions are tied directly to monetary rewards. Each student is given a set of instructions for the market in which he or she is participating. In these instructions, students are told how their decisions map into monetary rewards. However, they are not instructed on *how* to act in the market. Any money a participant earns is paid in cash to the student at the end of the experiment.

The results of oligopoly experiments are decidedly mixed. Several experiments have allowed participants to take the role of producer in the same market. The number of participants in the market makes a big difference in the results of these experiments.

When the number of participants in an experiment is two, collusion often results. Fouraker and Siegel, Dolbear et al., Holt, Phillips, Battalio, and Holcomb, and Beil have all found generally the same results in two-person quantity-setting experiments. Approximately 60 percent of the duopoly pairs are able to find and maintain a collusive action with nothing other than their output decisions to guide them. About 25 percent of the participants have market outcomes that are not statistically different from Cournot output levels. However, the Cournot result does not tend to be stable in the sense that participants produce the Cournot output level every time. Instead, output fluctuates around the Cournot level of output. It appears participants would like to move toward collusive outcomes but are unable to accomplish this. The remaining 15 percent of the participants are split equally between output levels that lie between Cournot and collusive and between Cournot and perfectly competitive solutions. When the number of participants in these experiments rises to three or more in each market, Cournot levels of output are almost always observed.

Sources: E. H. Chamberlain, "An Experimental Imperfect Market," *Journal of Political Economy* 56, 1948, pp. 95–108; L. E. Fouraker and S. Siegel, *Bargaining Behaviour* (New York: McGraw-Hill, 1963); F. T. Dolbear, L. B. Lave, G. Bowman, A. Lieberman, E. Prescott, F. Rueter, and A. Sherman, "Collusion in Oligopoly: An Experiment on the Effect of Numbers and Information," *Quarterly Journal of Economics* 82, May 1968, pp. 506–15; C. A. Holt, "An Experimental Test of the Consistent Conjectures Hypothesis," *American Economic Review* 76, June 1985, pp. 314–25; G. W. Harrison and M. McKee, "Monopoly Behaviour, Decentralized Regulation, and Contestable Markets: An Experimental Evaluation," *Rand Journal of Economics* 16, Spring 1985, pp. 51–69; O. R. Phillips, R. C. Battalio, and J. H. Holcomb, "Duopoly Behaviour with Market History," manuscript, University of Wyoming, 1990; R. O. Beil, "Collusive Behaviour in Experimental Oligopoly Markets," Ph.D. dissertation, Texas A&M University, 1988.

4. Total industry output is

$$Q = Q_1 + Q_2 = \frac{10}{3} + \frac{10}{3} = \frac{20}{3}$$

The price in the market is determined by the (inverse) demand for this quantity:

$$P = 10 - (Q_1 + Q_2)$$
$$= 10 - \frac{20}{3}$$
$$= \frac{10}{3}$$

| **FIGURE 9–4** | Effect of Decline in Firm 2's Cost on Cournot Equilibrium |

Initial equilibrium is E, and firm 2's *MC* declines and *MR* remains the same (at the given level of output). Firm 2's reaction function shifts up from r_2 to r_2^{**} due to its *MR* > *MC* making it optimal to produce more output for any given level of Q_1. The new Cournot equilibrium is F. Firm 2's output increases from Q_2^* to Q_2^{**} and firm 1's output decreases from Q_1^* to Q_1^{**}.

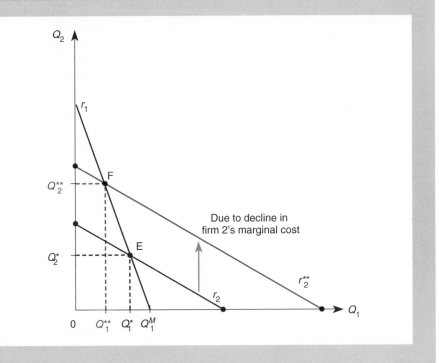

Changes in Marginal Costs

In a Cournot oligopoly, the effect of a change in marginal cost is very different than in a Sweezy oligopoly. To see why, suppose the firms initially are in equilibrium at point E in Figure 9–4, where firm 1 produces Q_1^* units and firm 2 produces Q_2^* units. Now suppose firm 2's marginal cost declines. At the given level of output, marginal revenue remains unchanged but marginal cost is reduced. This means that for firm 2, marginal revenue exceeds the lower marginal cost, and it is optimal to produce more output for any given level of Q_1. Graphically, this shifts firm 2's reaction function up from r_2 to r_2^{**}, leading to a new Cournot equilibrium at point F. Thus, the reduction in firm 2's marginal cost leads to an increase in firm 2's output, from Q_2^* to Q_2^{**}, and a decline in firm 1's output from Q_1^* to Q_1^{**}. Firm 2 enjoys a larger market share due to its improved cost situation.

The reason for the difference between the preceding analysis and the analysis of Sweezy oligopoly is the difference in the way a firm perceives how other firms will respond to a change in its decisions. These differences lead to differences in the way a manager should optimally respond to a reduction in the firm's marginal cost. If the manager believes other firms will follow price reductions but not price increases, the Sweezy model applies. In this instance, we learned that it may be optimal to continue to produce the same level of output even if marginal cost declines. If the manager believes other firms will maintain their existing output levels if the firm expands output, the Cournot model applies. In this case, it is optimal to expand output if marginal cost declines. The most important ingredient in making managerial decisions in markets characterized by interdependence is obtaining an accurate grasp of how other firms in the market will respond to the manager's decisions.

Collusion

Whenever a market is dominated by only a few firms, firms can benefit at the expense of consumers by "agreeing" to restrict output or, equivalently, charge higher prices. Such an act by firm is known as *collusion*. In the next chapter, we will devote considerable attention to collusion; for now, it is useful to use the model of Cournot oligopoly to show why such an incentive exists.

In Figure 9–5, point C corresponds to a Cournot equilibrium; it is the intersection of the reaction functions of the two firms in the market. Suppose, instead, that competition laws were relaxed so the two firms could collude. In this case, they would set their outputs to maximize their *joint* profit. The joint profit is maximized at a total (joint) level of output where marginal revenue equals marginal cost. This would occur when total output is $Q_1^M = Q_2^M$.

The algebraic solution for the joint (monopolist) profit-maximizing case can also be obtained. In particular, the monopolist's marginal revenue is

$$MR = a - 2bQ$$

where $Q = Q_1 + Q_2$. Setting MR equal to MC, c, which is derived from $TC(Q) = cQ$,

$$Q_M = \frac{a - c}{2b} = \frac{1}{2}\left(\frac{a - c}{b}\right) \tag{9–6}$$

Any combination of outputs Q_1 and Q_2 that adds up to Q_1^M ($= Q_2^M$) maximizes total industry profit. Therefore, the line that connects Q_1^M to Q_2^M is the locus of all pairs

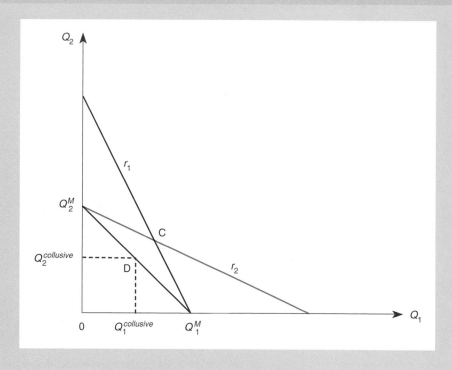

FIGURE 9–5 The Incentive to Collude in a Cournot Oligopoly

The line that connects Q_1^M to Q_2^M shows combinations of Q_1 and Q_2 that maximize joint profits. If the two firms collude and share profits equally, they will each produce $Q_1^{collusive} = Q_2^{collusive}$.

of output Q_1 and Q_2 that maximize joint profit. Assuming that total profits is split evenly, each firm's output would be half of total output, that is, $Q_1^{collusive}$ and $Q_2^{collusive}$ at point D. Notice that by colluding and maximizing their joint profit (like a monopoly), each firm would produce less output (than in a Cournot equilibrium) and would enjoy a greater profit. Note that aside from being considered illegal by competition laws, collusion is also ethically wrong since it harms consumers.

Below, we will repeat the example used in Demonstration Problem 9–4 to determine equilibrium in the presence of collusion.

Demonstration PROBLEM 9–5

Again suppose the inverse demand function for two Cournot duopolists is given by

$$P = 10 - (Q_1 + Q_2)$$

and their costs are zero.

1. What is the joint profit (collusive) equilibrium output?
2. What is the joint profit (collusive) equilibrium price?
3. Compare total profit and each individual firm's profit with that in Cournot equilibrium.

Answer

1.
$$TR = P \times Q = (10 - Q)Q = 10Q - Q^2$$

So

$$MR(Q) = 10 - 2$$

Setting MR equal to MC (that is, zero), we find total (joint) output.

$$MR(Q) = 10 - 2Q$$
$$MR(Q) = MC(Q)$$
$$10 - 2Q = 0$$
$$Q(= Q_1 + Q_2) = 5$$
$$Q_1 = Q_2 = 2.5$$

2. Equilibrium (collusive) price is $P = 10 - 5 = \$5$.
3. Total profit to be split evenly is

$$\pi = TR - TC = \$5 \times 5 - 0 = 25$$

where

$$\pi_1 = \pi_2 = \$12.5$$

In a Cournot situation,

$$\pi = TR - TC = \$\frac{10}{3}\left(\frac{20}{3}\right) - 0 = \$\frac{200}{9} = \$22.22$$

and $\pi_1 = \pi_2 = \$11.11$, which is less than that in the collusive case.

| FIGURE 9-6 | The Incentive to Renege on Collusive Agreements in Cournot Oligopoly |

When firms agree to collude, each will produce the collusive output, point D. Assuming that firm 2 produces $Q_2^{collusive}$, firm 1 has an incentive to cheat by expanding output, point G. At this point firm 1's profit is higher than that under collusive solution.

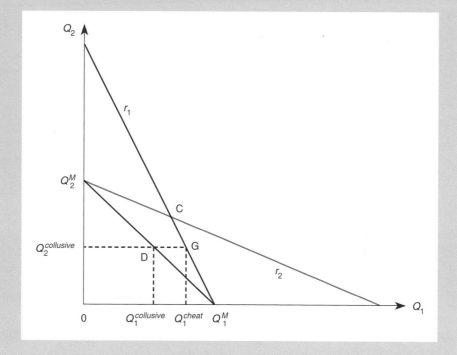

It is not easy for firms to reach such a collusive agreement, however. We will analyze this point in greater detail in the next chapter, but we can use our existing framework to see why collusion is sometimes difficult. Suppose firms agree to collude, each firm producing the collusive output associated with point D in Figure 9–6 to earn collusive profits. Given that firm 2 produces $Q_2^{collusive}$, firm 1 has an incentive to "cheat" on the collusive agreement by expanding output, Q_1^{cheat}, to point G. At this point, firm 1 earns even higher profits than it would by colluding. This suggests that a firm can gain by inducing other firms to restrict output and then expanding its own output to earn higher profits at the expense of its collusion partners. Because firms know this incentive exists, it is often difficult for them to reach collusive agreements in the first place. This problem is amplified by the fact that firm 2 in Figure 9–6 earns less at point G (where firm 1 cheats) than it would have earned at point C (the Cournot equilibrium).

Demonstration PROBLEM 9-6

Again suppose the inverse demand function for two Cournot duopolists is given by

$$P = 10 - (Q_1 + Q_2)$$

and their costs are zero.

1. What are firm 1's (collusive) and firm 2's (cheat) output?
2. How much profit is earned by each firm?
3. Compare these outcomes with those under collusion.

Answer

1. Firm 2 would continue to produce $Q_2^{collusive} = 2.5$, while firm 1 would now be producing

$$Q_2^{cheat} = 5 - \frac{1}{2}(2.5) = 3.75$$

2. To find the price that the oligopolists charge, we plug in for total Q (6.25) in the demand equation to obtain

$$P = 10 - 6.25 = \$3.75$$

Therefore, $\pi_2^{collusive} = \$9.375$ and $\pi_1^{cheat} = \$14.0625$.

3. Firm 2 is clearly worse off, not only in comparison to the outcome under the collusive scenario but also to that under Cournot.

The above analysis reveals the difficulty that firms face in deciding to cooperate and jointly maximize profit—collusion—or independently maximizing profit—Cournot. A comparison between the monopolists' solutions, Equation 9–6, and the Cournot duopoly, Equation 9–5, discussed above, reveals that when the number of firms increases from one to two, the output of the industry rises from $(1/2)\left(\dfrac{a-c}{b}\right)$ to $(2/3)\left(\dfrac{a-c}{b}\right)$. If we were to increase the number of the firms to three, the industry output would increase to $(3/4)\left(\dfrac{a-c}{b}\right)$, implying that when the industry consists of n identical firms the industry output will be

$$Q = \left(\frac{n+1}{n}\right)\frac{a-c}{b} \tag{9–7}$$

Needless to say, as the number of firms increases within the industry, the output price decreases. When the number of identical firms within the industry becomes very large, the industry approaches perfect competition, where

$$Q = \frac{a-c}{b} \tag{9–8}$$

and the output price equals c.

Stackelberg Oligopoly

Up until this point, we have analyzed oligopoly situations that are symmetric in that firm 2 is the "mirror image" of firm 1. In many oligopoly markets, however, firms differ from one another. In a **Stackelberg oligopoly**, firms differ with respect to when they make decisions. Specifically, one firm (the leader) is assumed to make an output decision before the other firms. Given knowledge of the leader's output, all other firms (the followers) take as given the leader's output and choose outputs that maximize profits. Thus, in a Stackelberg oligopoly, each follower behaves just like a Cournot oligopolist. In fact, the leader does not take the followers' outputs as given

Stackelberg oligopoly
An industry in which (1) there are few firms serving many consumers; (2) firms produce either differentiated or homogeneous products; (3) a single firm (the leader) chooses an output before rivals select their outputs; (4) all other firms (the followers) take the leader's output as given and select outputs that maximize profits given the leader's output; and (5) barriers to entry exist.

but instead chooses an output that maximizes profits given that each follower will react to this output decision according to a Cournot reaction function.

An industry is characterized as a Stackelberg oligopoly if

1. There are few firms serving many consumers
2. The firms produce either differentiated or homogeneous products
3. A single firm (the leader) chooses an output before all other firms choose their outputs
4. All other firms (the followers) take as given the output of the leader and choose outputs that maximize profits given the leader's output
5. Barriers to entry exist

To highlight a Stackelberg oligopoly, let us consider a situation where there are only two firms. Firm 1 is the *leader* and thus has a "first-mover" advantage; that is, firm 1 produces before firm 2. Firm 2 is the *follower* and maximizes profit given the output produced by the leader.

Because the follower produces after the leader, the follower's profit-maximizing level of output is determined by its reaction function. This is denoted by r_2 in Figure 9–7. However, the leader knows the follower will react according to r_2. Consequently, the leader must choose the level of output that will maximize its profits given that the follower reacts to whatever the leader does.

Suppose the leader's profit is maximized at point S in Figure 9–7, a situation consistent with the follower's reaction function. The leader would be producing Q_1^S and the follower observing this output would be producing Q_2^S. At this point the leader's profit is higher than that at C (Cournot equilibrium), whereas the follower's profit is

---

FIGURE 9-7 Stackelberg Equilibrium

Firm 2, the follower, produces after firm 1, the leader, and hence—taking output of firm 1 as a given— firm 2 behaves in a Cournot fashion. The leader, with this knowledge, produces at a point on the follower's reaction function, point S, which maximizes its profits. At this point, the leader produces Q_2^S and the follower Q_1^S.

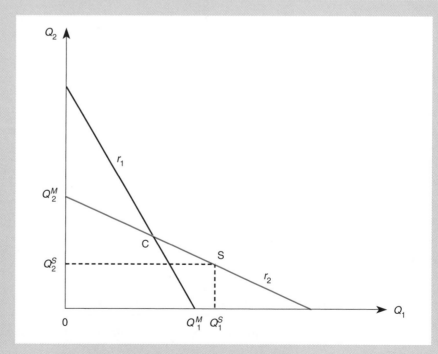

lower. Going first gives firm 1 an advantage. This kind of *first-mover advantage* happens in many strategic situations.

The algebraic solution for a Stackelberg oligopoly can also be obtained, provided firms have information about market demand and costs. In particular, recall that the follower's decision is identical to that of a Cournot model. For instance, with homogeneous products, linear demand, and constant marginal cost, the output of the follower is given by the reaction function

$$Q_2 = r_2(Q_1) = \frac{a - c_2}{2b} - \frac{1}{2}Q_1$$

which is simply the follower's Cournot reaction function. However, the leader in the Stackelberg oligopoly takes into account this reaction function when it selects Q_1. With a linear inverse demand function and constant marginal costs, the leader's profits are

$$\pi_1 = \left\{ a - b \left[Q_1 + \left(\frac{a - c_2}{2b} - \frac{1}{2}Q_1 \right) \right] \right\} Q_1 - c_1 Q_1$$

The leader chooses Q_1 to maximize this profit expression. It turns out that the value of Q_1 that maximizes the leader's profits is

$$Q_1 = \frac{a + c_2 - 2c_1}{2b}$$

Formula: Equilibrium Outputs in Stackelberg Oligopoly. For the linear (inverse) demand function

$$P = a - b(Q_1 + Q_2)$$

and cost functions

$$TC_1(Q_1) = c_1 Q_1$$
$$TC_2(Q_2) = c_2 Q_2$$

the follower sets output according to the Cournot reaction function

$$Q_2 = r_2(Q_1) = \frac{a - c_2}{2b} - \frac{1}{2}Q_1$$

The leader's output is

$$Q_1 = \frac{a + c_2 - 2c_1}{2b}$$

A Calculus ALTERNATIVE

To maximize profits, firm 1 sets output so as to maximize

$$\pi_1 = \left\{ a - b \left[Q_1 + \left(\frac{a - c_2}{2b} - \frac{1}{2}Q_1 \right) \right] \right\} Q_1 - c_1 Q_1$$

The first-order condition for maximizing profits is

$$\frac{d\pi_1}{dQ_1} = a - 2bQ_1 - \left(\frac{a - c_2}{2}\right) + bQ_1 - c_1 = 0$$

Solving for Q_1 yields the profit-maximizing level of output for the leader:

$$Q_1 = \frac{a + c_2 - 2c_1}{2b}$$

The formula for the follower's reaction function is derived in the same way as that for a Cournot oligopolist.

Demonstration PROBLEM 9–7

Suppose the demand and cost function are the same as those in Demonstration Problem 9–4 for two firms in a homogenous-product Stackelberg oligopoly. Firm 1 is the leader and firm 2 the follower.

1. What is firm 2's reaction function?
2. What is firm 1's output?
3. What is firm 2's output?
4. What is the market price?
5. What is each firm's profit level?

Answer

1. Firm 2's reaction function is the same as in Cournot, since 2 assumes the output of 1 as a given:

$$Q_2 = 5 - \frac{1}{2}Q_1$$

2. Firm 1, the leader, anticipating firm's 2 output from 2's Cournot reaction function, takes it into account when it selects Q_1. Using the formula given for the Stackelberg leader, we find

$$Q_1 = \frac{10 + 0 - 0}{2} = 5$$

3. By plugging the answer to part 2 into the reaction function in part 1, we find the follower's output to be

$$Q_2 = 5 - \frac{1}{2}(5) = 2.5$$

4. The market price can be found by adding the two firms' outputs together and plugging the answer into the inverse demand function:

$$P = 10 - (2.5 + 5) = \$2.5$$

5. The level of profit earned by each firm is:

$$\pi_{leader} = 5 \times \$2.5 = \$12.5 \text{ and}$$
$$\pi_{follower} = 2.5 \times \$2.5 = \$6.25$$

Bertrand Oligopoly

To further highlight the fact that there is no single model of oligopoly a manager can use in all circumstances and illustrate that oligopoly power does not always imply firms will make positive profits, we will next examine Bertrand oligopoly. The treatment here assumes the firms sell identical products and that consumers are willing to pay the (finite) monopoly price for the good.

An industry is characterized as a **Bertrand oligopoly** if

Bertrand oligopoly
An industry in which
(1) there are few firms
serving many consumers;
(2) firms produce
identical products at a
constant marginal cost;
(3) firms compete in
price and react optimally
to competitors' prices;
(4) consumers have
perfect information and
there are no transaction
costs; and (5) barriers to
entry exist.

1. There are few firms in the market serving many consumers
2. The firms produce identical products at a constant marginal cost
3. Firms engage in price competition and react optimally to prices charged by competitors
4. Consumers have perfect information and there are no transaction costs
5. Barriers to entry exist

From the viewpoint of the manager, Bertrand oligopoly is undesirable: it leads to zero economic profits even if there are only two firms in the market. From the viewpoint of consumers, Bertrand oligopoly is desirable: it leads to precisely the same outcome as a perfectly competitive market.

To explain more precisely the preceding assertions, we can use the cost and demand conditions from the Cournot model in Demonstration Problem 9–4 to explore the Bertrand market equilibrium. Recall that the inverse demand function for the two duopolists is given by $P = 10 - (Q_1 + Q_2)$ and their costs are zero. The Cournot equilibrium is found as

$$Q_1 = Q_2 = 10/3 \quad \text{and} \quad P_1 = P_2 = \$10/3$$

This is not, however, a Bertrand equilibrium. In this case, because consumers have perfect information and have zero transaction costs, and the products are identical, all consumers will purchase from the firm charging the lowest price. For concreteness we repeat the Demonstration Problem 9–4.

Demonstration PROBLEM 9–8

Suppose the inverse demand function for two Bertrand duopolists that produce identical products is given by

$$P = 10 - (Q_1 + Q_2)$$

and their costs are zero.

1. What is the equilibrium price?
2. What are the Bertrand equilibrium outputs?

Answer

1. If firm 1 believed that firm 2 will charge a price of $10/3, it would not wish to charge a price of $10/3. Firm 1 would realize that by slightly undercutting firm 2's price, say by charging a price of $3, it would get all of firm 2's business. Thus firm 1 believes that if $P_1 = \$3$ and $P_2 = \$10/3$ then $Q_1 = 7$ and $Q_2 = 0$. In this case, firm 1 expects to earn profits of $21, which is greater than the profit of $11.11 ($=10/3 \times \$10/3$) it would earn if it charged a price of $10/3.

   Of course, $P_1 = \$3$ and $P_2 = \$10/3$ is not an equilibrium, because in this situation firm 2 would wish to retaliate by undercutting firm 1. As long as both firms set prices above marginal costs, each will always have an incentive to corner the market by slightly undercutting the other.

When would this price war end? The only possible equilibrium could be $P_1 = P_2 = MC = \$0$. At these prices, neither firm can do better by changing its price. Given the price of the other firm, each would choose to lower its price, for then its price would be below marginal cost and it would take a loss. Also, no firm would want to raise its price, for then it would sell nothing.

2. At this perfectly competitive outcome, where $P_1 = P_2 = \$0$, the industry's volume of output $(Q_1 + Q_2) = 10$, and each firm's share of output $= 5$ units, while its profits would be equal to zero.

Chapters 10 and 11 provide strategies that managers can use to mitigate the cutthroat competition that ensues in homogeneous-product Bertrand oligopoly. As we will see, the key is to either raise switching costs or eliminate the perception that the firms' products are identical. The product differentiation induced by these strategies permits firms to price above marginal cost without losing customers to rivals. The appendix to this chapter illustrates that, under differentiated-product price competition, reaction functions are upward-sloping and equilibrium occurs at a point where prices exceed marginal cost. This explains, in part, why firms such as Kellogg's and General Mills spend millions of dollars on advertisements designed to persuade consumers that their competing brands of corn flakes are not identical. If consumers did not view the brands as differentiated products, these two makers of breakfast cereal would have to price at marginal cost.

Comparing Oligopoly Models

To see further how each form of oligopoly affects firms, it is useful to compare the models covered in this chapter in terms of individual firm outputs, prices in the market, and profits per firm. To accomplish this, we will use the same market demand and cost conditions that we used in the previous Demonstration Problems for each firm when examining results for each model. The inverse demand function is represented by

$$P = 10 - (Q_1 + Q_2)$$

and their costs are zero.

We will now see how outputs, prices, and profits vary according to the type of oligopolistic interdependence that exists in the market.

Cournot

We will first examine Cournot equilibrium. Recalling the profit function for the individual Cournot firm given the preceding inverse demand and cost functions,

$$\pi_i = [10 - (Q_1 + Q_2)]Q_1 - 0$$

and the reaction functions of the Cournot oligopolists are

$$Q_1 = r_1(Q_2) = 5 - \frac{1}{2}Q_2$$

$$Q_2 = r_2(Q_1) = 5 - \frac{1}{2}Q_1$$

Inside**BUSINESS**

9-2 Managerial Compensation in Bertrand and Cournot Oligopoly

The issue of executive compensation has received considerable attention from academics and the popular press. Much of the work in this area attempts to estimate the relationship between firm performance and executive compensation. Classical microeconomic theory suggests that managers will be rewarded for maximizing firm profits. In 1959, William Baumol proposed that firms benefit from increases in sales. Since then, analysts have attempted to analyze the relationship among executive pay, profits, and sales.

More recently, Chaim Fershtman and Kenneth Judd developed a model of compensation contracting that incorporates aspects of oligopoly theory. These authors argue that managers of perfectly competitive firms will be rewarded only for profits; however, they find that managers of oligopolistic firms may be rewarded or penalized for increases in firm sales. The model suggests that by carefully choosing the terms of compensation contracts, firm owners are able to influence the decisions of both their own manager and managers of competing firms. Whether managers are rewarded or penalized for increases in firm sales depends on whether firms interact in a Cournot (quantity-setting) or Bertrand (price-setting) environment.

For example, assume two firms, Acme and Mustang, are quantity setters. If Mustang's manager is rewarded only for increases in profits while Acme's manager is rewarded for increases in both profits and sales, Acme's manager will become a more aggressive seller. As a result, Acme's sales will increase and the market price of the

product will fall, which in turn will lead Mustang's manager to reduce output and sales. Acme will become the dominant firm. It can be shown that the best thing Mustang's owner can do, regardless of the contract written by Acme's owner, is to also reward his or her manager for increases in sales. It is interesting to note that when both managers are rewarded for increases in sales, both firms' profits and product prices decrease as sales increase.

In contrast, if these firms are price setters, owners will penalize their managers for increases in sales. When Acme's manager is penalized for sales, this signals to Mustang's manager a willingness to price less aggressively. Mustang's manager, in turn, will increase the price of her or his product. It can be shown that when managers are price setters, compensation contracts that penalize them for increases in sales are optimal. In this case, output will be lower, and profits and prices greater than in the Bertrand pricing game without contracting.

In each scenario just outlined, performance can be thought of as a linear combination of profits and sales, with owners choosing α:

Performance = α Profits + $(1 - \alpha)$ Sales

In a Cournot oligopoly $\alpha < 1$, while in a Bertrand oligopoly $\alpha > 1$.

Marc Chopin adapted this model to empirically examine executive compensation in oligopolies. The empirical model includes an estimate of the salary payment and the degree to which measured performance

Solving the two reaction functions for two unknowns,

$$Q_1 = Q_2 = \frac{10}{3}$$

$$P = \frac{\$10}{3}$$

$$\pi_1 = \pi_2 = TR - TC = \frac{\$10}{3}\left(\frac{10}{3}\right) - 0 = \frac{\$100}{9} = \$11.11$$

Collusion

With these demand and cost functions, we now determine the collusive outcome, which results when the firms choose output to maximize total (joint) industry profits. When firms collude, total industry output is the monopoly level, based on the market

TABLE 9-1	**Estimates of Owners' Choices of α and the Degree of Dependence of Compensation on Measured Performance for Retail Variety Stores**	

Firm	δ (*t*-statistic in parentheses)	α (standard deviation in parentheses)
Dayton-Hudson	517	1.056
	(3.57)	(0.009)
Kmart	170	1.035
	(2.27)	(0.010)
Woolworth	847	1.048
	(4.92)	(0.013)
Zayre	2,717	1.061
	(2.08)	(0.007)

affects compensation. The degree of dependence is represented as δ in the following equation:

$$\text{Pay} = \text{Salary} + \delta[\alpha \text{ Profits} + (1 - \alpha) \text{ Sales}]$$

Using this model, Chopin estimated the terms of incentive contracts for 233 firms competing in 50 industries and found significant differences in the terms of compensation contracts across firms. As Table 9–1 shows, retail variety stores appear to have almost homogeneous measures of performance, with the majority of the weight placed on profits and a small but significant disincentive for sales. As suggested by the estimates of δ, the effect of performance on pay varies significantly across firms.

For example, these estimates indicate that the CEO of Dayton-Hudson will receive an additional $545.95 for

each $1 million increase in profits (since $517 \times 1.056 = 545.95$), while cash compensation falls by $28.95 for each increase in sales of $1 million (since $517 \times (1 - 1.056) = -28.95$). When compared to Zayre's CEO, Dayton-Hudson's manager appears relatively insulated from performance. The CEO of Zayre earns additional cash compensation of $2882.74 for each $1 million increase in profits; cash compensation decreases by $165.74 for each $1 million increase in sales.

Sources: William J. Baumol, *Business Behaviour, Value and Growth* (New York: Macmillan, 1959); Marc C. Chopin, "Executive Compensation in Oligopolies: Sales, Profits, and Pay," *Advances in Applied Microeconomics* 9 (1999), pp. 101–22; Chaim Fershtman and Kenneth L. Judd, "Equilibrium Incentives in Oligopoly," *American Economic Review* 5, December 1987, pp. 927–40.

inverse demand curve. Deriving from the market demand curve its marginal revenue curve and setting $MR(Q) = MC(Q)$, we obtain

$$TR = P \times Q = (10 - Q)Q = 10Q - Q^2$$

$$MR(Q) = 10 - 2Q$$

$$MR(Q) = MC(Q)$$

$$10 - 2Q = 0$$

$$Q \ (= Q_1 + Q_2) = 5,$$

$$\text{and } Q_1 \text{ and } Q_2 = 5$$

Equilibrium (collusive) price is $P = 10 - 5 = \$5$ and total profit to be split evenly is

$$\pi = TR - TC = \$5 \times 5 - 0 = 25, \text{ where } \pi_1 = \pi_2 = \$12.5$$

Inside BUSINESS

9-3 Using a Spreadsheet to Calculate Cournot, Stackelberg, and Collusive Outcomes

The CD that accompanies this edition of *Managerial Economics and Business Strategy* includes three files located in the Chapter 9 directory of the CD. With a few clicks of a mouse, you can use these files to calculate the profit-maximizing price and quantity and the maximum profits for the following oligopoly situations.

COURNOT DUOPOLY

In a Cournot duopoly, each firm believes the other will hold its output constant as it changes its own output. Therefore, the profit-maximizing output level for firm 1 depends on firm 2's output. Each firm will adjust its profit-maximizing output level until the point where the two firms' reaction functions are equal. This point corresponds to the Cournot equilibrium. At the Cournot equilibrium, neither firm has an incentive to change its output, given the output of the other firm. Step-by-step instructions for computing the Cournot equilibrium outputs, price, and profits are included in the Chapter 9 directory of the learning CD in a file named CournotSolver.xls.

STACKELBERG DUOPOLY

The Stackelberg duopoly model assumes that one firm is the leader while the other is a follower. The leader has a first-mover advantage and selects its profit-maximizing output level, knowing that the follower will move second and thus react to this decision according to a Cournot reaction function. Given the leader's output decision, the follower takes the leader's output as given and chooses its profit-maximizing level of output. Step-by-step instructions for computing the Stackelberg equilibrium outputs, price, and profits are included in the Chapter 9 directory of the learning CD in a file named StackelbergSolver.xls.

COLLUSIVE DUOPOLY
(THE MONOPOLY SOLUTION)

Under collusion, duopolists produce a total output that corresponds to the monopoly output. In a symmetric situation, the two firms share the market equally, each producing one-half of the monopoly output. Step-by-step instructions for computing the collusive (monopoly) output, price, and profits are included in the Chapter 9 directory of the learning CD in a file named CollusionSolver.xls.

Stackelberg

With these demand and cost functions, the output of the Stackelberg leader is

$$Q_1 = \frac{10 + 0 - 0}{2} = 5, \text{ and}$$

$$Q_2 = 5 - \frac{1}{2}(5) = 2.5$$

Total output in the market thus is 7.5 units. Given the inverse demand function, this output yields a price of $2.5. Total market output is higher in a Stackelberg oligopoly than in a Cournot oligopoly. This leads to a lower price in the Stackelberg oligopoly than in the Cournot oligopoly. The profits for the leader are $12.5, while the follower earns only $6.25 in profits. The leader does better in a Stackelberg oligopoly than in a Cournot oligopoly due to its first-mover advantage. However, the follower earns lower profits in a Stackelberg oligopoly than in a Cournot oligopoly.

Bertrand

Finally, we will recall the Bertrand equilibrium price, quantities, and profits. Recall that firms that engage in Bertrand competition end up setting price equal to marginal cost. Therefore, with the given inverse demand and cost functions,

$$P_1 = P_2 = MC = \$0$$

FIGURE 9–8 | Alternative Models of Oligopoly Equilibrium

In Cournot equilibrium, C, each firm produces 10/3. If the firms collude and share profits equally, they will each produce 2.5, D. Under Bertrand, each firm will produce 5 and earn zero profit. Also shown is Stackelberg equilibrium, G, at which the leader, firm 1, produces 5 and the follower produces 2.5.

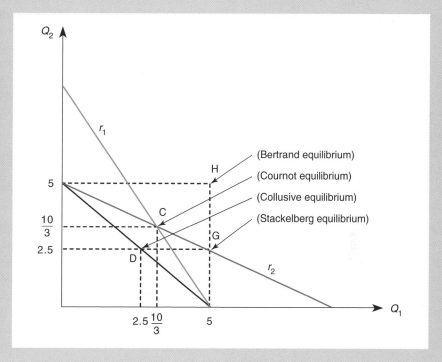

The industry's volume of output $(Q_1 + Q_2) = 10$, and each firm's share of output = 5 units. Each firm will earn zero profit.

Figure 9–8 captures all these oligopoly models.

Cournot equilibrium is represented by point C, where $Q_1 = Q_2 = 10/3$, the collusive equilibrium by point D, where $Q_1 = Q_2 = 2.5$, Bertrand equilibrium by point H, where $Q_1 = Q_2 = 5$, and finally Stackelberg equilibrium is represented by $Q_1 = 5$ and $Q_2 = 2.5$.

Comparison of the outcomes in these different oligopoly situations reveals the following. The highest market output is produced in a Bertrand oligopoly, followed by Stackelberg, then Cournot, and finally collusion. Profits are highest for the Stackelberg leader and the colluding firms, followed by Cournot, then the Stackelberg follower. The Bertrand oligopolists earn the lowest level of profits. If you become a manager in an oligopolistic market, it is important to recognize that your optimal decisions and profits will vary depending on the type of oligopolistic interaction that exists in the market.

The above analysis clearly indicates that all oligopoly outcomes except the Bertrand model tend to be less efficient than perfect competition and hence to entail a deadweight loss. This loss is largest with collusion, which is a case of monopoly, and smallest with Stackelberg.

A more thorough investigation of managerial decisions in oligopolistic markets, based on the game-theoretic approach, is made in Chapter 10. Chapter 13 gives more advanced coverage of strategy-based game theory analysis.

Contestable Markets

Thus far, we have emphasized strategic interaction among existing firms in an oligopoly. Strategic interaction can also exist between existing firms and potential entrants into a market. To illustrate the importance of this interaction and its similarity to Bertrand oligopoly, let us suppose a market is served by a single firm but there is another firm (a potential entrant) free to enter the market whenever it chooses.

Before we continue our analysis, let us make more precise what we mean by *free entry*. What we have in mind here is what economists refer to as a **contestable market**. A market is contestable if

contestable market
A market in which (1) all firms have access to the same technology; (2) consumers respond quickly to price changes; (3) existing firms cannot respond quickly to entry by lowering their prices; and (4) there are no sunk costs.

1. All producers have access to the same technology
2. Consumers respond quickly to price changes
3. Existing firms cannot respond quickly to entry by lowering price
4. There are no sunk costs

If these four conditions hold, incumbent firms (existing firms in the market) have no market power over consumers. This is true even if there is only one existing firm in the market.

The reason for this result follows. If existing firms charged a price in excess of what they required to cover costs, a new firm could immediately enter the market with the same technology and charge a price slightly below the existing firms' prices. Since the incumbents cannot quickly respond by lowering their prices, the entrant would get all the incumbents' customers by charging the lower price. Because the incumbents know this, they have no alternative but to charge a low price equal to the cost of production to keep out the entrant. Thus, if a market is perfectly contestable, incumbents are disciplined by the threat of entry by new firms.

An important condition for a contestable market is the absence of sunk costs. In this context, *sunk costs* are defined as costs a new entrant must bear that cannot be recouped upon exiting the market. For example, if an entrant pays $100 000 for a truck to enter the market for moving services, but receives $80 000 for the truck upon exiting the market, $20 000 represents the sunk costs of entering the market. Similarly, if a firm pays a nonrefundable fee of $20 000 for the nontransferable right to lease a truck for a year to enter the market, this reflects a sunk cost associated with entry. Or if a small firm must incur a loss of $2000 per month for six months while waiting for customers to "switch" to that company, it incurs $12 000 of sunk costs.

Sunk costs are important for the following reason. Suppose incumbent firms are charging high prices, and a new entrant calculates that it could earn $70 000 by entering the market and charging a lower price than the existing firms. This calculation is, of course, conditional upon the existing firms continuing to charge their present prices. Suppose that to enter, the firm must pay sunk costs of $20 000. If it enters the market and the incumbent firms keep charging the high price, entry is profitable; indeed, the firm will make $70 000. However, if the incumbents do not continue charging the high price but instead lower their prices, the entrant can be left with no customers. In this instance, the entrant loses the sunk cost of $20 000. In short, if a potential entrant must pay sunk costs to enter a market and has reason to believe incumbents will respond to entry by lowering their prices, it will find it unprofitable to enter even though prices are high. The end result is that with sunk costs, incumbents may not be disciplined by potential entry, and higher prices may prevail.

ANSWERING THE **Head**line

This is clearly a case of an oligopolistic market with differentiated (as opposed to homogenous) products, in which competition seems to be taking place on the basis of price. Typically, competition in a differentiated product market takes the form of price or quality competition. This case serves to highlight many aspects of oligopolistic market structure, including the challenges of competing on price. Consider that the majority of Mountain Crest's market share comes from competing on price, without advertising. Consider, too, that success in the beer industry comes from having a brand consumers associate with their lifestyle choice. (In recent years in Canada, premium and super-premium brands have been the only growing beer segment, while all other segments have either stagnated or lost market share.)

The first question that arises, then, is how sustainable Mountain Crest's market position is. If we assume that Mountain Crest's beer appeals to a segment of the population who choose not to purchase a similarly segmented brand because of the dollar differential, Mountain Crest's position is only sustainable as long as that segment is unable or unwilling to pay more for beer. Once the segment switches from regular brands to premium or super-premium beers, Mountain Crest loses customers. A product that owes its success entirely to its being cheaper—its dollar differential—is said to be *vertically differentiated* from regular brands and premium beers, that is, it represents an inferior product.

If, on the other hand, Mountain Crest beer is viewed as a good substitute for other beers even at equal prices, it is said to be *horizontally differentiated*. Horizontal differentiation is about sustainability. Therefore, Mountain Crest will have to forecast whether the growth in earning potential of their current customer base is equal to or more than the growth in customers who purchase beer primarily on the basis of price, in order to determine how sustainable their market position is. When firms sell horizontally differentiated products or services, they will have a downward-sloping demand curve, which tends to be flat when the demand is sensitive to its own price and to the prices of competitors and steep when the demand is less sensitive.

The second question that arises is what happens if Molson and/or Labatt choose to compete on price. (As was seen during the summer of 2003, Labatt chose to decrease prices on certain of its cases of beers, to attract sales; obviously, the company can do so without harming its overall financial position.) Once a large, deep-pocketed firm chooses to compete on price by, say, matching Mountain Crest's prices, it is very likely consumers will switch to a brand they know. When a firm's demand is sensitive to changes in the price of its product and price of competitors, that is, if a small decrease in the price of brand beers causes a large drop in demand for Mountain Crest beer, the horizontal differentiation is weak. (It cannot be overstated that success in the beer industry relies on the brands a given company owns.) As Mountain Crest appears not to have developed any brand identity other than "cheap beer," it has no platform on which to compete if the powers of the oligopoly choose to play its game.

The third question, then, is: What is Mountain Crest to do? If you were a manager for Mountain Crest, what would you advise? Should the company continue to compete on price while starting to build brand recognition? How would you protect against possible price competition waged by the large companies in your industry? These kinds of questions will be answered, indirectly, in the next chapter, as we turn to game theory and how managers can utilize it to understand their next move.

Summary

In this chapter, we examined several models of markets that consist of a small number of strategically interdependent firms. These models help explain several possible types of behaviour when a market is characterized by oligopoly. You should now be familiar with the Sweezy, Cournot, Stackelberg, and Bertrand models.

In the Cournot model, a firm chooses quantity based on its competitors' given levels of output. Each firm earns some economic profits. Bertrand competitors, on the other hand, set prices given their rivals' prices. They end up charging a price equal to their marginal cost and earn zero economic profits. Sweezy oligopolists believe their competitors will follow price decreases but will ignore price increases, leading to extremely stable prices even when costs change in the industry. Finally, Stackelberg oligopolies have a follower and a leader. The leader knows how the follower will behave, and the follower simply maximizes profits given what the leader has chosen. This leads to profits for each firm but much higher profits for the leader than for the follower.

The next chapter will explain in more detail how managers go about reaching equilibrium in oligopoly. For now, it should be clear that your decisions will affect others in your market and their decisions will affect you as well.

Key Terms and Concepts

Bertrand oligopoly 324
contestable market 330
Cournot equilibrium 312
Cournot oligopoly 310

oligopoly 306
reaction function 310
Stackelberg oligopoly 320
Sweezy oligopoly 308

Conceptual and Computational Questions

1. The graph that accompanies this question illustrates two demand curves for a firm operating in a differentiated product oligopoly. Initially, the firm charges a price of $60 and produces 10 units of output. One of the demand curves is relevant when rivals match the firm's price changes; the other demand curve is relevant when rivals do not match price changes.
   a. Which demand curve is relevant when rivals will match any price change?
   b. Which demand curve is relevant when rivals will *not* match any price change?

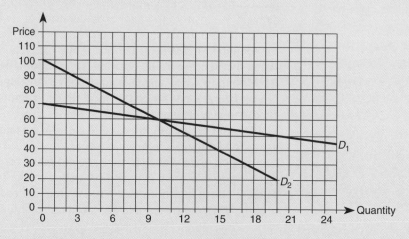

    c. Suppose the manager believes that rivals will match price cuts, but will not match price increases.
      (1) What price will the firm be able to charge if it produces 20 units?
      (2) How many units will the firm sell if it charges a price of $70?
      (3) For what range in marginal cost will the firm continue to charge a price of $60?

2. The inverse market demand in a homogeneous-product Cournot duopoly is $P = 100 - 2(Q_1 + Q_2)$ and costs are $TC_1(Q_1) = 12Q_1$ and $TC_2(Q_2) = 20Q_2$.
    a. Determine the reaction function for each firm.
    b. Calculate each firm's equilibrium output.
    c. Calculate the equilibrium market price.
    d. Calculate the profit each firm earns in equilibrium.

3. The inverse demand for a homogeneous-product Stackelberg duopoly is $P = 20\,000 - 5Q$. The cost structures for the leader and the follower, respectively, are $TC_L(Q_L) = 3000Q_L$ and $TC_F(Q_F) = 4000Q_F$.
    a. What is the follower's reaction function?
    b. Determine the equilibrium output level for both the leader and the follower.
    c. Determine the equilibrium market price.
    d. Determine the profits of the leader and the follower.

4. Consider a Bertrand oligopoly consisting of four firms that produce an identical product at a marginal cost of $100. The inverse market demand for this product is $P = 500 - 2Q$.
    a. Determine the equilibrium level of output in the market.
    b. Determine the equilibrium market price.
    c. Determine the profits of each firm.

5. Provide a real-world example of a market that approximates each oligopoly setting, and explain your reasoning.
    a. Cournot oligopoly
    b. Stackelberg oligopoly
    c. Bertrand oligopoly

6. Two firms compete in a market to sell a homogeneous product with inverse demand function $P = 400 - 2Q$. Each firm produces at a constant marginal cost of $50 and has no fixed costs. Use this information to compare the output levels and profits in settings characterized by Cournot, Stackelberg, Bertrand, and collusive behaviour.

7. Consider a homogeneous-product duopoly where each firm initially produces at a constant marginal cost of $100 and there are no fixed costs. Determine what would happen to each firm's equilibrium output and profits if firm 2's marginal cost increased to $110 but firm 1's marginal cost remained constant at $100 in each of the following settings:
    a. Cournot duopoly
    b. Sweezy oligopoly

Problems and Applications

8. Ford executives recently announced that the company would extend its most dramatic consumer incentive program in the company's long history—the Ford Drive America Program. The program provides consumers with either cash back or zero percent financing for new Ford vehicles. As the manager of a Ford/Lincoln/Mercury franchise, how would you expect this program to impact your firm's bottom line? Explain.

9. You are the manager of BlackSpot Computers, which competes directly with Condensed Computers to sell high-powered computers to businesses. From the two businesses' perspectives, the two products are indistinguishable. The large investment required to build production facilities prohibits other firms from entering this market, and existing firms operate under the assumption that the rival will hold output constant. The inverse market demand for computers is $P = 5100 - 0.5Q$ and both firms produce at a marginal cost of $750 per computer. Currently, BlackSpot earns revenues of $6.38 million and profits (net of investment, R&D, and other fixed costs) of $1 million. The engineering department at BlackSpot has been steadily working on developing an assembly method that would dramatically reduce the marginal cost of producing these high-powered computers and has found a process that allows it to manufacture each computer at a marginal cost of $500. How will this technological advance impact your production and pricing plans? How will it impact BlackSpot's bottom line?

10. BlackGold and the Richmond Hill Petroleum Company are retail gasoline franchises that compete in a local market to sell gasoline to consumers. BlackGold and Richmond Hill are located across the street from one another and can observe the prices posted on each other's marquees. Demand for gasoline in this market is $Q = 50 - 10P$, and both franchises obtain gasoline from their supplier at $0.80 per litre. On the day that both franchises opened for business, each owner was observed changing the price of gasoline advertised on its marquee more than ten times; the owner of Richmond Hill lowered its price to slightly undercut BlackGold's price, and the owner of BlackGold lowered its advertised price to beat Richmond Hill's price. Since then, prices appear to have stabilized. Under current conditions, how many litres of gasoline are sold in the market, and at what price? Would your answer differ if Richmond Hill had service attendants available to fill consumers' tanks but BlackGold was only a self-service station? Explain.

11. You are the manager of the only firm worldwide that specializes in exporting fish products to Japan. Your firm competes against a handful of Japanese firms that enjoy a significant first-mover advantage. Recently, one of your Japanese customers has called to inform you that the Japanese legislature is considering imposing a quota that would reduce the number of kilograms of fish products you are permitted to ship to Japan each year. Your first instinct is to call the trade representative of your country to lobby against the import quota. Is following through with your first instinct necessarily the best decision? Explain.

12. The opening statement on the website of the Organization of Petroleum Exporting Countries (OPEC) states "OPEC's eleven members are all developing countries whose economies are heavily reliant on oil export revenues. They therefore seek stable oil prices that are fair and reasonable for both producers and consumers of oil." To achieve this goal, OPEC attempts to coordinate and unify petroleum policies by raising or lowering their collective oil production. However, increased production by Russia, Oman, Mexico, Norway, and other non-OPEC countries has caused the price of crude oil to fall dramatically in recent years. To achieve its goal of stable and fair oil prices, what must OPEC do to maintain the price of oil at its desired level? Do you think this will be easy for OPEC to do? Explain.

13. Semi-Salt Industries began its operation in 1975 and remains the only firm in the world that produces and sells commercial-grade polyglutamate. While virtually anyone with a degree in college chemistry could replicate the firm's formula, due to the relatively high cost Semi-Salt has decided not to apply for a patent. Despite the absence of patent protection, Semi-Salt has averaged accounting profits of 5.5 percent on investment since it began producing polyglutamate—a rate comparable to

the average rate of interest that large banks paid on deposits over this period. Do you think Semi-Salt is earning monopoly profits? Why?

14. You are the manager of a firm that competes against four other firms by bidding for government contracts. While you believe your product is better than the competition, the government purchasing agent views the products as identical and purchases from the firm offering the best price. Total government demand is $Q = 750 - 8P$ and all five firms produce at a constant marginal cost of $50. For security reasons, the government has imposed restrictions that permit a maximum of five firms to compete in this market; thus entry by new firms is prohibited. A member of Parliament is concerned because no restrictions have been placed on the price that the government pays for this product. In response, she has proposed legislation that would award each existing firm 20 percent of a contract for 270 units at a contracted price of $60 per unit. Would you support or oppose this legislation? Explain.

15. The market for a standard-sized cardboard container consists of two firms: CompositeBox and Fibreboard. As the manager of CompositeBox, you enjoy a patented technology that permits your company to produce boxes faster and at a lower cost than Fibreboard. You use this advantage to be the first to choose its profit-maximizing output level in the market. The inverse demand function for boxes is $P = 800 - 4Q$, CompositeBox's costs are $TC_C(Q_C) = 40Q_C$, and Fibreboard's costs are $TC_F(Q_F) = 80Q_F$. Ignoring competition laws, would it be profitable for your firm to merge with Fibreboard? If not, explain why not; if so, put together an offer that would permit you to profitably complete the merger.

16. You are the manager of Taurus Technologies, and your sole competitor is Spyder Technologies. The two firms' products are viewed as identical by most consumers. The relevant cost functions are $TC(Q_i) = 2Q_i$, and the inverse market demand curve for this unique product is given by $P = 50 - Q$. Currently, you and your rival simultaneously (but independently) make production decisions, and the price you fetch for the product depends on the total amount produced by each firm. However, by making an unrecoverable fixed investment of $40, Taurus Technologies can bring its product to market before Spyder finalizes production plans. Should you invest the $40? Explain.

APPENDIX: Differentiated-Product Bertrand Oligopoly

The model of Bertrand oligopoly presented in the text is based on Bertrand's classic treatment of the subject, which assumes oligopolists produce identical products. Because oligopolists that produce differentiated products may engage in price competition, this appendix presents a model of differentiated-product Bertrand oligopoly.

Suppose two oligopolists produce slightly differentiated products and compete by setting prices. In this case, one firm cannot capture all of its rival's customers by undercutting the rival's price; some consumers will have a preference for a firm's product even if the rival is charging a lower price. Thus, even if firm 2 were to "give its products away for free" (charge a zero price), firm 1 generally would find it profitable to charge a positive price. Moreover, as firm 2 raised its price, some of its customers would defect to firm 1, and thus the demand for firm 1's product would increase. This would raise firm 1's marginal revenue, making it profitable for the firm to increase its price.

In a differentiated-product price-setting oligopoly, the reaction function of firm 1 defines firm 1's profit-maximizing price given the price charged by firm 2. Based on the above reasoning, firm 1's reaction function is upward-sloping, as illustrated in

FIGURE 9–9 Reaction Functions in a Differentiated-Product Bertrand Oligopoly

Here two Bertrand firms selling a differentiated product choose their prices at the same time, point A, where the two reaction functions intersect. At this point, firm 1 charges p_1^* and firm 2 charges p_2^*.

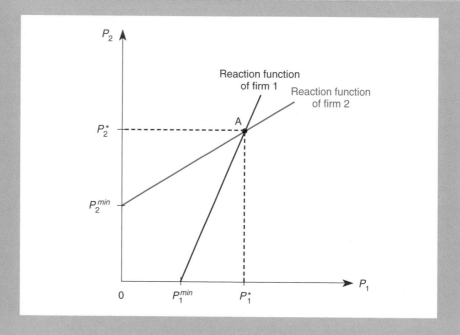

Figure 9–9. To see this, note that if firm 2 sets its price at zero, firm 1 will find it profitable to set price at $P_1^{min} > 0$, since some consumers will prefer its product to the rival's. Effectively, P_1^{min} is the price that maximizes firm 1's profits when it sells only to its brand-loyal customers (customers who do not want the other product, even for free). If the rival raises its price to, say, P_2^*, some of firm 2's customers will decide to switch to firm 1's product. Consequently, when firm 2 raises its price to P_2^*, firm 1 will raise its price to P_1^* to maximize profits given the higher demand. In fact, each point along firm 1's reaction function defines the profit-maximizing price charged by firm 1 for each price charged by firm 2. Notice that firm 1's reaction function is upward-sloping, unlike in the case of Cournot oligopoly.

Firm 2's reaction function, which defines the profit-maximizing price for firm 2 given the price charged by firm 1, also is illustrated in Figure 9–9. It is upward-sloping for the same reason firm 1's reaction function is upward-sloping; in fact, firm 2's reaction function is the mirror image of firm 1's.

In a differentiated-product Bertrand oligopoly, equilibrium is determined by the intersection of the two firms' reaction functions, which corresponds to point A in Figure 9–9. To see that point A is indeed an equilibrium, note that the profit-maximizing price for firm 1 when firm 2 sets price at P_2^* is P_1^*. Similarly, the profit-maximizing price for firm 2 when firm 1 sets price at P_1^* is P_2^*.

In a differentiated-product Bertrand oligopoly, firms charge prices that exceed marginal cost. The reason they are able to do so is that the products are not perfect substitutes. As a firm raises its price, it loses some customers to the rival firm, but not all of them. Thus, the demand function for an individual firm's product is downward-sloping, similarly to the case in monopolistic competition. But unlike in monopolistic competition, the existence of entry barriers prevents other firms from entering the market. This allows the firms in a differentiated-product Bertrand oligopoly to potentially earn positive economic profits in the long run.

Headline

Theoretically, strategic moves by a firm within an oligopolistic industry tend to draw rival responses that may precipitate either cooperative or noncooperative interactions. In the wide range of contributions made in the literature on this topic, oligopolists are shown to adopt dominant strategies within a game framework. Accordingly, these strategic moves are noncooperative, and the solution is Nash equilibrium because of the myopic perspectives of the players in the game. The fact remains, however, that each player achieves a relatively unsatisfactory payoff in such a warfare setting. Oligopolists would not choose the cooperative solution if they could not be more trusting of their rivals, and such a trusting relationship must be necessary for any lasting cooperative outcome.

In a study entitled "New Brunswick Gasoline Industry: An Oligopoly Tacit Collusion Under Consistent Conjectures?" Fidel Ezeala-Harrison develops a model that explains how despite the inherently noncooperative strategies of the players, who are resolved to maximizing their individual (rather than joint) profits, a cooperative solution can be sustained in New Brunswick's oligopolistic gasoline retail industry. Noting that, as shown in the table here, the implication of an ongoing state of competition within an oligopoly industry has not been compatible with observed industry conditions, the author rejects the competitive Cournot-Nash equilibrium, in which firms assume their rivals would not change their output in the future, in favour of a cooperative–tacitly collusive solution—in other words, quasi-cooperative.

Gasoline Price War Incidences/Frequency* in New Brunswick, 1983–1993

	1983	1984	1985	1986	1987	1988	1989	1990	1991	1992	1993
Moncton	1	1	0	1	0	1	1	0	0	0	1
Saint John	0	0	1	1	0	1	0	0	0	0	0
Fredericton	1	0	0	1	0	1	1	0	1	0	0.9

*Incidences/frequency defined as number of events.

Assume a two-player (duopoly) market, firm 1 and firm 2, in which each adopts either of the two strategies of cooperative moves (coop) with possible payoff 1 if rival adopts a similar strategy, or payoff −1 (losses) if rival plays noncooperatively (noncoop). Each player receives payoff 0 (indicating a bare breakeven condition) under a mutually aggressive (noncoop) play (a competitive warfare setting). Finally, a firm reaps payoff 2 should its rival play cooperatively while it plays aggressively.

Write the payoff matrix for the above game. What is the outcome if the rivalry between the gas retailers is a one-shot affair? Do the firms have a dominant strategy? How would your answer change in a repeated-game scenario? Why? On the basis of the evidence above, have the gas retailers been involved in price warfare or price fixing?

Source: Canadian Journal of Regional Science XIX(2), Fall 1996, available <www.lib.unb.ca/ Texts/CJRS/Fall96/contents.html>, accessed July 31, 2004.

Introduction

In this chapter we continue our analysis of strategic interaction. As we saw in the previous chapter, when only a few firms compete in a market, the actions of one firm will have a drastic impact on its rivals. For example, the pricing and output decisions of one firm in an oligopoly generally will affect the profits of other firms in the industry. Consequently, to maximize profits a manager must take into account the likely impact of his or her decisions on the behavior of other managers in the industry.

In this chapter we will delve more deeply into managerial decisions that arise in the presence of interdependence. We will develop general tools that will assist you in making a host of decisions in oligopolistic markets, including what prices to charge, how much advertising to use, whether to introduce new products, and whether to enter a new market. The basic tool we will use to examine these issues is *game theory*. Game theory is a very useful tool for managers. In fact, we will see that game theory can be used to analyze decisions within a firm, such as those related to monitoring and bargaining with workers.

Overview of Games and Strategic Thinking

Perhaps when you think of a game, a trivial game like tic-tac-toe, checkers, or *Wheel of Fortune* comes to mind. Game theory is actually a much more general framework to aid in decision making when your payoff depends on the actions taken by other players.

In a game, the players are individuals who make decisions. For example, in an oligopolistic market consisting of two firms, each of which must make a pricing decision, the firms (or, more precisely, the firms' managers) are the players. The planned decisions of the players are called *strategies*. The payoffs to the players are the profits or losses that result from the strategies. Due to interdependence, the payoff to a player depends not only on that player's strategy but also on the strategies employed by other players.

simultaneous-move game
Game in which each player makes decisions without knowledge of the other players' decisions.

sequential-move game
Game in which one player makes a move after observing the other player's move.

In the analysis of games, the order in which players make decisions is important. In a **simultaneous-move game**, each player makes decisions without knowledge of the other players' decisions. In a **sequential-move game**, one player makes a move after observing the other player's move. Tic-tac-toe, chess, and checkers are examples of sequential-move games (since players alternate moves), whereas matching pennies, duelling, and rock-paper-scissors are examples of simultaneous-move games. In the context of oligopoly games, if two firms must set prices without knowledge of each other's decisions, it is a simultaneous-move game; if one firm sets its price after observing its rival's price, it is a sequential-move game.

It is also important to distinguish between one-shot games and repeated games. In a *one-shot game,* the underlying game is played only once. In a *repeated game,* the underlying game is played more than once. For example, if you agree to play one, and only one, game of chess with a "rival," you are playing a one-shot game. If you agree to play chess two times with a rival, you are playing a repeated game.

Before we formally show how game theory can help managers solve business decisions, it is instructive to provide an example. Imagine that two gasoline stations are located side by side on the same block so that neither firm has a location advantage over the other. Consumers view the gasoline at each station as perfect substitutes and will purchase from the station that offers the lowest price. The first thing in the morning, the manager of a gas station must phone the attendant to tell him what price to put on the sign. Since she must do so without knowledge of the rival's price, this "pricing game" is a simultaneous-move game. This type of game often is called the *Bertrand duopoly game.* The concept of Bertrand oligopoly was discussed in Chapter 9. Note that the outcomes of various models of oligopoly, such as Cournot and Bertrand, can be captured within a simple payoff table (matrix) by Nash equilibrium.

Given the structure of the game, if the manager of station A calls in a higher price than the manager of station B, consumers will not buy any gas from station A. The manager of station A, therefore, is likely to reason, "I think I'll charge $0.70 per litre. But if station B thinks I will charge $0.70, they will charge $0.69, so I'd better charge $0.68. But if manager B thinks I think she'll charge $0.69, she will try to 'trick' me by charging $0.67. So I'd better charge $0.66. But if she thinks I think she thinks . . ." Perhaps you have gone through a similar thought process in trying to decide what to study for an exam ("The professor won't test us on this, but if he thinks we think he won't, he'll ask it to get us . . .").

Game theory is a powerful tool for analyzing situations such as these. First, however, we must examine the foundations of game theory. We will begin with the study of simultaneous-move, one-shot games.

Simultaneous-Move, One-Shot Games

This section presents the basic tools used to analyze simultaneous-move, one-shot games. Recall that in a simultaneous-move game, players must make decisions without knowledge of the decisions made by other players. The fact that a game is "one-shot" simply means that the players will play the game only once.

Knowledge of simultaneous-move, one-shot games is important to managers making decisions in an environment of interdependence. For example, it can be used to analyze situations where the profits of a firm depend not only on the firm's action but on the actions of rival firms as well. Before we look at specific applications of simultaneous-move, one-shot games, let us examine the general theory used to analyze such decisions.

Theory

We begin with two key definitions. First, a **strategy** is a decision rule that describes the actions a player will take at each decision point. Second, the **normal-form** representation of a game indicates the players in the game, the possible strategies of the players, and the payoffs to the players that will result from alternative strategies.

Perhaps the best way to understand precisely what is meant by *strategy* and *normal-form game* is to examine a simple example. The normal form of a simultaneous-move game is presented in Table 10–1. There are two players, whom we will call A and B to emphasize that the theory is completely general; that is, the players can be any two entities that are engaged in a situation of strategic interaction. If you wish, you may think of the players as the managers of two firms competing in a duopoly.

Player A has two possible strategies: He can choose *up* or *down*. Similarly, the feasible strategies for player B are *left* or *right*. Again, by calling the strategies *up*, *down*, and so on, we emphasize that these actions can represent virtually any decisions. For instance, *up* might represent raising the price and *down* lowering price, or *up* a high level of advertising and *down* a low level of advertising.

Finally, the payoffs to the two players are given by the entries in each cell of the matrix. The first entry refers to the payoff to player A, and the second entry denotes the payoff to player B. An important thing to notice about the description of the game is that the payoff to player A crucially depends on the strategy player B chooses. For example, if A chooses *up* and B chooses *left,* the resulting payoffs are 10 for A and 20 for B. Similarly, if player A's strategy is *up* while B's strategy is *right,* A's payoff is 15 while B's payoff is 8.

Since the game in Table 10–1 is a simultaneous-move, one-shot game, the players get to make one, and only one, decision and must make their decisions at the same time. For player A, the decision is simply *up* or *down*. Moreover, the players cannot make conditional decisions; for example, A can't choose *up* if B chooses *right* or *down* if B chooses *left.* The fact that the players make decisions at the same time precludes each player from basing his or her decisions on what the other player does.

What is the optimal strategy for a player in a simultaneous-move, one-shot game? As it turns out, this is a very complex question and depends on the nature of the game being played. There is one instance, however, in which it is easy to characterize the optimal decision—a situation that involves a dominant strategy. A strategy is a **dominant strategy** if it results in the highest payoff regardless of the action of the opponent.

In Table 10–1, the dominant strategy for player A is *up*. To see this, note that if player B chooses *left,* the best choice by player A is *up* since 10 units of profits are better than the -10 he would earn by choosing *down*. If B chose *right,* the best choice by A would be *up* since 15 units of profits are better than the 10 he would earn by choosing *down*. In short, regardless of whether player B's strategy is *left* or *right,* the best choice by player A is *up*. *Up* is a dominant strategy for player A.

TABLE 10–1 A Normal-Form Game

	Player B		
Player A	**Strategy**	**Left**	**Right**
	Up	10, 20	15, 8
	Down	−10, 7	10, 10

Principle	**PLAY YOUR DOMINANT STRATEGY**
	Check to see if you have a dominant strategy. If you have one, play it.

In simultaneous-move, one-shot games where a player has a dominant strategy, the optimal decision is to choose the dominant strategy. By doing so, you will maximize your payoff regardless of what your opponent does. In some games a player may not have a dominant strategy, as illustrated in Demonstration Problem 10–1.

Demonstration PROBLEM 10–1

In the game presented in Table 10–1, does player B have a dominant strategy?

Answer

Player B does not have a dominant strategy. To see this, note that if player A chose *up*, the best choice by player B would be *left,* since 20 is better than the payoff of 8 she would earn by choosing *right*. But if A chose *down,* the best choice by B would be *right,* since 10 is better than the payoff of 7 she would realize by choosing *left*. Thus, there is no dominant strategy for player B; the best choice by B depends on what A does.

secure strategy
A strategy that guarantees the highest payoff given the worst possible scenario.

What should a player do in the absence of a dominant strategy? One possibility would be to play a **secure strategy**—a strategy that guarantees the highest payoff given the worst possible scenario. As we will see in a moment, this approach is not generally the optimal way to play a game, but it is useful to explain the reasoning that underlies this strategy. By using a secure strategy, a player maximizes the payoff that would result in the "worst-case scenario." In other words, to find a secure strategy, a player examines the worst payoff that could arise for each of his or her actions and chooses the action that has the highest of these worst payoffs.

Demonstration PROBLEM 10–2

What is the secure strategy for player B in the game presented in Table 10–1?

Answer

The secure strategy for player B is *right*. By choosing *left* B can guarantee a payoff of only 7, but by choosing *right* she can guarantee a payoff of 8. Thus, the secure strategy by player B is *right*.

While useful, the notion of a secure strategy suffers from two shortcomings. First, it is a very conservative strategy and should be considered only if you have a good reason to be extremely averse to risk. Second, it does not take into account the optimal decisions of your rival and thus may prevent you from earning a significantly higher payoff. In particular, player B in Table 10–1 should recognize that a dominant strategy for player A is to play *up*. Thus, player B should reason as follows: "Player A will surely choose *up*, since *up* is a dominant strategy. Therefore, I should not choose my secure strategy (*right*) but instead choose *left*." Assuming player A indeed chooses the dominant strategy (*up*), player B will earn 20 by choosing *left*, but only 8 by choosing the secure strategy (*right*).

Principle	**PUT YOURSELF IN YOUR RIVAL'S SHOES**
	If you do not have a dominant strategy, look at the game from your rival's perspective. If your rival has a dominant strategy, anticipate that he or she will play it.

Nash equilibrium
A condition describing a set of strategies in which no player can improve her payoff by unilaterally changing her own strategy, given the other players' strategies.

A very natural way of formalizing the "end result" of such a thought process is captured in the definition of Nash equilibrium. A set of strategies constitute a **Nash equilibrium** if, given the strategies of the other players, no player can improve her payoff by unilaterally changing her own strategy. The concept of Nash equilibrium is very important, because it represents a situation where every player is doing the best he or she can given what other players are doing.

Demonstration PROBLEM 10–3

In the game presented in Table 10–1, what are the Nash equilibrium strategies for players A and B?

Answer

The Nash equilibrium strategy for player A is *up,* and for player B it is *left.* To see this, suppose A chooses *up* and B chooses *left.* Would either player have an incentive to change his or her strategy? No. Given that player A's strategy is *up,* the best player B can do is choose *left.* Given that B's strategy is *left,* the best A can do is choose *up.* Hence, given the strategies (*up, left*), each player is doing the best he or she can given the other player's decision.

Applications of One-Shot Games

Pricing Decisions

Let us now see how game theory can help formalize the optimal managerial decisions in a Bertrand duopoly. Consider the game presented in Table 10–2, where two firms face a situation where they must decide whether to charge low or high prices. The first number in each cell represents firm A's profits, and the second number represents firm B's profits. For example, if firm A charges a high price while firm B charges a low price, A loses 10 units of profits while B earns 50 units of profits.

While the numbers in Table 10–2 are arbitrary, their relative magnitude is consistent with the nature of Bertrand competition. In particular, note that the profits of both firms are higher when both charge high prices than when they both charge low prices, because in each instance consumers have no incentive to switch to the other firm. On the other hand, if one firm charges a high price and the other firm undercuts that price, the lower-priced firm will gain all of the other firm's customers and thus earn higher profits at the expense of the competitor.

TABLE 10–2 A Pricing Game

		Firm B	
	Strategy	Low price	High price
Firm A	Low price	0, 0	50, −10
	High price	−10, 50	10, 10

Inside**BUSINESS**

10–1   Hollywood's (Not So) Beautiful Mind: Nash or "Opie" Equilibrium?

Director Ron Howard scored a home run by strategically releasing *A Beautiful Mind* just in time to win four Golden Globe Awards in 2002. The film—based loosely on the life of Nobel Laureate John Forbes Nash, Jr., whose "Nash equilibrium" revolutionized economics and game theory—won best dramatic picture and best screenplay. Actor Russell Crowe also won a Golden Globe for his portrayal of the brilliant man whose battle with delusions, mental illness, and paranoid schizophrenia almost kept him from winning the 1994 Nobel Prize in Economics. While some know Ron Howard for his accomplishments as a director, he is best known as the kid who played Opie Taylor and Richie Cunningham in the popular TV shows *Andy Griffith* and *Happy Days*. For this reason, Eddie Murphy once dubbed him "Little Opie Cunningham" in a *Saturday Night Live* skit.

While *A Beautiful Mind* is an enjoyable film, its portrait of Nash's life is at odds with Sylvia Nasar's carefully documented and bestselling book of the same title. And what is more relevant to students of game theory, the film does not accurately illustrate the concept for which Nash is renowned. Translation: Don't rent the movie as a substitute for learning how to use Nash's equilibrium concept to make business decisions.

Hollywood attempts to illustrate Nash's insight into game theory in a bar scene in which Nash and his buddies are eyeing one absolutely stunning blonde and several of her brunette friends. All of the men prefer the blonde. Nash ponders the situation and says, "If we all go for the blonde, we block each other. Not a single one of us is going to get her. So then we go for her friends. But they will all give us the cold shoulder because nobody likes to be second choice. But what if no one goes for the blonde? We don't get in each other's way, and we don't insult the other girls. That's the only way we win." The camera shows a shot of the blonde sitting all alone at the bar while the men dance happily with the brunettes. The scene concludes with Nash rushing off to write a paper on his new concept of equilibrium.

What's wrong with this scene? Recall that a Nash equilibrium is a situation where *no player* can gain by changing his decision, given the decisions of the other players. In Hollywood's game, the men are players and their decisions are which of the women to pursue. If the other men opt for the brunettes, the blonde is all alone just waiting to dance. This means that the remaining man's best response, given the decisions of the others, is to pursue the lonely blonde! Hollywood's dance scene does not illustrate a Nash equilibrium, but the exact opposite: a situation where any one of the men could unilaterally gain by switching to the blonde, given that the other men are dancing with brunettes! What is the correct term for Hollywood's dance scene in which the blonde is left all alone? Personally, I like the term "Opie equilibrium," because it honours the director of the film and sounds much more upbeat than "disequilibrium."

Hollywood also uses the dance scene to spin its view that "Adam Smith was wrong." In particular, since the men are better off dancing with the brunettes than all pursuing the blonde, viewers are to conclude that it is never socially efficient for individuals to pursue their own selfish desires. While Chapter 14 of this book shows a number of situations where markets may fail, Hollywood's illustration is not one of them. Its "Opie equilibrium" outcome is actually *socially inefficient* because none of the men get to enjoy the company of the stunning blonde. In contrast, a real Nash equilibrium to the game entails one man dancing with the blonde and the others dancing with brunettes. Any Nash equilibrium to Hollywood's game not only has the property that each man is selfishly maximizing his own satisfaction, given the strategies of the others, but the outcome is also *socially efficient* because it doesn't squander a dance with the blonde.

We are considering a one-shot play of the game in Table 10–2, that is, a situation where the firms meet once, and only once, in the market. Moreover, the game is a simultaneous-move game in that each firm makes a pricing decision without knowledge of the decision made by the other firm. In a one-shot play of the game, the Nash equilibrium strategies are for each firm to charge the low price. The reason is simple. If firm B charges a high price, firm A's best choice is to charge a low price, since 50 units of profits are better than the 10 units it would earn if A charged the high price. Similarly, if firm B charges the low price, firm A's best choice is to charge the low price, since 0 units of profits are preferred to the 10 units of losses that would result if A charged the high price. Similar arguments hold from firm B's perspective.

Firm A is always better off charging the low price regardless of what firm B does, and B is always better off charging the low price regardless of what A does. To summarize, in the one-shot version of the above game, each firm's best strategy is to charge a low price regardless of the other firm's action. The outcome of the game is that both firms charge low prices and earn profits of zero.

Clearly, profits are less than the firms would earn if they colluded and "agreed" to both charge high prices. This point was illustrated in Chapter 9, Demonstration Problem 9–5. For example, in Table 10–2 we see that each firm would earn profits of 10 units if both charged high prices. This is a classic result in economics and is called a *dilemma* because the Nash equilibrium outcome is inferior (from the viewpoint of the firms) to the situation where they both "agree" to charge high prices.

Why can't firms collude and agree to charge high prices? One answer is that collusion is illegal in Canada and many other countries; firms are not allowed to meet and "conspire" to set high prices. There are other reasons, however. Suppose the managers did secretly meet and agree to charge high prices. Would they have an incentive to live up to their promises? Consider firm A's point of view. If it "cheated" on the collusive agreement by lowering its price, it would increase its profits from 10 to 50. Thus, firm A has an incentive to induce firm B to charge a high price so that it can "cheat" to earn higher profits. Of course, firm B recognizes this incentive, which precludes the agreement from being reached in the first place.

However, suppose the manager of firm A is "honest" and would never cheat on a promise to charge a high price. (She is "honest" enough to keep her word to the other manager, but not so honest as to obey the law against collusion.) What happens to firm A if the manager of firm B cheats on the collusive agreement? If B cheats, A experiences losses of $10. When firm A's stockholders ask the manager why they lost $10 when the rival firm earned profits of $50, how can the manager answer? She cannot admit she was cheated on in a collusive agreement, for doing so might send her to jail for having violated the law. Whatever her answer, she risks being fired or sent to prison.

Advertising and Quality Decisions

Our framework for analyzing simultaneous-move, one-shot games can also be used to analyze advertising and quality decisions. In oligopolistic markets, firms advertise and/or increase their product quality in an attempt to increase the demand for their products. While both quality and advertising can be used to increase the demand for a product, our discussion will use advertising as a placeholder for both quality and advertising.

An important issue in evaluating the consequences of advertising is to recognize where the increase in demand comes from. In most oligopolistic markets, advertising increases the demand for a firm's product by taking customers away from other firms in the industry. An increase in one firm's advertising increases its profits at the expense of other firms in the market; there is interdependency among the advertising decisions of firms.

A classic example of such a situation is the breakfast cereal industry, which has a four-firm concentration ratio of 86 percent; that is, four firms produce 86 percent of all breakfast cereals. By advertising its brand of cereal, a particular firm does not induce many consumers to eat cereal for lunch and dinner; instead, it induces customers to switch to its brand from another brand. This can lead to a situation where each firm advertises just to "cancel out" the effects of other firms' advertising, resulting in high levels of advertising, no change in industry or firm demand, and low profits.

Demonstration PROBLEM 10-4

Suppose your firm competes against another firm for customers. You and your rival know your products will be obsolete at the end of the year and must simultaneously determine whether or not to advertise. In your industry, advertising does not increase total industry demand but instead induces consumers to switch among the products of different firms. Thus, if both you and your rival advertise, the two advertising campaigns will simply offset each other, and you will each earn $4 million in profits. If neither of you advertises, you will each earn $10 million in profits. However, if one of you advertises and the other one does not, the firm that advertises will earn $20 million and the firm that does not advertise will earn $1 million in profits. Is your profit-maximizing choice to advertise or not to advertise? How much money do you expect to earn?

Answer

The description of the game corresponds to the matrix presented in Table 10–3. The game is a one-shot game. Note that the dominant strategy for each firm is to advertise, and thus the unique Nash equilibrium for the game is for each firm to advertise. Thus, the profit-maximizing choice by your firm is to advertise. You can expect to earn $4 million. Collusion would not work because this is a one-shot game; if you and your rival "agreed" not to advertise (in the hope of making $10 million each), each of you would have an incentive to cheat on the agreement.

TABLE 10-3 An Advertising Game

		Firm B	
	Strategy	Advertise	Don't Advertise
Firm A	Advertise	$4, $4	$20, $1
	Don't Advertise	$1, $20	$10, $10

Coordination Decisions

Thus far, our analysis of oligopoly has focused on situations where firms have competing objectives: One firm can gain only at the expense of other firms. Not all games have this structure, however.

Imagine a world where producers of electrical appliances have a choice of which type of electrical outlets to put on appliances: 90-volt, four-prong outlets or 120-volt, two-prong outlets. In an environment where different appliances require different outlets, a consumer who desires several appliances would have to spend a considerable sum wiring the house to accommodate all of the appliances. This would reduce the amount the consumer has available for buying appliances and therefore would adversely affect the profits of appliance manufacturers. In contrast, if the appliance manufacturers can "coordinate" their decisions (that is, produce appliances that require the same types of wiring), they will earn higher profits.

Table 10–4 presents a hypothetical example of what is called a *coordination game*. Two firms must decide whether to produce appliances requiring 120-volt or 90-volt outlets. If each firm produces appliances requiring 120-volt outlets, each firm will earn profits of $100. Similarly, if each firm produces appliances requiring 90-volt outlets, each firm will earn $100. However, if the two firms produce appliances requiring different types of outlets, each firm will earn zero profits due to the

TABLE 10–4 A Coordination Game

		Firm B	
	Strategy	120-Volt Outlets	90-Volt Outlets
Firm A	120-Volt Outlets	$100, $100	$0, $0
	90-Volt Outlets	$0, $0	$100, $100

lower demand that will result from consumers' need to spend more money wiring their houses.

What would you do if you were the manager of firm A in this example? If you do not know what firm B is going to do, you have a very tough decision. All you can do is "guess" what B will do. If you think B will produce 120-volt appliances, you should produce 120-volt appliances as well. If you think B will produce 90-volt appliances, you should do likewise. You will thus maximize profits by doing what firm B does. Effectively, both you and firm B will do better by "coordinating" your decisions.

The game in Table 10–4 has two Nash equilibria. One Nash equilibrium is for each firm to produce 120-volt appliances; the other is for each firm to produce 90-volt appliances. The question is how the firms will get to one of these equilibria. If the firms could "talk" to each other, they could agree to produce 120-volt systems. Alternatively, the government could set a standard that electrical outlets be required to operate on 120-volt, two-prong outlets. In effect, this would allow the firms to "coordinate" their decisions. Notice that once they agree to produce 120-volt appliances, there is no incentive to cheat on this agreement. The game in Table 10–4 is not analogous to the pricing or advertising games analyzed earlier; it is a game of coordination rather than a game of conflicting interests.

Monitoring Employees

Game theory can also be used to analyze interactions between workers and the manager. In Chapter 6, we discussed the principal-agent problem and argued that there can be conflicting goals between workers and managers. Managers desire workers to work hard, while workers enjoy leisure.

In our discussion of manager-worker principal-agent problems in Chapter 6, we noted that one way a manager can reduce workers' incentives to shirk is to engage in "random" spot checks of the workplace. Game theory provides a way of seeing why this can work. Consider a game between a worker and a manager. The manager has two possible actions: (1) monitor the worker or (2) don't monitor the worker. The worker has two choices: (1) work or (2) shirk. These possible actions and resulting payoffs are depicted in Table 10–6.

The interpretation of this normal-form game is as follows. If the manager monitors while the worker works, the worker "wins" and the manager "loses." The manager has spent time monitoring a worker who was already working. In this case, suppose the manager's payoff is -1 and the worker's payoff is 1. The payoffs are the same if the manager does not monitor the worker and the worker shirks; the worker wins because she gets away with shirking.

In contrast, if the manager monitors while the worker shirks, the manager wins 1 and the worker who gets caught loses 1. Similarly, if the worker works and the manager does not monitor, the manager wins 1 and the worker loses 1. The numbers in Table 10–6 are, of course, purely hypothetical, but they are consistent with the relative payoffs that arise in such situations.

Inside BUSINESS

10-2 Coordinating Activities: How Hard Is It?

An interesting area of study has arisen out of the question "Can firms coordinate their activities?" Russell W. Cooper and his associates recently published the results of several experiments that address this topic. In the experiments, volunteers participated in market situations where they had a chance to earn substantial amounts of money. The choices made by each participant along with the other participants in their group determined their earnings. In these coordination experiments, two or more Nash equilibria existed. The experiments were designed to test whether people choose the dominant ("best") equilibrium—the Nash equilibrium that has the highest payoff.

Cooper et al. conducted experiments with a payoff matrix like the one in Table 10–5. There are two pairs of Nash equilibrium strategies in this game: (1, 1) and (2, 2).

Participants would generally prefer to find themselves at equilibrium (2, 2), since it has the highest level of earnings of the two Nash equilibria. However, out of 110 opportunities, participants chose the Nash equilibrium (1, 1) 83 times, the Nash equilibrium (2, 2) 26 times, and the nonequilibrium cell (1, 3) once. The reason the Nash equilibrium with the higher payoff was selected so infrequently is that participants apparently placed a high probability that their opponent would choose the "cooperative strategy" of 3, which would lead to a payoff of 1000 if they chose 1.

Source: Russell W. Cooper, Douglas V. DeJong, Robert Forsythe, and T. W. Ross, "Selection Criteria in Coordination Games: Some Experimental Results," *American Economic Review* 80, March 1990, pp. 218–33.

TABLE 10–5 A Coordination Game

		Player B		
	Strategy	1	2	3
Player A	1	350, 350	350, 250	1000, 0
	2	250, 350	550, 550	0, 0
	3	0, 1000	0, 0	600, 600

Notice that the game in Table 10–6 does not have a Nash equilibrium, at least in the usual sense of the term. To see this, suppose the manager's strategy is to monitor the worker. Then the best choice of the worker is to work. But if the worker works, the manager does better by changing his strategy: choosing not to monitor. Thus, "monitoring" is not part of a Nash equilibrium strategy. The paradox, however, is that "not monitoring" isn't part of a Nash equilibrium either. To see why, suppose the manager's strategy is "don't monitor." Then the worker will maximize her payoff by shirking. Given that the worker shirks, the manager does better by changing the strategy to "monitor" to increase his payoff from -1 to 1. Thus, we see that "don't monitor" is not part of a Nash equilibrium strategy either.

The thing to notice in this example is that both the worker and the manager want to keep their actions "secret"; if the manager knows what the worker is doing, it will

TABLE 10–6 A Game with No Nash Equilibrium

		Worker	
	Strategy	Work	Shirk
Manager	Monitor	$-1, 1$	$1, -1$
	Don't Monitor	$1, -1$	$-1, 1$

mixed (randomized) strategy
A strategy whereby a player randomizes over two or more available actions in order to keep rivals from being able to predict his or her action.

be curtains for the worker, and vice versa. In such situations, players find it in their interest to engage in a **mixed (randomized) strategy**. What this means is that players "randomize" over their available strategies; for instance, the manager flips a coin to determine whether or not to monitor. By doing so, the worker cannot predict whether the manager will be present to monitor her and, consequently, cannot outguess the manager.

Those of you who have taken multiple-choice tests have had firsthand experience with randomized strategies. If your professor made *a* the correct answer more often than *b*, *c*, or *d*, you could gain by answering *a* in those instances when you did not know the correct answer. This would enable you to earn a higher grade than you deserved on the basis of your knowledge of subject matter. To prevent this strategy from working for you, professors randomize which option is the correct answer so that you cannot systematically guess the correct answer on an exam.

Nash Bargaining

The final application of simultaneous-move, one-shot games we will consider is a simple bargaining game. In a *Nash bargaining* game, two players "bargain" over some object of value. In a simultaneous-move, one-shot bargaining game, the players have only one chance to reach an agreement, and the offers made in bargaining are made simultaneously.

To be concrete, suppose management and a labour union are bargaining over how much of a $100 surplus to give to the union. Suppose, for simplicity, that the $100 can be split only into $50 increments. The players have one shot to reach an agreement. The parties simultaneously write the amount they desire on a piece of paper (either 0, 50, or 100). If the sum of the amounts each party asks for does not exceed $100, the players get the specified amounts. But if the sum of the amounts requested exceeds $100, bargaining ends in a stalemate. Let's suppose that the delays caused by this stalemate cost both the union and management $1.

Table 10–7 presents the normal form of this hypothetical bargaining game. If you were management, what amount would you ask for? Suppose you wrote down $100. Then the only way you would get any money is if the union asked for zero. Notice that if management asked for $100 and the union asked for $0, neither party would have an incentive to change its amounts; we would be in Nash equilibrium.

Before concluding that you should ask for $100, think again. Suppose the union wrote down $50. Management's best response to this move would be to ask for $50. And given that management asked for $50, the union would have no incentive to change its amount. Thus, a 50-50 split of the $100 also would be a Nash equilibrium.

Finally, suppose management asked for $0 and the union asked for the entire $100. This too would constitute a Nash equilibrium. Neither party could improve its payoff by changing its strategy given the strategy of the other.

TABLE 10–7	A Bargaining Game		
	Union		
Management Strategy	0	50	100
0	0, 0	0, 50	0, 100
50	50, 0	50, 50	−1, −1
100	100, 0	−1, −1	−1, −1

Thus, there are three Nash equilibrium outcomes to this bargaining game. One outcome splits the money evenly among the parties, while the other two outcomes give all the money to either the union or management.

This example illustrates that the outcomes of simultaneous-move bargaining games are difficult to predict because there are generally multiple Nash equilibria. This multiplicity of equilibria leads to inefficiencies when the parties fail to "coordinate" on an equilibrium. In Table 10–7, for instance, six of the nine potential outcomes are inefficient in that they result in total payoffs that are less than the amount to be divided. Three of these outcomes entail negative payoffs due to stalemate. Unfortunately, stalemate is common in labour disputes: agreements often fail or are delayed because the two sides ask for more (in total) than there is to split.

Experimental evidence suggests that bargainers often perceive a 50-50 split to be "fair." Consequently, many players in real-world settings tend to choose strategies that result in such a split even though there are other Nash equilibria. Clearly, for the game in Table 10–7, if you expect the union to ask for $50, you, as management, should ask for $50.

Demonstration PROBLEM 10–5

Suppose a $1 coin is to be divided between two players according to a simultaneous-move, one-shot bargaining game. Is there a Nash equilibrium to the bargaining game if the smallest unit in which the money can be divided is $.01? Assume that if the players ask for more in total than is available, they go home empty-handed.

Answer

Yes, in fact there are many Nash equilibria. Any amount the players ask for that sums to exactly 100 cents constitutes a Nash equilibrium. As examples, one player asks for $0.01 and the other asks for $0.99; one player asks for $0.02 and the other asks for $0.98; and so on. In each case, neither party can gain by asking for more, given what the other player has asked for.

Infinitely Repeated Games

From our analysis of one-shot pricing and advertising games, one might be led to believe that collusion is impossible in an industry. This conclusion is erroneous, however, and stems from the fact that firms in some industries do not play a one-shot game. Instead, they compete week after week, year after year. In these instances, the appropriate mode of analysis is to consider a situation where a game is repeated over time. In this section, we analyze a situation where players perpetually interact.

infinitely repeated game
A game that is played over and over again forever and in which players receive payoffs during each play of the game.

An **infinitely repeated game** is a game that is played over and over again forever. Players receive payoffs during each repetition of the game.

Theory

When a game is played again and again, players receive payoffs during each repetition of the game. Due to the time value of money, a dollar earned during the first repetition of the game is worth more than a dollar earned in later repetitions; players must appropriately discount future payoffs when they make current decisions. For this reason, we will review the key aspects of present value analysis before we begin examining repeated games.

Review of Present Value

The value of a firm is the present value of all future profits earned by the firm. If the interest rate is i, π_0 represents profits today, π_1 profits one year from today, π_2 profits two years from today, and so on, the value of a firm that will be in business for T years is

$$PV_{Firm} = \pi_0 + \frac{\pi_1}{1+i} + \frac{\pi_2}{(1+i)^2} + \cdots + \frac{\pi_T}{(1+i)^T} = \sum_{t=0}^{T} \frac{\pi_t}{(1+i)^t}$$

If the profits earned by the firm are the same in each period ($\pi_t = \pi$ for each period, t) and the horizon is infinite ($T = \infty$), this formula simplifies to

$$PV_{Firm} = \left(\frac{1+i}{i}\right)\pi$$

As we will see, this formula is very useful in analyzing decisions in infinitely repeated games.

Supporting Collusion with Trigger Strategies

Now consider the simultaneous-move Bertrand pricing game presented in Table 10–8. The Nash equilibrium in a one-shot play of this game is for each firm to charge low prices and earn zero profits. Let us suppose the firms play the game in Table 10–8 day after day, week after week, for all eternity. Thus, we are considering an infinitely repeated Bertrand pricing game, not a one-shot game. In this section, we will examine the impact of repeated play on the equilibrium outcome of the game.

When firms repeatedly face a matrix such as that in Table 10–8, it is possible for them to "collude" without fear of being cheated on. They do this by using trigger strategies. A **trigger strategy** is a strategy that is contingent on the past plays of players in a game. A player who adopts a trigger strategy continues to choose the same action until some other player takes an action that "triggers" a different action by the first player.

To see how trigger strategies can be used to support collusive outcomes, suppose firm A and firm B secretly meet and agree to the following arrangement: "We will each charge the high price, provided neither of us has ever 'cheated' in the past (that is, charged the low price in any previous period). If one of us cheats and charges the low price, the other player will 'punish' the deviator by charging the low price in every period thereafter." Thus, if firm A cheats, it pulls a "trigger" that leads firm B to charge the low price forever after, and vice versa. It turns out that if both firms adopt such a trigger strategy, there are conditions under which neither firm has an incentive to cheat on the collusive agreement. Before we show this formally, let us examine the basic intuition.

trigger strategy
A strategy that is contingent on the past play of a game and in which some particular past action "triggers" a different action by a player.

TABLE 10–8	A Pricing Game That Is Repeated	
	Firm B	
	Price	Low	High
Firm A	Low	0, 0	50, −40
	High	−40, 50	10, 10

If neither firm in Table 10–8 cheats on the collusive agreement, each firm will earn $10 each period forever. But if one firm plays according to the agreement, the other firm could cheat and earn an immediate profit of $50 instead of $10. Thus, there is still the immediate benefit to a firm of cheating on the agreement. However, because the firms compete repeatedly over time, there is a future cost of cheating. According to the agreement, if a firm ever cheats, the other firm will charge a low price in all future periods. Thus, the best the firm that cheated can do is earn $0 in the periods after cheating instead of the $10 it would have earned had it not broken the agreement.

In short, the benefit of cheating today on the collusive agreement is earning $50 instead of $10 today. The cost of cheating today is earning $0 instead of $10 in each future period. If the present value of the cost of cheating exceeds the one-time benefit of cheating, it does not pay for a firm to cheat, and high prices can be sustained.

Now let us formalize this idea. Suppose the firms agree to the collusive plan just outlined, and firm A believes firm B will live up to the agreement. Does firm A have an incentive to cheat and charge a low price? If firm A cheats by charging a low price, its profits will be $50 today but $0 in all subsequent periods, since cheating today will lead firm B to charge a low price in all future periods. The best choice of firm A when firm B charges the low price in these future periods is to charge the low price to earn $0. Thus, if firm A cheats today, the present value of its profits are

$$PV_{Firm\,A}^{Cheat} = \$50 + 0 + 0 + 0 + 0 + \cdots$$

If firm A does not cheat, it earns $10 each period forever. Thus, the present value of the profits of firm A if it "cooperates" (does not cheat) are

$$PV_{Firm\,A}^{Coop} = 10 + \frac{10}{1+i} + \frac{10}{(1+i)^2} + \frac{10}{(1+i)^3} + \cdots = \frac{10(1+i)}{i}$$

where i is the interest rate. Firm A has no incentive to cheat if the present value of its earnings from cheating is less than the present value of its earnings from not cheating. For the numbers in this example, there is no incentive to cheat if

$$PV_{Firm\,A}^{Cheat} = 50 \leq \frac{10(1+i)}{i} = PV_{Firm\,A}^{Coop}$$

which is true if $i \leq 1/4$. In other words, if the interest rate is less than 25 percent, firm A will lose more (in present value) by cheating than it will gain. Since firm B's incentives are symmetric, the same is true for firm B. Thus, when oligopolistic firms compete repeatedly over time, it is possible for them to collude and charge high prices to earn $10 each period. This benefits firms at the expense of consumers and also leads to a deadweight loss. This explains why there are laws against collusion.

Put differently, because firm B has much to gain by matching firm A's low price, and firm A's response incorporates this rational reaction of firm B, the two firms' strategies amount to what is known as **tit for tat**: a commitment that neither firm will be undersold. Firm A would be even more confident that firm B would match its price decrease if firm A also announced to firm B that, starting next period, its price in any given period would match the price firm B charges in the previous period. The outcome, therefore, corresponds to the monopoly outcome even though neither firm colludes.

tit for tat
A strategy in which cheating triggers punishment in the next period.

More generally, we may state the following principle:

Principle	**SUSTAINING COOPERATIVE OUTCOMES WITH TRIGGER STRATEGIES**

Suppose a one-shot game is infinitely repeated and the interest rate is i. Further, suppose the "cooperative" one-shot payoff to a player is π^{Coop}, the maximum one-shot payoff if the player cheats on the collusive outcome is π^{Cheat}, the one-shot Nash equilibrium payoff is π^N, and

$$\frac{\pi^{Cheat} - \pi^{Coop}}{\pi^{Coop} - \pi^N} \leq \frac{1}{i}$$

Then the cooperative (collusive) outcome can be sustained in the infinitely repeated game with the following trigger strategy: "Cooperate provided no player has ever cheated in the past. If any player cheats, 'punish' the player by choosing the one-shot Nash equilibrium strategy forever after."

The condition written in the preceding principle has a very intuitive interpretation. It can be rewritten as

$$\pi^{Cheat} - \pi^{Coop} \leq \frac{1}{i}(\pi^{Coop} - \pi^N)$$

The left-hand side of this equation represents the one-time gain of breaking the collusive agreement today. The right-hand side represents the present value of what is given up in the future by cheating today. Provided the one-time gain is less than the present value of what would be given up by cheating, players find it in their interest to live up to the agreement.

Demonstration PROBLEM 10–6

Suppose firm A and firm B repeatedly face the situation presented in Table 10–8 and the interest rate is 40 percent. The firms agree to charge a high price each period, provided neither firm has cheated on this agreement in the past.

1. What are firm A's profits if it cheats on the collusive agreement?
2. What are firm A's profits if it does not cheat on the collusive agreement?
3. Does an equilibrium result where the firms charge the high price each period?

Answer
1. If firm B lives up to the collusive agreement but firm A cheats, firm A will earn $50 today and zero forever after.
2. If firm B lives up to the collusive agreement and firm A does not cheat, the present value of firm A's profits is

$$10 + \frac{10}{1 + 0.4} + \frac{10}{(1 + 0.4)^2} + \frac{10}{(1 + 0.4)^3} + \cdots = \frac{10(1 + 0.4)}{0.4} = 35$$

3. Since $50 > 35$, the present value of firm A's profits is higher if A cheats on the collusive agreement than if it does not cheat. Since the matrix is symmetric, each firm has an incentive to cheat on the collusive agreement, even if it believes the other firm will not cheat. In equilibrium, each firm will charge the low price each period to earn profits of $0 each period.

Inside BUSINESS

10–3 Game-Theoretic Analysis of the Canada-U.S. Lumber Dispute

Canadian exports of softwood lumber to the United States have been a source of controversy since early 1960s. Since 1986, as a result of pressure from the U.S. Coalition for Fair Lumber Imports and the judgment of the International Trade Commission (ITC) that Canadian lumber producers were being subsidized, the trade scene between the two countries has witnessed a series of United States trade retaliatory initiatives. A series of countervailing duties—import taxes designed specifically to offset the competitive advantage provided by trading partners' export subsidies—and antidumping measures imposed by the United States against Canada's exports of lumber characterize this environment.

In 1995–96, the two governments concluded the Canada-U.S. Softwood Lumber Agreement (SLA), which employed a quota (quantitative restrictions) mechanism. The SLA ran from April 1, 1996 to March 31, 2001, and constrained annual lumber exports to the United States from four provinces (British Columbia, Alberta, Ontario, and Quebec), which in 1998 accounted for 87.4 percent of all softwood lumber exported by Canada to the United States. Since its expiration, the bitter dispute about the lower-priced softwood lumber imports from Canada has continued, and it is unlikely to disappear as long as weakness of the Canadian dollar, the high degree of public ownership of forest lands, and restrictions on log exports remain unchanged.

A paper by van Kooten provides some insights into this controversy, which has little to do with economic efficiency and everything to do with politics and the creation and distribution of economic rents. The author demonstrates that restrictions on softwood lumber trade will benefit producers on both sides of the border, as well as Canadian consumers, all at the expense of U.S. consumers. In the light of this, it helps to view the dispute from a game-theoretic perspective.

Consider a two-player game involving Canada and the United States. As long as both countries ignore the well-being of consumers, the solution to the trade dispute or to the game—Nash equilibrium—is straightforward: restrict imports of Canadian lumber into the U.S. market. From Canada's perspective, the best strategy is to encourage Canadian softwood lumber producers to form a joint profit-maximizing entity—a cartel—to sell a limited quantity of lumber to the United States. This provides the greatest benefits to Canadian producers; and U.S. producers would welcome such a cartel, even though their preferred solution (with the greatest producer surplus) would be no trade whatsoever. Alternatively, Canada could employ an export tax and directly collect the economic rent created by the trade restriction. Game theory suggests that the most troublesome solution would be a countervailing duty. The author demonstrates that such a duty results in large U.S. government revenues at the expense of Canadian lumber producers (with U.S. producers no better or worse off than under a quota or Canadian export tax).

Countervailing duties and export taxes have an impact on U.S. and Canadian consumers and U.S. producers similar to that of a quota scheme. Since a countervailing duty provides no benefits to Canada, Canada will always seek to get around it. It did this in 1987 and again in 1996 with the SLA.

Insights from the two-player game are limited, however, because the problem in Canada is to get agreement among provinces and producers. Provinces vigorously guard their autonomy over forestry policy and the wood products industry, making it difficult to agree on a method for allocating quotas.

In any event, Canada's position has favoured free trade. On the basis of his analysis, van Kooten concludes that Canada should make an effort to form a softwood lumber cartel to restrict lumber exports. U.S. producers should not oppose such a cartel, and may even support it since the U.S. companies produce lumber on both sides of the border. The eventual outcome of this "game" will be to either enhance the incomes of U.S. and Canadian lumber producers or bring the U.S. Justice Department into the fray. In the latter case, free trade will be the most likely outcome. While export taxes might be considered a second-best alternative, Canada should reject a countervailing duty under any circumstances.

Source: G. Cornelis van Kooten, "Economic Analysis of the Canada-United States Softwood Lumber Dispute: Playing the Quota Game," *Forest Science* 48, November 2002, pp. 712–721, available <http://web.uvic.ca/~kooten/Downloads/SLA.pdf>, accessed July 31, 2004.

In summary, in a one-shot game there is no tomorrow; any gains must be had today or not at all. In an infinitely repeated game there is always a tomorrow, and firms must weigh the benefits of current actions against the future costs of those actions. The principal result of infinitely repeated games is that when the interest rate is low, firms may find it in their interest to collude and charge high prices, unlike in the case of a one-shot game. The basic reason for this important result is this: if a player deviates from the "collusive strategy," he or she is punished in future periods long enough to wipe out the gains from having deviated from the collusive outcome. The threat of punishment makes cooperation work in repeated games. In one-shot games there is no tomorrow, and threats have no bite.

Factors Affecting Collusion in Pricing Games

It is easier to sustain collusive arrangements via the punishment strategies outlined earlier when firms know (1) who their rivals are, so they know whom to punish should the need arise; (2) who their rivals' customers are, so that if punishment is necessary they can take away those customers by charging lower prices; and (3) when their rivals deviate from the collusive arrangement, so they know when to begin the punishments. Furthermore, they must (4) be able to successfully punish rivals for deviating from the collusive agreement, for otherwise the threat of punishment would not work. These factors are related to several variables reflected in the structure and conduct of the industry.

Number of Firms

Collusion is easier when there are few firms rather than many. If there are n firms in the industry, the total amount of monitoring that must go on to sustain the collusive arrangement is $n \times (n - 1)$. For example, let the firms be indexed by A, B, C, ... If there are only two firms in the industry, then to punish a firm for deviating, each firm must know whether its rival has deviated and, if so, where its customers are so it can punish the rival by getting some of its customers. To do this, each must keep an eye on its rival. With two firms, this information may be obtained if A monitors B and B monitors A.

The total number of monitors needed in the market grows very rapidly as the number of firms increases. For example, if there are five firms, each firm must monitor four other firms, so the total number of monitors needed in the market is $5 \times 4 = 20$. The cost of monitoring rivals reduces the gains to colluding. If the number of firms is "large enough," the monitoring costs become so high relative to collusive profits that it does not pay to monitor the actions of other firms. Under these circumstances, the "threat" used to sustain the collusive outcome is not credible, and the collusion fails. This is one reason why it is easier for two firms to collude than it is for, say, four firms to do so.

It is important to note that a trigger strategy may not work well in the presence of "noise" in the marketplace. Under imperfect information, price is determined by a random component as well as output. In this environment, each firm knows the expected price and its own output but not the output of its rivals. When, for instance, a low price occurs, any one firm does not know whether it is because demand is very low or because a rival has cheated. Thus, in this model there is a fair chance that cheating may go undetected. However, if prices fall below a certain threshold all firms revert to the noncollusive equilibrium, whatever the reason for the price decline. In other words, firms may be punished even if there are no deviants! Firms sometimes respond to low prices by going into a punishment phase, not necessarily because someone has cheated, but because if low prices did not trigger punishment, firms would cheat and the cartel would break down.

Firm Size

Economies of scale exist in monitoring. Monitoring and policing costs constitute a much greater share of total costs for small firms than for larger firms. Thus, it may be easier for a large firm to monitor a small firm than for a small firm to monitor a

InsideBUSINESS

10-4 Trigger Strategies in the Waste Industry

For trigger strategies to work, players must be able to monitor their rivals' actions, so that they know whether to take punitive actions. For punishments to deter cheating, players do not actually have to punish cheaters forever. As long as they punish cheaters long enough to take away the profits earned by cheating, no player will find it profitable to cheat. In this case, players can achieve collusive outcomes. Real-world firms recognize these points.

Firms that pick up trash in Dade County, Florida devised a mechanism to use trigger strategies to enforce high prices in a Bertrand market. To ensure that competitors did not undercut their high prices, firms monitored one another quite closely.

One company hired several people to follow the trucks of rival firms to make sure they did not steal its customers by undercutting its price. What did the firm do if it found a competitor servicing one of its clients? It took away five or ten of the competitor's customers for every one that had been lost to punish the rival for stealing its customers. It accomplished this by offering these customers a more favourable price than the competitor offered. After awhile, its competitors learned that it did not pay to steal this firm's customers. In the end there was little cheating, and firms in the market charged collusive prices.

Before you decide to adopt similar methods, be aware that this example was taken from court transcripts in the U.S. District Court of Southern Florida, where those involved in the conspiracy were tried. In situations with repeated interaction, trigger strategies can be used to enhance profits—but it is illegal to engage in such practices.

Source: Docket No. 84-6107-Cr-KING (MISHLER), March 17, 1986. U.S. District Court of Southern Florida, Miami Division.

large firm. For example, a large firm (with, say, 20 outlets) can monitor the prices charged by a small competitor (with 1 outlet) by simply checking prices at the one store. But to check the prices of its rival, the smaller firm must hire individuals to monitor 20 outlets.

History of the Market

One key issue not addressed thus far is how firms reach an understanding to collude. One way is for the firms to explicitly meet and verbally warn their rivals not to steal their customers, or else they will be punished. Alternatively, firms might not meet at all but instead gain an understanding over time of the way the game is played and thus achieve "tacit collusion." *Tacit collusion* occurs when the firms do not explicitly conspire to collude but accomplish collusion indirectly. For example, in many instances firms learn from experience how other firms will behave in a market. If a firm observes over time that it is "punished" each time it charges a low price or attempts to steal customers from a rival, it eventually will learn that it does not pay to charge low prices. In these instances, tacit collusion will be the likely outcome.

In contrast, if a firm learns over time that its opponents are unable to successfully punish it for undercutting prices, tacit collusion will be unlikely to result. If firms never carry out their threats, the history of the industry will be such that collusion by threat of reprisal is not an equilibrium. But if firms observe that rivals indeed carry out their threats, this "history" ultimately will result in collusion.

Punishment Mechanisms

The pricing mechanisms firms use also affect their ability to punish rivals that do not cooperate. For example, in a posted-price market, where a single price is posted and charged to all of a firm's customers, the cost of punishing an opponent is higher than in markets in which different customers are quoted different prices. The reason is as follows. If a single price is charged to all customers, a firm that wishes to punish a rival by stealing its customers not only has to charge a low price to the rival's customers but also must lower its price to its own customers. This is essentially what a retailer must do to get customers away from another retailer. In contrast, in an industry in which different prices are quoted to different customers, a firm can punish its rival by charging the rival's customers a low price while continuing to charge its own customers a higher price. This, of course, substantially reduces the cost of engaging in punishment.

An Application of Infinitely Repeated Games to Product Quality

The theory of infinitely repeated games can be used to analyze the desirability of firm policies such as warranties and guarantees. Effectively, a game occurs between consumers and firms: consumers desire durable, high-quality products at a low price, while firms wish to maximize profits. In a one-shot game, any profits made by the firm must be made today; there is no prospect for repeat business. Thus, in a one-shot game, a firm may have an incentive to sell shoddy products. This is particularly true if consumers cannot determine the quality of the products prior to purchase.

To see this, consider the normal-form game in Table 10–9. Here the game is between a consumer and a firm. The consumer has two strategies: buy the product or don't buy it. The firm can produce a low-quality product or a high-quality product. In a one-shot play of the game, the Nash equilibrium strategy is for the firm to produce a low-quality product and for consumers to shun the product. To see this, note that if the consumer decided to buy the product, the firm would benefit by selling a low-quality product, since profits of 10 are better than the 1 it would earn by producing a high-quality product. Given a low-quality product, the consumer chooses not to buy, since 0 is better than losing 10 by purchasing a shoddy product. But since the consumer chooses not to buy, it does not pay for the firm to produce a high-quality product. In a one-shot game, the consumer chooses not to buy the product because he or she knows the firm will "take the money and run."

The story differs if the game is infinitely repeated. Suppose the consumer tells the firm "I'll buy your product and will continue to buy it if it is of good quality. But if it turns out to be shoddy, I'll tell all my friends never to purchase anything from you again." Given this strategy by the consumer, what is the best thing for the firm to do? If the interest rate is not too high, the best alternative is to sell a high-quality product. The reason is simple. By selling a shoddy product, the firm earns 10 instead of 1 that period. This is, in effect, "the gain to cheating" (selling a poor-quality product). The cost of selling a shoddy product, however, is to earn zero forever after, as the firm's reputation is ruined by having sold such a product. When the interest rate is low, the one-time gain will be more than offset by the lost future sales. It will not pay for the firm to "cheat" by selling shoddy merchandise.

The lesson to be drawn from this example is twofold. First, if your firm desires to be a "going concern," that is, infinitely lived, it does not pay to "cheat" customers if

TABLE 10–9 A Product Quality Game

		Firm	
	Strategy	Low-Quality Product	High-Quality Product
Consumer	Don't Buy	0, 0	50, −40
	Buy	−40, 50	10, 10

Inside BUSINESS

On July 17, 1996, the U.S. Department of Justice (DOJ) filed a civil action suit against one of the largest securities markets in the world, The NASDAQ Stock Market, Inc. (NASDAQ). In its suit, the DOJ alleged that 24 major brokerage firms that made markets in stocks traded on the NASDAQ implicitly colluded to increase the inside spread—the transaction cost for buying and selling NAS-DAQ stocks—to a level above what would be expected in a competitive market.

NASDAQ is an electronic securities exchange. Investors place orders to buy and sell through dealers belonging to the National Association of Securities Dealers (NASD), a self-regulatory organization that is responsible for regulating its member firms. The dealers, also known as market makers, are located throughout the United States and communicate via either a centralized computer system or telephone. To determine the price or quote of an individual NASDAQ stock, dealers simultaneously post (to the computer system) the prices at which they are willing to buy or sell particular securities, respectively, the "bid" and "ask" prices. The difference between the dealer's bid and ask price is called the dealer spread. The wider the spread, the more money it earns.

The DOJ's suit claimed that beginning as early as 1989 dealers came to a common understanding—a quoting convention—about the way bid and ask prices would be displayed on NASDAQ. Dealers not complying with the quoting convention were "punished" into compliance. Initially, telephone calls were made to dealers and traders not complying with the quoting convention. If the telephone call did not work, some dealers would threaten to stop dealing with certain rogue traders, something that is extremely painful for a dealer who needs to cover a position in a stock.

In 1997, the firms reached a settlement agreement, without admitting or denying the allegations, with the DOJ. The settlement requires firms to adhere to new oversight rules, including spot checks of trading activity and randomly taped trading desk conversations. Also, the settlement prohibits firms from engaging in the anticompetitive practices of spread manipulation or coercion by intimidation.

Sources: Deborah Lohse, "Judge Approves Settlement with 24 Big NASDAQ Dealers," *The Wall Street Journal Interactive Edition,* April 24, 1997; William G. Christie and Paul H. Schultz, "Policy Watch: Did NASDAQ Market Makers Implicitly Collude?" *Journal of Economic Perspectives* 9(3), Summer 1995, pp. 199–208; *United States v. Alex Brown & Sons Inc., et al.*

the one-time gain is more than offset by lost future sales. Notice that this is true even if your firm cannot be sued or if there are no government regulations against selling shoddy merchandise.

Second, you should recognize that any production process is likely to have "bad runs," in which some low-quality products are produced out of honest error. Notice in this example that even if the firm "tried" to produce high-quality merchandise but, due to an inadvertent error, one unit was defective, that error could ruin the firm. To guard against this, many firms offer guarantees that the product will be of high quality. That way, if an error occurs in production, the consumer can obtain a new item, be satisfied, and not "punish" the firm by spreading the news that it sells shoddy merchandise.

Finitely Repeated Games

So far we have considered two extremes: games that are played only once and games that are played infinitely many times. This section summarizes important implications of games that are repeated a finite number of times, that is, games that eventually end. We will consider two classes of *finitely repeated games:* (1) games in which players do not know when the game will end and (2) games in which players know when it will end.

TABLE 10–10	A Pricing Game That Is Finitely Repeated	

		Firm B	
	Price	**Low**	**High**
Firm A	**Low**	0, 0	50, −40
	High	−40, 50	10, 10

Games with an Uncertain Final Period

Suppose two duopolists repeatedly play the pricing game in Table 10–10 until their products become obsolete, at which point the game ends. Thus, we are considering a finitely repeated game. Suppose the firms do not know the exact date at which their products will become obsolete. Thus, there is uncertainty regarding the final period in which the game will be played.

Suppose the probability that the game will end after a given play is Θ, where $0 < \Theta < 1$. Thus, when a firm makes today's pricing decision, there is a chance that the game will be played again tomorrow; if the game is played again tomorrow, there is a chance that it will be played again the next day; and so on. For example, if $\Theta = 1/2$ there is a 50-50 chance the game will end after one play, a 1/4 chance it will end after two plays, a 1/8 chance that it will end after three plays, or, more generally, a $(½)^t$ chance that the game will end after t plays of the game. It is as if a coin is flipped at the end of every play of the game, and if the coin comes up heads, the game terminates. The game terminates after t plays if the first heads occurs after t consecutive tosses of the coin.

It turns out that when there is uncertainty regarding precisely when the game will end, the finitely repeated game in Table 10–10 exactly mirrors our analysis of infinitely repeated games. To see why, suppose the firms adopt trigger strategies, whereby each agrees to charge a high price provided the other has not charged a low price in any previous period. If a firm deviates by charging a low price, the other firm will "punish" it by charging a low price until the game ends. For simplicity, let us assume the interest rate is zero so that the firms do not discount future profits.

Given such trigger strategies, does firm A have an incentive to cheat by charging a low price? If A cheats by charging a low price when B charges a high price, A's profits are $50 today but zero in all remaining periods of the game. This is because cheating today "triggers" firm B to charge a low price in all future periods, and the best A can do in these periods is to earn $0. Thus, if firm A cheats today, it earns

$$\Pi_{Firm\ A}^{Cheat} = \$50$$

regardless of whether the game ends after one play, two plays, or whenever.

If firm A does not cheat, it earns $10 today. In addition, there is a probability of $1 - \Theta$ that the game will be played again, in which case the firm will earn another $10. There is also a probability of $(1 - \Theta)^2$ that the game will not terminate after two plays, in which case A will earn yet another $10. Carrying out this reasoning for all possible dates at which the game terminates, we see that firm A can expect to earn

$$\Pi_{Firm\ A}^{Coop} = 10 + (1 - \Theta)10 + (1 - \Theta)^2 10 + (1 - \Theta)^3 10 + \cdots = \frac{10}{\Theta}$$

if it does not cheat. In this equation, Θ is the probability the game will terminate after one play. Notice that when $\Theta = 1$, firm A is certain the game will end after one play; in this case, A's profits if it cooperates are $10. But if $\Theta < 1$, the probability the game will end after one play is less than 1 (there is a chance they will play again), and the profits of cooperating are greater than $10.

The important thing to notice is that when the game is repeated a finite but uncertain number of times, the benefits of cooperating look exactly like the benefits of cooperating in an infinitely repeated game, which are

$$PV^{Coop}_{Firm\,A} = 10 + \frac{10}{1+i} + \frac{10}{(1+i)^2} + \frac{10}{(1+i)^3} + \cdots = \frac{10(1+i)}{i}$$

where i is the interest rate. In a repeated game with an uncertain end point, $1 - \Theta$ plays the role of $1/(1 + i)$; players discount the future not because of the interest rate but because they are not certain future plays will occur.

In a finitely repeated game with an unknown endpoint, firm A has no incentive to cheat if it expects to earn less from cheating than from not cheating. For the numbers in our example, firm A has no incentive to cheat if

$$\Pi^{Cheat}_{Firm\,A} = 50 \le \frac{10}{\Theta} = \Pi^{Coop}_{Firm\,A}$$

which is true if $\Theta \le 1/5$. In other words, if after each play of the game the probability the game will end is less than 20 percent, firm A will lose more by cheating than it will gain. Since firm B's incentives are symmetric, the same is true for B. Thus, when oligopolistic firms compete a finite but uncertain number of times, it is possible for them to collude and charge high prices—to earn $10 each period—just as they can when they know the game will be played forever. The key is that there must be a sufficiently high probability that the game will be played in subsequent periods. In the extreme case where $\Theta = 1$, players are certain they will play the game only once. In this case, the profits of cheating ($50) are much greater than the profits of cooperating ($10), and collusion cannot work. This should come as no surprise to you; when $\Theta = 1$, the game is really a one-shot game, and the dominant strategy for each firm is to charge the low price.

Demonstration PROBLEM 10–7

Two cigarette manufacturers repeatedly play the following simultaneous-move billboard advertising game. If both advertise, each earns profits of $0 million. If neither advertises, each earns profits of $10 million. If one advertises and the other does not, the firm that advertises earns $20 million and the other firm loses $1 million. If there is a 10 percent chance that the government will ban cigarette sales in any given year, can the firms "collude" by agreeing not to advertise?

Answer

The normal form of the one-shot game that is to be repeated an uncertain number of times is presented in Table 10–11. Suppose the players have adopted a trigger strategy, whereby each agrees not to advertise provided the other firm has not advertised in any previous period. If a firm deviates by advertising, the other firm will "punish" the offender by advertising until the game ends. If firm A cheats on the agreement, its profits are $20 today but $0 in all subsequent periods until the game terminates. If firm A does not cheat, it can expect to earn

$$\Pi_{Firm\ A}^{Coop} = 10 + (0.90)10 + (0.90)^2 10 + (0.90)^3 10 + \cdots = \frac{10}{0.10} = 100$$

(this assumes the interest rate is 0). Since $20 < $100, firm A has no incentive to cheat. The incentives for firm B are symmetric. Thus, the firms can collude by using this type of trigger strategy.

TABLE 10–11 A Billboard Advertising Game			
		Firm B	
	Strategy	Advertise	Don't Advertise
Firm A	Advertise	0, 0	20, −1
	Don't Advertise	−1, 20	10, 10

Repeated Games with a Known Final Period: The End-of-Period Problem

Now suppose a game is repeated some known finite number of times. For simplicity, we will suppose the game in Table 10–12 is repeated two times. However, the arguments that follow apply even when a game is repeated a larger number of times (for example, 1000 times), provided the players know precisely when the game will end and the game has only one Nash equilibrium.

The important thing about repeating the game in Table 10–12 two times is that in the second play of the game there is no tomorrow, and thus each firm has an incentive to use the same strategy during that period that it would use in a one-shot version of the game. Since there is no possibility of playing the game in the third period, the players cannot punish their rival for actions it takes in the second period. For this game, this implies that each player will charge a low price in period 2; even if firm B thought firm A would "cooperate" by charging a high price during the second period, A would maximize its profits by charging a low price during the last period. There is nothing B could do in the future to "punish" A for doing so. In fact, A would be very happy if B charged a high price in the second period; if it did, A could charge a low price and earn profits of $50.

Of course, firm B knows firm A has an incentive to charge a low price in period 2 (the last period) and will likewise want to charge a low price in this period. Since both players know their opponent will charge a low price in the second period, the

TABLE 10–12 A Pricing Game			
		Firm B	
	Price	Low	High
Firm A	Low	0, 0	50, −40
	High	−40, 50	10, 10

first period is essentially the last period. There is a tomorrow, but it is the last period, and each player knows what the opponent will do in the last period. Thus, in period 1, each player has an incentive to choose the same strategy as in a one-shot version of the game, namely, charge a low price. In short, the Nash equilibrium for the two-shot version of the game in Table 10–12 is to charge a low price each period. Each player earns zero profits during each of the two periods.

In fact, collusion cannot work even if the game is played for 3 periods, 4 periods, or even 1000 periods, provided the firms know precisely when the game will end. The key reason firms cannot collude in a finitely repeated known endpoint version of the game in Table 10–12 is that eventually a point will come when both players are certain there is no tomorrow. At that point, any promises to "cooperate" made during previous periods will be broken, because there is no way a player can be punished tomorrow for having broken the promise. Effectively, a player has an incentive to break a promise in the second to the last period, since there is no effective punishment during the last period. Because all the players know this, there is effectively no tomorrow in the third period from the last. This type of "backward unravelling" continues until the players realize no effective punishment can be used during any period. The players charge low prices in every period, right up to the known last period.

Demonstration PROBLEM 10–8

You and a rival will play the game in Table 10–12 two times. Suppose your strategy is to charge a high price each period provided your opponent never charged a low price in any previous period. How much will you earn? Assume the interest rate is zero.

Answer

Given your strategy, your opponent's best strategy is to charge a high price the first period and a low price the second period. To see why, note that if she charges a high price each period, she will earn 10 the first period and 10 the second period, for a total of 20 units of profit. She does better by charging a high price the first period (earning 10 units) and a low price the second period (earning 50 units), for a total of 60 units of profit. You will earn 10 units the first period but lose 40 units the second period, for a total loss of 30 units. Since each of you knows exactly when the game will end, trigger strategies will not enhance your profits.

Applications of the End-of-Period Problem

When players know precisely when a repeated game will end, what is known as the *end-of-period problem* arises. In the final period there is no tomorrow, and there is no way to "punish" a player for doing something "wrong" in the last period. Consequently, in the last period, players will behave just as they would in a one-shot game. In this section, we will examine some implications of the end-of-period problem for managerial decisions.

Resignations and Quits

As we discussed in Chapter 6, one reason workers find it in their interest to work hard is that they are implicitly threatened with the prospect of being fired if they get caught not working. As long as the benefits of shirking are less than the cost to workers of getting fired, workers will find it in their interest to work hard.

When a worker announces that she or he plans to quit, say, tomorrow, the cost of shirking to the worker is considerably reduced. Specifically, since the worker does not plan to work tomorrow anyway, the benefits of shirking on the last day generally will exceed the expected costs. In other words, since the worker does not plan to show up tomorrow, the "threat" of being fired has no bite.

What can the manager do to overcome this problem? One possibility is to "fire" the worker as soon as he or she announces the plan to quit. While in some instances there are legal restrictions against this practice, there is a more fundamental reason why a firm should not adopt such a policy. If you, as a manager, adopt a strategy of firing workers as soon as they notify you they plan to quit, how will workers respond? The best strategy for a worker would be to wait and tell you at the end of the day he or she plans to quit! By keeping the plan to quit a secret, the worker gets to work longer than he or she would otherwise. Notice that the worker's incentive to shirk is just as strong as it would be if you did not adopt this policy. Consequently, you will not solve the end-of-period problem, but instead will be continually "surprised" by worker resignations, with no lead time to find new workers to replace them.

A better managerial strategy is to provide some rewards for good work that extend beyond the termination of employment with your firm. For instance, you can emphasize to workers that you are very well connected and will be pleased to write a letter of recommendation should a worker need one in the future. By doing this, you send a signal to workers that quitting is not really the end of the game. If a worker takes advantage of the end-of-period problem, you, being well connected, can "punish" the worker by informing other potential employers of this fact.

The "Snake Oil" Salesman

In old TV westerns, "snake oil" salesmen move from town to town, selling bottles of an elixir that is promised to cure every disease known to humankind. Unfortunately, buyers of the "medicine" soon learn that it is worthless and that they have been had. Nonetheless, these salesmen make a livelihood selling the worthless substance because they continue moving from town to town. By moving about, they ensure that buyers cannot "punish" them for selling worthless bottles of fluid. In contrast, if a local merchant were to sell worthless medicine, customers could have punished him or her by refusing to buy from the merchant in the future. As we saw earlier, this threat can be used to induce firms to sell products of good quality. But in the days of the "snake oil" salesman, no such threat was possible.

For punishments to work, there must be some way to link the past, present, and future as it relates to the seller. The inadequate communication networks of the Old West precluded consumers from spreading the word about the salesman to future customers; thus, the loss of his "reputation" was not a threat to him. However, over time consumers learned from past experience not to trust such salesmen, and when a new salesman came to town, they would "run him out."

Perhaps you have learned from experience that "sidewalk vendors" sell inferior merchandise. The reason, as you should now recognize, is that consumers have no way of tracking such vendors down in the event the merchandise is inferior. These salespeople indeed take advantage of the end-of-period problem.

Multistage Games

An alternative class of games is called *multistage games*. Multistage games differ from the class of games examined earlier in that timing is very important.

Theory

To understand how multistage games differ from one-shot and infinitely repeated games, it is useful to introduce the extensive form of a game. An **extensive-form game** summarizes who the players are, the information available to the players at each stage of the game, the strategies available to the players, the order of the moves of the game, and the payoffs that result from the alternative strategies.

Once again, the best way to understand the extensive-form representation of a game is by way of example. Figure 10–1 depicts the extensive form of a game. The circles are called *decision nodes*, and each circle indicates that at that stage of the game the particular player must choose a strategy. The single point (denoted A) at which all of the lines originate is the beginning of the game, and the numbers at the ends of the branches represent the payoffs at the end of the game. For example, in this game player A moves first. A's feasible strategies are *up* or *down*. Once player A moves, it is player B's turn. Player B must then decide whether to move *up* or *down*. If both players move *up*, player A receives a payoff of 10 and player B receives a payoff of 15. If player A moves *up* and player B moves *down*, both players receive a payoff of 5. Thus, the first number in parentheses reflects the payoff to player A (the first mover in the game), while the second number refers to the payoff of player B (the second mover).

As in simultaneous-move games, each player's payoff depends not only on his or her action but on the action of the other player as well. For example, if player A moves *down* and player B moves *up*, the resulting payoff to A is 0. But if player B moves *down* when player A moves *down*, A receives 6.

There is, however, an important difference between the sequential-move game depicted in Figure 10–1 and the simultaneous-move games examined in the previous sections. Since player A must make a decision before player B, A cannot make actions conditional on what B does. Thus, A can choose only *up* or *down*. In contrast, B gets to make a decision after A. Consequently, a strategy for player B will specify an action for both of his decision nodes. If player A chooses *up*, player B can choose either *up* or *down*. If A chooses *down*, B can choose either *up* or *down*. Thus, one example of a strategy for B is to choose *up* if A chooses *up*, and *down* if A chooses *down*. Notice that player B's strategy is allowed to depend on what player A has done, since this is a sequential-move game and B moves second. In contrast, there is no conditional "if" in player A's strategy.

FIGURE 10–1 A Sequential-Move Game in Extensive Form

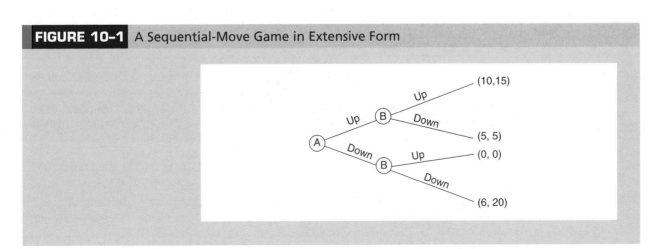

To illustrate how strategies work in sequential-move games, suppose player B's strategy is: "Choose *down* if player A chooses *up,* and *down* if player A chooses *down.*" Given this strategy, what is the best choice by player A? If A chooses *up,* she earns 5, since B will choose *down.* If A chooses *down,* she earns 6, since B will choose *down.* Given a choice between earning 5 and 6, player A prefers 6 and therefore will choose *down.*

Given that player A chooses *down,* does player B have an incentive to change his strategy? B's strategy specifies that he chooses *down* if A chooses *down.* By choosing down B earns 20, whereas he earns 0 by choosing *up.* We thus see that player B has no incentive to change his strategy given that player A chose *down.*

Since neither player has an incentive to change his or her strategies, we have found a Nash equilibrium to the game in Figure 10–1. These strategies are:

Player A: *down*

Player B: *down* if player A chooses *up,* and *down* if player A chooses *down*

The payoffs that result in this equilibrium are 6 for player A and 20 for player B.

You should ask yourself whether this is a reasonable outcome for the game. In particular, notice that the highest payoff for player A results when A chooses *up* and B chooses *up* as well. Why didn't player A choose *up?* Because player B "threatened" to choose *down* if A chose *up.* Should player A believe this threat? If she chooses *up,* player B's best choice is *up,* since the payoff of 15 is better for B than the payoff of 5 that results from choosing *down.* But if B chooses *up,* A earns 10. This is higher than the payoff that resulted in the Nash equilibrium we examined earlier.

What do we make of all this? There is, in fact, another Nash equilibrium to this game. In particular, suppose player B's strategy is "Choose *up* if player A chooses *up,* choose *down* if player A chooses *down.*" Given this strategy by player B, player A earns 10 by choosing *up* and 6 by choosing *down.* Clearly the best response by A to this strategy by B is *up.* Given that player A chooses *up,* player B has no incentive to change his strategy, and thus we have another Nash equilibrium. In this Nash equilibrium, player A earns 10 and player B earns 15.

Which of these two Nash equilibrium outcomes is the more reasonable? The answer is the second one. The reason is as follows. In the first Nash equilibrium, player A chooses *down* because player B threatened to play *down* if A chooses *up.* But player A should recognize that this threat is really not credible. If this stage of the game (decision node) were in fact reached, player B would have an incentive to renege on his threat to choose *down.* Choosing *down* at this stage of the game would result in lower profits for B than he would earn by choosing *up.* Player B therefore has no incentive to do what he said he would do. In the jargon of game theory, the Nash equilibrium in which player A earns 6 and player B earns 20 is not a subgame perfect equilibrium. A set of strategies constitutes a **subgame perfect equilibrium** if (1) it is a Nash equilibrium and (2) at each stage of the game (decision node) neither player can improve her payoff by changing her own strategy. Thus, a subgame perfect equilibrium is a Nash equilibrium that involves only credible threats. For the game in Figure 10–1, the only subgame perfect equilibrium is for player A to choose *up,* and player B to follow this move with *up.*

The analysis in this section typically is difficult for students to grasp on the first or second reading, so I encourage you to review this section if you are not clear on the concepts presented. Before you do so, or move on to the next section, let me provide a fable that may help you understand the notion of a subgame perfect equilibrium.

A teenager is given the following instructions by her father: "If you're not home by midnight, I'll burn down the house and you will lose everything you own." If the teenager believes her father, it will certainly be in her best interest to return before

subgame perfect equilibrium
A condition describing a set of strategies that constitutes a Nash equilibrium and allows no player to improve his own payoff at any stage of the game by changing strategies.

midnight, since she does not want to lose everything she owns. And if the teenager returns before midnight, the father never has to burn down the house; there is no cost to the father of threatening to do so. The threat of the father and the return of the daughter before midnight are Nash equilibrium strategies. However, they are not sub-game perfect equilibrium strategies. The father's threat to burn down the house, which is what led the teenager to choose to return before midnight, is not credible. The father will not find it in his interest to burn down his own house if his daughter returns late. If the daughter knows this, she knows that the threat is not credible and will not let it affect whether or not she returns home before midnight. Thus, since the Nash equilibrium is obtained by a threat that is not credible, it is not a subgame perfect equilibrium.

Applications of Multistage Games

The Entry Game

To illustrate the use of the theory of multistage games in a market setting, consider the extensive-form game presented in Figure 10–2. Here, firm B is an existing firm in the market and firm A is a potential entrant. Firm A must decide whether to enter the market (*in*) or stay out (*out*). If A decides to stay out of the market, firm B continues its existing behaviour and earns profits of $10 million, while A earns $0. But if A decides to enter the market, B must decide whether to engage in a price war (*hard*) or to simply share the market (*soft*). By choosing *hard,* firm B ensures that firm A incurs a loss of $1 million, but B makes only $1 million in profits. On the other hand, if firm B chooses *soft* after A enters, A takes half of the market and each firm earns profits of $5 million.

It turns out that there are two Nash equilibria for this game. The first occurs where firm B threatens to choose *hard* if A enters the market, and thus A stays *out* of the market. To see that these strategies indeed comprise a Nash equilibrium, note the following. Given that firm B's strategy is to choose *hard* if firm A enters, A's best choice is not to enter. Given that A doesn't enter, B may as well threaten to choose *hard* if A enters. Thus, neither firm has an incentive to change its strategy; firm A earns $0, and firm B earns profits of $10 million.

However, this Nash equilibrium involves a threat that is not credible. The reason firm A chooses not to enter is that firm B threatens to choose *hard* if A enters. Does B have an incentive to carry through its threat of choosing *hard* if firm A enters? The answer is no. Given that firm A enters the market, firm B will earn $5 million by choosing *soft* but only $1 million by choosing *hard*. If firm A enters, it is not in firm

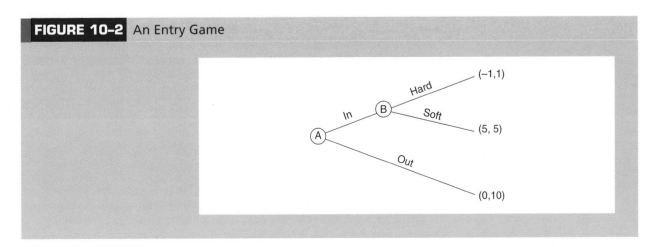

FIGURE 10–2 An Entry Game

B's best interest to play *hard*. Thus, the outcome in which firm A stays out of the market because firm B threatens to choose *hard* if it enters is a Nash equilibrium, but it is not a subgame perfect equilibrium. It involves a threat that is not credible, namely, the threat by firm B to engage in a price war if firm A enters.

The other Nash equilibrium for this game is for firm A to choose *in* and firm B to follow this move by playing *soft*. In particular, if firm A enters, firm B's best choice is to play *soft* (by playing *soft*, B earns 5 instead of the 1 it would earn by playing *hard*). Given that firm B plays *soft* if firm A enters, A's best choice is to enter (by choosing *in*, A earns 5 instead of the 0 it would earn by staying out). This is a subgame perfect equilibrium, because it is clearly in firm B's self-interest to play *soft* whenever A chooses to enter. Thus, while there are two Nash equilibria for the entry game, there is a unique subgame perfect equilibrium in which firm A chooses *in* and firm B plays *soft*.

Innovation

Our analysis of the entry game reveals an important lesson for future managers: It does not pay to heed threats made by rivals when the threats are not credible. We can also use the theory of sequential, or multistage, games to analyze innovation decisions, as the next problem illustrates.

Demonstration PROBLEM 10–9

Your firm must decide whether or not to introduce a new product. If you introduce the new product, your rival will have to decide whether or not to clone the new product. If you don't introduce the new product, you and your rival will earn $1 million each. If you introduce the new product and your rival clones it, you will lose $5 million and your rival will earn $20 million (you have spent a lot on research and development, and your rival doesn't have to make this investment to compete with its clone). If you introduce the new product and your rival does not clone, you will make $100 million and your rival will make $0.

1. Set up the extensive form of this game.
2. Should you introduce the new product?
3. How would your answer change if your rival has "promised" not to clone your product?
4. What would you do if patent law prevented your rival from cloning your product?

Answer

1. The new-product game is depicted in Figure 10–3. Note that this is a multistage game in which your firm (A) moves first, followed by your rival (B).
2. If you introduce the product, B's best choice is to clone, in which case your firm loses $5 million. If you don't introduce the product, you earn $1 million. Thus, your profit-maximizing decision is not to introduce the new product.
3. If you believe your rival's "promise" not to clone, you will earn $100 million by introducing the new product and only $1 million if you do not introduce it. However, B's promise is not credible; B would love you to spend money developing the product so that B could clone it and earn profits of $20 million. In this case, you stand to lose $5 million. Since the promise is not credible, you had better think twice about letting it affect your behaviour.
4. If you can obtain a patent on your new product, B will be forced by law to refrain from cloning. In this case, you should introduce the product to earn $100 million. This illustrates that the ability to patent a new product often induces firms to introduce products that they would not introduce in the absence of a patent system.

FIGURE 10–3 An Innovation Game

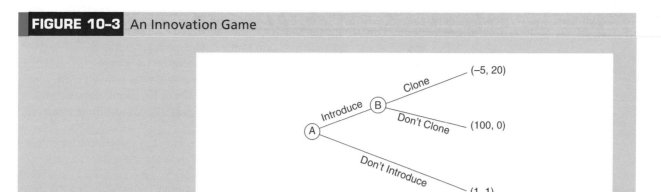

Sequential Bargaining

The final application of multistage games that we will consider is a *sequential-move bargaining game*. Specifically, suppose a firm and a labour union are engaged in negotiations over how much of a $100 surplus will go to the union and how much will go to management. Suppose management (M) moves first by offering an amount to the union (U). Given the offer, the union gets to decide to accept or reject the offer. If the offer is rejected, neither party receives anything. If the offer is accepted, the union gets the amount specified and management gets the residual. To simplify matters, suppose management can offer the union one of three amounts: $1, $50, or $99.

The extensive form of this game is depicted in Figure 10–4. Notice that the union gets to make its decision after it learns of management's offer. For instance, if management offers the union $1 and the union accepts the offer, management gets $99 and the union gets $1. If the union rejects the offer, both parties get $0.

Suppose you are management and the union makes the following statement to you before you make an offer: "Give us $99 or else we will reject the offer." What should you do? If you believe the union, then if you offered it a lower amount, it would reject the offer and you would get nothing. Given the union's strategy, your best choice is to give the union $99, since that action gives you a payoff of $1 instead of $0. And given that you offer the union $99, its best choice is to accept the offer.

FIGURE 10–4 A Sequential-Move Bargaining Game

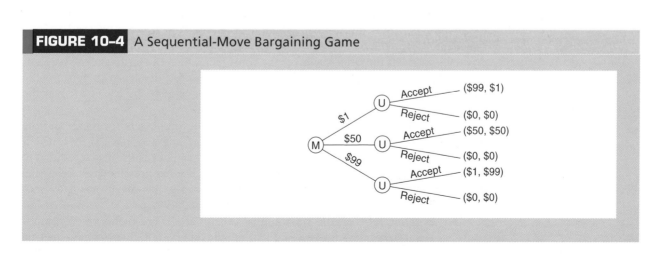

Thus, one Nash equilibrium outcome of this sequential bargaining process yields $1 for management and $99 for the union.

Does this mean that the optimal action for management is to give the union $99? The answer is no. Notice that this equilibrium is supported by a union threat that is not credible. According to the union, if management offered the union $1, the union would reject the offer. But by rejecting such an offer, the union would earn $0 instead of the $1 it could earn by accepting it. Thus, it is not in the union's best interest to reject the offer.

In fact, the unique subgame perfect equilibrium for this sequential bargaining game is for management to offer the union $1 and for the union to accept the offer. To see this, notice that if management offered the union $1, the union's best choice would be to accept, since $1 is preferred to the $0 it would earn by rejecting the offer. In this sequential-move bargaining game, the unique subgame perfect equilibrium is for management to get $99 and the union $1.

Demonstration PROBLEM 10–10

Consider the bargaining game just described, but suppose the order of play is reversed: the union gets to make an offer, and then management decides whether to accept or reject it. What is the subgame perfect equilibrium outcome of this bargaining process?

Answer

The profit-maximizing choice by management to any offer is to accept it if that yields more than the $0 management would earn by rejecting the offer. Therefore, the subgame perfect equilibrium is for the union to offer management $1 and keep $99 for itself. Given this offer, management's best choice is to accept it. Any threat by management to refuse an offer of $1 or $50 would not be credible.

This section has illustrated a remarkable feature of two-stage sequential bargaining games. Effectively, the first mover in the bargaining game makes a take-it-or-leave-it offer. The second mover can accept the offer or reject it and receive nothing. The player making the take-it-or-leave-it offer extracts virtually all of the amount bargained over. The following example illustrates this principle.

Suppose a consumer wishes to buy a car that the dealer values at $10 000. The consumer values the car at $12 000. Effectively, the bargaining game is over the $2000 difference between the consumer's valuation and the dealer's cost. Suppose the consumer makes the following take-it-or-leave-it offer to the dealer: "I'll pay you $10 001 for the car. If you don't accept it, I will buy a car from the dealer down the road." If the dealer believes the consumer's threat to terminate the bargaining process if the offer is rejected, he will accept the offer; the dealer prefers earning $1 to earning $0 by not selling the car. The consumer buys the car at $1 over the dealer's cost.

In contrast, suppose the order of the bargaining process is reversed, and the dealer tells the consumer: "Another buyer wants the car. Pay me $11 999, or I'll sell it to the other customer." In this case, if the buyer believes the dealer's threat to sell to another buyer is credible and has no other options, her best choice is to buy the car, since it costs $1 less than her valuation. In this case, the dealer makes a handsome profit.

In concluding this section, we note that several aspects of reality often complicate sequential-bargaining processes. First, the players do not always know the true payoffs to other players. For instance, if a car buyer does not know the dealer's cost of a car, he or she cannot make a take-it-or-leave-it offer and be assured of getting the car. Similarly, if a dealer does not know the maximum price a consumer will pay for a car, she or he cannot be assured of making a sale by making a take-it-or-leave-it offer. In bargaining processes, it is worthwhile to invest some time in learning about your opponent. This explains why there is a market for publications that specialize in providing information to consumers about the dealer cost of automobiles.

Second, an important assumption in the bargaining process analyzed in this section is that bargaining terminates as soon as the second player rejects or accepts an offer. If this were not the case, the person making the decision to accept or reject the offer might reason as follows: "If I reject the offer, perhaps the other party will make a new, more attractive offer." Effectively, this changes the game and can change the players' underlying decisions. On the other hand, a player who can credibly commit to making a take-it-or-leave-it offer will do very well in the bargaining game. But if the commitment is not credible, he or she may end up "eating crow" when the other party makes a counteroffer that the first player would prefer over walking away from the bargaining table.

Strategic Behaviour: Threats, Commitments, and Credibility

This section summarizes part of the earlier discussion pertaining to strategic behaviour of firms in oligopolistic market structures. Like most really powerful ideas, the basic notion of Nash equilibrium is very simple, even obvious. Its mathematical extensions and implications are not, however. The idea of this natural "sticking point" is that no single player can benefit from unilaterally changing his or her move—a noncooperative best-response equilibrium. Competitive markets come to rest at Nash equilibrium, and the special structure of competitive markets makes them efficient. But it is important to recognize that most Nash equilibria are noncooperative (inefficient). The famous example of inefficiency is the so-called "prisoner's dilemma," whose main message is not to get caught in it. Being in the dilemma means there are unconsummated wealth-creating transactions, and getting out of it means consummating them.

One way out of a prisoner's dilemma is to make a *strategic move*—one that influences the choice of your rival in a manner you find favourable. Strategic moves are also used by firms that engage in noncooperative strategic behaviour to harm their rivals and thereby benefit themselves. Firms use many techniques to prevent rivals from entering a market, to drive rivals out of a market, or to reduce the size of a rival.

Thomas Schelling initiated the formal study of strategic behaviour and introduced many of the important concepts in his path-breaking book *The Strategy of Conflict* (1973). He distinguishes between threats, promises, and commitments.

threats
Penalties to be imposed on a rival if she takes an action.

promises
A reward offered to the rival if she takes some actions.

commitment
A threat or promise, if carrying out the punishment or reward is in one's best interest.

Threats denote a penalty to be imposed on a rival if she takes some action. **Promises** involve a reward to be conferred on a rival if she takes some action. A threat or a promise becomes a **commitment** if carrying out the punishment or reward is in fact in one's best interest. The role of a strategic move is to convert a threat or promise into a commitment. This concept is elaborated on in Chapter 13.

A key issue for strategic analysis is whether these threats are credible. The threat is not credible if the firm's rival makes a wrong move and the firm finds out that it is not in its interest to carry out the threat. On the other hand, the firm's credibility is enhanced if it can *commit* to carrying out threats or promises. For a firm's strategic behaviour to work, it must demonstrate that it will follow its strategy regardless of the actions of its rivals, and that it will remain committed to the strategy for as long as necessary. For example, an incumbent firm may announce that it will do something drastic, such as produce large quantities of output, which in turn tends to drive down the price, if another firm enters its market. This way, the firm will develop a reputation for "punishing" aggressive rival behaviour. For example, after a rival's price cut it might price even lower. A rival, on the other hand, will look ahead and realize that if it cuts price, it will provoke punishment. If it believes it will be punished, it will not pursue such a course of action.

The more severe the threatened punishment, the less likely rivals will price low. However, the more severe the punishment, the less credible it is. What if the firm actually has to use it? If the threat is not credible, in the sense that other players do not believe this firm will actually carry it out, they will ignore it altogether.

An example of a *noncredible* threat is the game of "Chicken," in which two drivers align their automobiles on a collision course and then drive at high speed, and whoever swerves first is deemed the "loser." Both before and during this game, each driver is threatening the other: "You better swerve, because I won't." There is one sure way to win this game: convert the noncredible threat into a commitment.

The ability to effectively choose other people's beliefs in a strategic situation either by making credible announcements, committing future actions, or establishing a reputation for trustworthiness is valuable, because it allows one to influence their behaviour in desirable ways. In many situations it seems possible for reputation developed through repeated interaction to substitute for formal commitments.

Demonstration PROBLEM 10–11

Consider the game tree shown in Figure 10–5. In this game, players 1 and 2 have two strategic choices: price low and price high. Accordingly, firm 2 tells firm 1 that it will punish severely if firm 1 prices low. If firm 1 prices low and firm 2 follows through on its threat, both firms will incur a loss of $200, whereas if firm 2 does not punish, firm 1 will earn $60 and firm 2 will receive $30. On the other hand, if firm 1 prices high, firm 2 will also price high and each firm will earn $50. Is this threat credible?

Answer

If firm 1 believes firm 2, the equilibrium is attained when both price high. The more severe the punishment, the less likely rivals will price low. If firm 1 does price low, firm 2 would do better by not punishing firm 1; that is, the threat is not credible.

FIGURE 10–5 A Noncredible Game

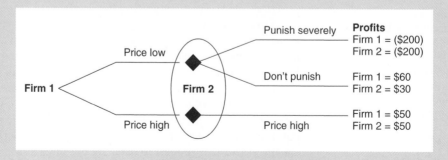

Inside BUSINESS

10-6 Strategic Commitment with R&D

A paper by Brander and Spencer, using a simple two-stage Nash duopoly model, demonstrated that when research and development (R&D) take place before the associated output is produced, imperfectly competitive firms may use R&D for strategic purposes rather than simply to minimize costs. A strategic use of R&D will increase the total amount of R&D undertaken, increase total output, lower industry profit, and raise net welfare.

R&D expenditures are typically regarded as up-front costs; that is, they are incurred before associated output is produced. When R&D levels are observable, which is very likely at least in repeated games, oligopolies may be empowered to use R&D expenditure to gain strategic advantages. In circumstances where firms' market shares depend on their own marginal costs as well as the marginal costs of their rivals, oligopolies might be motivated to shift additional resources to the overhead or sunk category in order to reduce marginal costs. Lower marginal costs in turn give rise to a greater market share. This strategic marginal cost reduction via the appropriate use of R&D is similar to the phenomena of "commitment" and "credible threat" in oligopolistic models that empha-

size the role of irreversible investments in establishing market power. If the game is played only one time, R&D levels cannot be revised once the firm engages in production. However, in a repeated game in which products are developed simultaneously—that is, no firm has a first-mover advanta—the two-step Nash equilibrium would be the oligopoly solution. In the two-step equilibrium, firms first choose R&D levels, which are made known to each other ahead of time or at least inferred, and then output levels are determined.

Nonetheless, in this environment, firms have incentives to undertake too much R&D, hence not minimizing costs. If one firm uses R&D strategically, it can increase both its output and its profit at the expense of other firms. On the other hand, if all firms attempt to do so, the industry's output will rise while firms' profits and prices fall, leading to higher net welfare of the society.

Source: J. A. Brander and B. J. Spencer, "Strategic Commitment with R&D: The Symmetric Case," *The Bell Journal of Economics*, Spring 1983, pp. 225–235.

Strategic Entry Deterrence

In addition to creating a positioning advantage over rival firms in the market, strategic investment is often used to make the entry of rival firms unprofitable. The incumbent firm earns higher profit as a monopolist than it does as a duopolist. It is said that entry is deterred if the incumbent firm can keep the entrant out by employing an entry-deterring strategy that allows the incumbent to earn positive economic profits, while making it unprofitable for newcomers to enter the industry. These barriers include actions by the incumbent to hold more (excess) capacity and to charge low prices before entry occurs.

Demonstration PROBLEM 10–12

Consider the game tree shown in Figure 10–6. In this game, players 1 and 2 have two strategic choices: enter or don't enter. Accordingly, firm 2 tells firm 1 that it will punish severely if firm 1 enters. If firm 1 enters and firm 2 follows through on its threat, both firms will incur a loss of $200, whereas if firm 2 does not punish, each firm will earn $50. On the other hand, if firm 1 does not enter, firm 2 will charge a high price to earn $100. Is this threat credible?

Answer

It is possible to apply the same logic to entry-deterring strategies. Here, if firm 1 believes firm 2 will punish it if it enters, the equilibrium is to not enter. But the punishment threat is

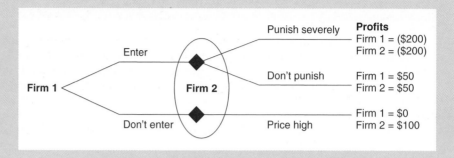

FIGURE 10–6 An Entry Deterrence Game

Firm 1

Enter → Firm 2

Punish severely — **Profits**
Firm 1 = ($200)
Firm 2 = ($200)

Don't punish — Firm 1 = $50
Firm 2 = $50

Don't enter → Firm 2

Price high — Firm 1 = $0
Firm 2 = $100

not credible, because if it did enter, firm 2 would accommodate (not punish) it. Note that if firm 1 is uncertain about what firm 2 will do, it might attach probabilities to each of the outcomes to determine the strategy that maximizes expected payoffs.

ANSWERING THE **Head**line

On the basis of the scenario stated in the Headline, the normal-form game facing the two firms is that shown in Table 10–13, where payoffs reflect the firms' payoffs in alternative scenarios.

Notice that the dominant strategy for each player in this game is not to cooperate (noncoop). Regardless of what its rivals do, each gas retailer is better off if it does not cooperate. If the two gas retailers opted for a cooperative strategy, each would earn a collusive profit of $1, but then each firm could gain customers and profits by going back to the noncooperative strategy, $2, if the other firm continued its cooperative attitude.

The prospects of this outcome in a repeated game compel the competitor to adopt a cooperative stance in the game. In a repeated game, the player could be sure of the tit-for-tat reaction down the horizon should it play aggressively at any stage. It is this possibility that compels players to play cooperatively, resulting in a cooperative solution in an otherwise inherently noncooperative game setting.

The information in the Headline with regard to the incidences/frequency over this 10-year period, reveal very low incidences reported in New Brunswick's major centres Saint John, Fredericton, and Moncton. The period before the early 1990s seems to have witnessed greater incidences of price competition in New Brunswick's cities, while the 1990s saw reduced competition.

TABLE 10–13 The Retail Gas Game

		Firm 2	
		coop	noncoop
Firm 1	coop	1, 1	−1, 2
	noncoop	2, −1	0, 0

Summary

This chapter opened with the study of Nash equilibrium in one-shot, simultaneous-move games. We learned that the resulting payoffs are sometimes lower than would arise if players colluded. The reason higher payoffs cannot be achieved in one-shot games is that each participant has an incentive to cheat on a collusive agreement. In many games, what primarily motivates firms to cheat is the fact that cheating is a dominant strategy. Dominant strategies, when they exist, determine the optimal decision in a one-shot game.

We also examined solutions to games that are infinitely repeated. The use of trigger strategies in these games enables players to enter and enforce collusive agreements when the interest rate is low. By adopting strategies that punish cheaters over long periods of time, collusive agreements can be self-enforcing when the game is infinitely repeated. Other factors that affect collusion are the number of firms, the history in the market, the ability of firms to monitor one another's behaviour, and the ability to punish cheaters. Similar features of repeated interaction also help consumers and businesses continue trading with each other and keep product quality high.

Finally, we covered finitely repeated games with both uncertain and known terminal periods, as well as sequential-move entry and bargaining games. When the interaction among parties is for a known time period, problems with cheating in the last period can unravel cooperative agreements that would have been supported by trigger strategies in infinitely repeated games or games with an uncertain endpoint. In sequential-move games, one must determine whether the threats to induce a particular outcome in the game are credible.

Key Terms and Concepts

commitment 369
dominant strategy 340
extensive-form game 363
infinitely repeated game 349
mixed (randomized) strategy 348
Nash equilibrium 342
normal-form game 340
promises 369

secure strategy 341
sequential-move game 339
simultaneous-move game 339
strategy 340
subgame perfect equilibrium 364
threats 369
tit-for-tat 351
trigger strategy 350

Conceptual and Computational Questions

1. Use the following one-shot, normal-form game to answer the questions below.

		Player 2		
	Strategy	D	E	F
Player 1	A	100, 125	300, 250	200, 100
	B	250, 0	500, 500	750, 400
	C	0, −100	400, 300	−100, 350

    a. Find each player's dominant strategy, if it exists.
    b. Find each player's secure strategy.
    c. Find the Nash equilibrium.

2. In a two-player, one-shot simultaneous-move game each player can choose strategy *A* or strategy *B*. If both players choose strategy *A*, each earns a payoff of $500. If both players choose strategy *B*, each earns a payoff of $100. If player 1 chooses strategy *A* and player 2 chooses strategy *B*, then player 1 earns $0 and player 2 earns $650. If player 1 chooses strategy *B* and player 2 chooses strategy *A*, then player 1 earns $650 and player 2 earns $0.
    a. Write the above game in normal form.
    b. Find each player's dominant strategy, if it exists.
    c. Find the Nash equilibrium (or equilibria) of this game.
    d. Rank strategy pairs by aggregate payoff (highest to lowest).
    e. Can the outcome with the highest aggregate payoff be sustained in equilibrium? Why or why not?

3. Use the following payoff matrix for a simultaneous-move one-shot game to answer the accompanying questions.

		Player 2			
	Strategy	C	D	E	F
Player 1	A	25, 15	4, 20	16, 14	28, 12
	B	10, 10	5, 15	8, 6	18, 13

    a. What is player 1's optimal strategy? Why?
    b. Determine player 1's equilibrium payoff.

4. Use the following normal-form game to answer the questions below.

		Player 2	
	Strategy	C	D
Player 1	A	10, 10	60, −5
	B	−5, 60	50, 50

    a. Identify the one-shot Nash equilibrium.
    b. Suppose the players know this game will be repeated exactly three times. Can they achieve payoffs that are better than the one-shot Nash equilibrium? Explain.
    c. Suppose this game is infinitely repeated and the interest rate is 5 percent. Can the players achieve payoffs that are better than the one-shot Nash equilibrium? Explain.
    d. Suppose the players do not know exactly how many times this game will be repeated, but they do know that the probability the game will end after a given play is Θ. If Θ is sufficiently low, can players earn more than they could in the one-shot Nash equilibrium?

5. Use the following normal-form game to answer the questions below.

		Player 2	
	Strategy	C	D
Player 1	A	1, 4 − x	2, 2
	B	2, 2	4 − x, 3

a. For what values of x is strategy D (strictly) dominant for player 2?

b. For what values of x is strategy B (strictly) dominant for player 1?

c. For what values of x is (B, D) the only Nash equilibrium of the game?

6. Consider a two-player, sequential-move game where each player can choose to play *right* or *left*. Player 1 moves first. Player 2 observes player 1's actual move and then decides to move *right* or *left*. If player 1 moves *right*, player 1 receives $0 and player 2 receives $15. If both players move *left*, player 1 receives −$10 and player 2 receives $8. If player 1 moves *left* and player 2 moves *right*, player 1 receives $10 and player 2 receives $10.

a. Write the above game in extensive form.

b. Find the Nash equilibrium outcomes to this game.

c. Which of the equilibrium outcomes is most reasonable? Explain.

7. Use the following extensive-form game to answer the questions below.

a. List the feasible strategies for player 1 and player 2.

b. Identify the Nash equilibria to this game.

c. Find the subgame perfect equilibrium.

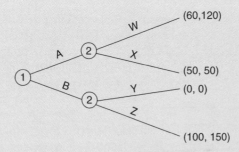

8. Use the following payoff matrix for a one-shot game to answer the following questions.

		Player 2	
	Strategy	X	Y
Player 1	A	5, 5	0, −200
	B	−200, 0	20, 20

a. Determine the Nash equilibrium outcomes that arise if the players make decisions independently, simultaneously, and without any communication. Which of these outcomes would you consider most likely? Explain.

b. Suppose player 1 is permitted to "communicate" by uttering one syllable before the players simultaneously and independently make their decisions. What should player 1 utter, and what outcome do you think would occur as a result?

c. Suppose player 2 can choose its strategy before player 1, that player 1 observes player 2's choice before making her decision, and that this move structure is known by both players. What outcome would you expect? Explain.

Problems and Applications

9. While there is a degree of differentiation among general department stores such as Sears and The Bay, weekly newspaper circulars announcing sales provide evidence that these firms engage in price competition. This suggests that Sears and The Bay simultaneously choose to announce one of two prices for a given product: a regular

price or a sale price. Suppose that when one firm announces the sale price and the other announces the regular price for a particular product, the firm announcing the sale price attracts 50 million extra customers to earn a profit of $5 billion, compared to the $3 billion earned by the firm announcing the regular price. When both firms announce the sale price, the two firms split the market equally (each getting an extra 25 million customers) to earn profits of $1 billion each. When both firms announce the regular price, each company attracts only its 50 million loyal customers and the firms each earn $3 billion in profits. If you were in charge of pricing at one of these firms, would you have a clear-cut pricing strategy? If so, explain why. If not, explain why not and propose a mechanism that might solve your dilemma. (*Hint:* General merchandise retailers like Zeller's and Wal-Mart guarantee "everyday low prices.")

10. On February 11, 2004, Honda Canada Inc. announced in a press release plans to expand its "Safety for Everyone" initiative. The "Safety for Everyone" concept is a comprehensive approach to vehicle safety that includes Front Side Airbags, Side Curtain Airbags, and Anti-Lock Brakes as standard equipment before the end of calendar year 2006. As well, all Honda and Acura light trucks, including all SUVs and minivans, will be equipped with Vehicle Stability Assist (VSA) and rollover sensors for side-curtain airbag deployment before the end of calendar year 2006. Furthermore, Honda's Advanced Compatibility Engineering (ACE) body structure, offering enhanced occupant protection with reduced "aggressivity" toward other vehicles, will be applied to all new vehicle platforms in Canada and globally over the next six to seven years.

    However, these new safety features will come with a catch, namely a price hike. Assume that these initiatives raise the average price of each vehicle by $2000. Assume also that if Honda's closest rival in Canada, Toyota, makes similar safety features standard equipment, each automaker will earn profits of $200 million. If Honda adopts the technology as standard equipment and Toyota does not, Honda will earn a profit of $300 million and Toyota will lose $150 million. If, however, Honda delays introducing new technology while Toyota adopts new technology, Honda will lose $150 million while Toyota will earn a profit of $200 million. If neither follows through on their plans, each will earn $100 million (due to lost sales to other automakers.)

    If you were a decision maker at Toyota, would you make these new initiatives standard features?

11. Coca-Cola and PepsiCo are the leading competitors in the market for cola products. In 1960 Coca-Cola introduced Sprite, which today is the worldwide leader in the lemon-lime soft drink market and ranks fourth among all soft drinks worldwide. Prior to 1999, PepsiCo did not have a product that competed directly against Sprite and had to decide whether to introduce such a soft drink. By not introducing a lemon-lime soft drink, PepsiCo would continue to earn a $200 million profit, and Coca-Cola would continue to earn a $300 million profit. Suppose that by introducing a new lemon-lime soft drink, one of two possible strategies could be pursued: (1) PepsiCo could trigger a price war with Coca-Cola in both the lemon-lime and the cola market or (2) Coca-Cola could acquiesce and each firm maintain its current 50-50 split of the cola market and split the lemon-lime market 30/70 (PepsiCo/Coca-Cola). If PepsiCo introduced a lemon-lime soft drink and a price war resulted, both companies would earn profits of $100 million. Alternatively, Coca-Cola and PepsiCo would earn $275 million and $227 million, respectively, if PepsiCo introduced a lemon-lime soft drink and Coca-Cola acquiesced and split the markets as listed above. If you were a manager at PepsiCo, would you try to convince your colleagues that introducing the new soft drink is the most profitable strategy? Why or why not?

12. The Canadian Auto Workers Union (CAW) reached a tentative labour contract agreement with Air Canada in May 2003. In the months preceding the agreement, bargaining teams for CAW and Air Canada met to negotiate a new contract. All contracts were to be ratified by the union members. Two of the issues on the table were job security and funding of airline retirement incentives. If you were an executive in charge of human resources issues at Air Canada during the negotiation phase, would you have, in the absence of hindsight, adopted the strategy of (*a*) letting the union bear the expense of crafting a document summarizing its desired compensation or (*b*) making the union a take-it-or-leave-it offer? Explain.

13. Price comparison services on the Internet (as well as "shopbots") are a popular way for retailers to advertise their products and a convenient way for consumers to simultaneously obtain price quotes from several firms selling an identical product. Suppose that you are the manager of Digital Camera Inc., a firm that specializes in selling digital cameras to consumers that advertises with an Internet price comparison service. In the market for one particular high-end camera, you have only one rival firm—The Camera Shop—with whom you've competed for the last four years by setting prices day after day. Being savvy entrepreneurs, the ease of using the Internet to monitor rival firms' prices has enabled you and your rival to charge extremely high prices for this particular camera. In a recent newspaper article, you read that The Camera Shop has exhausted its venture capital and that no new investors are willing to sink money into the company. As a result, The Camera Shop will discontinue its operations next month. Will this information alter your pricing decisions today? Explain.

14. You are the manager of a firm in Brampton, Ontario that manufactures front and rear windshields for the automobile industry. Due to economies of scale in the industry, entry by new firms is not profitable. Toyota Canada Inc., in Cambridge, Ontario, has asked your company and your only rival to simultaneously submit a price quote for supplying 100 000 front and rear windshields for its new Corolla. If both you and your rival submit a low price, each firm supplies 50 000 front and rear windshields and earns a zero profit. If one firm quotes a low price and the other a high price, the low-price firm supplies 100 000 front and rear windshields and earns a profit of $9 million and the high-price firm supplies no windshields and loses $1 million. If both firms quote a high price, each firm supplies 50 000 front and rear windshields and earns a $7 million profit. Determine your optimal pricing strategy if you and your rival believe that the new Corolla is a "special edition" that will be sold only for one year. Would your answer differ if you and your rival were required to resubmit price quotes year after year and if, in any given year, there was a 50 percent chance that Toyota Canada would discontinue the Corolla? Explain.

15. At a time when demand for ready-to-eat cereal was stagnant, a spokesperson for the cereal maker Kellogg's was quoted as saying "for the past several years, our individual company growth has come out of the other fellow's hide." Kellogg's has been producing cereal since 1906 and continues to implement strategies that make it a leader in the cereal industry. Suppose that when Kellogg's and its largest rival advertise, each company earns $0 billion in profits. When neither company advertises, each company earns profits of $8 billion. If one company advertises and the other does not, the company that advertises earns $48 billion and the company that does not advertise loses $1 billion. Under what conditions could trigger strategies be used by these firms to support the collusive level of advertising?

16. You are a pricing manager at Argyle Inc., a medium-sized firm that recently introduced a new product into the market. Argyle's only competitor is Baker Company, which is significantly smaller than Argyle. The management of Argyle has decided to pursue a short-term strategy of maximizing this quarter's revenues, and you are

in charge of formulating a strategy that will permit the firm to do so. After talking with an employee who was recently hired from the Baker Company, you are confident that (a) Baker is constrained to charge $10 or $20 for its product, (b) Baker's goal is to maximize this quarter's profits, and (c) Baker's relevant unit costs are identical to yours. You have been authorized to price the product at two possible levels ($5 or $10) and know that your relevant costs are $2 per unit. The marketing department has provided the following information about the expected number of units sold (in millions) this quarter at various prices to help you formulate your decision:

Argyle Price	Baker Price	Argyle Quantity (millions of units)	Baker Quantity (millions of units)
$ 5	$10	3	2
5	20	3	1
10	10	1	2
10	20	1	1

Argyle and Baker currently set prices at the same time. However, Argyle can become the first mover by spending $2 million on computer equipment that would permit it to set its price before Baker. Determine Argyle's optimal price and whether you should invest the $2 million.

17. You are the manager of Canadaone and must decide how many Internet hubs to produce to maximize your firm's profit. Canadaone and its only rival (NetWorks) sell dual-speed Internet hubs that are identical from consumers' perspectives. The market price for hubs depends on the total quantity produced by the two firms. A survey reveals that the market price of hubs depends on total market output as follows:

Combined Hub Production of Canadaone and NetWorks	Market Price of Hubs (per unit)
500 units	$120
750 units	100
1000 units	90

Canadaone and NetWorks each use labour, materials, and machines to produce output. Canadaone purchases labour and materials on an as-needed basis; its machines were purchased three years ago and are being depreciated according to the straight-line method. Canadaone's accounting department has provided the following data about its unit production costs:

Item	Canadaone's Unit Cost for an Output Of:	
	250 units	500 units
Direct labour	$40	$40
Direct materials	30	30
Depreciation charge	80	40

Reports from industry experts suggest that NetWork's cost structure is similar to Canadaone's and that technological constraints require each firm to produce either 250 hubs or 500 hubs. Identify the costs that are relevant for your decision, and then determine whether Canadaone should produce 250 hubs or 500 hubs.

Headline

When the new BMW-made Cooper Mini came on the market in Canada in late 2001, purchasers noticed that they were legally bound not to sell the vehicle in the United States. Now, it is quite possible that this resulted, in part, from the fact that the Cooper was at the time not available for purchase there. However, if one were to look further into the matter, one would have learned that there are a series of consequences for any U.S. purchasers of Canadian cars, either for the purchaser (not being able to use the car's warranty, for example), or the dealership (fines).

Automakers call the price differential "pricing to the market." They say they price cars lower in Canada—anywhere from 1 to 40 percent—because wages and economic conditions are below those in the United States, and taxes are higher. It's what the market will bear, they say. Plants in the United States and Canada generally make the same cars and trucks for both markets. For example, the Honda Odyssey minivan that a U.S. dealer sells for $26 750 costs about $6000 (Canadian dollars) less in Canada. A new loaded Dodge Caravan that costs $28 000 from the factory in the United States could be delivered to the customer's door from Canada for $19 500.

"Automakers price models for less in Canada than in the U.S. because Canadians won't or can't pay more. ... We can't have the same pricing in [Canada] as in the U.S. without losing [market] share. ... My issue is doing what it takes so that GM doesn't lose share," said Ron Sobrero, General Motors Corp.'s manager of dealer planning.

The case for this market differentiation is that Canada's market is much smaller and more price elastic than the U.S. market. Nevertheless, with price differentials that average $5000, there is a clear opportunity for arbitrage on the part of U.S. car dealers, and major savings for individual car buyers.

What are the implications for having two markets where almost identical products are marketed at significantly different prices? What factors might cause the price differences between the two markets? Is it just the exchange rate, or something more?

Sources: "Cheaper Cars Worth Drive: Canada's Prices Draw Americans Past Border, Leaving Detroit Angry," *Houston Chronicle*, June 2002; CarcostCanada.com <www.carcostcanada.com>; *Automotive News* <www.autonews.com>.

Introduction

In this chapter, we deal with pricing decisions by firms that have some market power: firms in monopoly, monopolistic competition, and oligopoly. As we learned in Chapter 8, firms in perfect competition have no control over the prices they charge for their products; prices are determined by market forces. Therefore, the pricing decision in perfect competition is simple: charge the same price other firms in the market charge for their products.

In contrast, firms with market power have some influence over the prices they charge. Therefore, it is important for you, as a manager, to learn some basic pricing strategies for maximizing a firm's profits. This chapter provides practical advice that you can use to implement such pricing strategies, typically using information that is readily available to managers. For instance, we will see how a manager can use publicly available information about demand elasticities to determine the profit-maximizing markup used to set product price.

The optimal pricing decisions will vary from firm to firm depending on the underlying market structure of the industry and the instruments (such as advertising) available. Thus, we will begin with basic pricing strategies used by firms in monopoly, monopolistic competition, and oligopoly to set the price that maximizes profits. Then we will develop more sophisticated pricing strategies that enable a firm to extract even greater profits. As you work through this chapter, remember that some of these more advanced pricing strategies would work in some situations but will not be viable in others. You should familiarize yourself not only with how to implement the strategies but also with the conditions under which each type of strategy is feasible.

Basic Pricing Strategies

In this section we will examine the most basic pricing strategy used by firms with market power: charge a single price to all customers such that marginal revenue equals marginal cost. We will begin with a review of the economic basis for such a pricing strategy and then discuss how it can be easily implemented in monopoly, monopolistic competition, and Cournot oligopoly.

Review of the Basic Rule of Profit Maximization

Firms with market power face a downward-sloping demand for their products. This means that by charging a higher price, the firm reduces the amount it will sell. Thus, there is a tradeoff between selling many units at a low price and selling only a few units at a high price.

In Chapter 8 we learned how the manager of a firm with market power balances off these two forces: output is set at the point where marginal revenue (MR) equals marginal cost (MC). The profit-maximizing price is the maximum price per unit that consumers will pay for this level of output. The following problem summarizes what we learned in Chapter 8 about the profit-maximizing pricing decision of a firm with market power.

Demonstration PROBLEM 11–1

Suppose the (inverse) demand for a firm's product is given by

$$P = 10 - 2Q$$

and the cost function is

$$TC(Q) = 2Q$$

What is the profit-maximizing level of output and price for this firm?

Answer

For this (inverse) demand function, marginal revenue is

$$MR = 10 - 4Q$$

and marginal cost is

$$MC = 2$$

Setting $MR = MC$ yields

$$10 - 4Q = 2$$

Thus, the profit-maximizing level of output is $Q = 2$. Substituting this into the inverse demand function yields the profit-maximizing price

$$P = 10 - 2(2) = \$6$$

A Simple Pricing Rule for Monopoly and Monopolistic Competition

As we saw in the previous section, in instances where a manager has estimates of the demand and cost functions for the firm's product, calculation of the profit-maximizing price is straightforward. In some cases, a manager lacks access to an estimated form of demand or cost functions. This is particularly true of managers of small firms that do not have research departments or funds to hire economists to estimate demand and cost functions.

Fortunately, all is not lost in these instances. It turns out that given minimal information about demand and costs, a manager can do a reasonably good job of determining what price to charge for a product. Specifically, most retailers have a rough estimate of the marginal cost of each item sold. For instance, the manager of a clothing store knows how much the store pays the supplier for each pair of jeans and thus has crude information about the marginal cost of selling jeans. (This information is "crude" because the cost to the firm of buying jeans will slightly understate the true marginal cost of selling jeans, since it does not include the cost of the sales force, etc.)

The clothing store manager also has some crude information about the elasticity of demand for jeans at its store. Chapter 7 provided tables with estimates of the elasticity of demand for a "representative firm" in broadly defined industries. For instance, Table 7–3 presented a study that estimated the own price elasticity of demand for a representative apparel firm's product to be -4.1. In the absence of better information, the manager of a clothing store can use this estimate to approximate the elasticity of demand for jeans sold at his or her store.

Thus, even small firms can obtain some information about demand and costs from publicly available information. All that remains is to show how this information can be used to make pricing decisions. The key is to recall the relation between the elasticity of demand for a firm's product and marginal revenue, which we derived in Chapter 8. This relation is summarized in the following formula.

Inside BUSINESS

11–1 Pricing Markups as Rules of Thumb

Many malls and flea markets sponsor shows to which home producers and do-it-yourselfers bring their products for fun and profit. Most of these small businesses are run by craftspeople with little or no knowledge of economics, yet they often reap large profits. One might ask how these artisans find a price that maximizes their profits—or do they?

If you ask them, you will find that most artists who frequent these shows use a rule-of-thumb markup strategy. They take the price of the materials, and add an hourly wage rate for themselves, then charge from 1.5 to 5 times their marginal cost. How do they determine the

price to charge? Through trial and error and word of mouth from artisan to artisan.

Who has higher markups, and who has lower markups? Those products that are extremely unique and show a high degree of crafting skill have the high markups, whereas the products that almost anyone with some free time could make have the low markups. This is exactly what economic theory would predict. The more unique products will have fewer substitutes and therefore will have a more inelastic demand than those that are easily copied. This fact, in turn, implies a higher profit-maximizing markup.

Formula: Marginal Revenue for a Firm with Market Power. The marginal revenue for a firm with market power is given by

$$MR = P \left[\frac{1 + E_F}{E_F} \right]$$

where E_F is the own price elasticity of demand for the firm's product and P is the price charged.

Since the profit-maximizing level of output is where marginal revenue equals marginal cost, this formula implies that

$$P \left[\frac{1 + E_F}{E_F} \right] = MC$$

at the profit-maximizing level of output. If we solve this equation for P, we obtain the profit-maximizing price for a firm with market power:

$$P = \left[\frac{E_F}{1 + E_F} \right] MC$$

In other words, the price that maximizes profits is a number K times marginal cost:

$$P = (K)MC$$

where $K = E_F/(1 + E_F)$. Remember from Chapter 7 that the relationship between P and MC is captured via the Lerner index (L) so that $K = 1/(1 - L)$, which is the markup factor. The number K can be viewed as the profit-maximizing markup factor. For the case of the clothing store, the manager's best estimate of the elasticity of demand is -4.1, so the markup factor $K = -4.1/(1 - 4.1) = 1.32$. In this instance, the profit-maximizing price is 1.32 times marginal cost:

$$P = (1.32)MC$$

Principle	**PROFIT-MAXIMIZING MARKUP FOR MONOPOLY AND MONOPOLISTIC COMPETITION**

The price that maximizes profit is given by

$$P = \left[\frac{E_F}{1 + E_F}\right] MC$$

where E_F is the own-price elasticity of demand for the firm's product and MC is the firm's marginal cost. The term in brackets is the optimal markup factor.

A manager should note two important things about this pricing rule. First, the more elastic the demand for the firm's product, the lower the profit-maximizing markup. Since demand is more elastic when there are many available substitutes for a product, managers that sell such products should have a relatively low markup. In the extreme case when the elasticity of demand is perfectly elastic ($E_F = -\infty$), this markup rule reveals that price should be set equal to marginal cost. This should come as no surprise, since we learned in Chapter 8 that a perfectly competitive firm that faces a perfectly elastic demand curve charges a price equal to marginal cost.

The second thing to notice is that the higher the marginal cost, the higher the profit-maximizing price. Firms with higher marginal costs will charge higher prices than firms with lower marginal costs, other things being the same.

Demonstration PROBLEM 11–2

The manager of a convenience store competes in a monopolistically competitive market and buys cola from a supplier at a price of $1.25 per litre. The manager thinks that because there are several supermarkets nearby, the demand for cola sold at her store is slightly more elastic than the elasticity for the representative food store reported in Table 7–3 in Chapter 7 (which is −3.8). On the basis of this information, she perceives that the elasticity of demand for cola sold by her store is −4. What price should the manager charge for a litre of cola to maximize profits?

Answer

The marginal cost of cola to the firm is $1.25, or 5/4 per litre, and $K = 4/3$. Using the pricing rule for a monopolistically competitive firm, the profit-maximizing price is

$$P = \left[\frac{4}{3}\right]\left[\frac{5}{4}\right] = \frac{5}{3}$$

or about $1.67 per litre.

A Simple Pricing Rule for Cournot Oligopoly

Recall that in Cournot oligopoly, there are few firms in the market servicing many consumers. The firms produce either differentiated or homogeneous products, and each firm believes rivals will hold their output constant if it changes its own output.

In Chapter 9 we saw that to maximize profits, a manager of a firm in Cournot oligopoly produces where marginal revenue equals marginal cost. We also saw how to calculate the profit-maximizing price and quantity given information about demand

and cost curves. Recall that this procedure requires full information about the demand and costs of all firms in the industry and is complicated by the fact that the marginal revenue of a Cournot oligopolist depends on the outputs produced by all firms in the market. Ultimately, the solution is based on the intersection of reaction functions.

Fortunately, we can also provide a simple pricing rule that can be used by managers in Cournot oligopoly. Suppose an industry consists of N Cournot oligopolists, each having identical cost structures and producing similar products. In this instance, the profit-maximizing price in Cournot equilibrium is given by a simple formula.

Principle	**PROFIT-MAXIMIZING MARKUP FOR COURNOT OLIGOPOLY**
	If there are N identical firms in a Cournot oligopoly, the profit-maximizing price for a firm in this market is

$$P = \left[\frac{NE_M}{1 + NE_M}\right] MC$$

where N is the number of firms in the industry, E_M is the market elasticity of demand, and MC is marginal cost.

A Calculus ALTERNATIVE

Instead of having to memorize this formula, we can simply substitute the relation between a Cournot oligopolist's own price elasticity of demand and that of the market into the formula for the markup rule for monopoly and monopolistic competition. In particular, for a homogeneous-product Cournot oligopoly with N firms, we will show that the elasticity of demand for an individual firm's product is N times that of the market elasticity of demand:

$$E_F = NE_M$$

When we substitute this for E_F in the pricing formula for monopoly and monopolistic competition, the result is the pricing formula for Cournot oligopoly.

To see that $E_F = NE_M$, we need a little calculus. Specifically, if

$$Q = \sum_{i=1}^{N} Q_i$$

is total industry output and industry demand is $Q = f(P)$, the own price elasticity of market demand is

$$E_M = \frac{dQ}{dP}\frac{P}{Q} = \frac{df(P)}{dP}\frac{P}{Q}$$

The demand facing an individual firm (say, firm 1) is

$$Q_1 = f(P) - Q_2 - Q_3 - \cdots - Q_N$$

Thus, since the firm views the output of other firms as fixed, the elasticity of demand for an individual firm is

$$E_F = \frac{\partial Q_1}{\partial P}\frac{P}{Q_1} = \frac{df(P)}{dP}\frac{P}{Q_1}$$

But with identical firms $Q_1 = Q/N$, so

$$E_F = \frac{df(P)}{dP} \frac{PN}{Q} = NE_M$$

which is what we needed to establish.

The pricing rule given for a firm in Cournot oligopoly has a very simple justification. When firms in a Cournot oligopoly sell identical products, the elasticity of demand for an individual firm's product is N times the market elasticity of demand:

$$E_F = NE_M$$

If $N = 1$ (monopoly), there is only one firm in the industry, and the elasticity of demand for that firm's product is the same as the market elasticity of demand ($E_F = E_M$). When $N = 2$ (Cournot duopoly), there are two firms in the market, and each firm's elasticity of demand is twice as elastic as that for the market ($E_F = 2E_M$). Thus, the markup formula for Cournot oligopoly is really identical to that presented in the previous section, except that we are using the relation between elasticity of demand for an individual firm's product and that of the market.

Three aspects of this pricing rule for Cournot oligopoly are worth noting. First, the more elastic the market demand, the closer the profit-maximizing price is to marginal cost. In the extreme case where the absolute value of the market elasticity of demand is infinite, the profit-maximizing price is marginal cost, regardless of how many firms are in the industry. Second, notice that as the number of firms increases, the profit-maximizing price gets closer to marginal cost. Notice that in the limiting case where there are infinitely many firms ($N = \infty$), the profit-maximizing price is exactly equal to marginal cost. This is consistent with our analysis of perfect competition: when many firms produce a homogeneous product, price equals marginal cost. Thus, perfect competition can be viewed as the limiting case of Cournot oligopoly, as the number of firms approaches infinity. Finally, notice that the higher the marginal cost, the higher the profit-maximizing price in Cournot oligopoly.

Demonstration PROBLEM 11–3

Suppose three firms compete in a homogeneous-product Cournot industry. The market elasticity of demand for the product is -2, and each firm's marginal cost of production is $50. What is the profit-maximizing equilibrium price?

Answer
Simply set $N = 3$, $E_M = -2$, and $MC = 50 in the markup formula for Cournot oligopoly to obtain

$$P = \left[\frac{(3)(-2)}{1 + (3)(-2)} \right] \$50 = \$60$$

Strategies That Yield Even Greater Profits

The analysis in the previous section demonstrated how a manager can implement the familiar $MR = MC$ rule for setting the profit-maximizing price. Given estimates of demand and cost functions, such a price can be computed directly. Alternatively, given publicly available estimates of demand elasticities, a manager can implement the rule by using the appropriate markup formula.

In some markets, managers can enhance profits above those they would earn by simply charging a single per-unit price to all consumers. As we will see in this section, several pricing strategies can be used to yield profits above those earned by simply charging a single price where marginal revenue equals marginal cost.

Extracting Surplus from Consumers

The first four strategies we will discuss—price discrimination, two-part pricing, block pricing, and commodity bundling—are strategies appropriate for firms with various cost structures and degrees of market interdependence. Thus, these strategies can enhance profits of firms in industries with monopolistic, monopolistically competitive, or oligopolistic structures. The pricing strategies discussed in this section enhance profits by enabling a firm to extract additional surplus from consumers.

Price Discrimination

price discrimination
The practice of charging different prices to consumers for the same good or service.

Up until this point, our analysis of pricing decisions presumes the firm must charge the same price for each unit that consumers purchase in the market. Sometimes, however, firms can earn higher profits by charging different prices for the same product or service, a strategy referred to as **price discrimination**. The three basic types of price discrimination—first-, second-, and third-degree price discrimination—are examined next. As we will see, each type requires that the manager have different types of information about consumers.

Ideally, a firm would like to engage in *first-degree price discrimination*—that is, charge each consumer the maximum price he or she would be willing to pay for each unit of the good purchased. By adopting this strategy, a firm extracts all surplus from consumers and thus earns the highest possible profits. Unfortunately for managers, first-degree price discrimination (also called perfect price discrimination) is extremely difficult to implement because it requires the firm to know precisely the maximum price each consumer is willing and able to pay for alternative quantities of the firm's product.

Nonetheless, some service-related businesses, including car dealers, mechanics, doctors, and lawyers, successfully practise a form of first-degree price discrimination. For instance, most car dealers post sticker prices on cars that are well above the dealer's actual marginal cost, but offer "discounts" to customers on a case-by-case basis. The best salespersons are able to size up customers to determine the minimum discount necessary to get them to drive away with the car. In this way they are able to charge different prices to different consumers depending on each consumer's willingness and ability to pay. This practice permits them to sell more cars and to earn higher profits than they would if they charged the same price to all consumers. Similarly, most professionals also charge rates for their services that vary, depending on their assessment of customers' willingness and ability to pay.

Panel (a) of Figure 11–1 shows how first-degree price discrimination works. Each point on the market demand curve reflects the maximum price that consumers would be willing to pay for each incremental unit of the output. Consumers start out with 0 units of the good, and the firm can sell the first incremental unit for $10. Since the demand curve slopes downward, the maximum price the firm can charge for each additional unit declines, ultimately to $4 at an output of 5 units. The difference between each point on the demand curve and the firm's marginal cost represents the

---

FIGURE 11–1 First- and Second-Degree Price Discrimination

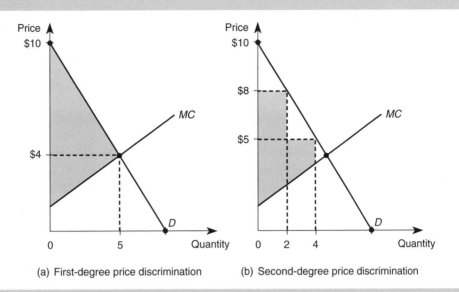

(a) First-degree price discrimination

(b) Second-degree price discrimination

(a) **First-degree price discrimination**
A first-degree price-discriminating firm charges each consumer the maximum price that she is willing to pay (as reflected by each point on the demand curve). In this case the maximum quantity that the firm sells is 5 (up to the point where marginal cost is equal to the maximum price that the consumer is willing to pay). The shaded area is the total profit of the firm, which is equal to the total surplus.

(b) **Second-degree price discrimination**
A second-degree price-discriminating firm does not know the exact maximum price that a consumer would be willing to pay. Therefore, the firm fixes a price schedule for different ranges of quantities. In this case, the firm charges $8 for quantities between 0 and 2 and $5 for quantities between 2 and 4. This way the firm manages to extract some surplus out of the consumers.

---

profits earned on each incremental unit sold. Thus, the shaded area between the demand curve and the firm's marginal cost curve reflects the firm's total profit when it charges each consumer the maximum price he or she will pay for small increments of output between 0 and 5 units. This strategy allows the firm to earn the maximum possible profits. Notice that consumers receive no consumer surplus on the 5 units they purchase: the firm extracts all surplus under first-degree price discrimination. As noted earlier, however, this favorable outcome (from the firm's perspective) can occur only if the manager has perfect information about the price that each consumer is willing and able to pay for each incremental unit of output.

Note that since the firm extracts the entire consumer surplus, which is the measure of the loss to the consumers, the firm's gains are exactly equal to consumers' losses. Therefore, the first-degree price discrimination that results only in a transfer from consumers to the producer entails no net (deadweight) loss to society.

In situations where the firm does not know the maximum price that each consumer will pay for a good, or when it is not practical to post a continuous schedule of prices for each incremental unit purchased, a firm might be able to employ second-degree price discrimination to extract part of the surplus from consumers. *Second-degree price discrimination* is the practice of posting a discrete schedule of declining prices for different ranges of quantities. This practice is very common in the electric utility industry, where firms typically charge a higher rate on the first hundred kilowatt-hours of electricity used than on subsequent units. The primary advantage of this strategy is that the firm can extract some consumer surplus from consumers without needing to know beforehand the identity of the consumers who will choose to purchase small amounts (and thus are willing and able to pay a higher price per unit). Given the posted schedule of prices, consumers sort themselves according to their willingness to pay for alternative quantities of the good. Thus, the firm charges different prices to different consumers, but does not need to know specific characteristics of individual consumers.

To illustrate how second-degree price discrimination works, suppose the Acme Floppy Disk Company charges consumers $8 per unit for the first two boxes of floppy disks purchased, and $5 per unit for boxes of disks purchased in excess of 2. The shaded region in panel (b) of Figure 11–1 shows the profits that Acme earns with this strategy. The first two units are sold at a price of $8, and the region between this price and the marginal cost curve reflects the firm's profits on the first two units. The second two units are priced at $5, so the region between that price and the marginal cost curve between 2 and 4 units of output reflects the firm's profits on the second two units sold. Notice that consumers end up with some consumer surplus, which means that second-degree price discrimination yields lower profits for the firm than it would have earned if it were able to perfectly price-discriminate. Nonetheless, profits are still higher than they would have been if the firm had used the simple strategy of charging the same price for all units sold. In effect, consumers purchasing small quantities (or alternatively, those having higher marginal valuations) pay higher prices than those who purchase in bulk.

The final type of price discrimination is commonly practised by firms that recognize that the demand for their product differs systematically across consumers in different demographic groups. In these instances firms can profit by charging different groups of consumers different prices for the same product, a strategy referred to as *third-degree price discrimination.* For example, it is common for stores to offer "student discounts" and for hotels and restaurants to offer "senior citizen discounts." These practices effectively mean that students and senior citizens pay less for some goods than do other consumers. Similarly, telephone companies charge lower rates on weekends than during the day, meaning that businesses may pay a higher price for telephone services than households. One might think that these pricing strategies are instituted to benefit students, senior citizens, and households, but there is a more compelling reason: to increase the firm's profits.

To see why third-degree price discrimination enhances profits, suppose a firm with market power can charge two different prices to two groups of consumers and the marginal revenues of selling to group 1 and group 2 are MR_1 and MR_2, respectively. The basic profit-maximizing rule is to produce output such that marginal revenue is equal to marginal cost. This principle is still valid, but the presence of two marginal revenue functions introduces some ambiguity.

It turns out that to maximize profits, the firm should equate the marginal revenue from selling output to each group to marginal cost: $MR_1 = MC$ and $MR_2 = MC$. To see why, suppose $MR_1 > MC$. If the firm produced one more unit and sold it to group 1, it would increase revenue by more than costs would increase. As additional output is sold to group 1, marginal revenue declines until it ultimately equals marginal cost.

Figure 11–2 illustrates the two-market situation, market 1, representing group 1, and market 2, representing group 2. Panel (a) shows D_1 and MR_1 (the demand and marginal revenue curves for the product that the firm sells in market 1), panel (b)

FIGURE 11–2 Third-Degree Price Discrimination

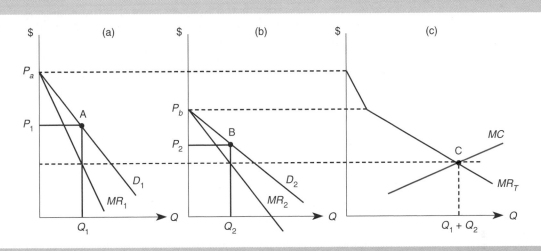

Part (a) shows D_1 and MR_1 (market 1), part (b) shows D_2 and MR_2 (market 2), and part (c) shows MR_T (the total marginal revenue) superimposed on its MC curve. The best level of output of the firm is $Q_1 + Q_2$, point C, where MC crosses MR_T. The firm sells Q_1 in market 1 and Q_2 in market 2 so that $MR_1 = MR_2 = MR_T = MC$. For Q_1 in market 1 the price charged is P_1, and for Q_2 in market 2 the price charged is P_2.

shows D_2 and MR_2 (the demand and marginal revenue curves for the product that the firm sells in market 2), and panel (c) shows MR_T (the total marginal revenue curve for the product that the firm sells in both markets together). The total marginal revenue curve (MR_T) is obtained from the horizontal summation of MR_1 and MR_2, $MR_T = MR_1 + MR_2$. Clearly, this curve must begin at price level P_a and kink at price level P_b, since below this level it is the horizontal sum of both MR curves rather than just the one.

Note that market (a) has the more inelastic demand situation, perhaps because of fewer competitors (less competition), or higher incomes of the buyers, or simply because of different taste patterns of the buyers in that market. If the firm were to start with its first unit, it would certainly sell this unit in market 1, at a price near P_a, since the marginal revenue of the first unit is higher there than in market 2. As the firm lowers its price to sell successive units, these units too will be sold in market 1 until price has reached P_b, where the marginal revenue from the sale of an additional unit is the same in both markets. Thus buyers in market 2 begin to enter market, and the firm should now allocate successive output units back and forth between market 1 and 2 to derive the greatest marginal revenue for each unit.

The firm's production level is established by the intersection of the firm's marginal revenue, MR_T with its marginal cost, MC. Extending a line at this level across to the panel for markets 1 and 2, we see that the firm should allocate Q_1 units to market 1 and Q_2 units to market 2, where $MC = MR_1 = MR_2$. In market 1, quantity Q_1 should be produced at price P_1, and quantity Q_2, will be sold at price P_2 in market 2, where $P_1 > P_2$. Note that the more inelastic market is charged the higher price, P_1, and more elastic market is charged the lower price, P_2. To see why, suppose the marginal revenue for group 1 is 10 and the marginal revenue for group 2 is 5. If one less unit were sold to group 2, revenue from that group would fall by 5. If the extra unit of output were sold to group 1, revenue would increase by 10. Thus, it pays for the firm to allocate output to the group with the greater marginal revenue. As additional output is allocated to the group, its marginal revenue falls until, in equilibrium, the marginal revenues to the two groups are exactly equal.

To understand the basis for third-degree price discrimination, suppose two groups of consumers have elasticities of demand of E_1 and E_2, and the firm can charge group 1 a price of P_1 and group 2 a price of P_2. Using the formula for the marginal revenue of a firm with market power, it follows that the marginal revenue of selling the product to group 1 at a price of P_1 is

$$MR_1 = P_1 \left[\frac{1 + E_1}{E_1} \right]$$

while the marginal revenue of selling to group 2 at a price of P_2 is

$$MR_2 = P_2 \left[\frac{1 + E_2}{E_2} \right]$$

As mentioned, a profit-maximizing firm should equate the marginal revenue of each group to marginal cost, which implies that $MR_1 = MR_2$. Using the formula for marginal revenue, this condition may be rewritten as

$$P_1 \left[\frac{1 + E_1}{E_1} \right] = P_2 \left[\frac{1 + E_2}{E_2} \right]$$

If $E_1 = E_2$, the terms in brackets are equal, and thus the firm will maximize profits by charging each group the same price. If the demand by group 1 is more inelastic than that by group 2, $E_2 < E_1 < 0$. In this instance, the firm should charge a higher price to group 1, since it has a more inelastic demand than group 2.

Thus, in order for third-degree price discrimination to enhance profits, differences must exist in the elasticity of demand of various consumers. In the examples cited earlier, there is reason to believe that senior citizens have a more elastic demand for a hotel room or a restaurant meal than other consumers. Most retired individuals are on fixed incomes and thus are much more sensitive to price than people who still work. The fact that they are charged lower prices for a hotel room is a simple implication of third-degree price discrimination, namely, charging a lower price to people with more elastic demands.

Another condition that must exist for third-degree price discrimination to be effective is that the firm must have some means of identifying the elasticity of demand by different groups of consumers; otherwise, the firm has no way of knowing to which group of consumers it should charge the higher price. In practice, this is not difficult to do. Hotels require individuals seeking a senior citizens' discount to present evidence of their age, such as a driver's licence. This effectively identifies an individual as likely to have a more elastic demand for a hotel room.

Finally, note that no type of price discrimination will work if the consumers purchasing at lower prices can resell their purchases to individuals being charged higher prices. In this instance, consumers who purchase the good at a low price could buy extra quantities and resell them to those who face the higher prices. The firm would sell nothing to the group being charged the higher price, because those consumers would save money by buying from consumers who purchased at the low price. In essence, the possibility of resale makes the goods purchased by the consumers charged the low price a perfect substitute for the firm's product. Those consumers can undercut the price the firm is charging the other group, thus reducing the firm's profits.

For example, students who purchase computer software at an educational discount are able to resell it. Note, however, that that while the possibility of resale typically applies to goods, it does not apply to services. Examples are Medicare, haircuts, etc.

Formula: Third-Degree Price Discrimination Rule. To maximize profits, a firm with market power produces the output at which the marginal revenue to each group equals marginal cost:

$$\underbrace{P_1 \left[\frac{1 + E_1}{E_1} \right] = MC}_{MR_1}$$

$$\underbrace{P_2 \left[\frac{1 + E_2}{E_2} \right] = MC}_{MR_2}$$

Demonstration PROBLEM 11–4

You are the manager of a pizzeria that produces at a marginal cost of $6 per pizza. The pizzeria is a local monopoly near campus (there are no other restaurants or food stores within 500 kilometres). During the day, only students eat at your restaurant. In the evening, while students are studying, faculty members eat there. If students have an elasticity of demand for pizzas of −4 and the faculty has an elasticity of demand of −2, what should your pricing policy be to maximize profits?

Answer

Assuming faculty would be unwilling to purchase cold pizzas from students, the conditions for effective price discrimination hold. It will be profitable to charge one price—say, P_L—on the "lunch menu" (effectively a student price) and another price, such as P_D, on the "dinner menu" (effectively a faculty price). To determine precisely what price to put on each menu, note that the people buying pizza off the lunch menu have an elasticity of demand of −4, while those buying off the dinner menu have an elasticity of demand of −2. The conditions for profit maximization require that the marginal revenue of selling a pizza to each group equal marginal cost. Using the third-degree price discrimination rule, this means that

$$P_L \left[\frac{1 + E_L}{E_L} \right] = MC$$

and

$$P_D \left[\frac{1 + E_D}{E_D} \right] = MC$$

Setting $E_D = -2$, $E_L = -4$, and $MC = 6$ yields

$$P_L\left[\frac{1-4}{-4}\right] = 6$$

$$P_D\left[\frac{1-2}{-2}\right] = 6$$

which simplifies to

$$P_L\left[\frac{3}{4}\right] = 6$$

$$P_D\left[\frac{1}{2}\right] = 6$$

Solving these two equations yields $P_L = \$8$ and $P_D = \$12$. Thus, to maximize profits, you should price a pizza on the lunch menu at \$8 and a pizza on the dinner menu at \$12. Since students have a more elastic demand for pizza than do faculty members, they should be charged a lower price to maximize profits.

Two-Part Pricing

two-part pricing
A pricing strategy in which consumers are charged a fixed fee for the right to purchase a product, plus a per-unit charge for each unit purchased.

Another strategy that firms with market power can use to enhance profits is **two-part pricing**. With two-part pricing, a firm charges a fixed fee for the right to purchase its goods, plus a per-unit charge for each unit purchased. This pricing strategy is commonly used by athletic clubs to enhance profits. Golf courses and health clubs, for instance, typically charge a fixed "initiation fee" plus a charge (either per month or per visit) to use the facilities. In this section, we will see how such a pricing strategy can enhance the profits of a firm.

Figure 11–3(a) provides a diagram of the demand, marginal revenue, and marginal cost for a firm with market power. Here the demand function is $Q = 10 - P$ and the cost function is $TC(Q) = 2Q$. If the firm adopted a pricing strategy of simply charging a single price to all consumers, the profit-maximizing level of output would be $Q = 4$ and the profit-maximizing price would be $P = 6$. This price-quantity combination corresponds to the point where marginal revenue equals marginal cost. Notice that the firm's profits are given by the shaded rectangle, which is

$$(\$6 - \$2)4 = \$16$$

Notice that the consumer surplus received by all consumers in the market—the value received but not paid for—corresponds to the upper triangle in Figure 11–3(a), which is

$$\frac{1}{2}[(\$10 - \$6)4] = \$8$$

In other words, consumers receive a total of \$8 in value from the four units purchased that they do not have to pay for.

Like first-degree price discrimination, two-part pricing allows a firm to extract all consumer surplus from consumers. In particular, suppose the demand function in

FIGURE 11–3 Comparisons of Standard Monopoly Pricing and Two-Part Pricing

(a) Standard monopoly pricing
The firm chooses the quantity for which marginal revenue and marginal cost are equal. The price per unit is then derived from the demand curve.
(b) Two-part pricing
The firm determines the amount of consumer surplus that would be generated when the market is in competitive equilibrium. Then the firm charges a fixed fee to extract the entire consumer surplus and a per-unit fee (set equal to *MC*) for each unit sold.

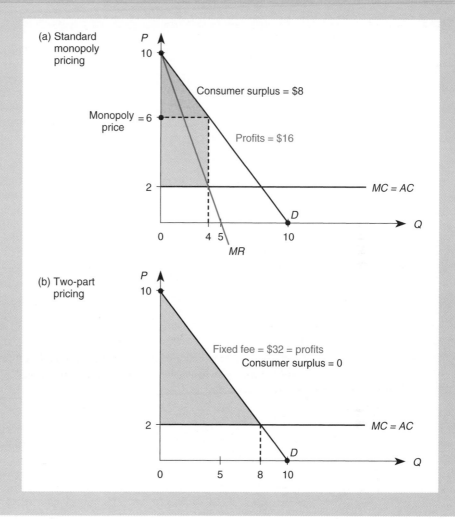

Figure 11–3(a) is that of a single individual and the firm uses the following pricing scheme: a fixed fee of $32 that gives the consumer the right to buy the product at a per-unit charge of $2. This situation is depicted in Figure 11–3(b) for the same demand and cost functions as in Figure 11–3(a). With a per-unit charge of $2, the consumer will purchase eight units and receive a consumer surplus of

$$\frac{1}{2}[(\$10 - \$2)8] = \$32$$

By charging a fixed fee of $32, the firm extracts all of this consumer's surplus. The firm sells each unit at its marginal cost of $2, and thus makes no profit on each unit sold at this price. But the firm also receives the fixed payment of $32, which is pure profit. The $32 in profits earned using the two-part pricing scheme is larger than the $16 the firm would earn by using a simple pricing strategy.

Inside BUSINESS

11-2 Price Discrimination (Differential Pricing) and Efficiency in Pharmaceuticals

Traditional economic analysis typically examines situations in which the prevalent technology involves no economies of scope and constant or decreasing returns to scale. In such industries the conventional wisdom "Set prices at marginal cost" is both efficient and economically viable. However, many important industries involve technologies that exhibit *increasing* returns to scale, large fixed and sunk costs, and significant economies of scope. An example is pharmaceuticals. In this industry, firms typically face high (R&D) fixed costs, significant joint costs, and low, even zero, marginal costs. Setting prices equal to marginal cost will generally not recoup sufficient revenue to cover the fixed costs, and the standard economic recommendation of "Price at marginal cost" is not economically viable. Some other mechanism for achieving efficient allocation of resources must be found.

The standard means to encourage innovation in any industry, including pharmaceuticals, is to provide patent rights. But patents work by enabling originator firms to charge prices above marginal cost, in order to recoup their investments in R&D. Thus, it appears that patents inevitably lead to high prices and that there is an inherent conflict between the objective of encouraging R&D and that of assuring access at affordable prices.

A recent study by Danzon focuses on the markets of developed and less-developed countries (LDC) for drugs. The author argues that price discrimination (differential pricing) is the key to resolving the potential conflict between patents, which are necessary to preserve incentives for R&D, and affordability of drugs in developing countries. Furthermore, differential pricing (price discrimination) may in fact increase efficiency by making everyone better off, if more drugs are more widely used in developing countries. The fact that current prices for some on-patent drugs may appear to be inappropriately high relative to income in some low-income countries may be due to current conditions not encouraging appropriate price differentials. Given the extent of current cross-market leakages, manufacturers would rationally be reluctant to grant low prices in low-income countries.

Differential pricing is defined as permitting the supplier (the pharmaceutical company in this case) to charge different prices in different markets. This is the same as the mechanism of the third-degree price discrimination, which is based on a principle that implies prices related to price sensitivity or demand elasticity.

In the absence of directly observable price elasticity, the author finds per capita income to be a good approximation. Casual evidence suggests that low income in LDCs makes demand highly elastic, in contrast to high income in developed countries that makes demand inelastic. A necessary condition for maintaining appropriate price differentials is that markets be separable, so that if manufacturers charge low prices in LDCs these prices do not spill over to high-income markets. In practice, however, the author argues, markets are not separate, because governments in many countries regulate their domestic prices on the basis of lower prices in other countries ("external referencing"), and intermediaries can import products from low- to higher-price countries ("parallel trade"). Given these linkages across markets, basic economics predicts that manufacturers will rationally seek to maintain much higher prices in LDCs than they would require if markets were separate and price leakages did not occur. Thus, as long as low prices offered to LDCs can spill over to other, potentially higher-price markets, manufacturers will rationally be reluctant to offer prices at marginal cost in LDCs, except when forced by political or other pressure.

A major conclusion of this study is that assuring low prices in LDCs requires that higher-income countries abstain from trying to "import" low LDC prices and that policies be established that enforce such market separation. Given enforceable barriers between markets, as discussed below, it will plausibly be in the self-interest of pharmaceutical manufacturers to charge prices close to marginal cost in LDCs, which would go a long way toward making drugs more affordable.

Firms, pursuing their own self-interest, will be led to set price differentials across markets that are socially appropriate. In theory, price discrimination is efficient, since all consumers with marginal value greater than marginal cost consume the product. Therefore, based on the evidence with regard to demand elasticities, a patent holder would rationally set prices near marginal cost in less-developed countries in the absence of leakages to less-elastic markets, while at the same time it would engage in an above-the-cost pricing strategy in developed countries. Differential pricing would thus go a long way toward making drugs developed for high-income countries available and affordable in LDCs, while preserving incentives for R&D. Differential pricing, viewed this way, is consistent with the criterion of economic efficiency. It is also consistent with standard norms of equity.

Source: P. M. Danzon and A. Towse, "Differential Pricing for Pharmaceuticals: Reconciling Access, R&D and Patents," *International Journal of Health Care Finance and Economics* 3, 2003, pp. 183–205, available <hc.wharton.upenn.edu/danzon/html/Journal_Articles.htm>, accessed August 1, 2004.

Inside BUSINESS

11-3 The Pricing Practices Provisions of the Competition Act

The Canadian law relating to price discrimination and predatory pricing traces its roots to the depression of the 1930s. The enactment of criminal prohibitions on these practices followed from a recommendation of the Royal Commission on Price Spreads in 1935.

The legislative history of what is now Section 50 of the Competition Act reveals the concern of that period in our economic history about "unfair competition" and the potential abuse by large firms such as department stores and chain stores of their market power to drive independent competitors out of the market and ultimately create monopoly or near-monopoly situations.

The difficulty with the notion of "unfair competition" is how to distinguish it from vigorous competition. That difficulty may be even greater when an industry is facing adjustments in the form of innovation, excess capacity, and the entry of new firms. How does one determine if a firm is the victim of predatory pricing or is simply paying the price for being a less-efficient or less-innovative player in the market?

PRICE DISCRIMINATION

The price discrimination provision in Subsection 50(1) of the Competition Act can be summarized as follows: It is an offence for a supplier to make a practice of discriminating, directly or indirectly, between purchasers who are in competition with one another and who are purchasing like quantity and quality of articles. The most important of elements of the offence of price discrimination are as follows:

- There are sales to two or more customers that can be compared.
- There is a discount, rebate, allowance, price concession or other advantage granted to one purchaser not available to another.
- The resulting discrimination is between purchasers who are in competition with one another.
- The sales are with respect to like quality and quantity of articles and are made at about the same time.
- There is a practice of discriminating.

- The supplier has knowledge that there is discrimination.

All of these elements must exist in order for there to be an offence. However, the following caveats should be born in mind:

- The section applies only to the sale of articles and not to services.
- It does not prevent or preclude suppliers from passing on to customers savings that might be achieved through sales of large quantities. Discounts or allowances based on volume of purchases are not illegal. (However, such discounts must be available to all competing purchasers with respect to sales of like quality and quantity.)
- The law does not prohibit granting special price concessions in the case of one-time events such as a store-opening special or a stock-clearance sale. There is only an offence if there is a practice of discrimination.
- The law does not require a cost justification for the volume discount. It is important to remember, though, that the volume discount must be available to all competing purchasers who may buy in the same quantity.
- The law does not preclude providing volume discounts in the form of rebates paid periodically based on quantities purchased over a reasonable period of time, provided once again, of course, that they are available to all competing purchasers.
- The question of like quality may require a careful examination in instances where products are sold under different brands—for example, the manufacturer's own brand and a private label. Presumably, there would be no issue when the products are treated differently by suppliers and purchasers in the market.
- Similarly, care should be taken with respect to other terms and conditions such as delivery charges and credit terms.

Principle	**TWO-PART PRICING**
	A firm can enhance profits by engaging in two-part pricing: charge a per-unit price that equals marginal cost, plus a fixed fee equal to the consumer surplus each consumer receives at this per-unit price.

We mentioned that athletic clubs often engage in two-part pricing. They charge an initiation fee, plus a per-unit fee for each visit to the facility. Notice that if the marginal cost is low, the optimal per-unit fee will be low as well. In the extreme case where marginal cost is zero, the profit-maximizing two-part pricing strategy of an athletic facility will be to charge $0 for each visit but a fixed initiation fee equal to a consumer's surplus. With two-part pricing, all profits are derived from the fixed fee. Setting the per-unit fee equal to marginal cost ensures that the surplus is as large as possible, thus allowing the largest fixed fee consistent with maximizing profits.

There are numerous other examples of two-part pricing strategies. Buying clubs are an excellent example. By paying a membership fee in a buying club, members get to buy products at "cost." Notice that if the membership fee is set equal to each consumer's surplus, the owner of a buying club actually makes higher profits than would be earned by simply setting the monopoly price.

Demonstration PROBLEM 11-5

Suppose the total monthly demand for golf services is $Q = 20 - P$. The marginal cost to the firm of each round is $1. If this demand function is based on the individual demands of 10 golfers, what is the optimal two-part pricing strategy for this golf services firm? How much profit will the firm earn?

Answer

The optimal per-unit charge is marginal cost. At this price, $20 - 1 = 19$ rounds of golf will be played each month. The total consumer surplus received by all 10 golfers at this price is thus

$$\frac{1}{2}[(20 - 1)19] = \$180.50$$

Since this is the total consumer surplus enjoyed by all 10 consumers, the optimal fixed fee is the consumer surplus enjoyed by an individual golfer ($180.50/10 = $18.05 per month). Thus, the optimal two-part pricing strategy is for the firm to charge a monthly fee to each golfer of $18.05, plus greens fees of $1 per round. The total profits of the firm thus are $180.50 per month, minus the firm's fixed costs.

Two-part pricing allows a firm to earn higher profits than it would earn by simply charging a price for each unit sold. By charging a fixed fee, the firm is able to extract consumer surplus, thus enhancing its profits. Unlike price discrimination, two-part pricing does not require that consumers have different elasticities of demand for the firm's product. By charging a per-unit fee for each unit purchased, consumers can vary the amounts they purchase according to their individual demands for the product.

The above analysis, however, applies to the case of homogeneous consumers. When there are two or more consumers with different demand curves, the firm may no longer wish to set the per-unit fee equal to marginal cost. The reason is that the firm can only set one fee for all its consumers. Only when consumers are homogenous, or at least similar in demand, does two-part pricing work well. When consumers have different demand curves, setting the per-unit fee equal to marginal cost forces the firm to charge a fixed fee that does not exceed the consumer surplus of the consumer with the smaller demand. If so, the firm will not be maximizing its profits. This is why we observe the wholesalers such as Sam's Club and Costco, who for instance cater to the needs of larger families, charging an entry fee, while ordinary supermarkets do not. Therefore, in order to maximize profits, the firm should set the per-unit fee above marginal cost and then set the fixed fee equal to the resulting consumer surplus of the consumer with the smaller demand. Note that there is no simple rule by which the manager can calculate the two-part price.

Block Pricing

block pricing
A pricing strategy in which identical products are packaged together in order to enhance profits by forcing customers to make an all-or-none decision to purchase.

Another way a firm with market power can enhance profits is to engage in **block pricing**. If you have purchased toilet paper in packages of four rolls or cans of soda in a six-pack, you have had firsthand experience with block pricing.

Let us see how block pricing can enhance a firm's profits. Suppose an individual consumer's demand function is $Q = 10 - P$ and the firm's costs are $TC(Q) = 2Q$. Figure 11–4 graphs the relevant curves. We see that if a firm charges a price of $2 per unit, it will sell eight units to the consumer. Notice, however, that the consumer receives a surplus of the upper triangle, which is equal to $32.

$$\frac{1}{2}[(\$10 - \$2)8] = \$32$$

This consumer's surplus reflects the value the consumer receives over and above the cost of buying eight units. In fact, in this case the consumer pays $2 × 8 = $16 to the firm for the eight units, but receives additional surplus of $32. The total value to the consumer of the eight units is $16 + $32 = $48.

Block pricing provides a means by which the firm can get the consumer to pay the full value of the eight units. It works very simply. Suppose the firm packaged eight units of its product and charged a price for the package. In this case, the consumer has to make an all-or-none decision between buying eight units and buying nothing. We just saw that the total value to the consumer of eight units is $48. Thus, so long as the price of the package of eight units is not greater than $48, this consumer will find it in her or his interest to buy the package.

Thus, the profit-maximizing price for the firm to charge for the package of eight units is $48. By charging this price for a package of eight instead of pricing each unit

FIGURE 11–4 Block Pricing

The firm earns more profits by packaging eight units of its product and charging a price of $48 for the package than by selling each unit separately at a simple per-unit price.

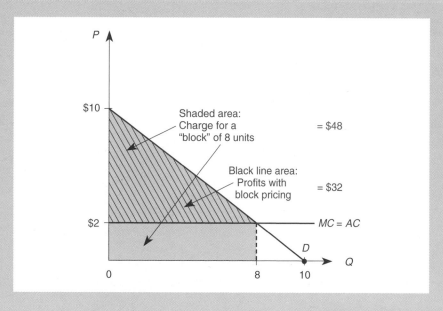

separately and letting the consumer choose how many units to buy, the firm earns $32 in profits—the value of the would-be consumer's surplus when the price is $2.

Principle	**BLOCK PRICING** By packaging units of a product and selling them as one package, the firm earns more than by posting a simple per-unit price. The profit-maximizing price on a package is the total value the consumer receives for the package, including consumer surplus.

Demonstration PROBLEM 11–6

Suppose a consumer's (inverse) demand function for gum produced by a firm with market power is given by $P = 0.2 - 0.04Q$ and the marginal cost is zero. What price should the firm charge for a package containing five pieces of gum?

Answer

When $Q = 5, P = 0$; when $Q = 0, P = 0.2$. This linear demand is graphed in Figure 11–5. Thus, the total value to the consumer of five pieces of gum is

$$\frac{1}{2}[(\$0.2 - \$0)5] = \$0.50$$

which corresponds to the shaded area in Figure 11–5. The firm extracts all of this surplus by charging a price of $0.50 for a package of five pieces of gum.

FIGURE 11–5 Optimal Block Pricing with Zero Marginal Cost

The firm extracts the entire consumer surplus by charging $0.50 for a package of five pieces of gum.

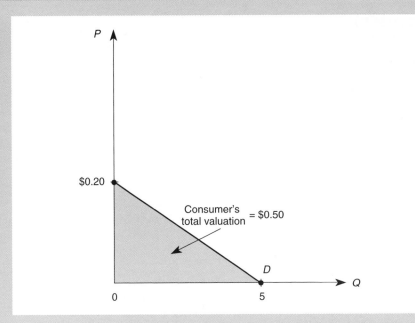

Block pricing enhances profits by forcing consumers to make an all-or-none decision to purchase units of a good. Unlike price discrimination, block pricing can enhance profits even in situations where consumers have identical demands for a firm's product.

Commodity Bundling

commodity bundling
The practice of bundling several different products together and selling them at a single "bundle price."

Another strategy managers can use to enhance profits is **commodity bundling**. Commodity bundling refers to the practice of bundling two or more different products together and selling them at a single "bundle price." For instance, travel companies often sell "package deals" that include airfare, hotel, and meals at a bundled price instead of pricing each component of a vacation separately. Computer firms bundle computers, monitors, and software and sell them at a bundled price. Many car dealers bundle options such as air conditioning, power steering, and automatic transmission and sell them at a "special package price." Let us see how these practices can enhance profits.

Suppose the manager of a computer firm knows there are two consumers who value its computers and monitors differently. Table 11–1 shows the maximum amount the two consumers would pay for a computer and monitor. The first consumer is willing to pay $2000 for a computer and $200 for a monitor. The second consumer is willing to pay $1500 for a computer and $300 for a monitor. However, the manager does not know the identity of each consumer; thus, she cannot price-discriminate by charging each consumer a different price.

Suppose the manager priced each component separately: one price for a computer, P_C, and another price for a monitor, P_M. (To simplify profit computations, suppose the cost to the firm of computers and monitors is zero.) If the firm charged $2000 for a computer, it would sell a computer only to consumer 1 and earn $2000, because consumer 2 is willing to pay only $1500 for a computer. If the firm charged $1500 for a computer, both consumers would buy a computer, netting the firm $3000. Clearly the profit-maximizing price to charge for a computer is $1500.

Similarly, if the firm priced monitors at $300, only consumer 2 would purchase a monitor, because consumer 1 would pay only $200 for a monitor. By pricing monitors at $200, it would sell two monitors and earn $400. The profit-maximizing price to charge for a monitor thus is $200.

On the surface, it appears that the most the firm can earn is $3400, by pricing computers at $1500 and monitors at $200. In this case, the firm sells two computers and two monitors. However, the firm can earn higher profits by bundling computers and monitors and selling the bundle at a price of $1800. To see why, notice that the total value to the first consumer of a computer and a monitor is $2000 + $200 = $2200, and the total value to the second consumer of a computer and a monitor is $1500 + $300 = $1800. By bundling a computer and a monitor and selling the bundle for $1800, the firm will sell a bundle to both consumers and earn $3600—a full $200 more than it would earn if it did not engage in commodity bundling.

This example illustrates that commodity bundling can enhance profits when consumers differ with respect to the amounts they are willing to pay for multiple

TABLE 11–1 Commodity Bundling

Consumer	Valuation of Computer	Valuation of Monitor
1	$2000	$200
2	1500	300

products sold by a firm. It is important to emphasize that commodity bundling can enhance profits even when the manager cannot distinguish between the amounts different customers are willing to pay for the firm's products. Note that the key as to why bundling the two products increases profits, as in the above illustrations, is the negative correlation between customers' demands. As you can see in Table 11–1, the preferences of group 1 and group 2 are inversely related. Group 1 is willing to pay more for the computer, whereas group 2 is willing to pay more for the monitor. By bundling them, the computer company is offering an incentive to the customers to take both products, while they may not have done so otherwise.

Recall that if the manager did know precisely how much each customer was willing to pay for each product, the firm could earn higher profits by engaging in price discrimination: charging higher prices to those consumers willing to pay more for its products.

Demonstration PROBLEM 11–7

Suppose three purchasers of a new car have the following valuations for options:

Consumer	Air Conditioner	Power Brakes
1	$1000	$500
2	800	300
3	100	800

The firm's costs are zero.

1. If the manager knows the valuations and identity of each consumer, what is the optimal pricing strategy?
2. Suppose the manager does not know the identities of the buyers. How much will the firm make if the manager sells brakes and air conditioners for $800 each but offers a special options package (power brakes and an air conditioner) for $1100?

Answer

1. If the manager knows the buyers' identities, he will maximize profits through price discrimination, since resale for these products is unlikely; charge consumer 1 $1500 for an air conditioner and power brakes; charge consumer 2 $1100 for an air conditioner and power brakes; and charge consumer 3 $900 for an air conditioner and power brakes. The firm's profits will be $3500. It makes no difference whether the manager charges the consumers a bundled price equal to their total valuation of an air conditioner and power brakes or charges a separate price for each component that equals the consumers' valuation.
2. The total value of a bundle containing an air conditioner and power brakes is $1500 for consumer 1, $1100 for consumer 2, and $900 for consumer 3. Thus, consumers 1 and 2 will buy the option package, because a bundle with an air conditioner and power brakes is worth at least $1100 to them. The firm earns $2200 on these consumers. Consumer 3 will not buy the bundle, because the total cost of the bundle is greater than the consumer's valuation ($900). However, consumer 3 will buy power brakes at the price of $800. Thus, the firm earns $3000 with this pricing strategy—$2200 comes from consumers 1 and 2, who each purchase the special options package for $1100, and $800 comes from consumer 3, who chooses to buy only power brakes.

Pricing Strategies for Special Cost and Demand Structures

The pricing strategies we will discuss in this section—peak-load pricing and cross-subsidization—enhance profits for firms that have special cost and demand structures.

Peak-Load Pricing

Many markets have periods in which demand is high and periods in which demand is low. Toll roads tend to have more traffic during rush hour than at other times of the day; utility companies tend to have higher demand during the day than during the late-night hours; and airlines tend to have heavier traffic during the week than during weekends. A good example of a toll road is the highway 407 ETR across the Greater Toronto Area to Hamilton that charges 13.95 cents per kilometre during peak hours (6–10 a.m., and 3–7 p.m.) and 13.10 cents per kilometer in off-peak hours and week-ends. When the demand during peak times is so high that the capacity of the firm cannot serve all customers at the same price, the profitable thing for the firm to do is engage in **peak-load pricing**.

Figure 11–6 illustrates a classic case of such a situation. Suppose the ETR's marginal cost is constant up to Q_H, where it becomes vertical. At this point, the firm is operating at full capacity and cannot provide additional units at any price.

The two demand curves in Figure 11–6 correspond to the ETR's peak and off-peak demand for the product: D_{Low} is the off-peak demand, which is lower than D_{High}, the peak demand. In general, where there are two types of demand, a firm will maximize profits by charging different prices to the different groups of demanders. In the case of peak-load pricing, the "groups" refer to those who purchase at different times during the day.

In Figure 11–6, for instance, demand during low-peak times is such that marginal revenue equals marginal cost at point Q_L. Thus, the profit-maximizing price during

peak-load pricing
A pricing strategy in which higher prices are charged during peak hours than during off-peak hours.

FIGURE 11–6 Peak-Load Pricing

With this strategy the monopolist charges a higher price during the time when the demand is high and a lower price during the time when the demand is low. The firm applies standard monopoly pricing strategy of equating marginal cost and marginal revenue based on the demand curve. In the figure, the firm charges P_H for quantity Q_H during high-demand time and price P_L and quantity Q_L during low-demand time.

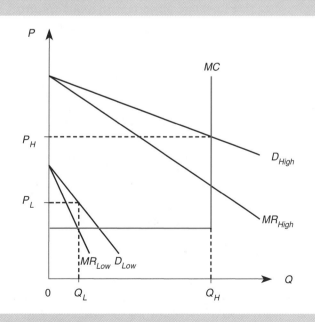

low-peak times is P_L (13.10 cents per kilometre). In contrast, during high-peak times, marginal revenue equals marginal cost at point Q_H, which corresponds to the firm's full capacity. The profit-maximizing price during high-peak times is P_H (13.95 cents per kilometre). Thus, as is the case in price discrimination, the firm charges two different prices: a low price during low-peak demand and a high price during high-peak demand.

Notice in Figure 11–6 that if the ETR charged a high price of 13.95 cents at all times of the day, no one would purchase during low-peak periods. By lowering the price during low-peak times but charging a high price during high-peak times, the firm increases its profits by selling to some consumers during low-peak times. Similarly, if the firm charged a low price during all times of the day, it would lose money during high-peak times, when consumers are willing to pay a higher price for services.

Principle	**PEAK-LOAD PRICING** When demand is higher at some times of the day than at other times, a firm may enhance profits by peak-load pricing: charge a higher price during peak times than is charged during off-peak times.

Demonstration PROBLEM 11–8

Airports typically charge a higher price for parking during holidays than they do during other times of the year. Why?

Answer

It pays for airports to engage in peak-load pricing. Since the demand for parking is much higher during holidays, when travellers spend extended periods with families, parking lots tend to fill up during that time. If airports charged a high price year-round, they would have empty spaces most of the time. If they charged low prices year-round, they would lose out on the additional amount consumers are willing to pay during holidays. Thus, with peak-load pricing, airports earn higher profits.

Cross-Subsidies

cross-subsidy
A pricing strategy in which profits gained from the sale of one product are used to subsidize sales of a related product.

The next pricing strategy we will discuss—cross-subsidies—is relevant in situations where a firm has cost complementarities and the demand by consumers for a group of products is interdependent. A firm that engages in a strategy of **cross-subsidies** uses profits made with one product to subsidize sales of another product.

For example, Adobe charges dramatically different prices for two of its products. One product—its Acrobat Reader—may be obtained "for free" by anyone willing to download the software from Adobe's Internet site. This software permits users to view documents created in portable document format (pdf). In contrast, individuals wishing to create pdf documents must *pay* for a software product called Adobe Acrobat.

Adobe engages in this cross-subsidization because complementaries in demand and costs make doing so profitable. More specifically, Adobe enjoys economies of scope and cost complementarities in making these two products jointly (it is cheaper to design and distribute both types of software within one firm). Furthermore these two products are complementary: the greater the number of people who use Acrobat Reader to view documents, the greater the amount they will be willing to pay to use Adobe Acrobat for document creation. In short, Adobe finds it profitable to price Acrobat Reader at or below cost because doing so stimulates demand for its comple-

Inside BUSINESS

11-4 Canadian Wheat Board: A Case of International Price Discrimination

The Canadian Wheat Board (CWB) is the single-desk seller of western Canadian wheat, feed barley, and malting barley for export destinations. In the domestic market, the CWB is the sole seller of western Canadian wheat and barley for human consumption, but operates alongside an open cash market for feed barley and feed wheat in western Canada. Acting as the sole and collective agent of western Canadian grain producers, the CWB is enabled to generate additional producer revenue by its ability to price-discriminate in international markets. By exercising a certain degree of market power in international markets, it can potentially earn larger returns for Canadian producers than would be possible under pure competition. As economic theory would dictate, this can be accomplished by holding back sales to certain price inelastic markets (such as Japan) and expanding sales in certain price elastic markets (such as Saudi Arabia).

As the only exporter of wheat, feed barley, and malting barley produced in western Canada, the CWB controls a significant portion of the export supply sought by importers. For example, the CWB controlled 26.9 percent of the world market share for barley in 1996–97. No wonder the CWB is often cast as a villain in the ongoing trade dispute between producers in the upper Midwestern United States and producers in Canada. United States protesters believe that the CWB purposely dumps grain into the U.S. market below cost, depressing U.S. prices. These same critics also argue that the CWB can extract monopoly rents through price discrimination across international markets, unfairly increasing the returns to Canadian wheat and barley producers at the expense of U.S. and other global competitors.

The results of this study indicate that the CWB realized an average price difference of $20.73/tonne between Japan and the rest of the world over the period 1980–81 through 1994–95. The CWB was not only able to price-discriminate during the period of the U.S. Export Enhancement Program (a farm subsidy program), 1985–86 through 1994–95, it was also able to price-discriminate between feed barley export markets prior to EEP (1980–81 through 1984–85). However, the magnitude of the differ-

ences in prices between markets increased as a result of EEP. For example, the CWB maintained a $13.99/tonne difference between Japan and the rest of the world prior to EEP (1980–81 through 1984–85). This price difference increased to an average of $23.70/tonne during the EEP period (1985–86 through 1994–95).

Nonetheless, the CWB's ability to price-discriminate in international markets does not by itself lead to the conclusion that producers in Canada have benefited from higher revenues as a result of its monopoly position. The link between price discrimination and market power in international barley markets is still the subject of intense debate in Canada and the United States. While current agricultural trade friction between Canada and the United States stems mostly from low commodity prices in 1998–99, U.S. critics focus on the unique nature of the CWB and uncertainty regarding its operations. Much of this debate may be political rhetoric aimed at simply reducing the volume of trade flows by using the CWB as a lightning rod. Interestingly, many U.S. policymakers argued for years that Canada's Western Grain Transportation Act (WGTA) subsidy that provided for grain shipments from the Prairies to the western and eastern Canadian ports was "unfair" because it resulted in increased exports of Canadian grain to the United States. However, when this subsidy was removed in 1995, Canadian grain exports to the United States actually increased. The U.S. became a relatively more attractive market because the cost of rail transportation over land to that country did not change, but transportation costs to the western and eastern ports for overseas exports actually increased. The U.S. experience with the elimination of the WGTA subsidy should be kept firmly in mind when attempting to determine the effect of the removal of a certain agricultural policy in another country on U.S. trade flows.

Source: H. Brooks and T. G. Schmitz, "Price Discrimination in the International Grain Trade: The Case of Canadian Wheat Board Feed Barley Exports," *Agribusiness* 15(3), August 26, 1999, pp. 313–22. Reprinted with permission of John Wiley and Sons, Inc.

mentary software product, thus permitting it to charge a significantly higher price for Adobe Acrobat than it would otherwise be able to charge. As we will see in Chapter 13, a number of similar pricing strategies (such as penetration pricing) can be used to enhance profits in strategic environments (including online auctions) where network effects are present.

More generally, the advantage of cross-subsidization for the firm is twofold. First, it permits the firm to sell multiple products, which leads to cost savings in the presence of economies of scope. Second, if the two products have demands that are interdependent, the firm can induce consumers to buy more of each product than they would otherwise.

Principle	**CROSS-SUBSIDIZATION**
	Whenever the demand for two products produced by a firm are interrelated through costs or demand, the firm may enhance profits by cross-subsidization: selling one product at or below cost and the other product above cost.

Transfer Pricing

transfer pricing
A pricing strategy in which a firm optimally sets the internal price at which an upstream division sells an input to a downstream division.

Thus far, our analysis of pricing decisions has presumed that a single manager is in charge of pricing and output decisions. However, most large firms have upstream and downstream managers who must make price and output decisions for their own divisions. For example, automakers like General Motors have upstream managers who control the production of inputs (like car engines) produced in *upstream divisions.* These inputs are "transferred" to *downstream divisions,* where downstream managers operate plants that use the inputs to produce the final output (automobiles). An important issue in this setting is optimal **transfer pricing**—the internal price at which an upstream division should sell inputs to the firm's downstream division in order to maximize the overall profits of the firm.

Transfer pricing is important because most division managers are provided an incentive to maximize their own division's profits. As we will see, if the owners of a firm do not set optimal transfer prices, but instead let division managers set the prices of internally manufactured inputs so as to maximize their division's profits, the result might be lower overall profits for the firm.

To illustrate, suppose there is no outside market for the input produced by the upstream division, and that divisional managers are instructed to maximize the profits of their divisions. In this case the upstream division manager has market power, and maximizes the profits of the upstream division by producing where the marginal revenue derived from selling to the downstream division equals the upstream division's marginal cost of producing the input. Because of the monopoly power enjoyed by the upstream division, the input is sold to the downstream division at a price that exceeds the firm's actual marginal cost. Given this input price, the downstream manager would then maximize divisional profits by producing where the marginal revenue it earns in the final product market (MR_d) equals its marginal cost. This implies that it, too, prices above marginal cost. Moreover, because the price the downstream division pays the upstream division for the input is higher than the true marginal cost of the input, the downstream division ends up charging a price for the final product that is actually higher than the price that maximizes overall firm profits. In short, when both divisions mark up prices in excess of marginal cost, *double marginalization* occurs and the result is less than optimal overall firm profits.

To circumvent the problem of double marginalization, transfer prices must be set that maximize the overall value of the firm rather than the profits of the upstream division. To see how this can be accomplished, suppose the downstream division requires one unit of the input (one engine, say) to produce one unit of the final output (one car). Assume that the downstream division has a marginal cost of assembling the final output, denoted MC_d, that is in addition to the cost of acquiring the input from the upstream division. In this case the overall profits of the firm are maximized when the upstream division produces engines such that its marginal cost, MC_u, equals the net marginal revenue to the downstream division (NMR_d):

$$NMR_d = MR_d - MC_d = MC_u$$

To see why, notice that it costs the firm MC_u to produce another unit of the input. This input can be converted into another unit of output and sold to generate additional revenues of MR_d in the final product market only after the downstream division expends an additional MC_d to convert the input into the final output. Thus, the actual marginal benefit to the firm of producing another unit of the input is NMR_d. Setting this equal to the marginal cost of producing the input maximizes overall firm profits.

Now that we know the necessary conditions for maximizing overall firm profits, we show how a firm can institute an incentive system that induces the divisional managers to indeed maximize overall firm profits. Suppose higher authorities within the firm determine that the level of final output that maximizes overall firm profits is Q^*. They set the transfer price, P_T, equal to the upstream division's marginal cost of producing the amount of input required by the downstream division to produce Q^* units of final output. According to this internal pricing scheme, the downstream manager can now purchase as many units of the input as it desires from the upstream division at a fixed price of P_T per unit. The upstream and downstream managers are instructed to maximize divisional profits, taking as given the transfer price set by higher authorities within the firm.

Since the upstream division now must sell the input internally at a fixed price of P_T per unit, it behaves like a perfectly competitive firm and maximizes profits by producing where price equals marginal cost: $P_T = MC_u$. Since one unit of input is required for each unit of output, the downstream division's marginal cost of producing final output is now $MC = MC_d + P_T$. The downstream divisional manager maximizes divisional profits by producing where marginal revenue equals marginal cost: $MR_d = MC_d + P_T$. Since $P_T = MC_u$, we may rewrite this as $MR_d - MC_d = MC_u$, which is exactly our condition for maximizing overall firm profits. Thus, we see that by setting the transfer price at the upstream division's marginal cost of producing the firm's profit-maximizing quantity of the input, the problem of double marginalization is avoided even though divisional managers operate independently to maximize their division's profits.

A concrete example will help illustrate how a firm can implement optimal transfer pricing. Suppose that the (inverse) demand for Aviation General's single-engine planes is given by $P = 15\ 000 - Q$. Its upstream division produces engines at a cost of $TC_u(Q_e) = 2.5Q_e^2$, and the downstream division's cost of assembling planes is $TC_d(Q) = 1000Q$. Let us derive the optimal transfer price when there is no external market for engines.

The optimal transfer price is set where the firm's net marginal revenue from engine production equals the upstream division's marginal cost of producing the engines. Downstream marginal revenue and marginal cost is $MR_d = 15\ 000 - 2Q$ and $MC_d = 1000$, respectively, while the upstream division's marginal cost of producing engines is $MC_u = 5Q_e$. Since it takes one engine to produce one plane ($Q = Q_e$), equating NMR_d and MC_u implies

$$NMR_d = 15\ 000 - 2Q_e - 1000 = 5Q_e$$

Solving for Q_e, we see that to maximize overall firm profits, the upstream division should produce 2000 engines. Since $Q_e = Q$, the downstream division should produce 2000 planes to maximize overall firm profits. The optimal transfer price is the upstream division's marginal cost evaluated at 2000 engines, or $P_T = \$10\,000$. Thus, the firm maximizes its overall profits when its accountants set the (internal) transfer price of engines at $\$10\,000$ per unit, and divisional managers are provided an incentive to maximize divisional profits given this price.

Pricing Strategies in Markets with Intense Price Competition

The final pricing strategies we will examine—price matching, trigger strategy and price wars, inducing brand loyalty, and randomized pricing—are valuable for firms competing in Bertrand oligopoly. Recall that firms in Bertrand oligopoly compete in price and sell similar products. As we learned in Chapters 9 and 10, in these instances price wars will likely result, leading to prices that are close to marginal cost and profits that are near zero. While the pricing strategies discussed in this section can be used in situations other than Bertrand oligopoly, they are particularly useful for mitigating the price wars that frequently occur in such a market.

Price Matching

In Chapters 9 and 10, we showed that when two or more firms compete in a homogeneous-product Bertrand oligopoly, the Nash equilibrium is for each firm to charge marginal cost and earn zero profits. However, in Chapter 10 we showed that if the game is infinitely repeated, firms can maintain collusive outcomes by adopting trigger strategies, which punish rivals that deviate from the high price. In an infinitely repeated game, punishments are threatened in the future if a firm cheats on a collusive agreement, and this can lead to a situation where firms end up charging high prices. However, recall that this strategy can work only if the interest rate is low and firms can effectively monitor the behaviour of other firms in the market.

In cases where trigger strategies do not work (because the game is not infinitely repeated or the firms cannot monitor other firms' behaviour), there is another way firms can attain higher profits: by advertising a price-matching strategy. A firm that uses a **price-matching** strategy advertises a price and a promise to "match" any lower price offered by a competitor.

To illustrate how such a strategy can enhance profits, suppose the firms in a market play a one-shot Bertrand pricing game. However, in addition to advertising a price, the firms advertise a commitment to match any lower price found in the market. Such an advertisement would look something like the following:

> Our price is P. If you find a better price in the market, we will match that price. We will not be undersold!

This sounds like a good deal for consumers; indeed, simply announcing this strategy may induce some consumers to buy from the firm to be "assured" of a great deal.

It turns out, however, that if all firms in the market announce such a policy, they can set the price (P) to the high monopoly price and earn large profits instead of the zero profits they would earn in the usual one-shot Bertrand oligopoly. How does this work?

Suppose all firms advertised the high monopoly price but promised to match any lower price found by consumers. Since all firms are charging the same high price, consumers can't find a better price in the market. The result is that firms share the market, charge the monopoly price, and earn high profits. Furthermore, notice that no firm has an incentive to charge a lower price in an attempt to steal customers from rivals. If a firm lowered its price, the rivals would match that price and gain back their share of the market. By lowering its price, a firm effectively triggers a price war,

price matching
A strategy in which a firm advertises a price and a promise to match any lower price offered by a competitor.

Inside**BUSINESS**

Page through almost any Sunday newspaper and you will find advertisements such as this one from Sears:

> We'll meet or beat the competition or double the difference! If our price does not beat the competition's advertised price on the identical item, we will meet it! If you find a lower competitor's advertised price within 30 days after purchase, we'll double the difference.[1]

This advertisement is an example of what economists call a *low-price guarantee* (LPG). An LPG contains either a price-matching guarantee (a promise to match any lower price) or a price-beating guarantee (a promise to beat competitors' prices). Notice that this Sears advertisement contains elements of both types of guarantees. If you present Sears with a lower-priced competitor's advertisement at the time of purchase, Sears will match the lower price (a price-matching guarantee). If you present Sears with a competitor's advertisement for a lower price within 30 days of your purchase at Sears, it will pay you double the difference between the two prices (a price-beating guarantee).

As noted in the text, LPGs permit firms to charge higher prices because the guarantees weaken the incentive for rivals to undercut any given store's price. Not surprisingly, LPGs are becoming increasingly popular among car dealers, office supply stores, electronics stores, supermarkets, and a variety of other retailers. Maria Arbatskaya, Morten Hviid, and Greg Shaffer, for instance, examined the frequency with which tire retailers use LPGs in their newspaper advertisements. Based on samples of over 500 tire advertisements across the country, over half contained LPGs.

[1]An excerpt from a Sears advertisement, *Sunday Herald-Times,* August 16, 1998.

Sources: Michael R. Baye, Dan Kovenock, and Casper G. de Vries, "How to Sell a Pickup Truck: Beat-or-Pay Advertisements as Facilitating Devices," *International Journal of Industrial Organization* 15, 1994, pp. 21–31; James D. Hess and Eitan Gerstner, "Price-Matching Policies: An Empirical Case," *Managerial and Decision Economics* 12, 1991, pp. 305–15; Maria Arbatskaya, Morten Hviid, and Greg Shaffer, "The Effects of Low-Price Guarantees on Tire Prices," *Advances in Applied Microeconomics* 8, 1999, pp. 123–38.

which results in no greater share of the market and lower profits. Thus, if all firms adopt price-matching strategies, the result is that each firm charges the monopoly price and shares the market to earn high profits.

An important aspect of price-matching policies is that the firms need not monitor the prices charged by rivals. This is in contrast to trigger strategies, in which firms must monitor rivals' prices to know whether to punish a rival that has charged a low price. With a price-matching strategy, it is up to a consumer to show the firm that some rival is offering a better deal. At that point, the firm can match the price for that consumer. The consumers who have not found a better deal continue to pay the higher price. Thus, even if some other firm happened to charge a low price, a firm using a price-matching strategy would get to price-discriminate between those consumers who found such a price and those who did not.

Before you choose to adopt a price-matching strategy, there are two things to consider. First, you must devise a mechanism that precludes consumers from claiming to have found a lower price when in fact they have not. Otherwise, consumers will have an incentive to tell you that another firm is "giving goods away" and ask you to match the lower price. One way firms avoid such deception is by promising to match prices that are advertised in some widely circulated newspaper. In this case, the consumer must bring in the advertisement before the price will be matched.

Second, you can get into trouble with a price-matching strategy if a competitor has lower costs than your firm. For instance, if your competitor's marginal cost is $300 for a television set and yours is $400, the profit-maximizing (monopoly) price set by your firm will be higher than that set by the rival. In such an instance, the monopoly price set by your rival may be lower than your cost. In this case, if you have to match your rival's price, you will incur losses on each unit sold.

Trigger Strategies and Price Wars

As discussed above, in many instances, repeating a strategic decision provides managers with a chance to punish cheaters through retaliation or to promise rewards through cooperation. While, in this case, players do not know the actions of their opponents in the current stage, they do know what their opponents did in all previous stages. Therefore, the strategy in each period is made contingent upon the history of the game. This strategy was referred to as the trigger strategy. More specifically, in a tit-for-tat strategy, the trigger strategy takes the form of punishing cheating in the next period and continuing to punish until cheating stops, which, in turn, triggers a return to cooperation in the following period. We also discussed that an effective way to reduce the benefit of cheating is to make a strategic commitment of price matching.

However, despite the fact that firms in an oligopolistic market structure recognize their interdependence, and that they clearly have an incentive to avoid ruinous price competition, in certain oligopolistic industries producers do engage in such competition—for example, fertilizer production in North America and gasoline retailer supply in Canada. Furthermore, volatility of prices appears to be characteristic of industries that consist of firms of sufficiently different sizes. Where the market players are numerous, with some large but the majority small, the outcome of trigger strategy is one of, not cooperative high market price, but rather a cyclical behaviour of retail pricing—a price war.

Inducing Brand Loyalty

Another strategy a firm can use to reduce the tension of Bertrand competition is to adopt strategies that induce *brand loyalty*. Brand-loyal customers will continue to buy a firm's product even if another firm offers a (slightly) better price. By inducing brand loyalty, a firm reduces the number of consumers who will "switch" to another firm if it undercuts its price.

Firms can use several methods to induce brand loyalty. One of the more common methods is to engage in advertising campaigns that promote a firm's product as being better than those of competitors. If advertisements make consumers believe that other products in the market are not perfect substitutes, higher profits can be earned by firms engaging in price competition. When a rival undercuts a firm's price, some customers will remain loyal to the firm, allowing it to charge a higher price and make positive profits.

Notice, however, that such an advertising strategy will not work if consumers believe products to be homogeneous. A self-service gasoline station would be hard pressed to convince consumers that its product is really "different" from the identical brand sold across the street. In these instances, firms can resort to alternative strategies to promote brand loyalty.

Some gasoline stations now have "frequent filler" programs, modelled after the frequent-flyer programs initiated by the airlines. Frequent-filler programs provide consumers with a cash rebate after a specified number of fill-ups. With this strategy, even though the products are identical, the consumer has an incentive to remain loyal to the same station to maximize the number of times he or she obtains a rebate. For example, suppose a station offers a $5 rebate after 10 fill-ups. If the consumer fills up at 10 different stations, he or she does not get the rebate, but if all 10 fill-ups are at the same station, the consumer gets $5. Thus, a frequent-filler strategy provides the consumer with an incentive to remain loyal to a particular station even though it offers products identical to its rivals.

Inside BUSINESS

11–6 Price Cycles in Retail Gasoline Markets: The Ontario Market

Consumer groups often point to the phenomenon of retail prices responding more rapidly to input price increases than to decreases as evidence of anti-competitive behaviour. Several recent studies have attempted to tackle the phenomenon of asymmetric behaviour of gasoline price in Canadian cities. They report sharp differences in pricing behaviour in retail gasoline prices across Canadian cities. Specifically, within Canada, between 1989 and 1999 three different pricing phenomena can be observed: cyclical, sticky, and normal. First, in the cyclical pattern, prices exhibit a rapidly cyclical and yet asymmetric pattern. The cycle starts with a large price increase from one week to the next followed a gradual decline in price over the next several weeks, which repeats itself over and over. The data for Windsor and Toronto exhibit a cyclical pattern that does not appear in wholesale prices. When the retail price gets too near the wholesale price, retail prices rise suddenly. They, however, fall gradually by a small amount every day or week until the price is sufficiently low that the cycle begins anew. The second pattern is one in which prices remain fixed (sticky) for months at a time. This is observed in St John's. Finally, the normal pattern is one in which retail prices more closely follow wholesale prices, where firms selling a homogenous good would set price equal to wholesale price plus the marginal cost of retailing. In Ottawa, the data indicate this normal pattern of pricing behaviour.

While the normal pricing observed in the data may be based on the a standard markup over the wholesale cost, the price cycle phenomenon can best be explained by a theoretical model known as Edgeworth cycle model, which is a dynamic Bertrand oligopoly model. According to this model, firms set prices alternately and each responds to its opponent's action from the previous period, resulting in two distinct sets of Nash equilibria. The first set of Nash equilibria is the focal markup equilibria supported under threat of retaliation. The sticky pricing phenomenon is consistent with a focal price and the normal pricing observed in the data could come from a standard, possibly competitive markup over the wholesale price.

The strong cyclical pattern observed in many cities, however, appears to be consistent with the second type of dynamic equilibria. In this environment, a firm has a strong incentive to undercut its rivals to realize a large immediate increase in market share before its rivals can respond. This swing in market shares forces the rivals to respond by matching or undercutting the rival. This undercutting continues until prices fall to the marginal cost (wholesale price), or to some lower bound that is a function of the wholesale price. At this point, one of the firms (typically a larger one) relents, sacrificing short-term profits by raising price, and initiates a new cycle that rivals will follow until a new cycle is initiated. Furthermore, a greater penetration of small firms leads to more cycling activity and less sticky pricing. In particular, the retail prices are insensitive to wholesale prices on the downward portion of the cycle when compared with the upward portion. This is consistent with the phenomenon that price decreases result when firms undercut each other for market share, but that the magnitude of price restorations are dependent on cost.

The authors also demonstrate that the welfare of consumers is greater under a cyclical pricing pattern than under the sticky pricing pattern. A simple comparison of (tax-exclusive) average markups over the full sample shows that markups are lower under price cycling than under sticky pricing or normal pricing. The markups are 1.02 cents per litre higher under sticky pricing regimes than under cycling regimes. Normal pricing markups are 0.96 cents higher than cycling markups. Consequently, unless consumers are unrealistically averse to short-term gas price volatility, the lower average markups in periods of cycling increase consumer welfare. To the extent that consumers can time purchases to periods of low prices, the gain is even greater.

There remains the question of why cycles are so common in Canada while, except for several western cities in the 1960s and 1970s, they have not occurred in the United States. Cycles appear to be best generated in markets with numerous small undercutting independents and at least one very large major firm capable of resetting the cycle. In some U.S. markets, there may be too few aggressive independents, or the more decentralized control of prices at branded outlets may make price resetting difficult. Perhaps historical price cycling in Canada has created price hypersensitivity of otherwise similar consumers in that country, which increases the propensity of cycles there.

Sources: M. Noel, "Edgeworth Price Cycles, Cost-Based Pricing and Sticky Pricing in Retail Gasoline Markets," Department of Economics Working Papers, December 10, 2003, University of California, San Diego, available <econ.ucsd.edu/papers/files/2004-04.pdf>, accessed August 1, 2004; M. Noel, "Edgeworth Price Cycles: Evidence from the Toronto Retail Gasoline Market," Department of Economics Working Papers, December 18, 2003, University of California, San Diego, available <www.econ.ucsd.edu/papers/files/2004-03.pdf>, accessed August 1, 2004; A. Eckert, "Retail Price Cycles and Response Asymmetry," *Canadian Journal of Economics*, 35(1), February 2002, pp. 52–77; A. Eckert and D. West, "Retail Gasoline Price Cycles and Cross-Sectional Price Dispersion," Department of Economics, University of Alberta, Edmonton, Alberta, November 2002, available <econ.ucalgary.ca/research/gaspaper5.pdf>, accessed August 1, 2004.

Inside BUSINESS

11-7 Randomized Pricing in the Airline Industry

There are over 215 396 changes in airfares each day. This translates into 150 changes per minute. Domestic airlines spend considerable sums of money in an attempt to monitor the prices of other firms. As noted by Marius Schwartz:

> Delta Airlines assigns 147 employees to track rivals' prices and select quick responses—on a typical day, comparing over 5,000 industry pricing changes against Delta's more than 70,000 fares. New fares filed the prior day with Air Tariff Publishing Co. are tracked by a Delta computer. "Secret" price changes that are deliberately withheld from the Air Tariff Publishing system for several days are tracked through local newspapers or calls to other airlines' reservation offices. Once Delta learns of a competitor's pricing move, it can put a matching fare into its reservation system within two hours.

Why do airlines take such drastic measures to learn the prices set by their rivals? The airlines compete in a Bertrand market. Firms need to know rivals' prices so that they can undercut them. Despite some brand loyalty created by frequent-flyer programs, a large number of airline customers choose a carrier based purely on price. To get these customers, an airline must succeed in charging the lowest price in the market. By continually monitoring rivals' prices, airlines are in a better position to set profit-maximizing prices.

Why do airfares change so frequently? Given the structure of the airline market, airlines find it profitable to "randomize" their prices so that rivals and consumers cannot learn from experience exactly what the price of a particular route is. By frequently changing its prices, an airline prevents rivals from learning the price they have to undercut to steal customers. With prices that vary randomly over time, an airline may be charging the highest price or lowest price in the market at a given instant. When it charges the lowest price, it sells tickets to both its price-conscious and loyal customers. When it charges high prices, it sells tickets only to its loyal customers, as the price-conscious flyers buy tickets from another airline.

Sources: Marius Schwartz, "The Nature and Scope of Contestability Theory," *Oxford Economic Papers,* Supplement 3, 1986, pp. 46–49; Michael R. Baye and Casper G. de Vries, "Mixed Strategy Trade Equilibrium," *Canadian Journal of Economics* 25, May 1992, pp. 281–93; *Travel and Leisure,* May 1992, p. 184.

Randomized Pricing

randomized pricing
A pricing strategy in which a firm intentionally varies its price in an attempt to "hide" price information from consumers and rivals.

The final strategy firms can use to enhance profits in markets with intense price competition is to engage in randomized-pricing strategies. With a **randomized-pricing** strategy, a firm varies its price from hour to hour or day to day. Such a strategy can benefit a firm for two reasons.

First, when firms adopt randomized pricing strategies, consumers cannot learn from experience which firm charges the lowest price in the market. On some days, one firm charges the lowest price; on another day, some other firm offers the best deal. By increasing the uncertainty about where the best deal exists, firms reduce consumers' incentive to shop for price information. Because one store offers the best deal today does not mean it will also offer the best deal tomorrow. To continually find the best price in the market, a consumer must constantly shop for a new deal. In effect, there is only a one-shot gain to a consumer of becoming informed; the information is worthless when new prices are set. This reduces consumers' incentive to invest in information about prices. As consumers have less information about the prices offered by competitors, firms are less vulnerable to rivals stealing customers by setting lower prices.

The second advantage of randomized prices is that they reduce the ability of rival firms to undercut a firm's price. Recall that in Bertrand oligopoly, a firm wishes to slightly undercut the rival's price. If another firm offers a slightly better deal, informed consumers will switch to that firm. Randomized pricing not only reduces the information available to consumers but it precludes rivals from knowing precisely what price to charge to undercut a given firm's price. Randomized-pricing strategies tend to reduce rivals' incentive to engage in price wars and thus can enhance profits.

We should point out that it is not always profitable to engage in randomized-pricing strategies. In many instances, other strategies, such as trigger or price-matching strategies, can be a more effective means of enhancing profits. Moreover, in some instances it may not be feasible to change prices as frequently as randomized-pricing strategies require. The cost of hiring personnel to continually change price tags can be prohibitive. Randomized pricing can work, however, when prices are entered in a computer and not directly on the products. It can also work when firms advertise "sales" in a weekly newspaper. In these instances, the prices advertised in the sales circular can be varied from week to week so the competition will not know what price to advertise to undercut the firm's price.

ANSWERING THE Headline

The average price differential of $5000 for the same car sold in Canada and the United States is considerable. All evidence indicates that exchanges rates have been the primary driver of this differential. Indeed, although no formal studies have been conducted, one would expect it to decrease, if not reverse, given the appreciation of Canada's exchange rate.

However, another factor certainly influences the gap. Canada's purchasing power party (PPP)–based GDP per capita for 2002 (the most recent year information is available for) was only US$29 400 while the United States' PPP-based GDP per capita was $37 600. This significant income gap indicates that Canadian spending capacity is smaller than that of their U.S. counterparts. As Americans are able to afford more, the fundamental law of economics dictates that prices will be higher in that market.

As automobile manufacturers must necessarily tailor their prices to the markets they are operating in, so must they guard against arbitrage. While there is an opportunity for a black market in automobile sales (and indeed news reports on the issue appear periodically), the laws punishing such cross-border traffic, and increased vigilance at the border, will be increasing the transportation costs of such vehicles. The result may be that automobile manufacturers will have effectively split the market, with cross-border shopping only a minor threat.

Source: World Facts and Figures site <www.worldfactsandfigures.com>.

Summary

This chapter presented pricing strategies used by firms with some market power. Unlike firms in a perfectly competitive market, when there are a small number of firms and products are slightly differentiated, a manager can use pricing strategies that will foster positive economic profits. These strategies range from simple markup rules to more complex two-part pricing strategies that enable a firm to extract all consumer surplus.

This chapter showed how markup rules come into existence. If a firm is monopolistic or monopolistically competitive, the elasticity from the firm's demand function can be used to find the markup factor that will maximize the firm's profits. If a manager operates in a Cournot oligopoly, the firm's own price elasticity is simply the number of firms in the market times the market elasticity. Knowing this, a manager in this kind of market can easily calculate the appropriate markup rule for his or her pricing strategies.

In some markets, the manager can actually do better than the single monopoly price. This can be accomplished through price discrimination or two-part pricing. Other pricing strategies that enhance profits include peak-load pricing, block pricing, commodity bundling, cross-subsidization, and optimal transfer pricing. The chapter concluded with descriptions of strategies that can help managers in a Bertrand oligopoly avoid the tendency toward zero economic profits.

Key Terms and Concepts

block pricing 397
commodity bundling 399
cross-subsidy 402
peak-load pricing 401
price discrimination 386

price matching 406
randomized pricing 410
transfer pricing 404
two-part pricing 392

Conceptual and Computational Questions

1. Based on the best available econometric estimates, the market elasticity of demand for your firm's product is −1.50. The marginal cost of producing the product is constant at $75, while average total cost at current production levels is $200. Determine your optimal per unit price if
   a. You are a monopolist
   b. You compete against one other firm in a Cournot oligopoly
   c. You compete against 19 other firms in a Cournot oligopoly

2. Based on the following graph (which summarizes the demand, marginal revenue, and relevant costs for your product), determine your firm's optimal price, output, and the resulting profits for each of the following scenarios:

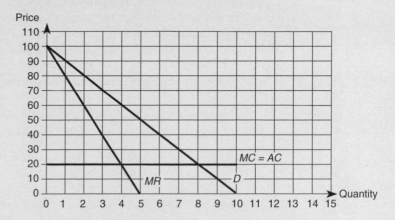

   a. You charge the same unit price to all consumers.
   b. You engage in first-degree price discrimination.
   c. You engage in two-part pricing.
   d. You engage block pricing.

3. You are the manager of a firm that charges customers $16 per unit for the first unit purchased, and $12 per unit for each additional unit purchased in excess of one unit. The accompanying graph summarizes your relevant demand and costs.
   a. What is the economic term for your firm's pricing strategy?

    b. Determine the profits you earn from this strategy.

    c. How much additional profit would you earn if you were able to perfectly price-discriminate?

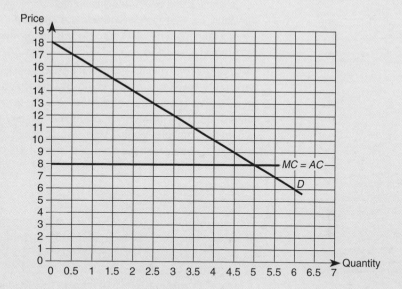

4. You are the manager of a monopoly that sells a product to two groups of consumers in different parts of the country. Group 1's elasticity of demand is -2, while group 2's is -6. Your marginal cost of producing the product is \$10.

    a. Determine your optimal markups and prices under third-degree price discrimination.

    b. Identify the conditions under which third-degree price discrimination enhances profits.

5. You are the manager of a monopoly. A typical consumer's inverse demand function for your firm's product is $P = 100 - 20Q$, and your cost function is $TC(Q) = 20Q$.

    a. Determine the optimal two-part pricing strategy.

    b. How much additional profit do you earn using a two-part pricing strategy compared with charging this consumer a per-unit price?

6. A monopoly is considering selling several units of a homogeneous product as a single package. A typical consumer's demand for the product is $Q^d = 50 - 0.25P$, and the marginal cost of production is \$120.

    a. Determine the optimal number of units to put in a package.

    b. How much should the firm charge for this package?

7. You are the manager of a firm that produces products X and Y at zero cost. You know that different types of consumers value your two products differently, but you are unable to identify these consumers individually at the time of the sale. In particular, you know there are three types of consumers (1000 of each type) with the following valuations for the two products:

Consumer Type	Product X	Product Y
1	\$60	\$ 50
2	50	125
3	25	140

    a. What are your firm's profits if you charge $25 for product X and $50 for product Y?

    b. What are your profits if you charge $60 for product X and $140 for product Y?

    c. What are your profits if you charge $110 for a bundle containing one unit of product X and one unit of product Y?

    d. What are your firm's profits if you charge $175 for a bundle containing one unit of X and one unit of Y, but also sell the products individually at a price of $60 for product X and $140 for product Y?

8. A large firm has two divisions: an upstream division that is a monopoly supplier of an input whose only market is the downstream division that produces the final output. To produce one unit of the final output, the downstream division requires one unit of the input. If the inverse demand for the final output is $P = 1000 - 80Q$, would the company's value be maximized by paying upstream and downstream divisional managers a percentage of their divisional profits? Explain.

Problems and Applications

9. You are the owner of a local Saturn dealership that competes against two other firms (Ford and Chrysler dealerships). Unlike other dealerships in the area, you take pride in your "No Hassles, No Haggle" sales policy. Last year, your dealership earned record profits of $1.5 million. However, according to the local chamber of commerce, your earnings were 10 percent less than either of your competitors. In your market, the price elasticity of demand for midsized Saturn automobiles is -4.5. In each of the last five years, your dealership has sold more midsized automobiles than any other Saturn dealership in the nation. This entitled your dealership to an additional 30 percent rebate off the manufacturer's suggested retail price (MSRP) in each year. Taking this rebate into account, your marginal cost of a midsized automobile is $11\ 000$. What price should you charge for a midsized automobile if you expect to maintain your record sales?

10. You are a pricing analyst for QuantCrunch Corporation, a company that recently spent $10\ 000$ to develop a statistical software package. To date, you only have one client. A recent internal study revealed that this client's demand for your software is $Q^d = 100 - 0.1P$ and that it would cost you $500 per unit to install and maintain software at this client's site. The CEO of your company recently asked you to construct a report that compares (1) the profit that results from charging this client a single per-unit price with (2) the profit that results from charging $900 for the first 10 units and $700 for each additional unit of software purchased. Construct this report, and include in your report a recommendation that would result in even higher profits.

11. You are the manager of a local sporting goods store and recently purchased a shipment of 60 sets of skis and ski bindings at a total cost of $30\ 000$ (your wholesale supplier would not let you purchase the skis and bindings separately, nor would it let you purchase fewer than 60 sets). The community in which your store is located consists of many different types of skiers, ranging from advanced to beginners. From experience, you know that different skiers value skis and bindings differently. However, you cannot profitably price-discriminate because you cannot prevent resale. There are about 20 advanced skiers who value skis at $350 and ski bindings at $250; 20 intermediate skiers who value skis at $250 and ski bindings at $375; and 20 beginning skiers who value skis at $175 and ski bindings at $325. Determine your optimal pricing strategy.

12. According to EMC, a leading researcher and publisher of intelligence about wireless markets, there are now more than 1 billion wireless phone subscribers world-

wide. In Canada, however, according to the Canadian Wireless Telecommunications Association (CWTA), Canadians currently use more than 16 million wireless devices on a daily basis, including 13.5 million wireless phones, more than 1.8 million pagers, 1 million mobile radios, and 10 000 mobile satellite phones. It is expected that by 2005 more than half of all Canadians be mobile phone customers. While the actual cost of basic wireless phone is about $75, most wireless carriers offer their customers a free phone with a one-year wireless service agreement. Is this pricing strategy rational? Explain.

13. The Canadian Baker's Association reports that annual sales of bakery goods last year rose 15 percent, driven by a 50 percent increase in the demand for bran muffins. Most of the increase was attributed to a report that diets rich in bran help prevent certain types of cancer. You are the manager of a bakery that produces and packages gourmet bran muffins, and you currently sell bran muffins in packages of three. However, as result of this new report, a typical consumer's inverse demand for your bran muffins is now $P = 3 - 0.5Q$. If your cost of producing bran muffins is $TC(Q) = Q$, determine the optimal number of bran muffins to sell in a single package and the optimal package price.

14. You are the owner of a hotel chain in Montreal. You recently read a report indicating that 80 percent of all tourists visit Montreal during the summer months in any given year. Travellers not planning ahead often have great difficulty finding hotel vacancies due to high demand. However, during non-summer months tourism drops dramatically and travelers have no problem securing hotel reservations. Determine the optimal pricing strategy, and explain why it is the best pricing strategy.

15. Blue Skies Aviation is a manufacturer of small single-engine airplanes. The company is relatively small and prides itself on being the only manufacturer of customized airplanes. The company's high standard of quality is attributed to its refusal to purchase engines from outside vendors, and it preserves its competitive advantage by refusing to sell engines to competitors. To achieve maximum efficiencies, the company has organized itself into two divisions: a division that manufactures engines and a division that manufactures airplane bodies and assembles airplanes. Demand for Blue Skies's customized planes is given by $P = 610\ 000 - 2000Q$. The cost of producing engines is $TC_e(Q_e) = 4000Q_e^2$, and cost of assembling airplanes is $TC_a(Q) = 10\ 000Q$. What problems would occur if the managers of each division were given incentives to maximize each division's profit separately? What price should the owners of Blue Skies set for engines in order to avoid this problem and maximize overall profits?

16. As a manager of a chain of movie theatres that are monopolies in their respective markets, you have noticed much higher demand on weekends than during the week. You therefore conducted a study that has revealed two different demand curves at your movie theatres. On weekends, the inverse demand functions is $P = 15 - 0.001Q$; on weekdays, it is $P = 10 - 0.001Q$. You acquire legal rights from movie producers to show their films at a cost of $20 000 per movie, plus a $2 "royalty" for each moviegoer entering your theaters (the average moviegoer in your market watches a movie only once). Devise a pricing strategy to maximize your firm's profits.

17. Many home entertainment and electronics retailers like Future Shop and Best Buy have low-price guarantee policies. At a minimum, these guarantees promise to match a rival's price, and some promise to beat the lowest advertised price by a given percentage. Do these types of pricing strategies result in cutthroat Bertrand competition and zero economic profits? If not, why not? If so, suggest an alternative pricing strategy that will permit these firms to earn positive economic profits.

CHAPTER 12

The Economics of Information

Headline

Bidding Opens for Wireless Spectrum in the 2300 MHz and 3500 MHz Bands

On February 9, 2004 Industry Canada through Spectrum Management and Telecommunications opened bidding for the 2300 MHz (in the WCS band) and 3500 MHz Band (in the FWA band) wireless spectrum.

Five licences in each of 172 service areas across the country (with the exception of the 3500 MHz licences for Vancouver Island), totalling 848 licences, are being auctioned. Following the publication of the spectrum auction policy on September 20, 2003, twenty-two companies made successful bids and are eligible to receive licences upon final payment. The bids are being conducted securely over the Internet using Canadian public key infrastructure encryption and digital signature technologies to ensure their confidentiality and authenticity.

Industry Canada on February 19, 2004 announced the provisional licence winners of this spectrum auction. Following the start of the auction on February 9, 2004, 392 licences were allocated with bids totalling over \$11.2 million. The allocation of this spectrum will enable carriers to extend and enhance wireless broadband access and services in both rural and urban areas throughout Canada. Why in your opinion has Industry Canada used an auction to assign this spectrum? What are the advantages of auctions? Do auctions mean higher prices for consumers?

Introduction

Throughout most of this book, we have assumed that participants in the market process—both consumers and firms—enjoy the benefits of perfect information. One need not look very hard at the real world to notice that this assumption is more fiction than fact. Nevertheless, our analyses in the preceding chapters can help us understand the market process. In fact, it is the basis for more complicated analysis that incorporates the effects of uncertainty and imperfect information.

More advanced courses in economics build on the foundations set forth in earlier chapters of this book by relaxing the assumption that people enjoy perfect information. While formal theoretical models of decision making in the presence of imperfect information are well beyond the scope and purpose of this book, it is useful to present an overview of some of the more important aspects of decision making under uncertainty. First, we will describe more formally what we mean by *uncertainty* and examine the impact of uncertainty on consumer behaviour. In this context, we will also discuss the utility analysis of risks and the concept of risk premium. Then we will briefly demonstrate means by which the manager can cope with risk. Finally, we will look at several important implications of uncertainty for the market process, including auction markets. Then we will briefly demonstrate means by which the manager can cope with risk. Finally, we will look at several important implications of uncertainty on the market process, including auction markets.

The Mean and the Variance

The easiest way to summarize information about uncertain outcomes is to use the statistical concepts of the mean and the variance of a random variable. More specifically, suppose there is some uncertainty regarding the value of some variable. The random variable, x, might represent profits, the price of output, or consumer income. Since x is a random variable, we cannot be sure what its actual value is. All we know is that with given probabilities, different values of the random variable will occur. For example, suppose someone promises to pay you (in dollars) whatever number comes up when a fair die is tossed. If x represents the payment to you, it is clear that you cannot be sure how much you will be paid. If you are lucky, you will roll a 6 and be paid \$6. If you are unlucky, you will roll a 1 and receive \$1. The probability that any number between 1 and 6 is rolled is 1/6, because there are six sides on the die. The expected value (or mean) of x is given by

$$Ex = \frac{1}{6}(\$1) + \frac{1}{6}(\$2) + \frac{1}{6}(\$3) + \frac{1}{6}(\$4) + \frac{1}{6}(\$5) + \frac{1}{6}(\$6) = \$3.50$$

In other words, even though you do not know for certain how much you will be paid when you roll the die, on average you will earn \$3.50.

mean (expected) value
The sum of the probabilities that different outcomes will occur multiplied by the resulting payoffs.

The **mean** or **expected value** of a random variable, x, is defined as the sum of the probabilities that different outcomes will occur times the resulting payoffs. Formally, if the possible outcomes of the random variable are $x_1, x_2, \ldots, x_n$ and the corresponding probabilities of the outcomes are $q_1, q_2, \ldots, q_n$, the expected value of x is given by

$$Ex = q_1x_1 + q_2x_2 + \ldots + q_nx_n$$

where $q_1 + q_2 + \ldots + q_n = 1$.

The mean of a random variable thus collapses information about the likelihood of different outcomes into a single statistic. This is a very convenient way of economizing on the amount of information needed to make decisions.

Demonstration PROBLEM 12–1

The manager of XYZ Company is introducing a new product that will yield $1000 in profits if the economy does not go into a recession. However, if a recession occurs, demand for the normal good will fall so sharply that the company will lose $4000. If economists project that there is a 10 percent chance the economy will go into a recession, what are the expected profits to XYZ Company of introducing the new product?

Answer

If there is a 10 percent chance of a recession, there is a 90 percent chance that there will not be a recession. Using the formula for the expected value of a random variable, the expected profits of introducing the new product are found to be

$$Ex = q_1x_1 + q_2x_2 = 0.1(-\$4000) + 0.9(\$1000) = \$500$$

Thus, the expected profits of introducing the new product are $500.

The mean provides information about the average value of a random variable but it yields no information about the degree of risk associated with the random variable. To illustrate the importance of considering risk in making decisions, consider the following two options:

Option 1: Flip a coin. If it comes up heads, you receive $1; if it comes up tails, you pay $1.

Option 2: Flip a coin. If it comes up heads, you receive $10; if it comes up tails, you pay $10.

Even though the stakes are much higher under option 2 than under option 1, each option has an expected value of zero. On average, you will neither make nor lose money with either option. To see this, note that there is a 50-50 chance the coin will land on heads. Thus, the expected value of option 1 is

$$E_{Option\ 1}[x] = \frac{1}{2}(\$1) + \frac{1}{2}(-\$1) = 0$$

and the expected value of option 2 is

$$E_{Option\ 2}[x] = \frac{1}{2}(\$10) + \frac{1}{2}(-\$10) = 0$$

The two options have the same expected value but are inherently different in nature. By summarizing information about the options using the mean, we have lost some information about the risk associated with the two options. Regardless of which option you choose, you will either gain money or lose money by flipping the coin. Under option 1, half the time you will make $1 more than the average and half the time you will make $1 less than the average. Under option 2, the deviation from the mean of the actual gain or loss is much greater: half the time you will make $10 more than the average, and half the time you will lose $10 more than the average. Since these deviations from the mean are much larger under option 2 than under option 1, it is natural to think of option 2 as being more risky than option 1.

While the preceding discussion provides a rationale for calling option 2 more risky than option 1, it is often convenient for the manager to have a number that summarizes the risk associated with random outcomes. The most common measure of *risk* is the variance, which depends in a special way on the deviations of possible outcomes from the mean. The **variance** of a random variable is the sum of the probabilities that different outcomes will occur times the squared deviations from the mean of the random variable. Formally, if the possible outcomes of the random variable are $x_1, x_2, \ldots, x_n$, their corresponding probabilities are $q_1, q_2, \ldots, q_n$, and the expected value of x is given by Ex, then the variance of x is given by

variance
The sum of the probabilities that different outcomes will occur multiplied by the squared deviations from the mean of the random variable.

$$\sigma^2 = q_1(x_1 - Ex)^2 + q_2(x_2 - Ex)^2 + \cdots + q_n(x_n - Ex)^2$$

standard deviation
The square root of the variance.

The **standard deviation** is simply the square root of the variance:

$$\sigma = \sqrt{\sigma^2} = \sqrt{q_1(x_1 - Ex)^2 + q_2(x_2 - Ex)^2 + \ldots + q_n(x_n - Ex)^2}$$

Let us apply these formulas to our coin tossing examples to see how the variance can be used to obtain a number that summarizes the risk associated with the options. In each case, only two possible outcomes occur with equal probabilities, so $q_1 = q_2 = 1/2$. The mean of each option is zero. Thus, the variance of option 1 is

$$\sigma^2_{Option\ 1} = \frac{1}{2}(1 - 0)^2 + \frac{1}{2}(-1 - 0)^2 = \frac{1}{2}(1) + \frac{1}{2}(1) = 1$$

The variance of option 2 is

$$\sigma^2_{Option\ 2} = \frac{1}{2}(10 - 0)^2 + \frac{1}{2}(-10 - 0)^2 = \frac{1}{2}(100) + \frac{1}{2}(100) = 100$$

Since

$$\sigma^2_{Option\ 1} = 1 < \sigma^2_{Option\ 2} = 100$$

option 2 is more risky than option 1. Since the standard deviation is the square root of the variance, the standard deviation of option 1 is 1 and the standard deviation of option 2 is 10.

Demonstration PROBLEM 12-2

Consider again the manager of XYZ Company who is introducing a new product that will yield $1000 in profits if the economy does not go into a recession. If a recession occurs, the company will lose $4000. If economists project that there is a 10 percent chance the economy will go into a recession, how risky is the introduction of the new product?

Answer

There is a 10 percent chance of a recession and a 90 percent chance of no recession. Thus, there is a 10 percent chance the firm will lose $4000 and a 90 percent chance it will make

$1000. We already calculated the expected profits to be $500. Using variance as a measure of risk,

$$\sigma^2 = 0.1(-4000 - 500)^2 + 0.9(1000 - 500)^2$$
$$= 0.1(-4500)^2 + 0.9(500)^2$$
$$= 2\ 025\ 000 + 225\ 000$$
$$= 2\ 250\ 000$$

The standard deviation is

$$\sigma = \sqrt{2\ 250\ 000} = 1500$$

Uncertainty and Consumer Behaviour

Now that you understand how to calculate the mean and variance of an uncertain outcome, we will see how the presence of *uncertainty* affects economic decisions of both consumers and managers.

Risk Aversion

In Chapter 4 we assumed consumers have preferences for bundles of goods, which were assumed to be known with certainty. We now will extend our analysis to preferences over uncertain outcomes.

Let F and G represent two uncertain prospects. F might represent the prospects associated with buying 100 shares of stock in company F, and G the prospects associated with buying 100 shares of stock in company G. When you purchase a stock, you are uncertain what your actual profits or losses will be; all you know is that there is some mean and variance in return associated with each stock. Different people exhibit different preferences for the same set of prospects. You may prefer F to G, while a friend prefers G to F. It simply is a matter of taste for risky prospects.

Because attitudes toward risk will differ among consumers, we must introduce some additional terminology to differentiate among these attitudes. First, a **risk-averse** person prefers a sure amount of $M to a risky prospect with an expected value of $M. A **risk-loving** individual prefers a risky prospect with an expected value of $M to a sure amount of $M. Finally, a **risk-neutral** individual is indifferent between a risky prospect with an expected value of $M and a sure amount of $M.

It is possible that for some prospects individuals will be risk loving, while for others they will be risk averse. For small gambles people typically are risk loving, whereas for larger gambles they are risk averse. You may be willing to bet a quarter that you can guess whether a flipped coin will come up heads or tails. The expected value of this gamble is zero. In this instance, you are behaving as a risk lover: you prefer the gamble with an expected payoff of zero to not playing (receiving zero for certain). If the stakes are raised to, say, $25 000, you will most likely choose not to bet. In this instance, you will prefer not betting (zero for certain) to the gamble with an expected value of zero.

risk averse
Preferring a sure amount of $M to a risky prospect with an expected value of $M.

risk loving
Preferring a risky prospect with an expected value of $M to a sure amount of $M.

risk neutral
Indifferent between a risky prospect with an expected value of $M and a sure amount of $M.

Managerial Decisions with Risk-Averse Consumers

For gambles with nontrivial outcomes, most individuals are risk averse. Here we will point out some implications of risk-averse consumers for optimal managerial decisions.

Product Quality. The analysis of risk can be used to analyze situations where consumers are uncertain about product quality. For instance, suppose a consumer regularly purchases a particular brand of car wax and thus is relatively certain about the underlying quality and characteristics of the product. If the consumer is risk averse, when will she be willing to purchase a car wax newly introduced to the market?

A risk-averse consumer prefers a sure thing to an uncertain prospect of equal expected value. Thus, if the consumer expects the new car wax to work just as well as the one she regularly purchases, then, other things equal, she will not buy the new product. The reason is that there is risk associated with using a new product; the new wax may make a car look much better than the old wax, or it may damage the paint on the car. When the consumer weighs these possibilities and concludes that the new wax is expected to be just as good as the wax she now uses, she decides not to buy the new product. The consumer prefers the sure thing (the current brand) to the risky prospect (the new product).

Firms use two primary tactics to induce risk-averse consumers to try a new product. First, the firm's manager may lower the price of the new product below that of the existing product to compensate the consumer for the risk associated with trying the new product. When firms send out free samples, they essentially use this technique because to the consumer the price of the new product is zero.

Alternatively, the manager can attempt to make the consumer think that the expected quality of the new product is higher than the certain quality of the old product. Typically firms do this using comparison advertising. For example, an advertisement might show 50 cars being waxed with a new wax and 50 cars being waxed with competitors' products; then the cars are repeatedly washed until only the 50 cars waxed with the new product still shine. If consumers are convinced by such an advertisement, they may go ahead and purchase the new product because its higher expected quality offsets the risk associated with trying a new product.

Chain Stores. Risk aversion also explains why it may be in a firm's interest to become part of a chain store instead of remaining independent. For example, suppose a consumer drives through Lethbridge, Alberta, and decides to eat lunch. There are two restaurants in the town: a local diner and a national hamburger chain. While the consumer knows nothing about this particular diner, his experience suggests that local diners typically are either very good or very bad. On the other hand, national hamburger chains have standardized menus and ingredients; the type and quality of product offered are relatively certain, albeit of average quality. Because the consumer is risk averse, he will choose to eat at the national chain, unless he expects the product of the local diner to be sufficiently better than the chain restaurant.

There is nothing special about the restaurant example; similar examples apply to retailing outlets, transmission shops, and other types of stores. While there are exceptions, out-of-town visitors typically prefer to make purchases at chain stores. Local customers are in a better position to know for certain the type and quality of products offered at stores in their town and may shop at the local store instead of the national chain. The key thing to notice is that even if the local store offers a better product than the national chain, the national chain can remain in business if the number of out-of-town customers is large enough.

Insurance. The fact that consumers are risk averse implies that they are willing to pay to avoid risk. This is precisely why individuals choose to buy insurance on their homes and automobiles. By buying insurance, individuals give up a small (relative to potential losses) amount of money to eliminate the risk associated with a catastrophic

Inside BUSINESS

12-1 The Likelihood of Business Failure

Thousands of businesses enter and exit the market place throughout the year. The best source of data in Canada is Statistics Canada's Employment Dynamics, which compares business in the base year with those in the year following. If a business is observed to exist in the year following year but not in the base year, it is considered an entry and vice versa for an exit of a business.

On the basis of the number in Figure 12–1, we see that for most of the 1980s the gross number of annual business entries remained around 150 000, while the number of exits increased steadily to a record in the period 1990–91; for once, the number of exits exceeded the number of entries. From a lower level after the recession of 1989–91, the number of entries grew again to nearly 150 000 by 1997–98. At the same time, the number of exits varied but generally decreased. From near-zero in 1991–92, the net number of entries remained low until 1996–97, when they again approached pre-recession levels.

Figure 12–1 also shows real GDP growth, a measure of the state of the economy. The business cycle is a key explanation for the variation of entries and exits over time. The number of entries increases when the economy expands, and drops in a slowdown, while the number of exits is inversely related to the state of the economy.

However, determining the probability of survival, defined as the percentage of new firms that continue to operate when they reach a given age, is a more useful way than determining average age of businesses because the majority of startup firms do not operate very long. The evidence for two size classes of businesses, *micro*, with fewer than five employees, and *small*, with five or more up to 99 employees, indicates that over the period 1984–96, the longest observable age was 11 years. The percentage of new firms that remain in business after one, two, or three years declines rapidly and consistently. That is, failure rates are high in the first few years after startup. This is even more so for micro businesses than it is for other small businesses. Beyond the first three years, survival rates of micro businesses continue to be well below those of larger small firms. Furthermore, the survival rates of new micro firms are consistently lowest in the Atlantic region for businesses of any age, and nearly the same holds for other small business. Small business survival rates are also low in the Prairies.

Source: Adapted from "Entries and Exits of Canadian Businesses up to 500 Employees, and GDP Growth," 1983–84 to 1998–99, available <http://strategis.ic.gc.ca/epic/internet/insbrp-rppe.nsf/vwapj/stats_may_e_01_updated.pdf/$file/stats_may_e_01_updated.pdf>, accessed August 1, 2004. Reproduced with the permission of the Minister of Public Works and Government Services, 2004.

FIGURE 12–1 Entries and Exits of Canadian Businesses up to 500 Employees, and GDP Growth, 1983–84 to 1998–99

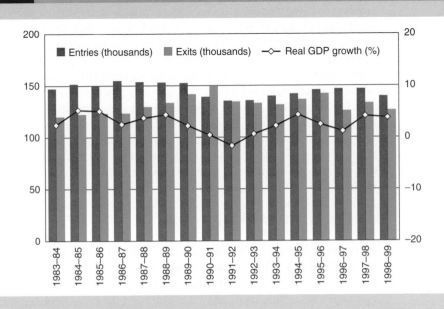

loss. For example, if a $100 000 house burns down, an uninsured homeowner loses $100 000; if it does not burn down, the homeowner loses nothing. Most homeowners are willing to pay several hundred dollars to avoid this risk. If the house burns down, the insurance company reimburses the homeowner for the loss. Thus, to a consumer, insurance represents a purchase of a "sure thing"—a house that is worth $100 000 regardless of whether or not it burns down.

Some firms give insurance to customers through "money-back guarantees." Other firms sell a form of insurance to customers. For example, many car manufacturers sell extended-warranty plans to customers whereby the company agrees to pay repair costs. This eliminates the risk associated with owning a car, thus making car ownership more attractive to risk-averse consumers.

The need for insurance occurs because people tend to be risk averse in many circumstances. As such, most of us are willing to pay for certainty. Those who satisfy this need for insurance, insurance companies for example, do so because they can pool risk. If insurance companies know the chance of some loss (an accident, illness, or whatever) and its cost, they can divide this cost among a large group of risk-averse types. The insurance company agrees to pay the cost of the loss and each of the risk-averse types pay a risk premium, but get the peace of mind that goes with certainty. **Risk pooling** is combining the uncertainty of individuals into a calculable risk for large groups. Risk pooling happens when many people get together and share their losses by averaging them together. Risk pooling works because of the "law of large numbers." As you average together more and more numbers in a certain range, the average becomes more and more stable. Unusually high or low numbers tend to cancel each other out.

For example, you may or may not get into a car accident. However, if you are thrown in with 99 999 other people, insurance companies will be able to predict that 1 percent of the group, or 1000 people, will get into an accident; the only uncertainty is that they do not know which 1000 people. This little bit of information is what makes risk pooling possible. If the cost is $1000 per accident, an insurance company can insure your 100 000-member group if they collect $1 000 000 ($1000 $\times$ 1000 accidents), or $10 per person. By agreeing to pay the cost of each accident in exchange for the $10 payments, the insurance company has effectively pooled the risk of the group.

Note that in order for risk pooling to work, the individual risks must be *independent*—they must go up and down at different times, not together, so that they tend to cancel each other out. Health care risks for individuals are generally independent, although contagious diseases or widespread disasters can change that. This is one reason why many life and property insurance policies exclude losses from catastrophic events such as war.

risk pooling
Many people getting together and sharing their losses by averaging them together.

Consumer Search

Up until now, we have assumed consumers know the prices of goods with certainty. The analysis is more complicated in situations where consumers do not know the prices charged by different firms for the same product.

Suppose consumers do not know the prices charged by different stores for some homogeneous commodity. Suppose there are numerous stores charging different prices for the same brand of watch. A consumer would like to purchase the product from the store charging the lowest price, but she does not know the prices being charged by individual stores. Let c denote the cost of obtaining information about the price charged by an individual store. For example, c might represent the cost of making a phone call, the cost of travelling to a store to find out what price it charges for a watch, or the cost of looking up a price in a catalogue.

Suppose that three-quarters of the stores in the market charge $100 for a particular brand of watch and one-quarter charge $40. If the consumer locates a store that sells a watch for $40, she clearly should stop searching; no store charges a price below $40.

What should a risk-neutral consumer do if she visits a store that charges $100? For simplicity, suppose the consumer searches with *free recall* and with *replacement*. By free recall we mean that the consumer is free to return to the store at any time to purchase the watch for $100. The fact that a consumer searches with replacement means that the distribution of prices charged by other firms does not change just because the consumer has learned that the one store charges $100 for a watch. Under these assumptions, if the consumer searches again, one-quarter of the time she will find a price of $40 and thus will save $100 − $40 = $60. But three-quarters of the time the consumer will find a price of $100, and the gains from having searched will be zero. Thus, the expected benefit of an additional search is

$$EB = \frac{1}{4}(\$100 - \$40) + \frac{3}{4}(0) = \$15$$

In other words, if the consumer searches for a price lower than $100, one-quarter of the time she will save $60, and three-quarters of the time she will save nothing. The expected benefit of searching for a lower price thus is $15.

The consumer should search for a lower price so long as the expected benefits are greater than the cost of an additional search. For example, if the cost of each search is $5, the consumer will find it in her interest to continue to search for a lower price. But if the cost of searching once more for a lower price is $20, it doesn't pay to continue searching for a better price.

This example reveals that the expected benefits of searching depend on the lowest price found during previous searches. If the lowest known price is p, the expected benefits (EB) from searching for a price lower than p slopes upward, as in Figure 12–2.

FIGURE 12-2 The Optimal Search Strategy

The expected benefit (EB) is represented by an upward-sloping relationship indicating that the higher the known price, the greater the expected benefit from an additional search. The cost per unit of search, c, is assumed as given and represented by a horizontal line. Where the benefit and cost of an additional search are equal—at the intersection point—the consumer is indifferent between purchasing at that price and searching for a better price.

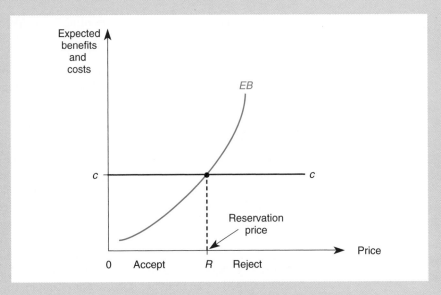

Inside BUSINESS

12-2 Risk Aversion and the Value of Selling the Firm: The St. Petersburg Paradox

Corporations often are sold at a price that seems much lower than the expected value of future profits. Before you conclude the market is not rational, ask yourself how much you would be willing to pay for the right to toss a coin when

- You receive 2 cents if the first heads is on the first flip
- You receive 4 cents if the first heads is on the second flip
- You receive 8 cents if the first heads is on the third flip
- More generally, you receive 2^n cents if the first heads is on the nth toss

Since coin flips are independent events, the expected value of participating in this coin toss gamble is

$$Ex = \left(\frac{1}{2}\right)2 + \left(\frac{1}{2}\right)^2 2^2 + \left(\frac{1}{2}\right)^3 2^3 + \left(\frac{1}{2}\right)^4 2^4 + \cdots$$
$$= 1 + 1 + 1 + 1 + \cdots$$
$$= \infty \text{ cents}$$

Thus, the expected value of this gamble is infinity: on average, you will make an infinite amount of money if you play this game. Of course, I know of no person willing to give up the world to play this particular game. I have found that in a class of 200 students, the most people will pay is about $2, which is considerably lower than the infinite expected value of the gamble. This outcome is known as the *St. Petersburg paradox.*

The answer to this paradox is that it is the utility individuals receive from winning a gamble, not the money itself, that is important. The satisfaction you derive from winning your first $1 million is much greater than that derived from winning your second $1 million, and so on. This diminishing marginal utility of income gives rise to risk aversion, meaning that individuals are willing to pay less than the expected value. For the case of the coin flip above, the difference between the expected value and the amount an individual is willing to pay is substantial. The same can be true when corporations are up for sale.

Intuitively, as lower prices are found, the savings associated with finding even lower prices diminish.

Figure 12–2 also illustrates the optimal search strategy for a consumer. The cost of each search is the horizontal line labeled c. If the consumer finds a price higher than R, the expected benefits of searching are greater than the cost, and the consumer should reject this price (continue to search for a lower price). On the other hand, if the consumer locates a price below R, it is best to accept this price (stop searching and purchase the product). This is because the expected benefits of searching for an even lower price are less than the cost of searching. If the consumer located a price of R, she would be indifferent between purchasing at that price and continuing to search for a lower price.

reservation price
The price at which a consumer is indifferent between purchasing at that price and searching for a lower price.

The **reservation price**, R, is the price at which the consumer is indifferent between purchasing at that price and searching for a lower price. Formally, if $EB(p)$ is the expected benefit of searching for a price lower than p, and c represents the cost per search, the reservation price satisfies the condition

$$EB(R) = c$$

Principle

THE CONSUMER'S SEARCH RULE
The optimal search rule is such that the consumer rejects prices above the reservation price (*R*) and accepts prices below the reservation price. Stated differently, the optimal search strategy is to search for a better price when the price charged by a firm is above the reservation price and stop searching when a price below the reservation price is found.

FIGURE 12–3 An Increase in Search Costs Raises the Reservation Price

An increase in the search cost causes the horizontal line to shift up. This tends to increase the reservation price, R^*, implying that consumers are less likely to search as intensively.

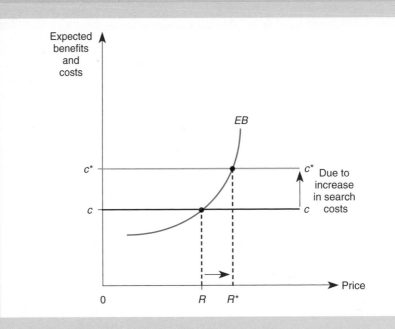

What happens if the cost of searching increases? As Figure 12–3 shows, an increase in search costs shifts up the horizontal line to c^*, resulting in a higher reservation price, R^*. This means the consumer will now find more prices acceptable and will search less intensively. Similarly, if the cost of searching for lower prices falls, the consumer will search more heavily for lower prices.

Our analysis of a consumer's decision to shop for lower prices can be used to aid managers in setting prices. In particular, when consumers have imperfect information about prices and search costs are low, the optimal prices set by a manager will be lower than when search costs are high. Moreover, managers must be careful not to price their products above consumers' reservation price; doing so will induce consumers to seek out lower prices at other firms. If you observe a large number of consumers "browsing" in your store but not making purchases, it may be a sign that your prices are set above their reservation price and that they have decided to continue to search for a lower price.

Utility, Risk Aversion, and Risk Premium

Suppose a job hunter in the field of management consulting is faced with two options. The first is a job offer from a large multinational company that promises to pay $50 000 a year. The second is an offer from a small but growing local company that promises to pay $20 000 a year plus a hefty $60 000 in commission assuming that the job hunter meets a million-dollar sales quota per year. Her assessment, however, shows that there is a 50 percent chance that she might meet this quota and 50 percent that she might not. The expected value of this lottery is

$$E(X) = 0.5(\$60\ 000) + 0.5(0) = \$30\ 000$$

On the basis of this calculation, which job would she choose?

If she chooses the job with the large multinational company, she is guaranteed $50 000, and if she accepts the job with the small local company, her expected income would be $50 000 ($20 000 salary plus $30 000 in expected commission). On the surface, it appears that both jobs offer the same income. However, it is very likely that she would choose the 100 percent salary job (certain outcome) with the multinational company over the local company's (risky) commission job. The reason is that the seemingly more exciting job with the local company may in fact end up paying her just $20 000, if our job hunter is unable to meet her quota. This suggests that most people, and that goes for firms' managers, faced with two alternative projects of equal expected value of profit but different coefficients of variation or risk, will generally prefer the less risky project (that is, the one with the smaller coefficient of variation). While it is true that some may very well choose the more risky project (that is, they are *risk seekers*) and some may be indifferent (that is, they are *risk neutral*), most managers are *risk averters*. The reason for this is to be found in the principle of diminishing marginal utility of money. The meaning of diminishing, constant, and increasing marginal utility of money will be explained with the aid of a reward structure that helps explain transformation of dollar payoffs into a more meaningful measurement. Utility is such a measurement, and it can be expressed in conceptual units called *utils*. Although it is difficult to establish a standard util by which one can perform a cardinal measurement of utility, it is nonetheless a useful concept.

Risk and Diminishing Marginal Utility

At this point, it is necessary to explain the relationship between risk and utility in a formal manner. To do so, profit and loss must be measured in terms of marginal utility rather than absolute dollar values. Marginal utility is defined as the change in total utility that takes place when one more unit of money is gained or lost.

The three ways in which utility may theoretically relate to income are depicted in Figures 12–4, 12–5, and 12–6. These figures depict behaviour of different types of investors when investment yield or income is increased by equal increments. Money income or wealth is measured along the horizontal axis while the utility or satisfaction of money (measured in utils) is plotted along the vertical axis. Each curve represents utility as a function of income, $U = U(I)$, where U stands for utils and I for income. The slope of each curve represents marginal utility, which is where our interest lies.

The most common behaviour, depicted in Figure 12–4, is that of a risk avoider (averter). The reason for risk aversion is *diminishing marginal utility*. It shows that with no investment there is no return. A given increment ($20 000) to income when income is low, zero, increases utility by 50 (vertical axis), $U($20 000$) = 50$, whereas the same increment to income when income is, say, $80 000 increases utility by a smaller amount, $U($100 000$) - U($80 000$) = (98 - 90) = 8$.

If, therefore, the total utility of the money curve is concave (or facing downward), doubling money income less than doubles utility. This is the basic explanation of risk and can be used to illustrate the behaviour of our job hunter.

Remember that our job hunter's salary at the established multinational company is $50 000, and as depicted in Figure 12–4 the level utility associated with this income, $U($50 000$)$, equals 78, point A. The job hunter's income at the less established local company, however, is one of the two cases. She either makes $20 000, in case she fails to make any commission income, when the corresponding utility would be 50, point B, or she makes $80 000, if she succeeds in meeting her quotas, when

FIGURE 12-4 The Utility Function of a Risk-Averse Individual

This is the case of the expected utility for a risk-averse decision maker, who loses more utility from a given drop in income than she gains for an increase in income of an equal magnitude. With zero income, there is no utility. Upon receipt of the $20 000, utility rises to 50, and when income rises to $80 000 (by four times), utility increases to 90. Clearly, marginal utility diminishes as income increases.

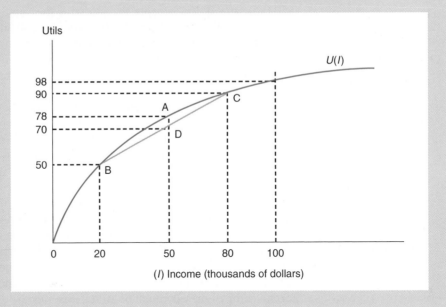

the corresponding utility would be 90, point C. Therefore, the job hunter's *expected utility* at the local company is the expected value of the utility levels she could receive if she worked for the local company:

$$0.50 \times U(\$20\ 000) + 0.50 \times U(\$20\ 000 + \$60\ 000)$$

$$= 0.5 \times 50 + 0.5 \times 90$$

$$= 70$$

This is depicted by point D in Figure 12–4.

The above analysis shows that although the local company offers the same expected salary as the established multinational company, the job hunter's expected utility at the local company, 70, is lower than the utility she would receive from the job with the multinational company, 78.

Thus, we see that the utility from the 100 percent salary job (risk-free) is greater than the expected utility from a commission-based job (risky) with equal expected value of income. Therefore, if our job hunter personality fits that represented by Figure 2–4, she will prefer the risk-free to the risky job. This is the preference of a decision maker who is *risk averse*.

In Figure 12–5, the utility function is a straight line, implying that doubling income doubles utility so that the marginal utility of money is constant. The straight-line utility function characterizes a person who is indifferent to risk, for whom marginal utility of a dollar lost is equal to that of a dollar gained.

Finally, in Figure 12–6, if the total utility of money curve is convex or faced down, doubling income more than doubles utility, so that the marginal utility of money income increases. This represents the case of compulsive gamblers, who put higher utility on dollars won than dollars lost. The more they win, the more important winning becomes.

FIGURE 12-5 | The Utility Function of a Risk-Neutral Individual

This is the case of the expected utility for a risk-neutral decision maker, who loses the same amount of utility from a given drop in income as she gains for an increase in income of an equal magnitude. With zero income, there is no utility. Upon receipt of the first $20 000, utility rises to 20. For the second $20 000 utility increases to 40. Clearly, marginal utility is constant. However, the individual represented by the solid line puts a greater utility on a dollar gained or lost than the individual represented by the dotted line.

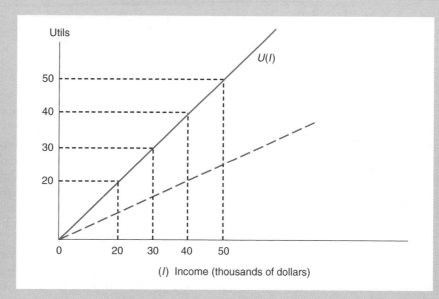

Most individuals are risk averters because their marginal utility of money diminishes; that is, they face a total utility curve that is concave or faces down. To see why this is so, consider the offer to engage in a bet to win $10 000 if a head turns up in the tossing of a coin or to lose $10 000 if a tail comes up. The expected value of the money won or lost is

$$E(I) = 0.5(\$10\ 000) + 0.5(-\$10\ 000) = 0$$

FIGURE 12-6 | The Utility Function of a Risk-Loving Individual

This is the case of the expected utility for a risk-loving decision maker, who loses less utility from a given drop in income than she gains for an increase in income of an equal magnitude. With zero income, there is no utility. Upon receipt of the $20 000, utility rises to 10, and when income doubles to $40 000, utility increases to 40 (quadruples). Clearly, marginal utility increase as income increases.

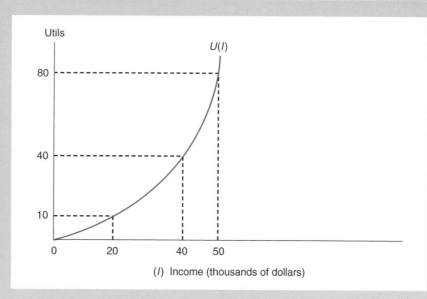

Risk Premium

Aversion to risk by managers and investors is manifest in many ways. The following are a few examples. Grade AA bonds sell for a higher price than grade B bonds. Investors diversify either by creating individual portfolios or by investing in mutual funds. People deposit their money in Treasury bills at low rates of interest rather than in bonds that may earn substantially more interest. And people buy all kinds of casualty and life insurance.

Why, then, if investors are averse to risk, do they put their money into common stocks, commodities, precious metals, collectibles, and other risky investments? The answer is that they do not do so unless they receive a **risk premium**. The investor wants to be compensated not only for the use of his or her money, but also for the risk that it may be lost. In other words, the investor demands a higher rate of return when risk is involved.

Accordingly, the *risk premium* is the minimum payment (compensation) to the risk-averse decision maker (our job hunter) to make her indifferent between the risky and risk-free events. In order to find the risk premium for our job seeker, let us ask the following question: At what level of sure (risk-free) income (with the multinational company) would the resulting level of utility be equal to the expected utility of the risky (commission-based) income? In Figure 12–7, the expected utility of the risky job that is expected to pay $50 000 is 70, point D. This is shown graphically by drawing a horizontal line to the vertical axis from point E (the risk-free income of $40 000 whose corresponding level of utility is also equal to 70), which bisects straight line BC, and hence representing an average of $20 000 and $80 000. Note that points E and D correspond to the same level of utility. Therefore, our job hunter would be indifferent between a $40 000 (all-salary) job with the multinational firm and a $50 000 risky (partly commission-based) job with the local company. Hence, the risk premium of the risky local company's offer is $10 000. Note that when risk increases so does the risk

---

FIGURE 12-7   The Risk Premium for a Risk-Averse Decision Maker

The expected utility of the risky job that is expected to pay $50 000 is 70, point D. Therefore, the risk-free income whose corresponding level of utility is also equal to 70 has to be about $40 000, at point E. Note that E and D correspond to the same level of utility. Our job hunter is indifferent between a $40 000 (all-salary) job with the multinational firm and a $50 000 risky job. Hence, the risk premium of the risky local company's offer is $10 000.

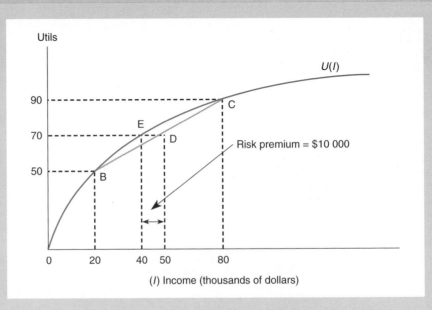

premium. More specifically, a doubling of the risk results in more than doubling the risk premium. This is due to the shape of the job hunter's utility function or curve, that is, the phenomenon of the diminishing marginal utility of income.

Demonstration PROBLEM 12–3

Suppose you have a utility function that is concave (faced down). Also suppose that you bet $100 on the flip of a coin at even odds. The probability of winning is 0.5 and the probability of losing is also 0.5. If you win, you will get $100 and if you lose you will lose $100. Should you take the bet?

Answer

Note that if you win, you get $100, and if you lose, you pay $100. We also know that if you win, you gain fewer utils of utility than you sacrifice if you lose $100. This is because of the shape of the utility function, diminishing marginal utility. Since the probability of winning or losing is the same, the expected value in utils is inevitably negative: 0.5(Utils gained) + 0.5(Utils sacrificed) < 0. This is so because utils gained are fewer than utils sacrificed. Clearly, the investor should not take this bet.

Demonstration PROBLEM 12–4

Suppose you have a utility function that is concave (faced down). Also suppose that you bet $100 on the flip of a coin at even odds. The probability of winning is 0.5 and the probability of losing is also 0.5. This time if you win, you will get $120 and if you lose you will lose $100. Should you take the bet?

Answer

It depends on the shape of your utility function. The $20 premium may or may not be sufficient to make you indifferent between the two possibilities. It may take more or less than $20 to take this bet. The curvature of the utility function speaks to this issue. The steeper the utility curve, the smaller the required risk premium, and vice versa.

Uncertainty and the Firm

We have seen that the presence of uncertainty has a direct impact on consumer behaviour and that the firm manager must take these effects into account to fully understand the nature of consumer demand. Uncertainty also affects the manager's input and output decisions. In this section, we will examine the implications of uncertainty for production and output decisions. It is important to point out that all of our analysis of the impact of uncertainty on consumer behaviour is directly applicable to the firm's manager. We will briefly discuss extensions of the analysis of uncertainty to highlight its direct influence on managerial decisions.

Risk Aversion

Just as consumers have preferences regarding risky prospects, so does the manager of the firm. A manager who is risk neutral is interested in maximizing expected profits; the variance of profits does not affect a risk-neutral manager's decisions. If the manager is risk averse, he or she may prefer a risky project with a lower expected value if it has lower risk than one with a higher expected value. Alternatively, if given a choice between a risky project with an expected return of $1 million and a certain return of $1 million, a risk-averse manager will prefer the sure thing. For the manager to be willing to undertake a risky project, the project must offer a higher expected return than a comparable "safe" project. Just how much higher depends on the manager's particular risk preferences.

Whenever a manager faces a decision to choose among risky projects, it is important to carefully evaluate the risks and expected returns of the projects and then to document this evaluation. The reason is simple. Risky prospects may result in bad outcomes. A manager is less likely to get fired over a bad outcome if she or he provides evidence that, based on the information available at the time the decision was made, the decision was sound. A convenient way to do this is to use mean-variance analysis, as the next Demonstration Problem illustrates.

Demonstration PROBLEM 12–5

A risk-averse manager is considering two projects. The first project involves expanding the market for bologna; the second involves expanding the market for caviar. There is a 10 percent chance of a recession and a 90 percent chance of an economic boom. During a boom, the bologna project will lose $10 000 whereas the caviar project will earn $20 000. During a recession, the bologna project will earn $12 000 and the caviar project will lose $8000. If the alternative is earning $3000 on a safe asset (say, a Treasury bill), what should the manager do? Why?

Answer

The first thing the manager should do is summarize the available information to document the relevant alternatives:

Project	Boom (90%)	Recession (10%)	Mean	Standard Deviation
Bologna	−$10 000	$12 000	−$ 7 800	6 600
Caviar	20 000	−8 000	17 200	8 400
Joint	10 000	4 000	9 400	1 800
T-bill	3 000	3 000	3 000	0

The "joint" option reflects what would happen if the manager adopted both the bologna and caviar projects. The entries under this option are obtained by vertically summing the payoffs of the individual options. For example, if the manager jointly adopted the caviar and bologna projects, during a boom the firm would lose $10 000 on the bologna project but make $20 000 on the caviar project. Thus, during a boom the joint project will result in a return of $10 000. Similar calculations reveal the joint project will yield a return of $4000 during a recession.

Based on the preceding table, what should a prudent manager do? The first thing to note is that the manager should not invest in a Treasury bill. The joint project will generate profits of $4000 during a recession and $10 000 during a boom. Thus, regardless of what happens to the economy, the manager is assured of making at least $4000 under the joint project, which is greater than the return of $3000 on the Treasury bill.

The second thing to notice is that the expected (mean) profits of the bologna project are negative. A risk-averse manager would never choose this project (neither would a risk-neutral manager). Thus, the manager should adopt either the caviar project or the joint project. Precisely which choice the manager makes will depend on his or her preferences for risk.

The returns associated with the joint project in the preceding problem reveal the important notion of *diversification,* which is taught in basic business finance courses. By investing in multiple projects, the manager may be able to reduce risk. This is merely a technical version of the adage, "Don't put all your eggs in one basket." As the example reveals, there are benefits to diversification, but whether it is optimal to diversify depends on a manager's risk preference and the incentives provided to the manager to avoid risk. Note that the main reason why mutual funds are so popular is that they achieve good diversity.

While many managers are risk averse, generally the owners of the firm (the stockholders) want the manager to behave in a risk-neutral manner. A manager who is risk neutral cares only about the expected value of a risky project, not the underlying task. More specifically, a risk-neutral manager's objective is to take actions that maximize the expected present value of the firm, that is, actions that maximize expected profits. A risk-neutral manager would choose a risky action over a sure thing provided the expected profits of the risky prospect exceeded those of the sure thing.

Why would shareholders want managers to take actions that maximize expected profits even when doing so might involve considerable risk? Shareholders can pool and diversify risks by purchasing shares of many different firms to eliminate the systematic risk associated with the firm's operation. It therefore is inefficient for managers to spend time and money attempting to diversify against risk when doing so will reduce the firm's expected profits. Thus, while the owners of a firm may be risk averse, they prefer managers who make risk-neutral decisions.

A simple example will illustrate why shareholders desire managers to behave in a risk-neutral manner. Suppose a manager must decide which of two projects to undertake. The first project is risky, with a 50-50 chance of yielding profits of $2 million or zero profits. The second project will yield a certain return of $900 000. The expected profits earned by the risky project are $1 million, which is greater than those of the project yielding a certain return. But the variance of the risky project is greater than that of the certain one; half of the time profits will be zero, half of the time they will be $2 million. Why would shareholders want the manager to undertake the risky project even though it has greater risk? The answer is that shareholders can purchase shares of many firms in the economy. If the managers of each of these firms choose the risky project, the projects will not pay off for some firms but will pay off for others. If the profits earned by one firm are independent of those earned by other firms, then, on average, the unfavourable outcomes experienced by some firms will be more than offset by the favourable outcomes at other firms. This situation is similar to flipping a coin: flip a coin once, and you cannot be sure it will turn up heads; flip a coin many times, and you can rest assured that half the flips will be heads. Similarly, when shareholders own shares of many different firms, each of which takes on risky projects, they can rest assured that half of the firms will earn $2 million.

For these reasons, as a manager you are likely to be given an incentive to maximize the expected profits of your firm. If you are provided with such incentives, you will behave in a risk-neutral manner even if you and the owners of the firm are risk averse.

Producer Search

Just as consumers search for stores charging low prices, producers search for low prices of inputs. When there is uncertainty regarding the prices of inputs, optimizing firms employ optimal search strategies. The search strategy for a risk-neutral manager will be precisely the same as that of a risk-neutral consumer. Rather than repeat the basic theory, it is more useful to illustrate these concepts with an example.

InsideBUSINESS

12-3 Searching for Workers

Managers spend considerable time searching for new employees. Thus, it is important for them to know when to continue searching for another employee and when to stop searching by hiring one who has already been interviewed. How many applicants does the average manager reject before finding an employee willing to work for an acceptable wage? How much time (a component of search costs) is spent engaging in these activities? A recent study provides answers to these questions.

The average manager searching for an employee sees about 3.7 applicants before finding a qualified worker willing to work at a wage below the firm's reservation price. The time cost of searching for workers is substantial; the average manager spends about 6.4 hours examining each applicant he or she sees. There is, however, considerable variation in these numbers for managers seeking different types of workers. For instance, managers tend to search more when hiring workers who require a lot of training. For each 10 percent increase in the amount of

training required, firms spend about 1.8 percent more time per applicant. Firms also search more heavily when hiring a manager or a professional worker—about 33 percent more time per application—than when hiring a blue-collar worker. Firms also search more intensely for permanent workers than for temporary or seasonal workers; in fact, firms spend about 24 percent less time per applicant when hiring temporary workers.

Larger firms also spend much more time searching than smaller firms: A firm with 500 employees spends about 80 percent more time per applicant than a firm with 100 employees. Thus, managers of large firms should expect to spend more time searching for workers than managers of smaller firms.

Source: John M. Barron, Dan A. Black, and Mark A. Loewenstein, "Job Matching and On-the-Job Training," *Journal of Labor Economics* 7, January 1989, pp. 1–19.

Demonstration PROBLEM 12–6

A risk-neutral manager is attempting to hire a worker. All workers in the market are of identical quality but differ with respect to the wage at which they are willing to work. Suppose half of the workers in the labour market are willing to work for a salary of $40 000 and half will accept a salary of $38 000. The manager spends three hours interviewing a given worker and values this time at $300. The first worker the manager interviews says he will work only if paid $40 000. Should the firm manager make him an offer, or interview another worker?

Answer

This is an optimal search problem with a search cost of $300. If the manager searches for another worker, half of the time she will find one willing to work for $38 000 and thus will save $2000. But half of the time the manager will find a worker just like the one she chose not to hire, and the effort will have been for nothing. Thus, the expected benefit of interviewing another worker is

$$EB = \frac{1}{2}(\$2000) + \frac{1}{2}(0) = \$1000$$

Since this is greater than the cost of $300, the manager should not hire the worker but instead search for a worker willing to work for $38 000.

Profit Maximization

The basic principles of profit maximization can also be modified to deal with uncertainty. To illustrate how the basic principles of profit maximization are affected by the presence of uncertainty, let us suppose the manager is risk neutral and demand is uncertain. Recall that the goal of a risk-neutral manager is to maximize expected profits.

The risk-neutral manager must determine what output to produce before she is certain of the demand for the product. Because demand is uncertain, revenues are uncertain. This means that to maximize expected profits, the manager should equate expected marginal revenue with marginal cost in setting output:

$$EMR = MC$$

The reason is simple. If expected marginal revenue exceeded marginal cost, the manager could increase expected profits by expanding output. The production of another unit of output would, on average, add more to revenue than it would to costs. Similarly, if expected marginal revenue were less than marginal cost, the manager should reduce output. This is because by reducing output, the firm would reduce costs by more than it would reduce expected revenue.

Thus we see that when the manager is risk neutral, profit maximization under uncertain demand is very similar to profit maximization under certainty. All that needs to be done is adjust the corresponding formula to represent what the manager expects marginal revenue to be.

Demonstration PROBLEM 12–7

Appleway Industries produces apple juice and sells it in a competitive market. The firm's manager must determine how much juice to produce before he knows what the market (competitive) price will be. Economists estimate that there is a 30 percent chance the market price will be $2 per gallon and a 70 percent chance it will be $1 when the juice hits the market. If the firm's cost function is $TC = 200 + 0.0005Q^2$, how much juice should be produced to maximize expected profits? What are the expected profits of Appleway Industries?

Answer

The profits of Appleway Industries are given by

$$\pi = pQ - 200 - 0.0005Q^2$$

Since price is uncertain, the firm's revenues and profits are uncertain. For a competitive firm, $MR = p$; thus, marginal revenue also is uncertain. Marginal cost is given by $MC = 0.001Q$. To maximize expected profits, the manager equates expected price with marginal cost:

$$Ep = 0.001Q$$

The expected price is given by

$$Ep = 0.3(2) + 0.7(1) = 0.60 + 0.70 = \$1.30$$

Equating this with marginal cost, we obtain

$$1.30 = 0.001Q$$

Solving for Q, we find that the output that maximizes expected profits is $Q = 1300$ gallons. Expected profits for Appleway Industries are

$$E\pi = EpQ - 200 - 0.0005Q^2$$
$$= 1.30(1300) - 200 - 0.0005(1300)^2$$
$$= 1690 - 200 - 845 = \$645$$

Thus, Appleway Industries can expect to make \$645 in profits.

While our analysis of profit maximization under uncertainty is far from exhaustive, it points out that much of our previous analysis can be easily extended to deal with uncertainty. In fact, these extensions are important topics in more advanced courses in economics.

Asymmetric Information, Moral Hazard, and Adverse Selection

The presence of uncertainty can have a profound impact on the ability of markets to efficiently allocate resources. In this section, we examine some problems created in markets when there is uncertainty. We also show how managers and other market participants can overcome some of these problems.

Asymmetric Information

When some people in the market have better information than others, the people with the least information may choose not to participate in a market. To see why this is so, suppose someone offers to sell you a box full of money. You do not know how much money is in the box, but she does. Should you choose to buy the box?

The answer is no. Since she knows how much money is in the box, she will never sell you the box unless you offer her more for the box than is in it. Suppose she knows the box contains \$10. If you offered her \$6 for the box, she would have no incentive to engage in the transaction. If you offered her \$12, she would gladly sell you the box, and you would lose \$2.

asymmetric information
A situation that exists when some people have better information than others.

As the preceding example reveals, **asymmetric information** can result in a situation where people with the least information rationally refuse to participate in the market. If you think of the box in the example as being a company whose stock is traded on the TSX or NASDAQ, it should be clear why there is so much concern over insider trading—the buying and selling of stocks by persons who have privileged information about a firm. If some people know for certain what a stock will sell for tomorrow (say, due to a takeover) and others do not, asymmetric information exists. The only time insiders will purchase stock is when they know it is selling at a price below what it is worth; the only time insiders will sell stock is when they know it is selling at a premium over what it is worth. If people know that insiders regularly trade in the stock market, people who are not insiders may rationally choose to stay out of the stock market to avoid paying too much for a stock or selling it for too little. In extreme cases, this situation can completely destroy the stock market, as no one is willing to buy or sell shares of firms' stock. For this reason, there are laws that restrict persons with privileged information about a firm from buying shares of that firm's stock.

Asymmetric information between consumers and the firm can affect firm profits. For example, suppose a firm invests in developing a new product that it knows to be superior to existing products in the market. Consumers, on the other hand, are unlikely to know whether the new product is truly superior to existing products or whether the firm is falsely claiming the product to be superior. If the degree of asymmetric information is severe enough, consumers may refuse to buy a new product even if it really is better than existing products. The reason is that they do not know the product is indeed superior.

Asymmetric information affects many other managerial decisions, including hiring workers and issuing credit to customers. In particular, job applicants have much better information about their own capabilities than does the person in charge of hiring new workers. A job applicant who claims to have excellent skills may be lying or telling the truth; the personnel manager has less information than the applicant. This is why firms spend considerable sums designing tests to evaluate job applicants, doing background checks, and the like. The basic reason for these types of expenditures is to provide the firm with better information about the capabilities and tendencies of job applicants. Similarly, a consumer who wishes to make a purchase on credit has much better information about his own ability to pay off the debt than does the creditor. Of course, every consumer seeking to purchase on credit will claim that he or she will pay off the debt. Asymmetric information makes it difficult for the firm to know whether a person actually will pay off the debt. In fact, firms pay sizable sums to credit bureaus to obtain better information about their credit customers. These expenditures reduce asymmetric information and make it more difficult for customers to take advantage of it.

With this overview of some problems that can arise in the presence of asymmetric information, we turn now to two specific manifestations of asymmetric information: adverse selection and moral hazard. These two concepts are often difficult to distinguish, so it is useful first to distinguish between the types of asymmetric information that generally lead to adverse selection and moral hazard.

Adverse selection generally arises when an individual has **hidden characteristics**—characteristics that she knows, but that are unknown by the other party in an economic transaction. In our example of the job applicant, for instance, the worker knows his own abilities but the employer does not. The worker's ability thus reflects a hidden characteristic. In contrast, moral hazard generally occurs when one party takes **hidden actions**—actions that it knows another party cannot observe. For example, if the manager of a firm cannot monitor a worker's effort, then the worker's effort represents a hidden action. Just as it is often difficult to distinguish between ability (a characteristic) and effort (an action), it is sometimes difficult to distinguish between adverse selection and moral hazard.

Adverse Selection

Adverse selection refers to a situation where a selection process results in a pool of individuals with economically undesirable characteristics. A simple example highlights the basic issues involved in adverse selection.

Consider an industry in which all firms allow their employees five days of paid sick leave. Suppose one firm decides to increase the number of paid sick leave days from five to ten to attract more workers. If the workers have hidden characteristics—that is, if the firm cannot distinguish between healthy and unhealthy workers—the plan will probably lure many workers away from other firms. But what type of workers is the firm most likely to attract? Workers who know they are frequently ill, and thus who value sick leave the most. Workers who know they never get sick will have little incentive to leave their current employers, but those who are frequently sick will. From the firm's point of view, the policy attracts undesirable workers. In economic terms, the policy results in adverse selection.

---

hidden characteristics
Things one party to a transaction knows about itself but which are unknown by the other party.

hidden action
Action taken by one party in a relationship that cannot be observed by the other party.

adverse selection
Situation where individuals have hidden characteristics and in which a selection process results in a pool of individuals with undesirable characteristics.

Adverse selection explains why people with poor driving records find it difficult to buy automobile insurance. Suppose there are two types of people with bad driving records: (1) those who are poor drivers and frequently have accidents and (2) those who are good drivers but, due purely to bad luck, have been involved in numerous accidents in the past. Past accidents by bad drivers are a result of their driving habits and are good indicators of the number of expected future accidents. Past accidents by good drivers, on the other hand, are not a good indicator of the expected number of future accidents; they merely reflect an unusual string of bad luck.

An insurance company has asymmetric information; it does not know whether a person with a bad driving record is truly a poor driver or whether past accidents were unusual events due to bad luck. Assuming that those who have poor driving records know their own type, we have a situation where one side of the insurance market has hidden characteristics. Suppose an insurance company decides to insure drivers with poor driving records, but at a very high premium to cover the anticipated future claims due to bad driving. The insurance company must charge all drivers with bad records the same insurance rate, since it cannot distinguish between those who are good drivers and those who are bad drivers. By charging the same price to both types of drivers, adverse selection results. As the insurance company raises insurance rates to cover the losses of bad drivers, the only people who will be willing to pay the higher price are those drivers who know they are most likely to have accidents. The good drivers, who know that their past accidents were unusual events, will not be willing to pay the high rate. Thus, the insurance company will end up selling policies only to the drivers most likely to wreck their cars. Since insurance works only when there are some drivers who pay premiums and do not wreck their automobiles, insurance companies typically find it in their interest to charge lower prices for insurance and refuse to insure any driver with a bad driving record. Doing otherwise would lead to adverse selection within the pool of drivers with poor records.

Asymmetric information also plays a significant role in other markets. For example, the distinguishing features of the market for used cars are: (a) considerable uncertainty about the quality of used cars, which varies wildly; and (b) information asymmetry, since sellers have much better information about the cars than buyers. As a result, the resale value of a car after leaving the showroom is considerably lower than its original price.

How can one explain this price differential? The explanation can be found in the concept of adverse selection. There is a wide range of quality; some cars are in excellent condition and some are **lemons**—which basically means they have persistent mechanical problems. The point is that the buyer, not knowing the true value of the cars, expects low-quality cars to be sold on the lot; and the seller, knowing full well the true value of the cars, does not sell high-quality cars. This asymmetric information gives rise to an equilibrium situation in which the market is dominated by low-quality cars.[1]

lemons
Vehicles with persistent mechanical problems.

moral hazard
A situation in which one party to a contract takes a hidden action that benefits him or her at the expense of another party.

Moral Hazard

Sometimes, one party agrees to insulate from economic loss the other party to a contract. If the contract induces the party that is insulated from loss to take a hidden action that harms the other party, we say that **moral hazard** exists.

---

[1]This discussion is based on the classic article by G. A. Akerlof, "The Market for 'Lemons': Quality Uncertainty and the Market Mechanism," *Quarterly Journal of Economics* 84(3), August 1970, pp. 488–500.

Consider, for instance, the principal-agent problem we first examined in Chapter 6. In this setting the owner hires a manager to operate the firm, which earns profits that vary randomly with economic conditions. Unfortunately, profits also depend on the manager's effort, which is unobservable to the owner. Thus, the effort of the manager represents a hidden action. Notice that if the owner agrees to pay the manager a fixed salary of $50 000 (the contract), then the manager is completely insulated from any economic loss that might arise due to random fluctuations in the firm's profits. The manager now has an incentive to spend less time at the office (the hidden action), and the reduced effort of the manager results in lower firm profits (and thus harms the owner). In other words, the fixed salary contract, coupled with the hidden action of the manager, results in moral hazard. As we learned in Chapter 6, the owner can overcome this problem by either monitoring the manager (taking away the hidden action) or by making the manager's pay contingent on the firm's profits (taking away the manager's insurance against economic loss).

As you might suspect, the nature of insurance markets makes insurance companies particularly vulnerable to the moral hazard problem. As we discussed earlier in this chapter, the fact that individuals are risk averse provides an incentive for them to purchase insurance against large losses. Most people have insurance on their homes and automobiles, and some form of health insurance. Usually the probability of a loss depends on the hidden effort expended by the insured to avoid the loss. Thus, a moral hazard exists: when individuals are fully insured, they have a reduced incentive to put forth effort to avoid a loss.

For example, suppose a company rents cars and fully insures renters against damage to the cars. Obviously, the company cannot observe the effort put forth by renters to avoid damages to rented vehicles. Since renters are fully insured and can take hidden actions that may result in damages to cars, they are indifferent between returning the car with a stolen radio and returning the car in perfect condition. If a radio is stolen, the replacement cost is paid for out of the company's pocket. Thus, when the car is fully insured, the driver has no incentive to take the time to lock the car or to avoid parking the car in areas where theft is likely. If the car were uninsured, the driver would have to replace stolen items with his or her own money and therefore would be much more careful with the car. Thus, if the company insures renters against damage, drivers will be less careful with cars than if they were not insured against damage. In economic terms a moral hazard exists.

One way car insurance companies attempt to reduce moral hazard is by requiring a deductible on all insurance claims. If the deductible is $200, the first $200 in losses is paid by the insured. This effectively means that the person buying insurance must pay something in the event of a loss and thus has an incentive to take actions to reduce the likelihood of a loss.

Under a public health system, such as that in Canada, individuals do not have to pay for the cost of medical services. As a consequence, individuals are more likely to visit a doctor when they have a minor illness (say a cold) than they would if they had to pay for the medical service. In this system, the moral hazard results in an increase in the demand for medical services, leading to a higher equilibrium price. This is because the basic care is free of charge and thus individuals use physicians' services more frequently than otherwise. Therefore, the moral hazard is the primary cause of rising medical costs in Canada in the past decade.

On the other hand, in a private health system, such as that in the United States, when individuals have health insurance or belong to a health maintenance organization, they do not pay for the full marginal cost of medical services, even though they do pay for a portion of the cost. In this system also, the moral hazard leads to a higher equilibrium price. However, here there is also a second problem. The rising medical costs tend to increase the cost of private medical insurance claims, prompting insurance companies to increase the rates they charge for medical insurance. This might lead those who know they are in good health to decide against insurance coverage, which means that the higher medical insurance premiums also lead to adverse selection. In this case, the insurance company is left to insure a pool of less healthy individuals, which exacerbates the problem. Thus, while a system of public heath, such as that in Canada, may be conducive to moral hazard, a private health system, such as that in the United States, is conducive to moral hazard as well as adverse selection.

The effect of this is twofold. First, the moral hazard results in an increase in the demand for medical services, leading to a higher equilibrium price of medical services. This is because individuals do not pay the full cost of a visit to a doctor and thus use physicians' services more frequently than they would if they were required to pay the full cost of each visit. Second, insurance companies must increase the rates they charge for medical insurance to cover the higher costs of insurance claims due to more frequent visits. This might lead those who know they are in good health to decide against insurance coverage, which means that the higher medical insurance premiums also lead to adverse selection. In this case the insurance company is left to insure a pool of less healthy individuals, which exacerbates the problem. Thus, moral hazard and adverse selection may be partially responsible for the recent increases in the cost of medical insurance.

Signalling and Screening

We learned that incentive contracts can be used to mitigate moral hazard problems that stem from hidden actions. We now show how managers and other market participants can use signalling and screening to mitigate some of the problems that arise when one party to a transaction has hidden characteristics.

signalling
An attempt by an informed party to send an observable indicator of his or her hidden characteristics to an uninformed party.

Signalling occurs when an informed party sends a signal (or indicator) of his or her hidden characteristics to an uninformed party in an attempt to provide information about these hidden characteristics. In product markets, firms use a host of devices to signal product quality to consumers: money-back guarantees, free trial periods, and packaging labels which indicate that the product has won a "special award" or that the manufacturer has been in business since 1933. In labour markets, job applicants attempt to signal their ability through résumés that tout their "pedigree" (the school at which they earned an undergraduate degree) or the fact that they have an advanced degree such as an M.B.A. or Ph.D.

For a signal to provide useful information to an otherwise uninformed party, the signal must be observable by the uninformed party. Moreover, the signal must be a reliable indicator of the underlying unobservable characteristic and difficult for parties with other characteristics to easily mimic. To be concrete, consider a manager who wishes to hire a worker from an employment pool that consists of two types of individuals: (1) unproductive workers, who produce nothing; and (2) productive workers, who each have a value marginal product of $80 000 per year. Obviously, if the labour market is perfectly competitive and the manager can observe the productivity of workers before hiring them, unproductive workers will earn a salary of zero and productive workers will earn a salary that equals their value marginal product—$80 000 per year.

The situation is dramatically different when managers cannot observe the productivity of a worker by simply looking at the worker. Suppose that at the time of the hiring decision, workers know whether or not they are productive, but managers do not.

Inside BUSINESS

12-4 Employment Insurance: A Case of Moral Hazard and Adverse Selection

The major declared objective of the Employment Insurance (EI) program is the provision of insurance against the interruption of earnings due to unemployment. This may be called the *insurance* or *efficiency objective*, in that the probable failure of private EI markets to exist on a comprehensive basis provides the fundamental efficiency rationale for publicly funded EI.

The extent to which the insurance objective can be achieved is constrained by two phenomena which exist in any insurance market: adverse selection and moral hazard. These two effects make the public provision of insurance more costly to society of operating such a program.

In the EI program, problems due to adverse selection are substantially minimized by having compulsory coverage. In Canada, where EI coverage is over 90 percent, the concern about adverse selection is mainly limited to the recent growth of non-standard employment (for example, part-time work, outsourcing, etc.) which at present is not covered. However, moral hazard effects remain a central concern for EI and these are an important focus of this study.

The extent to which the EI program meets the insurance objective depends on the level and duration of benefits received. The more generous the benefits (that is, the shorter the waiting period, the greater the benefit/wage replacement rate, and the longer the maximum benefit duration), the greater the value of EI as insurance, but also the greater the moral hazard effects. As a consequence, there is a tradeoff between meeting the insurance objective and minimizing costly side effects due to moral hazard.

EI has also evolved to have equity objectives relating to the distribution of income among individuals and regions. The extent to which EI should pursue equity objectives and the degree to which tradeoffs should be made between the insurance and distributional objectives are important issues in any overall evaluation of the program.

The larger study on the insurance or temporary income protection role of EI addresses a number of questions related to the tradeoffs that arise in meeting the insurance objective because of moral hazard effects and those that may exist between the insurance and equity objectives. These evaluation questions are intimately related to questions regarding the effects of EI parameters such as the benefit rate, the maximum duration of benefits and entrance requirement on labour force participation, and employment and non-employment durations.

The entrance requirements for EI are a key tool for battling moral hazard problems in EI use, and the focus of this particular analysis. Lengthening the entrance requirement will make it less likely that individuals enter the work force or lengthen job spells in order to qualify for EI. Setting very high entrance requirements may also discourage the use of EI to subsidize seasonal work patterns. Alternatively, a short entrance requirement may make it less costly for workers and firms to terminate poor job matches, allowing workers to expend more effort in searching for a better match. For both reasons, one would like to know whether the entrance requirement has a significant impact on employment durations and how individuals adjust to changes in the entrance requirement.

From the manager's perspective, there is a 50-50 chance that a given worker is productive or unproductive. Since the expected value marginal product of a worker is 0.5(0) + 0.5($80 000) = $40 000, a risk-neutral manager will only be willing to pay a salary of $40 000 to hire a worker with unobservable characteristics. Notice that the unproductive worker earns more than he would have earned if his characteristic were observable to the manager, and the productive worker earns less than he would have earned if the manager knew he was productive. The manager's lack of information, in this case, benefits unproductive workers at the expense of productive ones.

Since productive workers are harmed by the manager's lack of information, it is in their best interest to attempt to provide information to the manager that reveals that they are indeed productive; doing so will boost their salary from $40 000 to $80 000. How can they signal their productivity to the manager? You might think that it would be enough for productive workers to simply tell the manager that they are productive. The problem with this approach is that talk is cheap; if productive workers could boost their earnings by $40 000 by simply declaring "I'm productive," then unproductive workers could easily mimic this strategy to earn an extra $40 000. For this

Inside BUSINESS

12-5 Moral Hazards of No-Fault Insurance

The siren call of "pure" no-fault automobile insurance has been echoing across Canada. The imminent introduction of no-fault insurance raises familiar questions. "Is no-fault automobile insurance better than a tort liability system in containing premium costs, producing fairer awards, and reducing injuries?" The quick answer, based on empirical evidence of no-fault insurance and economic theory, is that no-fault does not deliver the benefits promised; it simply redistributes the costs, which may actually increase.

A tort liability system allows automobile injury victims full access to the courts to sue at-fault drivers and/or their insurance company for losses, economic or personal, beyond what is covered by the insurance of either or both parties. A pure no-fault insurance system does not allow injury victims to pursue compensation in the courts. Rather, all benefits are set by the insurer according to a predetermined scale. Variations of the no-fault regime include add-on insurance that sets a basic amount which injured parties receive whether or not they were at fault. Most provinces, including British Columbia, have some form of add-on no-fault insurance. Other mixed no-fault schemes allow victims to sue if they meet either a "verbal threshold," based on the severity of injuries sustained, or a "monetary threshold," based on the cost of care.

THE ORIGIN OF THE DEBATE

The origin of the current no-fault debate in Canada starts in British Columbia. New Zealand, however, was the first country to adopt a pure no-fault scheme, in 1974, followed by Australia's Northern Territory, in 1979. In Canada, limited add-on no-fault insurance schemes have been adopted by several Canadian provinces, starting with Saskatchewan in 1946. In 1978, Quebec was the first North American jurisdiction to move to a pure no-fault regime. Manitoba followed suit in 1994 and Saskatchewan in 1995. Ontario introduced no-fault insurance under a "verbal threshold" in 1990, graduated to a pure no-fault system in 1994, then returned to "verbal threshold" in 1996.

One of the most controversial issues is the impact of no-fault insurance on the rate of accidents, injuries, and fatalities. Evidence from Quebec points out that since 1978, both fatal accidents and accidents leading to injuries have increased. Findings in New Zealand and Australia's Northern Territory following their introduction of pure no-fault insurance schemes corroborate the evidence from Quebec. In any event, conclusions would be hard to draw given the prevalence of public monopoly insurers who often set premium levels by political rather than actuarial calculations. Still, it is worth noting the "coincidence" that the provinces that have had pure no-fault insurance since 1993 have witnessed the highest premium increases: Quebec by 35 percent, Ontario by 29.5 percent, and Manitoba by 12.9 percent.

The major financial effect of no-fault insurance—and hence its attraction—is that it imposes a cap on individual injury awards and on their associated transactional costs, for example legal counsel and court fees. To most economists, however, the potential problem with no-fault insurance is far greater than its perceived benefits. No-fault insurance may actually encourage antisocial behaviour, despite all the good intentions of its designers. In terms of automobile insurance, the antisocial behaviour

reason, a rational manager would ignore this idle chatter—everyone has an incentive to claim to be productive, so this message does not reveal anything about the true characteristics of workers.

For signalling to enhance the salaries of productive workers, they must send a signal that cannot be mimicked easily by unproductive workers. For instance, suppose productive workers have innate abilities that make it easy for them to earn a college degree, and unproductive workers have lower innate abilities that preclude them (or more generally, make it very costly for them) from earning a college degree. In this case, those individuals who know they are productive can earn a college degree to "signal" to managers that they are indeed productive. Since unproductive types cannot mimic this signal, managers can infer that workers with college degrees are the productive types. As a consequence, competitive pressures will result in college graduates earning $80 000. Signalling works because unproductive workers are unable (or more generally, unwilling to bear the cost required) to mimic this signal; managers know that anyone with a college degree is indeed a productive worker.

is, of course, reckless driving. Economists describe the effect as "moral hazard," and it can be particularly acute under the conditions of a public monopoly insurance provider.

A good way to illustrate "moral hazard" is by using the well-documented fact that restaurants with fire insurance burn down more often than restaurants without it. The reason is not that insured restaurant owners tend to be immoral arsonists, but rather that the owners, knowing that they have insurance, may not take due care to prevent fires. They may cut costs on sprinkler systems and grease-cleaning schedules.

Proponents of no-fault insurance, however, argue that moral hazard is not a factor in driving behaviour. They point out that driving is a complex activity, requiring practically hundreds of driver actions per minute; that "honest mistakes" rather than negligence account for most accidents; and, if we are all equally susceptible to accidents, it is unfair to discriminate against those who do get into accidents.

Can "moral hazard" exist in the relationship between driving and automobile insurance? Well, the empirical evidence from Quebec, New Zealand, and Australia does indicate a link. Economic theory also suggests there should be a connection because price and demand are inversely related: if you raise the cost of reckless driving, you will reduce the demand or the likelihood of bad driving; a driver will curtail the thrill of speeding or the convenience of driving home drunk if he or she knows the cost of an accident could prove catastrophic.

That some drivers are not constrained by price does not invalidate the existence of moral hazard. In theory, insurance companies adjust for the distribution of drivers on the risk-averse-to-reckless axis in their pricing of coverage premiums. They modify how their clients drive by raising the costs of coverage to the point where it deters antisocial behaviour, yet is still affordable. A well-informed insurance market estimates the optimum balance between risk and premiums by compiling information both on the risk characteristics of its clients and on the likely range of awards paid out when accidents do occur.

The problem with awards set under a no-fault insurance regime is that they fail to reflect the complete cost of injuries both to individuals and to society. This failure under no-fault insurance to generate complete information on costs can, in turn, lead insurers to underprice premiums, which in effect subsidizes reckless drivers. This is the moral hazard phenomenon.

However long the answer, both experience and theory suggests that no-fault insurance fails to meet the grade of equity and efficiency. Awards to victims are less than the true cost of their injuries. Hidden costs are passed on to either the least able, the victims themselves, or the least suspecting, the taxpayer. Bad drivers are subsidized at the expense of good drivers, and as a result risky driving is rewarded. As reckless drivers are unchecked, accidents increase, and everyone ends up paying more.

Source: Peter Sheldon, "The Health and Moral Hazards of No-Fault Insurance," *Public Policy Sources*, Fraser Institute, 2, 2001, available <oldfraser.lexi.net/publications/pps/2>, accessed August 1, 2004.

---

screening
An attempt by an uninformed party to sort individuals according to their characteristics.

self-selection device
A mechanism in which informed parties are presented with a set of options, and the options they choose reveal their hidden characteristics to an uninformed party.

Screening occurs when an uninformed party attempts to sort individuals according to their characteristics. This sorting may be achieved through a **self-selection device**: individuals who have information about their own characteristics are presented with a set of options, and the options they choose reveal their characteristics to the uninformed party.

A simple example will illustrate how an uninformed manager can use a self-selection device to gain information about the hidden characteristics of workers. Suppose two workers—Fred and Mitchell—have different characteristics: Fred is the best administrator, and Mitchell is the best salesman. Fred and Mitchell know what they do best, but their personnel director does not. Specifically, Fred knows the firm's profits would increase by $20 000 if he were employed as an administrator and that he would be unable to generate any sales if he were employed as a salesman. Mitchell knows the firm's profits would increase by $15 000 if he were employed as an administrator and that he could generate $1 million in sales if he were employed as a salesman. The personnel director, Natalie, wants to place each worker in the position that adds the most value to the firm, but she lacks the information needed to make these assignments.

Natalie can overcome her lack of information by offering Fred and Mitchell different employment options and letting them self-select into the job that is best for them as well as the firm. In particular, suppose Natalie uses a self-selection device whereby she announces the following compensation for administrators and salesmen: administrators earn a fixed salary of $20 000; salespersons receive a 10 percent sales commission. Confronted with these options, Fred realizes that he would earn $0 as a salesman and thus will self-select into his best-paying option: the administrative position. Mitchell will opt for the sales position, since the $100 000 he earns as a salesman (10 percent of the $1 million he generates in sales) exceeds the $20 000 he would earn as an administrator. Thus, even though Natalie does not know which of the two individuals would be the best administrator and the best salesman, the self-selection device sorts workers into the jobs she would have assigned if she had known Fred and Mitchell's characteristics.

Demonstration PROBLEM 12–8

Jetsgo Airlines has 100 customers and is the only airline servicing two small cities in the Maritime provinces. Half of Jetsgo's customers are leisure travellers, and half are business travellers. Business travellers are willing to pay $600 for a ticket that does not require a Saturday stayover and $100 for a ticket that requires a Saturday stayover. Leisure travellers are flexible, willing to pay $300 for a ticket regardless of whether it requires a Saturday stayover. Jetsgo is unable to determine whether a particular customer is a business or leisure traveller. Consequently, the airline's current pricing policy is to charge $300 for all tickets. As a pricing consultant for Jetsgo Airlines, can you devise a self-selection mechanism that will permit Jetsgo to increase revenues and continue to serve all its customers? Explain.

Answer

Yes. Jetsgo can offer two types of tickets: a $300 "supersaver" ticket that requires a Saturday stayover and a $600 "full fare" ticket that does not require a Saturday stayover. Given the options, leisure travellers will select the supersaver ticket and business travellers will select the full-fare ticket. This screening device not only sorts travellers by their characteristics but increases Jetsgo's revenues from $30 000 (computed as $100 \times \$300$) to $45 000 (computed as $50 \times \$300 + 50 \times \$600$).

Auctions

In an *auction,* potential buyers compete for the right to own a good, service, or, more generally, anything of value. Auctions are used to sell a variety of things, including art, Treasury bills, furniture, real estate, oil leases, corporations, electricity, and numerous consumer goods at auction sites on the Internet. When the auctioneer is a seller, as in an art auction, she or he wishes to obtain the highest possible price for the item. Buyers, on the other hand, seek to obtain the item at the lowest possible price. In some instances, the auctioneer is the person seeking bids from potential suppliers. For instance, a firm that needs new capital equipment may hold an auction in which potential suppliers bid prices that reflect what they would charge for the equipment. In auctions with multiple bidders, competition among bidders leads to more favourable terms for the auctioneer.

Auctions are important for managers to understand because in many instances, firms participate either as the auctioneer or as a bidder in the auction process. In other words, a firm may wish to sell a good in an auction or buy a good (or input) in an auction. For this reason it is important for managers to understand the implications of auctions for managerial decisions.

While the bidders' risk preferences can affect bidding strategies and the expected revenue the auctioneer receives, we will assume throughout this section that bidders are risk neutral. This assumption is satisfied in many auction settings, since bidders can mitigate their overall risk by participating in a large number of auctions. Before we explain how much a risk-neutral bidder should bid in an auction, we first describe the rules of some different types of auctions and the nature of the information bidders can have about the item for which they are competing.

Types of Auctions

There are four basic types of auction: English (ascending-bid); first-price, sealed-bid; second-price, sealed-bid; and Dutch (descending-bid) auctions. These auctions differ with respect to (1) the timing of bidder decisions (whether bids are made simultaneously or sequentially) and (2) the amount the winner is required to pay. Keep these two sources of differences in auctions in mind as we discuss each type of auction.

English Auction

English auction

An ascending sequential-bid auction in which bidders observe the bids of others and decide whether or not to increase the bid. The auction ends when a single bidder remains; this bidder obtains the item and pays the auctioneer the amount of the bid.

The type of auction you probably are most familiar with is the English auction. In an **English auction**, a single item is to be sold to the highest bidder. The auction begins with an opening bid. Given knowledge of the opening bid, the auctioneer asks if anyone is willing to pay a higher price. The bids continue to rise in a sequential fashion until no other participants wish to increase the bid. The highest bidder—the only bidder left—pays the auctioneer his or her bid and takes possession of the item.

Notice that in an English auction, the bidders continually obtain information about one another's bids. Given this information, if they think the item is worth more than the current high bid, they will increase their bids. The auction ends when no other bidder is willing to pay more for the item than the highest bid. For this reason, in an English auction the person who ends up with the item is the one who values the item the most.

To illustrate, suppose three firms are competing for the right to purchase a machine in an English auction at a bankruptcy sale. Firm A values the machine at $1 million, firm B values it at $2 million, and firm C values it at $1.5 million. Which firm will acquire the machine, and at what price?

All three firms will bid up to $1 million for the machine. Once the bid is slightly above this amount, firm A will drop out, since it values the machine at $1 million. When the bid reaches $1.5 million, firm C will drop out, which means firm B will acquire the machine for $1.5 million (or perhaps $1.5 million plus $0.01). Effectively, the winner of the auction simply has to top the second-highest valuation of the machine.

First-Price, Sealed-Bid Auction

first-price, sealed-bid auction

A simultaneous-move auction in which bidders simultaneously submit bids on pieces of paper. The auctioneer awards the item to the high bidder, who pays the amount bid.

In a **first-price, sealed-bid auction**, the bidders write their bids on pieces of paper without knowledge of bids made by other players. The auctioneer collects the bids and awards the item to the high bidder. The high bidder pays the auctioneer the amount he or she has written on the piece of paper.

Thus, in a first-price, sealed-bid auction, the highest bidder wins the item just as in an English auction. However, unlike in an English auction, the bidders do not know the bids of other players. As we will see, this characteristic can affect bidding behavior and, consequently, the price collected by the auctioneer.

Second-Price, Sealed-Bid Auction

second-price, sealed-bid auction
A simultaneous-move auction in which bidders simultaneously submit bids. The auctioneer awards the item to the high bidder, who pays the amount bid by the second-highest bidder.

A **second-price, sealed-bid auction** is similar to a first-price, sealed-bid auction in that bidders submit bids without knowledge of the bids submitted by others. The person submitting the highest bid wins, but has to pay only the amount bid by the second-highest bidder. Consider, for instance, the situation where a machine is auctioned off to one of three firms in a second-price, sealed-bid auction. If firm A bids $1 million, firm B bids $2 million, and firm C bids $1.5 million, then the high bidder—firm B—wins the item. But it pays only the second-highest bid, which is $1.5 million.

Dutch Auction

Dutch auction
A descending sequential-bid auction in which the auctioneer begins with a high asking price and gradually reduces the asking price until one bidder announces a willingness to pay that price for the item.

In a **Dutch auction**, the seller begins by asking for a very high price for the item (a price so high that she or he is certain no one will be willing to buy). The auctioneer gradually lowers the price until one buyer indicates a willingness to buy the item at that price. At this point, the auction is over: the bidder buys the item at the last announced price. Dutch auctions are used extensively in the Netherlands to auction flowers such as tulips. Car dealers sometimes use a Dutch auction to sell cars; a price for a particular car is posted each day on a marquee, and the price is lowered every day until someone purchases the car.

The information available to bidders in a Dutch auction is identical to that in a sealed-bid auction. In particular, no information is available about the bids of other players until the auction is over, that is, when the first bidder speaks up. Consequently, a Dutch auction is strategically equivalent to a first-price, sealed-bid auction. The reason is that in both types of auctions, bidders do not know the bids of other players. Furthermore, in each case the bidder pays what he or she bid for the item. In terms of optimal bidding behaviour and the profits earned by the auctioneer, the Dutch auction and the first-price, sealed-bid auctions are identical.

Principle	**STRATEGIC EQUIVALENCE OF DUTCH AND FIRST-PRICE AUCTIONS**
	The Dutch and first-price, sealed-bid auctions are strategically equivalent; that is, the optimal bids by participants are identical for both types of auctions.

Information Structures

The four basic types of auctions differ with respect to the information bidders have about the bids of other players. In the English auction, players know the current bid and can choose to raise it if they so desire. In the other three types of auctions, players make bids without knowledge of other players' bids; they cannot decide to increase their own bids based on bids made by others.

In analyzing an auction, it is also important to consider the information players have about their valuations of the item being auctioned. One possibility is that each bidder in an auction knows for certain what the item is worth, and furthermore, all players know the valuations of other players in an auction. For example, if a $5 bill were being auctioned off, every bidder would know that the item is worth $5 to each bidder. This is the case of *perfect information.*

Rarely do bidders in an auction enjoy perfect information. Even in situations in which each bidder knows how much he or she values the item, it is unlikely that other bidders are privy to this information. Moreover, individuals may be unsure of an item's true value and must rely on whatever information they have to form an estimate of its worth. These circumstances reflect situations of asymmetric information: each bidder has information about his or her valuation or value estimate that is unknown by other bidders. These information structures are discussed next.

Independent Private Values

Consider an antique auction in which the bidders are consumers who wish to acquire an antique for personal use. Thus, the bidders' valuations of the item are determined by their individual tastes. While a bidder knows his or her own tastes, he or she does not know the preferences of the other bidders. Thus, there is asymmetric information.

independent private values
Auction environment in which each bidder knows his own valuation of the item but does not know other bidders' valuations, and in which each bidder's valuation does not depend on other bidders' valuations of the object.

The auction just described is one in which bidders have **independent private values**. The term *private value* refers to the fact that the item's worth to an individual bidder is determined by personal tastes that are known only to that bidder. The fact that these private values are *independent* means that they do not depend on the valuations of others: even if a player could obtain information about other bidders' valuations, his or her valuation of the object would not change. This information might, however, induce him or her to bid differently in the auction.

To be concrete, imagine that the item is an antique desk, which you value at $200 because you know it would make studying managerial economics more enjoyable. You face another bidder who, unbeknown to you, values the desk at $50. (He only wants the desk for scrap lumber.) Notice the asymmetric information that is present regarding these private values—you each know how much you value the desk but do not know how much the other values it. These valuations are also independent: even if you knew the other bidder valued the desk at $50, it would not affect your own valuation of the desk. Of course, information about the other bidder's valuation might induce you to bid less aggressively for the antique desk.

Correlated Value Estimates

In many auction settings, bidders are unsure of an item's true valuation. Bidders may have access to different information about an item's actual worth and thus may form different estimates of the item's value. Consider an art auction, where the authenticity of the artist is uncertain. In this case, bidders will likely have different estimates of the painting's value for two reasons. First, individual tastes might lead some individuals to value the painting more than others. Second, bidders might have different estimates of the painting's authenticity. Furthermore, the bidders' estimates of the painting's value are likely to be interdependent. Your estimate of the painting's value would likely be higher if you knew others valued the painting, since you value owning a painting that is admired by others. Likewise, your valuation of the painting would likely be higher if you knew others valued the painting because of information they have about the painting's authenticity.

affiliated (or correlated) value estimates
Auction environment in which bidders do not know their own valuation of the item or the valuations of others. Each bidder uses his or her own information to estimate their valuation, and these value estimates are affiliated: the higher a bidder's value estimate, the more likely it is that other bidders also have high value estimates.

This example illustrates an environment in which bidders have **affiliated (or correlated) value estimates**. Each bidder must base his or her decision on an estimate (or guess) of his or her valuation of the item. Furthermore, the bidders' value estimates are correlated, or, more precisely, *affiliated:* the higher one bidder's value estimate, the more likely it is that other bidders also have high value estimates.

common value
Auction environment in which the true value of the item is the same for all bidders, but this common value is unknown. Bidders each use their own (private) information to form an estimate of the item's true common value.

A special case of this environment, the **common-value** auction, arises when the true underlying value of the item is the same for all bidders. In this case, individual tastes play no role in shaping the bidders' value estimates. The uncertainty stems purely from the fact that different bidders use different information to form their estimates of the common value of the item.

A good example of a common-value auction is the government's use of auctions to sell oil, gas, and mineral rights to prospective firms. The true value of these rights (the amount of oil, gas, or ore underneath the earth) is unknown to the bidders, but whatever the amount, the value is the same for all bidders. Each bidder forms an estimate of the true common value by taking seismic readings and performing other tests. Even though the true value is the same for all bidders, each bidder will likely obtain different estimates through their own tests.

Optimal Bidding Strategies for Risk-Neutral Bidders

This section presents the optimal bidding strategies for risk-neutral bidders, that is, strategies which maximize a bidder's expected profits. As we will see, a player's optimal bidding strategy depends not only on the type of auction but on the information available to the bidders when they make their bids.

Strategies for Independent Private Values Auctions

It is easiest to characterize optimal bidding strategies for environments in which the bidders have independent private valuations. In this case, each bidder already knows how much he or she values the item before the auction starts, so bidders learn nothing useful about their own valuations during the auction process.

Consider first an English auction, in which the auctioneer starts with a low price and gradually raises it until only one bidder remains. A bidder who remains in the auction after the price exceeds his valuation risks having to pay more for the item than it is worth to him. A bidder who drops out of the auction before the price reaches her valuation misses an opportunity to obtain the item at a price below her value. Thus, the optimal bidding strategy in an English auction is for each bidder to remain active until the price exceeds his or her own valuation of the object. Thus, the bidder with the highest valuation will win the object and pay an amount to the auctioneer that equals the second-highest valuation (the price at which the last competitor drops out).

Principle	**THE OPTIMAL BIDDING STRATEGY FOR AN ENGLISH AUCTION** A player's optimal bidding strategy in an English auction with independent, private valuations is to remain active until the price exceeds his or her own valuation of the object.

Next, consider a second-price, sealed-bid auction: the highest bidder wins and pays the amount bid by the second-highest bidder. In this case something remarkable happens: each player has an incentive to bid precisely his or her own valuation of the item. Since each player bids his or her own valuation, the amount actually paid by the highest bidder is the valuation of the second-highest bidder, just as in the English auction.

Why should players bid their true valuation in a second-price auction? The reason is quite simple. Since the winner pays the bid of the second-highest bidder, not his or her own bid, it does not pay for players to bid more or less than their own valuations. To see this, suppose a player bid more than the item was worth to him to increase the likelihood of being the high bidder. If the second-highest bid is less than his valuation, this strategy yields no additional returns; he also would have won had he bid his true valuation. If the second bid is above his valuation, then by bidding more than his valuation he may indeed win. But if he does win, he pays the second-highest bid, which we assumed is above his own valuation! In this case, he pays more for the item than the item is worth to him. Thus, it does not pay for a player to bid more than his or her valuation in a second-price auction. Will a player ever bid less than his valuation? No. A player who bids less merely reduces the chance of winning, since the player never pays his or her own bid! For this reason, the dominant strategy for bidders in a second-price, sealed-bid auction is to bid their valuations.

Principle	**THE OPTIMAL BIDDING STRATEGY FOR A SECOND-PRICE, SEALED-BID AUCTION** In a second-price, sealed-bid auction with independent private values, a player's optimal strategy is to bid his or her own valuation of the item. In fact, this is a dominant strategy.

Finally, consider a first-price auction (which as we have seen is strategically equivalent to a Dutch auction). In this case, the high bidder wins and pays his or her own bid. Since players do not know the valuations or bids of others and must pay their own bid if they win, players have an incentive to bid less than their own valuation of the item. By bidding less than his or her own valuation of the item, a player reduces the probability of submitting the highest bid. But the profits the bidder earns if he or she does win more than offsets the reduced probability of winning. The amount by which a bidder shades down his bid depends on how many other bidders are competing for the item. The more competitive the auction (that is, the greater the number of other bidders), the closer a player should bid to his or her true valuation. The following principle includes a formula that you can use to explicitly compute your optimal bid in situations in which you and other bidders perceive that the lowest possible valuation of other bidders is L and the highest possible valuation is H.

Principle	**THE OPTIMAL BIDDING STRATEGY FOR A FIRST-PRICE, SEALED-BID AUCTION** In a first-price, sealed-bid auction with independent private values, a bidder's optimal strategy is to bid less than his or her valuation of the item. If there are n bidders who all perceive valuations to be evenly (or uniformly) distributed between a lowest possible valuation of L and a highest possible valuation of H, then the optimal bid for a player whose own valuation is v is given by $$b = v - \frac{v - L}{n}$$ where b denotes the player's optimal bid.

In the above formula, notice that the greater the number of bidders (n) or the closer the bidder's valuation is to the lowest possible valuation of the other bidders (that is, the closer $v - L$ is to zero), then the closer the optimal bid (b) is to the player's actual valuation of the item (v). The following Demonstration Problem shows how you can use this formula to determine your optimal bid in both first-price and Dutch auctions.

Demonstration PROBLEM 12–9

Consider an auction where bidders have independent private values. Each bidder perceives that valuations are evenly distributed between $1 and $10. Sam knows his own valuation is $2. Determine Sam's optimal bidding strategy in (1) a first-price, sealed-bid auction with two bidders, (2) a Dutch auction with three bidders, and (3) a second-price, sealed-bid auction with 20 bidders.

Answer

1. With only two bidders, $n = 2$. The lowest possible valuation is $L = \$1$, and Sam's own valuation is $v = \$2$. Thus, Sam's optimal sealed bid is

$$b = v - \frac{v - L}{n} = 2 - \frac{2 - 1}{2} = \$1.50$$

2. Since a Dutch auction is strategically equivalent to a first-price, sealed-bid auction, we can use that formula to determine the price at which Sam should declare his willingness to buy the item. Here, $n = 3$, the lowest possible valuation is $L = \$1$, and Sam's own valuation is $v = \$2$. Thus,

$$b = v - \frac{v - L}{n} = 2 - \frac{2 - 1}{3} = \$1.67$$

Sam's optimal strategy is to let the auctioneer continue to lower the price until it reaches $1.67 and then yell "Mine!"
3. Sam should bid his true valuation, which is $2.

Strategies for Correlated Values Auctions

Optimal bidding strategies with affiliated (or correlated) values are more difficult to describe, for two main reasons. First, the bidders do not know their own valuations of the item, let alone the valuations of others. This not only makes it difficult for players to determine how much to bid, but as we will see, it makes them vulnerable to what is called the "winner's curse." Second, the auction process itself may reveal information about how much the other bidders value the object. When players' value estimates are affiliated, optimal bidding requires that players use this information to update their own value estimates during the auction process.

To illustrate, suppose 100 firms bid for the rights to an oil lease in a first-price, sealed-bid common-values auction. Thus, each bidder is uncertain about the true amount of oil underneath the earth, but nevertheless it is worth the same to each bidder. Before participating in the bidding process, each firm runs an independent test to obtain an estimate of the amount of oil in the ground. Naturally, these estimates vary randomly from firm to firm.

Suppose the differences in their estimates of the amount of oil in the ground are due purely to random variations in test procedures. Some firms think there is more oil in the ground than others, not because they are better informed but due purely to random chance. In this case, the firm that submits the winning bid is the firm with the most optimistic estimate of the amount of oil in the ground. Expressed differently, one of the spoils of victory in a common-values auction is the **winner's curse**: winning conveys news to the victor that all the other firms think the lease is worth less than he or she paid for it. The chance that the other 99 firms are wrong and the winner is right is slim indeed. Notice that if the bidders could "pool" their information and average it, they would have a more precise estimate of the true amount of oil in the ground.

winner's curse
The "bad news" conveyed to the winner that his or her estimate of the item's value exceeds the estimates of all other bidders.

The winner's curse presents a danger that prudent managers must avoid. To illustrate, suppose a geologist for one of the above firms estimated that the lease is worth $50 million. The manager of this firm, being naïve, ignores the fact that $50 million is only an estimate of the common value. In fact, he calculates his firm's bid by using the formula described earlier for a first-price, sealed-bid auction with independent private valuations. He knows the number of bidders ($n = 100$), recognizes that some firms might think there is no oil underneath the earth ($L = 0$), and sets $v = \$50\ 000\ 000$ in the formula to arrive at a bid of $49.5 million. He submits this bid and wins but then learns that the second-highest bid was only $40 million. By the rules of the auction, his firm must pay $49.5 million for a lease that his firm's geologist thinks is worth $50 million. Chances are, the lease is worth millions of dollars less than this estimate of $50 million since the other 99 firms were not willing to pay more than $40 million for the lease. He should have realized that the only way he could win with a bid of $49.5 million is if the other 99 firms obtained more pessimistic value estimates. For this reason, a player who submits a bid based purely on his or her initial value estimate will, on average, pay more for the item than it is worth. To avoid the winner's curse, a bidder must revise downward his or her value estimate to account for this fact.

Principle	**AVOIDING THE WINNER'S CURSE** In a common-values auction, the winner is the bidder who is the most optimistic about the true value of the item. To avoid the winner's curse, a bidder should revise downward his or her private estimate of the value to account for this fact.

The winner's curse is most pronounced in sealed-bid auctions because players do not learn anything about other players' value estimates until it is too late to act on it. In contrast, in an English auction the auction process provides information to the bidders. Each bidder shows up at the auction with an initial estimate of the item's value. During the auction process, each bidder gains information about the item's worth and can revise his or her value estimate accordingly. Specifically, as the price gets higher and higher and the other bidders continue to remain active, you should realize that the other bidders also estimate the object to be of high value—if their private information suggested the object was of low value, they would have already dropped out of the auction. By affiliation, you should revise upward your estimate of the item's worth, since higher-value estimates by other bidders make it more likely that the value to you is also high. Conversely, if you observe that many bidders dropped out at a low price, you should revise downward your private estimate. The optimal strategy in an English auction with affiliated value estimates is to continue to bid so long as the price does not exceed the value estimate you obtain based not only on your private information but on information gleaned through the auction process.

Expected Revenues in Alternative Types of Auctions

Now that you have a basic understanding of bidding strategies in auctions, we can compare the prices that result, on average, in each type of auction. In particular, suppose an auctioneer is interested in maximizing her expected profits. Which type of auction will generate the highest profits: English, second-price, first-price, or Dutch? As Table 12–1 shows, the "best" auction from the auctioneer's viewpoint depends on the nature of the information the bidders hold.

Inside BUSINESS

12-6 Auctions with Risk-Averse Bidders

Risk aversion affects bidder behaviour in some types of auctions but not in others. Consider the independent private values case. In an English auction, players know their own valuation and get to observe the bids of others. Therefore, risk aversion plays no real role in the analysis of bidding strategies: risk-averse bidders will remain active until the price exceeds their valuation and then drop out. The winner will pay an amount that equals the second-highest valuation. Likewise, in a second-price auction, it is a dominant strategy for a risk-averse bidder to bid his or her true valuation, so this type of auction also results in a price that equals the second-highest valuation.

In contrast, risk aversion induces players to bid more aggressively in a first-price auction with independent private values. To see why, recall that risk-neutral bidders shade down their bids in a first-price auction. This increases the chance that some other player outbids them, but risk-neutral bidders are willing to accept this risk because of the greater profits they get if they win. Risk-averse bidders are

less willing to accept this risk and therefore shrink their bids by a lower amount. Consequently, with risk-averse bidders and independent private values, the expected revenue of the auctioneer is greatest in first-price and Dutch auctions and lowest in English and second-price auctions:

First-price = Dutch > Second-price = English

What happens when risk-averse bidders have affiliated value estimates? Recall that the information revealed in an English auction lessens the winner's curse. This reduction in risk induces risk-averse bidders to bid more aggressively, on average, in an English auction than in a second-price auction. Consequently, the English auction always generates greater expected revenues than a second-price auction. It may, in fact, even generate higher revenues than a first-price or Dutch auction:

English > Second-price $\gtrsim$ First-price = Dutch

The first row in Table 12–1 indicates that, with independent private values, the auctioneer's expected revenues are the same for all four auction types. The reason for this result, known as *revenue equivalence,* is as follows.

With independent private values, players already know their own valuations and therefore learn nothing useful about the item's worth during the auction process. As we saw in the previous section, the price ultimately paid by the winner in an English auction is the second-highest valuation—the price at which the last competitor drops out. This is also the case in a second-price auction. In particular, each player bids his or her own value, and thus the price paid by the winner (the second-highest price) is the second-highest valuation. It follows that, with independent private values, the expected revenue earned by the auctioneer is the same in an English auction as a second-price auction.

In a first-price auction, each bidder has an incentive to shade his bid. In effect, each bidder estimates how far below his own valuation the next highest valuation is and then shrinks his or her bid by that amount. The player who wins the auction is the one with the highest valuation, and therefore he pays an amount to the auctioneer that is, on average, equal to the second-highest valuation. Thus, with independent private values, the expected revenue earned by the auctioneer in a first-price auction is identical to that in English and second-price auctions. Since the Dutch auction is strategi-

TABLE 12–1	Comparison of Expected Revenues in Auctions with Risk-Neutral Bidders
Information Structure	**Expected Revenues**
Independent private values	English = Second-price = First-price = Dutch
Affiliated value estimates	English > Second-price > First-price = Dutch

cally equivalent to a first-price auction, the expected revenues under the two auctions are the same. For these reasons, all four of these auctions generate the same expected revenues for the auctioneer when bidders have independent private values.

Table 12–1 shows that revenue equivalence does not hold for affiliated values. Players shrink their bids below what they would have bid based purely on their private value estimates in order to avoid the winner's curse. In an English auction, players gain the most information about the value estimates of others, and this additional information mitigates the winner's curse to some extent. Thus, bidders shrink their bids less in an English auction than in sealed-bid or Dutch auctions. In contrast, in first-price and Dutch auctions, players learn nothing about other players' value estimates during the auction process. Bidders thus shrink their bids most in first-price and Dutch auctions. In a second-price auction, bidders also learn nothing about the value estimates of others. However, the winner does not have to pay his or her own bid but rather the amount bid by the second-highest bidder. The fact that the second-highest bid is linked to information another bidder has about the item's valuation mitigates to some extent the winner's curse, thus inducing players to shrink their bids by less than they would in a first-price auction. As a result, with affiliated value estimates, the auctioneer earns greater expected revenues in an English auction than a second-price auction, and the lowest expected revenues in a first-price or Dutch auction.

Demonstration PROBLEM 12–10

Suppose your firm is in need of cash and plans to auction off a subsidiary to the highest bidder. Which type of auction will maximize your firm's revenues from the sale if: (1) The bidders are risk neutral and have independent private valuations? (2) The bidders are risk neutral and have affiliated value estimates?

Answer

1. With independent private valuations, all four auction types will lead to identical expected revenues under these conditions.
2. With affiliated value estimates and risk-neutral bidders, the English auction will yield the highest expected revenues.

ANSWERING THE **Head**line

According to Industry Canada, auctions offer a number of advantages, such as their ability to promote economically efficient use of spectrum, their openness and objectivity as an assignment mechanism, their procedural efficiency, and their ability to return appropriate compensation to Canadian taxpayers for the use of a public resource. Auctions represent a valuable new spectrum management tool for those situations in which it will be appropriate to rely on market forces for the selection of licensees.

Auctions are just one of the available tools at the government's disposal to assign licences when the demand for spectrum exceeds the available supply. They may be used when the Minister of Industry is confident that market forces can be relied upon to select licensees consistently with the public interest. They will not be used where the licensing involves priority users of the spectrum, for example, national defence, public safety, or essential government operations. Furthermore, the vast majority of licences will continue to be assigned on a first-come, first-served basis as the instances of mutually exclusive demand for spectrum tend to be the exception rather than the rule.

Prices for consumer services are typically set according to supply and demand in the consumer services marketplace. In a competitive market, if one firm raises its prices, consumers will switch to a competitor. Firms will base their bids upon, among other things, the prices at which they will be able to sell their services to consumers. Auction bids thus depend on consumer prices; consumer prices do not depend on auction bids.

Summary

In this chapter, we examined some of the problems uncertainty and asymmetric information add to managerial decision problems. It should be clear that in many instances, consumers and firms' managers have imperfect information about demand functions, costs, sources of products, and product quality. Decisions are harder to make because the outcomes are uncertain. If your information is probabilistic in nature, you should take the time to find the mean, variance, and standard deviation of outcomes that will result from alternative actions. By doing this, you can use marginal analysis to make optimal decisions.

Consumers and producers have different risk preferences. Some people like to go to the mountains to ski treacherous slopes, while others prefer to sit in the lodge and take in the scenery outside. Similarly, some individuals have a preference for risky prospects, while others are risk averse. If you or the firm you work for has a preference for not taking risks (that is, is risk averse), you will accept projects with low expected returns, provided the corresponding risk is lower than projects with higher expected returns. However, if risk taking excites you, you will be willing to take on riskier projects.

Risk structures and the use of the mean, variance, and standard deviation also help identify how customers will respond to uncertain prospects. For example, those individuals who most actively seek insurance and are willing to pay the most for it frequently are bad risks. This results in adverse selection. Moreover, once individuals obtain insurance, they will tend to take fewer precautions to avoid losses than they would otherwise. This creates a moral hazard. Incentive contracts, signalling, and screening can be used to reduce some of the problems associated with asymmetric information.

We described preferences of a risk-averse, a risk-neutral, and a risk-lover decision maker using a utility function. We showed that the risk premium is the difference between the expected value of a risky outcome and the payoff from a sure thing that makes the risk-averse decision maker indifferent between the risky and the safe outcome.

We also examined how consumers will react to uncertainty about prices or quality through search behaviour. Consumers will change their search for quality and "good" prices based on both their perceptions of the probability of finding a better deal and the value of their time. Putting this information to work can help you keep more of your customers. When your customers have a low value of time, you know you will need to lower prices to keep them, because their opportunity cost of searching is low.

Finally, we examined auctions, which play a central role in capitalistic economies. We covered four types of auctions: the English auction, the Dutch auction, the first-price, sealed-bid auction, and the second-price, sealed-bid auction. Bidding strategies and expected revenues vary across auction types depending on the type of auction and whether bidders have independent private values or affiliated value estimates.

Key Terms and Concepts

adverse selection 437
affiliated (or correlated) value
  estimates 447
asymmetric information 436
common value 447
Dutch auction 446
English auction 445
first-price, sealed-bid auction 445
hidden action 437
hidden characteristics 437
independent private values 447
lemons 438
mean (expected) value 417
moral hazard 438

reservation price 425
risk averse 420
risk loving 420
risk neutral 420
risk pooling 423
risk premium 430
screening 443
second-price, sealed-bid auction 446
self-selection device 443
signalling 440
standard deviation 419
variance 419
winner's curse 450

Conceptual and Computational Questions

1. Consider the two options in the following table, both of which have random outcomes

Option 1		Option 2	
Probability of Outcome	Possible Outcomes ($)	Probability of Outcome	Possible Outcomes ($)
1/16	100	1/5	80
4/16	200	1/5	170
6/16	500	1/5	1000
4/16	200	1/5	170
1/16	100	1/5	80

   a. Determine the expected value of each option.
   b. Determine the variance and standard deviation of each option.
   c. Which option is most risky?

2. For each of the following scenarios, determine whether the decision maker is risk neutral, risk averse, or risk loving.
   a. A manager prefers a 10 percent chance of receiving $1000 and a 90 percent chance of receiving $100 to receiving $190 for sure.
   b. A shareholder prefers receiving $775 with certainty to a 75 percent chance of receiving $1000 and a 25 percent chance of receiving $100.
   c. A consumer is indifferent between receiving $550 for sure and a lottery that pays $1000 half of the time and $100 half of the time.

3. Your store sells an item desired by a consumer. The consumer is using an optimal search strategy; the graph here shows the consumer's expected benefits and costs of searching for a lower price.

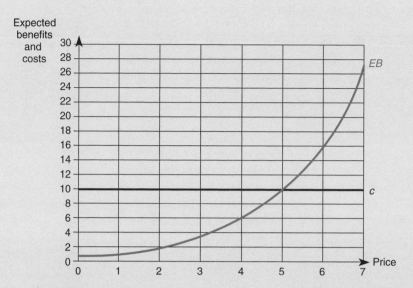

a. What is the consumer's reservation price?

b. If your price is $3 and the consumer visits your store, will she purchase the item or continue to search? Explain.

c. Suppose the consumer's cost of each search rises to $16. What is the highest price you can charge and still sell the item to the consumer if she visits your store?

d. Suppose the consumer's cost of each search falls to $2. If the consumer finds a store charging $3, will she purchase at that price or continue to search?

4. You are the manager of a firm that sells a "commodity" in a market that resembles perfect competition, and your cost function is $TC(Q) = Q + 2Q^2$. Unfortunately, due to production lags, you must make your output decision prior to knowing for certain the price that will prevail in the market. You believe that there is a 60 percent chance the market price will be $100 and a 40 percent chance it will be $200.

a. Calculate the expected market price.

b. What output should you produce in order to maximize expected profits?

c. What are your expected profits?

5. A risk-neutral consumer is deciding whether to purchase a homogeneous product from one of two firms. One firm produces an unreliable product, and the other a reliable product. At the time of the sale, the consumer is unable to distinguish between the two firms' products. From the consumer's perspective, there is an equal chance that a given firm's product is reliable or unreliable. The maximum amount this consumer will pay for an unreliable product is $0, while she will pay $50 for a reliable product.

a. Given this uncertainty, what is the most this consumer will pay to purchase one unit of this product?

b. How much will this consumer be willing to pay for the product if the firm offering the reliable product includes a warranty that will protect the consumer? Explain.

6. You are a bidder in an independent private values auction, and you value the object at $2500. Each bidder perceives that valuations are uniformly distributed between $1000 and $10 000. Determine your optimal bidding strategy in a first-price, sealed-bid auction when the total number of bidders (including you) is

a. 2

b. 10

c. 100

7. You are one of five risk-neutral bidders participating in an independent private values auction. Each bidder perceives that all other bidders' valuations for the item are evenly distributed between $50 000 and $80 000. For each of the following auction types, determine your optimal bidding strategy if you value the item at $75 000.

    a. First-price, sealed-bid auction
    b. Dutch auction
    c. Second-price, sealed-bid auction
    d. English auction

8. The text points out that asymmetric information can have deleterious effects on market outcomes.

    a. Explain how asymmetric information about a hidden action or a hidden characteristic can lead to moral hazard or adverse selection.
    b. Discuss a few tactics that managers can use to overcome these problems.

Problems and Applications

9. Industry Canada has hired you as a consultant to design an auction to sell wireless spectrum rights. Industry Canada indicates that its goal of using auctions to sell these spectrum rights is to generate revenue. Since most bidders are large telecommunications companies, you rationally surmise that all participants in the auction are risk neutral. Which auction type—first-price, second-price, English, or Dutch— would you recommend if all bidders value spectrum rights identically, but have different estimates of the true underlying value of spectrum rights? Explain.

10. As the manager of Smith Construction, you need to make a decision on the number of homes to build in a new residential area where you are the only builder. Unfortunately, you must build the homes before you learn how strong demand is for homes in this large neighbourhood. There is a 50 percent chance of low demand and a 50 percent chance of high demand. The corresponding (inverse) demand functions for these two scenarios are $P = 200\,000 - 250Q$ and $P = 400\,000 - 250Q$, respectively. Your cost function is $TC(Q) = 110\,000 + 200\,000Q$. How many new homes should you build, and what profits can you expect?

11. Life insurance companies require applicants to submit to a physical examination as proof of insurability prior to issuing standard life insurance policies. In contrast, credit card companies offer their customers a type of insurance called "credit life insurance" which pays off the credit card balance if the cardholder dies. Would you expect insurance premiums to be higher (per dollar of death benefits) on standard life or credit life policies? Explain.

12. The Yukon Books is an online book retailer that also has 10 000 "bricks and mortar" outlets worldwide. You are a risk-neutral manager within the Corporate Finance Division and are in dire need of a new financial analyst. You only interview students from the top M.B.A. programs in your area. Thanks to your screening mechanisms and contacts, the students you interview ultimately differ only with respect to the wage that they are willing to accept. About 5 percent of acceptable candidates are willing to accept a salary of $60 000, while 95 percent demand a salary of $110 000. There are two phases to the interview process that every interviewee must go through. Phase 1 is the initial one-hour on-campus interview. All candidates interviewed in Phase 1 are also invited to Phase 2 of the interview, which consists of a five-hour office visit. In all, you spend six hours interviewing each candidate and value this time at $750. In addition, it costs a total of $4250 in travel expenses to

interview each candidate. You are very impressed with the first interviewee completing both phases of Yukon's interviewing process, and she has indicated that her reservation salary is $110 000. Should you make her an offer at that salary or continue the interviewing process? Explain.

13. Since 1997, more than 25 U.S. steel companies have filed for bankruptcy. A combination of low prices with strong competition by foreign competitors and so-called "legacy costs" of unions are cited as the primary reasons why so many steel companies are filing for bankruptcy in that country. In 2002, as Brownstown Steel Corp. was in the process of restructuring its loans to avoid bankruptcy, its lenders requested that the firm disclose full information about its revenues and costs. Explain why Brownstown's management was reluctant to release this information to its lenders.

14. This past year, Used Imported Autos sold very few cars and lost over $500 000. As a consequence, its manager is contemplating two strategies to increase its sales volume. The low-cost strategy involves changing the dealership name to Quality Used Imported Autos to signal to customers that the company sells high-quality cars. The high-cost strategy involves issuing a 10-point auto inspection on all used cars on the lot and offering consumers a 30-day warranty on every used car sold. Which of these two strategies do you think would have the greatest impact on sales volume? Explain.

15. Pelican Point Financial Group's clientele consists of two types of investors. The first type of investor makes many transactions in a given year and has a net worth of over $1 million. These investors seek unlimited access to investment consultants and are willing to pay up to $10 000 annually for no fee-based transactions, or alternatively, $25 per trade. The other type of investor also has a net worth of over $1 million but makes few transactions each year and therefore is willing to pay $100 per trade. As the manager of Pelican Point Financial Group, you are unable to determine whether any given individual is a high- or low-volume transaction investor. Design a self-selection mechanism that permits you to identify each type of investor.

16. Oshawa Inc. is a local manufacturer of conveyor systems. Last year, Oshawa Inc. sold over $2 million worth of conveyor systems that netted the company $100 000 in profits. Raw materials and labour are Oshawa Inc.'s biggest expenses. Spending on structural steel alone amounted to over $500 000, or 25 percent of total sales. In an effort to reduce costs, Oshawa now uses an online procurement procedure that is best described as a first-price, sealed-bid auction. The bidders in these auctions utilize the steel for a wide variety of purposes, ranging from art to skyscrapers. This suggests that bidders value the steel independently, although it is perceived that bidder valuations are evenly distributed between $5000 and $20 000. You are the purchasing manager at Oshawa and are bidding on three tonnes of 2 metre hot-rolled channel steel against five other bidders. Your company values the three tonnes of channel steel at $12 000. What is your optimal bid?

Advanced Topics in Business Strategy

13

Head*line*

Barkley and Sharpe to Announce Plans at Trade Show

Barkley Enterprises has been battling Sharpe Products in the market for high-end digital recording equipment. Most experts agree that the market will ultimately support only one firm, and that the final shakeout will occur this year. Industry analysts are waiting for the two firms to announce whether their latest products will be marketed to professional users or households. Such announcements are traditionally made at the annual trade show. This year's trade show takes place in six months in Phoenix, Arizona. All bets are on Sharpe, which is expected to earn $100 million with its promotion strategy.

Roger Planter, a marketing executive at Barkley, is now looking over a spreadsheet that has been e-mailed to him. He does not like what he sees. Based on the numbers, it appears that even if Barkley adopts its dominant strategy and announces at the trade show that the company is targeting households, the company will lose $2 million. Suddenly, Roger sees a way out. He picks up the phone and begins the conversation: "I've got a plan that will earn us $10 million and drive Sharpe out of the market, but we have to move quickly!" What is Roger's plan? (The profit figures Roger has been examining are summarized below.)

		Sharpe	
	Marketing Target	Professional Users	Households
Barkley	Professional Users	$10, −$10	−$10, −$20
	Households	$20, $3	−$2, $100

Inside BUSINESS

13-1 Business Strategy at Microsoft

On May 18, 1998, the United States Department of Justice filed suit against Microsoft—the world's largest supplier of computer software for personal computers—under Sections 1 and 2 of the Sherman Antitrust Act. The government alleged that Microsoft employed a number of anticompetitive business strategies, including tying other Microsoft software products to Microsoft's Windows operating system; exclusionary agreements precluding companies from distributing, promoting, buying, or using products of Microsoft's software competitors or potential competitors; and exclusionary agreements restricting the right of companies to provide services or resources to Microsoft's software competitors or potential competitors.

According to the government, Netscape enjoyed a 70 to 80 percent share of the Internet browser market during the early 1990s. Microsoft invested hundreds of millions of dollars to develop, test, and promote Internet Explorer, but it faced the serious challenge of getting consumers to switch from Netscape Navigator to Internet Explorer. According to the government, a top executive at Microsoft—its vice-president of the Platforms Group—summarized the company's strategy thusly: "We are going to cut off their air supply. Everything they're selling, we're going to give away for free." The government also alleged that Bill Gates made threats to Netscape and said, "Our business model works even if all Internet software is free . . . We are still selling operating systems. What does Netscape's business model look like? Not very good."

A lot has happened since 1998. Microsoft lost the suit; Netscape merged with America Online; and America Online later merged with Time-Warner. Ultimately, only time will tell if Microsoft's strategies were successful.

Sources: Antitrust Complaint: *United States of America v. Microsoft Corporation*, May 18, 1998; *Wall Street Journal Online Edition*, Front Page, October 9, 2001.

Introduction

In our examination of the quest for profitable business strategies, we have generally taken the business environment (the number of competitors, the timing of decisions, and more generally, the decisions of rivals) as given and outside of the manager's control. This chapter changes all that. We identify strategies managers can use to change the business environment in order to enhance the firm's long-run profits. In short, this chapter's theme is: "If you don't like the game you're playing, look for strategies to change the game."

The first part of this chapter identifies three strategies that managers can use to change the business environment. Two pricing strategies—limit pricing and predatory pricing—are identified as potential tools for reducing the number of competitors. A third strategy lessens competition by raising rivals' fixed or marginal costs. Unfortunately, all of these strategies involve economic tradeoffs. Before implementing a given strategy, a manager must determine whether the potential benefits of the strategies exceed the associated costs.

The second part of this chapter focuses on first- and second-mover advantages and explains when it is profitable to change the business environment by altering the timing or sequence of decisions. We conclude by showing why first-mover advantages are typically strong in network industries (such as telecommunications, airlines, and the Internet). Penetration pricing is a strategy entrants can use to "change the game" in order to overcome these potential obstacles.

Limit Pricing to Prevent Entry

One of the unfortunate consequences of successful management is that it often leads to imitation or entry into the market by other firms. Of course, entry by competitors adversely affects the profits of existing firms. Faced with the threat of entry, a manager might consider a strategy like limit pricing. Limit pricing changes the business environment by reducing the number of competitors.

More formally, **limit pricing** occurs when a monopolist (or other firm with market power) prices below the monopoly price to prevent other firms from entering a market. As we will see, limit pricing is not always a profitable business strategy, and extreme care must be exercised when adopting such a strategy.

Theoretical Basis for Limit Pricing

Consider a situation in which a monopolist controls the entire market. The demand curve for the monopolist's product is D^M in Figure 13–1. Monopoly profits are maximized at the price P^M, and monopoly profits are given by π^M. Unfortunately for this incumbent, if a potential entrant were to learn about this profit opportunity and possess the technological know-how to produce the product at the same cost as the incumbent, the profits enjoyed by the monopolist would be eroded if the potential entrant could profitably enter the market. Entry would move the industry from monopoly to duopoly and reduce the incumbent's profits. Over time, if additional firms entered the market, profits would be further eroded.

One strategy for an incumbent is to charge a price below the monopoly price in an attempt to discourage entry. To see the potential merits of this strategy, suppose for the moment that the entrant's costs are identical to those of the incumbent and that the entrant has complete information about the incumbent's costs as well as the demand for the product. In other words, imagine that the potential entrant knows all of the information enjoyed by the incumbent.

limit pricing
A strategy in which an incumbent maintains a price below the monopoly level in order to prevent entry.

FIGURE 13–1 Monopoly Pricing

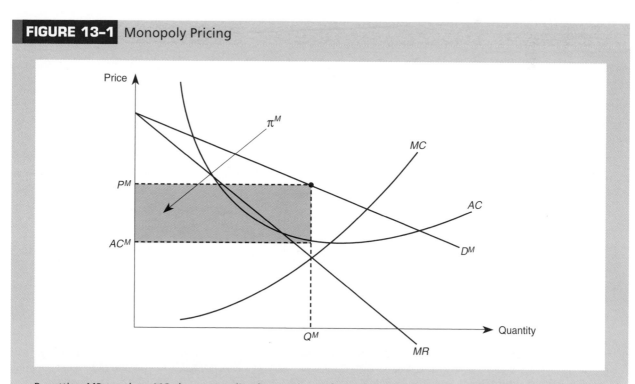

By setting *MR* equals to *MC*, the monopolist charges the profit-maximizing price P_M and produces the corresponding quantity of Q_M.

To limit price, the incumbent produces Q^L (which exceeds the monopoly output of Q^M) and charges a price P^L that is lower than the monopoly price. This situation is shown in Figure 13–2. If the potential entrant believes the incumbent will continue to produce Q^L units of output if it enters the market, then the *residual demand* for the entrant's product is simply the market demand, D^M, minus the amount (Q^L) produced by the incumbent. This difference, $D^M - Q^L$, is the entrant's residual demand curve and is sketched in Figure 13–2. The entrant's residual demand curve starts out at a price of P^L (since $D^M - Q^L$ is zero at this price). For each price below P^L, the horizontal distance between the entrant's residual demand curve and the monopolist's demand curve is Q^L at each price.

Since the entrant's residual demand curve in Figure 13–2 lies below the average cost curve, entry is not profitable. To see this, note that the entrant loses money if it enters and produces more output or less output than Q units. By entering and producing exactly Q units, total market output increases to $Q + Q^L$. This pushes the price down to the point where $P = AC$ for the entrant, so its economic profits are zero. Thus, the entrant cannot earn positive profits by entering the market. Furthermore, if entry involves any extra costs whatsoever (even one cent), the entrant will have a strict incentive to stay out of this market. Thus, limit pricing prevents entry and the incumbent earns higher profits than those earned in the presence of entry (but profits under limit pricing are lower than if it were an uncontested monopoly).

Limit Pricing May Fail to Deter Entry

Now that you understand the basic rationale for limit pricing, let's take a more critical look at this strategy. In our example, the potential entrant was assumed to have

FIGURE 13–2 Limit Pricing and Residual Demand

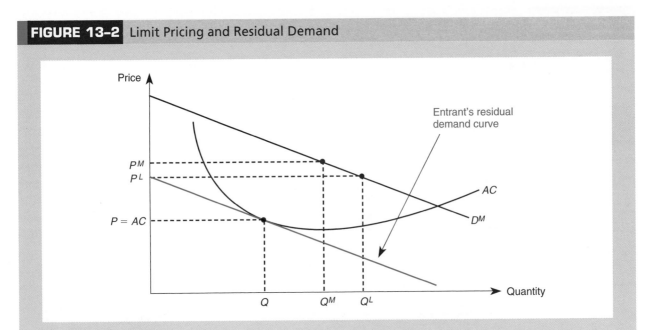

The monopolist concerned about losing its profit to new entrants sets a price, P_L, below the profit-maximizing price, P_M, and produces quantity of Q_L that is greater than Q_M. Faced with this low (limit) price, the entrant at best can break even at Q, where the AC equals the residual demand curve (Market demand $-Q_M$). It will face an economic loss if it produces above or below the Q.

complete information about demand and costs, so the strategy of limit pricing did not "hide" anything about the profitability of the incumbent's line of business. In fact, the low price charged by the incumbent played no real role in preventing entry: the entrant opted to stay out because it believed the incumbent would produce at least Q^L units if it entered.

In light of this observation, a better strategy for the incumbent would be to charge the monopoly price (P^M) and produce the monopoly output (Q^M), but *threaten* to expand output to Q^L if entry occurs. If the potential entrant believes this threat and stays out of the market, the incumbent will earn higher profits from this strategy than under limit pricing. Unfortunately, it is not credible for the incumbent to produce an output of Q^L if entry occurs. In particular, entry reduces the incumbent's marginal revenue, leading to an optimal output that is less than Q^L. Thus, the incumbent has an incentive to renege on its threat to produce Q^L if entry occurs. Recognizing this, a rational entrant would find it profitable to enter the market if the incumbent sets its price at P^L.

This is related to our earlier discussion of Nash subgame perfect equilibrium in Chapter 10. A subgame perfect equilibrium is a Nash equilibrium that involves only credible threats. Since in the limit pricing case discussed here, the entrant recognizes that the incumbent's threat is not credible, the Nash equilibrium obtained is not subgame perfect.

In order to actually prevent entry, the incumbent must engage in an activity that lowers the post-entry profits of the entrant. In the simple example considered above, post-entry profits are completely independent of the pre-entry price charged by the incumbent. This, coupled with the fact that the "threat" to maintain output at Q^L in the face of entry is not credible, means that limit pricing will not protect an incumbent's profits unless other factors are present that link pre-entry prices to post-entry profits.

Principle	**EFFECTIVE LIMIT PRICING** In order for limit pricing to effectively prevent entry by rational competitors, the pre-entry price must be linked to the post-entry profits of potential entrants.

Linking the Pre-entry Price to Post-entry Profits

In many real-world business settings, the pre-entry price may be linked to post-entry profits through commitments made by incumbents, learning curve effects, incomplete information, or reputation effects. As discussed below, limit pricing may be profitable if one or more of these conditions are met, but care must be taken in evaluating the dynamic effects of limit pricing to ensure that deterring entry is actually the best strategy.

Commitment Mechanisms

In Chapter 10, we discussed the concept of commitment. Here, we expand on it. Returning to the example in Figure 13–2, the pre-entry price is not linked to post-entry profits because rational entrants recognize that the incumbent does not have an incentive to maintain a post-entry output of Q^L. The incumbent can overcome this problem by committing to produce at least Q^L units of output. More specifically, if the entrant can somehow "tie its own hands" and credibly commit to not reducing output in the face of entry—and if this commitment is known by the potential entrant—then the strategy will indeed block entry.

The incumbent might make such a commitment by building a plant that is incapable of producing less than Q^L units of output. In this case, the incumbent may be able to produce more than Q^L units; the key is that all potential entrants know it cannot produce *less* than this amount. The incumbent can then set its price at P^L (which corresponds to the output Q^L), so that the pre-entry price is linked (through Q^L) to the post-entry profits of the entrant. Since entrants realize that the incumbent will continue to produce at least Q^L units of output after entry, their residual demand curve lies below average costs. Therefore, it is not profitable for potential entrants to enter the market.

It may seem strange that the incumbent earns higher profits by "tying its hands" and committing to produce at least Q^L instead of maintaining the flexibility to adjust output as it sees fit should entry occur. To better understand why commitment is a profitable strategy, consider the extensive form representation of the entry game presented in Figure 13–3. Here, the incumbent has a first-mover advantage that permits it to decide whether to (1) commit by building a plant that is incapable of producing less than Q^L units of output or (2) not commit by building a plant that can produce any range of output. Once this decision is made, the entrant decides to enter or not, given the decision of the incumbent. The payoffs in parentheses represent the profits earned by the incumbent and entrant, respectively, in each possible scenario. For instance, if the incumbent does not commit to Q^L and the potential entrant does not enter, then the incumbent earns profits of $100 (the monopoly profits) and the potential entrant earns $0.

Notice in Figure 13–3 that the monopoly payoff of $100 is the highest possible payoff for the incumbent. However, any attempt by the incumbent to realize this payoff (by not committing to Q^L) provides the entrant an incentive to enter, since entry nets the entrant $40 instead of the $0 earned by not entering. Thus, we see that if the incumbent does not commit, it will earn $40 instead of the monopoly profits of $100 because it will end up sharing the market with the other firm.

In contrast, if the incumbent commits to produce Q^L, it alters the incentives confronting the potential entrant in a way that favorably changes the business environment. More specifically, commitment changes the post-entry payoffs of the entrant and makes entry an unprofitable strategy. To see this, suppose the incumbent makes an irreversible decision to commit to produce Q^L. The potential entrant now earns a payoff of $-\$10$ if it enters and $0 if it stays out of the market. In this case, the

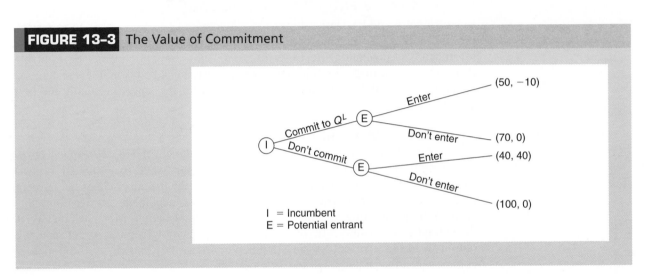

FIGURE 13-3 The Value of Commitment

I = Incumbent
E = Potential entrant

rational strategy by the entrant is to not enter, since this is better than the $10 loss that will occur if it enters the market. In the vernacular of game theory, the unique sub-game perfect Nash equilibrium for the game in Figure 13–3 results in no entry; the incumbent earns an equilibrium payoff of $70 by committing to produce Q^L. While the incumbent's payoff is lower than the monopoly payoff of $100 (which cannot be achieved in equilibrium), it is greater than the $40 payoff that would have been earned absent commitment by the incumbent.

Learning Curve Effects

learning curve effects
A firm's enjoyment of lower costs due to knowledge gained from its past production decisions.

In some production processes, the cost of producing a good or service depends on the firm's level of experience. Firms with greater historical levels of output have more experience and can produce more efficiently than firms with little or no past experience in producing the good. These effects are known as **learning curve effects**.

Learning curve effects provide a link between the pre-entry price and post-entry profits, and therefore may permit an incumbent to use limit pricing to block entry. To be concrete, consider an incumbent who has a one-period jump on a potential entrant. This first-mover advantage permits the incumbent to produce and sell output for one period before the entrant has a chance to enter the market. In this case, the incumbent may find it profitable to produce more than the monopoly output in the first period. Doing so leads to lower first-period profits, but this extra output gives the firm more experience and therefore permits it to produce in the second period at a lower cost. If these learning curve effects are sufficiently strong, this cost advantage may induce the potential entrant to stay out of the market. Notice that by producing more output in the first period, the incumbent drives down the first-period price. Since this lower price is linked to post-entry profits (through output and the learning curve effect), this form of limit pricing can be effective in discouraging entry.

Incomplete Information

The assumption that the entrant and incumbent enjoy complete information is clearly not applicable in all situations. It is usually costly for entrepreneurs and other potential entrants to find profitable business opportunities. To the extent that pre-entry prices or profits are a signal that lowers potential entrants' costs of identifying profitable opportunities, a link between price and post-entry profits may be forged. Limit pricing may help "hide" information about profits from potential entrants, and this may delay or (in rare cases) completely eliminate entry, depending on how costly it is for potential entrants to obtain information from other sources.

To be concrete, imagine a small town with one attorney who is a monopolist in the local market for legal services. In the absence of entry, the attorney is able to earn a handsome salary of $500 000 per year. If the attorney has an impressive collection of sports cars and regularly travels to exotic places (because she charges the monopoly price), hometown kids who graduate from law school may decide to come back home to get a piece of this action. On the other hand, if the attorney lives a more modest lifestyle (because she charges less than the monopoly price), she is less likely to attract such attention. In this latter case, the attorney is practising limit pricing in an attempt to "hide" information from potential entrants. To the extent that this tactic makes it more costly for new graduates from law school to recognize the excellent profit opportunities in this small town, the strategy may delay or eliminate entry.

Alternatively, consider a situation in which the potential entrant does not know for certain the incumbent's costs. If the potential entrant knows that the incumbent has high costs, it will find it profitable to enter the market. If the potential entrant knows the incumbent's costs are low, on the other hand, it will find the market unprofitable to enter. If the entrant does not know the incumbent's costs, it has an incentive to use whatever information is available to infer the incumbent's costs. For instance, when the incumbent charges a low price, the entrant might infer that costs are low and conclude that it does not pay to enter the market. In situations such as these, the incumbent may be able to induce the potential entrant to stay out of the market by pricing below the monopoly price. In this case, there is a link between the pre-entry price and post-entry profits, and limit pricing can be used to profitably deter entry.

Reputation Effects

We learned in Chapter 10 that incentives in one-shot games are different than in repeated games. In games that are indefinitely repeated, trigger strategies link the past behaviour of players to future payoffs. In the context of entry, such *reputation effects* can provide a link between the pre-entry price charged in a market and post-entry profits. Permitting entry today is likely to encourage entry in future periods by other potential entrants. Depending on the relative costs and benefits of future entry, it may pay for a firm to invest in a reputation for being "tough" on entrants in order to deter future entry by other firms. To the extent that charging a low price today (to punish an entrant) discourages entry by other firms, such a strategy may increase long-run profits.

Dynamic Considerations

Even if the incumbent can forge a link between the pre-entry price and post-entry profits to prevent entry, it may earn higher profits by allowing entry to occur. To see this, recall that when the interest rate is i and π^M represents the current profits a monopolist earns by charging P^M, the present value of current and future profits if the firm maintains its monopoly status indefinitely is

$$\Pi^M = \pi^M + \left(\frac{1}{1+i}\right)\pi^M + \left(\frac{1}{1+i}\right)^2\pi^M + \left(\frac{1}{1+i}\right)^3\pi^M + \ldots$$

$$= \left(\frac{1+i}{i}\right)\pi^M$$

Suppose that, upon observing the current period price (P^M), a new entrant decides to enter the market to compete with the (incumbent) monopolist. Entry fosters competition in the product market during the second and following periods, and this reduces the incumbent's profits from the monopoly level (π^M) to the duopoly level (π^D). While different oligopoly settings will lead to different duopoly profits, in all cases the duopoly profits are less than those enjoyed under monopoly: $\pi^D < \pi^M$. If entry occurs, the present value of the incumbent's current and future profits falls to

$$\Pi^{MD} = \pi^M + \left(\frac{1}{1+i}\right)\pi^D + \left(\frac{1}{1+i}\right)^2\pi^D + \left(\frac{1}{1+i}\right)^3\pi^D + \ldots$$

$$= \pi^M + \frac{\pi^D}{i}$$

In particular, the incumbent earns the monopoly profit during the first period, but this induces entry—which reduces profits to π^D in all remaining periods. The term

π^D/i reflects the present value of the perpetuity of duopoly profits. It is clear that $\Pi^{MD} < \Pi^M$, so entry harms the incumbent.

Suppose that (through commitment, learning curve effects, incomplete information, or reputation effects) the incumbent can successfully thwart entry by charging a limit price. Is such a strategy profitable? Under the limit pricing strategy, the incumbent earns profits of π^L during each period, where $\pi^L < \pi^M$. Thus, under limit pricing, the present value of the firm's profit stream is

$$\Pi^L = \pi^L + \left(\frac{1}{1+i}\right)\pi^L + \left(\frac{1}{1+i}\right)^2\pi^L + \left(\frac{1}{1+i}\right)^3\pi^L + \ldots$$

$$= \left(\frac{1+i}{i}\right)\pi^L$$

A necessary condition for limit pricing to be an optimal strategy is for the present value of profits under limit pricing to exceed those under entry: $\Pi^L > \Pi^{MD}$. Rearranging the above equations for Π^L and Π^{MD} reveals that limit pricing is profitable ($\Pi^L > \Pi^{MD}$) whenever

$$\frac{(\pi^L - \pi^D)}{i} > \pi^M - \pi^L$$

The left-hand side of this inequality represents the present value of the benefits of limit pricing, and the right-hand side represents the up-front costs of limit pricing. Notice that a necessary condition for profitable limit pricing is for the per-period profits under limit pricing (π^L) to exceed the per-period duopoly profits (π^D). However, this alone is not enough to warrant limit pricing. In addition, the present value of these benefits must exceed the up-front costs of generating the profit stream. In this case, the up-front cost is the profit forgone by limit pricing in the first period rather than charging the monopoly price.

Based on this analysis, it is clear that limit pricing is more attractive in situations where (*a*) the interest rate is low, (*b*) profits under the limit price are close to the monopoly price, and (*c*) duopoly profits are significantly lower than profits under the limit price. Absent these conditions, it will not be in a firm's best interest to fight entry by limit pricing. When a firm faces entrants but opts against limit pricing, its price will gradually decline over time as more and more firms enter the market. Chapters is an example of a firm that did not find it profitable to fight entry by limit pricing.

Demonstration PROBLEM 13–1

Baker Enterprises operates a midsized company that specializes in the production of a unique type of memory chip. It is currently the only firm in the market, and it earns $10 million per year by charging the monopoly price of $115 per chip. Baker is concerned that a new firm might soon attempt to clone its product. If successful, this would reduce Baker's profit to $4 million per year. Estimates indicate that, if Baker increases its output to 28 000 units (which would lower its price to $100 per chip), the entrant will stay out of the market and Baker will earn profits of $8 million per year for the indefinite future.

1. What must Baker do to credibly deter entry by limit pricing?
2. Does it make sense for Baker to limit price if the interest rate is 10 percent?

Inside BUSINESS

13-2 Dynamic Limit Pricing

In 1901, the United States Steel Corporation controlled almost 70 percent of the U.S. market and enjoyed profits (as a percentage of sales) of 25 percent. Rather than protect this market share through limit pricing, U.S. Steel adopted a strategy of setting the profit-maximizing price each period and enjoyed the higher short-term profits associated with such a strategy. As one would expect, this strategy resulted in entry by smaller firms who essentially took the price set by U.S. Steel as given and maximized their own profits. Over time, as the size of this competitive fringe grew, U.S. Steel gradually found it optimal to lower its price—not as a limit pricing strategy, but because its reduced market share and more elastic demand resulted in a lower optimal price. By the 1930s, U.S. Steel's market share had dropped to about 30 percent and its profits (as a percentage of sales) had fallen to less than 10 percent.

Looking at the discounted cash flows, most economists agree that U.S. Steel's policy of charging a high price and accepting entry by other firms was probably its best strategy. Among other things, U.S. Steel did not enjoy any significant cost advantages over rivals and could not credibly commit to maintain a high market share in the face of entry. Consequently, attempts to thwart entry by limit pricing would have reduced the firm's immediate profits without substantially retarding entry. More recently, McCraw and Reinhardt have pointed out another reason why U.S. Steel did not attempt to limit price: it was concerned that legal (antitrust) actions would have resulted if it aggressively fought entry.

Sources: T. K. McCraw and F. Reinhardt, "Losing to Win: U.S. Steel's Pricing, Investment Decisions, and Market Share, 1901–1938," *Economic History* 49, 1989, pp. 593–619; H. Yamawaki, "Dominant Firm Pricing and Fringe Expansion: The Case of the U.S. Iron and Steel Industry, 1907–1930," *The Review of Economics and Statistics*, 67(3), 1985, pp. 429–37.

Answer

1. Baker must "tie its hands" to prevent itself from cutting output below 28 000 units if entry occurs, and this commitment must be observable to potential entrants before they make their decision to enter or not enter.
2. Limit pricing is profitable if

$$\frac{(\pi^L - \pi^D)}{i} > \pi^M - \pi^L$$

or in this case

$$\frac{(\$8 - \$4)}{0.1} > \$10 - \$8$$

Since this inequality holds, limit pricing is profitable: The present value of the benefits of limit pricing (the left-hand side) is $40, while the up-front costs (the right-hand side) are only $2 million.

Predatory Pricing to Lessen Competition

predatory pricing
A strategy in which a firm temporarily prices below its marginal cost to drive competitors out of the market.

While limit pricing changes the business environment by preventing *potential* competitors from entering a market, predatory pricing lessens competition by eliminating *existing* competitors. More formally, **predatory pricing** arises when a firm charges a price below its own marginal cost in order to drive a rival out of business. Once the "prey" (the rival) leaves the market, the "predator" (the firm engaging in predatory pricing) can raise its price to a higher level, thanks to the dampened competition. Thus, predatory pricing involves a tradeoff between current and future profits: it is profitable only when the present value of the higher future profits offsets the losses required to drive rivals out of the market.

Since predatory pricing hurts not only the prey but also the predator, its success critically depends on the presumption that the predator is "healthier" than the prey. A firm engaging in predatory pricing must have "deeper pockets" (greater financial resources) than the prey in order to outlast it. Reputation effects enhance the benefits of predatory pricing. Taking tough actions today to drive a competitor out of the market may, in a repeated play context, make it easier to drive future competitors out of the market. Establishing a reputation for playing tough against existing firms may induce other firms to stay out of the market. It may also provide smaller rivals an incentive to "sell out" to a large firm at a bargain price rather than risk being driven out of the market through predation.

A number of counter-strategies on the part of the prey can significantly reduce the profitability of predatory pricing. Since the predator is selling the product below its own cost, the prey might stop production entirely (in which case the predator will lose more money each period than the prey) or purchase the product from the predator and stockpile it to sell when predatory pricing ceases. The point is that a strategy of predatory pricing is typically more costly for the predator than for the prey. It is unlikely to be a profitable way of eliminating a rival that is similarly situated (in terms of size, costs, financial resources, and product appeal), but it can be successful in driving a small competitor (with "empty pockets") out of the market.

While businesses engaging in predatory pricing are vulnerable to prosecution under the Competition Act (the Sherman Antitrust Act in the United States), predatory pricing is often difficult to prove in court.

Many economists (and judges) believe that a number of practices that might be deemed "predatory" under legal definitions are, in fact, legitimate business practices. Entry generally heightens competition and results in more competitive pricing. In situations where there are substantial fixed costs, the end result of fierce price competition will be the departure of the weakest firms, and the surviving firm will raise its price. Efforts to prevent such competition would encourage entry by inefficient firms. Even worse, strict enforcement of rules against predatory pricing could lead to a collusive situation in which firms would be afraid to compete because such actions might be construed as predatory and lead to prosecution.

In addition, firms attempting to penetrate a market with a new product often find it advantageous to sell the product at a low price or even give it away for free initially, raising the price once consumers become aware of the product's value. As we will see toward the end of this chapter, the strategy of selling products below cost need not be motivated by a desire to drive rivals out of business. Quite to the contrary, such strategies are sometimes essential for new entrants to successfully compete against well-established firms.

We conclude by noting that the technical (legal) definition of predatory pricing requires the predator to price below its own marginal cost (and thus sustain losses in order to inflict damage on its prey). However, similar strategies can be used when the predator has a cost advantage over its prey. In this case, the predator does not have to price below its own marginal cost in order to drive a less efficient rival out of the market; it merely needs to set its price below the rival's cost. Similarly to predatory pricing, the more efficient firm can raise its price after the less efficient firm exits the market.

Illegal Trade Practices

In 2002, the Competition Bureau released a draft document *Enforcement Guidelines on Illegal Trade Practices: Unreasonably Low Pricing Policies* (here referred to as

"Draft Guidelines") for public comment, which signalled a renewed approach to predatory pricing. Prior to that, in the early 1990s, the Bureau had issued two enforcement guidelines on criminal provisions addressing pricing which continue in effect today. Prior to the publication of the 1992 *Predatory Pricing Guidelines* ("1992 Guidelines") the Bureau's examination of predatory pricing complaints focused on the complicated and time-consuming analysis of price-cost relationships as opposed to the likely competitive effects of the low pricing behaviour.

The 1992 Guidelines follow the classic model of predation. They were heavily influenced by the jurisprudence arising out of the U.S. courts in *Matsushita Electric Industrial Co. v. Zenith Radio Corp.* and the paper by Paul L. Joskow and Alvin K. Klevorick *A Framework for Analyzing Predatory Pricing Policy*, which proposed a two-stage process for analyzing predation.

The classic form of predation involves an actual or near-monopolist selling at below-cost prices, and thus incurring losses, in the short run to eliminate competitors, typically a new entrant, and subsequently recouping losses by charging higher, non-competitive prices in the market. Short-run profits are sacrificed, but the economy is harmed in the long run, as the resulting high prices decrease output and exclude some consumers from the market.

Much of the literature on predation focuses on how to distinguish predatory pricing from aggressive competition. The well-known Areeda-Turner test focuses on price-cost relationships. In theory, only prices below marginal cost should be condemned as predatory, since the sale of each additional unit only adds to losses and makes no contribution to fixed costs. In practice, the accounting concept of average variable costs, that is, costs that vary directly with production, are used as a proxy for marginal costs. When prices are above average variable costs but less than average total costs, determining predation becomes more complex. Prices below average variable costs were deemed to be unreasonable, while prices between average variable and average total costs would fall into the "grey range." In the "grey range," the Bureau would delve into the surrounding circumstances such as industry conditions, business objectives underlying the below-cost prices, and whether the firm had passed over opportunities to increase prices.

Section 50 of the Competition Act, introduced into Canada's competition law in 1935, addressing predation states

> Everyone engaged in a business who engages in a policy of selling products in any area of Canada at prices lower than those exacted by him elsewhere in Canada, having the effect or tendency of substantially lessening competition or eliminating a competitor in that part of Canada, or designed to have that effect, or engages in a policy of selling products at prices unreasonably low, having the effect or tendency of substantially lessening competition or eliminating a competitor, or designed to have that effect, is guilty of an indictable offence and liable to imprisonment for a term not exceeding two years.

Paragraph 50(1)(b) (geographic price discrimination) and paragraph 50(1)(c) (predatory pricing) address two types of harm to competition: (1) effect, tendency, or design to substantially lessening competition and (2) low pricing policies, effect, tendency, or design to eliminating a competitor.

The competitive effects test of "substantially lessening competition" is sufficiently close to the test of prevent or lessen competition substantially found in the merger and abuse of dominance provisions of the Competition Act that it falls within the mainstream concerns about market power. However, the same cannot always be said of the "eliminating a competitor" element of the offence. This presents a long-standing conundrum for antitrust enforcers. The Competition Act seeks to protect

Inside BUSINESS

13-3 Competition Bureau: What Constitutes Predatory Pricing

The Competition Act seeks to protect competition and not individual competitors, yet in certain markets the presence of individual competitors can be vitally important to maintaining and encouraging a competitive market.

Carnation (1968) is the only significant case under paragraph 50(1)(b). The company was charged with geographic price discrimination, as it charged lower prices for condensed milk in British Columbia than it did in Alberta to counter a new competitor in the British Columbia market. The Court ruled that the pricing conduct was not illegal—it is permissible to react to new competition by cutting prices. There have been few cases under that provision since the *Carnation* decision.

There have been four significant cases under section 50.1(c): *Producers Dairy Ltd.* (1966), *Hoffman LaRoche* (1980), *Consumers Glass* (1981), and *Boehringer v. Bristol-Myers Squibb* (1981). In *Producers Dairy* the court found that two days of low pricing activity was not of a sufficient duration to constitute a policy. Similar complaints would not likely merit more than a few minutes' consideration at the Bureau today.

In *Hoffman LaRoche*, the accused was convicted for selling valium at a zero price to hospitals in response to the entry of a new competitor. The court found that the giveaway program had no adverse impact on competition and that the target firm was not seriously impeded in its ability to compete, but convicted on the basis that the policy was designed to substantially lessen competition. The trial decision provides considerable insight into the meaning of "unreasonable." The court ruled that above-cost prices can never be unreasonable, but rejected a purely price-cost approach to determining whether prices are unreasonable. Rather, all relevant factors need to be considered by courts, such as the duration of the below-cost prices and the business objectives underlying the policy. The company was fined $50 000, far less than the Crown's recommendation of $1 million. The court noted that Hoffman LaRoche's policy did not ultimately succeed in excluding competitors and cost the company more than $1 million. In delivering its sentence, the court also commented on the rarity of predatory pricing in the economy compared to conspiracy and price fixing, the defensive nature of Hoffman LaRoche's policy, the fact that a penalty for intention to harm should be less severe than actual harm, and other well-established factors.

In *Consumers Glass*, Portion, a wholly owned subsidiary of Consumers Glass that manufactured disposable cup lids, cut prices below average total costs in response to the entry of a new competitor formed by former employees. The company was acquitted on the basis that, at a time of industry overcapacity, the company was minimizing losses by selling at above average variable cost. The court essentially endorsed the Areeda-Turner test, though it did consider the underlying intent of Portion's business objectives in determining that Portion's prices were not unreasonable.

Boehringer v. Bristol-Myers Squibb was a private prosecution under Section 36 of the Competition Act. The case is notable for affirming that price matching, even if it is below cost, is not unreasonable.

The two-stage analysis introduced in the 1992 *Predatory Pricing Guidelines* radically changed the Bureau's approach to predation. In stage one, market power on the part of the predator must be established using high market share and barriers to entry as well as the ability to recoup losses as indicators. Only if the market power requirement is satisfied would the Bureau move to the second stage and examine the relationship between price and costs.

Predatory pricing can also be the subject of an application to the Competition Tribunal under the "civil abuse of dominance" provisions. The recent Enforcement Guidelines on these provisions contain a section on predation. The Bureau has incorporated, and the Competition Tribunal has considered, allegations of predatory conduct in two abuse cases: *Nutrasweet* and *Teledirect*.

In *NutraSweet* (1990), the Competition Tribunal dismissed the Commissioner's allegation that the NutraSweet Company was selling at prices below "acquisition cost" which is identified as an anticompetitive act in paragraph 78(i). The Tribunal held that the Commissioner did not present a consistent or coherent case as to the proper measurement of cost, and then went on to endorse the Areeda-Turner rule, pricing below average variable cost, as the appropriate standard for determining predation.

The other case in which the Tribunal addressed predatory conduct was *Teledirect*. The Tribunal rejected the argument that *Teledirect*'s responses to entry initiatives were predatory. In the judgment, the Tribunal expressed concerns about drawing proper distinctions between pro- and anticompetitive pricing behaviour and expressed concerns about the law being used to discourage aggressive competition. In both cases, the Tribunal concluded that evidence of probable recoupment is an essential element to support an allegation of predation.

competition and not individual competitors, yet in certain markets the presence of individual competitors can be vitally important to maintaining and encouraging a competitive market.

Demonstration PROBLEM 13–2

Baker Enterprises operates a midsized company that specializes in the production of a fairly unique type of memory chip. If Baker was a monopolist, it could earn $10 million per year for an indefinite period of time by charging the monopoly price of $115 per chip. While Baker could have thwarted the entry of potential rivals by limit pricing (see Demonstration Problem 13–1), it opted against doing so, and it is now in a duopoly situation, earning annual profits of $4 million per year for the foreseeable future. If Baker drops its price to $68 per chip and holds it there for one year, it will be able to drive the other firm out of the market and retain its monopoly position indefinitely. Over the year in which it engages in predatory pricing, however, Baker will lose $60 million. Ignoring legal considerations, is predatory pricing a profitable strategy? Assume the interest rate is 10 percent and, for simplicity, that any current period profits or losses occur immediately (at the beginning of the year).

Answer

If Baker does not engage in predatory pricing, the present value of its earnings (including its current $4 million in earnings) will be Π^D, where

$$\Pi^D = \$4 + \left(\frac{1}{1 + 0.1}\right)(\$4) + \left(\frac{1}{1 + 0.1}\right)^2(\$4) + \left(\frac{1}{1 + 0.1}\right)^3(\$4) + \ldots$$

$$= \left(\frac{1 + 0.1}{0.1}\right)(\$4)$$

$$= (11)(\$4)$$

$$= \$44 \text{ million}$$

If Baker uses predatory pricing, the present value of its current and future profits will be

$$\Pi^P = -\$60 + \left(\frac{1}{1 + 0.1}\right)(\$10) + \left(\frac{1}{1 + 0.1}\right)^2(\$10) + \left(\frac{1}{1 + 0.1}\right)^3(\$10) + \ldots$$

$$= -\$60 + \frac{\$10}{0.1}$$

$$= -\$60 + \$100$$

$$= \$40 \text{ million}$$

Since $\Pi^P < \Pi^D$, Baker earns less by engaging in predatory pricing than it does by not using predatory pricing (that is, maintaining its duopoly situation). It does not pay to use predatory pricing because it costs too much to drive the other firm out of the market.

Raising Rivals' Costs to Lessen Competition

raising rivals' costs
A strategy in which a firm gains an advantage over competitors by increasing their costs.

Another way a manager may be able to profitably change the business environment is by **raising rivals' costs**. By increasing rivals' costs, a firm distorts rivals' decision-making incentives, and this can ultimately affect their prices, output, and entry decisions. Provided the costs of implementing such a strategy are sufficiently low, the firm that raises rivals' costs may gain at the expense of other firms.

For instance, consider a large software manufacturer that is the sole producer of the most popular operating system. This firm also has a presence in other software markets; it competes against smaller rivals who sell different brands of word processing software. The large software maker might attempt to raise the costs of rivals who produce competing word processing software by making it difficult for them to access the operating system's code. In extreme cases, the large firm might refuse to release the operating system's code to firms that compete in other software markets. In both cases, this increases the cost to rivals of creating and updating their own word processing software, with little or no increase in the large firm's costs. In addition to increasing the rivals' fixed cost of producing software, this strategy may also increase the rivals' marginal cost of marketing their software, as customers are more likely to require their technical support to resolve conflicts and other problems.

A firm can also raise its rivals' costs by making it more costly for other firms to distribute their products through the retail chain. For instance, in the famous Microsoft case, the government alleged that Microsoft entered into exclusive contracts with PC suppliers, precluding them from loading Netscape's Internet browser on PCs loaded with the Windows operating system. This strategy presumably raised Netscape's cost of distributing its browser software relative to Microsoft's cost of distributing its own browser.

Strategies Involving Marginal Cost

To illustrate how a firm can gain by raising a rival's marginal cost, consider Figure 13–4, which shows a Cournot duopoly (see Chapter 9). Recall that r_1 and r_2 are the reaction functions of the two competing firms. The firms produce outputs of Q_1 and Q_2, and the reaction functions summarize each firm's profit-maximizing output given the output produced by the rival. For example, r_1 identifies the profit-maximizing output of firm 1 for each potential level of output by firm 2. These reaction functions are downward-sloping because each firm produces its output simultaneously, and the market price adjusts to clear whatever output is brought to market. The greater the amount of output firm 2 brings to market, the lower the resulting market price and thus the lower the optimal output of firm 1.

Point A in Figure 13–4 represents the initial Cournot equilibrium, at which point firm 1's profits are π_1^A. These profits are clearly lower than the profits that would result if firm 1 were a monopolist (the point where firm 1 produces Q_1^M units of output and firm 2 produces zero units of output).

Now suppose that firm 1 uses a business tactic that raises its rival's marginal cost of production. Due to the higher cost, firm 2 now has an incentive to produce less output than before. Geometrically, by raising its rival's marginal cost, firm 1 shifts its rival's reaction function down to r_2^* in Figure 13–4. The new equilibrium moves to point B. Due to its higher marginal cost, firm 2 reduces its output. This has the effect of raising the market price, and firm 2 takes advantage of this higher price by expanding its own output. Ultimately, firm 1 ends up with more market share and higher profits. In particular, notice that firm 1's profits at point B are π_1^B. Since this level of profits is closer to the monopoly point, firm 1 has benefited by raising its rival's marginal cost.

Strategies Involving Fixed Costs

A firm may also gain by raising its rivals' fixed costs. Perhaps surprisingly, such benefits may accrue to a firm even when the strategy also raises the firm's own costs. To see

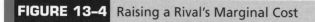

FIGURE 13-4 Raising a Rival's Marginal Cost

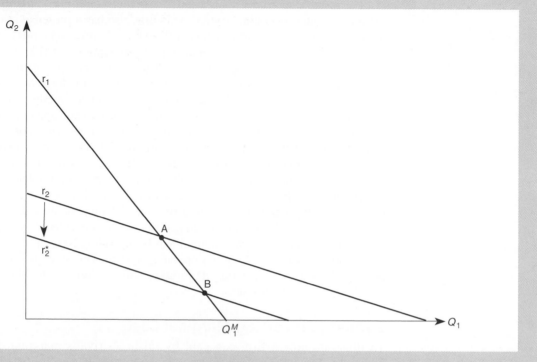

The initial Cournot equilibrium is represented by point A, where firm 1 and firm 2's reaction functions intersect. If firm 1 manages, through a business tactic, to raise firm 2's marginal cost, firm 2's reaction function will shift down to r_2^*, representing a drop in firm 2's production and an increase in production by firm 1.

this, consider an incumbent that earns monopoly profits of $200 if no other firms enter the market. However, if a rival enters the market, the competition that ensues reduces the incumbent's profit to $70, with the entrant also earning $70. Since the entrant earns zero if it does not enter but earns $70 by entering, the monopolist will be unable to sustain its monopoly profit unless it can successfully change the business environment.

Suppose the incumbent successfully lobbies for a regulation requiring any firm operating in the market (including itself) to obtain a licence from the government that costs $90. Notice that the incumbent has raised its own fixed costs by $90, but more importantly, it also has raised its rival's costs by $90. Now if the rival enters the market it loses $20 (the original $70 less the $90 licence fee). Since the rival earns $0 by not entering, this strategy of raising all firms' costs by $90 changes the rival's entry decision, and the incumbent maintains its monopoly position. Notice that the resulting profits of the incumbent are $110 (the original $200 monopoly profit less the $90 licence fee). While this is not as profitable as before the licence was required and the firm enjoyed a monopoly ($200), it is better than the $70 that would be earned if no licence was required and the rival entered.

This strategy has a significant implication for international trade policies. In the international context, governments tend to take initiatives to assist domestic firms to outcompete their foreign rivals in order to gain greater market shares. These initiatives are known as strategic trade policies.

This scenario is depicted in the extensive form shown in Figure 13–5. Here, the incumbent has two strategies: support a $90 licence fee, or do not support it. The

FIGURE 13-5 Raising a Rival's Fixed Cost

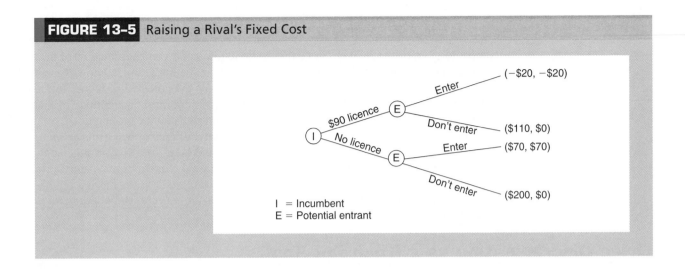

potential entrant gets to observe whether there is a fee before making its entry decision. In the absence of a fee, the entrant has an incentive to enter and thus the incumbent earns profits of only $70. If the incumbent supports the $90 fee, the entrant's best strategy is to stay out of the market (since $0 > −$20). In this case the incumbent earns $110. This is clearly the best strategy for the incumbent, and we see that the incumbent earns $110 in the unique subgame perfect equilibrium to this game.

Strategies for Vertically Integrated Firms

In Chapter 6 we learned that vertically integrated firms produce in both the upstream (input) market and the downstream (output) market. A vertically integrated firm with market power in an upstream market may be able to exploit this market power in order to raise rivals' costs in downstream markets. In particular, actions taken by the vertically integrated firm to increase input prices in the upstream market will increase the costs of rivals competing in downstream markets. In what follows, we discuss two strategies of this sort: vertical foreclosure and the price-cost squeeze.

Vertical Foreclosure

vertical foreclosure
A strategy wherein a vertically integrated firm charges downstream rivals a prohibitive price for an essential input, thus forcing rivals to use more costly substitutes or go out of business.

An extreme form of raising rivals' costs, called **vertical foreclosure**, occurs when a firm that controls an essential upstream input competes against other firms in the downstream market. By refusing to sell other downstream firms the needed input, it forces them to seek out less efficient substitutes. This increases their cost of production. When no substitutes are available, the rivals are completely driven out of the downstream market because they are unable to acquire the essential input.

While vertical foreclosure may be profitable in some instances, it is not always the most profitable strategy. In particular, by charging input prices so high that it drives nonintegrated firms out of the market, the vertically integrated firm forgoes upstream profits from the sale of the input. Vertical foreclosure is profitable only when the higher profits earned in the downstream market (due to the increased market power) more than offset the profits lost in the upstream input market.

The Price-Cost Squeeze

price-cost squeeze
A tactic used by a vertically integrated firm to squeeze the margins of its competitors.

Another way a vertically integrated firm can potentially benefit from raising rivals' costs is through a **price-cost squeeze**. Here, the vertically integrated firm raises rivals' costs on the input side while holding constant (or even lowering) the price charged for the final product. This squeezes the margins of downstream competitors. The ultimate effect of a severe price-cost squeeze is similar to that under predatory pricing: It drives competitors out of the market. Since this tactic requires the vertically integrated firm to charge prices that do not maximize current profits in the upstream and downstream markets, the firm trades off lower short-term profits for the potential of higher future profits once rivals exit the downstream market. Depending on the magnitude of this tradeoff and the level of interest rates, a price-cost squeeze may be profitable.

Price-cost squeezes also can be used by large vertically integrated firms to "punish" rivals who do not participate in market-sharing and other collusive arrangements in downstream markets. While the vertically integrated firm may lose short-term profits by using price-cost squeezes to discipline rivals, this investment in a reputation for being "tough" can generate higher future profits in markets where there is repeated interaction.

Price Discrimination as a Strategic Tool

The profitability of predatory pricing, limit pricing, and raising rivals' costs depends on the relative benefits and costs of such strategies. The relative attractiveness of these tactics is enhanced when the perpetrator can effectively price-discriminate among its various customers. Recall that price discrimination (discussed in detail in Chapter 11) is the practice of charging different customers different prices for the same product.

In the absence of price discrimination, it is more costly for a firm to engage in limit pricing or predatory pricing. By lowering its price to prevent entry or to drive a competitor from the market, a nondiscriminating firm must lower its price to all of its customers. In contrast, if the firm can price discriminate, it can "target" the price cuts to those consumers or markets that will inflict the most damage to the rival (in the case of predatory pricing) or potential entrants (in the case of limit pricing). Meanwhile, it can continue to charge the monopoly price to its other customers.

Likewise, a price-discriminating firm using vertical foreclosure or a price-cost squeeze can target increases in input prices to those firms that pose the most serious threats in downstream markets. At the same time, it can continue to charge lower input prices to input buyers that pose no threat in downstream markets. This permits the firm to maximize profits from input sales to nonthreatening customers while raising the costs for those firms who are rivals in the downstream market.

For these reasons, price discrimination can be used as a strategic tool to facilitate limit pricing, predatory pricing, or raising rivals' costs.

Changing the Timing of Decisions or the Order of Moves

Another way a manager can profitably change the business environment is by changing the timing of decisions or the order of moves. We formally illustrate this below.

First-Mover Advantages

A *first-mover advantage* permits a firm to earn a higher payoff by committing to a decision before its rivals get a chance to commit to their decisions. The Stackelberg model of oligopoly we examined in Chapter 9 is a classic example of a strategic environment in which the first mover enjoys an advantage. Recall that, in this setting, one firm (called the Stackelberg leader) gets to commit to a higher level of output before its rivals (followers) make their own output decisions. The Stackelberg leader earns higher profits than it would if it did not have the opportunity to move first.

TABLE 13–1	Simultaneous-Move Production Game	

		Firm B	
Strategy		**Low Output**	**High Output**
Firm A	**Low Output**	$30, $10	$10, 15
	High Output	$20, $5	$1, $2

The rationale for changing the timing of decisions to achieve a first-mover advantage can be easily illustrated. Consider two firms (firm A and firm B) who must make output decisions (low or high). We will consider two scenarios. In the first situation, both firms make their decisions simultaneously (and thus there is no scope for a first-mover advantage). We will see that the outcome of the game changes in the second situation, where firm A makes its decision before firm B.

The normal form representation for the simultaneous-move version of the game is presented in Table 13–1. For each pair of strategies by firm A and firm B, the first number in each cell represents the payoff to firm A, while the second entry represents firm B's payoff. For instance, if firm A produces a low level of output and firm B produces a low level of output, then firm A earns $30 and firm B earns $10.

In this simultaneous-move game, firm A has a dominant strategy: Regardless of whether firm B produces a low or high level of output, firm A's profits are highest if it produces a low level of output. Firm B, being rational, recognizes this and has an incentive to produce the high output (since the $15 earned from doing so exceeds the $10 that would be earned if it produced a low output). We conclude that the unique Nash equilibrium in this simultaneous-move production game is for firm A to produce a low output and firm B to produce a high output. In equilibrium, firm A earns profits of $10 and firm B earns profits of $15.

Now suppose firm A changes the timing of its decision so that it gets to move before firm B. Just as importantly, assume firm B actually observes firm A's decision before it makes its own decision, and firm A knows this. The extensive form for this sequential-move production game is given in Figure 13–6. Notice that the payoffs at the end of the game tree are identical to those in Table 13–1. The only difference between these two games is that, in Figure 13–6, firm A gets to move first and firm B gets to observe A's decision before making its own decision.

FIGURE 13–6	Sequential-Move Production Game

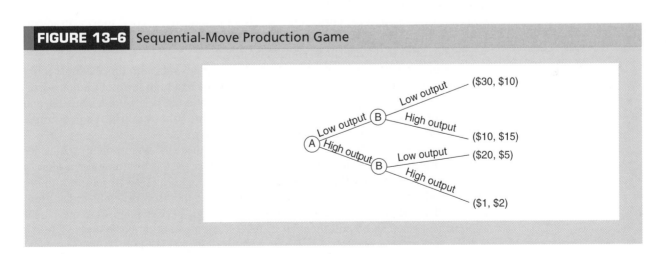

InsideBUSINESS

13-4 First to Market, First to Succeed? Or First to Fail?

During the early era of personal computers, companies were inaccurate in forecasting PC demand. As a result, many firms lost sales to competitors or were stuck with unsold inventories. This all changed in 1984, when Michael Dell founded the Dell Computer Corporation. Dell's business model permitted it to sell a 12 megahertz computer for $1995, compared to the price of $3995 that IBM was charging for a 6 megahertz machine. Ultimately, Dell pioneered the direct sales model for computers (selling computers directly to end users) and later expanded his direct sales model to the Internet. While many other businesses have attempted to imitate this strategy (Compaq began selling direct in 1998), Dell's first-mover advantage placed it at the top of the industry by the year 2000 in terms of sales and profit growth. Dell is an example of a firm that successfully capitalized on its first-mover advantage (although due to entry, the industry is becoming more and more competitive each day).

Unfortunately, being the first to market an idea or product does not guarantee success. A number of well-known companies have been first to introduce new prod-

ucts, but being first has not always formed the basis for an "advantage." The first disposable diaper—a product called Chux—lost out to Procter & Gamble, which later introduced Pampers. A company called Ampex pioneered the video recorder, but most remember Sony as being the first mover when it introduced VCRs based on the now-defunct Beta format. Ultimately, JVC won the market with its VHS format. Prodigy Services was the main visionary regarding the online computer business, but America Online now dominates the market. Apple was the first company to introduce PCs (the Apple) and hand-held devices (the Newton) to home users, but IBM-compatible machines (sold by Dell and other companies) and Palm compatible PCs and hand-held devices now dominate these two product markets.

Get the picture? Being first is not always an advantage; sometimes it pays to be patient.

Sources: "Being There First Isn't Good Enough," *Wall Street Journal*, June 8, 1996; Michael Dell, *Direct from Dell* (New York: Harper Business, 1999); various company Internet sites.

What should firm A do when it gets to move first? If it chooses a low level of output, firm B's best response would be to produce a high level of output. If it does so, firm A earns a payoff of $10. However, if firm A chooses a high level of output, firm B's best response is to produce a low level of output. In this case, firm A earns a payoff of $20. Thus, in the unique subgame perfect equilibrium to the game in Figure 13–6, firm A produces a high level of output. Firm B observes this and responds with a low level of output. Firm A's equilibrium payoff is $20, and firm B's equilibrium payoff is $5.

The fact that firm A's equilibrium payoff is higher ($20) when it gets to move first compared to its equilibrium payoff in the simultaneous-move game ($10) represents a first-mover advantage. In effect, the ability to move first gives firm A an advantage over its rival. In contrast, notice that firm B suffers from a second-mover disadvantage: it earns $5 when it moves second, which is lower than the $15 that is earned when both firms make decisions simultaneously.

It is important to stress that firm A's first-mover advantage in this example relies on three crucial things: (1) firm A's decision to produce a high level of output is irreversible, (2) firm B observes this decision before making its own output decision, and (3) both of these facts are common knowledge (firm B knows firm A's decision is irreversible, firm A knows firm B knows this, and so on).

First-mover advantages are common in many business environments. Consider an innovator who is the first to market a new product. Being first may permit her to enjoy monopoly profits throughout the life of the patent. Due to learning curve effects, additional first-mover benefits may accrue in the form of lower costs. First-mover advantages due to learning curve effects can persist long after the patent expires, and also can be present even if there is not a patent in the first place. In the last part of this chapter, we will see that first-mover advantages are particularly strong in industries with significant network effects.

Second-Mover Advantages

Being first is not always advantageous; sometimes *second-mover advantages* are even greater. For example, being the second to introduce a new product can yield higher payoffs than being first if it permits the second mover to free-ride on investments made by the first mover. This permits the second mover to produce at a lower cost than the firm that moves first. In addition, a second mover may gain an advantage because it can learn from the first mover's mistakes. In this case, the second mover may be able to produce a better product at a lower cost than the firm that moves first. Inside Business 13–4 documents that, while many firms have benefited from being the first mover, some have benefited from being the second mover.

Demonstration PROBLEM 13–3

Determine how much you would be willing to pay for the privilege of moving first in these two different games:[1]

1. There are two players, you and a rival. The player announcing the larger positive integer gets a payoff of $10, while the other player gets $0.
2. There are two players, you and a rival. The player announcing the smaller positive integer gets a payoff of $20, while the other player gets $2.

Answer

1. This game has a second-mover advantage; the second player can guarantee a payoff of $10 by simply announcing a positive integer that is larger than that announced by the first mover. Since there is not a first-mover advantage, you should not be willing to pay anything to move first (but note that you would be willing to pay up to $10 for the right to move second).
2. This game has a first-mover advantage; the first mover can guarantee a payoff of $20 by announcing "1." Since there is a first-mover advantage and you stand to earn $18 more by moving first rather than second, you should be willing to pay up to $18 for the right to move first in this game.

Penetration Pricing to Overcome Network Effects

In many industries (including airlines, electric power, and Internet auction markets), phenomena known as network effects give incumbents first-mover advantages that are difficult for potential entrants to overcome. In light of the growing importance of networks in the global economic landscape, we conclude with an overview of networks and explain why network externalities lead to significant first-mover advantages. We also show how entrants can use penetration pricing strategies to change the business environment and potentially overcome obstacles created by network externalities.

---

[1] In working out this problem, note that the positive integers consist of the numbers $\{1, 2, 3, 4, \ldots\}$, and "infinity" is not an integer.

What Is a Network?

A *network* consists of links that connect different points (called *nodes*) in geographic or economic space. Networks play a profound role in the organization of many industries, including railroads, airlines, trucking, telecommunications, and a host of other sectors of the "new" economy, such as the Internet.

The simplest type of network is a *one-way network* in which services flow in only one direction. Residential water service is a commonly used example of a one-way network: water typically flows one way from the local water company to homes. Not surprisingly, one-way networks can lead to first-mover advantages because of economies of scale or scope. Since a network provider (the local water company) often enjoys economies of scale in creating a network to deliver service to its customers, new entrants typically find it difficult to build a network that supplants the network services of a well-established incumbent. The distinguishing feature of a one-way network is that its value to each user does not *directly* depend on how many other people use the new network.

As we will see, this is not the case for two-way networks (such as telephone systems, e-mail, or many facets of the Internet including instant messages). In a *two-way network*, the value to each user depends *directly* on how many other people use the network. This may permit an existing two-way network provider to enjoy significant first-mover advantages even in the absence of any significant economies of scale.

An example of a two-way network is the *star network* shown in Figure 13–7. The points C_1 through C_7 represent nodes—for example, consumers who own a telephone. The point in the middle (denoted H) represents the *hub*—for example, a switch owned by the telephone company. Consumer C_1 can call consumer C_2 through the connection C_1HC_2. Star networks are common not only in telecommunications, but also in other sectors of the economy, including the airline industry. For example, a consumer wishing to fly from Windsor to Vancouver on Air Canada first flies from Windsor to Toronto (one of Air Canada's hubs) and then from Windsor to Vancouver.

direct network externality
The direct value enjoyed by the user of a network because others also use the network.

Network Externalities

Two-way networks that link users exhibit positive externalities called **direct network externalities**: the per-unit value of the services provided by a network increases as

---

FIGURE 13–7 A Star Network

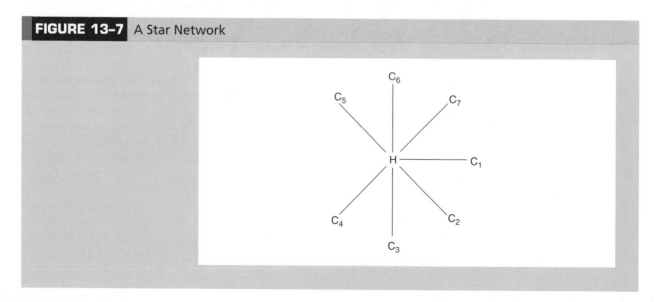

the size of the network grows. A telephone network with only one user is worthless. A telephone network that connects two users is more valuable, but worth less to each consumer than a network that connects three users, and so on. With only two users, there are two potential connection services created by the network: user 1 can call user 2, and user 2 can call user 1. Adding one more user increases the number of potential connection services from two to six: user 1 can call user 2, user 1 can call user 3, user 2 can call user 1, user 2 can call user 3, user 3 can call user 1, and user 3 can call user 2. More generally, if there are n users, there are $n(n-1)$ potential connection services. Adding one user to the network directly benefits all users by adding $2n$ potential connections.

Principle	**DIRECT NETWORK EXTERNALITIES** A two-way network linking n users provides $n(n-1)$ potential connection services. If one new user joins the network, all of the existing users directly benefit because the new user adds $2n$ potential connection services to the network.

indirect network externality The indirect value enjoyed by the user of a network because of complementarities between the size of a network and the availability of complementary products or services.

network complementarities Indirect externalities that stem from the growing use of a particular network.

In addition to these direct externalities present in two-way networks, **indirect network externalities** also can exist. Indirect externalities that stem from the growing use of a particular network are called **network complementarities** and can arise in both one-way and two-way networks. For instance, the growing use of the Internet has led to many complementary products and services, such as teleconferencing software. Due to the sizable fixed costs required to develop such software, a large number of Internet users is needed to justify the associated software development costs. As more and more software is developed for use on the Internet, the associated network complementarities make the Internet even more valuable to each user.

Similarly, the growing use of electricity in the early twentieth century led to the development of millions of different types of electrical appliances. The availability of these appliances and the associated network complementarities increased the value of electricity networks. Analogous indirect externalities arise in non-network industries. For example, the growing popularity of DVD players has led to an increase in the number of movie titles released on DVDs that may be rented or purchased in the marketplace.

Negative externalities such as *bottlenecks* also can arise in networks. As the size of a network grows, it may eventually reach a point where the existing infrastructure cannot handle additional users. Beyond this point, additional users create congestion. This makes it harder for users to make network connections, and the value per user of the services provided by the network declines. Examples of bottlenecks include traffic jams on highway networks, delays at airports, busy signals on telecommunication networks, slow server responses on the Internet, and power outages on local electricity networks.

First-Mover Advantages Due to Consumer Lock-In

Because of network externalities, it is often difficult for new networks to replace or compete with existing networks—even if the new network is technologically superior to the existing one. In particular, since the established network is likely to have many users and complementary services, the total value of the existing network will be greater for each user (due to direct and/or indirect network externalities) than a new network with relatively few users or complementary services.

FIGURE 13-8 Entry Creates a Competing (but Exclusive) Network

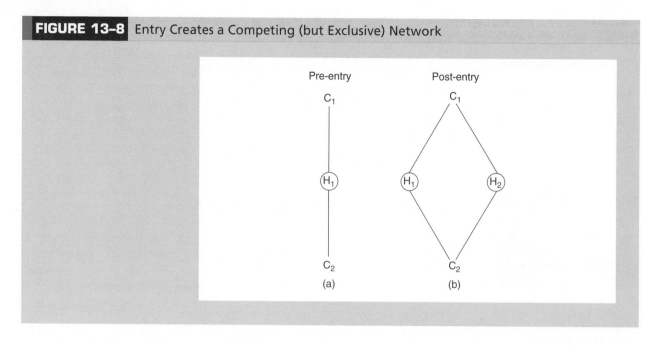

To see the nature of the problem, consider the simple two-way network shown in Figure 13–8(a) providing connection services between users C_1 and C_2. Imagine that this network is owned by the monopolist identified as the hub H_1 and that each user values these network services at $10 per month.

Now suppose another firm decides to enter the market to compete against the existing monopoly network. Since creating such a network will likely involve substantial fixed costs, let us suppose that the new firm has a superior technology such that, at full capacity, each user values the new network at $20 per month. Once the new network is built, the situation looks like that in Figure 13–8(b), where H_1 and H_2 represent the duopolists' hubs. In this figure, the two networks are exclusive. This means that both consumers must subscribe to the same network in order for the services of that network to be useful (see Inside Business 13–5).

Will the new entrant be able to enter the market with its superior technology? Table 13–2 illustrates the underlying issues. The players in this game are users who must choose a network provider. Both users are initially using network provider H_1, thanks to its first-mover advantage. In the initial situation, each user receives $10 in value each month from the network. Notice that, when the new network becomes available, neither user has a unilateral incentive to change network providers. Given the choice of the other user, neither user has an incentive to change to H_2, even though, if both consumers switched simultaneously, each would be better off. This is

TABLE 13-2 A Network Game

	Network Provider	User 2 H_1	User 2 H_2
User 1	H_1	$10, $10	$0, $0
	H_2	$0, $0	$20, $20

Inside**BUSINESS**

13-5 Network Externalities and Penetration Pricing by Yahoo! Auctions

Online auctions are a classic example of an *exclusive network*. In particular, companies like eBay may be viewed as hubs that provide connections for buyers and sellers. The more buyers that visit the site, the more valuable the site is to sellers. Similarly, the more sellers that list items for sale at the site, the more valuable the site is to buyers.

Once a first-mover like eBay establishes itself as "the site" for buying and selling items on the Internet, it can be very difficult for a new entrant to gain a foothold with a competing auction site. After all, if no sellers list their products at the new site, buyers have no incentive to visit the site. And if no buyers visit the site, sellers have no incentive to pay for the privilege of listing items for sale at the new site. In this manner, a first mover into online auctions (such as eBay) may be able to sustain market power through network effects and its first-mover advantage.

This exact scenario presented a challenge for Yahoo! in the late 1990s. Yahoo! wanted to enter the market for online auctions to compete against eBay. Recognizing the problem of network effects and eBay's first-mover advantage, Yahoo! adopted a penetration pricing strategy, allowing both buyers and sellers to use its auction site for free. It reasoned that, since eBay was charging sellers a fee, this strategy would permit the Yahoo! auction site to grow to its critical mass. Once a sufficiently large number of buyers and sellers had begun using the site, the network effects would kick in and Yahoo! would be able to charge fees for its auction services.

This strategy apparently worked to some extent; on January 10, 2001, Yahoo! began charging all sellers a listing fee when they submit an auction through its network.

Sources: Michael R. Baye and John Morgan, "Information Gatekeepers on the Internet and the Competitiveness of Homogeneous Product Markets." *American Economic Review* 91(3), June 2001, pp. 454–74; Yahoo! Auction site <help.yahoo.com/help/auctions/asell> on October 6, 2001.

a classic coordination problem (see Chapter 10). The network externalities create a consumer *lock-in:* the consumers are stuck in a situation (equilibrium) where they are using the inferior network.

Using Penetration Pricing to "Change the Game"

While a lock-in with only two users might be easily resolved by communication between the two users (each consumer agreeing to switch to the other network), the transaction costs of such a strategy make it unfeasible when there are hundreds or potentially millions of users who do not know one another. In these more realistic settings, what can a business like firm 2 do to establish its network?

penetration pricing
Charging a low price initially to penetrate a market and gain a critical mass of customers; useful when strong network effects are present.

One strategy, called **penetration pricing**, entails charging an initial price that is very low—potentially even giving the product away for free or *paying* customers to try out the new product—to gain a critical mass of customers. This protects users from the risk that other users will not switch to the new technology: users can maintain their use of the existing network while experimenting with the new network.

To see how a penetration pricing strategy can help firm 2 attract a critical mass of users on its network, notice that the value to users of having access to both networks is at least as large as the value of using either network individually. Consequently, if the new network provider actually pays users a small amount (say $1) to try out its service, then during this "trial" period the game facing consumers would change from the one in Table 13–2 to the one in Table 13–3. In this case, each consumer has an incentive to try the new network since the choice "H_1 & H_2" is a dominant strategy for each user.

Once consumers try the two networks, they will soon realize that H_2 is best and eventually quit using H_1. Once a critical mass of users (in this case, both users) begins using H_2, the owner of network H_2 can eliminate the $1 payment (and ulti-

TABLE 13–3 The Network Game with Penetration Pricing

	Network Provider	User 2	
		H_1	H_1 & H_2
User 1	H_1	$10, $10	$10, $11
	H_1 & H_2	$11, $10	$21, $21

mately increase the price charged for access to its network), since each consumer now receives $20 in benefits from H_2, compared to the $10 in benefits when both consumers used H_1. In this manner, the new entrant can use penetration pricing to overcome the incumbent's first-mover advantage that stems from these network externalities. Looking again at Table 13–2, penetration pricing is exactly the tool needed to move consumers from the equilibrium in the top left cell to the bottom right cell.

Demonstration PROBLEM 13–4

A firm is contemplating the establishment of a potential two-way network linking 100 users. A feasibility study reveals that each user is willing to pay an average of $1 for each potential connection service provided by the network. If the total cost of establishing the network is $500 000, should the firm establish the network? Explain.

Answer

A network linking 100 users provides $100(100 - 1) = 9900$ potential connection services. Valued at an average of $1 each, the firm can generate revenues of $9900 from each user who subscribes to the network. If the firm gets all 100 users to subscribe to the network, its total revenues would be $990 000, which clearly exceeds the $500 000 in costs required to establish the network. However, note that the firm earns the $490 000 in profits only if all 100 users subscribe. Due to network effects and consumer lock-in, there is no guarantee that these profits will be realized. Penetration pricing or some other method will likely be needed to jump-start the network. This will obviously impact the firm's revenues and profits in the short run.

ANSWERING THE Headline

Roger's plan is to attempt to change the game from a simultaneous-move game (in which Barkley and Sharpe simultaneously announce their marketing strategies at the annual trade show) to a sequential-move game in which Barkley moves first. As shown in Figure 13–9, this will give Barkley a first-mover advantage. By announcing as early as possible its plan to target professionals (and credibly committing to such a strategy), it will get the jump on Sharpe. Once Sharpe observes this commitment, it will be too late: its best response will be to also target professionals, since this will minimize its loss ($-$10 > -20). Obviously, this plan critically depends on Barkley's ability to move very quickly (the trade show is in six months) as well as its ability to credibly commit to such a strategy. If Barkley can do this, it will likely earn profits of $10 million and force Sharpe out of business.

FIGURE 13-9 First-Mover Advantage in Marketing

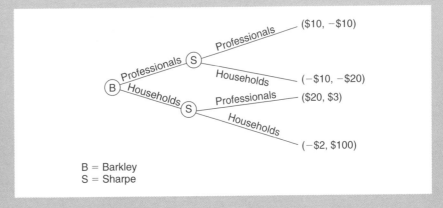

B = Barkley
S = Sharpe

Summary

In this chapter, we explored several strategies that businesses can use to change the environment in which they operate. Strategies such as limit pricing and predatory pricing are designed to eliminate competition in the market. For limit pricing to be effective, a firm must be able to link its pre-entry price to the post-entry profits of potential entrants. Similarly, predatory pricing can be used to reduce the number of existing competitors. Both limit pricing and predatory pricing involve tradeoffs between current and future profits, and therefore the profitability of such strategies depends on the interest rate and other variables.

We also learned that, in situations where it is not possible to eliminate competition, other tactics may be used to change the environment in a manner that increases profits. Examples of such strategies include raising rivals' costs to lessen competition, changing the timing of decisions to create first- or second-mover advantages, and penetration pricing. Penetration pricing is particularly useful in network industries, where consumer lock-in due to direct and indirect network externalities gives existing firms a substantial advantage over new entrants.

Key Terms and Concepts

direct network externality 480
indirect network externality 481
learning curve effects 465
limit pricing 461
network complementarities 481

penetration pricing 483
predatory pricing 468
price-cost squeeze 475
raising rivals' costs 472
vertical foreclosure 475

Conceptual and Computational Questions

1. A potential entrant can produce at the same cost as the monopolist illustrated in the figure below. The monopolist's demand curve is given by D^M, and its average cost curve is AC.

a. What level of output does the monopolist have to produce in order for the entrant to face the residual demand curve, D^R?

b. How much profit will the monopolist earn if it commits to the output that generates the residual demand curve, D^R?

c. Can the monopolist profitably deter entry by committing to a different level of output? Explain?

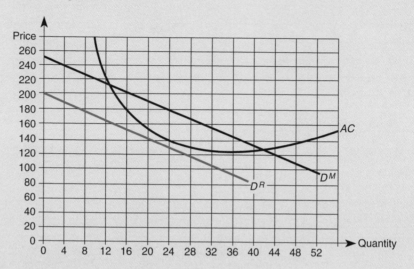

2. A monopolist earns $40 million annually and will maintain that level of profit indefinitely, provided that no other firm enters the market. However, if another firm enters the market, the monopolist will earn $40 million in the current period and $10 million annually thereafter. The opportunity cost of funds is 20 percent, and profits in each period are realized at the beginning of each period.

a. What is the present value of the monopolist's current and future earnings if entry occurs?

b. If the monopolist can earn $8 million indefinitely by limit pricing, should it do so? Explain.

3. Consider the following simultaneous-move game:

	Strategy	Player 2	
		Yes	No
Player 1	Yes	200, 225	400, 100
	No	100, 100	350, 200

a. What is the maximum amount player 1 should be willing to pay for the opportunity to move first instead of moving at the same time as player 2? Explain carefully.

b. What is the maximum amount player 2 should be willing to spend to keep player 1 from getting to move first?

4. A firm is considering building a two-way network that links 10 users. The cost of building the network is $6000.

a. How many potential connection services does this network provide?

b. If each user is willing to pay $100 to connect to the network, will the firm profit by building the network?

    c. If each user is willing to pay an average of $10 for each potential connection service provided by the network, will the firm profit by building the network?

    d. What happens to the number of potential connection services if one additional user joins the network?

5. Two firms compete in a Cournot fashion. Firm 1 successfully engages in an activity that raises its rival's marginal cost of production.

    a. Provide two examples of activities that might raise rivals' marginal costs.

    b. In order for such strategies to be beneficial, is it necessary for the manager of firm 1 to enjoy hurting the rival? Explain.

6. The market for taxi services in a Quebec town is monopolized by firm 1. Currently, any taxi services firm must purchase a $40 thousand licence from the city in order to offer its services. A potential entrant (firm 2) is considering entering the market. Since entry would adversely affect firm 1's profits, the owner of firm 1 is planning to call her friend (the mayor) to request that the city change the licence fee by $F thousand. The extensive form representation of the relevant issues is summarized in the graph here (all payoffs are in thousands of dollars and include the current licence fee of $40 thousand). Notice that when $F > 0$, the licence fee is increased and profits decline; when $F < 0$, the fee is reduced and profits increase.

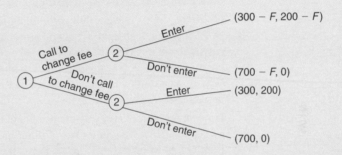

    a. What are firm 1's profits if it does not call to change the fee (that is, if it opts for a strategy of maintaining the status quo)?

    b. How much will firm 1 earn if it convinces the mayor to *decrease* the licence fee by $40 thousand ($F = -\$40$) so that the licence fee is entirely eliminated?

    c. How much will firm 1 earn if it convinces the mayor to *increase* the licence fee by $300 thousand ($F = \$300$)?

    d. Determine the change in the licence fee that maximizes firm 1's profits.

    e. Do you think it will be politically feasible for the manager of firm 1 to implement the change in (*d*)? Explain.

7. Two firms compete in a homogeneous-product market where the inverse demand function is $P = 10 - 2Q$ (quantity is measured in millions). Firm 1 has been in business for one year, while firm 2 just recently entered the market. Each firm has a legal obligation to pay one year's rent of $1 million regardless of its production decision. Firm 1's marginal cost is $2, and firm 2's marginal cost is $6. The current market price is $8 and was set optimally last year when firm 1 was the only firm in the market. At present, each firm has a 50 percent share of the market.

    a. Why do you think firm 1's marginal cost is lower than firm 2's marginal cost?

    b. Determine the current profits of the two firms.

    c. What would happen to each firm's current profits if firm 1 reduced its price to $6 while firm 2 continued to charge $8?

d. Suppose that, by cutting its price to $6, firm 1 is able to drive firm 2 completely out of the market. After firm 2 exits the market, does firm 1 have an incentive to raise its price? Explain.

e. Is firm 1 engaging in predatory pricing when it cuts its price from $8 to $6? Explain.

8. In this chapter's Headline, we learned that Barkley Enterprises benefits by announcing well in advance of the trade show that its new marketing plan will target professionals. Suppose you are an executive at Sharpe, and by lucky electronic happenstance, your cell phone picks up Roger Planter's call. As a result, you learn that Barkley will announce its plan to target its latest product to professional users in two months. What plan of action should you take? Explain.

Problems and Applications

9. UNIX (short for UNiversal Internet eXchange) is a powerful multiuser operating system designed for use with servers. UNIX's popularity has grown since it was developed by Bell Labs in 1969, as record numbers of users are logging onto the Internet. More recently, however, a branded version of another operating system has become available. This product, called Red Hat Linux, is a potential replacement for UNIX and other well-known operating systems. If you were in charge of pricing at Red Hat, what strategy would you pursue? Explain.

10. Ever since the onslaught of several small low-cost carriers, Air Canada has repeatedly reduced its price and increased service on selected routes. As a result, one of the low-cost carriers stopped service, which led Air Canada to increase its price. Why do you think a lawsuit was filed against Air Canada, and why Air Canada prevailed at trial?

11. For several years, Palm was the dominant manufacturer of PDAs (personal digital assistants). However, a number of other manufacturers, including Waterloo-based Research in Motion, have since entered the market, eroding Palm's market share and profits. Suppose that prior to other firms entering the market, Palm earned profits amounting to $100 million per year. By reducing its price of PDAs by 50 percent, Palm could discourage entry into "its" market, but doing so would cause its profits to sink to −$5 million. By pricing such that other firms would be able to enter the market, Palm's profits would drop to $75 million for the indefinite future. In the light of these estimates, do you think it would have been profitable for Palm to engage in limit pricing? Is any additional information needed to formulate an answer to this question? Explain.

12. During the early days of the Internet, most dot-coms were driven by revenues rather than profits. A large number were even driven by "hits" to their site rather than revenues. This all changed in early 2000, however, when the prices of unprofitable dot-com stocks plummeted on all stock exchanges, including the major Canadian ones. Most analysts have attributed this to a return to rationality, with investors focusing once again on fundamentals like earnings growth. Does this mean that, during the 1990s, dot-coms that focused on "hits" rather than revenues or profits had bad business plans? Explain.

13. A number of professional associations, such as the Canadian Medical Association and the Canadian Bar Association, support regulations that make it more costly for their members (for example, doctors and lawyers) to practise their services. While some of these regulations may stem from a genuine desire for higher-quality medical and legal services, self-interest may also play a role. Explain.

14. Barnacle Industries was awarded a patent over 15 years ago for a unique industrial-strength cleaner that removes barnacles and other particles from the hulls of ships. Thanks to its monopoly position, Barnacle has earned more than $160 million over the past decade. Its customers—spanning the gamut from cruise lines to freighters—use the product because it reduces their fuel bills. The annual (inverse) demand function for Barnacle's product is given by $P = 220 - 0.000006Q$, and Barnacle's cost function is given by $C(Q) = 200Q$. Thanks to subsidies stemming from an energy bill passed by Parliament nearly two decades ago, Barnacle does not have any fixed costs: The federal government essentially pays for the plant and capital equipment required to make this energy-saving product. Absent this subsidy, Barnacle's fixed costs would be about $9 million annually. Knowing that the company's patent will soon expire, Marge, Barnacle's manager, is concerned that entrants will qualify for the subsidy, enter the market, and produce a perfect substitute at an identical cost. With interest rates at 5 percent, Marge is considering a limit-pricing strategy. If you were Marge, what strategy would you pursue? Explain.

15. During the late 1990s, several mergers among brokerage houses resulted in the acquiring firm paying a premium on the order of $100 for each of the acquired firm's customers. Is there a business rationale for such a strategy? Do you think these circumstances are met in the brokerage business? Explain.

16. Argyle is a large, vertically integrated firm that manufactures sweaters from a rare type of wool produced on its sheep farms. Argyle has adopted a strategy of selling wool to companies that compete against it in the market for sweaters. Explain why this strategy may, in fact, be rational. Also, identify at least two other strategies that might permit Argyle to earn higher profits.

17. You are the manager of ATI Technologies Inc. in Richmond Hill, Ontario—a large imaging company that does graphics work for Disney and other companies. You and your only competitor are contemplating the purchase of a new 3-D imaging device. If only one of you acquires the device, that firm will earn profits of $15 million and the other firm will lose $10 million. Unfortunately, there is only one 3-D imaging device in the world, and additional devices will not be available for the foreseeable future. Recognizing this fact, an opportunistic salesperson for the company that makes this device calls you. She indicates that, for an additional up-front payment of $24 million (not included in the above figures), her firm will deliver the device to your company's premises tomorrow. Otherwise, she'll call your competitor and offer it the same deal. Should you accept or decline her offer? Explain.

A Manager's Guide to Government in the Marketplace

Headline

Competition Bureau Seeks Order Against Anticompetitive Practices by Air Canada

On March 5, 2001, the Competition Bureau asked the Competition Tribunal for an order prohibiting Air Canada from engaging in anticompetitive practices directed against low-cost carriers WestJet and CanJet. In an application under the abuse-of-dominance provisions of the Competition Act (Section 79), the Bureau seeks an order prohibiting Air Canada from operating flights on routes in eastern Canada at fares that do not cover its "avoidable cost" of providing the service. The application follows a detailed investigation of Air Canada's response to the entry of WestJet Airlines and CanJet Airlines into the eastern Canadian market. The routes involved are Halifax–Montreal, Halifax–Ottawa, Halifax–St. John's, Toronto–Moncton, Toronto–Saint John, Toronto–Fredericton, and Toronto–Charlottetown. The Bureau believes Air Canada's pricing and capacity management would result in WestJet and CanJet abandoning these routes. It is concerned their exit will result in higher prices in the long term. In the light of the rules of Canada's anti-predatory pricing, why do you think Air Canada was found guilty of abuse of dominance?

Introduction

Throughout most of this book, we have treated the market as a place where firms and consumers come together to trade goods and services with no intervention from government. But as you are aware, rules and regulations that are passed and enforced by government enter into almost every decision firms and consumers make. As a manager, it is important to understand the regulations passed by government, why such regulations have been passed, and how they affect optimal managerial decisions.

We will begin by examining four reasons why free markets may fail to provide the socially efficient quantities of goods: (1) market power, (2) externalities, (3) public goods, and (4) incomplete information. Our analysis includes an overview of government policies designed to alleviate these "market failures" and an explanation of how the policies affect managerial decisions. The power of politicians to institute policies that affect the allocation of resources in markets provides those adversely affected with an incentive to engage in lobbying activities. We will illustrate the underlying reasons for these types of rent-seeking activities. Finally, we will examine how these activities can lead politicians to impose restrictions such as quotas and tariffs in markets affected by international trade.

Market Failure

One of the main reasons for government involvement in the marketplace is that free markets do not always result in the socially efficient quantities of goods at socially efficient prices. In this section, we will consider why markets do not always lead to socially efficient outcomes and examine how government policies designed to correct "market failures" affect managerial decisions. We will begin by examining market failure due to the presence of market power.

Market Power

market power
The ability of a firm to set its price above marginal cost.

A firm has **market power** when it sells output at a price that exceeds its marginal cost of production. In such instances, the value to society of another unit of the good is greater than the cost of the resources needed to produce that unit; there would be a net gain to society if additional output were produced. In these instances, government may intervene in the market and regulate the actions of firms in an attempt to increase *social welfare*.

To see the potential benefits of government intervention in a market, consider a market serviced by a monopoly. Figure 14–1 shows the monopolist's demand, marginal cost, and marginal revenue curves. Assuming the monopolist must charge the same price to all consumers in the market, the profit-maximizing output is Q^M units, and these units are sold at the monopoly price of P^M. At this price, consumers pay more for the last unit of output than it cost the producer to manufacture and sell it. As discussed in Chapter 9, total social welfare under monopoly is the sum of producer and consumer surplus, which is the region labelled W in Figure 14–1.

Notice in Figure 14–1 that the area of triangle ABC is the *deadweight loss* of the monopoly—welfare that would have accrued to society if the industry were perfectly competitive but is not realized because of the market power the monopolist enjoys. The failure of the market to fully maximize social welfare is due to market power; the deadweight loss triangle provides a measure of this welfare loss to society—which, as discussed in Chapter 8, consists of the lost consumer surplus, the triangle BCD, and the lost producer surplus, the triangle ACD.

FIGURE 14-1 Welfare and Deadweight Loss Under Monopoly

In a competitive situation the equilibrium should be at point C. But the monopolist produces quantity that is less than the competitive output, Q^C, and charges a higher price than P^C. As a result, consumers lose some surplus, the triangle BCD, and the lost producer surplus is the triangle ACD. The shaded area ABC is the deadweight loss or the loss in total surplus, which cannot be recovered if a monopoly price is charged.

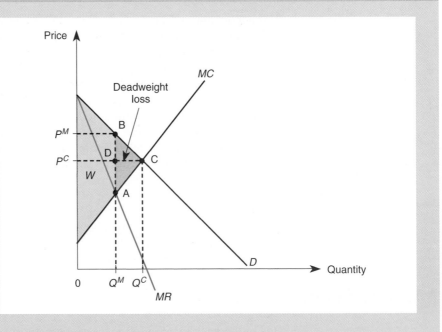

The government uses antitrust policy to enact and enforce laws that restrict the formation of monopolies. The rationale for these policies is that by preventing monopoly power from emerging, the deadweight loss of monopoly can be avoided. In some instances, however, the presence of economies of scale makes it desirable to allow the formation of a monopoly. In these cases, government attempts to reduce the deadweight loss by regulating the price charged by the monopolist.

The Competition Bureau's Role and Mandate and the Competition Act[1]

Competition Act

Competition Act
Government policies designed to promote competition and efficiency in the marketplace.

The **Competition Act** is designed to promote competition and efficiency in the Canadian marketplace. It forms a major part of the economic legislative framework for the conduct of business in Canada, applying with few exceptions to all industries and levels of trade. The Act contains both criminal and non-criminal provisions. In terms of enforcement, the *Director of Investigation and Research* has a statutory responsibility to carry out investigations under the Act and, where grounds exist, to

[1]Competition Tribunal <www.ct-tc.gc.ca/english/welcome.html>; Competition Bureau: (1) "Our Legislation" <strategis.ic.gc.ca/epic/internet/incb-bc.nsf/en/h_ct01252e.html>, (2) "Changes to the Competition Act" <strategis.ic.gc.ca/epic/internet/incb-bc.nsf/en/ct02392e.html>, (3) "International Antitrust Cooperation: Bilateralism or Multilateralism?" <strategis.ic.gc.ca/epic/internet/incb-bc.nsf/en/ct02240e.html>, (4) "Anti-Trust Law in Canada" <strategis.ic.gc.ca/epic/internet/incb-bc.nsf/en/ct01410e.html>, (5) "Merger Enforcement Guidelines" <strategis.ic.gc.ca/epic/internet/incb-bc.nsf/en/ct01026e.html>. All accessed August 10, 2004.

forward criminal matters to the Attorney General for prosecution before the courts or, in the case of the civil matters, to apply to the *Competition Tribunal* for remedial orders. Criminal offences include conspiracy, bid rigging, discriminatory and predatory pricing, price maintenance, misleading advertising, and deceptive marketing practices. The courts may impose fines, order imprisonment, issue prohibition orders and interim injunctions, or perform any combination of these remedies.

Non-criminal or "reviewable matters" include mergers, abuse of dominant position, refusal to deal, consignment selling, exclusive dealing, tied selling, market restriction, and delivered pricing. To address these issues, the *Commissioner of Competition* can apply to the Competition Tribunal for an interim order or final order to stop certain activities or requiring a person to take certain steps that the Tribunal considers necessary to prevent injury to competition.

Competition policy is founded on the belief that competitive market forces should act as the engine of growth for our economy. Sectors of the economy in which competition is not the driver should be the exception, not the norm. In a mixed economy such as ours it is essential to constantly reexamine and reassess the continuing need for, and the costs associated with, sector-specific regulation.

It may come as no surprise that the Competition Bureau strongly favours the elimination of regulation in favour of competition wherever possible. First, competition is better than regulation at creating incentives for innovation and the development of new products, services, and methods of doing business. Competition is more effective in minimizing the costs at which products and services are brought to consumers. This is particularly true in telecommunications, where rapid technological innovation is creating an explosion of new products and services at increasingly lower prices. Second, market forces drive the prices of goods and services toward their relative costs of production and minimize the misallocation of resources. This in turn enhances economic efficiency, increasing overall benefit to the Canadian economy.

The Competition Tribunal Act

The *Competition Tribunal Act* establishes the Competition Tribunal and sets out the powers and jurisdiction of the Tribunal. The Tribunal is a specialized court that is independent of government. It is chaired by a judge and includes lay members who bring a business and economic perspective to the proceedings. The Act also provides the Tribunal with the ability to make rules as to how proceedings brought before it will be conducted.

Promoting Conformity with the Competition Act

The Commissioner of Competition heads the Competition Bureau at Industry Canada and promotes conformity with the legislation for which they are responsible. The Bureau provides the administrative and enforcement support to carry out the Commissioner's statutory responsibilities.

When the Bureau becomes aware of a possible offence under the Competition Act, the Commissioner investigates, and if he or she concludes that there are reasonable grounds to believe an offence has been or is about to be committed, or that grounds exist for the Tribunal to make an order, the Bureau launches a formal inquiry. Once an inquiry has begun, the Commissioner may use formal investigative tools to gather information, such as court-authorized search and seizure powers and the power to question witnesses under oath. All inquiries under the Act are conducted in private.

Where the Bureau believes a criminal offence has occurred, the matter is referred to the Attorney General for prosecution before criminal courts. To address reviewable matters, the Commissioner may apply to the Tribunal for an interim or final order. In addition to fulfilling an enforcement role, the Commissioner may appear before provincial regulators and before any federal board, commission, or other tribunal when issues concerning competition policy arise in regulated industries.

Proposed Amendments

The Competition Act was amended in 1999 and specific airline industry amendments added in 2000. The 1999 amendments overhauled the misleading advertising provisions and added a new criminal offence of deceptive telemarketing. There were also changes in the areas of prohibition orders, wiretapping, whistle-blowing, and merger prenotification.

The new bill amends the Competition Act and the Competition Tribunal Act. The purpose of the amendments is to increase Canada's ability to effectively enforce and administer competition policy in the face of a changing global economy so as to build a more efficient and competitive Canadian marketplace. The amendments would

- Facilitate co-operation with foreign competition authorities regarding evidence for civil competition matters
- Prohibit the deceptive notice of winning a prize aimed at the general public and sent through the mail and Internet
- Streamline the Competition Tribunal process by providing for cost awards, summary dispositions, and references
- Broaden the scope under which the Competition Tribunal may issue temporary orders

These amendments were developed in close consultation with stakeholders and on the basis of the principles contained in four private members' bills to amend the *Merger Enforcement Guidelines.*

Merger Enforcement Guidelines

These guidelines are issued to provide general guidance. Parties are encouraged to enter into early contact with the Bureau to discuss proposed transactions. The particular facts will determine how the Bureau assesses any proposed transaction. Parties contemplating a merger or acquisition should obtain appropriate legal advice when contemplating a possible transaction. The final interpretation of the Competition Act rests with the Competition Tribunal and the courts.

In general terms, *Section 91* deems a "merger" to occur when direct or indirect control over, or significant interest in, all or part of the business of another person is acquired or established.

In general, a merger will be found to be likely to prevent or lessen competition substantially when the parties to the merger would more likely be in a position to exercise a materially greater degree of market power in a substantial part of a market for two years or more, than if the merger did not proceed in whole or in part. In the assessment of the extent to which market power will likely be acquired or entrenched as a result of a merger, the focus is primarily upon the price dimension of competition. Nevertheless, competition can be substantially prevented or lessened with respect to service, quality, variety, advertising, or innovation, where rivalry in the market in respect of these dimensions of competition is important.

In *Part 1*, the Guidelines address the Director's enforcement policy regarding Section 91 of the Act, which sets forth the definition of the term "merger." In general terms, Section 91 deems a "merger" to occur when direct or indirect control over, or significant interest in, all or part of the business of another person is acquired or established.

Part 2 deals with the Director's enforcement policy regarding the statutory standard set forth in *Section 92(1)* of the Act. In general, a merger will be found to be likely to prevent or lessen competition substantially when the parties to the merger would more likely be in a position to exercise a materially greater degree of market power in a substantial part of a market for two years or more, than if the merger did not proceed in whole or in part.

Part 4 addresses the various evaluative criteria that are analyzed in the determination of the likely effects of a merger on competition in a relevant market. The first matter discussed is the significance of information relating to market share and concentration. Mergers generally will not be challenged on the basis of concerns relating to the unilateral exercise of market power where the *post-merger market share* of the merged entity would be less than 35 percent. Similarly, mergers generally will not be challenged on the basis of concerns relating to the interdependent exercise of market power, where the share of the market accounted for by the largest four firms, the *four-firm concentration ratio*, in the market post-merger would be less than 65 percent. Notwithstanding that market share of the largest four firms may exceed 65 percent, the Director generally will not challenge a merger on the basis of concerns relating to the interdependent exercise of market power where the merged entity's market share would be less than 10 percent. These thresholds merely serve to distinguish mergers that are unlikely to have anticompetitive consequences from mergers that require further analysis of various qualitative assessment criteria such as those highlighted in Section 93. No inferences regarding the likely effects of a merger on competition are drawn from evidence that relates solely to market share or concentration. In all cases, an assessment of market shares and concentration is only the starting point of the analysis.

Enhancing Cooperation

Like the United States, Canada has developed ties, both formal and informal, with its foreign counterparts that have stood us in good stead when it comes time to consider matters of mutual interest. For over a decade now, Canada and the United States have had in place the *Mutual Legal Assistance Treaty* and enabling legislation which allows for "hard" cooperation in cartel and other criminal antitrust matters. The Bureau and its counterparts also utilize, almost on a daily basis, our "soft" cooperation agreement, the 1995 Canada-U.S. Agreement, to facilitate cooperation and coordination in cases involving, among other things, cross-border mergers, monopolization, and deceptive marketing scams.

And, while the United States is Canada's most important trading partner, and thus its most important partner for cooperation and coordination on antitrust matters, steps are taken to broaden cooperation with other jurisdictions that are important to Canada, in particular: with the European Union, through the *1999 Cooperation Agreement*; through the interagency cooperation agreement with Australia and New Zealand, and the ongoing interchange program with Australia; with one of Canada's free-trade partners, Chile, through an interagency agreement; and with several other jurisdictions, with whom Canada is at various stages of discussion with a view to commencing the negotiation of cooperation agreements.

Price Regulation

In the presence of large economies of scale (as is often the case for utility companies), it may be desirable for a single firm to service a market. In these instances, government may allow a firm to exist as a monopoly but choose to regulate its price to reduce the deadweight loss. In this section, we will see how such regulation affects managerial decisions and social welfare.

Consider the situation depicted in Figure 14–2, where an unregulated monopolist produces Q^M units of output at a price of P^M. A competitive industry would produce Q^C units, where marginal cost intersects the demand curve. Suppose the government imposed and enforced a regulated price of P^C, which corresponds to the price a competitive industry would charge for the product given identical demand and cost conditions. How should the manager respond to maximize the firm's profits?

The monopolist cannot legally charge a price above P^C, so the maximum price it can charge for units less than Q^C is P^C. For units above Q^C, the maximum price it can charge is the price along the inverse demand curve, since the amount consumers are willing to pay is less than the ceiling. As a consequence, the effective inverse demand curve of the monopolist is given by $P^C BD$. Notice that for points to the left of B, the demand curve is horizontal, just as it is for a perfectly competitive firm. But if the monopolist wishes to sell more than Q^C units of output, it can do so only by lowering price below P^C.

Since the monopolist can sell each unit up to Q^C at a price of P^C, the marginal revenue for these units is simply P^C: Each additional unit of output up to Q^C adds exactly P^C to the firm's revenue. In effect, the ceiling creates a situation where the demand curve the monopolist faces is just like that of a perfectly competitive firm for these output levels. To maximize profits, the regulated monopolist will produce where the marginal revenue of the effective demand curve (P^C) equals marginal cost,

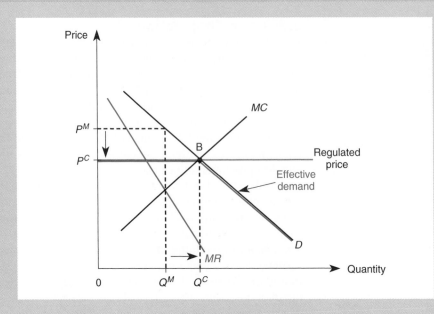

FIGURE 14–2 Regulating a Monopolist's Price at the Socially Efficient Level

In an unregulated environment, the monopolist applies standard monopoly pricing strategy and charges a higher price, P^M, than the competitive price, P^C. The regulatory body can impose competitive pricing to ensure that there is no deadweight loss. If the regulated price is same as competitive price, P^C, the firm produces the quantity that it would produce in a competitive market situation, Q^C.

which is at point B. This corresponds to an output of Q^C. Thus, when the monopolist's price is regulated at P^C in Figure 14–2, the firm maximizes profits by producing Q^C units and selling them at the regulated price of P^C.

Notice that the impact of the price regulation is to induce the profit-maximizing monopolist to produce the perfectly competitive output at the perfectly competitive price. The result of the price regulation is to completely eliminate the deadweight loss of the monopoly. The government policy thus reduces monopoly profits but increases social welfare.

On the basis of Figure 14–2, one might be tempted to conclude that it is always beneficial to regulate the price charged by a monopolist. This is not the case, however. To see why, consider the monopoly situation in Figure 14–3. Suppose the government regulates the price at the level P^*. Given the regulated price, the effective demand curve for the monopolist is now P^*FD, and the corresponding marginal revenue curve for units produced below Q^* is given by line P^*F. To maximize profits, the regulated monopolist will produce where the marginal revenue of the effective demand curve (P^*) equals marginal cost, which is at point G. This corresponds to an output of Q^R, which is less than the output the monopolist would have produced in the absence of regulation. Moreover, the quantity demanded at a price of P^* is Q^*, so there is a shortage of $Q^* - Q^R$ units under the regulated price. Furthermore, the deadweight loss under this regulated price (regions $R + W$) is actually larger than the deadweight loss in the absence of regulation (region W). If the government lacks accurate information about demand and costs, or for some other reason regulates the price at too low a level, it can actually reduce social welfare and create a shortage of the good.

It is very important to note that the analysis in Figures 14–2 and 14–3 suppresses the position of the average total cost curve. To see why it is important to consider the position of the average total cost curve before reaching conclusions about the welfare

FIGURE 14–3 Regulating a Monopolist's Price Below the Socially Efficient Level

If the regulatory body imposes a price, P^*, that is below the socially efficient level, then the deadweight loss, $(R + W)$, is greater than if the monopolist applies standard pricing strategy (W). In this case, given the very low level of price, the firm produces less output and thus the loss in surplus is higher.

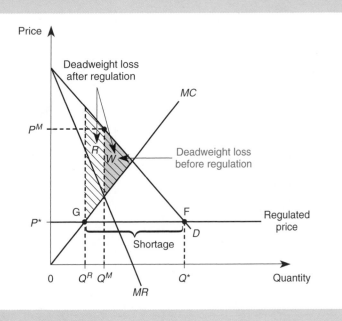

loss arising from monopoly, consider the situation in Figure 14–4, where the monopolist is just breaking even at point A. In this instance, an unregulated monopolist would produce Q^M units and charge a price of P^M. Since price is equal to the average total cost of production, this monopolist earns zero economic profits in the absence of regulation.

Now suppose the price is regulated at P^C. In the long run, how much output will the firm produce? The answer is zero output. To see why, note that under the regulated price, average total cost lies above the regulated price, so the monopolist would experience a loss if it produced. Thus, in the long run the monopolist in Figure 14–4 would exit the market if the price were regulated at P^C, and everyone in the market would be made worse off (there would be no product to consume). To keep this from happening, the government would have to subsidize the monopoly by agreeing to compensate it for any losses incurred. These funds would come from taxes, and thus consumers would indirectly be paying for the lower price through higher taxes. Moreover, the manager of a subsidized monopoly would have no incentive to keep costs low; any losses that resulted would be subsidized by the government. Consequently, the manager would have an incentive to spend enormous sums of money on plush offices, corporate jets, and the like, since losses would be reimbursed by the government.

The analysis in Figure 14–4 points up a very important caveat regarding comparisons of monopoly and perfect competition. One key source of monopoly power is the presence of economies of scale. These economies of scale may render it impossible for output to be produced in a competitive industry. For example, a competitive industry could not sustain an output of Q^C in Figure 14–4, because the intersection of the marginal cost and demand curves lies below the average total cost curve.

FIGURE 14–4 A Case Where Price Regulation Drives the Monopolist Out of Business

The unregulated monopolist produces Q^M, charges P^M, and earns zero economic profits. If the regulated price, P^C, is below the monopolist's price, then $ATC > P^C$ and the monopolist would experience a loss if it produced. Therefore, in the long run, the firm would leave the business, even if the regulated price is the same as the competitive equilibrium price, and everyone would be worse off.

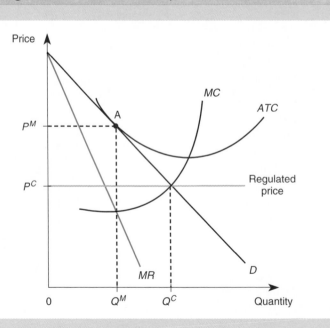

Inside BUSINESS

14-1 Price Regulation: The CRTC and the Pricing of Canadian Basic Cable Television Services

In 1986 the Canadian Radio-television and Telecommunications Commission (CRTC) adopted a new approach to the regulation of basic cable television services. Before then, applications for rate increases were evaluated by the Commission under a set of discretionary criteria—guidelines rather than requirements. But in 1986 the practices that had arisen over previous years of regulatory experience were codified into a set of pricing rules.

A study by Stephen Law[1] examines the pricing behaviour of cable television firms (CATV) under the new rules. To evaluate costs and conduct in the CATV industry, he determines how far apart marginal costs are from average costs and how close realized prices are to marginal costs in each year. While the comparison between the prices and marginal costs reveals the presence or absence of the firms' ability to mark up—monopoly pricing—the comparison of marginal with average costs indicates whether marginal cost pricing would allow cable television companies to cover costs. A natural monopoly is an instance in which marginal cost pricing would fail the CATV operators as well as the test of efficiency. If the CATV firms are natural monopolies, cost structures in the industry should exhibit returns to scale that are large relative to the market, that is, the downward-sloping average and marginal cost curves with the latter lying below the former. Therefore, applying the marginal cost pricing rule in this case would cause the firms to incur losses unless they were offered subsidies to cover the difference between average and marginal cost.

Comparing prices with marginal costs over the period 1985–91, the author shows that the CATV firms, regardless of their sizes, do not practise marginal cost pricing. Average markups of price over marginal cost range from 12 to 30 percent, and the ratio of price to marginal cost is always significantly greater than one. To the extent that the CATV firms are monopolies in their licensed service areas constrained only by competition from other signal sources, such as rented videos or broadcast antennas, the degree to which prices exceed marginal cost reflects the degree to which the CRTC has left the CATV firms with some market power.

The estimates of marginal cost pricing (P/MC), however, suggest that the largest cable operators (those with more than 6000 subscribers) closed in on marginal cost pricing in 1990 relative to earlier years, while for the medium-size operators (those with fewer than 6000 subscribers) this decline in P/MC did not occur until the following year. The small market operators have been exempt from the rate regulations.

To determine whether the regulator could feasibly impose marginal cost pricing, however, the author evaluates the degree of returns to scale for the CATV systems. Clearly, firms operating under increasing returns to scale could not be restricted to "competitive" pricing levels without incurring losses. If marginal cost is below average cost, as is the case under increasing returns to scale, price must exceed marginal cost for the firm to break even but not to exceed average cost.

The divergence of price from marginal cost, therefore, can have two different interpretations. It might be a sign of some sort of monopoly power and the markup ability on part of the CATV firms, or it might be due to economies of scale and the need for nonnegative profit or due to a reluctance of the CRTC to limit market power. The important question that the author attempts to answer is whether it is better to (1) follow the rules, under which prices were higher than marginal cost, but not exceeding average cost, or (2) to restrain the firms to charge a rate equal to marginal cost and subsidize any losses from tax revenues. One way to answer this question is to compare the efficiency cost of the two alternative policies. An estimate of the marginal cost of subsidization provides a benchmark against which one can measure the marginal efficiency cost of the realized prices and hence the ability of the CRTC's rules to constrain static allocative efficiency losses.

The results of this study indicate some improvement in this measure of regulatory performance between 1985 and 1991 for large and mid-sized operations. Even though rules do not consistently promote greater efficiency, regulated CATV prices fell more closely into line with efficiency concerns by the end of sample period, at least for the larger firms. Furthermore, the market power left to the larger operations remained relatively constant until 1990, when this power was reduced by one-third. For small operations, which are not regulated, market power rose over the sample period. The results also demonstrate that the CRTC could have restricted the average large and medium-size cable operators to marginal cost pricing without any requirement for subsidy if the CRTC's goal was to maximize simple static efficiency. As a whole, the pricing rules were moderately successful, but needed adjustments.

[1]"Holding the Line: The CRTC and the Pricing of Canadian Basic Cable Television Services," *Canadian Journal of Economics* 32(3), May 1999, pp. 630–653, available Ideas site, University of Connecticut <ideas.repec.org>.

Inside**BUSINESS**

14-2 Prescription Drug Pricing: A Case of Price Regulation

Are drug price differences attributable to differences in the costs of production?

An investigation by the U.S. General Accounting Office has revealed that the apparent drug price differential in the United States in comparison with Canada and Mexico cannot be attributed to differences in the costs of production and distribution.

Recently the U.S. House of Representatives' Committee on Government Reform and Oversight released a report that compared prescription drug prices in the state of Vermont with drug prices in Canada and Mexico. The report found that senior citizens and other consumers in Vermont who lack insurance coverage for prescription drugs paid far more for prescription drugs than consumers in Canada and Mexico. The report concluded that these price differentials by the drug manufacturers reflected "cost shifting" and did not constitute an "efficient differential pricing" system based on income differential or inverse price elasticity. They charge low prices to consumers in Canada and Mexico and appear to make up the difference by charging far higher prices to senior citizens and other individual consumers in the United States.

This study investigates the pricing of the ten brand-name prescription drugs with the highest dollar sales to the elderly in the United States. The study compares the prices senior citizens who buy their own prescription drugs must pay in the state of Vermont with the prices consumers who buy their own drugs must pay in Canada

or Mexico. The study finds that the average prices senior citizens in Vermont must pay are 81 percent higher than the average prices Canadian consumers pay and 112 percent higher than the average prices Mexican consumers pay. For the drugs Zocor, Ticlid, Prilosec, and Relafen, the U.S. prices were at least twice as high as the Canadian prices. The highest price differential among the top ten drugs was 149 percent, for Zocor, a cholesterol medication manufactured by Merck.

For other drugs, price differentials were even higher. Synthroid is a hormone treatment manufactured by Knoll Pharmaceuticals. For this prescription drug, senior citizens in Vermont pay an average retail price of $28.27, while consumers in Canada pay only $9.25—a price differential of 205 percent. Similarly, for Micronase, a diabetes drug manufactured by Upjohn, Vermont senior citizens pay prices that are 210 percent higher than Canadian consumers.

In the United States, drug manufacturers are allowed to discriminate in drug pricing. They have historically raised prices to private customers to compensate for the discounts they grant to managed-care customers. Under this practice, drugs sold to wholesale distributors and pharmacy chains for the individual physician/patient are marked at the higher end of the scale.

The governments of Canada and Mexico do not allow drug manufacturers to engage in price discrimination. In Canada, approximately 35 percent of prescription drugs are paid for by the government for beneficiaries of

Demonstration PROBLEM 14-1

Many firms that sell in small markets are effectively monopolies; they are the sole provider of a good in their area. Most of these firms earn positive economic profits, yet they are allowed to operate as monopolies without regulation by government. Why?

Answer

In situations where economies of scale are large relative to market demand, only a single firm will be able to service the market. In these instances, it is not desirable to break the firm up into smaller firms using antitrust policy. There would, however, be a potential gain in social welfare if the firm's price were regulated at the socially efficient level. This gain must be weighed against the cost of setting up a regulatory body to administer the regulation. If the cost of setting up and running the regulative body exceeds the deadweight loss of monopoly—as it likely will in small markets—there will be a net loss in social welfare by regulation. In these instances, social welfare would be better served by leaving the firm alone even though it creates a deadweight loss. In effect, it would cost more to fix the problem than would be gained by eliminating the deadweight loss.

government health care programs. In Mexico, 30 percent of prescription drugs are paid for by the government under similar circumstances. The rest of the population in these two countries must either buy their own drugs or obtain prescription drug insurance coverage. To prevent the drug companies from charging individual consumers excessive prices, both the Canadian and the Mexican government regulate prices for patented prescription drugs. Drug manufacturers do not have to sell their products in Canada or Mexico, but if they do they cannot sell their drugs at prices above the government maximums.

The regulatory system in Canada protects individual consumers who buy their own drugs. The Patent Medicine Price Review Board (PMPRB), established under the Ministry of Health by a 1987 law, regulates the maximum prices at which manufacturers can sell patented medicines. If the Board finds that the price of a patented drug is excessive, it may order the manufacturer to lower it, and may also take measures to offset any revenues it has received from the excess pricing. Pharmacy dispensing fees for individual retail customers are not controlled by the government. Every pharmacy sets its usual and customary dispensing fee and must register this fee with provincial authorities.

In order to determine the prices the elderly are paying for prescription drugs in Vermont, the Congressional office of the congressperson from Vermont conducted a survey of eleven pharmacies—six independent stores and five chain stores—in Vermont. Rep. Bernard Sanders represents

Vermont's At Large seat in the House of Representatives. Retail prices for prescription drugs in Canada and Mexico were determined via a survey of four pharmacies in Canada and three pharmacies in Mexico. In Canada, pharmacies were surveyed in three provinces: Ontario, British Columbia, and Nova Scotia. In Mexico, pharmacies were surveyed in Ciudad Juarez, which is just across the border from El Paso, Texas. No significant price differences were observed between prices at different pharmacies in Canada; similarly, no significant price differences were observed between prices at different pharmacies in Mexico. Prices from Canadian pharmacies were determined in Canadian dollars, and prices from Mexican pharmacies were determined in pesos. All prices were converted to U.S. dollars using exchange rates in effect on October 5, 1998.

Interestingly enough, the U.S. General Accounting Office found that drug costs—such as research and development—are not allocated to specific countries, and the costs of production and distribution make up only a small share of the cost of any drug. The study concluded that production and distribution costs cannot be a major source of price differentials.

Source: "Prescription Drug Pricing in Vermont: An International Price Comparison," prepared for Rep. Bernard Sanders, Minority Staff Report, Committee on Government Reform and Oversight, U.S. House of Representatives, November 1, 1998, available Congressman Bernie Sanders site <bernie.house.gov/prescriptions/international.asp>, accessed August 10, 2004.

Externalities

Unfortunately, some production processes create costs for people who are not part of the production or consumption process for the good. These external costs are called **negative externalities**.

negative externalities
Costs borne by parties who are not involved in the production or consumption of a good.

The most common example of a negative externality is pollution. When a firm creates wastes that either do not easily biodegrade or have harmful effects on other resources, it does not pay the full cost of production. For example, a firm that produces textiles usually creates waste products that contain dioxin, a cancer-causing chemical. When a textile manufacturer can dispose of this waste "for free" by dumping it into a nearby river, it has an incentive to dump more waste into the river than is socially optimal. While the firm benefits from dumping waste into the river, the waste reduces the oxygen content of the water, clogs normal waterway routes, and creates reproduction problems for birds, fish, reptiles, and aquatic animals. These results negatively affect people who are not involved in the production or consumption process.

To see why the market fails to provide the efficient level of output when there are externalities in production, consider Figure 14–5. If a firm emits pollutants into the

FIGURE 14–5 The Socially Efficient Equilibrium in the Presence of External Costs

If externalities are present, the free-market equilibrium is not socially efficient. In case of negative externalities, discussed here, the marginal cost of externalities would have to be incorporated in setting the price. The socially efficient level is determined by the intersection point, point C, between the demand curve and the total marginal cost curve (that is, the firm's marginal cost plus the marginal cost of externalities).

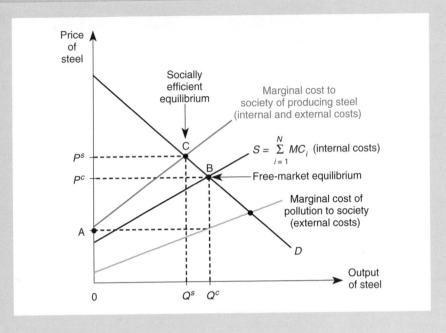

water as a byproduct of producing steel, a cost, or negative externality, is borne by members of society. Figure 14–5 shows the negative externality as the marginal cost of pollution to society. This cost represents the cost to society of dirtier water due to increases in steel production. The production of only a little steel results in only minor damage to water, but as increasing amounts of steel are produced, more and more pollutants collect in the water. The marginal cost of pollution to society thus increases as more steel is produced.

Assuming the market for steel is perfectly competitive, the market supply curve is S in Figure 14–5, which is the sum of the marginal costs of the firms producing in the industry. The supply curve is based on the costs paid by the steel firms; thus, if they are allowed to dump pollutants into the water for free, the market equilibrium is at point B, where the market demand and supply curves intersect. The result is that Q^c units will be produced and purchased at a price of P^c per unit of steel.

However, at this quantity of output, society pays a marginal price of A, on top of the price of P^c paid to the steel firms. This amount is the additional cost to society of the pollution. In particular, since the firms are dumping pollutants into the water for free, the cost of pollution is not internalized by those who buy and sell steel; rather, society pays for the dumping of pollutants by having to endure polluted water. If the firms were to take into account the cost of pollution to society, the sum of their marginal cost curves would be the vertical sum of the supply curve and the marginal cost of pollution to society. This sum is shown as the marginal cost to society of producing steel in Figure 14–5. The socially efficient level of output, which takes into account all the costs and benefits of producing steel, is at point C, where the marginal cost to society of producing steel intersects the market demand curve. The socially efficient level of steel output is Q^s, which is less than the output produced in the perfectly competitive market. The socially efficient price of steel is P^s, which is greater than the perfectly competitive price of P^c. In other words, in the presence of external costs, the market equilibrium output is greater than the socially efficient level, and the market price is below the socially efficient level. In effect, consumers get to purchase too much output at too low a price.

The basic reason for the "market failure" is the absence of well-defined *property rights;* the steel firms believe they have the right to use the river to dump waste, and environmentalists believe they have the right to a clean river. This failure often can be solved when government defines itself to be the owner of the environment. It can then use its power to induce the socially efficient levels of output and pollution.

To induce the socially efficient level of output, government may force firms to internalize the costs of emitting pollutants by enacting policies that shift the internal cost of production up to where it actually equals the social cost of production. A prime example of a government policy designed to do this is the Canadian Environmental Protection Act (CEPA).

Canadian Environmental Protection Act

The Canadian Environmental Protection Act, 1999 (CEPA 1999) contributes to sustainable development through pollution prevention and protects the environment and human health from the risks associated with toxic substances, pollutants, and wastes. Through the CEPA 1999, the Government of Canada is committed to implementing pollution prevention as a national goal and as the priority approach to environmental protection; is committed to implementing the precautionary principle; recognizes the importance of cooperating with provinces, territories, and Aboriginal people for protecting the environment; recognizes that the risk of toxic substances in the environment is a matter of national concern; and acknowledges the need to virtually eliminate the most persistent and bioaccumulative toxic substances and the need to control and manage pollutants and wastes.

Health Canada works in collaboration with Environment Canada to determine whether substances are toxic under the Act and to develop control options. The Act also allows the regulation of disposal at sea; nutrients; export, import, transit, and interprovincial movement of hazardous wastes; fuels; emissions from engines and vehicles; and other threats to Canada's ecosystems and biological diversity.

A firm in an industry covered by the CEPA is required to obtain a permit to be able to pollute. These permits are limited in availability and require the firm to pay a fee for each unit of pollutants emitted. For an existing firm, these permits increase both the fixed and variable costs of producing goods. They are a variable cost because as output increases, the level of pollutants emitted rises, and a fee must be paid on each of these units of pollution. The fixed-cost component is the fee required to obtain a permit in the first place. Along with the permit, the CEPA requires new entrants into an industry to match or improve on the most effective pollution removal system used in the industry. Existing firms must follow suit and upgrade within three years. Once purchased from the government, the permits may be bought from and sold to other firms.

The CEPA causes firms to internalize the cost of emitting pollutants, since a fee must be paid for each unit emitted. This raises each firm's marginal cost and therefore induces them to produce less output. As shown in Figure 14–6, this leads to a decrease in the market supply of the good; less of the product is available in the market at any price. Consequently, the CEPA ultimately decreases the market equilibrium quantity from Q_0 to Q_1 in Figure 14–6 and raises the market price from P_0 to P_1. The change caused by the permits is exactly what is called for in Figure 14–5 to solve the negative externality of pollution: less output at a higher price.

Inside BUSINESS

14-3 Potential Use of Kyoto Protocol Mechanisms with Different Types of Domestic Policies

The Kyoto Protocol establishes emissions limitation or reduction commitments for 38 wealthier countries (Annex I), including Canada. The emissions limitation or reduction commitments apply to each country's aggregate emissions of six greenhouse gases during the period 2008–12. Canada's commitment is to limit its average annual emissions during the period 2008–12 to 94 percent of its baseline emissions, a reduction of 6 percent from the baseline and of 20–30 percent from projected emissions in 2010.

The Kyoto Protocol includes three mechanisms a country can use to help meet its commitment:

(1) International emissions trading (IET) between Annex I parties (Article 17) involves transfers of assigned amount between Annex I countries. (2) Joint implementation (JI) between Annex I parties (Article 6) involves transfers of emission reduction units created by emission reduction or sequestration actions in one Annex I country with financial assistance from another Annex I country. (3) Clean development mechanism (CDM) (Article 12) involves transfers to Annex I parties of certified emission reduction credits created through emission mitigation projects implemented in developing countries with financial and other assistance from Annex I countries.

The Government of Canada can use the Kyoto Protocol mechanisms to help achieve the national commitment regardless of the policies implemented domestically. But the ability of individual sources of greenhouse gas emissions to use the mechanisms depends upon the nature of the domestic policies with which they must comply.

POTENTIAL USE BY THE GOVERNMENT OF CANADA

The Government of Canada might buy the assigned amount or JI emission reduction units from other Annex I

parties. It might also purchase certified emission reduction credits created by CDM projects in developing countries. The purchases of these instruments and their use to help achieve compliance with the national commitment would, of course, be subject to the rules adopted for the mechanisms. The Government might also sell surplus assigned amount or approve JI projects that reduce emissions in Canada. Some of the emission reductions achieved by such projects would be exported and reduce Canada's assigned amount accordingly. Such purchases and sales are possible regardless of the policies implemented domestically.

POTENTIAL USE BY INDIVIDUAL EMISSION SOURCES IN CANADA

To meet its national commitment, Canada needs to adopt policies to limit greenhouse gas emissions by individual sources. The ability of a specific source of greenhouse gas emissions to use the Kyoto Protocol mechanisms depends on the domestic policies with which it must comply. Possible domestic policies to manage greenhouse gas emissions fall into four categories: domestic emissions trading, emission fee or tax, regulations, and other policies.

A Canadian source might wish to purchase an assigned amount of JI emission reduction units or certified CDM credits to help achieve compliance with its domestic obligations. If the source is a participant in a domestic emissions trading program, it should be allowed to purchase such instruments and to use them. Thus, a source might provide the regulator with a combination of domestic allowances or credits and Kyoto Protocol instruments equal to its actual emissions. Title to the Protocol instruments would be transferred to the Government of Canada so that it could use them toward compliance with its national commitment.

An interesting aspect of this new legislation is the fact that permits can be sold by one firm to another both within and across industries. This does two things that allow the market to reduce pollution. First, it allows new firms to enter an industry when demand increases. Second, it provides an incentive for existing firms to invest in new technology to create cleaner production methods.

To see this, suppose demand in a nonpolluting industry increases. As a result, the price increases, economic profits will be earned in the short run, and in the long run new firms will enter the market until economic profits return to zero. However, in a polluting industry that is not allowed to buy and sell permits to pollute, entry cannot occur; the fixed number of pollution permits are already allocated, and new entrants face a barrier to entry because of their inability to obtain a permit. In contrast, if the permits can be traded across industries, a potential entrant can purchase these rights

CANADIAN OPPOSITION TO THE KYOTO PROTOCOL

In Canada, the Alberta provincial government has led the opposition to the Kyoto Protocol. Understandably, most large oil companies are against the Protocol. Large industry groups, such as the Canadian Chamber of Commerce, also initially opposed it. On the other hand, Manitoba, Quebec, Nunavut, and the Northwest Territories have been supportive from the outset. It is also likely British Columbia will be on side, because it will benefit from its large hydroelectric resources. Environmentalism groups such as Greenpeace Canada support ratification of the Protocol. Many insurance companies support it, since extreme weather events cost them money, and some banks support it because of possible business from the global emissions trading market. Some arguments against Canada ratifying the Protocol are that the costs are not yet known, and will be too high, and that it would add a financial burden to Canadian companies that their U.S. counterparts do not face.

However, it looks like the campaign to keep Canada a Kyoto-free zone is running out of momentum. The federal negotiators are reporting remarkable progress in obtaining agreements on greenhouse gas emission caps and trading schemes from a broad range of industries. And the oil and gas industry is among them. A federal-provincial agreement on measuring and registering the amount of greenhouse gas emissions is already in place; Statistics Canada will administer this program. The forestry industry has an emissions agreement with the government, and the oil and gas industry is working on one. An Emissions Trading Scheme (ETS), similar to that used in the EU, will cap the emissions of greenhouse gases such as carbon dioxide. Companies, such as electricity

producers, that exceed the target will have two choices. They can buy carbon credits on the market or install the technology and conservation measures (such as turning off lights) to get them below the target. Companies that are under the target can make a profit by selling surplus credits on an exchange. Banks and other financial intermediaries are naturally great fans of ETS because it gives them a brand-new commodity—carbon dioxide—that can be bought, sold, financed, and otherwise traded like so much wheat or coal.

But this being Canada, it's going more slowly. This is not a bad thing. The slower pace will allow the big greenhouse gas emitters, dominated by the petroleum, power-generating, and manufacturing sectors, more time to build consensus with the government and develop a glitch-free trading system. The goal is fairly modest—a 15 percent reduction in emissions by about 2010. This is not a real reduction, but a reduction in what the emissions would otherwise have been by that date, absent Kyoto.

Sources: "Possible Policies to Manage Greenhouse Gas Emissions; Section 6: Potential Use of Kyoto Protocol Mechanisms with Different Types of Domestic Policies," Departmental Electronic Publications, Agriculture and Agri-Food Canada, Policy Branch <www.agr.gc.ca/cal/epub/2034e/2034-0011_e.html>; (2) "Canada and the Kyoto Protocol," Climate Change site, Government of Canada <www.climatechange.gc.ca/cop/cop6_hague/english/overview_e.html>; (3) Eric Reguly, "Stop Whining, Kyoto's Here to Stay, So Learn to Love Emissions Trading," *The Globe and Mail*, July 15, 2004, available <www.globeinvestor.com/servlet/ArticleNews/story/GAM/20040715/RREGULY15/stocks/news?back_url=yes>. All accessed August 10, 2004.

from a firm in another industry or bring less polluting technology into the existing industry and buy some of the rights to pollute from existing firms. Thus, by making the pollution rights marketable, new firms can enter markets when consumer preferences indicate that more of the good is desired. Firms wishing to enter an industry that produces a highly valued product can purchase permits from firms that produce products that consumers do not value as highly.

The ability to sell the permits also provides an incentive for firms to develop and innovate new technologies that produce less pollution. In particular, a firm that develops a pollution-reducing technology can sell the pollution rights it no longer needs to firms in industries where the technology is not available. This allows the innovating firm to recover a portion of the cost of developing pollution-reducing technologies.

FIGURE 14-6 Impact of the Canadian Environmental Protection Act

The CEPA forces the firms to take the cost of externalities into account. Thus the marginal cost curve of the firm shifts up to S_1, the competitive equilibrium price rises to P_1, and the quantity falls to Q_1. This results in less production (and consumption) of the polluting goods, which is socially more desirable.

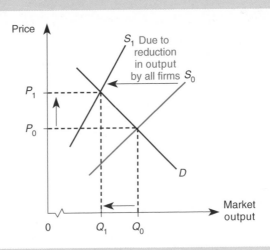

Demonstration PROBLEM 14–2

Suppose the external marginal cost of producing steel is

$$MC_{External} = 3Q$$

and the internal marginal cost is

$$MC_{Internal} = 6Q$$

The inverse demand for steel is given by

$$P = 100 - Q$$

1. What is the socially efficient level of output?
2. How much output would a competitive industry produce?
3. How much output would a monopoly produce?

Answer

1. The socially efficient level of output occurs where the marginal cost to society of producing another unit equals demand. The social marginal cost is

$$MC_{Social} = MC_{External} + MC_{Internal} = 3Q + 6Q = 9Q$$

   Equating this with price yields

$$9Q = 100 - Q$$

   or $Q = 10$ units.

2. A competitive industry produces where the internal marginal cost equals price:

$$6Q = 100 - Q$$

or about $Q = 14.3$ units. Thus, a competitive industry produces too much steel, because it ignores the cost society pays for the pollution.

3. A monopolist produces where marginal revenue equals the internal marginal cost. Since $MR = 100 - 2Q$, we have

$$100 - 2Q = 6Q$$

or $Q = 12.5$ units. Thus, given these demand and cost functions, a monopolist will produce more than the socially efficient level of steel with these cost conditions. Note, however, that since the monopolist has a tendency to restrict output, given these cost and demand functions it produces closer to the socially efficient level than does a competitive industry.

positive externalities
Benefits to society exceeding those to the firm or the individual.

Externalities can be positive. **Positive externalities** exist when the marginal benefit to society of production and or consumption exceeds the marginal benefit to the firm or the individual; that is, production and/or consumption generate external benefits that may go undervalued by the market. There are numerous examples of economic activities that can generate positive externalities, including research and development, education, and health care. Research into new technologies, for example, can later be disseminated for use by other producers. These spillover effects help to reduce the costs of other producers, and cost savings might be passed onto consumers through lower prices. Similarly, a well-educated labour force can increase efficiency and produce other important social benefits. Finally, improved health provision and health care reduces absenteeism from work and creates a better quality of life and higher living standards.

Where positive externalities exist, the good or service may be underconsumed or underprovided, since the free market may fail to take into account their effects. This is because the marginal benefits to society of consuming the good are greater than the marginal benefits to the individual. In the case of external benefits from production, the marginal benefits to the society would be greater than marginal benefits to the firm.

Public Goods

public good
A good that is nonrival and nonexclusionary in consumption.

Another source of market failure is the provision of **public goods**—goods that are nonrival and nonexclusionary in nature and therefore benefit persons other than those who buy the goods. Public goods differ from most goods you consume, which are rivalrous in nature. This simply means that when you consume the good, another person is unable to consume it as well. For example, when you buy and wear a pair of shoes to protect your feet, you prevent someone else from wearing the same pair; the consumption of shoes is rivalrous in nature.

nonrival consumption
A good is nonrival in consumption if the consumption of the good by one person does not preclude other people from also consuming the good.

Nonrival goods include radio signals, lighthouses, national defence, and protecting the environment. When you receive a radio signal in your car, you do not prevent other drivers from picking up the same station in their cars. This is in sharp contrast to your purchasing a pair of shoes.

nonexclusionary consumption
A good or service is nonexclusionary if, once provided, no one can be excluded from consuming it.

The second aspect of a public good is that it is **nonexclusionary**: once a public good is made available, everyone gets it; no one can be excluded from enjoying the good. Most goods and services are by nature exclusionary. For example, when a car manufacturer produces a car, it can keep people from using the car by putting a lock on the door and giving the key only to the person who is willing to pay for the car.

Goods and services such as clean air, national defence, and radio waves are nonexclusionary goods. For example, when the air is clean, everyone gets to consume the clean air; it cannot be allocated to a single person.

What is it about public goods that leads the market to provide them in inefficient quantities? The answer is that since everyone gets to consume a public good once it is available, individuals have little incentive to purchase the good; rather, they prefer to let other people pay for it. Once it becomes available, they can "free ride" on the efforts of others to provide the good. But if everyone thinks this way, no one will buy the good and it will not be available. One person alone may be unable to afford to purchase the good.

Demonstration PROBLEM 14–3

Every time you go to your firm's lounge to get a cup of coffee, the pot is empty. Why?

Answer

There is a free-rider problem caused by the public-goods nature of making a pot of coffee. If you make a pot when it is empty, you benefit by getting a cup, but so do the next seven people who come into the lounge after you. Thus, people typically wait to let someone else make the coffee, which results in an empty coffee pot.

A concrete example will help you see why public goods are not provided in the socially efficient quantity. Suppose individuals value streetlights in their neighbourhood because streetlights help prevent crime. Three people live in the neighbourhood: A, B, and C. All three individuals have identical inverse demand functions for streetlights: $P_A = 30 - Q$, $P_B = 30 - Q$, and $P_C = 30 - Q$. The inverse demand curves reveal how much each person values another streetlight.

Because streetlights are nonexclusionary and nonrival in nature, everyone benefits once a streetlight is installed. For this reason, the total demand for a public good such as streetlights is the vertical sum of the individual inverse demand curves; it reveals the value of each additional streetlight to everyone in the neighbourhood. Given A's, B's, and C's individual demands, the total demand for streetlights is given by

$$P_A + P_B + P_C = 90 - 3Q$$

The individual and total demand curves are graphed in Figure 14–7. Notice that the total demand curve is the vertical sum of all three individual demand curves, and thus every point on it is three times higher than each point on the individual demand curves.

The socially efficient level of streetlights is at point A in Figure 14–7, where the marginal cost of producing streetlights exactly equals the total demand for streetlights. Algebraically, if the marginal cost of providing streetlights is $54 per light, the socially efficient quantity of streetlights is the quantity that equates

$$54 = 90 - 3Q$$

which is 12 lights.

Since the marginal cost of each streetlight is $54 and lies above each individual's demand curve for streetlights in Figure 14–7, none of them will be willing to pay for even one streetlight on their own. However, if each person paid $18 per light, together they would pay $54 per light and could afford to purchase the socially efficient quantity of lights. The only way the people in this neighborhood can achieve the

FIGURE 14–7 The Demand for a Public Good

The marginal cost of producing the good is higher than any individual's demand curve, $54 per light, and thus no one person will pay for the good. However, if the total demand (that is, the vertical sum of each individual's demand) is considered, producing the good is feasible. This allows the producer of the public good to charge each individual $18 per light that she would be willing to pay for the given quantity.

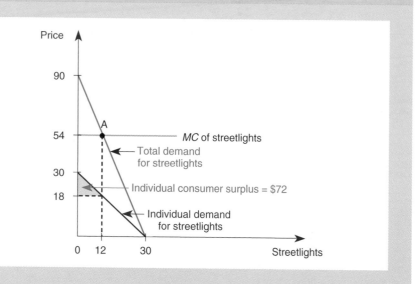

socially efficient quantity of lights is to pool their resources. If they accomplish this and each pays $18 per light, each will enjoy a consumer surplus of the shaded region in Figure 14–7, which is $72.

The problem, however, is that each individual would be better off by letting the other two install the streetlights. In particular, it is strategically advantageous for each person to misrepresent his or her true personal demand function (valuation of the public good). If A claimed she did not want streetlights, and let the others pay for them, she would get to enjoy the lights for free (due to the nonrival and nonexclusionary nature of the good). This is similar to "cheating" on a cooperative agreement and is called *free riding*.

To illustrate this idea, suppose that instead of revealing her true demand for streetlights, A stated that she does not value streetlights at all. If A is the only one who did this, the revealed demand function would be the vertical sum of B's and C's inverse demand functions, which is shown in Figure 14–8(a). Since this demand curve intersects the $54 marginal cost at three streetlights, B and C would each pay $27 per light and purchase three lights. A, on the other hand, would get to enjoy the three streetlights for free, because she misrepresented her true demand for streetlights. By consuming three streetlights for free, she would enjoy a consumer surplus of $85.50, which corresponds to the shaded region in Figure 14–8(b). In contrast, if she had truthfully revealed her demand for streetlights, her consumer surplus would be only $72—the shaded region in Figure 14–7. Thus A is better off by misrepresenting her true preferences for streetlights and letting B and C buy them.

Of course, the same is true of the other two individuals: If they think the others will contribute to buying streetlights, they are better off claiming not to want them. And if they think no one else will pay for streetlights, they will not pay for even one, since the cost is greater than their own individual demand. In the end, no streetlights are provided; the market has failed to provide the public good.

Government solves the public-goods problem by forcing everyone to pay taxes regardless of whether or not a given taxpayer claims to want government services.

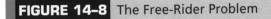

FIGURE 14–8 The Free-Rider Problem

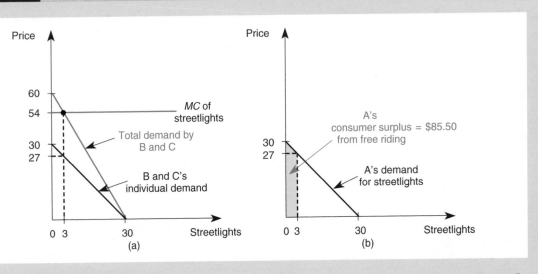

If consumer A does not reveal her demand curve (for example, she can claim not to have any demand for the good), the revealed demand function (B's + C's) intersects the $54 marginal cost where B and C would each pay $27 per light, and A would enjoy streetlights for free since the good is a public good. The free rider, A, extracts $85.50 of surplus without paying for the good.

Government then uses this revenue to fund public projects such as streetlights and national defence, which would not be provided in the absence of government intervention in the marketplace. Thus, while few of us enjoy paying taxes, it does provide a means for obtaining funds for public goods.

It is important to note that government may not provide the socially efficient quantity of public goods; it may in fact provide too much of them. The reason is that when a government official asks a citizen how much of a public good she or he desires, the person may misrepresent the quantity desired. Since most people believe their tax bill is an extremely small percentage of the total funds used to provide public goods, they perceive that the personal cost of the goods is zero and report to the official how many units of the public good they would desire if it were free. In our streetlight example, this means that all three people would tell the official they wanted 30 streetlights—more than twice the socially efficient quantity.

Demonstration PROBLEM 14–4

A firm has 20 employees, each of whom desires a more pleasant work environment. Accordingly, they are considering planting shrubs near the firm's parking lot. Each employee has an inverse demand for shrubs of $P = 10 - Q$, where Q is the number of shrubs. The marginal cost of planting shrubs is $20 each.

1. What is the socially efficient quantity of shrubs to plant?
2. How much would each person have to pay per shrub to achieve the efficient quantity?
3. How many shrubs are likely to be planted? Why?

Answer

1. The total demand for shrubs (a public good) is

$$P = 200 - 20Q$$

Equating this with the marginal cost of planting shrubs yields the socially efficient quantity of shrubs:

$$200 - 20Q = \$20$$

or $Q = 9$ shrubs.

2. If each person paid his or her marginal valuation of another shrub, which is

$$P = 10 - 9 = \$1$$

the 20 employees together would pay $20 for each shrub.

3. Since there is a free-rider problem, no shrubs are likely to be planted unless the boss exerts "moral suasion" and collects $9 from each employee to plant nine shrubs.

We conclude by pointing out that it may be advantageous for a firm to contribute to public goods in its market area. Doing things such as cleaning up a local park or giving money to public television creates goodwill toward the firm and as a result may create brand loyalty or increase the demand for the firm's product. Since public goods are nonrival and nonexclusionary, $1 spent on cleaning up a park or subsidizing public TV is $1 spent on everyone who finds a clean park or public TV appealing. This makes the provision of public goods an inexpensive way for a firm to "benefit" numerous consumers and thus may be a useful advertising strategy in some situations. Another advantage is that it may put the firm on more favourable terms with politicians, who have considerable latitude in affecting the environment in which the firm operates. Unfortunately, there is no easy way to explicitly calculate the optimal amount that a firm should voluntarily contribute to public goods. But ultimately, if the firm's goal is to maximize profits, the last dollar spent on contributions to public projects should bring in one additional dollar in revenue.

Incomplete Information

For markets to function efficiently, participants must have reasonably good information about things such as prices, quality, available technologies, and the risks associated with working in certain jobs or consuming certain products. When participants in the market have *incomplete information* about such things, the result will be inefficiencies in input usage and in firms' output.

Consider the consumption of cigarettes. If individuals are not told that cigarettes are hazardous, some people who currently do not smoke because of the known health risks would smoke out of ignorance of the dangers of smoking. The decision to smoke would be based on incomplete information about the dangers of smoking. For reasons such as these, government serves as a provider of information in many markets, dispensing information to consumers about the ingredients of certain foods, the dangers of certain products and drugs, and the like. Firms print some of this information on the labels of their products due to regulations imposed by government. Government even regulates the work environment by ensuring that workers are aware of the dangers of chemicals such as asbestos and the benefits of precautions such as wearing hard hats in construction jobs. In these instances, the regulations are carried out by Occupational Health and Safety.

One of the more severe causes of market failure is asymmetric information, a situation where some market participants have better information than others. As we saw in Chapter 12, the presence of asymmetric information can lead buyers to refuse to purchase from sellers out of fear that the seller is willing to get rid of the product because it is worth less than they are willing to pay. In the extreme case, the market can collapse altogether. For this reason, several government policies are designed to alleviate the problems caused by asymmetric information. A few of the policies that affect managers are discussed next.

Rules Against Insider Trading

One example of a government regulation designed to alleviate market failures due to asymmetric information is the law against *insider trading* in the stock market. The purpose of the law is to ensure that asymmetric information (better information by insiders) does not destroy the market by inducing outsiders to stay out of it.

For example, suppose Jane Insider has just learned that her research staff has made a discovery that will revolutionize the industry. If Jane can keep the discovery quiet for a short time while she purchases some of her company's stock at its present price, she will make a bundle. When the announcement of the discovery is made public and the market price of the stock increases dramatically, she can resell the stock and make a large profit. Unfortunately, if potential investors believe the market is dominated by insiders who buy and sell stock based on inside information, they will stay out of the market. The only time the insiders will sell is when they know the price will fall, and they will buy only when they know the price will rise. There is no way for outsiders to earn money in a market dominated by insiders, and they will refuse to buy or sell stock. This reduces the marketability of assets in markets dominated by insiders, which decreases the welfare of all potential market participants.

To prevent insider trading from destroying the market for financial assets, the government has enacted rules against insider trading. In Canada, the federal and provincial governments (as well as securities regulators) share responsibility for enforcing laws pertaining to corporate and securities activities. In response to the recent spate of corporate scandals that have plagued the United States and weakened investor confidence in capital markets around the world, the federal government has introduced a new Criminal Code offence (Section 382.1 of the Code, added by clause 5 of Bill C-46) creating new criminal offences with respect to prohibited insider trading and tipping inside information. While improper insider trading has been prohibited under provincial securities law and the Canada Business Corporations Act, the new Criminal Code offence is used for cases that merit the more severe responses available through the criminal law. The government has also set up nine Integrated Market Enforcement Teams, which will include RCMP investigators, federal lawyers, and other experts. The teams are based in Toronto, Montreal, Vancouver, and Calgary.

Certification

Another policy government uses to disseminate information and reduce asymmetric information is the certification of skills and/or authenticity. The purpose of *certification* is to centralize the cost of gathering information. All licensing done by the government falls under certification; this includes all nonprofit organizations, such as charities. Certification can also be a set of minimum standards, such as those for schools and physicians. The purpose is to assure consumers that the products or services have been certified as meeting a certain set of minimum standards. Without a central authority to fulfill this information-gathering role, each individual would have to pay the cost of gaining knowledge about the quality of a product or service. This would lead to inefficiencies due to duplication of information-gathering efforts.

Schools are an example of a potential asymmetric information problem. Without the government certifying a school as satisfying some minimum standard, anyone could open a school. Parents who wanted to educate their children would choose a school based on appearance, cost, proximity to their home, advertising, and reputation. When the school first opens, it may look like a very good deal. But to save money, the school might choose to use unsafe equipment, hire undereducated teachers, and crowd classrooms far beyond a size that is conducive to learning. In the long run, the market would correct these problems; their reputation for poor quality would drive bad schools out of business. In the short run, however, parents who had enrolled their children would lose their investment in education, and the students would have wasted potentially valuable time.

Physician certification is another example of the short-run benefits of government certification. In the absence of physician certification, some less than reputable person could hang a sign stating "Medical Service Here." If improperly trained, this person might prescribe a medicine that could make a patient worse, cause a drug addiction, or even lead to death. In the presence of a government-enforced set of standards, however, this short-run scenario is less likely to happen.

Misleading Advertising

The Competition Act, which is administered by the Bureau of Competition Policy, part of Consumer and Corporate Affairs Canada, is the only federal statute of general application to all Canadian media advertising.[2] In Canada, the first major impetus toward effective misleading advertising laws came in 1960, due to pressure from businesses. They were concerned that misleading regular-price comparisons were making the genuine advertising of sales less credible to consumers and that these misrepresentations were giving their originators an unfair competitive advantage.

In general, these provisions apply to anyone promoting, directly or indirectly, the supply or use of a product or service, or any business interest, by any means. This does not include advertisements or representations made *solely* for a political or charitable purpose. All methods of making representations, including printed or broadcast advertisements, written or oral representations, and audiovisual promotions and illustrations, are within the general scope of the Act.

The Act refers to representations made "to the public." It has been held that a representation to just one person constitutes a representation to the public. It should also be noted that it is not necessary for the Crown to prove that any person was in fact misled; all that is required is that the representation be capable of misleading.

Any representation relating to a product being offered for sale should contain all the information necessary to enable a reasonable purchaser to make a sound purchasing decision. This heading deals with testimonials and endorsements, the nondisclosure of material information, hidden charges, and the use of illustrations. Since these matters generally fall within the scope of Section 52(1), the general-impression test will apply. The onus is on advertisers to ensure that claims about the performance,

---

[2]"Misleading Advertising Guidelines," Competition Bureau site <strategis.ic.gc.ca/epic/internet/incb-bc.nsf/en/ct01299e.html#a>, accessed August 10, 2004.

Inside BUSINESS

14-4   Custom Home Developer: Ordinary Selling Price

In July 2003, the Competition Bureau received a complaint alleging that the product pricing policies of a custom home developer were not in compliance with the Competition Act. The complaint alleged that the company was constantly offering a discounted or sale price without ever selling the products at the "regular" price, giving the consumer the impression of a bargain when no real discount was offered.

Under the civil provisions of the Act, Section 74.01(1), it is an offence for retailers to make a representation to the public that is false or misleading in a material respect. It is also illegal, under the ordinary selling provisions in Section 74.01(3), for retailers to make regular price claims without selling a substantial volume of the product, or offering the product, at that price or a higher price for a substantial amount of time.

During the investigation, Bureau staff met with legal counsel for the company to discuss the complaint, its findings, and the company's explanation. As a result of those discussions, the company provided written assurance that it would refrain from making any representation to the public that was false or misleading in a material respect; ensure that any representation to the public made in respect to the ordinary selling price of its products satisfied the volume and time tests of the Act and considered the content of the Bureau's Ordinary Price Claims Information Bulletin; and ensure that all officers, employees, and agents of the company would be informed in writing of the requirements of the Act and that procedures would be developed to ensure compliance. The issue was resolved in February 2004.

Source: "Alternative Case Resolutions (ACRs)," Competition Bureau site <strategis.ic.gc.ca/epic/internet/incb-bc.nsf/en/h_ct 02071e.html>, accessed August 10, 2004.

efficacy, or length of life of their products have been substantiated by an "adequate and proper test." The test must have been concluded before the representation is made. In other words, a subsequent substantiating test would not exempt an advertiser from liability under this provision.

Any information that would likely have a tendency to affect a purchasing decision should be included. Examples include 8 percent mortgages, when they are in fact 11 percent mortgages reduced to 8 percent by means of a CMHC interest reduction loan; or a photocopier priced at $2995, when an integral part of the copier is not included in the price; or vehicles advertised for sale with "free insurance," when the insurance is only included if the full asking price is paid.

Enforcing Contracts

Another way government solves the problems of asymmetric information is through *contract enforcement*. In Chapters 6 and 10, we learned that contracts are written to keep the parties from behaving opportunistically in the final period of a game. For example, suppose your boss "promised" you payment for labour services at the end of the month. After you have worked for a month, your boss refuses to pay you—in effect gaining a month's worth of your labour for free. In Chapters 6 and 10 we saw that these types of problems do not arise when reputation is important or when there is the potential for repeated interaction among the parties. In these instances, the one-time gain to behaving opportunistically will be more than offset by future losses.

In short-term relationships, however, one or more parties may take advantage of the "end period" by behaving opportunistically. If you knew your boss would not pay you at the end of the month, you would refuse to work. The problem, however, is that you do not know what your boss will do at the end of the month—only she does. In effect, you are uncertain whether your boss is "honest" (will keep a promise) or dishonest (will break a promise). This asymmetric information can destroy the ability of individuals to use contracts to solve the problem of opportunism.

Inside BUSINESS

14-5 Consumer Ministers Advance Initiatives to Protect Consumers in a Marketplace Without Borders

On January 16, 2004 the federal, provincial, and territorial ministers responsible for consumer affairs met for the sixth time under the auspices of the Agreement on Internal Trade in Winnipeg to deal with consumer protection issues associated with a rapidly changing and increasingly open marketplace. Chapter 8 of the Agreement calls upon the federal, provincial, and territorial governments, through their consumer ministers, to cooperate in the enforcement of consumer protection measures. Consumer ministers accomplish this objective through regular meetings and through the work of their officials on the Consumer Measures Committee (CMC). Over the past number of years, ministers' decisions have expanded and strengthened the level of consumer protection by: promoting harmonized regulations and policies; enhancing information sharing among enforcement agencies via mechanisms such as CANSHARE; and by providing reliable consumer information via the Canadian Consumer Handbook and the Canadian Consumer Information Gateway website. This most recent meeting continued a tradition of developing cooperative solutions to pressing consumer issues.

Following that meeting, the ministers announced agreement on a series of cooperative initiatives to promote consumer protection in the following areas: electronic commerce, identity theft, credit card chargebacks, interjurisdictional transactions, short-term credit markets, and the launch of new consumer information products.

The Canadian Code of Practice for Consumer Protection in Electronic Commerce was endorsed by the ministers. The Code, developed cooperatively with business, consumer groups and governments, sets out good business practices for merchants conducting online commercial activities. Important consumer issues, such as a provision of clear information, payment security, contract formation, and complaint handling are addressed.

Furthermore, serious concerns were expressed about threats that identity theft poses for consumers, leaving victims with a poor credit rating, a ruined reputation, and money losses. It was agreed, as a first step, to harmonize information efforts to bring consumers the most reliable and complete information on how to reduce the risk of being victimized.

Ministers also endorsed a proposal to ensure that, in future, the credit card chargeback provisions now applicable to Internet sales would also be applied to other forms of distance sales, such as mail order or telephone selling. This would allow consumers to reverse charges should a merchant fail to meet certain obligations. To further the previous consultations on chargebacks with consumer and business stakeholders, the ministers have asked officials to consult with the credit card industry to determine the most effective way to achieve these objectives and to report back in six months regarding progress.

Consumers are increasingly buying goods and services from suppliers outside their jurisdiction. A coordinated approach is needed to protect consumers and resolve disputes across borders. The ministers welcomed the model legislation developed by a working group of federal, provincial, and territorial representatives and the Uniform Law Conference of Canada (ULCC), and acknowledged the clarity it provides on consumer protection in cross-border transactions. Each jurisdiction is reviewing the model to determine applicability to its situation.

Recognizing the need for improved consumer protection in a legitimate, viable marketplace for short-term credit—for example, payday loans, cheque cashing, vehicle pawn lenders—a group of ministers have formed a task force to work with officials to establish a consumer protection framework, including measures to address the issue of rollovers of loans, concurrent loans from multiple lenders, and the habitual use of payday loans. This work would entail the establishment of best practices for the industry, encouraging the traditional financial institutions (that is, banks and credit unions) to improve consumers' access to financial services, as well as the development of a public education program to raise awareness of the full costs of, and alternatives to, small, short-term loans.

Source: "Backgrounder, Consumer Ministers' Meeting, Winnipeg, Manitoba, January 15–16, 2004," Canadian Intergovernmental Conference Secretariat site, available <www.scics.gc.ca/cinfo04/830807005_e.html>, accessed August 10, 2004.

Rent Seeking

The preceding analysis shows how government policies can improve the allocation of resources in the economy by alleviating the problems associated with market power, externalities, public goods, and incomplete information. It is important to note, however, that government policies generally benefit some parties at the expense of

rent seeking
Selfishly motivated
efforts to influence
another party's decision.

others. For this reason, lobbyists spend considerable sums in attempts to influence government policies. This process, which was also discussed in Chapter 8, is known as **rent seeking**.

To illustrate rent seeking and its consequences, suppose a politician has the power to regulate the monopoly in Figure 14–9. The monopoly currently charges a price of P^M, produces Q^M units of output, and earns profits described by the shaded region A. At the monopoly price and output, consumer surplus is given by triangle C.

If consumers could persuade the politician to regulate the monopolist's price at the competitive level (P^C), the result would be an output of Q^C. If this happened, the monopoly would lose all of its profits (rectangle A). Consumers, on the other hand, would end up with total consumer surplus of regions A, B, and C.

Since the monopolist stands to lose rectangle A if the regulation is imposed, it has an incentive to lobby very hard to prevent the regulation from being imposed. In fact, the monopolist is willing to spend up to the amount A to avoid the regulation. These expenditures may be in the form of legal activities, such as campaign contributions or wining and dining the politician, or illegal activities such as bribes.

Notice that the consumers in Figure 14–9 also would be willing to spend money to persuade the politician to regulate the monopoly. In fact, as a group they would be willing to spend up to A + B to impose the competitive solution, since this is the additional consumer surplus enjoyed when the price is P^C. Of course, each individual consumer stands to gain much less than the group (regulation is a public good in that it benefits all consumers). Consequently, each consumer has an incentive to "free ride," and in the end the amount the consumers spend as a group will be very low. The monopolist, on the other hand, is a single entity. Avoiding regulation is not a public good to the monopolist; the monopolist will receive private gains if it can avoid the legislation. As a result, the monopolist generally will spend much more on lobby-

---

FIGURE 14–9 The Incentives to Engage in Rent-Seeking Activities

Area A is the surplus the monopolist enjoys by applying market power. The regulatory body can force the firm to sell at the competitive equilibrium price of P^C. The monopolist will be willing to pay up to the amount A in order to stop this regulation. Therefore, this situation creates an incentive for the regulatory body to seek rent up to the amount A from the firm.

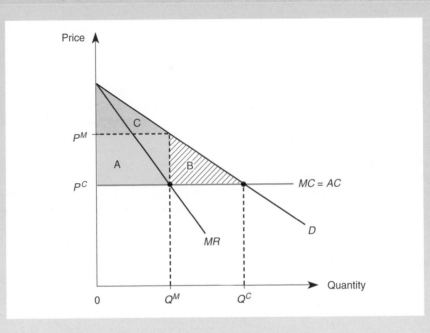

ing activities than the consumers and thus will often avoid legislation by engaging in rent-seeking activities.

Demonstration PROBLEM 14–5

You are the manager of a monopoly that faces an inverse demand curve of $P = 10 - Q$ and has a cost function of $TC(Q) = 2Q$. The government is considering legislation that would regulate your price at the competitive level. What is the maximum amount you would be willing to spend on legal lobbying activities designed to stop the regulation?

Answer

If the regulation passes, your firm's price will be regulated at marginal cost ($2) and the firm will earn zero profits. If not, the firm can continue to produce the monopoly output and charge the monopoly price. The monopoly output is determined by the point where $MR = MC$:

$$10 - 2Q = 2$$

Solving for Q yields the monopoly output of $Q^M = 4$ units. The monopoly price is obtained by inserting this quantity into the demand function to obtain

$$P^M = 10 - (4) = 6$$

Thus, your firm stands to lose monopoly profits of $P^M Q^M - TC(Q^M) = \$16$ if the regulation is imposed. The most you would be willing to spend on legal lobbying activities thus is $16.

Cost-Benefit Analysis

In a world in which the environment and sustainable economic development have become major policy issues, evaluative techniques such as cost-benefit analysis (CBA) must increasingly be included as part of the standard tool kit of government departments and regulatory agencies. However, all organizations, be they commercial entities or government agencies, are faced with decisions on how best to pursue their objectives: What to do? How? When? To guide investment decisions of this kind, organizations use evaluation techniques that focus on options and search for the option that maximizes the payoff. The main difference between private and public sector organizations lies not so much in the evaluation principles as in the frame of reference.

The frame of reference for a commercial entity is the firm itself. The payoff is internal to the firm and comes in the form of the return on investment. A firm's evaluation of a project would focus on the impact of that project on its financial accounts, even though the options under consideration would often have effects extending beyond those accounts. For example, the location of a new plant for a manufacturing enterprise would have an impact on congestion on adjacent roadways. In evaluating alternative locations, the manufacturer would likely limit its concern about congestion effects to the estimated impact on its own operations and profitability (for example, by affecting deliveries to, or shipments from, the plant).

The frame of reference for a federal government organization is society at large. While government agencies are concerned with the effect of project options on their own financial accounts, their interest goes further, extending to the costs and benefits to be realized by society. For example, if Transport Canada were to consider the construction of a new runway at an airport to relieve congestion, it would take into account the benefits and costs to all parties affected, not just itself. Values would be put on benefits such as fuel savings to airlines and time savings for passengers, as well as on negative effects such as increased noise experienced by individuals living or working in the vicinity of the airport.

The applications of CBA are prevalent, including several recent Environmental Assessment Regulations Projects (EARP) processes, such as the expansion (construction of new parallel runways) of Vancouver International Airport and Toronto Pearson International Airport, for which the benefits would consist of reductions in passengers and aircraft delay, and the costs include costs of capital, land costs, and social cost of externalities, that is, the noise level increase.

Government Policy and International Markets

Sometimes rent seeking manifests itself in the form of government involvement in international markets. Such policies usually take the form of tariffs or quotas that are designed to benefit specific firms and workers at the expense of others. In this section, we will examine how government tariff and quota policies affect managerial decisions.

Quotas

In Chapter 2, we showed how government policies in international markets, such as tariffs, affect the market equilibrium outcome. A quota is another tool of government policy.

quota
A restriction that limits the quantity of imported goods that can legally enter the country.

The purpose of a **quota** is to limit the number of units of a product that foreign competitors can bring into the country. For example, a quota on Japanese automobile imports limits the number of cars Japanese automakers can sell in Canada. This reduces competition in the domestic automobile market, which results in higher car prices, higher profits for domestic firms, and lower consumer surplus for domestic consumers. Domestic producers thus benefit at the expense of domestic consumers and foreign producers.

To see why these results occur, consider Figure 14–10, which shows the domestic market for a product. Before the imposition of a quota, the domestic demand curve is D, the supply curve for foreign producers is $S^{Foreign}$, the supply curve for domestic producers is $S^{Domestic}$, and the market supply curve—the horizontal summation of the foreign and domestic supply curves—is S^{F+D}. Equilibrium in the absence of a quota is at point K, where the equilibrium price is P^{F+D} and the equilibrium quantity is Q^{F+D}.

Now suppose a quota is imposed on foreign producers that restricts them from selling more than the quota in the domestic market. Under the quota, foreign supply is $GAS^{F\ Quota}$, while the supply by domestic firms remains at $S^{Domestic}$. Thus, market supply in the domestic market after the quota is GBC, resulting in an equilibrium at point M. The quota increases the price received by domestic producers to P^{Quota}, and domestic firms now earn higher profits. The shaded triangle in Figure 14–10 represents the deadweight loss due to the quota. Total welfare declines as a result of the quota even though domestic producers earn higher profits. The reason for the decline in total welfare is that domestic consumers and foreign producers are harmed more than domestic producers gain from the quota. Domestic producers therefore have a strong incentive to lobby for quotas on foreign imports into their market.

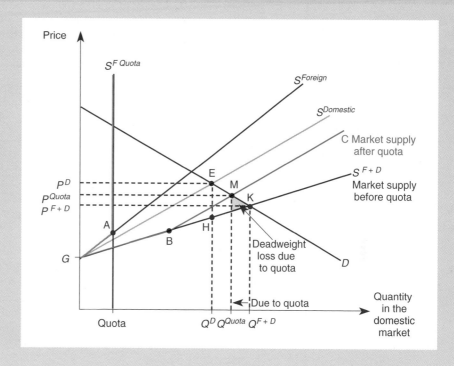

FIGURE 14-10 The Impact of a Foreign Import Quota on the Domestic Market

In the absence of any quota, the total supply curve is the horizontal summation of the foreign supply curve and the domestic supply curve, S^{F+D}. The import quota $S^{F\,Quota}$ increases the price received by domestic producers to P^{Quota} and their profits. However, this creates a deadweight loss for the society equal to the shaded triangle.

Demonstration PROBLEM 14–6

Suppose domestic producers in Figure 14–10 successfully persuaded politicians to completely ban sales by foreign manufacturers in the domestic market. What would be the resulting price and deadweight loss?

Answer

In the absence of foreign supply, the supply curve in the domestic market in Figure 14–10 is $S^{Domestic}$ and equilibrium is at point E. The resulting price is P^D. The deadweight loss of the ban on foreign producers is given by the triangle HEK.

Demonstration PROBLEM 14–7

Suppose the supply of a good by domestic firms is $Q^{SD} = 10 + 2P$ and the supply by foreign firms is $Q^{SF} = 10 + P$. The domestic demand for the product is given by $Q^d = 30 - P$.

1. In the absence of a quota, what is the total supply of the good?
2. What are the equilibrium price and quantity of the good?
3. Suppose a quota of 10 units is imposed. What is the total supply of the product?
4. Determine the equilibrium price in the domestic market under the quota of 10 units.

Answer

1. The total supply is the sum of foreign and domestic supply, which is

$$Q^T = Q^{SD} + Q^{SF} = (10 + 2P) + (10 + P) = 20 + 3P$$

2. Equilibrium is determined by equating total demand and supply:

$$30 - P = 20 + 3P$$

Solving for P yields the equilibrium price of $P = \$2.50$. Given this price, domestic firms produce

$$Q^{SD} = 10 + 2(2.5) = 15 \text{ units}$$

and foreign firms produce

$$Q^{SF} = 10 + 2.5 = 12.5 \text{ units}$$

for a total equilibrium output of $Q^T = 27.5$ units.

3. With a quota of 10 units, foreign firms will sell only 10 units in the domestic market. Thus, total supply is

$$Q^T = Q^{SD} + Q^{SF} = (10 + 2P) + 10 = 20 + 2P$$

4. Equilibrium is determined by equating total demand and total supply under a quota:

$$30 - P = 20 + 2P$$

Solving for P yields the equilibrium price of $P = \$3.33$. The quota increases the price of the good in the domestic market due to the reduction in foreign competition.

Tariffs

Tariffs, like quotas, are designed to limit foreign competition in the domestic market to benefit domestic producers. As shown in Chapter 2, the benefits to domestic producers accrue at the expense of domestic consumers and foreign producers.

We will address two types of tariffs: lump-sum tariffs and excise or per-unit tariffs. A **lump-sum tariff** is a fixed fee that foreign firms must pay the domestic government to be able to sell in the domestic market. In contrast, the more familiar **per-unit** or **excise tariff** requires the importing firms to pay the domestic government a fee on each unit they bring into the country.

lump-sum tariff
A fixed fee that an importing firm must pay the domestic government in order to have the legal right to sell the product in the domestic market.

per-unit (excise) tariff
The fee an importing firm must pay to the domestic government on each unit it brings into the country.

Lump-Sum Tariffs

Figure 14–11 shows the marginal and average cost curves for an individual foreign firm before and after the imposition of a lump-sum tariff. The first thing to notice about the lump-sum tariff is that it does not affect the marginal cost curve. This is because the importer must pay the same amount of tariff regardless of how much of the product it brings into the country. Since the lump-sum tariff raises average costs from AC^1 to AC^2, an importer is unwilling to pay the tariff to enter the domestic market unless the price in the domestic market is at least P^2.

Figure 14–12 shows the effect of a lump-sum tariff on the market. Before the tariff is imposed, the supply curve for foreign competitors is ES^F, that for domestic producers is ES^D, and the market supply curve—the summation of domestic and foreign

FIGURE 14–11 | Impact of a Lump-Sum Tariff on a Foreign Firm

The imposition of a lump-sum tariff does not affect the foreign firm's marginal cost curve. However, the average cost curve shifts up by the amount of tariff to AC^2. Consequently, the importer will not be willing to pay the tariff to enter the market unless the price is at least as high as P^2.

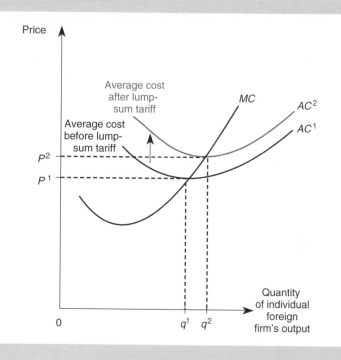

FIGURE 14–12 | Impact of a Lump-Sum Tariff on Market Supply

When a lump-sum tariff is imposed on the foreign firms, the foreign supply curve becomes AS^F and the market supply curve becomes $EBCS^{D+F}$. P^2 is the price below which only domestic firms make a production and foreign firms do not supply. At P^2 and higher, the quantity the foreign firm is willing to supply is added. The coloured line is the new supply curve after imposition of a lump-sum tariff on the foreign firms.

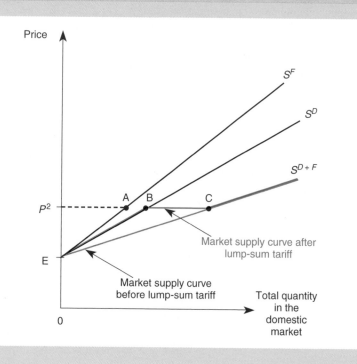

Inside BUSINESS

14-6 Motorcycle Tariffs

Harley-Davidson was the king of the road when it came to big motorcycles. From its beginnings in 1903, Harley-Davidson made the largest, fastest bike in the world. Its success came from a diehard group of bikers who knew that a Harley was indestructible. However, in the early 1960s Harley got lax; quality started to slide, and Japanese imports started making inroads into its market. By 1979, Harley had only 5 percent of the overall motorcycle market and was down to 21 percent of the market for large bikes. By 1983, its share of the market had slipped to 9 percent.

The Japanese had come to compete in the market. Harley still had only two engine blocks, and they were extremely heavy. On top of that, quality had slipped to the point where once devoted fans of Harley-Davidson said they would never buy another Harley. Instead, customers were going to Japanese makers of large bikes like Kawasaki, Honda, Yamaha, and Suzuki. Harley's competition had 14 different models to choose from; also, they were lighter, faster, and higher in quality.

In 1981 Vaughn Beals, a vice-president of Harley, organized a leveraged buyout and purchased Harley-Davidson. The first thing Beals noticed was that labour was extremely lax; the second was that the manufacturing equipment was old and worn out. So Beals launched a pep-squad-style management team and put quality control in the hands of line workers. Then he borrowed and invested $160 million in retooling and redesigning the Harley.

The boldest thing Beals did was ask the International Trade Commission for an excise tariff of 49.4 percent on Japanese imports of bikes with 700cc and larger engines. Despite President Reagan's then-recent pledge to open up markets and do away with tariffs and quotas, the ITC and the president got behind Harley's proposal. What was it about the proposal that brought the Reagan administration around?

Beals explained to the ITC that Harley's problem was a short-term one and the firm would need the tariffs for only five years to become competitive again. He proposed that the tariff decline from 49.4 percent in 1983 to 29.4 percent in 1988 and then be removed completely. This was a chance for American business to show it could be competitive in world markets when times were getting tough. So the Reagan administration backed the plan completely.

Did the tariff work? Japanese sales of motorcycles larger than 750cc dropped from 88 000 in the first half of 1983 to under 21 000 in the first half of 1984. Of course, this had the Japanese producers calling foul, but it gave Harley some time to reorganize. Sales of Harley bikes rose, and so did their prices. But the tariffs alone would not save Harley-Davidson. With retooling in progress, along with 12 new models and quality control that was even tighter than that of the Japanese manufacturers, Harley-Davidson was able to rebound.

In an effort to break the tariffs, the Japanese responded by producing a 699cc machine that performed better than their earlier 750cc models. They also moved a large number of their plants to the United States to avoid the tariff. But this plan took a couple of years to implement and proved to be too little too late. By 1987 Harley was back in the black. Its market share had increased to 46.5 percent of the large-bike market in the United States and was gaining ground in Europe and Japan.

The success of the temporary reprieve and reorganization was so swift that Harley asked for the tariff to be removed ahead of schedule. The ITC obliged. Even though the tariff protection was gone, by 1992 Harley couldn't produce enough motorcycles to keep up with demand. Over the past decade, Harley has continued to enjoy phenomenal earnings growth. Adjusting for numerous stock splits, its shareholders have seen the value of their company increase from less than $3 per share in 1992 to over $50 per share in 2001.

Sources: S&P Reports, 2001; Harley-Davidson site <www.harley-davidson.com>, accessed December 5, 2001; Michael Kolbenschlag, "Harley-Davidson Takes Lessons from Arch-Rivals' Handbook," *International Management*, February 1985, pp. 46–48; Vineeta Anand, "Japanese Management Style Puts Harley-Davidson on the Road Again," *Global Trade Executive*, May 1986, pp. 66–68; Peter C. Reid, *Well Made in America: Lessons from Harley-Davidson on Being the Best* (New York: McGraw-Hill, 1990).

supply—is ES^{D+F}. After the lump-sum tariff is imposed, the foreign supply curve becomes AS^F, because importers will not pay the lump-sum tariff to enter the domestic market unless the price is above P^2. Thus, the market supply curve in the presence of a lump-sum tariff is given by $EBCS^{D+F}$. The overall effect of this policy is to remove foreign competitors from the domestic market if the demand curve crosses the domestic supply curve at a price below P^2. A lump-sum tariff increases the profits of domestic producers if demand is low but has no effect on their profits if demand is high.

FIGURE 14–13 Impact of an Excise Tariff on Market Supply

An excise tariff increases the marginal cost of the foreign producers by the amount of tariff per unit, which in turn decreases (leftward shift) the supply of all foreign firms from S^F to S^{F+T}. The overall market supply is now ACS^{D+F+T}, and the resulting market equilibrium is at point E. At this point, the total quantity supplied is lower and the price is higher. The domestic firms make more profit at the expense of foreign firms.

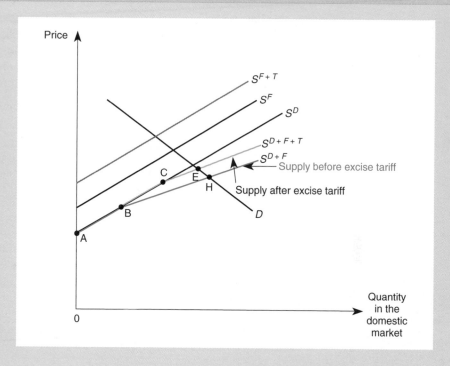

Excise Tariffs

If an excise tariff is imposed on foreign producers instead of a lump-sum tariff, domestic producers benefit at all levels of demand. To see this, consider Figure 14–13, which shows the effect of an excise tariff. S^F is the supply by foreign producers before the tariff, S^D is the supply by domestic producers, and ABS^{D+F} is the market supply curve before an excise tariff. Equilibrium in the absence of a tariff is at point H.

When a tariff of T is imposed on each unit of the product, the marginal cost curve for foreign firms shifts up by the amount of the tariff, which in turn decreases the supply of all foreign firms to S^{F+T} in Figure 14–13. The market supply under a per-unit tariff is now ACS^{D+F+T}, and the resulting equilibrium is at point E. The tariff raises the price domestic consumers must pay for the product, which raises the profits of domestic firms at the expense of domestic consumers and foreign producers.

ANSWERING THE Headline

Section 50 of the Competition Act introduced into Canada's competition law in 1935 addressing predation states

> Everyone engaged in a policy of selling products at prices unreasonably low, having the effect or tendency of substantially lessening competition or eliminating a competitor, or designed to have that effect, is guilty of an indictable offence and liable to imprisonment for a term not exceeding two years.

The test of this focuses on price-cost relationships to detect predatory pricing. Accordingly, prices below average (avoidable) variable costs are deemed to be unreasonable. In the Bureau's view, the "avoidable costs," or "variable costs" in this case, consist of those incurred to provide airline services: fuel, aircraft costs, pilots, crews, tickets and meals, etc., which would be avoided if the service were not provided. These are essentially the costs associated with operating flights, but they do not include all ground or terminal costs or corporate overhead. As it turns out, the variable cost calculated this way will exceed the airfare charged by Air Canada on the proposed routes, indicating Air Canada's practice of predatory pricing.

Summary

In this chapter, we focused on government's activity in the market to correct market failures caused by market power, externalities, public goods, and incomplete information. The government's ability to regulate markets gives market participants an incentive to engage in rent-seeking activities, such as lobbying, to affect public policy. These activities may extend to international markets, where government imposes tariffs or quotas on foreign imports to increase the profits of special interests.

In Canada, as in many other countries, the government influences markets through devices such as antitrust legislation, price regulation, and truth-in-advertising/truth-in-lending regulations, as well as policies designed to alleviate market failure due to externalities or public-goods problems. The rules that affect the decisions of future managers are spelled out in documents such as the Sherman Antitrust Act and the Canadian Environmental Protection Act.

Key Terms and Concepts

Competition Act 492
lump-sum tariff 520
market power 491
negative externalities 501
nonexclusionary consumption 507
nonrival consumption 507

per-unit (excise) tariff 520
positive externalities 507
public good 507
quota 518
rent seeking 516

Conceptual and Computational Questions

1. You are the manager in a market comprising five firms, each of which has a 20 percent market share. In addition, each firm has a strong financial position and is located within a 100 kilometre radius of its competitors.
    a. Calculate the pre-merger C_4 (four-firm concentration ratio) for this market.
    b. Suppose that any two of these firms merge. What is the post-merger C_4?
    c. On the basis of on the information contained in this question and on the Canadian Competition Bureau merger guidelines described in this chapter, do you think the Bureau would attempt to block a merger between any two of the firms? Explain.

2. Use the following graph to answer the questions.

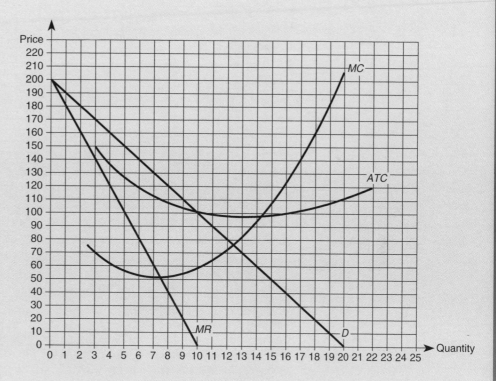

a. Suppose this monopolist is unregulated.
   (1) What price will the firm charge to maximize its profits?
   (2) What is the level of consumer surplus at this price?
b. Suppose the firm's price is regulated at $80.
   (1) What is the firm's marginal revenue if it produces 7 units?
   (2) If the firm is able to cover its variable costs at the regulated price, how much output will the firm produce in the short run to maximize its profits?
   (3) In the long run, how much output will this firm produce if the price remains regulated at $80?

3. You are an industry analyst that specializes in an industry where the market inverse demand is $P = 100 - 5Q$. The external marginal cost of producing the product is $MC_{External} = 10Q$, and the internal cost is $MC_{Internal} = 20Q$.
   a. What is the socially efficient level of output?
   b. Given these costs and market demand, how much output would a competitive industry produce?
   c. Given these costs and market demand, how much output would a monopolist produce?
   d. Discuss actions the government could take to induce firms in this industry to produce the socially efficient level of output.

4. There are two workers. Each worker's demand for a public good is $P = 20 - Q$. The marginal cost of providing the public good is $24. The following graph summarizes the relevant information.

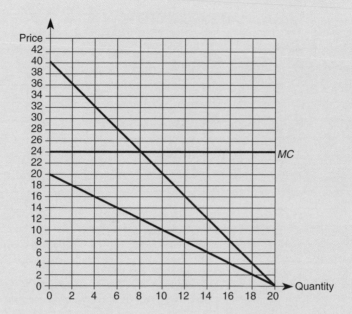

a. What is the socially efficient quantity of the public good?
b. How much will each worker have to pay per unit to provide the socially efficient quantity?
c. Suppose the two workers contribute the amount needed to provide the quantity of public good you identified in parts (a) and (b). A third worker values the public good just like the two contributing workers, but she claims *not* to value the good because she wants to "free ride" on the payments of the other two workers.
   (1) Given the three workers' true demands for the public good, is the amount of the public good provided by the two workers socially efficient?
   (2) Compare the level of consumer surplus enjoyed by these three workers. Which worker(s) enjoys the most surplus?

5. As the manager of a monopoly, you face potential government regulation. Your inverse demand is $P = 25 - Q$, and your costs are $C(Q) = 5Q$.
   a. Determine the monopoly price and output.
   b. Determine the socially efficient price and output.
   c. What is the maximum amount your firm should be willing to spend on lobbying efforts to prevent the price from being regulated at the socially optimal level?

6. Consider a competitive market served by many domestic and foreign firms. The domestic demand for these firms' product is $Q^d = 500 - 1.5P$. The supply function of the domestic firms is $Q^{SD} = 50 + 0.5P$, while that of the foreign firms is $Q^{SF} = 250$.
   a. Determine the equilibrium price and quantity under free trade.
   b. Determine the equilibrium price and quantity when foreign firms are constrained by a 100-unit quota.
   c. Are domestic consumers better or worse off as a result of the quota?
   d. Are domestic producers better or worse off as a result of the quota?

7. Suppose that the government gets legislation passed through Parliament that imposes a one-time lump-sum tariff on the product that a foreign firm exports to Canada.
   a. What happens to the foreign firm's marginal cost curve as a result of the lump-sum tariff?
   b. Will the lump-sum tariff cause the foreign firm to export more or less of the good? Explain carefully.

8. The diagram below depicts a monopolist whose price is regulated at $10 per unit. Use the figure to answer the questions that follow.

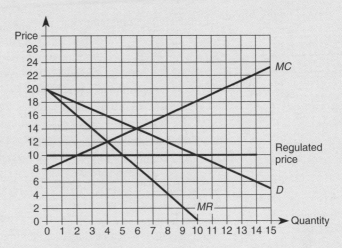

 a. What price will an unregulated monopoly charge?
 b. What quantity will an unregulated monopoly produce?
 c. How many units will a monopoly produce when the regulated price is $10 per unit?
 d. Determine the quantity demanded and the amount produced at the regulated price of $10 per unit. Is there a shortage or a surplus?
 e. Determine the deadweight loss to society (if any) when the regulated price is $10 per unit.
 f. Determine the regulated price that maximizes social welfare. Is there a shortage or a surplus at this price?

Problems and Applications

9. Molson and Labatt, Quebec's two main breweries, market nearly 90 percent of the beer sold in Quebec. The remaining 10 percent is sold by microbreweries. In 2000, Competition Bureau received complaints from certain microbreweries regarding Molson Canada (Molson) and La Brasserie Labatt Ltée (Labatt). The complainants maintained that the two breweries were engaged in various anticompetitive acts in the Quebec beer market. Specifically, they asserted that the introduction of new brands and agreements entered into by Molson and Labatt with licensed establishments were harmful to the development of the complainants' business activities. Among the offending contract clauses were exclusivity and shelf-space allocation clauses. What category of offences did the complainants allege the two major breweries were engaged in?

10. In 2001, the Competition Bureau received a complaint that Canadian manufacturers had pressured sewer pipe distributors in one province to refuse to deal in pipe imported from the United States. The allegations were examined under Section 45 and 61 of Competition Act.

 Evidence of violation of the Act under these two sections was found inconclusive. Subsequently, the U.S. pipe manufacturer was able to establish a distribution network in the province and the prices for the affected pipe fell more than 20 percent. In addition, all of the manufacturers had agreed to create or reinforce programs within their companies to ensure compliance with the Act. What aspect of the Act do you believe the complainants were trying to accuse the manufacturer of violating?

11. The Competition Bureau received a complaint in June 2003 alleging that a telecommunications provider's advertisements were not in compliance with the Competition Act. The advertisements in question, which appeared on the Internet, claimed that the provider's pay-per-view movies were the "latest and greatest hit Hollywood movies." A Bureau examination conducted under Subsection 74.01(1)(a) of the Act revealed that pay-per-view movies are regularly released approximately two months after their release date in video rental stores. This is due to a movie industry practice known as "windowing"—releasing movies through a progressive series of outlets at different price points. Feature films debut in movie theatres before moving to home video sales and rental, pay-per-view, and cable. What provision of the Act did the complainant allege the advertisements violating?

12. On July 19, 2002, the Competition Tribunal issued a consent order to remedy competition concerns raised by Bayer AG's acquisition of Aventis CropScience. It required Bayer AG to divest three key agricultural chemical products and to license a fourth in its crop protection division. The Tribunal had issued an interim consent order on June 6, 2002 to ensure that the designated assets were separated and managed independently from Bayer's other business operations. On January 21, 2003, the Bureau announced that Bayer AG had complied with the consent order, and the Bureau approved the following divestitures: Arvesta Corporation would acquire certain assets of the flucarbazone business (including Everest, a spring wheat herbicide); BASF AG would acquire certain assets of the triticonazole business (including Charter, a cereal seed treatment); and Nippon Soda Co. Ltd. would acquire certain assets of the acetamiprid business, including a licence for Iprodione. In partnership with a Canadian licensee, Nippon would then be able to manufacture and develop Assail, a fruit and vegetable insecticide, and Assail ST, a canola seed treatment. Why in your opinion were these divestitures required, and what did they accomplish?

13. According to a *Toronto Star* report, the Ontario Securities Commission (OSC), Canada's main stock regulator, was investigating almost 400 cases involving investors who bought companies' special warrants before they were sold to the public. The cases, which dated from January 1, 2000, involved companies that raised millions of dollars by selling special warrants, or discounted shares, to a small group of institutional investors, the newspaper said. Michael Watson, the regulator's director of enforcement, told the *Star* that the probe focused on whether money managers who were offered the warrants used information from sales presentations to trade shares in the companies trying to raise the money. The Commission alleged that some fund mangers sold stock before the warrant sales were completed and disclosed to the public. A company whose shares trade at C$10 might offer investors the chance to buy special warrants at C$9 each, giving a fund manager a chance to sell its shares at C$10 and replace them at the cheaper price. Why did the OSC allege this to be a violation of laws? According to the OSC, what laws might have been violated?

14. Electricity North is a monopoly provider of residential electricity in a region of northern Manitoba. Total demand by its 2 million households is $Q^d = 1000 - P$, and Electricity North can produce electricity at a constant marginal cost of $2 per megawatt hour. Consumers in this region of Manitoba have recently complained that the company is charging too much for its services. In fact, a few consumers are so upset that they're trying to form a coalition to lobby the local government to regulate the price it charges. If all the consumers of this region joined the coalition against the company, how much would each consumer be willing to spend to lobby the local government to regulate its price? Do you think the consumers will be successful in their efforts? Explain.

15. China's entry into the World Trade Organization (WTO) is likely to create more competition between local and foreign firms, as well as provide China greater access to the market for exports. This is particularly true in the market for rubber, since China is the world's second-largest consumer of rubber. According to the WTO, China plans to eliminate its import quota on rubber over the next five years. What impact is the import quota reduction likely to have on the price of rubber and the quantity of rubber exchanged in China? What implications will the elimination of the quota on rubber have on China's social welfare?

APPENDIX: Antitrust Policy

antitrust policy
Government policy designed to keep firms from monopolizing their markets.

Antitrust policy attempts to eliminate the deadweight loss of monopoly by making it illegal for managers to engage in activities that foster monopoly power, such as price-fixing agreements and other collusive practices. The cornerstone of U.S. antitrust policy is contained in Sections 1 and 2 of the *Sherman Antitrust Act* of 1890:

Sec. 1
Every contract, combination in the form of trust or otherwise, or conspiracy, in restraint of trade or commerce among the several states, or with foreign nations, is hereby declared to be illegal. Every person who shall make any such contract or engage in any such combination or conspiracy shall be deemed guilty of a felony, and, on conviction thereof, shall be punished by fine not exceeding five thousand dollars (one million dollars if a corporation, or, if any other person, one hundred thousand dollars) or by imprisonment not exceeding one (three) years, or by both said punishments, in the discretion of the court.

Sec. 2
Every person who shall monopolize, or attempt to monopolize, or combine or conspire with any person or persons, to monopolize any part of the trade or commerce among the several States, or with foreign nations, shall be deemed guilty of a felony, and, on conviction thereof, shall be punished by fine not exceeding five thousand dollars (one million dollars if a corporation, or, if any other person, one hundred thousand dollars) or by imprisonment not exceeding one (three) years, or by both said punishments, in the discretion of the court.[1]

Among other things, the Sherman Act makes it illegal for managers of U.S. firms to collude with other domestic or foreign firms. Thus, even though OPEC is not bound by U.S. law (it is composed of foreign nations), the manager of a U.S. oil company cannot legally participate in the OPEC oil cartel.

The interpretation of antitrust policy is largely shaped by the courts, which rule on ambiguities in the law and previous cases. For example, the first successful use of the Sherman Antitrust Act was in 1897, when the Supreme Court held that rate agreements are illegal in *United States v. Trans-Missouri Freight Association*. This ruling was again upheld in *United States v. Joint Traffic Association* (1898). The court extended its interpretation to include collusive bidding in *Addyston Pipe & Steel Company v. United States* (1899). The full power of the Sherman Antitrust Act was

---

[1]The penalties have been amended twice, in 1955 and in 1970. The penalties in parentheses represent the 1970 change.

not realized until the conclusion of *United States v. Standard Oil of New Jersey* in 1911. The last case is interesting and provides useful caveats to future managers.

Standard Oil of New Jersey, along with Standard Oil of Ohio, was charged with attempting to fix the prices of petroleum products and the prices at which the products would be shipped. Standard Oil, in particular, was accused of numerous activities designed to enhance monopoly power: using physical threats to shippers and other producers, setting up bogus companies, using espionage by bribing employees of other companies, engaging in restraint of trade, and making several attempts to monopolize the oil industry. Managers, of course, should avoid all of these practices; as a result of these actions, the court dissolved Standard Oil into 33 subsidiaries, many of which survive today under the names Exxon, Mobil, Chevron, Amoco, and BP America. More important than breaking up the Standard Oil Trust, however, was the Supreme Court's new *rule of reason,* as defined in Justice White's majority opinion:

> Thus not specifying, the indubitably contemplating and requiring a standard, it follows that it was intended that the standard of reason which had been applied at the common law and in this country in dealing with subjects of the character embraced by the statute was intended to be the measure used for the purpose of determining whether, in a given case, a particular act had or had not brought about the wrong against which the statute provided.

The rule of reason has since become the code of decision making used by the court for determining antitrust cases. Effectively, the rule of reason stipulates that not all trade restraints are illegal; rather, only those that are "unreasonable" are prohibited. For example, in applying this rule, the courts determined that the size of a firm alone is not sufficient evidence to convict a firm under Section 2 of the Sherman Act:

> To hold to the contrary would require the conclusion either that every contract, act, or combination of any kind or nature, whether it operated in restraint of trade or not, was within the statute.

Effectively, this means that a firm must take an explicit action designed to lessen competition before it can be found guilty of violating Section 2 of the Sherman Act. For example, the rule of reason was used in the decision against American Tobacco, which was found guilty of monopolizing the U.S. cigarette market by engaging in predatory pricing—pricing explicitly designed to harm other firms and thus enhance the firm's own monopoly power.

The problem with the rule of reason is that it makes it difficult for managers to know in advance whether particular pricing strategies used to enhance profits are in fact violations of the law. Congress attempted to clarify its intent by more precisely defining illegal actions in the Clayton Act (1914) and its amendment, the Robinson Patman Act (1936). For example, Section 2(a) of the Robinson Patman Act amends Section 2 of the Clayton Act and makes price discrimination illegal if it is designed to lessen competition or create a monopoly:

> **Sec. 2(a)**
> That it shall be unlawful for any person engaged in commerce, in the course of such commerce, either directly or indirectly, to discriminate in price between different purchasers of commodities of like grade and quality, . . . where such discrimination may be substantially to lessen competition or tend to create a monopoly in line of commerce, or to injure, destroy, or prevent competition.

Price discrimination that arises because of cost or quality differences is permitted under the act, as is price discrimination when it is necessary to meet a competitor's price in a market. Still, there is considerable ambiguity regarding whether a particular type of price discrimination is illegal under the law.

The Clayton Act contains more than 20 sections that, among other things, make it illegal for firms to (1) hide kickbacks as commissions or brokerage fees; (2) use rebates unless they are made available to all customers; (3) engage in exclusive dealings with a supplier unless the supplier adds to the furnishing of the buyer and/or offers to make like terms to all other potential suppliers; (4) fix prices or engage in exclusive contracts if such a practice will lead to lessening of competition or monopoly; and (5) acquire one or more other firms if such an acquisition will lead to a lessening of competition.

The Cellar-Kefauver Act (1950) strengthened Section 7 of the Clayton Act by making it more difficult for firms to engage in mergers and acquisitions without violating the law:

Sec. 7

That no corporation engaged in commerce shall acquire, directly or indirectly, the whole or any part of the stock or other share capital and no corporation subject to the jurisdiction of the Federal Trade Commission shall acquire the whole or any part of the assets of another corporation engaged also in commerce, where in any line of commerce in any section of the country, the effect of such acquisition may be substantially to lessen competition, or to tend to create a monopoly.

Merger policy changed, however, when new horizontal merger guidelines were written in 1982, amended in 1984, and revised in 1992 and in 1997. The guidelines are based on the *Herfindahl-Hirschman index (HHI),* which is the sum of the squared shares of the market for every firm in a particular market times 10 000:

$$HHI = 10\ 000 \sum_{i=1}^{N} w_i^2$$

Under the *Horizontal Merger Guidelines,* a merger can be challenged if (1) the *HHI* in an industry is greater than 1800, or would be after merger, or (2) the *HHI* is between 1000 and 1800, in which case the merger is to be carefully examined. It is important to stress that these are only guidelines; mergers are often allowed even when *HHI* indexes are large, provided there is significant foreign competition, an emerging new technology, increased efficiency, or one of the firms has financial problems.

The main theme of the *Horizontal Merger Guidelines* is summarized as follows:

The primary benefit of mergers to the economy is their efficiency potential, which can increase the competitiveness of firms and result in lower prices to consumers. . . . In the majority of cases, the Guidelines will allow firms to achieve efficiencies through mergers without interference from the Department.[2]

The 1997 revision to the *Horizontal Merger Guidelines* recognizes that efficiencies are difficult to verify and quantify. However, it requires merging firms to substantiate any efficiency claims; "vague or speculative" claims do not count.

The *Antitrust Division of the Department of Justice (DOJ)* and the *Federal Trade Commission (FTC)* are charged with the task of enforcing antitrust regulations. The

[2]Department of Justice, *Horizontal Merger Guidelines,* 1984, sec. 1.

Hart-Scott-Rodino Antitrust Improvement Act of 1976 requires that parties to an acquisition notify both the DOJ and the FTC of their intent to merge, provided that the dollar value of the transaction exceeds a certain threshold (currently $50 million). Following this premerger notification, the parties must wait 30 days before they may complete the merger. If the DOJ or FTC decides that further examination of the merger is warranted, a so-called second request is issued: The parties are asked to provide additional information to the government. A second request automatically extends the waiting period. Once the parties comply with the second request, the government has 30 days to review the information and either file a complaint to block the merger or permit the merger to take place.

In practice, less than 3 percent of all premerger notifications lead to a second request. In those cases where a second request is issued, the government and the parties usually reach an agreement before going to court. Typically, the firms sell to third parties certain market assets where there is considerable business overlap. This eliminates the government's antitrust concerns and allows the parties to consummate the merger. If the government and the parties cannot come to an agreement about which assets will be divested, the government may file suit to block the merger.

Answers to Selected End-of-Chapter Problems

Chapter 1

1. Consumer–consumer rivalry best illustrates this situation. Here, Levi Strauss & Co. is a buyer competing against other bidders for the right to obtain the antique blue jeans.

4. *a.* The value of the firm before it pays out current dividends is

$$PV_{firm} = \$550\ 000\left(\frac{1 + 0.08}{0.08 - 0.05}\right)$$

$$= \$19.8 \text{ million}$$

6. *a.* Profits are maximized at $Q = 108$.

8. *a.* Her accounting profits are $180\ 000$. These are computed as the difference between revenues ($200\ 000$) and explicit costs ($20\ 000$).

Chapter 2

1. *a.* Since X is a normal good, an increase in income will lead to an increase in the demand for good X (the demand curve for good X will shift to the right).

3. *a.* 50 units.

4. *b.* X is a normal good.

5. *b.* $12\ 800$.

Chapter 3

2. *a.* The own price elasticity is -0.44, so the demand for good X is inelastic at this price. The firm's revenue would fall if it charged a price below $154.

3. *c.* The income elasticity is 1, so good X is a normal good.

4. *a.* The quantity demanded of good X will decrease by 10 percent.

5. Decrease by 10 percent.

Chapter 4

1. *a.* −0.25.
2. *a.* $Y = 25 - 0.5X$.
6. *c.* 6 units.
7. *a.* The consumption of good X will decrease and the consumption of good Y will increase.

Chapter 5

1. *c.* $L = 16$.
2. *a.* Labour is the fixed input while capital is the variable input.
4. *a.* $FC = \$50$.
7. *b.* Cost complementarities exist since $a = -0.25 < 0$.

Chapter 6

3. *a.* Contract.
5. *a.* Human capital.
8. *a.* Reduces the benefits of vertical integration.

Chapter 7

1. $C_4 = 0.55$.
3. −1.5.
4. *a.* $100.
7. In general, a merger between two firms with market shares w_i and w_j will increase the *HHI* by $2(10\ 000)w_iw_j$.

Chapter 8

2. *b.* $80.
4. *a.* $Q = 20$ units.
6. *b.* $Q = 4; P = \$60$.
7. *a.* $P = 10 - 0.5Q$.

Chapter 9

1. *a.* D_2.
4. *b.* $P = MC = \$100$.
5. *c.* Competitive bidding by identical contractors.
7. *a.* Firm 1's output and profit would increase. Firm 2's output and profit would decrease.

Chapter 10

1. *a.* Player 1's dominant strategy is B. Player 2 does not have a dominant strategy.
3. *b.* Player 1's equilibrium payoff is 5.
4. *b.* No.
5. *a.* $x > 2$.

Chapter 11

1. *a.* $P = \$225$.
5. *a.* Charge a fixed fee of $160, plus a per-unit charge of $20.
6. *b.* $3200.
7. *a.* $225 000.

Chapter 12

2. *a.* Risk loving.
3. *a.* $5.
5. *a.* $25.
6. *a.* $1750.

Chapter 13

2. *b.* No.
4. *a.* 90.
5. *b.* No. The benefits stem from the fact that by raising rivals' costs, your rivals reduce their own output. This tends to increase the market price, thus permitting you to expand your own output (and market share) and enjoy higher profits.
6. *a.* Firm 2 will enter, so firm 1 earns profits of $300 000.

Chapter 14

1. *a.* $C_4 = 0.80$.
3. *a.* $Q = 100/35$.
5. *a.* $Q = 10$ and $P = \$15$.
7. *a.* Nothing.

APPENDIX B   Selected Readings

Chapter 1

Anders, Gary C.; Ohta, Hiroshi; and Sailors, Joel, "A Note on the Marginal Efficiency of Investment and Related Concepts." *Journal of Economic Studies* 17(2), 1990, pp. 50–57.

Clark, Gregory, "Factory Discipline." *Journal of Economic History* 54(1), March 1994, pp. 128–63.

Fizel, John L. and Nunnikhoven, Thomas S., "Technical Efficiency of For-Profit and Non-profit Nursing Homes." *Managerial and Decision Economics* 13(5), Sept.–Oct. 1992, pp. 429–39.

Gifford, Sharon, "Allocation of Entrepreneurial Attention." *Journal of Economic Behavior and Organization* 19(3), December 1992, pp. 265–84.

McNamara, John R., "The Economics of Decision Making in the New Manufacturing Firm." *Managerial and Decision Economics* 13(4), July–August 1992, pp. 287–93.

Mercuro, Nicholas; Sourbis, Haralambos; and Whitney, Gerald, "Ownership Structure, Value of the Firm and the Bargaining Power of the Manager." *Southern Economic Journal* 59(2), October 1992, pp. 273–83.

Parsons, George R. and Wu, Yangru, "The Opportunity Cost of Coastal Land-Use Controls: An Empirical Analysis." *Land Economics* 67, Aug. 1991, pp. 308–16.

Phillips, Owen R.; Battalio, Raymond C.; and Kogut, Carl A., "Sunk Costs and Opportunity Costs in Valuation and Bidding." *Southern Economic Journal* 58, July 1991, pp. 112–28.

Pindyck, Robert S., "Irreversibility, Uncertainty, and Investment." *The Journal of Economic Literature* 29, Sept. 1991, pp. 1110–48.

Chapter 2

Ault, Richard W.; Jackson, John D.; and Saba, Richard P., "The Effect of Long-Term Rent Control on Tenant Mobility." *Journal of Urban Economics* 35(2), March 1994, pp. 140–58.

Espana, Juan R., "Impact of the North American Free Trade Agreement (NAFTA) on U.S. Mexican Trade and Investment Flows." *Business Economics* 28(3), July 1993, pp. 41–47.

Friedman, Milton, *Capitalism and Freedom.* Chicago: University of Chicago Press, 1962.

Katz, Lawrence F. and Murphy, Kevin M., "Changes in Relative Wages, 1963–1987: Supply and Demand Factors." *Quarterly Journal of Economics* 107(1), February 1992, pp. 35–78.

Olson, Josephine E. and Frieze, Irene Hanson, "Job Interruptions and Part-Time Work: Their Effect on MBAs' Income." *Industrial Relations* 28(3), Fall 1989, pp. 373–86.

O'Neill, June and Polachek, Solomon, "Why the Gender Gap in Wages Narrowed in the 1980s." *Journal of Labor Economics* 11(1), January 1993, pp. 205–28.

Simon, Herbert A., "Organizations and Markets." *Journal of Economic Perspectives* 5(2), Spring 1991, pp. 25–44.

Smith, Vernon L., "An Experimental Study of Competitive Market Behavior." *Journal of Political Economy* 70(2), April 1962, pp. 111–39.

Williamson, Oliver, *The Economic Institutions of Capitalism.* New York: Free Press, 1985.

Chapter 3

Chiles, Ted W., Jr. and Sollars, David L., "Estimating Cigarette Tax Revenue." *Journal of Economics and Finance* 17(3), Fall 1993, pp. 1–15.

Crandall, R., "Import Quotas and the Automobile Industry: The Cost of Protectionism." *Brookings Review* 2(4), Summer 1984, pp. 8–16.

Houthakker, H. and Taylor, L., *Consumer Demand in the United States: Analyses and Projections,* 2nd ed. Cambridge: Harvard University Press, 1970.

Maxwell, Nan L. and Lopus, Jane S., "The Lake Wobegon Effect in Student Self Reported Data." *American Economic Review* 84(2), May 1994, pp. 201–05.

Pratt, Robert W., Jr., "Forecasting New Product Sales from Likelihood of Purchase Ratings: Commentary." *Marketing Science* 5(4), Fall 1986, pp. 387–88.

Sawtelle, Barbara A., "Income Elasticities of Household Expenditures: A U.S. Cross Section Perspective." *Applied Economics* 25(5), May 1993, pp. 635–44.

Stano, Miron and Hotelling, Harold, "Regression Analysis in Litigation: Some Overlooked Considerations." *Journal of Legal Economics* 1(3), December 1991, pp. 68–78.

Williams, Harold R. and Mount, Randall I., "OECD Gasoline Demand Elasticities: An Analysis of Consumer Behavior with Implications for U.S. Energy Policy." *Journal of Behavioral Economics* 16(1), Spring 1987, pp. 69–79.

Chapter 4

Baumol, William J., *Business Behavior, Value and Growth.* New York: Macmillan, 1959.

Battalio, Raymond C.; Kagel, John H.; and Kogut, Carl A., "Experimental Confirmation of the Existence of a Giffen Good." *American Economic Review* 81(4), September 1991, pp. 961–70.

Davis, J., "Transitivity of Preferences." *Behavioral Science,* Fall 1958, pp. 26–33.

Evans, William N. and Viscusi, W. Kip, "Income Effects and the Value of Health." *Journal of Human Resources* 28(3), Summer 1993, pp. 497–518.

Gilad, Benjamin; Kaish, Stanley; and Loeb, Peter D., "Cognitive Dissonance and Utility Maximization: A General Framework." *Journal of Economic Behavior and Organization* 8(1), March 1987, pp. 61–73.

Lancaster, Kelvin, *Consumer Demand: A New Approach.* New York: Columbia University Press, 1971.

MacKrimmon, Kenneth and Toda, Maseo, "The Experimental Determination of Indifference Curves." *Review of Economic Studies* 37, October 1969, pp. 433–51.

Smart, Denise T. and Martin, Charles L., "Manufacturer Responsiveness to Consumer Correspondence: An Empirical Investigation of Consumer Perceptions." *Journal of Consumer Affairs* 26(1), Summer 1992, pp. 104–28.

Chapter 5

Anderson, Evan E. and Chen, Yu Min, "Implicit Prices and Economies of Scale of Secondary Memory: The Case of Disk Drives." *Managerial and Decision Economics* 12(3), June 1991, pp. 241–48.

Carlsson, Bo; Audretsch, David B.; and Acs, Zoltan J., "Flexible Technology and Plant Size: U.S. Manufacturing and Metalworking Industries." *International Journal of Industrial Organization* 12(3), 1994, pp. 359–72.

Eaton, C., "The Geometry of Supply, Demand, and Competitive Market Structure with Economies of Scope." *American Economic Review* 81, September 1991, pp. 901–11.

Ferrier, Gary D. and Lovell, C. A. Knox, "Measuring Cost Efficiency in Banking: Econometric and Linear Programming Evidence." *Journal of Econometrics* 46(12), October/November 1990, pp. 229–45.

Gold, B., "Changing Perspectives on Size, Scale, and Returns: An Interpretive Survey." *Journal of Economic Literature* 19(1), March 1981, pp. 5–33.

Gropper, Daniel M., "An Empirical Investigation of Changes in Scale Economies for the Commercial Banking Firm, 1979–1986." *Journal of Money, Credit, and Banking* 23(4), November 1991, pp. 718–27.

Kohn, Robert E. and Levin, Stanford L., "Complementarity and Anticomplementarity with the Same Pair of Inputs." *Journal of Economic Education* 25(1), Winter 1994, pp. 67–73.

Mills, D., "Capacity Expansion and the Size of Plants." *Rand Journal of Economics* 21, Winter 1990, pp. 555–66.

Chapter 6

Alchian, Armen A. and Demsetz, Harold, "Production, Information Costs, and Economic Organization." *American Economic Review* 62, December 1972, pp. 777–95.

Antle, Rick and Smith, Abbie, "An Empirical Investigation of the Relative Performance Evaluation of Corporate Executives." *Journal of Accounting Research* 24(1), Spring 1986, pp. 1–39.

Coase, R. H., "The Nature of the Firm." *Economica,* November 1937, pp. 366–405.

Gibbons, Robert and Murphy, Kevin J., "Relative Performance Evaluation for Chief Executive Officers." *Industrial and Labor Relations Review* 43, February 1990, pp. 30–51.

Jensen, Michael C., "Takeovers: Their Causes and Consequences." *Journal of Economic Perspectives* 1, Winter 1988, pp. 21–48.

Jensen, Michael C. and Murphy, Kevin J., "Performance Pay and Top Management Incentives." *Journal of Political Economy* 98(2), April 1990, pp. 225–64.

Klein, Benjamin; Crawford, Robert G.; and Alchian, Armen A., "Vertical Integration, Appropriable Rents, and the Competitive Contracting Process." *Journal of Law and Economics* 21(2), October 1978, pp. 297–326.

Koss, Patricia A., "Reciprocal Exposure and Hold-Up in Fisheries: Implications of Fisheries Management Policy." Proceedings of the International Institute of Fisheries Economics and Trade Conference, Corvallis, OR, July 10–14, 2000.

Lewis, Tracy R. and Sappington, David E. M., "Incentives for Monitoring Quality." *Rand Journal of Economics* 22(3), Autumn 1991, pp. 370–84.

Williamson, Oliver E., "Markets and Hierarchies: Some Elementary Considerations." *American Economic Review* 63, May 1973, pp. 316–25.

Winn, Daryl N. and Shoenhair, John D., "Compensation Based (Dis)incentives for Revenue Maximizing Behavior: A Test of the 'Revised' Baumol Hypothesis." *Review of Economics and Statistics* 70(1), February 1988, pp. 154–58.

Chapter 7

Conant, John L., "The Role of Managerial Discretion in Union Mergers." *Journal of Economic Behavior and Organization* 20(1), January 1993, pp. 49–62.

Dansby, R. E. and Willig, R. D., "Industry Performance Gradient Indexes." *American Economic Review* 69, 1979, pp. 249–60.

Davis, Douglas D. and Holt, Charles A., "Market Power and Mergers in Laboratory Markets with Posted Prices." *Rand Journal of Economics* 25(3), Autumn 1994, pp. 467–87.

Golbe, Devra L. and White, Lawrence J., "Catch a Wave: The Time Series Behavior of Mergers." *Review of Economics and Statistics* 75(3), August 1993, pp. 493–99.

Hirschman, Albert O., "The Paternity of an Index." *American Economic Review* 54(5), September 1964, p. 761.

Johnson, Ronald N. and Parkman, Allen M., "Premerger Notification and the Incentive to Merge and Litigate." *Journal of Law, Economics and Organization* 7(1), Spring 1991, pp. 145–62.

Kim, E. Han and Singal, Vijay, "Mergers and Market Power: Evidence from the Airline Industry." *American Economic Review* 83(3), June 1993, pp. 549–69.

Lerner, A. P., "The Concept of Monopoly and the Measurement of Monopoly Power." *Review of Economic Studies,* October 1933, pp. 157–75.

O'Neill, Patrick B., "Concentration Trends and Profitability in U.S. Manufacturing: A Further Comment and Some New (and Improved) Evidence." *Applied Economics* 25(10), October 1993, pp. 1285–86.

Rothschild, K. W., "The Degree of Monopoly." *Economica* 9, 1942, pp. 24–39.

"Symposia: Horizontal Mergers and Antitrust." *Journal of Economic Perspectives* 1(2), Fall 1987.

Chapter 8

Gal Or, Esther and Spiro, Michael H., "Regulatory Regimes in the Electric Power Industry: Implications for Capacity." *Journal of Regulatory Economics* 4(3), September 1992, pp. 263–78.

Gius, Mark Paul, "The Extent of the Market in the Liquor Industry: An Empirical Test of Localized Brand Rivalry, 1970–1988." *Review of Industrial Organization* 8(5), October 1993, pp. 599–608.

Lamdin, Douglas J., "The Welfare Effects of Monopoly Versus Competition: A Clarification of Textbook Presentations." *Journal of Economic Education* 23(3), Summer 1992, pp. 247–53.

Malueg, David A., "Monopoly Output and Welfare: The Role of Curvature of the Demand Function." *Journal of Economic Education* 25(3), Summer 1994, pp. 235–50.

Nguyen, Dung, "Advertising, Random Sales Response, and Brand Competition: Some Theoretical and Econometric Implications." *Journal of Business* 60(2), April 1987, pp. 259–79.

Simon, Herbert A., "Organizations and Markets." *Journal of Economic Perspectives* 5(2), Spring 1991, pp. 25–44.

Stegeman, Mark, "Advertising in Competitive Markets." *American Economic Review* 81(1), March 1991, pp. 210–23.

Zupan, Mark A., "On Cream Skimming, Coase, and the Sustainability of Natural Monopolies." *Applied Economics* 22(4), April 1990, pp. 487–92.

Chapter 9

Alberts, William W., "Do Oligopolists Earn 'Noncompetitive' Rates of Return?" *American Economic Review* 74(4), September 1984, pp. 624–32.

Becker, Klaus G., "Natural Monopoly Equilibria: Nash and von Stackelberg Solutions." *Journal of Economics and Business* 46(2), May 1994, pp. 135–39.

Brander, James A. and Lewis, Tracy R., "Oligopoly and Financial Structure: The Limited Liability Effect." *American Economic Review* 76(5), December 1986, pp. 956–70.

Caudill, Steven B. and Mixon, Franklin G., Jr., "Cartels and the Incentive to Cheat: Evidence from the Classroom." *Journal of Economic Education* 25(3), Summer 1994, pp. 267–69.

Friedman, J. W., *Oligopoly Theory.* Amsterdam: North Holland, 1983.

Gal-Or, E., "Excessive Retailing at the Bertrand Equilibria." *Canadian Journal of Economics* 23(2), May 1990, pp. 294–304.

Levy, David T. and Reitzes, James D., "Product Differentiation and the Ability to Collude: Where Being Different Can Be an Advantage." *Antitrust Bulletin* 38(2), Summer 1993, pp. 349–68.

Plott, C. R., "Industrial Organization Theory and Experimental Economics." *Journal of Economic Literature* 20, 1982, pp. 1485–1527.

Ross, Howard N., "Oligopoly Theory and Price Rigidity." *Antitrust Bulletin* 32(2), Summer 1987, pp. 451–69.

Showalter, Dean M., "Oligopoly and Financial Structure: Comment." *American Economic Review* 85(3), June 1995, pp. 647–53.

Chapter 10

Bolton, Gary E., "A Comparative Model of Bargaining: Theory and Evidence." *American Economic Review* 81(5), December 1991, pp. 1096–136.

Buckley, N., Chan, K., Chowhan, J., Mestelman, S., and Shehata, M., "Value Orientations, Income and Displacement Effects, and Voluntary Contributions." *Experimental Economics*, October 2001, pp. 183–195.

Friedman, James W., ed., *Problems of Coordination in Economic Activity.* Boston: Kluwer Academic, 1994.

Gardner, Roy and Ostrom, Elinor, "Rules and Games." *Public Choice* 70(2), May 1991, pp. 121–49.

Gilbert, Richard J., "The Role of Potential Competition in Industrial Organization." *Journal of Economic Perspectives* 3(3), Summer 1989, pp. 107–28.

Green, E. J. and Porter, R. H., "Noncooperative Collusion Under Imperfect Price Information." *Economica*, January 1984, pp. 87–100.

Hansen, Robert G. and Samuelson, William F., "Evolution in Economic Games." *Journal of Economic Behavior and Organization* 10(3), October 1988, pp. 315–38.

Morrison, C. C. and Kamarei, H., "Some Experimental Testing of the Cournot-Nash Hypothesis in Small Group Rivalry Situations." *Journal of Economic Behavior and Organization* 13(2), March 1990, pp. 213–31.

Muller, R. A. and Sadanand, " Order of Play, Forward Induction, and the Presentation Effects in Two-Person Games." *Experimental Economics*, June 2003, pp. 5–25.

Rasmusen, Eric, *Games and Information: An Introduction to Game Theory.* New York: Basis Blackwell, 1989.

Rosenthal, Robert W., "Rules of Thumb in Games." *Journal of Economic Behavior and Organization* 22(1), September 1993, pp. 1–13.

Schelling, Thomas C., *The Strategy of Conflict.* Cambridge, MA: Harvard University Press, 1973.

Chapter 11

Adams, William J. and Yellen, Janet I., "Commodity Bundling and the Burden of Monopoly." *Quarterly Journal of Economics* 90, August 1976, pp. 475–98.

Baum, T. and Mudambi, R., "An Empirical-Analysis of Oligopolistic Hotel Pricing." *Annals of Tourism Research* 22 (1995), pp. 501–16.

Cain, Paul and Macdonald, James M., "Telephone Pricing Structures: The Effects on Universal Service." *Journal of Regulatory Economics* 3(4), December 1991, pp. 293–308.

Carroll, K. and Coates, D., "Teaching Price Discrimination: Some Clarification." *Southern Economic Journal* 66, October 1999, pp. 466–80.

Jeitschko, T. D., "Issues in Price Discrimination: A Comment on and Addendum to 'Teaching Price Discrimination' by Carroll and Coates." *Southern Economic Journal* 68, July 2001, pp. 178–86.

Karni, Edi and Levin, Dan, "Social Attributes and Strategic Equilibrium: A Restaurant Pricing Game." *Journal of Political Economy* 102(4), August 1994, pp. 822–40.

Masson, Robert and Shaanan, Joseph, "Optimal Oligopoly Pricing and the Threat of Entry: Canadian Evidence." *International Journal of Industrial Organization* 5(3), September 1987, pp. 323–39.

McAfee, R. Preston, McMillan, John, and Whinston, Michael D., "Multiproduct Monopoly, Commodity Bundling, and Correlation of Values." *Quarterly Journal of Economics* 104(2), May 1989, pp. 371–83.

Oi, Walter Y., "A Disneyland Dilemma: Two-Part Tariffs for a Mickey Mouse Monopoly." *Quarterly Journal of Economics* 85, February 1971, pp. 77–96.

Romano, Richard E., "Double Moral Hazard and Resale Price Maintenance." *Rand Journal of Economics* 25(3), Autumn 1994, pp. 455–66.

Scitovsky, T., "The Benefits of Asymmetric Markets." *Journal of Economics Perspectives* 4(1), Winter 1990, pp. 135–48.

Chapter 12

Akerlof, G. A., "The Market for Lemons: Quality Uncertainty and the Market Mechanism," *Quarterly Journal of Economics*, 1970, pp. 488–500.

Bikhchandani, Sushil, Hirshleifer, David, and Welch, Ivo, "A Theory of Fads, Fashion, Custom, and Cultural Change in Informational Cascades." *Journal of Political Economy* 100(5), October 1992, pp. 992–1026.

Cummins, J. David and Tennyson, Sharon, "Controlling Automobile Insurance Costs." *Journal of Economic Perspectives* 6(2), Spring 1992, pp. 95–115.

Hamilton, Jonathan H., "Resale Price Maintenance in a Model of Consumer Search." *Managerial and Decision Economics* 11(2), May 1990, pp. 87–98.

Kagel, John, Levine, Dan, and Battalio, Raymond, "First Price Common Value Auctions: Bidder Behavior and the 'Winner's Curse.'" *Economic Inquiry* 27, April 1989, pp. 241–58.

Lind, Barry and Plott, Charles, "The Winner's Curse: Experiments with Buyers and with Sellers." *American Economic Review* 81, March 1991, pp. 225–346.

Lucking-Reiley, David, "Auctions on the Internet: What's Being Auctioned, and How?" *Journal of Industrial Economics* 48 (3), September 2000, pp. 227–52.

Machina, Mark J., "Choice Under Uncertainty: Problems Solved and Unsolved." *Journal of Economic Perspectives* 1, Summer 1987, pp. 121–54.

McAfee, R. Preston and McMillan, John, "Auctions and Bidding." *Journal of Economic Literature* 25(2), June 1987, pp. 699–738.

McMillan, John, "Selling Spectrum Rights." *Journal of Economic Perspectives* 8(3), Summer 1994, pp. 145–62.

Milgrom, Paul, "Auctions and Bidding: A Primer." *Journal of Economic Perspectives* 3(3), Summer 1989, pp. 3–22.

Riley, John G., "Expected Revenues from Open and Sealed-Bid Auctions." *Journal of Economic Perspectives* 3(3), Summer 1989, pp. 41–50.

Salop, Steven, "Evaluating Uncertain Evidence with Sir Thomas Bayes: A Note for Teachers." *Journal of Economic Perspectives* 1, Summer 1987, pp. 155–59.

Chapter 13

Bental, Benjamin and Spiegel, Menahem, "Network Competition, Product Quality, and Market Coverage in the Presence of Network Externalities." *Journal of Industrial Economics* 43(2), June 1995, pp. 197–208.

Bolton, Patrick and Dewatripont, Mathias, "The Firm as a Communication Network." *Quarterly Journal of Economics* 109(4), November 1994, pp. 809–39.

Brueckner, Jan K., Dyer, Nichola J., and Spiller, Pablo T., "Fare Determination in Airline Hub-and-Spoke Networks." *RAND Journal of Economics* 23(3), Autumn 1992, pp. 309–33.

Economides, N., "The Economics of Networks." *International Journal of Industrial Organization* 14, October 1996, pp. 673–99.

Gabel, David, "Competition in a Network Industry: The Telephone Industry, 1894–1910." *Journal of Economic History* 54(3), September 1994, pp. 543–72.

Gilbert, Richard J., "The Role of Potential Competition in Industrial Organization." *Journal of Economic Perspectives* 3(3), Summer 1989, pp. 107–27.

LeBlanc, Greg, "Signaling Strength: Limit Pricing and Predatory Pricing." *RAND Journal of Economics* 23(4), Winter 1992, pp. 493–506.

Liebowitz, S. J. and Margolis, Stephen E., "Network Externality: An Uncommon Tragedy." *Journal of Economic Perspectives* 8(2), Spring 1994, pp. 133–50.

MacKie-Mason, Jeffrey K. and Varian, Hal, "Economic FAQs About the Internet." *Journal of Economic Perspectives* 8(3), Summer 1994, pp. 75–96.

Milgrom, Paul and Roberts, John, "Limit Pricing and Entry Under Incomplete Information: An Equilibrium Analysis." *Econometrica* 50(2), March 1982, pp. 443–60.

Salop, Steven C., "Exclusionary Vertical Restraints Law: Has Economics Mattered?" *American Economic Review* 83(2), May 1993, pp. 168–172.

Strassmann, Diana L., "Potential Competition in the Deregulated Airlines." *Review of Economics and Statistics* 72(4), November 1990, pp. 696–702.

Vickers, John, "Competition and Regulation in Vertically Related Markets." *Review of Economic Studies* 62(1), January 1995, pp. 1–17.

Weinberg, John A., "Exclusionary Practices and Technological Competition." *Journal of Industrial Economics* 40(2), June 1992, pp. 135–46.

Chapter 14

Economides, Nicholas and White, Lawrence J., "Networks and Compatibility: Implications for Antitrust." *European Economic Review* 38(34), April 1994, pp. 651–62.

Elzinga, Kenneth and Breit, William, *The Antitrust Penalties: A Study in Law and Economics.* New Haven: Yale University Press, 1976.

Formby, John P.; Keeler, James P.; and Thistle, Paul D., "X-Efficiency, Rent Seeking and Social Costs." *Public Choice* 57(2), May 1988, pp. 115–26.

Gradstein, Mark; Nitzan, Shmuel; and Slutsky, Steven, "Private Provision of Public Goods Under Price Uncertainty." *Social Choice and Welfare* 10(4), 1993, pp. 371–82.

Inman, Robert P., "New Research in Local Public Finance: Introduction." *Regional Science and Urban Economics* 19(3), August 1989, pp. 347–52.

McCall, Charles W., "Rule of Reason Versus Mechanical Tests in the Adjudication of Price Predation." *Review of Industrial Organization* 3(3), Spring 1988, pp. 15–44.

Rivlin, A. M., "Distinguished Lecture on Economics in Government: Strengthening the Economy by Rethinking the Role of Federal and State Governments." *Journal of Economic Perspectives* 5(2), Spring 1991, pp. 3–14.

Steiner, R. L., "Intrabrand Competition—Stepchild of Antitrust." *Antitrust Bulletin,* 36(1), Spring 1991, pp. 155–200.

Glossary

A

adverse selection Situation where individuals have hidden characteristics and in which a selection process results in a pool of individuals with undesirable characteristics.

affiliated (or correlated) value estimates Auction environment in which bidders do not know their own valuation of the item or the valuations of others. Each bidder uses his or her own information to estimate their valuation, and these value estimates are affiliated: the higher a bidder's value estimate, the more likely it is that other bidders also have high value estimates.

asymmetric information A situation that exists when some people have better information than others.

attribute space Possible combinations of attributes that can be possessed by products, conceived as a graph in several dimensions.

average fixed cost (*AFC*) Fixed costs divided by the number of units of output.

average product (*AP*) A measure of the output produced per unit of input.

average variable cost (*AVC*) Variable costs divided by the number of units of output.

B

Bertrand oligopoly An industry in which (1) there are few firms serving many consumers; (2) firms produce identical products at a constant marginal cost; (3) firms compete in price and react optimally to competitors' prices; (4) consumers have perfect information and there are no transaction costs; and (5) barriers to entry exist.

block pricing A pricing strategy in which identical products are packaged together in order to enhance profits by forcing customers to make an all-or-none decision to purchase.

brand equity The additional value added to a product because of its brand.

budget line The bundles of goods that exhaust a consumer's income.

budget set The bundles of goods a consumer can afford.

C

change in demand Changes in variables other than the price of a good, such as income or the price of another good, lead to a change in demand. This corresponds to a shift of the entire demand curve.

change in quantity demanded Changes in the price of a good lead to a change in the quantity demanded of that good. This corresponds to a movement along a given demand curve.

change in quantity supplied Changes in the price of a good lead to a change in the quantity supplied of that good. This corresponds to a movement along a given supply curve.

change in supply Changes in variables other than the price of a good, such as input prices or technological advances, lead to a change in supply. This corresponds to a shift of the entire supply curve.

Cobb-Douglas production function A production function that assumes some degree of substitutability among inputs.

commitment A threat or promise, if carrying out the punishment or reward is in one's best interest.

commodity bundling The practice of bundling several different products together and selling them at a single "bundle price."

common value Auction environment in which the true value of the item is the same for all bidders, but this common value is unknown. Bidders each use their own (private) information to form an estimate of the item's true common value.

comparative advertising A form of advertising in which a firm attempts to increase the demand for its brand by differentiating its product from competing brands.

Competition Act Government policies designed to promote competition and efficiency in the marketplace.

complements Goods for which an increase (decrease) in the price of one good leads to a decrease (increase) in the demand for the other good.

constant returns to scale Exist when long-run average costs remain constant as output is increased.

consumer equilibrium The equilibrium consumption bundle—the affordable bundle that yields the greatest satisfaction to the consumer.

consumer surplus The value consumers get from a good but do not have to pay for.

contestable market A market in which (1) all firms have access to the same technology; (2) consumers respond quickly to price changes; (3) existing firms cannot respond quickly to entry by lowering their prices; and (4) there are no sunk costs.

contract A formal relationship between a buyer and seller that obligates the buyer and seller to exchange at terms specified in a legal document.

cost complementarity The marginal cost of producing one type of output decreasing when the output of another good is increased.

Cournot equilibrium A situation in which neither firm has an incentive to change its output given the other firm's output.

Cournot oligopoly An industry in which (1) there are few firms serving many consumers; (2) firms produce either differentiated or homogeneous products; (3) each firm believes rivals will hold their output constant if it changes its output; and (4) barriers to entry exist.

cross-price elasticity A measure of the responsiveness of the demand for a good to changes in the price of a related good; the percentage change in the quantity demanded of one good divided by the percentage change in the price of a related good.

cross-subsidy A pricing strategy in which profits gained from the sale of one product are used to subsidize sales of a related product.

cubic cost function Considering costs as a cubic function of output provides a reasonable approximation to virtually any cost function.

D

Dansby-Willig (DW) performance index Ranks industries according to how much social welfare would improve if the output in an industry were increased by a small amount.

deadweight loss of monopoly The consumer and producer surplus that is lost due to the monopolist charging a price in excess of marginal cost.

decreasing (diminishing) marginal returns Range of input usage over which marginal product declines.

demand function A function that describes how much of a good will be purchased at alternative prices of that good and related goods, alternative income levels, and alternative values of other variables affecting demand.

direct network externality The direct value enjoyed by the user of a network because others also use the network.

diseconomies of scale Exist when long-run average costs rise as output is increased; exist whenever average total costs increase as output increases.

dominant strategy A strategy that results in the highest payoff to a player regardless of the opponent's action.

Dutch auction A descending sequential-bid auction in which the auctioneer begins with a high asking price and gradually reduces the asking price until one bidder announces a willingness to pay that price for the item.

E

economic profits The difference between total revenue and total opportunity cost.

economics The science of making decisions in the situation of scarce resources.

economies of scale Exist whenever long-run average costs decline as output is increased.

economies of scope Exist when the total cost of producing two products within the same firm is lower than when the products are produced by separate firms.

efficiency frontier The outer boundary of the attainable combinations of attributes in attribute space.

elastic demand Demand is elastic if the absolute value of the own price elasticity is greater than 1.

elasticity A measure of the responsiveness of one variable to changes in another variable; the percentage change in one variable that arises due to a given percentage change in another variable.

English auction An ascending sequential-bid auction in which bidders observe the bids of others and decide whether or not to increase the bid. The auction ends when a single bidder remains; this bidder obtains the item and pays the auctioneer the amount of the bid.

extensive-form game A representation of a game that summarizes the players, the information available to them at each stage, the strategies available to them, the sequence of moves, and the payoffs resulting from alternative strategies.

F

firm demand curve The demand curve for an individual firm's product; in a perfectly competitive market, it is simply the market price.

first-price, sealed-bid auction A simultaneous-move auction in which bidders simultaneously submit bids on pieces of paper. The auctioneer awards the item to the high bidder, who pays the amount bid.

fixed *and* variable factors of production Fixed factors are the inputs the manager cannot adjust in the short run. Variable factors are the inputs a manager can adjust to alter production.

fixed costs Costs that do not change with changes in output; include the costs of fixed inputs used in production.

four-firm concentration ratio The fraction of total industry sales generated by the four largest firms in the industry.

full economic price The dollar amount paid to a firm under a price ceiling, plus the nonpecuniary price.

G

green marketing A form of niche marketing in which firms target products toward consumers who are concerned about environmental issues.

H

Herfindahl-Hirschman index (*HHI*) The sum of the squared market shares of firms in a given industry multiplied by 10 000.

hidden action Action taken by one party in a relationship that cannot be observed by the other party.

hidden characteristics Things one party to a transaction knows about itself but which are unknown by the other party.

I

import tariff A tax on imports in the form of either a percentage or dollars per unit.

incidence of tax Where the burden of a tax falls.

income effect The movement from one indifference curve to another that results from the change in real income caused by a price change.

income elasticity A measure of the responsiveness of the demand for a good to changes in consumer income; the percentage change in quantity demanded divided by the percentage change in income.

increasing marginal returns Range of input usage over which marginal product increases.

incremental costs The additional costs that stem from a yes-or-no decision.

incremental revenues The additional revenues that stem from a yes-or-no decision.

independent private values Auction environment in which each bidder knows his own valuation of the item but does not know other bidders' valuations, and in which each bidder's valuation does not depend on other bidders' valuations of the object.

indifference curve A curve that defines the combinations of two or more goods that give a consumer the same level of satisfaction.

indirect network externality The indirect value enjoyed by the user of a network because of complementarities between the size of a network and the availability of complementary products or services.

inelastic demand Demand is inelastic if the absolute value of the own price elasticity is less than 1.

inferior good A good for which an increase (decrease) in income leads to a decrease (increase) in the demand for that good.

infinitely repeated game A game that is played over and over again forever and in which players receive payoffs during each play of the game.

isocost line A line that represents the combinations of inputs that will cost the producer the same amount of money.

isoquant Defines the combinations of units that yield the same level of output.

L

law of diminishing marginal rate of technical substitution A property of a production function stating that as less of one input is used, increasing amounts of another input must be employed to produce the same level of output.

learning curve effects A firm's enjoyment of lower costs due to knowledge gained from its past production decisions.

least squares regression The line that minimizes the sum of squared deviations between the line and the actual data points.

lemons Vehicles with persistent mechanical problems.

Leontief production function A production function that assumes inputs are used in fixed proportions.

Lerner index A measure of the difference between price and marginal cost as a fraction of the product's price.

limit pricing A strategy in which an incumbent maintains a price below the monopoly level in order to prevent entry.

linear demand function A representation of the demand function in which the demand for a given good is a linear function of prices, income levels, and other variables influencing demand.

linear production function A production function that assumes a perfect linear relationship between all inputs and total output.

linear supply function A representation of the supply function in which the supply of a given good is a linear function of input prices and other variables affecting supply.

log-linear demand Demand is log-linear if the logarithm of demand is a linear function of the logarithms of prices, income, and other variables.

long-run average cost curve A curve that defines the minimum average cost of producing alternative levels of output, allowing for optimal selection of both fixed and variable factors of production.

lump-sum tariff A fixed fee that an importing firm must pay the domestic government in order to have the legal right to sell the product in the domestic market.

M

manager A person who directs resources to achieve a stated goal.

managerial economics The study of how to direct scarce resources in the way that most efficiently achieves a managerial goal.

marginal (incremental) cost The cost of producing an additional unit of output.

marginal product The change in total output attributable to the last unit of an input.

marginal profits The change in net profits that arises from a one unit change in Q.

marginal rate of substitution (*MRS*) The rate at which a consumer is willing to substitute one good for another good and still maintain the same level of satisfaction.

marginal rate of technical substitution (*MRTS*) The rate at which a producer can substitute between two inputs and maintain the same level of output.

marginal revenue The change in revenue attributable to the last unit of output; for a competitive firm, *MR* is the market price.

market demand curve A curve indicating the total quantity of a good all consumers are willing and able to purchase at each possible price, holding the prices of related goods, income, advertising, and other variables constant.

market power The ability of a firm to set its price above marginal cost.

market rate of substitution The rate at which one good may be traded for another in the market; the slope of the budget line.

market structure Factors that affect managerial decisions, including the number of firms competing in a market, the relative size of firms, technological and cost considerations, demand conditions, and the ease with which firms can enter or exit the industry.

market supply curve A curve indicating the total quantity of a good that all producers in a competitive market would produce at each price, holding input prices, technology, and other variables affecting supply constant.

mean (expected) value The sum of the probabilities that different outcomes will occur multiplied by the resulting payoffs.

mixed (randomized) strategy A strategy whereby a player randomizes over two or more available actions in order to keep rivals from being able to predict his or her action.

monopolistically competitive market A market in which (1) there are many buyers and sellers; (2) each firm produces a differentiated product; and (3) there is free entry and exit.

monopoly A market structure in which a single firm serves an entire market for a good that has no close substitutes.

moral hazard A situation in which one party to a contract takes a hidden action that benefits him or her at the expense of another party.

multiproduct cost function A function that defines the cost of producing given levels of two or more types of outputs assuming all inputs are used efficiently.

N

Nash equilibrium A condition describing a set of strategies in which no player can improve her payoff by unilaterally changing her own strategy, given the other players' strategies.

negative externalities Costs borne by parties who are not involved in the production or consumption of a good.

negative marginal returns Range of input usage over which marginal product is negative.

net present value (NPV) The present value of the income stream generated by a project minus the current cost of the project.

network complementarities Indirect externalities that stem from the growing use of a particular network.

niche marketing A marketing strategy in which goods and services are tailored to meet the needs of a particular segment of the market.

nonexclusionary consumption A good or service is nonexclusionary if, once provided, no one can be excluded from consuming it.

nonrival consumption A good is nonrival in consumption if the consumption of the good by one person does not preclude other people from also consuming the good.

normal-form game A representation of a game indicating the players, their possible strategies, and the payoffs resulting from alternative strategies.

normal good A good for which an increase (decrease) in income leads to an increase (decrease) in the demand for that good.

O

oligopoly A market structure in which there are only a few firms, each of which is large relative to the total industry.

opportunity cost The cost of the explicit and implicit resources that are forgone when a decision is made.

own price elasticity A measure of the responsiveness of the quantity demanded of a good to a change in the price of that good; the percentage change in quantity demanded divided by the percentage change in the price of the good.

P

peak-load pricing A pricing strategy in which higher prices are charged during peak hours than during offpeak hours.

penetration pricing Charging a low price initially to penetrate a market and gain a critical mass of customers; useful when strong network effects are present.

per-unit (excise) tariff The fee an importing firm must pay to the domestic government on each unit it brings into the country.

perfectly competitive market A market in which (1) there are many buyers and sellers; (2) each firm produces a homogeneous product; (3) buyers and sellers have perfect information; (4) there are no transaction costs; and (5) there is free entry and exit.

perfectly elastic demand Demand is perfectly elastic if the own price elasticity is infinite in absolute value. In this case the demand curve is horizontal.

perfectly inelastic demand Demand is perfectly inelastic if the own price elasticity is zero. In this case the demand curve is vertical.

positive externalities Benefits to society exceeding those to the firm or the individual.

predatory pricing A strategy in which a firm temporarily prices below its marginal cost to drive competitors out of the market.

present value (PV) The amount that would have to be invested today at the prevailing interest rate to generate the given future value.

price ceiling The maximum legal price that can be charged in a market.

price-cost squeeze A tactic used by a vertically integrated firm to squeeze the margins of its competitors.

price discrimination The practice of charging different prices to consumers for the same good or service.

price floor The minimum legal price that can be charged in a market.

price matching A strategy in which a firm advertises a price and a promise to match any lower price offered by a competitor.

producer surplus The amount producers receive in excess of the amount necessary to induce them to produce the good.

production function A function that defines the maximum amount of output that can be produced with a given set of inputs.

profit sharing Mechanism used to enhance workers' efforts that involves tying compensation to the underlying profitability of the firm.

promises A reward offered to the rival if she takes some actions.

public good A good that is nonrival and nonexclusionary in consumption.

Q

quota A restriction that limits the quantity of imported goods that can legally enter the country.

R

raising rivals' costs A strategy in which a firm gains an advantage over competitors by increasing their costs.

randomized pricing A pricing strategy in which a firm intentionally varies its price in an attempt to "hide" price information from consumers and rivals.

reaction function A function that defines the profit-maximizing level of output for a firm for given output levels of another firm.

relationship-specific exchange A type of exchange that occurs when the parties to a transaction have made specialized investments.

rent seeking Selfishly motivated efforts to influence another party's decision.

reservation price The price at which a consumer is indifferent between purchasing at that price and searching for a lower price.

revenue sharing Mechanism used to enhance workers' efforts that involves linking compensation to the underlying revenues of the firm.

risk averse Preferring a sure amount of M to a risky prospect with an expected value of M.

risk loving Preferring a risky prospect with an expected value of M to a sure amount of M.

risk neutral Indifferent between a risky prospect with an expected value of M and a sure amount of M.

risk premium The amount a risk-averse person would pay to avoid taking a risk.

risk pooling Many people getting together and sharing their losses by averaging them together.

Rothschild index A measure of the sensitivity to price of a product group as a whole relative to the sensitivity of the quantity demanded of a single firm to a change in its price.

S

screening An attempt by an uninformed party to sort individuals according to their characteristics.

second-price, sealed-bid auction A simultaneous-move auction in which bidders simultaneously submit bids. The auctioneer awards the item to the high bidder, who pays the amount bid by the second-highest bidder.

secure strategy A strategy that guarantees the highest payoff given the worst possible scenario.

self-selection device A mechanism in which informed parties are presented with a set of options, and the options they choose reveal their hidden characteristics to an uninformed party.

sequential-move game Game in which one player makes a move after observing the other player's move.

short-run cost function A function that defines the minimum possible cost of producing each output level when variable factors are employed in the costminimizing fashion.

signalling An attempt by an informed party to send an observable indicator of his or her hidden characteristics to an uninformed party.

simultaneous-move game Game in which each player makes decisions without knowledge of the other players' decisions.

specialized investment An expenditure that must be made to allow two parties to exchange but has little or no value in any alternative use.

spot exchange An informal relationship between a buyer and seller in which neither party is obligated to adhere to specific terms for exchange.

Stackelberg oligopoly An industry in which (1) there are few firms serving many consumers; (2) firms produce either differentiated or homogeneous products; (3) a single firm (the leader) chooses an output before rivals select their outputs; (4) all other firms (the followers) take the leader's output as given and select outputs that maximize profits given the leader's output; and (5) barriers to entry exist.

standard deviation The square root of the variance.

strategy In game theory, a decision rule that describes the actions a player will take at each decision point.

subgame perfect equilibrium A condition describing a set of strategies that constitutes a Nash equilibrium and allows no player to improve his own payoff at any stage of the game by changing strategies.

substitutes Goods for which an increase (decrease) in the price of one good leads to an increase (decrease) in the demand for the other good.

substitution effect The movement along a given indifference curve that results from a change in the relative prices of goods, holding real income constant.

sunk cost A cost that is forever lost after it has been paid.

supply function A function that describes how much of a good will be produced at alternative prices of that good, alternative input prices, and alternative values of other variables affecting supply.

Sweezy oligopoly An industry in which (1) there are few firms serving many consumers; (2) firms produce differentiated products; (3) each firm believes rivals will respond to a price reduction but will not follow a price increase; and (4) barriers to entry exist.

T

tariff A tax on imports or exports.

threats Penalties to be imposed on a rival if she takes an action.

tit for tat A strategy in which cheating triggers punishment in the next period.

total product The maximum level of output that can be produced with a given amount of inputs.

transaction costs Costs associated with acquiring an input that are in excess of the amount paid to the input supplier.

transfer pricing A pricing strategy in which a firm optimally sets the internal price at which an upstream division sells an input to a downstream division.

trigger strategy A strategy that is contingent on the past play of a game and in which some particular past action "triggers" a different action by a player.

t-**statistic** The ratio of the value of a parameter estimate to the standard error of the parameter estimate.

two-part pricing A pricing strategy in which consumers are charged a fixed fee for the right to purchase a product, plus a per-unit charge for each unit purchased.

U

unit-elastic demand Demand is unit-elastic if the absolute value of the own price elasticity is equal to 1.

V

value marginal product The value of the output produced by the last unit of an input.

variable costs Costs that change with changes in output; include the costs of inputs that vary with output.

variance The sum of the probabilities that different outcomes will occur multiplied by the squared deviations from the mean of the random variable.

vertical foreclosure A strategy wherein a vertically integrated firm charges downstream rivals a prohibitive price for an essential input, thus forcing rivals to use more costly substitutes or go out of business.

vertical integration A situation where a firm produces the inputs required to make its final product.

W

winner's curse The "bad news" conveyed to the winner that his or her estimate of the item's value exceeds the estimates of all other bidders.

Name Index

Subject Index